'The editors present an encompassing, innovative and challenging view of the field. They manage to demonstrate the pertinence of the field to local and international issues as well as to historically persistent problems.'
— Irma Serrano-García, *University of Puerto Rico, Puerto Rico*

'The second edition was outstanding. Graduates often say that this is the only book they keep and take with them into their professional lives because it is so relevant - and the third edition promises to be even more relevant.'
— Dawn Darlaston-Jones, *The University of Notre Dame, Australia*

'Packed with useful tools to promote collective well-being, this significant contribution is my textbook of choice. It includes global perspectives, and illustrative, concrete examples that support student learning. Importantly, this text focuses on power, centers issues of social (in)justice, and calls for critical approaches within (and beyond) our field.'
— Erin Rose Ellison, *California State University, Sacramento, USA*

'In this excellent new edition, the authors have introduced important material on community psychology that will shape theory, research and action.'
— Enoch Teye-Kwadjo, *University of Ghana, Ghana*

'A provocative text packed with information, diverse examples and up to date resources that encourages students to observe the world around them and think critically about how it functions.'
— Niki Harré, *The University of Auckland, New Zealand*

'The third edition is indeed well beyond an updated version of this modern academic classic in community psychology. The addition of a broader, more diverse team of collaborators brings new life and vibrancy to this edition. This text provides unique and novel opportunities for personal reflection throughout, heightening reflexivity and dynamic learning.'
— Katie Wright-Bevans, *Keele University, UK*

'This edition adds impressive new members and perspectives to the already powerful scholarship of its original authors. This is both a visionary introduction to the field and a valuable addition to the library of established scholars, activists and researchers.'
— Julian Rappaport, *University of Illinois at Urbana-Champaign, USA*

'It is clear that this work is derived from a community of authors who are steeped in active participation and passionate about their endeavours. I believe this text will become a key resource, both for students across various levels of study and for practitioners seeking conceptual and strongly values-informed bases for their work.'
— Jacqueline Akhurst, *Rhodes University, South Africa*

'This book should be part of any psychology degree. It covers all the pertinent topics, including some of the special features of community-based research not covered in most courses on psychology methods, and is made accessible to students through clear writing, thoughtful questions and extra materials to use in classes.'
— Bernard Guerin, *University of South Australia, Australia*

'This text is comprehensive with its inclusion of Indigenous and settler voices of key issues from both historical and contemporary perspectives. Well done.'
— Bridgette Masters-Awatere, *University of Waikato, New Zealand*

'Providing comprehensive and incisive coverage of a range of contemporary social issues and drawing on a range of international perspectives, this textbook is an invaluable resource for students, instructors and practitioners.'
— Norman Duncan, *University of Pretoria, South Africa*

'A commanding and inspiring presentation of our past achievements! Most importantly, this book also advocates continuing to access and collaborate with governments and local community resources with imagination and vigor and long term commitments.'
— James G Kelly, *Univ*

D1268433

Other Books by the Authors

Also by Scotney D. Evans:

From Amelioration to Transformation in Human Services: Towards Critical Practice (2012)

Also by Geoffrey Nelson:

Shifting the Paradigm in Community Mental Health Towards Empowerment and Community (2001)
(with J. Lord & J. Ochocka)

Partnerships for Prevention: The Story of the Highfield Community Enrichment Project (2005)
(with S. Mark Pancer, K. Hayward, & R. DeV. Peters)

Also by Isaac Prilleltensky:

Critical Psychology: An Introduction (1997, 1st Ed.) (with D. Fox)

The Morals and Politics of Psychology: Psychological Discourse and the Status Quo (1994)

Promoting Well-being: Linking Personal, Organizational, and Community Change (2006) (with O. Prilleltensky)

Critical Psychology: An Introduction (2009, 2nd Ed.) (with D. Fox & S. Austin)

The Laughing Guide to Well-being: Using Humor and Science to Become Happier and Healthier (2016)

Also by Geoffrey Nelson and Isaac Prilleltensky:

Doing Psychology Critically: Making a Difference in Diverse Settings (2002)

Promoting Family Wellness and Preventing Child Maltreatment: Fundamentals for Thinking and Action (2001) (with L. Peirson)

Also by Stephanie M. Reich, Manuel Riemer, and Isaac Prilleltensky:

International Community Psychology: History and Theories (2007) (with M. Montero)

Community Psychology

IN PURSUIT OF LIBERATION AND WELLBEING

Third edition

Manuel Riemer
Stephanie M. Reich
Scotney D. Evans
Geoffrey Nelson
Isaac Prilleltensky

BLOOMSBURY ACADEMIC
LONDON • NEW YORK • OXFORD • NEW DELHI • SYDNEY

BLOOMSBURY ACADEMIC
Bloomsbury Publishing Plc
50 Bedford Square, London, WC1B 3DP, UK
1385 Broadway, New York, NY 10018, USA
29 Earlsfort Terrace, Dublin 2, Ireland

BLOOMSBURY, BLOOMSBURY ACADEMIC and the Diana logo
are trademarks of Bloomsbury Publishing Plc

First edition published in 2005 by Palgrave Macmillan
This edition published in 2020 by Red Globe Press
Reprinted by Bloomsbury Academic in 2022

A catalogue record for this book is available from the British Library.

A catalog record for this book is available from the Library of Congress.

ISBN: PB: 978-1-1374-6409-5
ePDF: 978-1-1374-6410-1

Printed and bound in Great Britain

To find out more about our authors and books visit
www.bloomsbury.com and sign up for our newsletters.

Brief Contents

Contents

List of Figures and Tables

Figures

Tables

About the Authors

Manuel Riemer is Professor of Psychology in the Community Psychology program at Wilfrid Laurier University. He is Director of the Viessmann Centre for Engagement and Research in Sustainability (VERiS) and the Community, Environment, and Justice Research Group (CEJRG). Professor Riemer applies community psychology principles, theories, and tools to address issues related to sustainability, including global climate change mitigation and resiliency, with a special interest in engagement and promoting a culture of sustainability in organizations and communities. His contributions to the application of community psychology to global climate change and sustainability were recognized by the Society for Community Research and Action's Early Researcher Award.

Stephanie M. Reich is Professor in the School of Education, with additional appointments in Psychological Science and Informatics, at the University of California, Irvine. Trained as a community psychologist with an emphasis on child development and program evaluation, her research interests focus on child development with the explicit goals of understanding children's social lives and how to promote healthy development. The bulk of her work explores direct and indirect influences on the child, specifically through the family, peers, school, and media. She is the recipient of the Society for Community Research and Action's Early Researcher Award and the Distinguished Early Career Applied Contributions to Media Psychology and Technology Award. She is also an elected fellow of the American Psychological Association and the Society for Community Research and Action.

Scotney D. Evans is Associate Professor in the Department of Educational and Psychological Studies in the School of Education and Human Development at the University of Miami. He is a community-engaged researcher working to understand and support the role of community-based organizations, networks, and coalitions in building collective power to promote community well-being, social change, and social justice. Scot is the editor of the open-access journal *Collaborations: A Journal of Community-Based Research and Practice*.

Geoffrey Nelson is Professor Emeritus of Psychology at Wilfrid Laurier University. He served as Co-lead for the qualitative research for Canada's five-city At Home/Chez Soi Housing First study. Professor Nelson was the recipient of the McNeill Award for Innovation in Community Mental Health in 1999 and the award for Distinguished Contributions to Community Psychology Theory and Research in 2013, both from the Society for Community Research and Action of the American Psychological Association. His research has focused on housing, homelessness, community mental health, and prevention.

Isaac Prilleltensky is the former Dean of the School of Education and Human Development at the University of Miami, where he currently serves as Professor of Educational and Psychological Studies and Vice Provost for Institutional Culture. He is the recipient of the Distinguished Contribution to Theory and Research Award, the Seymour B. Sarason Award, and the John Kalafat Applied Community Psychology Award, all from the Division of Community Psychology of the American Psychological Association (APA). He is also the recipient of the Lifetime Achievement Award of the Prevention Section of the Division of Counseling Psychology of APA. He is interested in wellbeing, humor, mattering, and the relationship between wellness and fairness.

Contributing Authors

Ronnelle Carolissen is a clinical psychologist and Professor of Community Psychology in the Department of Educational Psychology, and also Vice-Dean (Teaching and Learning) in the Faculty of Education at Stellenbosch University, South Africa. Her research expertise and publications explore feminist social justice and critical community psychology perspectives on equity in higher education contexts. She has published numerous journal articles in these areas and is co-editor of three books: *Community, Self and Identity: Educating South African University Students for Citizenship* (HSRC Press, 2012), *Discerning Critical Hope in Educational Practices* (Routledge, 2013), and *Transforming Transformation in Teaching and Research in Higher Education* (2018).

Glynis Clacherty has worked for many years doing research with vulnerable children in eastern and southern Africa for a number of international and local NGOs such as UNICEF, UNHCR, Soul City, CARE, PLAN, and Save the Children. She teaches creative, qualitative research methodology and does qualitative research that uses an innovative arts-based approach that seeks to allow children, men, and women to share their lived experience in an ethical way. She is also a writer of educational material, children's books, and story texts.

Natasha Afua Darko is a second year Masters student in the Community Psychology program at Wilfrid Laurier University. Natasha is a Black cis female and the daughter of Ghanaian immigrants. Her experiences with anti-Black racism have shaped her personal and professional experiences. Her community work and research is focused primarily on health interventions for Black and racialized youth. Darko is deeply committed to anti-oppressive practices and inclusion.

Pat Dudgeon is from the Bardi people in Western Australia and works at the School of Indigenous Studies at the University of Western Australia. Her area of research includes Indigenous social and emotional wellbeing and suicide prevention. She is the director of the Centre of Best Practice in Aboriginal and Torres Strait Islander Suicide Prevention. She is also the lead chief investigator of a national research project, Generating Indigenous Patient-centred, Clinically and Culturally Capable Models of Mental Health Care, that aims to develop approaches to Indigenous mental health services that promote cultural values and strengths as well as empowering users.

Susan Eckerle is a knowledge broker at the Centre for Addiction and Mental Health in Toronto, Ontario. Susan's work focuses on the social determinants of mental health and addiction, and she has worked on projects including the Mental Health Commission of Canada's At Home/Chez Soi, Turning the Key, and Aspiring Workforce projects. Susan is passionate about social justice, health equity, and including the voice of people with lived experience in program and policy development and implementation.

Suzette Fromm Reed serves as Associate Professor, Founding Director/Chair of National Louis University's (NLU) PhD program in Community Psychology and research consultant to the Resilient Belmont Cragin Community Collaborative. Prior to NLU, she led research and evaluation for non-profit, child welfare organizations at both the national and local levels. She holds an MA in Clinical Psychology and a PhD in Psychology in the Public Interest. Her research, recent publications, and community trainings focus on the buffering role of community/organizational resilience between Adverse Childhood Experiences (ACEs) and mental and physical health, as well as academic and employment outcomes.

Marewa Glover is a Māori behavioral scientist and former Massey University Professor of Public Health. Marewa has led and collaborated on many studies resulting in over 100 scientific publications. Her dedication to reducing tobacco smoking harm and advocating for a harm reduction approach to smoking was recognized in 2019 when she was named one of three finalists in the prestigious New Zealander of the Year Award. In 2018, Marewa established her own *Centre of Research Excellence: Indigenous Sovereignty & Smoking*, which aims to reduce harms associated with tobacco use among Indigenous people worldwide. Elucidating the role of loss of sovereignty and the health implications of institutional racism is a key focus of her research.

Heather Gridley is an Honorary Fellow at Victoria University in Melbourne, Australia. Her interest in feminist and community psychology developed as she became increasingly aware of the limitations of interventions directed solely at individuals. Heather has held national positions in both the APS College of Community Psychologists and Women and Psychology Interest Group. After serving two terms on the APS Board of Directors, she took up a management role in the Public Interest domain of the national office. In 2019, she was awarded an Order of Australia Medal for services to community health.

Brianna Hunt is a white cisgender woman who calls Treaty 1 territory her home and currently resides on the traditional territory of the Anishinaabe, Wendat, and Haudenosaunee in Toronto, Ontario. As an uninvited visitor on Turtle Island, Hunt works to acknowledge, analyze, and navigate her privilege within her academic and community work. As a queer author, Hunt's reflexive practice involves ongoing inquiry into the ways that her own identity shapes her work toward meaningful allyship with communities of color. In addition to her scholarly work, Hunt works as a Program Coordinator within Toronto's non-profit sector.

Ingrid Huygens is a Pākehā (White) New Zealander of Dutch immigrant descent. Her PhD investigated the impact of education about the Treaty of Waitangi for non-Indigenous New Zealanders (University of Waikato, 2007). She co-authored the landmark report Ngāpuhi Speaks (2012) about Indigenous expectations of the treaty relationship with settler-colonisers, from evidence presented to a national Indigenous claims Tribunal. Ingrid is a registered community psychologist, and national coordinator for the Tangata Tiriti – Treaty People education program.

Rich Janzen is Co-Executive Director of the Centre for Community Based Research (CCBR), a non-profit social enterprise established in 1982 in Waterloo, Ontario, Canada. Rich has been involved in over 130 community-based research and knowledge mobilization projects at CCBR, leading both academically and non-academically funded studies. Increasingly he is helping community groups to build their own research and evaluation capacity, and training academics to do community-based research with excellence. Rich has an MA and PhD in Community Psychology and is adjunct associate professor at Renison University College at the University of Waterloo.

Judith A. Kent is Associate Professor and faculty in the Community Psychology doctoral and Psychology bachelors' programs at National Louis University (NLU) in Chicago. Previously, she had taught English as a foreign language and second language in Florence, Italy and at NLU, respectively. Language, culture, and identity is a focus of her research, specifically their correlation with persistence through higher education among Latino emerging adults. Currently a research consultant for Resilient Belmont Cragin Community Collaborative (RBCCC), Kent is also a

Collaborative steering committee member. She conducts research and training and has published on Adverse Childhood Experiences (ACEs) and community resilience.

Bret Kloos is Professor of Psychology and Clinical-Community Doctoral Program Director at the University of South Carolina. Along with students and community partners, his research and action have focused on housing issues for persons with psychiatric disabilities, social inclusion, and promoting mutual help approaches to mental health. A developing area of his work seeks to support community-based structures that sustain people's wellbeing and can address stigma and discrimination.

Mariah Kornbluh is a Critical Community Psychologist, and an Assistant Professor in Clinical-Community Psychology at the University of South Carolina. Her research focuses on involving young people and historically silenced groups (i.e. immigrants, housing insecure, etc.) in democratic processes to address health inequities. She utilizes mixed methods, participatory research, and network analysis to document and inform social change efforts. Her work has been published in numerous community psychology journal outlets (*American Journal of Community Psychology, Global Journal of Community Practice,* and *Journal of Community and Applied Social Psychology*) and book chapters (*Handbook of Methodological Approaches to Community-Based Research* and *Handbook of System Science*).

Thilo Kroll is Professor of Health Systems Management at University College Dublin (UCD). He has a PhD in Psychology and over 27 years of interdisciplinary research and academic experience. Before coming to Ireland, he was Professor of Disability and Public Health at University of Dundee and Co-Director of the interdisciplinary Social Dimensions of Health Institute (SDHI) of Universities of Dundee and St Andrews. He has conducted interdisciplinary research and published widely with a focus on disability- and health-related topics and inclusive methodologies across the life span in Germany, Norway, England, Scotland, the US, and Ireland. In his youth, he worked as an advocate for young people with arthritis. His PhD focused on social inclusion and school re-entry of children and adolescents with cancer in Germany. In the US, he worked with young people with spinal injuries surviving gun violence. He is passionate about the inclusion of seldom heard groups in co-designing and conducting research. Currently, he supports the implementation of Public and Patient Involvement in health and social care-related work at UCD and beyond as part of the HRB-funded PPI Ignite Initiative.

Fernando Lacerda Jr obtained his doctoral degree at Pontifical Catholic University of Campinas. He is an Associate Professor at the Faculty of Education/Federal University of Goiás, Brazil and has published papers about social movements, critical history of psychology, Marxism, political psychology, liberation psychology, and community psychology.

Kien S. Lee is Principal Associate and Vice President at Community Science, a research and development organization in Gaithersburg, Maryland. Kien provides organizations in the private, public, and nonprofit sectors with research, evaluation, and strategy development services in the areas of equity, inclusion, and cultural competency, as they pertain to issues such as health disparities, immigrant integration, food security, civic participation, leadership development, and community and systems change. Kien is recipient of the 2013 award for Distinguished Contributions to Practice in Community Psychology.

Monica Eviandaru Madyaningrum is a full-time lecturer at the Faculty of Psychology, Sanata Dharma University, Yogyakarta, Indonesia. Currently, she is the Course Coordinator for the undergraduate program. Her research and teaching interests include community empowerment, disability studies, and qualitative methodologies. In addition to her teaching roles, Monica is actively involved in a local disability organization in Yogyakarta which works with families of children with multiple disabilities. Monica studied Community Psychology at Victoria University, where she completed her PhD on disability organizations as empowering settings.

Lauren Munro is a PhD candidate in the Community Psychology program at Wilfrid Laurier University whose personal and professional life is driven by a commitment to social justice. She has collaborated on various projects related to LGBTQ2S+ communities, including research focused on microaggressions, sexual health and HIV vulnerability, Gay–Straight Alliances, and challenges facing LGBTQ2S+ immigrant and refugee youth. Lauren strongly believes in the importance of integrating academia and grassroots activism to create projects that challenge the status quo. Beyond her work on LGBTQ2S+ health, Lauren's research cuts across a variety of disciplines including Fat Studies, Mad Studies, and Disability Studies.

Leslea Peirson has a long history of designing, managing, conducting, and disseminating applied, multidisciplinary, community-based, and community-engaged research, evaluation, and demonstration projects focused on promoting and protecting child and family wellbeing. Her collaborators have included government agencies, organizations, service providers, service users and community groups that focus on mental health, developmental services, child welfare, income security, education, criminal justice, public health, and primary health care. Leslea also has expertise and experience in knowledge translation, evidence informed decision-making, systematic reviews, and enhancing system level capacity for the organization and delivery of health and social services.

Shauna Reddin obtained a Masters in Community Psychology from Wilfrid Laurier University in 2007, which prepared her for a career in research, evaluation, program development, and policy analysis for mental health, addiction services, and education programs in Canada's smallest province. She lives near the fictional home of Anne of Green Gables on a red dirt road with her husband and two daughters, and is enrolled in a doctorate in clinical psychology at the University of Prince Edward Island.

David Reville, now retired, taught Mad People's History for 11 years for the School of Disability Studies at Ryerson University in Toronto. His chapter in *Mad Matters: A Critical Reader in Canadian Mad Studies* (2013) edited by LeFrancois, Menzies and Reaume, poses the question "Is mad studies emerging as a new field of inquiry?" Currently, he's asking himself whether he is writing a memoir.

Mariolga Reyes Cruz is a Puerto Rican community psychologist, ethnographer, and documentarist engaged in efforts to build power for social and climate justice from a decolonial-ecosocialist-feminist perspective. She is particularly interested in a praxis that focuses on the social reproduction and contestation of social injustice; the coloniality of power, knowledge and being; and the transformation of the dominant political culture towards the common good. Mariolga holds a PhD in Community Psychology and Qualitative Inquiry from the University of Illinois, Urbana-Champaign. Her work has been published in peer-reviewed journals and magazines, book chapters, and a book on education organizing with undocumented immigrants. Mariolga and her partner produced an EMMY nominated series of 30 short documentaries on the sustainable agriculture movement in the archipelago of Puerto Rico and a documentary feature film. She has taught as contingent faculty at the University of Puerto Rico and is currently dedicated to grassroots work, writing, and raising her son.

James Rudyk Jr. is Executive Director of Northwest Side Housing Center (NWSHC) and Adjunct Faculty in the Department of Sociology, DePaul University. His work focuses on the intersections of race, equality, and community organizing and development. Since joining the NWSHC in 2012, James has helped the NWSHC grow from a small housing counseling agency to a nationally recognized two-million-dollar organization. James' academic interests relate to the role of community organizing in the creation and preservation of affordable housing and anti-gentrification housing movements.

Christiane Sadeler is the Executive Director of the Waterloo Region Crime Prevention Council (WRCPC), which is a partnership between community and local government for crime prevention through social development. Her passion, and by extension much of her work, is often focused on those who live at the margins of our communities. In working collaboratively with diverse service providers, grass roots groups, enforcement and justice services, and with all orders of government, Christiane shows a strong preference for community based solutions and upstream prevention approaches that challenge us to think about old problems in new ways.

Amandeep Kaur Singh is a PhD candidate in the Community Psychology program at Wilfrid Laurier University and the Lab Coordinator for the Access and Equity Research Interest Group supervised by Dr. Ciann L. Wilson. She is a South Asian (Punjabi-Sikh) cisgender woman, born and raised in Canada (Treaty 7). Her community and professional work focus on the experiences of racialized and marginalized communities in the access and accessibility of educational, cultural, and health services. She hopes to foster a collective space within her community and research for uplifting silenced voices in the opposition of White hegemonic narratives while recognizing the interconnected oppressions of racialized peoples and communities.

Tod Sloan served as Professor of Counseling Psychology at Lewis and Clark Graduate School for Education and Counseling in Portland, Oregon from 2004 to 2018. He identified professionally as a community psychologist and was an internationally-recognized advocate for critical psychology. He is the author of two books: *Life Choices: Understanding Dilemmas* and *Decisions and Damaged Life: The Crisis of the Modern Psyche*, and edited the book *Critical Psychology: Voices for Change*, a collection of reflections by critical psychologists on the relations between psychology and social change. Tod passed away in 2018.

Audrey Stillerman is Medical Director, School Health Centers, at the University of Illinois at Chicago (UIC). She is Clinical Assistant Professor in the UIC Department of Family Medicine; Acting Medical Director of PCC Community Wellness Center, Steinmetz High School; and Co-Founder of the Center for Collaborative Study of Trauma Health Equity and Neurobiology. Audrey is a double board certified Integrative Family Physician engaged in patient care, teaching, and advocacy for traditionally marginalized Chicagoans in public and private practice settings. Certified in the Child Trauma Academy's Neurosequential Model of Therapeutics, Audrey is committed to sharing the science regarding the impact of childhood experience on health and wellbeing across the lifespan to co-create strategies for prevention and healing in communities.

Robb Travers is an interdisciplinary social scientist with degrees in Psychology and Public Health Sciences. He is a Professor of Health Sciences at Wilfrid Laurier University and the Co-Director of the Social Inclusion and Health Equity Research Group. Dr. Travers maintains an active community-based research program that investigates discrimination/marginalization and its effects on the health and wellbeing of gender and sexual minorities. He is an advocate for community-based research as a tool of community empowerment and social change.

Colleen Turner is Operations Manager of programs at VICSEG New Futures, a not-for-profit organization providing support and training to refugee and other culturally diverse communities in Melbourne. Her career journey spans three decades in applied research and community-based practice, bridging the divides between activism, service provision, community development and social policy. Her work within the trade union sector, HIV and AIDS prevention and treatment, aged and disability services, migrant women's health, and family and children's services, indicates the breadth and grounded nature of her experience. Colleen also served a term on the APS Board as Director of Social Issues.

Sherine Van Wyk is a counseling psychologist and lecturer in the Department of Psychology at Stellenbosch University, South Africa. She teaches Critical Community Psychology and group interventions at an undergraduate and postgraduate level. She also supervises students in the Clinical Masters program who facilitate adolescent girls' groups as part of their community placements. Her research interests are adolescent femininities and masculinities, and adolescent girls' embodiment and friendships. In addition, she facilitates adolescent girls' groups in under-resourced communities on the Cape Flats in Cape Town.

Glen W. White has been involved in the rehabilitation and independent living field for over 30 years. Until his recent retirement, he directed the Research and Training Center on Independent Living at the University of Kansas, served as Principal Investigator of the NIDILRR-funded Research and Training Center on Community Living, and as Professor in the Department of Applied Behavioral Science at the University of Kansas. Dr. White has had numerous opportunities to work with consumers with disabilities in identifying, developing, and shaping on-going disability research. For the past several years he developed a systematic line of research in the area community participation of people with disabilities. Other research interests include prevention of secondary health conditions, and disaster planning and emergency response for people with disabilities. On an international level, Dr. White has conducted research and training activities in Korea, Japan and Vietnam, and prevention of secondary health conditions in Perú. He is past president of the National Association of Rehabilitation Research and Training Centers, and past chair of the American Public Health Association's Section on Disability. Dr. White currently serves as chair of the Advisory Board on Disability for Delta Air Lines.

Melissa L. Whitson is Associate Professor of Psychology at the University of New Haven, Coordinator of the Community Psychology MA program, and a licensed psychologist. Her research is on risk and protective factors, as well as service effectiveness, for low-income children and their families, with a particular focus on children who have been exposed to traumatic events. She also serves as an evaluation consultant for several youth-serving agencies and programs. Melissa supervises internships, mentors student research, and teaches undergraduate and graduate students in courses covering community psychology, research, counseling, child development, and consultation.

Ciann L. Wilson is Associate Professor in Community Psychology at Wilfrid Laurier University. Ciann is of Afro-, Indo- and Euro-Jamaican ancestry. Her research interests build off her community-engaged work to include critical race theory, anti-/de-colonial theory, African diasporic and Indigenous community health, sexual and reproductive wellbeing, and community-based research approaches. Her body of work aims to utilize research as an avenue for sharing the stories and realities of African diasporic, Indigenous, and racialized peoples and improving the health and wellbeing of these communities.

Preface

Welcome to the third edition of *Community Psychology: In Pursuit of Liberation and Wellbeing*! We are glad you found your way to this book about our unique field of research, learning, and action that we, as authors and editors, are excited to share with you. This third edition represents a transition in the authorship team and with that change come new perspectives and ideas from a different generation of community psychologists. Thus, we begin this preface by introducing the extended team. We then talk about the people for whom this book is intended, that is, you (hopefully). Following that, we share our goals for the book and conclude with an overview of its structure.

About Us

While the general idea of a textbook like this is to provide an introduction to and overview of a specific field or topic area, the way that is done is very much influenced by the people who write and/or edit the book. Thus, before we introduce our goals and the way we organized this book, we would like to introduce our team. This introduction is started by Geoff and Isaac, the original authors of the first two editions, who have invited Manuel, Stephanie, and Scot to join them for this third edition.

The Old Guard

Geoff. My concern with social justice came at an early age from my mother and father, and I became active in social justice work when I attended the University of Illinois as an undergraduate from 1968 to 1972. This was the era of the Vietnam War and I was involved in anti-war protests. I was in the first class of students to take a new course in community psychology (CP) introduced by Julian Rappaport. Sometimes people take a university course that makes a lifelong impression and serves as a turning point in their life journey. That's what happened to me. This course brought together my interests in psychology, mental health, and working with people and my views about politics and the need for social change. I obtained a PhD in Clinical-Community Psychology from the University of Manitoba, which included a one-year internship at the Mendota Mental Health Institute, a very progressive, community-oriented and research-oriented program in Madison, Wisconsin. I moved to Kitchener-Waterloo, Ontario in 1979 to take a faculty position in a CP program at Wilfrid Laurier University. This position was a very good "fit" for me. I had the good fortune to work with colleagues and graduate students in CP and community members, with whom I share many values, experiences and interests. I was able to pursue my research and action interests in community mental health, housing, and prevention – some of the main areas of focus of CP. After 38 years at Laurier, I recently retired. But I continue to be involved in social justice work locally and in other parts of Canada.

Over the past two decades, I have become increasingly concerned about growing economic inequality and the degradation of the natural environment through climate change. These larger global issues are having an enormous impact on the issues, people, and interventions that are the concern of CP. I believe that education about these issues, civic participation, and political action must become part of the mainstream of CP.

Isaac. I was born in Argentina and grew up during turbulent times. There was constant and consistent persecution of social and political activists and there was marked anti-Semitism. As a young Jewish boy I remember going to school and reading graffiti on walls imploring fellow Argentinians "To be a patriot, kill a Jew." I joined a Zionist Socialist youth movement from a young age. We were taught how to decipher the news and the media and to become political actors in a highly charged environment. My sister was one of the people who were made to "disappear" by the military dictatorship. Luckily, she was one of the very few people who ended up in exile and not killed or thrown from an airplane into the Atlantic.

I lost my parents when I was eight years old and spent a lot of my time with friends in the youth movement. We discussed politics, injustice, and the fate of some of our friends and relatives who were "disappeared." I emigrated to Israel in 1976 with a group of friends. Paradoxically, I had a couple of very quiet years while I was finishing high school there. Compared to Argentina, Israel was an oasis of peace and quiet. I met Ora, my wife, during my MA studies and we moved together to Canada. In Winnipeg, our port of landing, I completed a PhD at the University of Manitoba and worked for the Child Guidance Clinic of Winnipeg for six years. Upon completion of my PhD, I joined the faculty of the Community Psychology program at Wilfrid Laurier University, where I worked for nine years. I moved with my family to Melbourne, Australia, in 1999, and then to Nashville, Tennessee in 2003. In 2006 I became Dean of the School of Education and Human Development at the University of Miami, where we established three programs in community psychology, an undergraduate program called Human and Social Development, a master's program in Community and Social Change, and a PhD program in Community Wellbeing. I stepped down from the deanship in 2017 and since then I have been serving as Vice Provost for Institutional Culture at the University of Miami and have gone back to teaching, which I love.

The New Guard

After completing the first two editions of this text, we [Geoff and Isaac] decided it was time to inject new blood into the next edition. We asked three terrific junior colleagues to assume the primary responsibility for putting together the third edition – Manuel, Stephanie, and Scot. Isaac knew these three when they were graduate students in the Community Psychology program that Isaac directed at Vanderbilt University, and Geoff had met them all as well. Furthermore, Geoff had the good fortune of working directly with Scot and Manuel in their first academic positions at Wilfrid Laurier University. Now all three are tenured Associate or Full Professors and each is already making substantial contributions to community psychology. We are delighted that they took up our invitation to revise this text.

As the new guard, it has been a daunting task for us [Manuel, Stephanie, and Scot] to step into the giant shoes of Geoff and Isaac, two of the most influential community psychologists of our time. But, being able to shape this book is a privilege that we could not pass up. The book had such a critical impact in our field and has influenced the understanding of community psychology for so many of us. It has been a long journey and steep learning curve and we are glad to finally be able to share the product of the last few years with you. But first, we will share a little bit about who we are.

Manuel. As a White, cisgender, straight, able-bodied male of European descent who grew up in one of the wealthiest countries in the world (Germany) with a fantastic and accessible healthcare and free educational system, I have lived an extremely privileged life. But, from early on, my parents and teachers have instilled a strong value for social justice and social responsibility in me. My parents' generation grappled with the recent horrible past of Nazi Germany and tried to find ways of raising our and following generations in a way that ensured that something like that would never happen again. I remember very vividly learning about the resistance movement during the Nazi regime. The courage these people showed to stand up against extreme forms of injustice, even if they could pay with their lives for speaking out (many of whom did), motivated me to become engaged with social justice causes myself and find a way to contribute to social change.

When I was 19, I moved to New York City to volunteer for 18 months as a children's counselor for the afterschool program in a domestic violence shelter in the South Bronx. Through this experience I matured very quickly and my eyes were opened to the level of inequality, injustice, and racism that could exist within one of the wealthiest countries in the world. It was a true culture shock. This experience drew me to study Kritische Psychologie (Critical Psychology) at the Free University of Berlin.

In 2000, I moved back to the US to pursue a Masters and PhD degree in psychology (Quantitative Methods of Psychology and CP) at Vanderbilt University in Nashville. This is where I met Isaac, Stephanie, and Scot and, at some point, also Geoff. In 2006, I saw a film about the looming climate change crisis, *An Inconvenient Truth* by Al Gore. When I watched that film, it became suddenly clear to me there is currently no greater and more urgent threat to social justice and wellbeing than this crisis. This started my activism (first working for Al Gore's climate change team) and research focus on climate change and sustainability and advocacy for this issue within community psychology. Since 2008, I have been Professor of CP and Sustainability Science at Wilfrid Laurier University and had the privilege to work alongside and learn from Geoff. After six years as the director of the Centre for Community Research, Learning, and Action, I am now directing the new Viessmann Centre for Engagement and Research in Sustainability, which is focused on fostering cultures of sustainability and sustainability justice.

Stephanie. My parents, in their late adolescence, found themselves unexpectedly pregnant and decided to give marriage a try. This was beneficial to me, as I was the second of three children born from that short union. Having such young parents taught me some very valuable lessons. First, I learned to place high importance on education. I watched my parents struggle to be the first in their families to earn a college degree. Juggling work, school, and children, my parents stressed the importance of learning and the opportunities that education affords. While it was clear that there were no financial resources for school, there was an expectation that I would go to college no matter what. It was a privilege of expectation and hope for the future that none of my cousins seemed to share. Second, I learned to value family. As my daily care often involved grandparents and other extended family, I was raised to value family connections and to see individual processes as collective struggles and successes. It is this family-strengths orientation that I bring to all my studies with families and programs that serve them. Third, I learned to see culture as a strength and challenge. I spent much of my early years with my paternal grandparents, both Hungarian immigrants and holocaust survivors. From them, I learned to value our family's language, food, and traditions, as well as exercise caution with whom we shared our Jewish-Hungarian roots. This awareness of difference was reified by my father's strong belief that his children act

"American" and not suffer the hardships he endured not knowing English and having to adjust to two countries (Australia and US). Thus, I began to appreciate how one's culture can simultaneously engender feelings of closeness and isolation.

Given these early experiences, it is no surprise that I chose to pursue a high level of education and to work in an educational setting that enables me to partner with communities and support children and their families. I grew up in California, attending college at the University of California, Los Angeles. After a few years of international travel and work, I returned to the US to pursue my PhD at Vanderbilt University, where I met Isaac, Manuel, and Scot, and eventually Geoff. In 2007, I took a job at the University of California, Irvine, where I have the pleasure of working with a very diverse student body. My research is dedicated to identifying, shaping, and improving the social context of children's lives. Most often I do this work with families, schools, and digital spaces.

Scotney. All I really ever wanted to do was play in a band. Never in a million years would I have imagined, as a young student in high school and college, that I would one day have a PhD in Community Psychology and be a tenured professor, teacher, mentor, and researcher at the University of Miami. You see, for a good part of my early adult life, I was a bass player, harmony vocalist, and writer/arranger (driver, cook, bookkeeper, musician wrangler) for a touring rock and roll band. After completing my undergraduate degree in music theory, I spent all of my 20s and part of my 30s in a Ford Club Wagon with two other long-haired dudes driving around the US to perform at festivals, concert halls, night clubs, and college campuses (I like how I made that sound glamorous). And when we weren't touring, we were in the studio writing songs and making records (before vinyl was cool). That was the life! All of my earthly belongings could fit into the trunk of a car. I was broke as dirt, but happy. So who am I and how did I get *here*?

When my professional music career slowed and I found myself at home in Nashville, Tennessee more often, I began volunteering at a youth organization that served runaway and homeless youth. I answered the crisis line, helped with shelter operations, and later was hired full-time as a coordinator for a youth peer education program. Mind you, I had no real training or credentials whatsoever for this gig, but they saw something in me that made them take a chance. This experience opened the door to the second phase of my adult life where music became my hobby (and side hustle) and research and teaching became my vocation.

I too am a White, cisgender, straight, able-bodied male of European descent. For all of my life, I have benefitted from patriarchy, White privilege, and the White supremacy culture of organizations and institutions. In my late 30s, I decided to get my master's degree in Human Development Counseling at Vanderbilt University while also working full time at the youth shelter. I had no interest in a PhD until I met a community psychologist named Bob Newbrough who introduced me to a little thing called action research after I somehow made it through a master's program never hearing of such a thing. Intrigued, I returned to Vanderbilt for my PhD in Community Research and Action where I met Manuel, Stephanie, and Isaac. Post PhD I had the incredible privilege to get my first academic job at Wilfrid Laurier University in 2006 where I had the opportunity to work closely with Geoff. I've been at the University of Miami for 12 years now and still feel like an imposter. I've grown to dislike much of what goes on in academia – the crushing workload, power dynamics, student debt, increasing neoliberal influence, etc. – but gain energy and inspiration from the incredible students I get to learn from every day.

About You

Many of you reading this book are students in a course in Community Psychology (CP) for which this book is the assigned text. Welcome to CP! We hope you find not just information and wisdom from what you read, but also inspiration and maybe even personal transformation. As we will argue throughout the book, being a community psychologist goes beyond the boundaries of our universities and work places into the way we act in our personal lives. Thus, this book will not only provide you with a thorough introduction to CP but also with many opportunities for personal reflection.

You may also be in a course or program in a related field, such as social work, social justice studies, public health, or education. An increasing number of community psychologists are working and teaching in these areas that share values and core theories with CP, just like Stephanie. CP is a very interdisciplinary field due to its ecological framing and has a lot to learn from, but also contribute to, these other disciplines. With this new edition, we specifically had you in mind.

Others of you reading the book are experienced community psychologists who are contemplating whether or not to adopt this book as a text for a course. We hope this book suits your needs. As you will see, we are introducing some topics and perspectives that are a little different from other CP texts. Yet we have tried to balance these new topics and perspectives with a faithful adherence to the roots and core concepts that have guided the field. We have also put effort towards capturing some of the more recent and diverse developments in CP. We hope you find our perspective and the topics covered to be valuable and re-invigorating.

And last but not least, there is everybody else. Maybe you are considering CP as an area of study and want to get an idea what this field is about, or you are preparing yourself for advanced studies and want a good review of the core theories, or you are a practitioner who is interested in reviewing the latest developments in this field. We certainly had you in mind as our target audience for this book as well.

The Goals of the Book

As the world is becoming increasingly complex and the human-caused crises are producing increasingly negative impacts on the wellbeing of people and our planet, the need for a field that has an ecological framing at its core and a strong value base in social justice, anti-oppression, and wellbeing has never been more critical. Crises are also opportunities for significant social transformations. We need people who are able to make the connection between individual needs and psychological experiences and larger political, economic, and cultural developments. We also need people who are committed to social justice and the promotion of wellbeing and want to hone their skills in working with diverse communities in pursuing a society that is fair and provides conditions under which everybody can thrive. Since its inception, CP, unlike other sub-disciplines of psychology, has been motivated by a set of values (Rappaport, 1977) and scientific evidence. Thus, our first goal with this book is to share with you how CP, as a field, is navigating the complexity of the issues it is dealing with, how our values drive a rigorous scientific enterprise, and how our theories and research findings provide guidance to the important applied and practical work that many of us are engaging in.

We have also been concerned that in its research and practice, CP has focused more on personal and relational values, such as wellbeing and collaboration, than on collective values, such as social justice and transformation. This is reflected in the theory, research and action base of CP. Thus, a second goal of the book is to re-invigorate the discussion of social injustice and the need for social action and social change. We want to inject critical, liberation, and human rights perspectives into CP, perspectives that have coalesced into critical and liberation psychology as well as a call for a critical community psychology (Evans, Duckett, Lawthom, & Kivell, 2017; Fox, Prilleltensky & Austin, 2009; Kagan et al., 2011; Prilleltensky & Nelson, 2002; Watts & Serrano-García, 2003). More explicitly, we want to advance a CP that is critical of the status quo and that actively pursues social justice and the reduction of inequities in power and resources in its theory, research, and action. Part and parcel of this social justice agenda is situating CP, the problems it studies and the interventions it pursues, in the larger context of global capitalism and the increased power of transnational corporations. With this third edition, we emphasize considerations of power at multiple ecological levels even more explicitly and strongly than we have in previous editions. This is reflected in a new chapter specifically focused on power, empowerment, and depowerment as well as discussions of power related to most issues discussed in this book.

A third goal of the book is to provide a text with an international perspective, drawing upon the work of community psychologists, allied professionals, and community activists from around the world (Reich, Riemer, Prilleltensky, & Montero, 2007). We have experience as CP academics inside and outside the US. We have constructed a book that can be used as a text, not just in the US, but in Canada, the UK, South Africa, Australia and New Zealand, and perhaps even in other parts of the world. We have done this by including examples of work done in many different countries and by including chapter authors and commentators from countries around the world. The chapter authors and practice commentators come from a variety of countries including Australia, Canada, Germany, Indonesia, Ireland, New Zealand, Puerto Rico (which, if not colonized, would be a country), South Africa, the UK and the US. One limitation of the book is that there is limited coverage of Africa, Asia, and Latin and South America, where much of the world lives. This reflects the state of the field, as CP as a formal field of study is only in its formative stages of development in some continents and language can serve as a barrier in others. We believe that the diversity of contexts, viewpoints and experiences of community psychologists from around the globe provides a rich base from which to learn.

A fourth goal of the book is to emphasize the reflexive and subjective nature of the field as well as the increased presence of voices from CP practitioners. There is a danger when well-respected academic authors write a book, that students and others will take what is written as gospel, when in fact the views of authors are shaped by their location and historical context and should be open to scrutiny, critique, and alternative viewpoints. Towards this end, many of the chapters in the first part of this book include a commentary written by practitioners from different parts of the world. Our intention with these commentaries was to incorporate diverse voices and viewpoints into the book and provide examples of how the topics and theoretical frameworks presented in these chapters are applied in practice. Also, the construction of the book was designed to include many voices. We wrote the first half of the book (Chapters 1–13) to provide the reader with a common framework regarding the foundations of CP, while the second half of the book (Chapters 14–21) was written by contributing authors. When possible, these chapters were co-written by both senior and junior community psychologists and/or authors from different countries to capture different perspectives within each chapter.

Another goal was to make this book accessible to a broad audience and relevant to current issues that concern many of us in the contemporary context. For that reason, we introduce three important social issues in the first chapter that serve as illustrative examples for the application of the different topics, theories, and issues addressed in the remainder of the book. These issues are affordable housing and homelessness, global climate change and sustainability, and immigration. Including these three issues does not imply that they are more important than other issues community psychologists concern themselves with. They were selected because they connect well to many of the issues and theories covered in this book. Other issues have full chapters devoted to them in the second half of the book. Sadly, given space concerns, we could not include more targeted topics – as there are many that CP addresses.

Community psychology is also a field that is going through interesting transitions. CP originally emerged across the world as a critical response to the shortcomings of mainstream approaches in psychology (Reich et al., 2007). Now, several decades later, mainstream psychology looks different and CP also has transcended the boundaries of psychology. New approaches (e.g., community-based participatory research) and areas of study (e.g., social justice studies and applied social psychology) have emerged that share a lot of values and theoretical frameworks with CP. As mentioned previously, many people trained in CP now work and teach in these related areas rather than in CP programs within psychology departments. This development blurs the boundaries of CP as a (sub-)discipline and with that its identity. Therefore, our final goal for this book was to be considerate of this professional shift and write the book in a way that makes it relevant to both those who work within traditional CP programs and those who work outside of those types of settings. For that reason, we have also strived to bring an interdisciplinary emphasis to the book. While most of the authors of the chapters are community psychologists, all the authors draw their sources from many different disciplines. Thus, this book is as much an introduction to a discipline as it is a guide and source for reflection for community-engaged researchers and practitioners who are interested in contributing to transformative change towards optimal conditions of social justice in which all people can thrive.

The Structure of the Book

We designed the book to provide a thorough introduction to a variety of core concepts, theoretical frameworks, and different types of interventions, research, and social issues with which community psychologists engage. With that, we tried to capture some of the classic discussions within our field as well as some of the more recent developments. The book has four major parts, which we briefly describe in the following section.

Part I (Chapters 1–7) provides a detailed introduction to some of the most important and commonly referenced theoretical frameworks and concepts in CP. We also present a review of the general framing (Chapter 1), history (Chapter 2), and core values (Chapter 3) of our field. Chapter 4 contains the detailed discussion of issues related to power, depowerment, and empowerment. Chapter 5 is devoted to theoretical and practical considerations related to system transformation, an important aim for many community psychologists. This chapter includes a review of ecological thinking and the ecological model, which are core to CP framing of social issues. There also have been some exciting theoretical developments in this area over the last several years, which we have tried to capture in this chapter. In Chapter 6, we explore the classic concepts of prevention, promotion, and social change and how they relate to the distinction between ameliorative and transformative change toward wellbeing and thriving. Chapter 7 then is focused on questions related to community, networks, social capital, and sense of community, which are all defining aspects of our field. Together, these seven chapters provide the historical–theoretical foundation upon which the following chapters build.

The details of the following chapters are introduced at the beginning of each respective part. Here, we provide only a very broad overview. Part II (Chapters 8–11) is focused on different aspects of interventions that community psychologists may engage with, including social and community, organizational, and group and individual-level interventions. Part III (Chapters 12 & 13) is a review of the historical-political context and the practice of community-engaged research. Finally, in Part IV (Chapters 14–21) our contributing authors share their insights about some of the most common social issues community psychologists engage with, which provide a good starting point and directions for diving deeper into each of these issues.

We do not claim that our book's introduction to CP does justice to the richness of this field, which has now been in existence for many decades but is also continuing to evolve, including exciting developments around the world (see Chapter 2). We can think of CP as a journey. In putting this book together, we have strived not only to tell the story of where CP comes from and where it is now, but also where we believe it should be headed. Thus, we think of this book as a "work in progress," rather than a definitive statement. We are now inviting you to join us on this journey.

Note to Instructors and Students

A range of teaching and learning resources can be found on this book's companion website: https://www.bloomsburyonlineresources.com/community-psychology-3e. Lecturers can obtain a sample of multiplechoice, short-answer, and essay questions for each of the chapters in this text. We have also prepared exercises for students that can be used in class.

Manuel Riemer
Stephanie M. Reich
Scotney D. Evans
Geoffrey Nelson
Isaac Prilleltensky

Acknowledgements

Manuel, Stephanie, and Scot, first of all, thank Geoff and Isaac for giving us the opportunity to build upon the great work they have done with the first two editions. Having worked on this third edition certainly made us appreciate the amount of effort, time, knowledge, and wisdom those two have put into this book. We are grateful for the guidance, mentorship, and support they have provided to us throughout this process.

We are appreciative of the encouragement, enthusiasm, and guidance of Luke Block and Verity Rimmer, our editors for the third edition. We are also thankful for the guidance and support provided by Paul Stevens and Stephanie Farano, who worked with us during the first phase of this edition, as well as Frances Arnold and Andrew McAleer, the editors for the first edition, and Jamie Joseph, the editor for the second edition.

We would also like to thank all of our contributors of the different chapters and commentaries. One of the strengths of this book is the different voices that are represented from different parts of the world. We greatly value your contributions. We would like to specifically acknowledge Tod Sloan, who is the lead author for Chapter 14 on globalization and poverty. Tod died during the process of finishing the book. He is remembered by us and many others as a true critical community psychologist and change agent who lived his social justice values not only in his work but also in his life, especially through his advocacy and action for social change. He was also a terrific person and delightful to have a great conversation with and a good laugh over a bottle of wine. Tod, you are missed.

Thank you also to the students and staff who helped us with literature reviews, compiling of references, and editing, including Brittany Spadafore, Jillian Zitars, Jovan Poposki, Stephanie Whitney, Leigh Rauk, Ignacio Barrenecha, and Ela Desmarchelier. We would also like to thank the students in the community psychology program at Wilfrid Laurier University and the external reviewers who have provided us with valuable feedback.

Finally, we would like to thank our partners and families who have been very patient as we have spent many early mornings, evenings, and weekends working to bring this book to completion. We are very appreciative of your support.

The publisher and authors would like to thank the organizations and people listed below for permission to reproduce material from their publications:

American Psychological Association
Angus Maguire
Australian Institute of Family Studies
Canadian Scholars' Press
Center for Story-Based Strategy
Global Fund for Women
Institute of Development Studies
International Women's Development Agency
Joe Mills

Joel Pett
John Wiley & Sons
Judy Horacek
McGraw Hill Higher Education
Oxford University Press
SAGE
Springer Nature
Steve Kelley
Young Lives

FRAMING COMMUNITY PSYCHOLOGY: HISTORY, VALUES, AND KEY CONCEPTS

COMMUNITY PSYCHOLOGY
RESEARCH AND ACTION FOR SOCIAL CHANGE AND WELLBEING

Warm-up Questions

Before you begin reading this chapter, we invite you to reflect on the following questions:

1 What motivated you to learn about community psychology (CP)?

2 What are some of your core values?

3 What are current social issues you care about? Is there any issue you feel especially passionate about? Reflect on why is it that you care about this specific issue. What are the kinds of things that you would like to see changed in regard to this issue? How could you possibly contribute to that change?

Learning Objectives

The goal of this chapter is to provide you with an introduction to CP. While CP is a distinct field with professional societies, graduate programs, practitioners, and textbooks, it is also a specific way of thinking about the world. This chapter will introduce you to that way of thinking so that you know what to expect as you embark on the journey through this book. Chapter 2 will provide you with an overview of how CP developed as a distinct field.

In this chapter you will learn about

- How CP can be defined
- Some key features of CP
- How community psychologists frame social issues using three examples:
  1 Immigration
  2 Homelessness and stable housing
  3 Environmental sustainability

Introduction to Community Psychology

Welcome to community psychology (CP)! Many students of CP find their way to this academic (sub-) discipline and field of practice from different and often complex paths. Maybe you are interested in psychological questions but are dissatisfied with the way psychology conceptualizes and deals with certain issues. Or, perhaps you value the balancing of theory, research, and action and are attracted by the combination of science and practice. It could also be that you are interested in one of the many critical social issues that community psychologists focus on, such as community mental health, immigration, or the rights of those who do not fit common sex and gender norms. Whatever the reason for studying CP, the goal of this chapter and the rest of this book is to get you excited about this vibrant field.

So, what is CP? A good starting point in understanding CP is the vision and mission of the Division of Community Psychology of the American Psychological Association, the Society for Community Research and Action (SCRA). SCRA's vision is to have a "strong, global impact on enhancing wellbeing and promoting social justice for all people by fostering collaboration where there is division and empowerment where there is oppression." SCRA's mission describes the organization as "devoted to advancing theory, research, and social action. Its members are committed to promoting health and empowerment and to preventing problems in communities, groups, and individuals" (Society for Community Research and Action, n.d.).

In one of the first CP textbooks, Julian Rappaport (1977) argued that CP is difficult to define precisely because it is more of a new paradigm, perspective, or way of thinking than a distinct and fixed entity. In discussing what CP is, Rappaport wrote about its ecological nature (the fit between people and their environments), attention to cultural relativity and diversity ("an attempt to support every person's right to be different without risk of suffering material and psychological sanctions," p. 1) and focus on social change ("toward a maximally equitable distribution of psychological as well as material resources," p. 3). Moreover, Rappaport (1977) argued that CP is concerned with human resource development, political activity and scientific inquiry, three elements that are often in conflict with one another.

UK community psychologists Mark Burton and Carolyn Kagan provide a useful and relatively comprehensive definition of CP:

> Community psychology offers a framework for working with those marginalised by the social system that leads to self-aware social change with an emphasis on value-based, participatory work and the forging of alliances. It is a way of working that is pragmatic and reflexive, whilst not wedding to any particular orthodoxy of method. As such, community psychology is one alternative to the dominant individualistic psychology typically taught and practised in the high-income countries. It is *community* psychology because it emphasises a level of analysis and intervention other than the individual and their immediate interpersonal context. It is community *psychology* because it is nevertheless concerned with how people feel, think, experience, and act as they work together, resisting oppression and struggling to create a better world. (Burton & Kegan, n.d. Cited in Burton, Boyle, Harris & Kagan, 2007, p. 219)

The name "community psychology" suggests that it is a sub-discipline of psychology and Kagan and Burton provide a good explanation of how the two are linked. As hinted above, many scholars and practitioners of CP, however, are not connected to psychological departments. You, reading this book, may not be a student in a psychology program. Thus, just as Rappaport suggested 40 years ago, it is best to consider CP a perspective or way of thinking that brings people together who share some key values that are applied in their research and action. With this book, we want to provide you with an opportunity to learn this way of thinking so that you feel comfortable in applying it in your own research and action.

Further, below we will provide you with some examples of how community psychologists approach three current issues: immigration; homelessness and stable housing; and environmental sustainability. Before we explore these issues, however, it is useful to first provide you with an introduction to some of the key assumptions and practices of CP that you will find present in the discussion of the three social issues (see Table 1.1 for an overview). Please note that each of these concepts will be elaborated in the following chapters of this book.

First, CP is a value-driven field (see Chapter 3). Our *values* of social justice, wellbeing and respect for diversity, for example, influence what issues we focus on (such as those three social issues mentioned above), how we frame those issues, and how we work with affected communities in addressing those issues through research, learning, and action. We use the values as guidelines for our work and critically reflect on an ongoing basis to what degree our actions align with those values. Many people find their way to CP because they share these values and find it important that those values be reflected in their work in academia or in practice. You may be one of them.

By *framing*, we refer to the main ideas or stories that provide meaning to certain events and issues (Gamson & Modigliani, 1987; Pan & Kosicki, 1993). In other words, how do we, as professionals and academics, classify, organize, and interpret the issues with which we are dealing. People experiencing homelessness with mental health challenges, for example, can be viewed either as citizens or community members with rights or as the objects of custodial care or professional intervention (Nelson & MacLeod, 2017). The way issues are framed (e.g., focused on the individual rather than ecological factors in the broader context) has a big impact on how these issues are investigated and interventions developed (e.g., targeted at the individual level or the community level, done to individuals or with individuals). We return to the concept of framing in more detail in Chapter 6.

Table 1.1 Framing and practices of community psychology

Framing and Practices	Community Psychology
Guiding principles	Key values such as social justice, wellbeing, and respect for diversity
Levels of analysis	Ecological (individual, relational, community/organizations, macro)
Problem definition	Problems are framed in terms of social context, cultural diversity, and social power
Approach to addressing social issues	Emphasis on transformative social change, prevention, and promotion of competencies, strengths, and self-determination, collaborative
Types of intervention	Multilevel, policy change, self-help, community development, social action
Role of professional	Resource collaborator (scholar-activist)
Research	Applied and action-oriented, focused on impact on social issues, participatory, community-based, diversity of methods
Ethics	Emphasis on social ethics, emancipatory values, self-determination, and social change

Source: Adapted from Nelson & Prilleltensky (2010).

CP is also the study of people and context. There is a holistic, *ecological analysis* of the person within multiple social systems, ranging from micro-systems (e.g., the family) to macro-sociopolitical structures (e.g., racism, income inequality). There is a strong belief that people cannot be understood apart from their context, nor can contexts be understood apart from the influence of people. When problems are defined in terms of individualistic conceptions of human nature, this can lead to a stance of "blaming the victim" (Ryan, 1971). Whether intentional or not, victim blaming is a practice that holds individuals responsible for the causes and solutions to their problems. However, when problems are reframed in terms of their social context and seen as arising from degrading social conditions, this tendency of blaming individuals is reduced (Caplan & Nelson, 1973). A focus on racism in the context of immigration challenges, or on housing policies in the context of homelessness, are examples of this contextual and ecological way of framing social issues. Chapter 5 provides an introduction to the *ecological model*, which is a key guiding theoretical framework for community psychologists.

Community psychologists emphasize the importance of considering *social power* in understanding root causes of social issues as well as in finding fair and empowering solutions. Predominately White, wealthy, and well-connected communities, for example, are able to use their social power to prevent toxic industry from settling in close proximity to their community, while marginalized and racialized communities have less power and resources to do that. Working with immigrant groups to develop social capital can help them to empower themselves to take more control over those factors that affect their wellbeing. Power and empowerment are important concepts in CP that are discussed in greater detail in Chapter 4.

Moreover, CP's approach to addressing individual problems and social issues is to focus on the relevant contextual factors with an emphasis on *transformative social change* and *prevention*. This often requires developing strong and effective collaborations among members of different disciplines, professions, and societal sectors (e.g., university, government, and community organizations). Community psychologists also aim to promote the *strengths* of people living in adverse conditions as well as the strengths of communities, rather than focusing on individual or community "deficits" (Rappaport, 1977). Focusing on problems puts people in a subordinate position to whoever is making such a categorization or diagnosis and suggests that they need monitoring and correction, whereas focusing on strengths enables people to build upon their pre-existing resources, capacities, and talents. In addition, there is an emphasis on developing new *capacities* among individuals and communities (e.g., capacity to advocate for yourself). In regard to the types of interventions and action, CP has a goal of promoting competence and wellbeing through self-help, consciousness-raising, community development, and social and political action. From a CP perspective, behavior is not viewed as maladaptive. People are viewed as adapting in the best ways they can to oppressive and stressful conditions. CP emphasizes active *participation*, choice, and *self-determination* of the participants in any intervention, assuming that people know best what they need and that active participation in individual and collective change is healthy and desirable. Community psychologists eschew the traditional role of the helper as the "expert" who knows best and who is well versed in the science and practice of assessment, diagnosis and treatment. Instead, community psychologists typically function as resources and collaborators, who bring both science and social activism to their community work.

Research in CP is not conducted just for the sake of developing new knowledge; research is conducted to create knowledge and change social conditions. As such, research in CP tends to be applied and action-oriented. Since most community psychologists do not believe in the "expert" approach of some traditional fields, community stakeholders often participate in the creation of knowledge, and in some cases are the key drivers of the research while the university or center-based researcher serves as a resource in the research process. Furthermore, the complexity of the issues CP research is trying to address and the nature of the questions that guide the research requires knowledge and application of a diversity of methods, as we will discuss in more detail in Chapters 12 and 13. Traditionally, the ethics of social science research is focused on the individual research participant and emphasize values such as informed consent, confidentiality, and lack of coercion. CP also abides by such individual ethics, but it goes further to consider social ethics (O'Neill 2005a, b) and values that promote social justice. Traditional psychology, for example, often claims to be "value neutral" when it comes to social ethics, but such a position often provides tacit acceptance of unjust social conditions. Community psychologists also consider potential negative implications of their research for the target community, such as when negative stereotypes about racialized groups are re-emphasized through research.

Finally, the emphasis on complex multilevel interventions and research questions and collaborative approaches naturally leads community psychologists to develop interdisciplinary ties with a variety of fields and professions, especially those with critical perspectives in a range of social and health science and humanities disciplines that focus on the interface between people and social environments (Davidson et al., 2006). There are many commonalities with other disciplines that motivate many community psychologists to work within allied fields such as public health, education, social work, urban studies, and anthropology to name just a few. When community psychologists do work in these related areas, they often contribute a specific perspective of looking at social issues and developing complex solutions that are informed by their CP background.

Three Illustrative Social Issues

While what we have described above may resonate with you in general, it may also be quite new for you to think in these terms, especially if you come from disciplines such as psychology, which often frame social issues in different ways. In the following chapters we will elaborate on these concepts in more detail. Also, in order to help you to see how all of these concepts are linked with each other, we have selected three different social issues that community psychologists have been working on. These issues are: immigration, homelessness and stable housing, and climate change and environmental sustainability. These three topics were selected as illustrative examples to help make theories, values, and practices more concrete throughout the book and help you link concepts from different chapters together. This does not mean, however, that these issues are more central or important than any of the many other social issues community psychologists are trying to address in their work. As we elaborate some of the important CP concepts, theories, and practices we will refer to some of these other issues. Additionally, some of the later chapters will feature some of those issues in greater detail.

As we introduce you to these three illustrative social issues, we use CP as a lens with which to view them. This includes how the issues are framed and how some of our field's core values influence the work we do as well as what approaches and methods we use to understand and address these issues. The main purpose of this section is to briefly introduce each of these three social issues using a CP way of framing. We will come back to each of these issues throughout the book to illustrate some of the core concepts, values, and theories of CP and to demonstrate how community psychologists conduct research and develop intervention for these and similar social issues.

Social Issue I: Immigration

Case 1: Isaac (Uganda/Italy)

Isaac, a social worker and gay activist from Uganda, often thinks back to the text message that caused him to leave the country where he grew up: "Go away! We know who you are. We don't want you in our country. If we see you, we'll burn you to death." This was just a few days after Uganda's notorious anti-homosexuality bill came into effect. Since that time, the flow of threats towards Isaac and his partner have been constant. With the help of a professional human smuggler Isaac managed to make it safely into Italy. He has no legal documents, however, that officially allow him to stay in Italy. There was no time to get those documents and, in addition, Uganda is considered a "safe country." "Safe countries" are those determined by the United Nations (UN) Refugee Agency as either being non-refugee-producing countries or as being countries in which refu-gees can enjoy asylum without any danger (United Nations High Commissioner for Refugees, 1991). In general, if you are a person from a "safe country," it is unlikely that you will be granted asylum in another country.

Reflection Questions

1   What types of challenges do you think Isaac may face in Italy?
2   What do you think could be done to support Isaac and others in similar situations?
3   How do you think the community where Isaac is staying in Italy will respond to him being there?
4   What is your reaction to how communities have responded to newcomers like Isaac?

At the time we started to write this chapter, European and several other countries on other continents were struggling with how to deal appropriately with the arrival of an increasing number of unauthorized immigrants. To escape the terrible war-torn conditions in their home country (e.g., Syria, Afghanistan, Iraq, Kosovo), many of these immigrants were willing to risk their lives and face uncertain legal status in their target countries. In many cases they depended on rogue smugglers who took refugees under horrendous conditions to the coastal European countries on boats that were in urgent need of repair. A disturbingly high number of these refugees did not make it to the coast alive (Smale, Eddy, & Fahim, 2015). In their target countries (i.e., where they were moving to), many asylum seekers were denied legal immigration status and also faced increasing hostility by some local citizens, such as in Germany where several apartment buildings for asylum seekers were intentionally set on fire (Smale et al., 2015). At the same time in the US, the Republican presidential candidate at that time, Donald Trump, gained significant support in the polls after referring to Mexican immigrants as "criminals and rapists" and resurrecting the idea of building a wall along the US–Mexican border (Corasaniti, 2015). After taking office, he erected detention centers, frequently removing children from their parents. Globally, climate scientists were predicting that within the next several decades millions of people living in coastal areas, especially in Asia, will be forced to find a new home due to increasing sea levels that will lead to significant flooding (Intergovernmental Panel on Climate Change (IPCC), 2014). These are just a few of the many recent developments that make it clear that migration within and between nations is one of the most pertinent social issues that societies across the globe are facing, which is one of the reasons we made this a featured issue for this book. Just as there are those negative reactions to immigration mentioned above, there are also many very positive examples of how host communities have worked on the inclusion and wellbeing of newcomers. The way this issue is framed can make all the difference to how we work towards the integration of newcomers.

Problem Definition and Guiding Principles

Immigration or *migration* – the act of moving permanently or for a significant period of time (e.g., a year) to a foreign country – is a complex issue that is riddled with community dynamics, power relations, and challenges to people's wellbeing (Prilleltensky, 2008a). Even though migration has always been present in human history, it is increasingly becoming an issue of worldwide concern as the number of people leaving their home community to find a new one is rising quickly. While the vast majority of people move within, rather than between, countries there were 232 million international immigrants in 2013 compared to 154 million in 1990 (Pew Research Center, 2013).

There are many different reasons why people migrate. Some leave their countries because of political persecution, conflicts, economic problems, environmental degradation, or a combination of these reasons; while others do so in search of conditions for survival or wellbeing that do not exist in their place of origin (UNESCO, n.d.). In general, a distinction is made between immigrants, who have made a relatively free choice to relocate from one country to another, and refugees, who are forced to move because their survival is threatened by forces such as war, disasters, or persecution (Sonn & Fisher, 2010). Furthermore, "sojourners" are considered immigrants who move to another country to achieve certain objectives within a specific time frame and intend to return home; such as international students, diplomats, military personnel and business people with international postings (and the families who travel with them). The experience of the immigration process can differ significantly depending on a person's reason for migration. A person who fled because of possible prosecution by a totalitarian regime in a war-torn country, for example, is likely to have a more challenging experience than a manager of a global company who is moving for two years to another country with her family to open up a new international office. In this chapter, and throughout the book, we will refer to all of these groups as newcomers while acknowledging this diversity in immigration backgrounds.

Another important difference among newcomers that can significantly affect their experience of the immigration process and their wellbeing is whether they have the required legal documentation and authorization for their immigration. Those newcomers who lack such authorization are referred to as **undocumented/unauthorized immigrants** (some people have also referred to them as "illegal aliens" or "illegal immigrants"; see Box 1.1 for a critical perspective on this). In 2012, for example, it is estimated that there were 11.4 million unauthorized immigrants in the US, which represents almost a third (28 percent) of the 40.8 million immigrants living in the US at that time (Migration Policy Center, 2017).

Figure 1.1 Immigration

Source: Steve Kelley Editorial Cartoon is used with the permission of Steve Kelley and Creators Syndicate. All rights reserved.

Box 1.1 The Power of Words

Language contains manifestations of power and oppression (Foucault, 1982). Therefore, it is important to be sensitive to the meaning and impact of terms we use. For example, to refer to unauthorized individuals as "illegal aliens" not only communicates that the newcomers are unfamiliar and different from the existing residents but it also suggests that somehow a person does not have a legal existence. There has been a broad movement advocating the use of a more appropriate term, such as "unauthorized immigrants." A common slogan of this movement is: "No one is illegal." This movement was not only about changing the use of the specific term but also about raising awareness about the many challenges and suffering many unauthorized immigrants face.

The term "unauthorized" communicates that the status of these immigrants has to do with a legal and administrative process that are temporary and are not characteristics of the person. For similar reasons, we use the term "people experiencing homelessness" rather than "the homeless."

Throughout this book we try to use terminology that is inclusive and sensitive to these power issues. We may have not been fully successful in our efforts, or perhaps new and better terms have been identified by the time you are reading this book. We encourage you, as the reader, to be reflective about these issues and let us know if you find that there are better terms to use for the next edition of this book.

The goal of many community psychologists is to improve the wellbeing of immigrants by understanding and changing risk and protective factors affecting newcomer communities. The aim is to engage in an empowering process to transform both structural conditions (e.g., challenging problematic immigration laws or advocating for more culturally appropriate services) and the communities themselves (e.g., developing social ties with people from the host community) (García-Ramírez, de la Mata, Paloma, & Hernández 2011; Prilleltensky, 2008a). *Risk factors* are any attributes, characteristics or exposure to certain conditions that increase the likelihood of individuals experiencing decreased physical and/or mental wellbeing. People experiencing poverty for an extended period of time, for example, are more likely to develop health problems such as diabetes (Chaufan, Constantino, & Davis 2011). Migrants' wellbeing has both objective (e.g., physical health) and subjective (e.g., sense of control) dimensions. Research by a variety of community psychologists and other social scientists has shown that the wellbeing of migrants is multilevel, dynamic, and value dependent (Prilleltensky, 2008a; Sonn & Fisher, 2010). It is multilevel because their wellbeing is affected by individual, relational, and collective conditions and processes; it is dynamic because these conditions and processes interact in positive and negative ways with the objective and subjective dimensions of wellbeing; and, it is value dependent because the likelihood of migrants becoming fully accepted members of their host society depends to a large degree on the social justice norms within that society (Prilleltensky, 2008a). *Social justice*, one of the key values of CP, and a critical lens by which the field is framing social issues, can be understood as the fair and equitable allocation of burden, resources, and power in society (Nelson & Prilleltensky, 2010).

Levels of Analysis

All people who relocate to another country are faced with settlement challenges. In addressing these challenges, it is easy to simply focus on the individual newcomers as they are trying to adapt to the dominant culture in their new country or community. This process is commonly referred to as "acculturation" – although, in its original meaning acculturation was understood as a bidirectional adaptation of two cultural groups to each other (Berry, 2001). *Culture* in this context is commonly understood as a set of values, beliefs, norms, symbols, and language as well as common practices shared within a group of people with similar ethnic heritage. In a popular model of the psychology of immigration, Berry (1997, 2001) suggested that there are four possible strategies in the acculturation process: assimilation, integration, separation and marginalization. *Assimilation* implies that the newcomers give up their own cultural heritage in favor of adopting the dominant culture of the receiving community. In contrast, *separation* means that the person prefers to hold onto their own culture and avoid interacting with the dominant culture. If the newcomer tries to both maintain their own culture and engage with the new one, then one refers to *integration*. Most mainstream psychological research has focused on the newcomers in their struggle to find the "right" way to adapt to their new environment. *Marginalization* is the process by which certain individuals or groups (e.g., people with disabilities, people who identify as lesbian or gay) are assigned a lower status in society and, as a consequence, are provided with less access to social power, resources, and the ability to be productive members of society (Kagan & Burton, 2010). As such, marginalization is a manifestation of social injustice. An example of a marginalizing practice in the context of migration is when newcomers with a strong accent are told on the phone that an apartment is no longer for rent even though it is actually still available. Experiences of discrimination and social exclusion are common for members of marginalized groups.

Community psychologists, such as García-Ramírez et al. (2011), Sonn and Fisher (2010), and Prilleltensky (2008a), however, argue that it is important to view immigration from an ecological perspective. This means that one considers how different levels of analysis – such as the individual, the community, and the economy – interact in complex ways to create challenges for both the newcomers and the receiving community. For example, consider the political decision by a local government to settle war refugees from a predominantly Muslim country in an economically deprived neighborhood with a history of racial tensions. This decision, in combination with media portrayals of racial stereotypes of Muslims with brown skin color, can be the cause of settlement problems for the refugees rather than their psychological challenges in adapting to the new culture. If one only considers the immigration process from the perspective of newcomers there is a danger of simplifying the situation and of seeing the external factors that influence the experience of the newcomers as overly deterministic. This often leads to *victim blaming* (Ryan, 1971); that is, the newcomers are seen as responsible for their failure to integrate within their new community. By using an ecological perspective, community psychologists try to avoid blaming the victim and instead focus on the people, structures, policies, and practices affecting immigrants and their new community.

In most cases, the dominant culture has a lot of power in pressuring newcomers to adopt the acculturation strategy that they see as preferable. For example, some countries, such as Canada, have adopted a multicultural framework for the co-location of different ethnic groups. Within this framework, the co-existence and integration of multiple cultural traditions within a country or region is accepted and promoted through respective laws, public policies, and social support practices. Providing access to culturally appropriate mental health services and supporting the reunification of families by supporting family sponsored visas are two examples of how host communities can support the cultural integration of newcomers. However, there are also dominant cultures that put pressure on the immigrants to assimilate ("the melting pot") or separate (segregation). Many immigrants experience marginalization if they are not willing to assimilate.

While many immigrants experience great improvements in their economic situation, political freedom, or personal safety by relocating to another country, many newcomers also struggle with significant settlement challenges. This can include dealing with the loss of friends and family, one's home, familiar surroundings, employment, and social status or with the stressful memories of horrific wars and persecution. Those who settle without authorization or documentation face these challenges as well as diminished economic opportunity, few legal protections (e.g., housing, work, crime), and fear of deportation. The struggles immigrants experience can also be caused by the reaction of the receiving community (exclusion, discrimination, laws and public policies that are intended to discourage unwanted immigration). For example, professionals from certain countries, especially those considered to be economically developing, are not able to practice at their level of qualification in Canada and other wealthy Western countries without significant additional schooling and licensing, often at prohibitive costs to these immigrants (Basran & Zong, 1998). This may force them to take a job significantly below their skill level, which may result in loss of social status and self-worth. The frequently invoked example is the taxi driver who used to be a medical doctor in India or an engineer in Ethiopia. Many newcomers experience significant mental health issues as a result (Kennedy & McDonald, 2006).

It is also important to not consider immigrants to be a homogeneous group. There are many different sub-cultures often intersecting with other types of cultures such as those characterized by sexual orientation or socioeconomic class, making the acculturation process even more complex and challenging. Racism, for example, is a prevalent social factor influencing the receiving community's reaction to the immigrants. People who look different from the dominant ethnic group – especially in regard to their skin color – are often more likely to experience discrimination than those who are physically similar (Viruell-Fuentes, Miranda, & Abdulrahim, 2012; see also Chapter 21).

Approach to Addressing Social Issues, Types of Intervention and the Role of the Professional

When social issues are framed in an individualistic way, then the ways these issues are being approached also tend to be individualistic, such as providing counseling services for newcomers. While these types of support can be of value to newcomers, a key value for community psychologists is to work with marginalized groups as allies in a process of empowerment that enables marginalized communities to shift power structures and transform their oppressive contexts into fair multicultural ones. Being an ally means to recognize your own relative privilege and to use your social power to support marginalized groups. In this role you work in partnership with the communities recognizing the importance of the communities' agency in leading their own liberation and empowerment process. Community psychologists García-Ramírez et al. (2011) see this process as critical for acculturative integration, which they define "as a liberating journey to citizenship, an empowerment process based on the acquisition of rights and responsibilities to be politically active members contributing to the development of the new society" (p. 89). They describe acculturative integration as a multilevel process where at the intrapersonal level the individual develops critical thinking. Through reflection and evaluation there is a renewed awareness that social change is possible. At the interpersonal level, the process is related to developing new social ties, organizations, and social networks that increase immigrants' access to resources and capacities to create change and respond to injustice. This can be described as building social capital (see discussion of this concept in Chapter 7). In Canada, for example, refugees can be sponsored by individuals or groups, who are held responsible to ensure that the newcomers have the necessary resources (housing, employment, language training, etc.) that will help them settle successfully. While these sponsorships officially only last a year, the social ties that are developed during that time often last a lifetime. Finally, at the citizenship level, the process results in civic actions promoting social change (see Chapter 6). Together, this complex process results in a shift from exclusion to inclusion, from isolation to participation, and from hopelessness to psychological wellbeing.

Research

The way social issues are framed also has a significant impact on how research is conducted on these issues. If immigration challenges are framed as a result of individual characteristics, for example, the focus of the research will likely be to link those characteristics to a presumed state of immigration success. As the discussion above shows, however, social issues are very multi-layered. In CP we tend to use methods that better capture that complexity, such as qualitative methods, mixed-method case studies, and multilevel analysis (Christens & Perkins, 2008; see also Chapter 13 for more details). Paloma, García-Ramírez, and Camacho (2014), for example, studied the wellbeing of Moroccan newcomers living in southern Spain using a multilevel analysis. In doing this, they found that wellbeing is closely determined by the following: (a) the level of social justice in the receiving context (openness to diversity of receiving communities, cultural sensitivity of community services, and residential integration); and (b) the individual strengths of the population (use of active coping strategies, satisfaction with the receiving context, and temporal stability in the new environment). Another important issue when conducting research on immigration is to work closely with specific immigration communities both in developing the research and in conducting it. This assures that the research is conducted in a culturally sensitive and appropriate way and is relevant to the community. Ideally, the researcher functions here as an ally to the community.

Social Issue II: Homelessness and Stable Housing

Case 2: Million Dollar Murray (US)

In 2006, Malcolm Gladwell, a writer for the magazine *The New Yorker*, published an article he titled "Million Dollar Murray: Why problems like homelessness may be easier to solve than to manage." The protagonist of his story is Murray Barr, an ex-marine who had been living on the streets of the US city Reno for over 15 years. He was well known to the local police and the nurses in the emergency rooms of the local hospitals. His serious drinking problem resulted in both significant physical and mental health issues. His drinking binges frequently ended in jail or in the emergency room; sometimes multiple times a day. Over the years, his treatment costs added up to hundreds of thousands of dollars with no long-term improvement. One time he was assigned to

a detoxification treatment program where he had a lot of structure and close monitoring. He worked hard and thrived in this program. Then, he "graduated" from the program and was back on the street without any support. He quickly returned to his old habits – and jail and the emergency room.

Reflection Questions

1 What do you think may have led Murray to experience homelessness?

2 What do you think should be the focus of an intervention to help Murray?

3 Do you think Murray's situation could have been prevented? If so, how?

Murray (see Case 2) is probably the type of case you have in your mind when you think about people experiencing homelessness. We see them on the street panhandling or sleeping over a heating vent. But, one of the points that Gladwell is trying to get across is that people who experience *chronic homelessness*, like Murray, make up only a relatively small proportion of the homeless population (see also Kuhn & Culhane, 1998). Many people who experience homelessness do so for only a relatively short period of time (a couple of days or weeks). They often stay temporarily with family or friends or live in sub-standard housing, in their cars, domestic violence shelters, or other types of transitional shelters. An increasing number of the homeless population is families and youth (Kilmer, Cook, Crusto, Strater, & Haber, 2012) and many of them lose their home due to some catastrophic event (e.g., the loss of a job, the foreclosure of their house, a large medical bill, fire, escape from a violent partner; Kuhn & Culhane, 1998).

In most cases, the episode of homelessness that these people experience could have been prevented if affordable housing was available and protective social policies and support were in place. If Margaret, for example (see Case 3), had lived in the US instead of Germany, she would have likely lost her apartment and experienced homelessness.

Case 3: Margaret (Germany)

Margaret is a 45 year-old technician who has worked in the coal industry in the Ruhr area in Germany for most of her life. She is a single mom of a 13 year-old daughter. Five years ago the coal mine she had worked in for the last fifteen years closed due to the shift toward the use of renewable energy in Germany. The timing of this job loss was unfortunate because she had also developed a chronic health condition that required an expensive drug treatment. Fortunately, the Arbeitslosengeld (a type of social insurance payment that employees who lose their job can receive for a certain period of time to help them transition into a new position) she received for a year allowed her to keep her apartment and support her daughter without too many significant changes. Her rent is very reasonable due to the availability of rental supplements and rent control by the government. The public insurance system that she is part of covers the cost of her medical bills, which has kept her health condition under control and allows her to continue working. Margaret took advantage of job training provided by the ministry of labor and within eight months of losing her job she found a new position at an insurance company.

Reflection Questions

1 What are some key differences between Margaret's and Murray's stories?

2 What prevented Margaret to experience homelessness even though she was facing significant life and financial challenges?

3 How can individuals like you contribute to creating and maintaining conditions that support people in difficult situations like the ones described in this case study?

Problem Definition and Guiding Principles

A focus on prevention and on the contextual factors that shape a person's lived experience and wellbeing is at the heart of CP (see Chapters 5 and 6). Just like migration, homelessness and housing are complex social issues that can be framed in very different ways. It is easy, for example, to focus on Murray's individual life history and immediate mental health needs by providing professional services. Many of us who are drawn to fields such as social work and psychology are compassionate people who want to help those in need. The solutions to such problems, however, need to match the complexity of the issue, and, in many cases, this requires getting to the root of the problem and working towards transformative system changes (see Chapter 6 for more details on transformative social change).

A good way of framing the issue can be found in *The Canadian Definition of Homelessness* released by the Canadian Homelessness Research Network in 2012:

> Homelessness describes the situation of an individual or family without stable, permanent, appropriate housing, or the immediate prospect, means and ability of acquiring it. It is the result of systemic or societal barriers, a lack of affordable and appropriate housing, the individual/household's financial, mental, cognitive, behavioral or physical challenges, and/or racism and discrimination. Most people do not choose to be homeless, and the experience is generally negative, unpleasant, stressful and distressing. (Gaetz et al., 2012, p. 1)

Unsplash/evstyle

Levels of Analysis

In understanding the causes of homelessness, community psychologist Shinn (2007) points to an interplay between individual, sociocultural, and policy factors. Levels of homelessness within a country or city have mostly to do with cultural, economic, and political factors (e.g., values for social justice, housing costs, and the availability of social housing or rental support); whereas which groups of people are most vulnerable to become homeless has to do with the level of support available for specific groups (e.g., social housing for families), social exclusion (e.g., racism), and individual risk factors (e.g., job loss). The US and Great Britain, for example, tend to have significantly higher rates of people who have experienced homelessness compared to countries in Continental Europe such as Germany, Italy, and Belgium (Shinn, 2007; Toro et al., 2007). The US and Great Britain also have more unequal income distribution and social programs that do less to reduce poverty compared to these other countries (Shinn, 2007). Germany, for example, which has the lowest rate of homelessness among those countries, has one of the most comprehensive social welfare systems in the world, including benefits such as a guaranteed minimum income, affordable public health care, comprehensive unemployment benefits, and rigorous tenants' rights (Toro et al., 2007). Comparing developments of homelessness in North America over time, one can also observe that increasing inequality, rising rents, and cuts in social spending correspond with growing levels of people experiencing precarious housing situations or literal homelessness (Kuhn & Culhane, 1998). It is also noticeable that the US has the highest rate of families experiencing homelessness among economically developed countries, while devoting only about one-fifth as much as Western Europe to social spending on families (relative to the Gross Domestic Product [GDP]; Shinn, 2007).

These differences among countries in regard to income distribution and social policies can be linked to differences in cultural attitudes of personal responsibility (Shinn, 2007). In a comprehensive study by Toro et al. (2007), the authors found less compassionate public attitudes toward homelessness in the US and Great Britain compared to Germany, Belgium, and Italy. Similarly, Alesina and Glaeser (2004) reported that public attitudes toward social welfare are important. The belief that poverty is society's fault explained 82 percent of the variance in social welfare spending among nations with per capita GDP of over $15,000 in 1998.

Racism and social exclusion play into some of these differences as well. In a comparison between states within the US, Alesina and Glaeser (2004) found an inverse correlation between the percentage of state residents who are Black and maximum welfare benefits available to residents – meaning that in states with more Blacks, fewer benefits are available. Stigmatized and excluded minority groups, such as racialized immigrant groups, are more likely to become homeless than non-excluded groups in most countries (Shinn, 2007). "Racialization is the very complex and contradictory process through which groups come to be designated as being of a particular 'race' and on that basis subjected to differential and/or unequal treatment" (Calgary Anti-Racism Education, n.d.).

A racialized group is, thus, one that is categorized by the dominant group as being part of a specific race, which historically were people of color and Indigenous people. Firdion and Marpsat (2007) report that African newcomers in France, for example, are more likely to become homeless compared to the general, mostly White French population. Shinn (2007) proposes that social exclusion in regard to employment, wealth, housing, and imprisonment are important mechanisms that lead to overrepresentation of minority groups. People convicted of felonies (and their families) often lose access to income and when released from prison are often excluded from certain social benefits and struggle to secure housing and employment, increasing their risk of becoming homeless (Shinn, 2007).

Besides the economic, policy, and socio-cultural causes of homelessness, there are also individual characteristics that put certain people at higher risk of becoming homeless (Shinn, 2007). These are related to a person or family's income and wealth, the strength of the social network (e.g., gay youth may be thrown out of the house by their unaccepting parents), education, skills, and experience that help secure jobs, poor physical and mental health, unauthorized immigration status, and substance abuse problems. As discussed, being part of a racialized minority and/or being an immigrant also increases the risk of social exclusion and, thus, homelessness. As we have discussed in the context of immigration, newcomers often find it more challenging to find jobs, especially in their original profession.

Approach to Addressing Social Issues, Types of Intervention, and the Role of the Professional

It is clear from the discussion above that most cases of homelessness can be prevented through economic and social policies that ensure people have access to affordable housing. These include minimum wages, rent control and rent supplements, public and affordable health care, and appropriate unemployment benefits (Shinn, 2007). Addressing more fundamental societal issues such as racism and basic social values is also a form of prevention. While that is the case, there are also people like Murray, who experience chronic homelessness. A lot of community psychologists have focused on this group in thinking about appropriate social interventions. People in that situation are the most challenging and costly for society to support as they have often been homeless for many years and often have to deal with personal challenges such as substance abuse problems, disabilities and mental or physical illness (Kuhn & Culhane, 1998). They are very entrenched in the shelter system and face significant barriers to finding employment and stable housing. The transition out of homelessness for people like Murray is complex and multi-layered (Toro, 2007). Housing people with serious mental illness, therefore, requires complex social interventions (Nelson, Goering, & Tsemberis, 2012).

In the last few decades the framing of these interventions has shifted significantly (Ridgway & Zipple, 1990). Nelson and MacLeod (2017), for example, report that in the 1960s–80s the interventions for people with serious mental health were mostly framed within a medical model of care and illness management rather than rehabilitation and skill building. The professionals providing the services were considered the experts and mental health consumers the chronic patients. There was little self-determination for the consumers and almost no collaboration and participation in their treatment planning or choice of housing. Common housing practices for mental health consumers included custodial housing (e.g., board-and-care homes) and supportive housing (e.g., halfway houses, group home, supervised apartments). This medical or professional model of framing interventions was also common in many other areas during that time (e.g., support for people with physical disabilities; Nelson & Riemer, 2014).

In Chapter 11 we discuss the Housing First model, which has significantly contributed to shifting the framing of homelessness and mental health, and first gained prominence through the work of community psychologist Sam Tsemberis (2010). In this model, the focus is on first providing appropriate housing without any specific requirements of the person (e.g., not using drugs) and then providing ongoing support to help the person retain stable housing over time (Nelson, Goering, & Tsemberis, 2012). Chapter 20 presents other examples of community-based intervention and prevention approaches for people who are dealing with mental health and additional challenges.

Research

A variety of studies on homelessness and housing conducted by, or in partnership with, community psychologists are intended to understand the multi-layered factors that contribute to people either becoming homeless or remaining in stable housing. In a recent longitudinal study by a Canadian team (Aubry, Duhoux, Klodawsky, Ecker, & Hay, 2016), for example, several risk and protective factors that affect homeless individuals' ability to achieve housing stability were examined at multiple levels. The findings from this study suggest that having a larger social support network, access to subsidized housing, and greater income seem to be important factors in achieving housing stability. Several other studies of this kind are referenced above. With this information in place, specific programs and policies can be developed to prevent homelessness and help those already experiencing homelessness regain housing. In many cases these studies are done in close collaboration with social services and government agencies as well as people with lived experience of homelessness.

Community psychologists are also often involved in the evaluation of innovative social programs. That is, they use social science research methods to establish empirical support for the effectiveness of these programs. In some cases they demonstrate that a program does not have the intended impact and needs further development. One example of a multi-site longitudinal evaluation of an innovative program is the research related to Housing First (HF), which has been widely implemented in countries around the world. As mentioned above, Housing First incorporates many CP principles and values, especially self-determination and consumer choice. One of the most comprehensive studies was conducted in Canada (Aubry, Nelson, & Tsemberis, 2015). This study looked at the implementation of ten HF programs in five cities. The research team evaluated their impact on housing, wellbeing, and a variety of other outcomes by randomly assigning participants to either a HF program or treatment as usual. A variety of methods such as qualitative interviews, surveys, document review, and observation were used to study the implementation and the outcomes of the HF programs. The results of this study and previous studies clearly indicate that the HF model works (Mental Health Commission of Canada, 2014).

One exciting aspect of doing this type of research is that it often has a direct impact on policy, community development, and the lives of individuals. To facilitate this kind of impact, community psychologists often engage in specific activities that mobilize the knowledge generated by the research. For the Housing First study, for example, the team developed an Integrated Knowledge Translation (IKT) strategy (Macnaughton, Nelson, Goering, & Piat, 2016). This included the development of an online toolkit, creation of a national network, presentations in several cities in Canada and other countries, and information sessions with government officials. As a result of the study and these knowledge mobilization activities, additional funding for Housing First was made available, more programs were implemented, and additional research conducted (Aubry et al. 2016). Consequently, more people experiencing homelessness will achieve stable housing and have more choice and improved wellbeing.

Social Issue III: Environmental Sustainability

Case 4: Aamjiwnaang First Nation Reserve (Canada)

Ada Lockridge, a member of the Aamjiwnaang First Nation reserve in Canada, had been an environmental activist for several years when Manuel first met her in 2011 as part of a judicial case against the Ontario Department of the Environment and the oil company Suncor. Ada became an activist when word got around that Shell was planning to build a large ethanol plant close to her reserve in Sarnia, Ontario. According to Ada, there had been no consultation about this plant with the members of her First Nation reserve. While most people generally prefer not to have a chemical plant right next to their house (with the exception of those who are hoping for additional employment), this case was especially questionable because there were already 14 petrochemical plants in close proximity to her house. In many

cases when provincial governments in Canada gave permission to pollute, they did not consider other existing polluters in the area. Often the area around Aamjiwnaang, commonly referred to as "Chemical Valley," experienced chemical releases and other potentially dangerous incidents such as explosions. Ada and the others in this community never knew if the sirens that frequently sounded through the air (often multiple times a week) indicated another dangerous release or just another test. Experiences of anxiety and depression were common for Ada. The unusual birth rates in her community (two girls for every boy) and unusually high numbers of rare cancers, including many deaths of close friends and family, compelled Ada into action. Eventually, when the Ontario Director of Environment made a questionable decision about a pollution permit for Suncor, Ada and her friend Ron Plain saw an opportunity to bring their case to court and force the government to consider cumulative pollution (i.e., the interactive effects of multiple polluters in the same area) when giving out new pollution permits. They received pro-bono legal support from the environmental law organization Ecojustice, who, in turn, requested expert opinions from Manuel and fellow community psychologist Terry Mitchell. With their activism, Ada and her fellow activists were not asking for all of the industry to be removed. All they were asking for was the right to breathe clean air.

To find out more about Chemical Valley and the situation of the Aamjiwnaang reserve, we recommend that you watch the following free documentary: www.vice.com/en_ca/video/the-chemical-valley-part-1

Reflection Questions

1 What are your general reactions to hearing about Ada's situation?

2 What are ways that people in academia could support Ada and her community?

3 What are some other environmental issues that may affect local communities that are at the margin of society (e.g., low-income communities, racialized communities, and Indigenous communities)?

The scientific community has warned that environmental degradation and global climate change are threatening the wellbeing of millions of people (Intergovernmental Panel on Climate Change (IPCC) 2014). Many places around the world are already experiencing higher temperatures, rising sea levels, less predictable seasons, increased rates of diseases and more frequent and intense droughts, storms and floods. For example, the US and Mexico experienced record heat waves and devastating droughts in 2012 (Worldwatch Institute, 2013). Other environmental degradation includes the increase of toxins in the environment, increasing deforestation and forest fires, and rapid species extinction (Worldwatch Institute, 2013). Nearly one in five Americans, for example, live in areas with unhealthy year-round levels of particulate pollution, which can contribute to asthma, chronic bronchitis, cardiovascular disease, and in utero developmental disorders (Speth, 2008).

Problem Definition and Guiding Principles

For most of the past century, environmental degradation, such as pollution and global climate change, was not an issue that received much attention from psychologists, including those within CP. Today, there is an increasing understanding that environmental issues are, in fact, human issues (Scott, Amel, Koger, & Manning, 2016). Not only are human actions the cause of these environmental problems, their consequences are also closely linked to human wellbeing and to social justice issues such as inequality, poverty, and marginalization (Riemer & Van Voorhees, 2014). Many communities that have existed for decades, if not centuries, are broken up by natural (e.g., hurricanes) and technical (e.g., nuclear reactor leaking) disasters resulting in an increasing number of environmental migrants (IPCC, 2014). Those who are already at the margin of society, such as people experiencing homelessness, or those living in economically developing countries, are especially vulnerable to the negative impacts of these anthropogenic changes, even though they contributed the least to them (Riemer, 2010). It is also not by chance that a lot of heavy industry is in close proximity to low-income and/or First Nation communities such as Aamjiwnaang. In Canada, similar to many other colonized countries, Indigenous communities have traditionally been carrying an unjust burden of industrial pollution (Agyeman, Cole, Haluza-Delay, and O-Riley 2009).

In the US, toxic waste sites can often be found in close proximity to predominantly Black or low-income neighborhoods (Bullard, Mohai, Saha, & Wright, 2007).

The rising potential for conflicts and use of violence is another concern related to environmental degradation. The exploitation and pollution of our natural environment and the resulting climate changes have led, and will continue to lead, to significant reductions in fish, agricultural land, forest, and water. For example, it is predicted that by 2025 at least 3.5 billion people will live in areas that will not have enough water to meet their needs (Hossay, 2006). Lake Chad, once the sixth largest lake in the world (about the size of Lake Erie), has shrunk to one-twentieth of its original size, causing famine for millions of people in neighboring African countries such as Sudan and Niger (Gore, 2006). While the reasons for the genocide in Darfur are complex, it is conceivable that this situation contributed to the conflict.

In 2007, a severe drought in the South-eastern region of the US caused a water shortage in Atlanta, Georgia. This led to a conflict with cities downriver and the state of Florida as Atlanta city officials contemplated reducing the amount of water released downriver from Lake Lanier to supply the water demand of Atlanta, a fast growing metropolis. In 1995, Ismail Serageldin from the World Bank predicted that "many of the wars this century were about oil, but those of the next century will be over water" (cited in Hossay, 2006, p. 39). People at the margins of society are often the most vulnerable to the impacts of these types of conflicts and wars. As a consequence, many of them are forced to migrate, and are then confronted with the immigration challenges described earlier in this chapter. The recent refugee crisis related to the war in Syria, for example, was preceded by a record five-year draught in that region (Kelley, Mohtadi, Cane, Seager, & Kushnir, 2015).

Considering the concerns we have discussed above, it is critical that societies across the world go through significant transformations toward environmental sustainability (Speth, 2008). Sustainability would imply a world in which the above environmental problems are mostly overcome and people have fulfilling lives without destroying the natural resources needed to provide for current and future generations (Munger & Riemer, 2014; Parris & Kates, 2003).

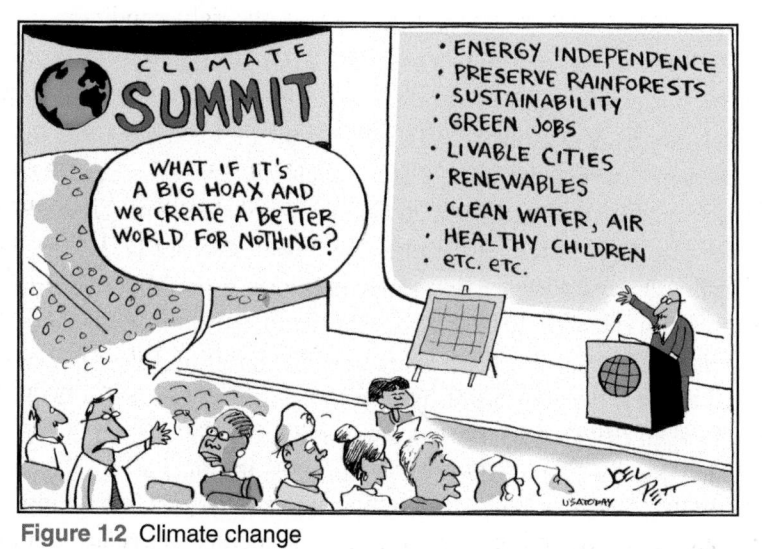

Figure 1.2 Climate change

Source: Joel Pett Editorial Cartoon is used with the permission of Joel Pett and the Cartoonist Group. All rights reserved.

Levels of Analysis

In the transition toward sustainability many people have turned to mostly technological solutions, such as harvesting renewable energy. Several psychologists and others have rightly pointed out, however, that human desires, values, thoughts, emotions, and actions are at the core of the problem and, consequently, also need to be part of the changes needed (Gifford, 2007; Harré, 2018; Swim et al., 2009). This has inspired a burst of research and the development of psychological strategies promoting pro-environmental behaviors and lifestyle changes (McKenzie-Mohr, 2000; Swim et al., 2009). In most cases, these represent a very individualistic approach and, to some degree, can be considered a form of victim blaming. Over many years, industry and their supporters in government have created conditions that cause us to act in non-sustainable ways. For example, the way that many North American cities are built forces people to drive a car rather than use public transportation or a bike. Asking people to change their transportation behaviors without addressing the issue of city development, thus, does not seem fair. Within CP a more ecological approach in working toward sustainability is taken (Riemer & Harré, 2017). People's behaviors are considered in their social, cultural, economic, and political context. This leads to approaches that emphasize people's participation in change processes that will change those contextual factors (Hickman, Riemer, & the YLEC Collaborative, 2016).

Approach to Addressing Social Issues, Types of Intervention and the Role of the Professional

Transformation toward sustainability requires engaged citizens, that is, people who are aware of their rights and responsibilities and actively participate in shaping their respective societies (Riemer, Lynes, & Hickman, 2014). These citizens need to be able to apply an ecological perspective to see how different parts of the system (e.g., environment and economy) interact in complex ways to influence their lives and those around them. And, they need to have the knowledge and the skills to individually and collectively influence those system components (Riemer et al., 2014; Hickman et al., 2016).

In addition to engaging people in civic actions, Harré (2016) also sees a need for helping people to change their own personal practices to be more sustainable (e.g., eat more local and seasonal food). The emphasis here is on providing individuals with the right conditions and tools that will support them in their efforts to make changes. A community psychologist may reflect with a work team on how they can avoid unsustainable food options during their work meetings.

Empowerment of local communities is another important area of work for CP. Community psychologists have found that public participation processes related to environmental disputes (e.g., related to nuclear and industrial waste sites) are strongly influenced by dimensions of social power. Power determines who has control over resources and who has the authority to set the agenda (Culley & Angelique, 2011; Culley & Hughey, 2008). In situations like these, local residents often lack power in advocating for their causes. This is also the kind of situation where the private and political actions of community psychologists often align with their academic pursuits. Two community psychologists, Culley and Angelique, who have been working in issues of nuclear power and citizen participation, for example, did not just research this issue, but have also been engaged in helping local residents organize and build social power.

These are just some of several examples of how community psychologists apply their theories, methods, and strategies to the critical issues of environmental degradation and sustainability (for comprehensive reviews see Dreyer & Riemer, 2018; Riemer, 2010; Riemer & Harré, 2017; Riemer & Reich, 2011).

Research

Research in CP is often very action-oriented. The need for change is large for any of the social issues we are dealing with, including sustainability. Thus, it is important for societies around the world to understand how to enact that change, especially through grassroots and community-based efforts and in ways that are socially just. By conducting action-oriented and participatory research, community psychologists are contributing to that type of knowledge. For example, a team of university-based scholars, representatives from environmental community-based organizations, and environmental youth leaders from six countries (Bangladesh, Canada, Germany, India, Uganda, and the US) got together to develop and empirically test a strategy for engaging young people in environmental action (Riemer & Dittmer, 2016). Based on a theory of engagement (Hickman et al., 2016), the team developed a workshop series grounded in the principle of **environmental justice** (which applies social justice in an environmental context). Several concepts from CP were used in developing the content of these workshops, such as the ecological model. The workshops were then implemented in the six countries and evaluated using a longitudinal, mixed-method, comparison-group design (Riemer et al., 2016). The longitudinal design is important because change happens over a certain period of time. Using a variety of methods such as qualitative interviews and surveys helps with understanding complex phenomena like the youth engagement process, which is the focus of this study. Having a comparison group helps with ruling out some alternative explanations for observed effects. In general, community psychologists work hard to find the most rigorous design that will best answer the research question and that is both feasible and acceptable to the groups we are doing the research with (see more details in Chapter 13).

Your Journey

This concludes our introduction to the way we, as community psychologists, frame, address, and research social issues. We invite you now to join us on the journey through this book, which may be your first introduction to CP. You will learn about the formal origins of CP, its mission, its founders, key ideas, and applications. This journey may be bumpy, jarring, and upsetting, both emotionally and intellectually, as we consider the gaps between our own privilege and the disenfranchisement and pain of those with whom we work. In this book, we challenge the field of CP to expand its boundaries and to consider new ways of thinking and acting. For those who read this book as students taking a course in CP, we hope you are able to consider and apply these ideas to your field placement experience as part of your course or other research experience, in which you will come face-to-face with the issues that we discuss and the disadvantaged people with whom we work.

We encourage you to go gently into what may be uncharted waters for you, listening respectfully to disadvantaged people, suspending judgment, and constantly reflecting on your thoughts, actions, and experiences. Do not take everything that we or other authors or commentators say as "the truth." The ability to think critically, challenge ideas, question assumptions, and develop alternative arguments based on experiences, values, and evidence is fundamental to CP. Additionally, we encourage you to question your own values, beliefs, and vision, as well as the sources and situations of your own privilege. Remember that social change movements have often started with student activism. What follows in the book and in your journey may be very sobering, disturbing, or eye-opening for those of you who are new to the field of CP. At the same time, however, we want to convey a message of hope and inspiration that change is possible and suggest ways that you can contribute to personal and collective change.

Key Terms

Acculturation: The process of how people from different cultures adapt to the dominant culture in their new country or community or, more generally, of how two cultural groups adapt to each other.

Acculturative integration: A multilevel empowerment and liberation process for immigrants toward full citizenship based on the acquisition of rights and responsibilities.

Ally: Recognition of one's own relative privilege and use of one's social power to support marginalized groups in their efforts to gain power and create meaningful social change.

Culture: A set of values, beliefs, norms, symbols and language, as well as common practices shared within a group (e.g., people with shared ethnic heritage).

Ecological perspective: Consideration of how different levels of analysis – such as the individual, the community and the economy – interact in complex ways and influence each other.

Environmental justice: The fair distribution of environmental burdens and benefits across groups and individuals within a country or globally, as well as the fair and meaningful access to power to influence the development, implementation, and enforcement of environmental laws, regulations, and policies.

Framing: Central organizing idea or story line that provides meaning to events related to an issue. That is, the way professionals and academics classify, organize, and interpret the issues they are dealing with.

Homelessness: The situation of an individual or family without stable, permanent, appropriate housing, or the immediate prospect, means, and ability of acquiring it.

Immigration: The act of moving permanently or for a significant period of time (e.g., a year) to a foreign country.

Marginalization: The process by which certain individuals or groups are assigned a lower status in society and, as a consequence, are provided with less access to social power, resources, and the ability to be productive members of society.

Migration: The act of moving permanently or for a significant period of time either within the same country or a foreign country.

Multicultural framework: The co-existence and integration of multiple cultural traditions within a country or region is accepted and promoted through respective laws, public policies and social support practices.

Racialization: A complex and contradictory process through which groups come to be designated as being of a particular 'race' and on that basis subjected to differential and/or unequal treatment.

Refugee: A person who is forced to migrate because their survival is threatened by forces such as war, disasters, or persecution.

Risk factor: Risk factors are any attributes, characteristics, or exposure of an individual that increases the likelihood of experiencing decreased physical and/or mental wellbeing.

Social justice: The fair and equitable allocation of burden, resources, and power in society.

Sustainability: A world in which current environmental problems are mostly overcome and people have fulfilling lives without destroying the natural resources needed to provide for current and future generations.

Undocumented/unauthorized immigrant: Immigrant who does not have the required legal documentations and authorization for their stay in the host country.

Victim blaming: A person being held responsible for the causes of and solutions to their problem.

Resources

General Community Psychology

Books

Below are a variety of books that provide introductions to CP and a collection of topical chapters related to key concepts and issues in CP.

Bond, M. A., Serrano-García, I., & Keys, C. (Eds.). (2017). *Handbook of community psychology – Volume 1: Theoretical foundations, core concepts, and emerging challenges.* Washington, DC: APA Press.

Bond, M. A., Serrano-García, I., & Keys, C. (Eds.) with B. Shinn (Associate Ed. for Research Methods) (2017). *Handbook of community psychology – Volume 2: Methods of community psychology in research and applications.* Washington, DC: APA Press.

Kagan, C., Burton, M., Duckett, P., Lawthom, R., & Siddiquee, A. (2011). *Critical community psychology.* Oxford, UK: Wiley.

Kelly, J. K. (2006). *Becoming ecological: Expedition into community psychology.* New York: Oxford.

Klos, B., Hill, J., Thomas, E., Wandersman, A., Dalton, J., & Elias, M. (2012). *Community psychology: Linking individuals and communities* (3rd ed.). Independence, KY: Cengage.

Nelson, G., Kloos, B., & Ornelas, J. (2014). *Community psychology and community mental health: Towards transformative change.* New York: Oxford University Press.

Nelson, G., & Prilleltensky, I. (2010). *Community psychology: In pursuit of liberation and wellbeing* (2nd ed.). London: Red Globe Press.

O'Donnell, C., & Ferrari, J. R. (2000). *Employment in community psychology.* New York: Routledge.

Reich, S. M., Riemer, M., Prilleltensky, I., & Montero, M. (Eds.). (2007). *International community psychology: History and theories.* New York: Springer.

Scott, V., & Wolfe, S. M. (2014). *Community psychology: Foundations for practice*. Washington, DC: SAGE Publications.

For additional relevant books go to: www.scra27.org/publications/other-community-psychology-books/

Websites

The following websites provide great information on CP and many useful resources:

- Society for Community Research and Action (Div. 27 of the American Psychological Association): www.SCRA27.org
- Australian Psychology Association College of Community Psychologists: https://groups.psychology.org.au/ccom/
- Community Toolbox: http://ctb.ku.edu/en
- European Community Psychology Association: www.ecpa-online.eu/
- Community psychology value proposition: www.gjcpp.org/pdfs/v2i3-0005-SpecSession-final.pdf
- Careers in Psychology - Community Psychology: http://careersinpsychology.org/becoming-a-community-psychologist/
- Introduction to community psychology by Dr. Douglas D. Perkins: https://my.vanderbilt.edu/perkins/2011/09/intro-to-community-psychology/
- Community Psychology UK: http://communitypsychologyuk.ning.com/

Journals and Newsletters

The following journals and newsletters cover many topics often written by community psychologists or are relevant to our work:

- Action Research
- American Journal of Community Psychology
- Collaborations: A Journal of Community-based Research and Practice
- Global Journal of Community Psychology Practice
- Community Development
- Community Psychology in Global Perspective
- Community Mental Health Journal
- Journal of Community and Applied Social Psychology
- Journal of Community Psychology
- Journal of Rural Community Psychology
- Journal of Social Issues
- Psychological Intervention/Intervenión Psicosocial (English/Spanish)
- Rivista di Psicologia di Communità (Italian)
- The Australian Community Psychologist
- The Community Psychologists

For additional relevant journals see: www.scra27.org/publications/other-journals-relevant-community-psychology/

Homelessness

Books and Articles

To learn more about housing, homelessness, and the Housing First approach, read these books and articles:

Padgett, D. K., Henwood, B.F., & Tsemberis, S. (2016). *Housing First: Ending homelessness, transforming systems, and changing lives.* New York: Oxford University Press.

Pleace, N. (2017). The Action Plan for Preventing Homelessness in Finland 2016-2019: The culmination of an integrated strategy to end homelessness. *European Journal of Homelessness, 11*(2), 95–115.

Sylvestre, J., Nelson, G., & Aubry, T. (Eds.). (2017). *Housing, citizenship, and communities for people with serious mental illness: Theory, research practice, and policy perspectives.* New York: Oxford University Press.

Tsemberis, S. (2015). *Housing First: The Pathways model to end homelessness for people with mental illness and addiction* (2nd ed.). Center City, MN: Hazelden.

Websites

To learn more about homelessness, check out the Homeless Hub, the largest repository of information on this subject in the world: www.homelesshub.ca/

Have a look at the website of the Society for Community Research Action and their work on homelessness, mental health, and Housing First: www.scra27.org/who-we-are/interest-groups/transformative-change/homelessness-mental-health-and-housing-first/

What is Housing First and how can it end homelessness for people with complex health issues? Check out this TED talk by award-winning community psychologist, Sam Tsemberis, the founder of Housing First: www.youtube.com/watch?v=HsFHV-McdPo

Read about how Finland has become the first country in the world to virtually end homelessness: www.huffingtonpost.ca/entry/homelessness-finland-housing-first_n_5c503844e4b0f43e410ad8b6

Read about how two Canadian provincial networks are dedicated to ending homelessness by building local capacity and changing social policy, one in Alberta called the Seven Cities: www.7cities.ca/, and one in Ontario called the Housing First Community of Interest: http://eenet.ca/initiative/housing-first-community-interest#about

What is happening in Europe to end homelessness? Check out this website: www.feantsa.org/en, and the *European Journal of Homelessness*: www.feantsaresearch.org/en/publications/european-journal-of-homelessness

The Mental Health Commission of Canada supported the largest study of Housing First in the world to end homelessness for people with mental illness and addictions. Read about this amazing five-city Canadian study: www.mentalhealthcommission.ca/English/at-home

Did you know that Housing First holds a biennial conference in the US? Have a look at the agenda for the 2020 conference in Seattle: www.hfpartnersconference.com/. And there is also an International Housing First conference: www.dpss.unipd.it/Housing-First-Conference/Home

Have a look at the on-line Housing First toolkit:

Polvere, L., MacLeod, T., Macnaughton, E., Caplan, R., Piat, M., Nelson, G., ... Goering, P. (2014). *Canadian Housing First toolkit: The At Home/Chez Soi experience.* Calgary and Toronto: Mental Health Commission of Canada and the Homeless Hub. Retrieved from http://housingfirsttoolkit.ca/

Immigration

Book Chapters and Articles

Here are a few articles and chapters written by community psychologists on the topic of immigration and inclusion:

García-Ramírez, M., de la Mata, M. L., Paloma, V., & Hernández, S. (2011). A liberation psychology approach to acculturative integration of migrant populations. *American Journal of Community Psychology, 47*, 86–97.

Paloma, V., García-Ramírez, M., & Camacho, C. (2014). Well-being and social justice among Moroccan migrants in southern Spain. *American Journal of Community Psychology, 54.* 1–11.

Patel, S. G., Tabb, K., & Sue, S. (2017). Diversity, multiculturalism, and inclusion. In M. A. Bond, I. Serrano-García, C. B. Keys, & M. Shinn (Eds.), *APA handbook of community psychology – Volume 1: Theoretical foundations, core concepts, and emerging challenges.* Washington, DC: American Psychological Association.

Prilleltensky, I. (2008). Migrant well-being is a multilevel, dynamic, and value dependent phenomenon. *American Journal of Community Psychology, 42*(3–4), 359–64.

Sonn, C. C., & Fisher, A. T. (2010). Immigration and settlement: Confronting the challenges of cultural diversity. In G. Nelson & I. Prilleltensky (Eds.), *Community psychology: In pursuit of liberation and well-being* (2nd ed., pp. 498–516). London: Red Globe Press.

Next are some general articles on the topic that provide useful background information:

Berry, J. W. (2001). A psychology of immigration. *Journal of Social Issues, 57*, 615–31.

Kennedy, S. & McDonald, J. T. (2006). Immigrant mental health and unemployment, *Economic Record, 82*(259), 445–59.

Viruell-Fuentes, E. A., Miranda, P. Y., & Abdulrahim, S. (2012). More than culture: Structural racism, intersectionality theory, and immigrant health. *Social Science Medicine, 75*(12), 2099–106.

Websites

Finally, here are a few websites that provide interesting statistics and other useful information on immigration:

International Migration Research Centre: https://researchcentres.wlu.ca/international-migration-research-centre/index.html

Migration Policy Center: www.migrationpolicy.org

Pew Research Center: www.pewsocialtrends.org

UNESCO: www.unesco.org/new/en/social-and-human-sciences/themes/international-migration/glossary/migrant/

UN: https://www.un.org/en/development/desa/population/migration/

Climate Change and Environmental Sustainability

Books

Harré, N. (2018). *Psychology for a better world*. Auckland, New Zealand: Department of Psychology, University of Auckland.

Hossay, P. (2006). *Unsustainable: A primer for global environmental and social justice*. New York: Zed Books.

Speth, J. G. (2008). *The bridge at the edge of the world: Capitalism, the environment, and crossing from crisis to sustainability*. New Haven, CT: Yale University Press.

Two special issues by community psychologists have been published:

Riemer, M., & Dittmer, L. (2016). Youth leading environmental change. *Ecopsychology* (Special Issues), *8*(3).

Riemer, M., & Reich, S.M. (2011). Community psychology and global climate change [Special Section]. *American Journal of Community Psychology*, *47*(3–4).

Book Chapters

Dreyer, B., & Riemer, M. (2018). Community and participatory approaches to the environment. In K. O'Doherty & D. Hodgetts (Eds.), *Handbook of applied social psychology*. London: SAGE Publications.

Munger, F., & Riemer, M. (2013). Sustainability. *Encyclopedia of Critical Psychology*. Available at: www.springerreference.com/

Riemer, M., & Harré, N. (2016). Environmental degradation and sustainability: A community psychology perspective. In: M. A. Bond, C. Keys, & I. Serrano-García (Eds.), *APA handbook of community psychology: Vol.2.* (pp. 441–55). Washington, DC: American Psychological Association.

Riemer, M., & Van Voorhees, C. W. (2014). Sustainability and social justice. In C. Johnson, H. Friedman, J. Diaz, B. Nastasi, & Z. Franco (Eds.), *Praeger handbook of social justice and psychology*. (pp. 49–66). Westport, CT: Praeger Publishers.

Riemer, M. (2010). Community psychology, the natural environment, and global climate change. In G. Nelson & I. Prilleltensky (Eds.), *Community psychology: In pursuit of liberation and well-being* (2nd ed., pp.498–516). London: Red Globe Press.

Websites

- http://grist.org/
- https://www.treehugger.com/
- http://www.realclimate.org/
- http://www.ipcc.ch/

HIGHLIGHTS OF THE HISTORY OF COMMUNITY PSYCHOLOGY

2

Learning Objectives

The aim of this chapter is to present an overview of the development of community psychology (CP).

In this chapter you will learn about

- The catalysts for the establishment of CP
- Allied disciplines in CP's development (past and present)
- CP as a value-driven field
- Key topics that CP has historically addressed
- Intellectual colonization in CP

Why Study History?

As Chapter 1 described, CP is a value-driven, action-oriented field, focused on reducing oppression and supporting individual, group, and collective **wellbeing** (Prilleltensky, 2003). Currently, CP is a small but active field existing on all inhabited continents. Though the genesis of the discipline varies from country to country, sometimes being imported from another region and other times evolving from the local **context**, CP is universally grounded in concerns with inequality and injustice. To try to understand what CP is and what it does, it helps to learn more about how it started and developed over its relatively brief history. Given that this is one small chapter in a textbook, we will highlight some of the contributors to the development of the field and briefly describe the current status of the discipline in different areas of the world. We will also discuss the values that underlie CP, as it is a value-driven science. For more detailed histories, please see some of the recommended reading listed at the end of the chapter.

History is about the roots of a subject, where it comes from and why. As Rappaport and Seidman (2000) stated in the introduction to their *Handbook of Community Psychology*, "every field requires a narrative about itself – a vision of its possibilities, a story that explains why it studies what it deems to be important" (p. 1). In the case of CP, a historical review provides an analysis of the development of the identity of the field and the values it embraces. In order to look forward to the future of CP, we need first to look backwards to our history and the lessons that we have learnt from the past. However, "history" is a story and like all stories, is dependent on the storyteller. So please consider that what is highlighted here may or may not be what would have been illuminated by another storyteller.

Important Issues and Allied Disciplines

Have you ever thought about how a field develops? What contributes to its theories, values, practices, and professionalization? What should be included as the "start" or described as contributors? It is clear that CP arose in different areas of the world at different times and often with different names (e.g., community psychology, Psicología Social Comunitaria, **community mental health**). Across these different histories are some common elements – the social issues that sparked the field and the handful of allied disciplines that supported its development. Though the contexts are varied in different countries, there are several issues that historical writings have noted as being important catalysts for the emergence of CP. These issues were around the importance of social context and civil rights for a variety of groups such as women, racial minorities, and people living with mental illness, different physical and mental abilities, or non-heterosexual orientations, to name just a few.

Mental Illness and Community Mental Health

The wars, conflicts, and economic depression of the early 1900s had heavy tolls on the mental health of people around the world. In the aftermath of World War II, numerous countries were faced with veterans and refugees returning (and rebuilding) home with considerable mental health issues, and for many countries, these issues persisted into the next conflict – the Vietnam War.

Different countries responded differently to these widespread, post-war health issues. In the US, the Mental Health Act was passed in 1946 and in the early 1960s, the Veteran's Administration (VA) hospitals and Community Mental Health Centers were established. In Canada, the Canadian Adult Community Mental Hygiene Program was launched in 1974, with increasing interest in the delivery of mental health services (Davidson, 1981). Increasingly, mental health systems in North America were taxed, especially with newer waves of veterans from the Vietnam War, and more individuals were having difficulty functioning in their communities. During this time, there was an increasing awareness that mental health was connected to how individuals fit their environments and that some environments did not fit people well. Research was increasingly documenting the influence of settings on mental health, such as consistent findings that mental illness rates were greatest in poor and disorganized communities (Dohrenwend & Dohrenwend 1969; Hollingshead & Redlich, 1958).

Further, people began to appreciate that the *label* of mental illness and the *context* of treatment for those with that label can greatly influence the wellbeing of people. During this time, studies of psychiatric institutions started to question whether these facilities, as a specific type of environment, elicited such dysfunctional behaviors, rather than curb them (Szasz, 1960). In one classic study, *Being Sane in Insane Places*, eight people (a pediatrician, a psychiatrist, a graduate student, a house painter, a housewife, and three psychologists) made an appointment at one of five psychiatric hospitals (Rosenhan, 1973). After pretending to have delusions, all eight were immediately hospitalized. Upon admission, the pseudopatients acted as they normally would. Although other patients viewed them as "sane," the hospital staff did not and their hospitalizations lasted from 7 to 52 days (average 19 days). Interestingly, typical behaviors like writing were viewed as signs of pathology and the powerlessness of being hospitalized made many of the pseudopatients doubt their own sanity. This study provided evidence that mental health and illness were dependent on context. At the time, this study drew much concern about our treatment of mental illness and clearly highlighted the role of perception and context in mental health. As Chapters 3 and 4 will describe, the influences of both context and power are important components of CP.

In addition to the awareness of the importance of context in mental health and its treatment, interest in the prevention of mental illness heightened, as did the desire to promote mental health. For instance in Canada, Health Minister Lalonde's 1974 policy paper argued for the need to focus on prevention, **self-help** (sometimes called **mutual aid**), and community interventions, noting that the Canadians most in need of services were in the rural areas and Indigenous reserves, rather than urban centers. The Lalonde Policy Paper stressed sustainable community programs and created a government policy with a community focus (Davidson, 1981). From these efforts, there was a gradual transition of some from clinical psychology, to community mental health, to CP/clinical-CP.

Europe experienced a similar process of questioning psychiatry and clinical psychology with movements around "anti-psychiatry" in England, "democratic psychiatry" in Italy, "community psychiatry" in Germany (Bergold & Seckinger, 2007) and "social psychiatry" in Norway (Carlquist, Nafstad, & Blakar, 2007). In Argentina and Uruguay, in the 1950s and 60s a "psychology of every day life" was developed, connecting clinical psychology/psychiatry with education, social work, and community organizations (Saforcada et al., 2007 p. 105). As Beaglehole (1950) wrote in the textbook, *Mental Health in New Zealand*, environmental contexts such as "strained personal, social and economic conditions, together with unsuitable or unsatisfactory employment"

Box 2.1 Jane Addams and Hull-House

One important setting between 1890 and 1914 was the settlement house, which provided support to immigrants to the US who were living in large cities. But settlement houses dealt with much more than immigration issues; they served as a base for community organization, social action, education, the labor movement, and the peace movement. In her book *Twenty Years at Hull-House*, community developer and social activist Jane Addams (Addams & Wald, 1910) describes Hull-House, a settlement house on the west side of Chicago which consisted of several different ethnic enclaves (Italians, Polish and Russian Jews, Irish). All these groups lived in slum conditions. The description of Hull-House is strikingly similar to contemporary community-driven prevention projects or neighborhood organizations with a community development, prevention, and social change focus. Hull-House operated a coffee house, a gymnasium, a coal cooperative, cooperative housing, a day nursery, and much more. When workers at Hull-House learnt that women and children were working from dawn until late in the evening in sweatshops, they advocated successfully for labor legislation that included an 8-hour day and a minimum age limit of 14 for young people to work. For people like Jane Addams, social issues of women, children, poverty, education, health, and social justice were interrelated and thus action was called for on several fronts and at several different levels. Addams went on to found the Women's International League for Peace and Freedom and she won the Nobel Peace Prize in 1931.

Many feel that Hull-House and the work of Jane Addams and Ellen Gates Starr, embody the values and practices of CP and as such are often viewed as the precursor to the field. Through collective action, social support, and self-help, groups of the most disenfranchised members of society (impoverished immigrants) were able to support one another, educate their children, and be politically involved. The actions of collective members of Hull-House improved the lives of the residents as well as many other poor Chicago residents.

(p. 47) contributed to mental health problems. Throughout much of the world, there was mounting awareness of the importance of context in mental health and the need to consider the collective, rather than just the individual, for societal wellbeing. Further, health promotion and illness prevention increasingly relied on interdisciplinary teams from social work, public health, education, sociology, epidemiology, and medicine. As such, the history of CP has strong ties to clinical psychology but also to these allied fields. It is interesting to note the more recent development of CP (1980s or later) in other countries like South Africa, Japan, France, Poland, and Greece has been closely tied to mental health and clinical psychology (Reich et al., 2017; Reich, Riemer, Prilleltensky, & Montero, 2007).

Mental Health and Self-Help

As helping professions began to appreciate the need for prevention and health-promotion, many focused on ways to capitalize on strengths and promote sustainability. Community psychologists do not view themselves as experts who can fix a social problem or "cure" a person. Instead, we view the community and its members as the experts. After all, they live with the social problems (e.g., mental illness, poverty, racism) and know what resources are available to them, from individuals with specific skills to physical structures and modes of communication. As community psychologists, we may help these experts identify their resources and strengths, connect pieces, or provide insights into structure, policies, or ways to assess impacts, but our hope is to facilitate change that makes us no longer needed.

A great example of how community mental health led to CP is our work in self-help. Self-help describes "individuals taking personal responsibility for their recovery or coping, usually with the aid of a group" (Dalton, Elias, & Wandersman, 2001 p. 197). Applying self-help to people living with mental illness, George Fairweather, in the 1960s, gathered a group of people in a psychiatric facility to form a small, self-governing patient group that could support each other. Although this group was beneficial while in the hospital, the members struggled when they left the facility. It became clear that adaptive living needed to involve supports in the community and not be dependent on dichotomous labels such as "sick" and "well" (Levine & Perkins, 1997). Fairweather, therefore, established the first Fairweather Lodge, a communal living arrangement for four to six people with serious mental health problems. The lodge was self-governing and each resident contributed to the expenses and home responsibilities. Like a family, everyone had duties to fulfill in the home and many had community jobs to support the costs. Professional/staff presence in the home was minimal, with the role of mentor, advisor, mediator, and counselor. The lodge was highly successful in reducing rates of re-admittance to the hospital and increasing rates of employment and stable housing (Fairweather, Sanders, Maynard, & Cressler, 1969). This self-help arrangement demonstrated the strength and expertise of community members in supporting each other and the utility of moving towards collective solutions. Fairweather Lodges are still in operation throughout the US and often called "community lodges" (www.theccl.org/FairweatherLodge.aspx). Self-help is, and had always been, an essential component of CP and examples are found throughout this book.

Social Justice and Civil Rights

The core of CP is a value of social justice and the desire to end oppression. As such, it is not surprising that CP grew as a value-directed, action-oriented field. In some countries, CP emerged to tackle tremendous social and physical oppression such as Apartheid in South Africa and coups, dictators, and death squads in Latin America. In other regions, it was a response to inequality for specific groups such as women, non-Whites, students, Indigenous/First People, non-heterosexuals, and those with different physical and mental abilities (e.g., North America, Australia, New Zealand, Europe and most recently, the Middle East), with most of the activism initiating in the 1970s. In all cases, CP was action-oriented, unlike most other branches of psychology.

Historical writings about the development of CP in Latin America have described it as arising from the "necessity to transform dissatisfaction into action" (Saforcada et al., 2007, p. 66). Closely aligned with social psychology, education, and critical sociology, CP developed in Latin America to address unequal power and resources and the basic needs of its people. With low literacy, food and housing insecurity, and physical persecution, CP developed as a connection between values and practices to immediately address needs. Drawing from the critical and liberation theorists such as Ignacio Martín-Baró, Paulo Freire, and Orlando Fals Borda, Latin American CP has always viewed the community as a strength and questioned the unequal allocation of resources, especially power, to an elite few. For instance, **Popular Education** linked education with emancipation and promoted **conscientization** – an awareness of the psychological and sociopolitical circumstances causing oppression – and **praxis** – critical reflection and action upon the world to transform it (Freire, 2006; Montero & Varas-Díaz, 2007). Maritza Montero (1996) has asserted that while the development of CP was impeded in Latin American countries in which there were or are repressive dictatorships, such conditions also "forged a powerful and lasting link between CP and political causes related to the development of social consciousness" (p. 593). Latin American community and social psychologists have been practicing research that is participatory and action oriented for many years, and they have been influenced by critical, alternative philosophies of science (Montero, 2008).

CP in Latin America is distinctly political. Unlike North America, where there is more of a pull towards mainstream psychology, in Latin America the political and the professional are closely intertwined. This is why there is a close affinity between community and political psychologists in that continent. The political overtures of CP in Latin America have much to offer to the practice of the field in other areas of the world.

In New Zealand, oppression of the Maori, the Indigenous people, was a large contributor to the development of CP. The colonization of New Zealand involved great conflicts with the Maori, who were not easily dominated. In 1840, the Treaty of Waitangi (Te Tiriti o Waitangi) was signed in which the Maori recognized the newly established New Zealand government and the government recognized Maori property rights. Further, the treaty offered all Maori the rights of British citizenship. This treaty provided legal support for the Maori, as the colonizers attempted to seize land or limit their rights. With the strong Indigenous presence in New Zealand, psychologists began to question whether the discipline could be culture-free and as CP developed to address such inequality it adopted a transdisciplinary approach (psychology, anthropology and sociology), with Indigenous theoretical influences and a focus on social justice (Robertson & Masters-Awatere, 2007).

In Australia, the rights of the Indigenous, Aborigines, has impacted the development of CP, but with little of the successes experienced with the Maori (Reich et al., 2017). Aboriginal rights and health were some of several catalysts to the start of CP in Australia. Similar to the US, the rights of people living with mental illness also factored into the development of the field, as did the discrimination of homosexuals and increasing frustration with the country's support of the Vietnam War (on behalf of the US) (Gridley & Breen, 2007). In Australia, CP emerged with a frustration with mainstream and institutional approaches of psychology to address these social issues (Gridley & Breen, 2007).

Throughout Europe and North America, civil rights issues were also key contributors to the development of CP. In Europe, the rights of specific groups (e.g., women, students, those with disabilities) and the questioning of government practices and policies promoted the development of the field. For instance, in Germany, student protests ranging from questioning the employment of former members of the Nazi regime in administrative and political positions to the country's involvement in the Vietnam War helped spark the field. In Italy, students, women, mental health patients, and health professionals worked together in "powerful political movements to obtain new rights" (Francescato, Arcidiacono, Albanesi, & Mannarini, 2007 p. 264). In Portugal, the fight for civil rights encompassed more groups as the country had been under a dictatorial regime from 1926–74. Early community activism and work focused on basic needs of education, healthcare, and freedom of speech (Menezes, Teixeira, & Fidalgo, 2007).

The development of CP in Africa occurred later than it did on many other continents, starting mostly in South Africa in response to extreme inequality and oppression. In South Africa, "all institutions, including academic institutions were controlled by whites" (Bhana, Petersen, & Rochat, 2007 p. 379) and as such, White values, rights, and interests dominated academia with no local influence or access. With the end of Apartheid, greater activism and access flourished, focusing on racial, gender, and class inequalities, contributing to the field of CP.

CP in India, Hong Kong, and Japan also developed as a response to injustice and inequality. India's awareness of inequality was complicated by the caste system and belief in **karma** – the view that good and bad deeds accumulate from previous lives and determine the level of suffering and joy of the current life – as a predetermined state for each individual and that health is not just a physical state but also includes mental and spiritual health (**prsasannanmedriyamanah**). Thus, the challenge for the emergence of CP was to address inequalities that many viewed as deserved due to karma and the need for interventions that promoted whole person health. As such, CP and community mental health grew to be interchangeable terms that work to tackle issues affecting the whole person (Bhatia & Sethi, 2007). Similarly in Hong Kong and Japan, CP developed alongside community mental health to address issues of resource, gender, and class inequality (Cheng & Mak, 2007; Sasao & Yasuda, 2007). In Asia, CP's presence is still somewhat nascent.

Three Social Issues from the Start

Interestingly, the development of CP around the world has addressed the three social issues featured in this book – housing, immigration, and climate change. Housing (lack of and quality of) has been an important issue for many countries ranging from basic housing needs for those with few financial resources (e.g., Africa, Europe, Latin America, North America) to those whose homes have been stolen (e.g., Indigenous on all continents), and those who have been deprived the right to select where they live (e.g., institutionalized, interned). Immigration has been a key issue for many community psychologists, who have worked on the rights and supports for those that immigrate by choice and those by need (e.g., refugees). The area of climate change was not labeled that in early work, but CP, since its inception, has focused on environmental issues, such as the disproportionate placement of environmental toxins (mining, toxic dumps) in areas of poverty, the destruction of Indigenous lands, and the health consequences of environmental degradation on people (see Box 2.2).

Box 2.2 Love Canal Homeowners Association

Love Canal is a small community in upper New York State. The community is built near, and the elementary school on top of, a site where chemical waste was buried by a local factory, Hooker Chemical Company. Residents of the area "complained from time to time of yawning holes that filled with dark, foul-smelling matter ... and of fetid materials seeping into their yards and basements" (Levine & Perkins, 1997 pgs. 402–4), however no action was taken. In 1978, Lois Gibbs, in response to her son developing allergies and kidney and neurological problems, asked her neighbors to sign a petition to close the school. When the Health Department suggested at a meeting (300 miles away) that pregnant women and young children should move out of the area, Lois and her neighbors banded together to form the Love Canal Homeowners Association (LCHA).

Initially, the state government purchased the houses on and immediately adjacent to the former dump site, noting that toxins were seeping through and that there was an elevated level of miscarriages for women living there. However, families across the street were forced to remain (as no one would purchase homes near a toxic dump and the families could not afford to live elsewhere). This prompted Gibbs and the LCHA to start marking a map for every home where a person was experiencing a health problem. Based on the pattern, they noted that toxins must be spreading via the underground swales (ditches). The LCHA then conducted a phone health survey, which found that illnesses were clustered around historically wet areas of Love Canal. Although dismissed as poor science done by housewives, the Health Department agreed to relocate pregnant women in wet areas. This

did not protect those with older children, adults, or couples planning to conceive. The partial acknowledgement of the problem caused house values to plummet, prohibiting residents from being able to sell and relocate.

In 1980, the Environmental Protection Agency (EPA) recommended evacuation after finding evidence that the chemical toxins caused chromosomal damage. However, the Office of Management and Budget feared setting a precedent for purchasing homes after a disaster and refused to relocate the residents. In response, the members of the LCHA told their story via media outlets (e.g., news, talk shows) and protested locally and at the Democratic Convention in New York City, where President Carter was seeking support for reelection. Following that protest, Gibbs was interviewed on a national talk show about the issue and the governments' lack of response. Two weeks later, President Carter gave all residents the option of relocating. Through persistence and ingenuity, this community was able to convince the US government to take action.

The LCHA is a clear demonstration of all that CP values – that the community is the expert, that there is greater power through the collective, and that social justice means combatting inequality and supporting those with less voice (e.g., children). This community change occurred because residents, predominately women/mothers, were dedicated to learning about nuclear disposal and health consequences, policies, and procedures of the Environmental Protection Agency and Health Department, and how to gather credible evidence. When asked why they were so dedicated, one mother responded, "It's the love that we feel for our kids and we can go the long haul" (Culley & Angelique, 2003 p. 454).

Formalization and Growth

In many areas of the world, CP was able to truly establish itself as a field when it had critical mass and mechanisms for sharing information and communicating with others. CP is interested in people and their connections to others. Therefore, it is not surprising that for many countries, CP grew out of face-to-face meetings that were held as part of a larger conference or were organized solely for the purpose of discussing CP. Japanese CP, for example, traces its start to a meeting held at the annual Japanese Psychological Association conference in 1969. Similarly, a symposium at the 1979 Canadian Psychological Association annual meeting is credited as a key catalyst to the field's establishment in Canada (Reich et al., 2017) and the creation of a CP taskforce at the 1979 Interamerican Congress of Psychology in Lima, Peru brought together researchers from Brazil, Colombia, Dominican Republic, El Salvador, Panamá, Perú, Puerto Rico, and Venezuela to help establish the Latin American form of social-CP (Reich et al., 2017).

In the US, two conferences are credited as the clear start of the field. The first was the Swampscott Conference in Massachusetts in 1965, which brought together community mental health researchers and prevention scientists (38 male and 1 female) who were interested in being "social change agents" (Rickel, 1987 p.511). At this meeting, the label "community psychology" was formally applied. However, the participants could not agree on a definition for the new field (Bennett et al., 1966). Nonetheless, this meeting is considered the birthplace of CP in the US. The second meeting was held a decade later in Austin, Texas, bringing together 100 US and Puerto Rican scholars and practitioners (about 25 percent were women; Nelson & Lavoie, 2010) to talk about the field of CP and expand its scope beyond its community mental health orientation to focus more on social justice, prevention, social competence, and diversity (Dalton et al., 2001; Iscoe, Bloom, & Spielberger, 1977).

Box 2.3 Marie Jahoda and Marienthal

A precursor to CP in Europe was the collaborative, interdisciplinary, and participatory work of Marie Jahoda and colleagues in Marienthal. Marienthal is the pseudonym for a town in Austria that experienced extreme unemployment in the 1930s following the closure of the main sources of income for the residents (spinning mills, printing works, and bleaching plants all closed within two years). The aims of the study were to focus on the unemployed community, not the individuals. Rather than describe character traits or psychopathology, the study attempted to describe daily life in an unemployed community (Jahoda, 1983) by using a naturalistic design. "Jahoda and colleagues, like community psychologists, focused on a whole, self-defining community unlike researchers who focus on individuals, cohorts or samples" (Fryer, 2008 p. 578). Researchers lived in the community and residents assisted with data collection. For instance, teachers recorded the contents of children's lunches, farmers reported the number of missing crops, and vendors noted the sales of newspapers. The entire inquiry was collective, with researchers and residents working together to analyze and interpret data. From the prolonged engagement, the team found that sustained unemployment led to a state of apathy in which residents stopped using the few opportunities available to them. As these opportunities reduced, so did the aspirations of the community. Thus, poverty became demoralizing and greatly affected the health and wellbeing of the collective. The ideas of this project, from the question formation to the participatory process to the findings of collective impacts, are all foundational components of the field of CP. That is why this work is often noted as early CP (Fryer, 2008) and credited as part of the foundation of CP in Europe.

In Europe, the development of CP occurred largely within countries before it connected between countries on the continent. In Britain, much CP work was being done, but that term was not used until it was applied in North America (Burton, Boyle, Harris, & Kagan, 2007). Although CP was being practiced in Britain in different regions and universities, there were few connections between those researchers and practitioners. However, once CP was more formalized in Britain, its publications and activities spread throughout Western Europe and the field evolved to have a more critical flavor – that is a questioning of how much of the field was unquestioning, if not supportive, of the **status quo**. Italy, Portugal, Germany, Norway, and Spain (and later France and Poland) all developed CP in their national context before joining together to form a European Community Psychology Association. See Box 2.3 for early community-based work in Europe.

National and International Organizations and Journals

Another clear marker of the establishment of CP is the formalization of a professional organization and a regular mechanism for sharing information such as peer-reviewed journals and books. Currently, there are over a dozen national CP organizations in such places as Argentina, Australia, Brazil, Canada, Columbia, France, Germany, India, Italy, Japan, New Zealand, Norway, Portugal, Spain, South Africa, the UK, and the US, and several international associations (e.g., the European Community Psychology Association (ECPA) and the Interamerican Society of Psychology in Latin America). The US established the first CP division (division 27) within the American Psychological Association (renamed, Society for Community Research and Action) in 1966. There are also numerous journals, books and textbooks dedicated to CP. Some of the well recognized ones in the field are the *American Journal of Community Psychology*, *Australian Community Psychologist*, *Community Development Journal*, *Journal of Community Psychology*, and *Journal of Community and Applied Social Psychology*. There is also growing effort to provide free, online, and easily accessible resources such as the Community Tool Box (http://ctb.ku.edu/en), *Global Journal of Community Psychology Practice* (www.gjcpp.org/en/), *Community Psychology in Global Perspective* (www.siba-ese.unisalento.it/index.php/cpgp), and social media campaigns on targeted issues such as self-help and transformation in mental health.

Diversity of Perspectives

In thinking about the history of CP internationally, it is worthwhile to consider the ways in which gender and ethnicity disproportionately contributed to its development in some countries and not others. In Australia, Canada, England, and the US, early CP writing and leadership were disproportionately White and male. A critique that has been noted globally (e.g., Angelique & Culley, 2007; Bond & Mulvey, 2000) and in response to the conceptualizations of specific theories within the field (e.g., Riger, 1993). For instance, the Swampscott conference in the US, often referenced as the birthplace of the field in that country, included only one female participant who played a largely secretarial/organizational role. Similarly, Australia's development was largely based on the contribution of several men, mainly ex-patriots from the US, who helped spark the field.

In other regions, women have had a larger and more documented presence, with some fields being launched by female scholars. For instance, Italy and South Africa are two countries where two women (Italian Donata Francescato and South African Sandra Lazarus) returned from training in the US to initiate the fields in their own countries. In Latin America, women have always been key contributors to the development of the field. The first core CP textbooks were written in Spanish by a Venezuelan woman (Martiza Montero) and half of the members of the first taskforce on CP for the Interamerican Congress of Psychology (in 1979) were women. Further, women also contributed to the first graduate program (in Puerto Rico) (Reich et al., 2017).

North American (US and Canada) and British CP have greatly influenced the field in other countries through outreach, collaboration, and intellectual colonization. With more journals, presses, and graduate programs, these English-speaking, industrialized countries have succeeded in disseminating CP work and training international scholars. Although this contributed greatly to the emergence of CP worldwide, it has caused many to question how the field has developed and whether Indigenous ideas have been displaced or silenced through this importation (Reich et al., 2007). For some countries, the poor fit of imported CP led to extreme modifications and evolution into a more relevant and supportive field for their context (e.g., Francescato et al., 2007; Reich et al., 2017). In some countries, the North American and British versions of CP have been critiqued as being too deficit focused. For example, in Cameroon, imported CP has largely been rejected in favor of Indigenously developed CP (Nsamenang, Fru, & Browne, 2007), and in South Africa, two types of CP are taught; one version that is similar to the imported version and another version of critical CP that critiques the process, theories, and practices of the field (Reich et al., 2017). As international connections flourish, North American CP is increasingly influenced by the work in other countries. Although there is increasing discussion of differences and similarities of CP in different countries, the ways in which gender, race, ethnicity, ability, and orientation have impacted the field are not explicitly addressed. This is an interesting gap, as CP is predicated on the value of respecting diversity. Yet, the ways in which androcentric and ethnocentric processes have impacted the field's development, including the lens, theories, and practices it utilizes, are not well explored. In the subsequent chapters we try to consider how race and gender might contribute to the theories, values and activities of CP.

Language and Influence

In considering the development of CP internationally, it is important to note that language seems to have had a greater impact on the spread of the field than geographical proximity. Not surprisingly, countries with common languages shared intellectual resources, while those in close proximity but with language differences influenced each other less. For instance, CP in Mexico, although bordering the US, has been influenced most by the work happening in Venezuela, Puerto Rico, and Argentina. Similarly, Portuguese CP has been influenced greatly by the work in Brazil, even though CP was more strongly established in neighboring European countries. After the end of almost 50 years of a dictatorship, community psychologists in Portugal drew on Freire's **alphabetization** as a way to combat illiteracy and support economic stability (Menezes et al., 2007), rather than more local theories of CP.

While language has been a strong facilitator for the sharing of information, it has also served as a barrier for some. In Canada, the English-speaking community psychologists have had reciprocal communication with other English-speaking countries like the US, Australia, and the UK. However, these English-speaking Canadian community psychologists have had less communication with French-speaking community psychologists in their own country (Nelson, Lavoie, & Mitchell, 2007). For monolingual countries like the US, information is easily disseminated to others through many publishing and conference outlets, but there are few ways to receive information about work in other, non-English speaking countries. Thus, language impacts the spread and development of CP worldwide and, even within the same country, language is a huge contributor to the development of the field.

Chapter Summary

CP is relatively new, with formalization of the field occurring within the last 50 years or so. Through the help of allied fields and sub-disciplines such as social work, education, medicine, public health, anthropology, public policy, social psychology and clinical psychology, CP has grown into a well-established field with professional organizations and undergraduate and graduate programs throughout the world. In some countries, like Norway, CP is well known, with CP courses being a core requirement in many undergraduate programs.

Interestingly, increasingly academic community psychologists are not working in traditional psychology departments, with more and more gravitating to education, social work, family studies, public health, and other aligned fields. Further, many community psychologists have bypassed academia and are focused on practice. In Chapters 8–11 we discuss career options for community psychologists in more detail, which include such areas as academia, civil service, consultation, activism, organizing, and evaluation. Core catalysts that sparked the start of CP on almost every continent were indignation over inequality and desire to improve the lives of others. As such, the development and evolution of CP has been based on clear values that drive research and practice.

From this brief history, one can appreciate how CP grew from dissatisfaction with the status quo and an indignation with the oppression of many. As the field has progressed, it has questioned inequity, worked towards civil rights, appreciated the role and power of the collective, identified key skills and lenses to be honed through education and training, and articulated its values towards promoting individual, relational, and collective wellbeing. To date, CP is a framework, value-system, and a field – and one can opt to embrace any or all three of these components.

Key Terms

Alphabetization: To promote conscientization and the critical awareness of daily problems and the understanding of the world and the knowledge of social reality.

Community mental health: The provision of services to people in their community, rather than through institutionalization. A less stigmatizing way to support mental health/treat mental illness, while reducing social exclusion and promoting social integration.

Context: The social, cultural, natural, or built environments that surround our lives and affect our cognitions, emotions, and behaviors.

Conscientization: An awareness of the psychological and sociopolitical circumstances causing oppression.

Karma: A belief that the total of a person's actions in this and previous states of existence, determine their fate in future existences.

Praxis: Reflection and action upon the world to transform it. Reflection alone is not enough, but must work towards change.

Popular Education: The concept that education is based on experiences and desires to bring political and social change. Education is empowering and all are teachers and learners.

Prsasannanmedriyamanah: Indian concept of health being a state of delight, or a feeling of spiritual, physical, and mental wellbeing.

Self-help/mutual aid: Individuals taking personal responsibility for their recovery or coping, usually with the aid of a group.

Status quo: The current state of the sociocultural, political, and economic situation and conditions in society.

Wellbeing: A positive state of affairs, brought about by the satisfaction of personal, relational and collective needs.

Resources

Additional Readings on CP by Region

Global

Perkins, D. D. (2009). International community psychology: Development and challenges. *American Journal of Community Psychology, 44,* 76–9.

Reich, S. M., Bishop, B., Carolissen, R., Dzidic, P., Portillo, N., Sasao, T., & Stark, W. (2017). Catalysts and connections: The (brief) history of community psychology throughout the world. In M. A. Bond, I. Serrano-García, and C. B. Keys (Eds.), *APA handbook of community psychology: Vol. 1. Theoretical foundations, core concepts, and emerging challenges* (pp. 22–66). Washington, DC: American Psychological Association.

Reich, S. M., Riemer, M., Prilleltensky, I., & Montero, M. (Eds.). (2007). *International community psychology: History and theories.* New York: Springer.

Africa

Amer, M., El-Sayeh, S., Fayad, Y., & Khoury, B. (2015). Community psychology and civil society: Opportunities for growth in Egypt and Lebanon. *Journal of Community Psychology, 43*(1), 49–62.

Carolissen, R., Rohleder, P., Swartz, L., Leibowitz, B., & Bozalek, V. (2010). 'Community psychology is for poor, black people': Pedagogy and teaching of community psychology in South Africa. *Equity and Excellence in Education, 43*(4), 495–510.

Carolissen, R., & Swartz, L. (2009). Removing the splinters from our own eyes: A commentary on identities and power in South African community psychology. *Feminism and Psychology, 19*(3), 407–13.

Painter, D., Terre Blanche, M., & Henderson, J. (2006). Critical psychology in South Africa: Histories, themes and prospects. *Annual Review of Critical Psychology, 5,* 212–35.

Seedat, M., Duncan, N., & Lazarus, S. (2001). *Community psychology: Theory, method and practice – South African and other perspectives.* Cape Town: Oxford University Press.

Seedat, M., & Lazarus, S. (2011). Community psychology in South Africa: Origins, developments, and manifestations. *Journal of Community Psychology, 39*(3), 241–57.

Asia

Ando, N. (1989). Community psychology in Japan: A historical review. *Applied Psychology: An International Review, 38,* 397–408.

Chan, C. (2010). Community psychology in Chinese societies. In M. B. Bond (Ed.), *Oxford handbook of Chinese psychology.* Oxford: Oxford University Press.

Japanese Society of Community Psychology. (2007). *Japanese Handbook of Community Psychology.* Tokyo: University of Tokyo Press.

Tapanya, S. (1989). Community psychology in Thailand. *American Journal of Community Psychology, 17*(1), 109–19.

Yu, H., & Yang, Y. (2008). Review of community psychology research in China. *Journal of Shandong Institute of Commerce and Technology, 8,* 13–18.

Australia and New Zealand

Gridley, H., Fisher, A., Thomas, D., & Bishop, B. (2007). Development of community psychology in Australia and Aotearoa/New Zealand. *Australian Psychologist, 42*(1), 15–22.

Thomas, D., & Veno, A. (1992). *Community psychology and social change: Australian and New Zealand perspectives.* Palmerston North: Dunmore.

Europe

Burton, M., & Kagan, C. (2003). Community psychology: Why this gap in Britain? *History and Philosophy of Psychology, 4*(2), 10–23.

Francescato, D., & Zani, B. (2010). Community psychology in Europe: More needed, less wanted. *Journal of Community and Applied Social Psychology, 20,* 445–55.

Orford, J. (2008). *Community psychology: Challenges, controversies, and emerging consensus.* London: Wiley.

Ornelas, J. (2008). *Psicologia comunitaria.* Lisboa: Fim de Seculo.

Latin America

Ardila, R. (1998). *La psicología en América Latina. Pasado, presente y futuro.* Mexico, DF: Siglo XXI.

Montero, M., & Serrano-García, I. (2011). *Historias de la psicología comunitaria en América Latina. Participación y transformación.* Buenos Aires: Editorial Paidós.

Serrano-García, I. (2010). Retos en la formación del psicólogo/a comunitario/a en las Américas. *Ciencia Psicológica, 4,* 225–34.

Wiesenfeld, E., & Sánchez, E. (Eds.). (1995). *Psicología social comunitaria. Contribuciones latinoamericanas.* Caracas: Fondo Editorial Tropykos.

Zaiter, J. (2011). La psicología comunitaria en la República Dominicana: Antecedentes socio-históricos y perspectivas. In M. Montero & I. Serrano-García (Eds.), *Historias de la psicología comunitaria en América Latina. Participación y transformación* (pp. 383–421). Buenos Aires: Paidós.

North America

Davidson, P. O. (1981). Some cultural, political and professional antecedents of community psychology in Canada. *Canadian Psychology, 22*(4), 315–20.

Nelson, G., & Lavoie, F. (2010). Contributions of Canadian community psychology. *Canadian Psychology, 51*(2), 79–88.

Rappaport, J., & Seidman, E. (2000). *Handbook of community psychology.* New York: Springer.

Rickel, A. (1987). The 1965 Swampscott Conference and future topics for community psychology. *American Journal of Community Psychology, 15*(5), 511–13.

Walsh-Bowers, R. (1998). Community psychology in Canadian psychological family. *Canadian Psychology, 39*(4), 280–7.

Online Resources for CP internationally:

Africa

Blog for Community and Social Psychology Division, PSySSA: http://psyssacns.blogspot.com/2013/05/at-this-years-psyssa-congress-scholarly.html

Blog for Southern Psychologies, critical psychology: http://southernpsychologies.wordpress.com/

Community, self and identity: Educating South African university students for citizenship (free download): www.hsrcpress.ac.za/product.php?productid=2299&cat=26&page=1

NGO networks in South Africa: www.ngopulse.org/about

Psychology in Africa: www.psychologyafrica.com

University of South Africa's Institute for Social and Health Sciences: www.unisa.ac.za/Default.asp?Cmd=ViewContent&ContentID=23334

US and Canada

Society for Community Research and Action (Div 27 of APA): www.scra27.org

Community Psychology section of the Canadian Psychological Association: www.cpa.ca/aboutcpa/cpasections/communitypsychology/

Community Tool Box: http://ctb.ku.edu/en/default.aspx

American Journal of Community Psychology: http://link.springer.com/journal/10464

Canadian Journal of Community Mental Health: www.cjcmh.com/journal/cjcmh

Journal of Community & Applied Social Psychology: http://onlinelibrary.wiley.com/journal/10.1002/(ISSN)1099-1298

Europe

European Community Psychology Association: www.ecpa-online.eu/

French Association of Community Psychology: www.psychologie-communautaire.fr/cmsmadesimple/

German Society for Research and Practice in Community Psychology: www.ggfp.de/

Italian Society for Community Psychology: www.sipco.it/

Polish Community Psychology Information: www.psychologia.uni.opole.pl/community/index.php?lang=en

Portuguese Society for Community Psychology: www.sppc.pt/cgi-sys/suspendedpage.cgi

UK Community Psychology Network: www.compsy.org.uk/

Latin America

Interamerican Society of Psychology: www.sipsych.org

Network of Scientific Journals from Latin America, the Caribbean, Spain, and Portugal (Psychology Section): www.redalyc.org/area.oa?id=15&tipo=coleccion

Latin American Community Psychology Training Network: http://red.pucp.edu.pe/psicologia-comunitaria

Latin American Union of Psychology Entities: http://ulapsi.org/portal

Association for the Advancement of Psychological Science: www.cienciapsicologica.org

Asia

Asian Association of Social Psychology: www.victoria.ac.nz/cacr/aasp-site/aasp/

Japanese Society of Community Psychology: http://jscp1998.jp/index.html

Hong Kong Community Psychological Medicine Association: http://hkcpma.com

Korean Health Psychological Association: www.healthpsy.org.kr

Korean Association for Industrial and Organizational Psychology: www.ksiop.or.kr

Australia and New Zealand

College of Community Psychologists, Australian Psychological Society: www.groups.psychology.org.au/ccom/

Community Psychology Australia: www.communitypsychologyaustralia.com.au

Institute of Community Psychology, New Zealand Psychological Society: www.psychology.org.nz/IComPA

The Australian Community Psychologist: www.groups.psychology.org.au/GroupContent.aspx?ID=4395#current

COMMUNITY PSYCHOLOGY VALUES AND VISION

3

Warm-up Questions

Have you ever heard of or been asked to make a vision board? It's a collage of things you hope for yourself in the future. Such boards could include images of good health, peaceful sleep, a new car, success in a new hobby, a romantic relationship, or perhaps a published book. Explicit in this is a vision of the future. Implicit in this are one's values (e.g., relations, health, materialism, professional success) and actions needed (e.g., join a dating site, make time to write or exercise each day) to obtain these goals. As community psychologists, vision, values, and actions are foundational for working towards a just society.

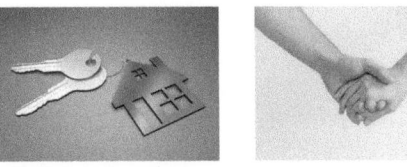

Goals +
Effort =
Success

Figure 3.1 Vision board

Image credits, clockwise from top left: Image by Shahid Abdullah from Pixabay; Photo by Roman Kraft on Unsplash; Image by OpenClipart-Vectors from Pixabay; Image by mohamed Hassan from Pixabay; Photo by Arteum.ro on Unsplash; Image by Clker-Free-Vector-Images from Pixabay; Yoga Photo by Carl Newton on Unsplash; Photo by Frank Vessia on Unsplash.

Learning Objectives

In this chapter you will learn about

- How vision, values, context, needs and action connect to community psychology (CP) research and practice
- How to weigh out, support, and promote individual, relational, and collective wellbeing
- How a value-driven science can work towards social justice

Values and Vision in Community Psychology

What would your ideal society look like? If you could design your own community, what would it be like? Would there be a government? If so, how would it be selected? What power would it have? If not, how would decisions be made? How would you balance personal decision-making with societal best interest? How would basic needs like housing, food, health care, etc. be allocated and their provision continued?

Thinking about an ideal society can help identify key **values** that underlie a **vision** for society. It also brings to light many of the tensions and trade-offs when working towards these goals. For example, should stable housing be a right for all? Should everyone be provided with the same home? What if one family is especially large or has members with special needs? What if some family members are very old? What if someone dreams of designing their own home? What if someone is a criminal or has addiction issues? What types of variations might some families receive in housing? What are the problems to a society if housing is not guaranteed to all?

Identifying our own values and vision for the future is useful for thinking through our actions, goals, beliefs, and practices. It helps us understand what we do, why we do it, and sometimes, what we should be doing instead. For CP, awareness of our values is an essential part of being a researcher, practitioner, and community partner.

Values for a Value-Driven Science and Practice

CP, worldwide, developed to address issues of injustice and oppression and to work towards justice, equality, and wellbeing. As such, values are a core component of the field. Values can "serve as guiding principles in the life of a person or other social entity" (Schwartz, 1994, p. 21). They are also "enduring prescriptive or proscriptive beliefs that a specific mode of conduct (instrumental value) or end state of existence (terminal value) is preferred to another mode of conduct or end state" (Mayton, Ball-Rokeach, & Loges, 1994, p. 3). Values are principles to guide action, lenses through which we see the world, and the scale by which we view the importance and worth of things, people, places, and interactions. We invoke them when we have a conflict with a friend or when we take a stand on a political issue. Should governments provide fiscal support to people experiencing homelessness? Will curbing manufacturing to reduce carbon emissions damage the economy? What is your position regarding Syrian refugees in Europe? Would you boycott a movie theatre because there is no access there for your friend who has a mobility impairment? Each time you take a stand you are invoking a value. For instance, a person who values independence highly would not be likely to support public housing programs, while a person who values *inter*dependence (the connection between people) would likely support government-financed housing programs. The question is, how do we choose values and are we aware of the values we have chosen? We suggest basing our values on vision, context, needs, and action.

Vision

Moral and political philosophers debate visions of the best possible society. Philosophers contribute to the discussion on values by portraying an *ideal vision* of what we should strive for. They can provide a blueprint of a better society in which values of autonomy and community are mutually enhanced (Etzioni, 1960).

Liberalism and liberal philosophers, for example, emphasize autonomy, self-determination, and the rights of the individual. As such, they fear that too much state intervention could end up dictating how private citizens run their lives, such as in the former Soviet Union (Brighouse, 2004). **Communitarian** thinkers, on the other hand, claim that we have gone too far in meeting the needs of individuals and that we have sacrificed our social obligations in the pursuit of private satisfaction (Etzioni, 1960; Lerner, 1996). They may point to countries like the US where there is great disparity in wealth and where people fear others enough to choose to live in gated communities to protect themselves.

Each position poses risks as well as benefits (Mulhall & Swift, 1996). People's desire for greater voice and autonomy may challenge oppressive social norms and regulations, but can also lead to unmitigated **individualism**, selfishness, and materialism (Etzioni, 1996). "When people pursue private goals, the risk is that they may never acquire an ennobling sense of a purpose beyond the self" (Damon, 1995, p. 66). This risk is very apparent in market societies where state intervention is minimal and the powerful are free to seek pleasure at the expense of others (Sen, 1999a; 1999b). Indeed, we hear that to climb the corporate ladder you may need to trample on some people. Not everyone in society has the same amount of power and those with less power have fewer opportunities to advocate for themselves.

Communitarian thinking, on the other hand, believes that individuals must cooperate to achieve their personal goals. By strengthening social and communal institutions we promote not only the good of the collective but also the good of the individual, since strong communities provide better environments for wellbeing than weak ones (Putnam, 2000a; Roffey, 2013). But communitarian thinking is not without risks either. **Collectivist societies** are known for expecting great sacrifices from their members for the benefit of the public good. Citizens can feel coerced to do things they do not like and may experience state intervention as oppressive (Brighouse, 2004; Weiner, 2008). For example, many countries' governments exercise the right of eminent domain, in which governments can seize private property. Historically, this is frequently done to use the land for public needs (e.g., path of a train or road, building housing) or to right historical wrongs (e.g., the illegal seizure of land from Indigenous people or ethnic or religious minorities), but abuses exist and, oftentimes, land owners view this legal action to be oppressive. Thus, an ever-present danger in philosophical discourse is its detachment from the social conditions in which people live. To counteract this risk, we need to explore the contextual circumstances that complement philosophical considerations.

Context

This set of considerations explores *the actual state of affairs* in which people live. Community psychologists and social scientists strive to understand the social, economic, cultural, and political conditions of a specific community. This line of inquiry helps us to determine social norms and cultural trends influencing people's choices and behavior (Neal & Christens, 2014; Partanen, 2016; Trickett, 1996).

A contextual assessment is necessary to understand the subjective experience of the residents of a particular community. Individualist and collectivist societies differ with respect to socialization, customs, and visions. Poor and rich communities ascribe different values to basic necessities. Eric Wiener, a journalist with National Public Radio in the US, decided to explore the meaning of happiness in ten different countries. He traveled to the Netherlands, Switzerland, Bhutan, Qatar, Iceland, Moldova, Thailand, Great Britain, India and the US. Not surprisingly, his travels convinced him that context is essential for understanding the vast array of conceptions of wellbeing and happiness people hold. In Moldova, the basic necessities become all consuming. In Iceland, self-expression reigns. Weiner (2008) claims:

> [H]appiness is not inside of us but out there. Or, to be more precise, the line between out there and in here is not as sharply defined as we think ... In other words, where we are is vital to who we are. By 'where,' I'm speaking not only of our physical environment but also of our cultural environment. (p. 3)

The meaning of self-determination in an individualist society is vastly different from its meaning in a collectivist environment. In a totally collectivist society, citizens may yearn for more autonomy and resent state and communal intrusion. In a totally individualist environment, on the other hand, citizens might desire a stronger sense of community and less selfishness. Unless we know the context, we cannot really know what values to promote (D'Andrade, 2008; Moritsugu, Vera, Wong, & Duffy, 2013).

Needs

Visions of the good society have to be validated with the lived experience and the needs of community members (Hultman & Gellerman, 2002; Kraut, 2007). Needs are important for considering values. Needs address key questions: What is missing? What is a desirable state of affairs? This source of values pays explicit attention to the voice of the people with whom we partner to improve community wellbeing. CP aims to identify and help address the needs of people, especially those in positions of disadvantage. By asking people what they want, need, and consider meaningful in life, we learn about the ingredients of an appealing vision (Fals Borda, 2001). This does not mean that whatever people say should be acceptable. For history has shown that majorities can endorse vicious attitudes. Human wishes should be subjected to ethical scrutiny to ensure that the needs and desires expressed by people are not immoral or unethical. As community psychologists, we must explore our own beliefs and values.

Action

Action concerns *feasible change*. Unlike previous deliberations, which asked what is, what is missing, or what should be, the main question answered by this set of considerations is what could be done? This question is meant to bridge the gap between the actual and the ideal states of affairs. Feasible change draws our attention to what social improvements can be realistically achieved (Fals Borda, 2001).

Agents of change translate values and community input into action. These are the professionals, paraprofessionals, politicians, volunteers, and activists who combine values with human experience to improve the welfare of a particular population. Agents of change strive to promote wellbeing by combining values with knowledge of what people want, need and regard as important in life. Agents of change bridge the abstract notions of philosophers and the lived experience of community members. They try to adapt ideals of the good society to specific contexts (Szakos & Szakos, 2007) and acknowledge the interconnections (i.e., **heterarchy**) of social systems with connected and overlapping components and networks (Tebes, 2012; Tebes, Thai, & Matlin, 2014). Throughout the history of the field, community psychologists have strived to be change agents and to support community members to be agents of change too.

Interdependence of Visions, Values, Context and Action

Without a vision, we do not know what we are working towards, without a contextual analysis we lack an understanding of social forces, without a needs assessment we lack an idea of what people want and, finally, without action we cannot move towards our vision. The interdependence of these sources makes it clear that we cannot rely on single sources of values (Hultman & Gellerman, 2002). Table 3.1 connects vision, context, needs, and action.

Values in Context and Practice

After considering what can contribute to values, we need to consider how these values connect to theoretical and grounded input, understanding and action, processes and outcomes, and differing and unequal voices. A balance between *theoretical* and *grounded input* is needed to complement analytical with experiential approaches to knowledge. Philosophical analyses of what values can lead to a good life and a good society are useful but limited. What is the use of a philosophical framework that does not reflect the living realities of people (Fowers, 2014)? On the other hand, what is the point of knowing people's needs and aspirations if that knowledge is not translated

Table 3.1 Sources of values for holistic and accountable practice in CP

Sources	Key Question	Situation Explored	Tools for Developing Values	Contribution to CP
Vision	What should be?	Ideal vision	Moral, spiritual and political thinking	Vision of wellbeing and liberation
Context	What is?	Actual state	Social science studies of individuals and communities	Understanding of social conditions
Needs	What is missing?	Desirable state	Experiences of community members	Identification of human needs
Action	What can be done?	Feasible change	Theories of change	Strategies for change

Source: Adapted from Prilleltensky (2001). Copyright © 2001, John Wiley and Sons.

into action? Theories of values have to be validated with lived experience and lived experience has to be interpreted meaningfully and converted into action.

A balance between *understanding* and *action* is also needed to ensure that knowledge does not end up on a shelf. To make an impact in the world, our theoretical sophistication has to be followed by action. Imagine what an incredible waste of resources it would be to generate a lot of knowledge about a social issue and not implement any of it in action. Pairing research and action ensures that knowledge generation is tied to program or policy implementation. At the same time, action should always occur with reflection. We need to reflect on the risks and benefits of pursuing one course of action over another. Whereas one set of values may be appropriate to one social context, it may be inappropriate in another. Thus, while we promote more autonomy and control for disadvantaged people in oppressively controlling environments, we do not want to push for more self-determination of violent people. Blind adherence to any value, from personal empowerment to sense of community (terms described in Chapter 4 and 7), is risky. However, action should strive to help build capabilities of individuals, collectives, and communities. As Shinn (2015) points out, "capabilities are freedoms to engage in valued social activities and roles – what people can do and be given both their capacities and the opportunities and constraints in their environments" (p. 234). As we think about understanding and action, we should take a capabilities approach (Sen, 1999b; Shinn, 2015).

A balance between *processes* and *outcomes* is needed to ensure that dialogue is not an end in itself and that the ends do not automatically justify any means. If the object of an intervention is to uphold the rights of a minority group, do we justify any means? On the other hand, can we justify endless talk when the lives of vulnerable children and families in conflict zones are at risk? These tensions between valid processes and just outcomes should be reflected in any framework of values.

Lastly, a balance between *differing* and *unequal voices* is needed. Social policies and programs are typically formulated by powerful politicians, educated government officials and privileged academics. Efforts by community psychologists to work in partnership with disadvantaged members of society are not typical of social and environmental policy formation (Nelson, Prilleltensky, & Hasford, 2013). On the contrary, most social and environmental policies are conceived in the absence of meaningful input from those most affected by them (Glucker, Driessen, Kolhoff, & Runhaar, 2013; Lord & Hutchison, 2007). Hence, a framework of values should be attentive to differing voices, and in particular to those who are often rendered invisible by the political process. Unequal power and unequal representation must be considered in proposing values. Values that are based on the voice of the powerful will usually perpetuate the status quo, whereas values that are based on the voice of the powerless have a better chance of promoting change (Cook, 2014; Lord & Hutchison, 2007).

Community Psychology Values

On every continent, CP has developed with explicit awareness of values. Unlike many forms of science that place a high worth on objectivity, CP supports rigorous scientific methods, but believes that objectivity, as typically understood, is an illusion (Myrdal, 1969). As researchers and practitioners, our values shape the questions we ask, the way we answer them, our connection to the communities we study and serve, and the impacts we hope our work will have. As such, CP is explicit about its values and encourages processes throughout its research and practice to question and critique its values. One way to consider these values is to consider them as:

- values for personal wellbeing
- values for relational wellbeing
- values for collective wellbeing.

Wellbeing is a positive state of affairs, brought about by the balanced satisfaction of personal, relational and collective needs (Prilleltensky et al., 2015; Prilleltensky & Prilleltensky, 2006). Our definition is consistent with Tyler's definition of a prosocial community. According to him, "a prosocial community is one in which everyone is committed to working together for their own well-being, each other's well-being, and that of the community, the society, and ultimately the world" (Tyler, 2007, p. 6). As a vision, wellbeing is an ideal state of affairs for individuals and communities. To achieve it, we have to know the context, the needs of people and groups, and the best available strategies. Wellbeing consists of individual components (personal, relational, and collective needs) and of the **synergy** created by all of them together. In the absence of any one component, wellbeing cannot really be achieved. To make this dictum an integral part of our values, we invoke the meta-value of holism. As Cowen (1996) observed, "optimal development of well-being ... requires integrated sets of operations involving individuals, families, settings, community contexts and macro-level societal structures and policies" (p. 246). Table 3.2 shows the diverse needs and values required to achieve wellbeing at different levels.

Table 3.2 Selected values for personal, relational, and collective wellbeing

	Wellbeing is achieved by holistic practice that attends to the following domains:						
	Personal Wellbeing			**Relational Wellbeing**		**Collective Wellbeing**	
Values	Self-determination	Caring and compassion	Health	Respect for diversity	Participation and collaboration	Support for community structures	Social justice and accountability
Objective	Creation of opportunities for self and others to pursue chosen goals in life without excessive frustration	Expression of care and concern for the physical and emotional wellbeing of self and others	Protection of physical and emotional health of self and others	Promotion of respect and appreciation for diverse social identities and for people's ability to define themselves	Promotion of fair processes whereby children and adults can have meaningful input into decisions affecting their lives	Promotion of vital community structures that facilitate the pursuit of personal and communal goals	Promotion of fair and equitable allocation of bargaining powers, obligations and resources for the oppressed
Needs Addressed	Mastery, control, self-efficacy, voice, choice, skills, growth, autonomy	Love, attention, empathy, attachment, acceptance, positive regard	Emotional and physical wellbeing	Identity, dignity, self-respect, self-esteem, acceptance	Participation, involvement, mutual responsibility	Sense of community, cohesion, formal support	Economic security, shelter, clothing, nutrition, access to vital health and social services

Source: Adapted from Prilleltensky & Nelson (2002).

Values for Personal Wellbeing

Values for personal wellbeing are those that serve the needs of the person. Self-determination, caring and compassion, and personal health advance the wellbeing of individual community members. Self-determination or autonomy refers to the ability of the individual to pursue chosen goals in life without excessive frustration. For instance, the Fairweather Lodge (described in Chapter 2) promoted personal wellbeing by allowing people with mental illness to live in their community (rather than psychiatric institutions), create their own social supports, be employed, and participate in their communities. Personal wellbeing is similar to theories of *empowerment* (discussed in the next chapter), in which individuals and groups strive to gain control over their lives (Zimmerman & Eisman, 2017). Personal health, in turn, is a state of physical and emotional wellbeing that is intrinsically beneficial and extrinsically instrumental in pursuing self-determination. The values of caring and compassion meet the need for empathy, understanding and solidarity. When people are the beneficiaries of these values their personal wellbeing is enhanced. But for them to enjoy these values, they have to engage in relationships that support them and they have to live in communities that care about these values (Partanen, 2016). Caring and compassion are based on sensitive relationships and self-determination is based on resources and opportunities. Without caring relationships there is no mutual understanding and without public resources there is little chance of fulfilling personal goals, especially for the poor and disadvantaged (Narayan, Patel, Schafft, Rademacher, & Koch-Schulte, 2000).

Values for Relational Wellbeing

Following his ten-country journey in the pursuit of happiness, Weiner reflects: "Of all the places I visited, of all the people I met, one keeps coming back to me again and again: Karma Ura, the Bhutanese scholar and cancer survivor. 'There is no such thing as personal happiness,' he told me. 'Happiness is one hundred percent relational'" (Weiner, 2008, p. 324). Weiner agrees: "Our happiness is completely and utterly intertwined with other people: family and friends and neighbours and the woman you hardly notice who cleans your office. Happiness is not a noun or verb. It's a conjunction. Connective tissue" (p. 324). This relationality can induce pleasure but also pain.

When conflicts between individuals or groups arise, it is crucial to have collaborative processes to resolve them. Otherwise, it is just a matter of the powerful imposing their will on others. Relational values remind us that self-determination must have limits. My wishes and desires have to take into account your wishes and desires. If they conflict, we have to have a process to resolve our differences. We have to be able to appreciate diversity and to respect it, and we should not romanticize communities and expect everyone to show caring and compassion for others.

Respect for a person's identity is, according to Canadian philosopher Charles Taylor (1992), "not just a courtesy we owe people. It is a vital human need" (p. 26). When we affirm people's identities, we help them affirm themselves (Bogart, 2015; Romero, Edwards, Fryberg, & Orduña, 2014). When we respect their defining human qualities, we help them respect themselves. Conversely, "a person or group of people can suffer real damage," Taylor says, "if the people or society around them mirror back to them a confining or demeaning or contemptible picture of themselves. Non-recognition or misrecognition can inflict harm, can be a form of oppression" (Taylor, 1992, p. 25). Appreciation for diverse social identities serves as a protective factor, whereas lack of respect constitutes a definite risk factor (Steele, 2011; Yoshino, 2007). In Canada and Australia as well as other countries, Aboriginal peoples have been subjected to demeaning and racist treatment that has led to serious emotional and community problems (Dudgeon, Garvey, & Pickett, 2000; Paradies, 2016; Short, 2016).

Values for Collective Wellbeing

Collective values complement individual aims, for the attainment of personal objectives requires the presence of social resources. **Distributive justice**, or the fair and equitable allocation of bargaining powers, resources, and obligations in society (Fondacaro & Weinberg, 2002; Evans, Rosen, & Nelson, 2014), is a prime example of a collective value. Support for societal structures and for the environment is another key value. Both of these values enable the achievement of personal and communal wellbeing.

Community psychologists have long recognized that people need resources to enjoy good health, to reach their potential, and to nurture their identity (Kloos et al., 2012). This is why the pursuit of **social justice** is so decisive. Without it, the prospects of personal and relational wellbeing remain elusive (Prilleltensky, 2012). To place social justice at the forefront of our priorities, we link it to the meta-value of accountability. Together, social justice and accountability to the oppressed are top priorities for CP.

Pursuit of Wellbeing

How could we pursue wellbeing in the absence of institutions such as public health, schools or transportation systems? Can you think of healthy development in a toxic environment? What about the cultivation of good health and happiness of poor children, single parents, and the very old without government supports (Marmot, 2015a; Putnam, 2016a)? Societal structures that look after people and the environment are essential for the promotion of health and wellbeing. Research on social determinants of health provides convincing evidence that environmental factors, broadly defined, influence our level of wellbeing in multiple ways (Marmot & Allen, 2014; Scribner, Simonsen, & Leonardi, 2017; World Health Organization, 2008). Physical, cultural, political, economic, and psychological factors combine to promote or decrease personal and collective health. There is a great deal of research showing that inequality and lack of control are conducive to poor outcomes (e.g., poor mental and physical health and less longevity), not only for the poor but also for middle-class people (Keating & Hertzman, 1999; Pickett & Wilkinson, 2015; Wilkinson, 1996). This is why we need to uphold the values of social justice and support for public institutions.

Publicly funded institutions perform a critical role in preventing disempowering chain reactions for people at risk. But their virtue goes beyond supporting the needy, for these organizations enhance the health and welfare of the population at large. Strong community structures afford us stable housing, clean water, sewage systems, child-care (in countries where it is publicly funded), recreational opportunities, libraries, unemployment insurance, pension plans, free primary and secondary education, access to health care and many other social goods (Marmot, 2015b; Nelson et al., 2013; Prilleltensky, 2012; Putnam 2016).

The Synergy of Values

Wellbeing comes about in the combination of personal, relational and collective values. The net effect of all the values combined is called *synergy*. This is reflected in our meta-value of holism. What is unique about CP is that it seeks to integrate the three sets of values. As we can see in Fig. 3.2, wellbeing is at the intersection of the three domains. Traditional approaches to psychology have concentrated on the personal and relational domains, to the exclusion of the collective. As a result, psychologists neglected to consider the powerful impact of the psychosocial environment; not only on physical, but also on emotional health.

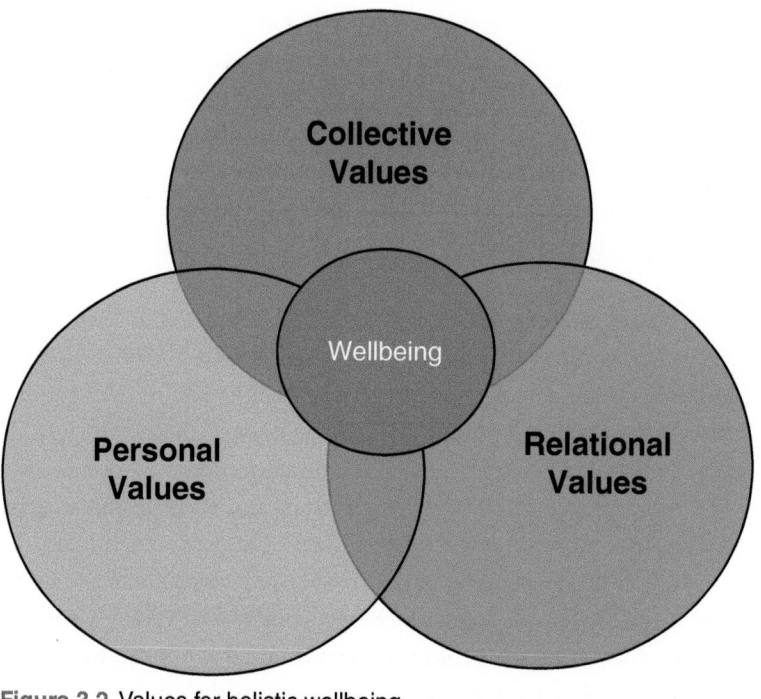

Figure 3.2 Values for holistic wellbeing

Consider, for example, the impact of inequality. Most societies with higher levels of inequality have poorer outcomes for the entire population, not just for the poor and disadvantaged:

> Differences in equity of income distribution is [*sic*] one of the principal determinants of differing health status among wealthy societies. Countries with highly unequal income distributions have poorer health status than those with more equitable income distributions ... This pattern suggests that health status (as a measure of human well-being) may be embedded in collective factors in society, not just in individual factors ... These findings led us to the conclusion that the underlying factors that determine health and well-being must be deeply embedded in social circumstances. (Keating & Hertzman, 1999, p. 6–7)

Given this evidence, we cannot accept definitions of wellbeing that are based exclusively on individual factors. The problem is that these definitions are psycho-centric – they concentrate on the cognitive and emotional sources and consequences of suffering and wellbeing, to the exclusion of the political roots of power and wellbeing. While beliefs and perceptions are important, they cannot be treated in isolation from the cultural, political, and economic environment (Eckersley, 2000, 2001). Instead, CP focuses on collective wellbeing as a value, and to do this, issues of power are foundational (which we will discuss more in the next chapter). Let's consider Margaret, the coal worker, described in Chapter 1. She lost her job due to economic strains and changing technology. Her unemployment and subsequent risk to stable housing was not due to individual failure, but larger, collective (national) issues. If Margaret and others like her who worked with her became homeless, the impact could have cascading effects ranging from decreased personal health (e.g., physical and mental health) to impacts at the community level (e.g., decreasing property values, loss of commerce to local businesses when the plant closed) and national level (unemployment, lower national domestic product). Fortunately, Margaret was in Germany with policies that provided housing support and job skill training. How collectives are organized and the values the individuals and groups hold within those configurations impact synergies greatly. We are interconnected and therefore must consider wellbeing at multiple levels.

Jack Tebes and colleagues have noted that science is a relational process that involves processes and structures, people, policies, and practices that are interconnected and dynamically interact with each other (Tebes, 2012; Tebes et al., 2014). These *heterarchies* involve all levels of relationships to include "individuals acting dynamically in various interconnected groups (e.g., families, peers, neighborhoods), specific regulatory processes in living cells, and [even] Wikipedia" (Tebes et al., 2014, p. 478). Community psychologists are interconnected to the people, places, and processes with inquiry linking individuals with social processes and connecting theory, research and practice (Tebes, 2017).

Amartya Sen, the Nobel Laureate economist, describes wellbeing in terms of capabilities (what individuals are able to be and do) and entitlements (Sen, 1999a, 1999b). Without the latter the former cannot thrive. Entitlements such as preventive health care and educational opportunities are not only means to human development but are also ends in their own right. Wellbeing at the collective level is not measured only by the health and educational outcomes of a group of individuals but also by the presence of enabling institutions and societal infrastructures. Hence, we define wellbeing in broad terms that encompass social progress and human development. We cannot talk about psychological wellbeing in the absence of interpersonal and collective wellbeing. The three kinds are mutually reinforcing and interdependent core values within CP.

The presence or absence of health-promoting factors at all levels can have positive or negative synergistic effects. When collective factors such as social justice and access to valued resources combine with a sense of community and personal empowerment, chances are that psychological and political wellbeing will ensue. When, on the other hand, injustice and exploitation reign, the result is suffering and oppression (Schwalbe, 2008).

Social Justice

When you read research articles, great efforts are typically made to describe the methods and types of analyses conducted. However, seldom are sections devoted to articulating the researchers' values (Prilleltensky, Nelson, & Peirson, 2001). Yet, for CP, values are foundational and achieving social justice is the goal. In this book we define *social justice* as the "fair and equitable allocation of bargaining powers, resources, and obligations in society in consideration of people's differential power, needs, and abilities to express wishes" (Prilleltensky, 2001 p. 754; see also Prilleltensky, 2012). Social justice is a core value of CP because it guides our vision, context, needs, and actions towards the promotion of individual, relational, and collective wellbeing.

Although social justice is a core tenet of CP, the specific label of *social justice* was not present in early CP texts (Fondacaro & Weinberg, 2002). As the field has evolved, so has our thinking about the concept of social justice, as both an outcome and a process (Evans et al. 2014a). Social justice involves not just the rights and benefits of people but also the ways in which these are provided. *Distributive justice* is the fair allocation of opportunities, resources, obligations, and power (Prilleltensky et al., 2001), *to* each unit (such as individuals, families, organizations, communities), according to their abilities, needs, efforts, opportunities and power, and *from* each unit, according to their abilities, needs, efforts, duties, opportunities and privilege (Evans et al., 2014a; Prilleltensky & Nelson, 2009). In the US, Canada, and many other countries, the burden (or obligation) of dealing with environmental pollution resulting from industrial production, for example, is disproportionally put on poor and marginalized communities such as Indigenous communities (Riemer & Van Voorhees, 2009).

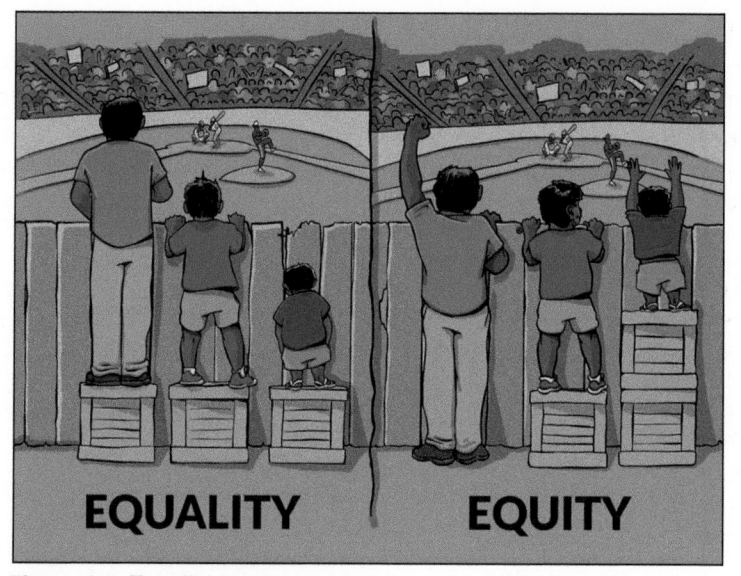

Figure 3.3 Equality versus equity

Image credit: Interaction Institute for Social Change interactioninstitute.org | Artist: Angus Maguire madewithangus.com.

Procedural justice involves transparent, fair, respectful, inclusive, and participatory decision-making processes (Prilleltensky, 2012; Prilleltensky, Nelson, & Peirson 2001). Culley and Hughey (2008), for example, found that the participation of citizens in decision-making processes related to local hazardous waste disputes was limited by their relative lack of social power (described in Chapter 4), which caused barriers to participation and agenda setting. In addition, it shaped conceptions about what participation was necessary or possible. Procedural justice is the process while distributive justice is the outcome of obtaining fairness. What is important to consider is that fairness does not mean the same or equal goods for everyone. CP is focused on equity more than equality (See Fig. 3.3 for an example). What is available and what is needed are very important components of fairness. For example, imagine that you have a barrel of apples to distribute across a village of hungry people. Would you divide the barrel so that everyone gets the same number of apples or would you consider the caloric needs of each person (e.g., a baby, a large man, a pregnant woman)? In a just society, we expect all to have access to such things as shelter, economic security, clothing, nutrition, health care, social services, self-determination, and voice (Nelson & Prilleltensky, 2005).

In the next chapter and throughout the book, the value of social justice and the power differentials associated with injustice will be highlighted. For community psychologists to work towards social justice, we must always be aware of and question power structures and the status quo (Prilleltensky & Nelson, 2009).

Chapter Summary

CP's goal is the pursuit of social justice in the service of personal, relational, and collective wellbeing. In order to work towards this vision, we must identify our values and how they interact with context, processes, and actions. From that awareness we can work towards the end of oppression and injustice and towards a just and thriving community.

PRACTITIONER COMMENTARY

Sticking to Our Vision and Values Can Sometimes Be Hard

Kien Lee, Community Science, USA

Community Science is a professional practice of social scientists and practitioners (some of whom identify as community psychologists) who work with organizations in the public, philanthropic, and nonprofit sectors to connect knowledge to social change. We believe that having community – both a feeling and a set of relationships among people, formed and maintained to meet their needs – is essential for our wellbeing. We strive to create strong and capable communities where all members – regardless of race, ethnicity, or culture – have the opportunity to reach their fullest potential. We research community change strategies, evaluate community change initiatives, and build the capacity of public agencies, foundations, and nonprofit organizations to solve social problems that weaken community.

As a community psychologist in a leadership position at Community Science, I work to ensure that our values and vision are integrated into all aspects of our policies, operations, and contracted work. We believe that relationships matter, and this value can generate both opportunity and tension in our interactions with funders, program partners, and community leaders. We also believe that we should *do no harm* through our work and always keep in mind the wellbeing of communities and the public in general. Last but not least, our work features an explicit commitment to equity and social justice, which can cause some to question our objectivity and mistakenly conclude that such a commitment hinders scientific rigor.

These values have different implications for us in different contexts. I have encountered situations where staying true to these values, which guide our actions in service of equity and social justice, was a rocky road. In such circumstances, we strived to balance:

- what we believed was an ethical decision, but not necessarily a smart financial decision for our professional practice
- how to be collaborative and supportive of our clients and partners, who shared our commitment to equity and social justice, while being critical about their strategies and, sometimes, performance – especially when we operated in an evaluator role
- how to maintain scientific rigor and cultural competency when there were insufficient funds to build relationships (and to ensure there were enough funds left for data collection, analysis, and reporting) and we had little control over the implementation timeline.

Several years ago, for instance, Community Science evaluated a regional initiative that consisted of multiple grant cycles and support from an organization that was contracted by the funder to manage the initiative's implementation ("the managing organization"). At the end of every year, we presented our evaluation findings and recommendations to inform the initiative's continual improvement.

As our nation faced a declining economy, the funder was forced to cut its budget, starting with its evaluation contracts. The funder asked us how likely it was that the evaluation would reveal a different set of outcomes in the coming year. Our response was negative because to date, our recommendations had not been implemented. This meant that our evaluation contract was most likely going to be terminated (a loss of several hundred thousand dollars), and a difficult conversation had to occur with the funder and the managing organization about why the initiative's implementation had not been adjusted and improved based on the evaluation findings and recommendations. This conversation surfaced the oversight and performance issues of the funder and the managing organization, respectively, and created an uncomfortable situation for everyone. Nevertheless, we knew that the ethical thing to do was to be honest about the low probability of a different set of outcomes and the reasons for it. Community Science's values and vision guided our actions through this difficult period.

In another instance, when we were contracted to evaluate a statewide, complex community change initiative, we had to persuade the funder and program partner to engage grantees, and determine what was considered success and how to measure community change. We raised questions about what constituted "community engagement," "community collaboration," "systems," and "equity." The answers to these questions were essential for us in designing the appropriate evaluation, building the grantees' capacity to participate in the evaluation, and using data to inform and improve their work.

During the discussions, we encountered the following issues, for which there were no easy resolutions:

- the tension between the funder's desire to not "overburden" grantees with reporting requirements and still be able to fully understand the change process and outcomes effected by them
- questions about whose equity in the grantee communities was at stake and the role of philanthropic institutions in facilitating the answers while being a part of the power structure
- misperceptions about evaluation, in particular the notion that our objectivity was compromised when we spoke about our commitment to equity and social justice.

During the evaluation process, we also encountered, and sometimes even generated, conflicts. The program partner and Community Science were expected to work collaboratively. However, this goal was often not operationalized, and the funder assumed that the two parties would work out any differences among ourselves – because after all, we shared similar values about the importance of relationships, community change, equity, and social justice. Sometimes, we resolved our differences amicably, and sometimes, we did not. For instance, the program partner came to believe that grantees had successfully "engaged the community" based on conversations they had during site visits. In contrast, we found that "community engagement" was really limited, or even lacking, through our interviews with various groups of stakeholders in each grantee community and through the systematic analysis of the data. This difference in our respective conclusions about the grantees' degree of community engagement – a crucial aspect of the initiative – became a contentious issue, which affected the relationship. The funder was consulted; they shared the program partner's belief because of exchanges with the grantee representatives. We stood by our conclusion based on the data (after we went back and double-checked the data and our analysis because the disagreement made us second-guess our findings), which led to lengthy discussions to work out the differences, taking time and resources away from other aspects of everyone's work. The funder's lack of acknowledgement about the power it holds over the relationship between the program partner and Community Science – in large part due to the way philanthropy and the consulting industry are structured to encourage competition and not collaboration – did not help.

In a third example, we were asked by the funder to revise an evaluation report to highlight their initiative's impact on promoting inclusiveness and equity. Our findings had suggested that while the initiative helped to diversify certain organizations' board membership – no doubt an important step toward inclusiveness – the organizations participating in the initiative did not have a common or clear understanding about what the funder meant by "inclusiveness" and "equity."

Also, the initiative's results were mixed. Some of the organizations implemented a series of diversity trainings with no concrete results related to inclusiveness and equity. Studies have shown that diversity trainings are not an effective solution for building the cultural competency of organizations or for sustaining equitable practices. On the other hand, a few organizations succeeded in institutionalizing a policy to dedicate a certain number of board positions for community leaders. They reported, however, the initiative was not solely responsible for this result but helped to accelerate their decision.

We informed the funding agency's program officer that we would not revise the report to reflect a favorable perspective, as that was not an accurate portrayal of the initiative. What we agreed to do, however, was to cite the program officer's perspective in the report, explaining the reasons for her opinion. This allowed us to maintain the rigor of our evaluation design while giving voice to the program officer's unique perspective. This decision aligned with our values.

In summary, at Community Science, we are clear about how our values and vision guide our actions. In reality, our actions based on these values and vision can cause tensions, test relationships, and sometimes even harm our organization financially. Additionally, holding to these values can affect our personal wellbeing, as we struggle individually to reconcile what we believe is right with the pressures we experience from external factors, the norms and practices of organizations on which we rely for support, and the communities in which we work.

Nevertheless, I cannot imagine engaging in a professional practice that is committed to building healthy and strong communities, and ultimately a nation, without such values. The experiences described in this short essay are reminders that as we strive to act as "professional helpers" building the capacity of communities, we too must continually build our own capacity to be mindful of how our actions – intentional or unintentional – could harm communities.

Key Terms

Collectivism (collectivist society): A belief in the importance of groups and communities that shapes attitudes and behaviors of citizens.

Communitarianism: A school of thought that strives to restore citizens' responsibilities towards the collective as a means of advancing social wellbeing.

Distributive justice: The fair allocation of opportunities, resources, obligations, and power.

Heterarchy: A biological or social organizational system that consists of an interconnected and overlapping network of components that operate dynamically to both emerge from and govern the interactions of constituent components. For example, individuals are connected to and a part of families, schools, communities, jobs, etc. They are not only influenced by these systems but also influence the systems.

Individualism (individualist society): A belief in the importance and supremacy of individuals over groups or collectives.

Liberalism: A school of thought that upholds the rights of the individual in society and espouses individual solutions to problems in life.

Procedural justice: Transparent, fair, respectful, inclusive, and participatory decision-making processes.

Social Justice: The fair and equitable allocation of bargaining powers, resources, and obligations in society in consideration of people's differential power, needs, and abilities to express wishes.

Synergy: The positive effect of multiple forces coming together.

Values: A set of principles, based on moral reasoning, which guide behavior.

Vision: An image of a desired state of affairs worth striving for.

Resources

Society for Community Research and Action's Values and Mission Statement: www.scra27.org/who-we-are

European Community Psychology Association's Vision:
www.ecpa-online.eu/AboutECPA/Vision/tabid/76/language/en-US/Default.aspx

Australian Psychological Society College of Community Psychology's objectives:
www.groups.psychology.org.au/ccom/about_us/

The New Zealand Psychological Society Institute of Community Psychology: www.psychology.org.nz/membership/member-groups/institute-of-community-psychology/?#.WYjvpKOZOEI

Red Latinoamericana de Formacíon en Psicología Communitaria (Latin American Community Psychology Training Network): www.red.pucp.edu.pe/psicologia-comunitaria/conoce-la-red/objetivos-y-caracteristicas/

Values Position published in the Global Journal of Community Psychology Practice: www.gjcpp.org/pdfs/v2i3-0005-SpecSession-final.pdf

POWER, EMPOWERMENT, AND DEPOWERMENT

4

Warm-up Questions

Before you begin reading this chapter, we invite you to reflect on the following questions:

1   How would you define power?

2   Is power an individual construct or a relational one?

3   Is power absolute? Does it vary in situations and among different people?

Learning Objectives

In this chapter, we introduce you to some conceptualizations of power and the challenges of defining the construct and recognizing it in practice.

In this chapter you will learn about

- The relational and situational aspects of power
- The complexity of power
- The different dimensions of power
- The concept of empowerment
- What contributes to "mattering"
- Why community psychologists must always consider issues of power when working with communities and towards social change

Opening Thinking: Power Dynamics in Daily Activities

Read the following vignette and consider how **power** plays a role in the interactions, behaviors, and feelings of the people. Part way through the chapter, we will consider how concepts of power apply to this example.

> For my mother, being ready for school means being presentable and respectful. Although we have already spent two hours in the fields today, my mother does not offer breakfast until I have scrubbed my face and hands and changed into clean clothes. As she braids my long black hair, she asks about what I will be learning in class today and reminds me to be polite to my teacher. She is clear that I must treat my teacher

with the same honor and respect that I show my parents. When she finishes my hair, I help my three little sisters so my mom can finish the tortillas. It is my job to check the girls' homework, help pack their assignments into their backpacks, and make sure they look presentable. Once we finish breakfast, the five of us pile into our truck and head for school. A few blocks into our drive, I hear my mom gasp and turn unexpectedly to the right. Before I ask why she is heading the wrong direction, I notice the police car drive past the street behind us. Although it is unlikely the officer would have pulled her over, one traffic stop could result in deportation. (My sisters and I are citizens, born here. But my mother came here without a visa or government permission.) Soon after our detour, we arrive at school. My mother walks us to class, taking time to kiss the littlest one on each cheek before she runs into her kindergarten classroom. My mother smiles at me as she turns and walks past a couple of mothers also dropping their children off. As she passes the group, the tall one mutters as she raised her latte to her lips, "Wetback." Her friend nods, and then says, "All these illegals! Stealing our jobs and ruining our schools." I watch as the smile falls from her face and my proud mother seems to shrink a few inches. This is the ways we start our mornings.

The Power of Thinking about Power

Have you ever wondered why things are the way they are? Why all people face the doors when they enter an elevator, rather than each other? Why students don't (usually) yell at their professors when they receive a failing grade? Why people seem especially serious and polite when talking to the police officer that just pulled them over for speeding? There are many contributors to these patterns, but foundational to them all are issues of power – power differentials between people (e.g., student/professor, driver/police officer) and societal norms and expectations with consequences (e.g., laughed at/shunned for facing the wrong way, expensive ticket or even deportation). This chapter will introduce different conceptualizations of power, identify ways in which power is not equally or fairly distributed, and describe theories and efforts for redistributing power (**empowerment** and **depowerment**).

What Is Power?

Defining power has been a challenge for many, as it is inherent in all social interactions and embedded in our social norms, structures, and cultural activities. Max Weber (1978) defined power as "the probability that one actor within a social relationship will be in a position to carry out his own will despite resistance" (Weber, 1978 p. 53). Although this definition is individualistic, explicit in this statement is that one person has power to do something. Also implicit in the statement is that others do not have power to stop their will or power over the person's ability to act. Robert Dahl (1957) observed "that some people have more power than others is one of the most palpable facts of human existence" (p. 201). In describing power, he noted that it is *relational*, meaning that one cannot demand power without others acknowledging it. For example, we could stand on a corner and yell for cars to pull over. It is unlikely that any would. However, if one of us was to dress as a police officer, it is quite probable that cars would pull over. Power is *relative*, often unequally balanced.

Thus, one could compare power between people and/or groups. When a father tells his five-year-old daughter to take his hand before crossing the street and she immediately complies, his greater power in their relationship is clear. Similarly, when a group of African-American boys cease their laughing when a police officer walks past them on the street, the boys' lesser power in that setting is clear. Power is also *limited* and *never absolute*. A person or group may have more or less power than another person or group, but they never have complete power. That same five-year-old girl could throw a tantrum and refuse to cross the street, exerting power over her father. Similarly, a boss may have much power over her employees, but those same people could work poorly, sabotage production, anger customers, or go on strike by refusing to work (Kagan, Burton, Duckett, Lawthom, & Siddiquee, 2011). Thus, no one ever has complete power and no one is ever completely powerless. Power can never exist in isolation – it is inherently a social process (Foucault, 1983). That is why people often refer to it as *social power*.

Several theorists have explored ways in which power enables or inhibits people. Much of this writing has described people or groups as having differing power relations to one another. This includes:

- *Power Over* – This is the explicit or implicit control over the actions of others. This level of dominance enables a person/people to affect the opportunities, actions, and thoughts of those with less power (Gaventa, 2006). For example, by not allowing women to vote, governments exercise power over women's ability to participate in government or affect policies regarding their rights or the rule of the country.

- *Power With* – This involves more egalitarian relationships that involve power sharing. As Gaventa (2006) described, this includes a "synergy which can emerge through partnerships and collaboration with others, or through processes of collective action and alliance building" (p. 24). For example, in the US, much of the agricultural work is done by immigrants, many of whom are unauthorized to work in the country. Historically, when these workers argued for better work conditions or higher pay, they were threatened with deportation or replaced by another ethnic immigrant group. In 1965, Filipino American grape workers went on strike and asked for support from the largely Hispanic American National Farm Worker Association (NFWA). Although the NFWA did not feel ready to mobilize a strike, they knew that their collective power would be stronger if they joined forces. The Filipino and Hispanic strikers worked together, forming picket lines and sharing strike kitchens and union halls. They also created the shared United Farm Workers union. The striking workers also urged a boycott of grapes by visiting families throughout Canada and the US, telling people their story, and requesting that no grapes be purchased. Their non-violent protest and collective action resulted in the first union contract, granting workers better pay, benefits, and protections (www.ufw. org). Their voice and impact were *powered with* each other.

- *Power To* – This means that individuals have opportunities to act more freely within some "realms of their lives, through power sharing, or what is commonly called empowerment" (Hollander & Offerman, 1990, p. 174) (described later in the section). *Power to* involves "the capacity to act; to exercise agency and to realise the potential of rights, citizenship or voice" (Gaventa 2006, p. 24). For instance, many immigrants must compete with other disadvantaged people for jobs, while often overcoming language barriers and acculturation challenges. In a study of African immigrants in Spain, García Ramírez et al. (2005) found that successful employment and perceptions of power to work were greatly enhanced through social support and feelings of empowerment.

- *Power Within* – This form of power is a more internalized process by which there are increases in confidence, a sense of identity, and awareness that action is needed (Gaventa, 1980, 1995). Conceptually, *power within* is related to critical consciousness (discussed in Chapter 5). Increases of power within are often observed through participatory action research (described in Chapter 13), in which people realize that they have the capacity to change aspects of unequal power in their lives. For example, in a recent project my colleagues and I [Stephanie] did with low-income, Latinx middle-schoolers, the students realized that although school lunches were provided for free, they could still have voice in what was served. Through their data collection about lunch consumption and classmate preferences, coupled with an understanding of the process of reimbursement (i.e., schools would lose tremendous amounts of money if food was not picked up by students), the students realized that they had the power within that could bring about change (Reich, Kay, & Lin, 2015).

- *Power From* – This involves individuals or groups having "the ability to resist the power of others by effectively fending off their unwanted demands" (Hollander & Offerman, 1990 p. 179). Familiar demonstrations of *power from* are strikes and protests from groups that are unwilling to accept efforts to disempower them. From Mahatma Ghandi's prison hunger strikes in India to the freedom riders' sit-ins at segregated restaurants in the Southern US to Mkhuseli Jack's call for local boycotts and Desmond Tutu's call for international boycotts in South Africa, these people and their supporting groups refused to accept that they were not offered the same privileges and freedoms as their White counterparts. They worked for *power from* these oppressive systems and processes (see the end of chapters for recommendations on where to read more about these movements).

Power in Context

In thinking about power, we may have power over, with, to, within and from in different settings, with different people. In considering the vignette from the chapter's start, who has the most power? Who has more power in which settings? What types of power does the mother have at home, with her daughters, at her children's school, while driving, with policies related to immigration, or with employment opportunities? As we progress through the book, you will find that power is a foundational component of all that community psychologists do and the values we hold. In learning more about the field, it is important to focus your lens on the way power flows between people, places, and practices. As part of this understanding, it is important to consider power as a multidimensional construct. Next, we describe some of these dimensions.

The Multidimensional Nature of Power

Early conceptualizations of power often employed a simple dichotomized view, based on who has the larger and most recognized power compared to others. As Lukes (1974) described, the powerful are "those who prevail in decision making" (p. 111). Gaventa (1995) clarified that "power is understood as the product of who wins and who loses on key, clearly recognized issues, in a relatively open system" (p. 29). According to this view, power is demonstrated as having *power over* others. In such systems, decision-making is based on having superior resources to advocate for oneself or cause, be that at the interpersonal level or larger political level. This conceptualization may explain why Person A has power over Person B in a specific context (Dahl, 1957) but does not explain why Person B accepts Person A's decisions (Gaventa, 1980). Viewing power along a single dimension does not explain either why disadvantaged groups behave differently in different contexts. Why is it that protests and actions towards civil rights for Black Americans occurred in some Southern States long before they occurred elsewhere in the South? In considering power, a one-dimensional view is insufficient.

Over the years, scholars such as Gaventa (1995), Lukes (1974), and VeneKlasen and Miller (2002) have identified three key forms of power[1], which together provide a deeper understanding of the complexity of power. Culley and Hughey (2008), based on Gaventa's earlier work, refer to each of these three forms as: (1) superior bargaining resources; (2) control of participation and debate; and (3) shaping interests. More recently, VeneKlasen and Miller (2002), followed by Gaventa (2006), describe these three forms of power as visible, hidden, and invisible. Let's use the game of Monopoly as a way of illustrating these three forms of power. Generally, people play Monopoly with the goal of winning the game. The three dimensions of power can be compared to three complementary strategies for winning the game. The first strategy is to ensure you have more resources (money, streets, houses, etc.) and/or skills than anybody else. If you dominate these resources, you obviously have a much better chance of winning. This first form (*superior bargaining resources/visible*) relates to the early conceptualization of power described above and is the form of power that is most obvious in its execution.

The second strategy is to change the rules of the games (e.g., you never have to go to prison) and decide who gets to play (e.g., only allowing inexperienced players). Clearly, those players who are not invited to play will not be able to win the game, even if they do have superior skills. This second form of power (*control of participation and debate/hidden*), which Lukes (1974) referred to as "agenda-making situations" (p. 111), considers more of the context of how and what decisions are made as well as who makes those decisions. This view of power is focused not only on the roles of Person A and Person B in a given context of decision-making, but also why Person C was not involved. This hidden face of power is "not about who won and who lost on key issues, but was about keeping issues and actors from getting to the table in the first place" (Bachrach & Baratz, 1970, cited in Gaventa, 1980). This form of power plays out by controlling agendas, determining participation, and writing procedures and regulations.

A current example of this is the establishment of governmental regulations (from local to national), which are typically established by appointed officials. These regulators were not elected to their position nor typically consult with citizens about how such regulations affect residents' daily life (Crow, Albright, & Koebele, 2016). Instead, the establishment of these regulations and appointment of the people that oversee them are often influenced by elected officials, lobbyists, and businesses. This is a common practice for the fuel industries (e.g., petroleum, natural gas, coal), where regulators set parameters around mining that do not involve the people who live near these sites – often Indigenous people – and suffer the environmental and health consequences (Hilson, 2002).

---

[1]   Gaventa and others have referred to these three forms as "dimensions" or "faces" of power. To avoid confusion with the three dimensions of the power cube, which we will introduce a little further down, we will use the term "form of power" here, which relates to one of the three dimensions/faces of the power cube.

The third form of power then (*shaping interests/invisible*) is to manipulate the thinking of other players in a way that provides you with an advantage (e.g., convincing them to exchange their superior property with your inferior one or making them believe that they actually don't want to win the game). When the rules of the game are complex and a player has more resources than others, this strategy is easier to employ and more effective. This third form of power relates to legitimacy that is afforded consciously or unconsciously by others. Person A may exercise power over B by getting him to do what she wants. She may also be exercising power when she influences, shapes, or determines what Person B wants (Gaventa, 1980). This view incorporates not just the interpersonal interactions between winners and losers, or the rules of the game, but also the ideological, social, and historical forces that contribute to the legitimacy of the status quo. For example, if Person A always gets her way, Person B may over time stop trying to make decisions, which can result in an unconscious pattern of withdrawal by B, "maintained not by fear of power of A but a sense of powerlessness within B" (Gaventa, 1980 p. 17). This sense of powerlessness (a reduction of *power to* and *power from*) can generalize to other decisions between A and B and could possibly be passed down to those similar or related to B. The internalized legitimacy approach explains historical and institutionalized forms of **oppression** and power inequality. Indigenous people, for example, have been made to believe that they are somehow inferior to their colonizers, and thus, deserve to be exploited. This leads to a feeling of powerlessness and despair, with many negative consequences for generations of Indigenous people, while allowing their colonizers to continue to exploit and destroy their land (see Chapter 15). While this is a very consequential form of power, it is often invisible. It is manifested in the language that we use, in cultural practices, in learning material, and in our way of thinking. It requires significant consciousness-raising to become aware of how power is embedded in these different aspects of our life and to start questioning their legitimacy.

Power Cube

To account for additional complexity in the analysis of power, Gaventa (2006) proposed a "power cube" model, for which he added two dimensions of power (levels and spaces) to the forms of power discussed above (see Fig. 4.1). One side of the cube (the levels dimension) describes the differing layers of decision-making and authority including the local, national and global contexts. A lot of local decision-making related to environmental protection, for example, are significantly limited by international treaties, that were drafted by appointed officials with little to no input of local stakeholders and often benefit the profit interests of global corporations. The next side addresses potential arenas for participation and action, which are referred to as closed, invited, and claimed spaces. Some spaces are closed with decision-making done by the elite (more empowered/power over). Some spaces are invited spaces in which certain people are allowed to participate in decision-making and others are not (power to and power from). Lastly, other spaces are claimed/created spaces. These are more organic spaces that emerge or are claimed from the more powerful (power with). Cooperatives, for example, are democratic forms of worker-owned businesses that reclaim power from the profit-driven capitalistic global corporations. Within these different types of spaces that exist at different levels, there are varying forms of power that are visible, hidden, or invisible. Visible power often involves structures, procedures, authorities, and formal rules for decision-making. Hidden power is power often used by the elite to control and maintain unequal decision-making and maintain inequitable power distribution. Invisible power is described

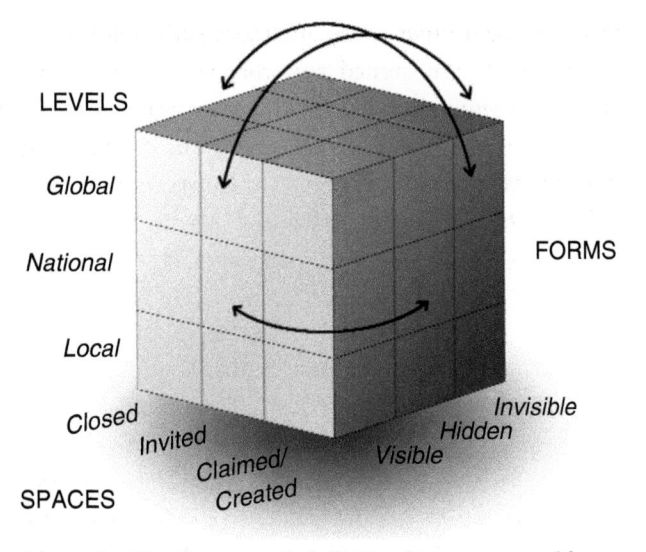

Figure 4.1 The "power cube": the levels, spaces, and forms of power (Gaventa, 2006)

Reproduced with permission from the Institute of Development Studies.

as "probably the most insidious of the three dimensions of power, invisible power shapes the psychological and ideological boundaries of participation" (Gaventa, 2006, p. 26).

Gaventa's conceptualizations of power and the placement of these three dimensions (levels, spaces, and forms) in a cube is an attempt to highlight the multifaceted nature of power. Much like a Rubik's cube, many configurations of power are possible, depending on who participates, the openness of the space, the levels of focus, and awareness of power dynamics for those involved or left out. The power cube is a way to visualize the dynamic and relational nature of power (see www.powercube.net for more details and examples).

Power and Community Work

As community researchers and practitioners, it is important that we consider issues of power. However, these issues are complex. There are historical patterns of power distribution that influence how we interact and the ways we feel our power, over, to, with, from, and within in every social situation. Think about a one-on-one interaction you might have with another person. How do the differences in your age, skin color, gender, physical ability, sexual orientation, accent, education, etc. influence the ways in which you interact with each other? How do these differences affect your comfort and ability to speak freely and honestly? To disagree with the other? To compromise or be unyielding? In a simple interpersonal interaction, all these dimensions of power are at play. Now consider how these power issues impact interactions with larger groups, corporations, communities, cities, or countries, with a greater diversity of personal characteristics, values, agendas, and authority.

Brazilian liberation theologian Paulo Freire (1970) acknowledged that when all of these power dynamics are considered, oppression dehumanizes the suppressed as well as their oppressors. That is to say that large power differentials result in inequity and such injustice is bad for all – including those with disproportionate power. For example, countries with high levels of inequality tend to have lower levels of mutual trust, which is related to lower levels of community cohesion and wellbeing, which affects both the relatively poor and the wealthy (although not equally; Wilkinson & Pickett, 2009). Freire (1970) also argued that through resisting oppression, the supressed (those with less power) free themselves and their oppressors (those with more power). He further describes a critical pedagogy of the oppressed, that is education and thinking that goes beneath surface meanings, dominant views, and patterns to understand root causes, social context discourse and ideology (Shor, 1980), as having two distinct stages:

> In the first, the oppressed unveil the world of oppression and through the praxis commit themselves to its transformation. In the second stage, in which the reality of the oppression has already been transformed, this pedagogy ceases to belong to the oppressed and becomes a pedagogy of all people in its process of permanent liberation. (Freire, 1970, p. 54)

Important is the idea that to work towards liberation and social justice, people must question the how, why, and by whom they are oppressed. They must consider the role of power in interpersonal interactions as well as within structures (such as who has access to an education, who has a roof over their head at night) and processes (like why generations of some are illiterate while others obtain graduate degrees, why some feel comfortable speaking and are typically listened to while others are silenced). By questioning the game, who gets to play it, and who usually wins (i.e., the visible, hidden, and invisible forms of power), people gain awareness of the issues and insight into what is needed to enact meaningful change.

Let's think about the building of a nuclear power plant. These plants are never built in high-income neighborhoods. Instead, they are typically erected in impoverished areas with high unemployment and lower average community education (Blowers & Leroy, 1994). Once they are built, housing prices in these neighborhoods go down (Davis, 2010). Even though there are documented health risks to nuclear waste and the threat of meltdown, these struggling communities often welcome the new business and accompanying jobs. The new jobs are relatively low paying in comparison to the energy company executives that profit highly from the plant but never risk nuclear exposure. In Freire's model, the residents must question why their community shoulders most of the environmental and health risks, but receives the smallest amount of money (visible power). Additionally, why the community members can work at the plant but not have a voice in its operation (hidden power). Further, why the school has a vocational program for working at the plant but not an engineering or physics course on nuclear power, technological innovation, or conservation (invisible power). The residents must question why property values have gone down since the nuclear power plant became operational and why, consequently, there are fewer forms of employment outside the plant. Only through this increase in awareness of the issues can power be redistributed.

In considering Gaventa's power cube, we can consider which spaces are invited, closed, or claimed and how these processes impact local community and national and global finance, trade, and environment. Further, we can consider these issues along the three forms of power of who gets to make the decisions and who benefits the most or is hurt by the decision (superior bargaining resources), selects who participates or is excluded from decision-making (control of participation and debate), and who withdraws from the decision-making because they feel their voice is never heard (shaping interests).

Freire's writings align well with a famous French theorist, Michel Foucault's, writing about conceptualizations of power. While Freire believed that critical consciousness was essential (awareness and understanding of power inequality), Foucault argued that knowledge and power are interconnected (Gordon, 1980). As such, academic disciplines, governments, and social institutions (e.g., prisons, schools) are systems by which power is exercised (Foucault, 1980, 1983). Thus, knowledge can ensure unequal power (by limiting who has access to knowledge or not) or be used to redistribute power (by increasing access to knowledge and promoting empowerment). This is even more critical in an era in which knowledge is the driving economic force, which is why it is often referred to as the "knowledge economy."

However, Freire argued that transformation and liberation could only occur when power is seized by the oppressed. As mentioned above, he believed that inequality and oppression dehumanizes both the oppressors and the oppressed. When the dominant (oppressors) hand over power, it is still an act of privilege and dominance and humanization is not restored. Freire believed that only the oppressed have the strength to change existing power structures in a way that fully restores humanity to both the oppressed and the oppressors. The heart of a liberation movement is, therefore, always within the oppressed groups in society. It is important to note that Freire was shaping his thoughts and writing during a time when many Latin American countries were controlled by dictators and highly oppressive military regimes. Foundational to Freire and others' ideas is whether power is a finite resource that can be reallocated but not diminished or increased, or whether power is infinite, with more power being created, shared, and stored. If power is finite, as Freire believed, then the empowerment of some must come from the depowerment of others. However, if power is infinite, then no power needs to be removed from some in order for others to have more.

Privilege/Overpowerment

Since power is relational, in most interactions some enjoy more power than others. This is called *privilege*. When some enjoy a high level of privilege compared to others, this is also referred to as **overpowerment** (Prilleltensky, Nelson, & Peirson, 2001). At times, people actively seek out power, but in most cases, there are structures in place that ensure the perpetuation of privilege. These structures range from social norms and values (related to such things as race, gender, mental and physical ability, age, sexuality, social class) as well as political and economic systems. Here is a personal example: as a sixth grader, I [Stephanie] was one of four White, English-only speaking students in a predominately low-income Latino and Black elementary school class. Although I was an ethnic minority at school, I was aware that I had privilege. Even my nickname of "White Girl/Blanca," was said affectionately. Although economically similar, the color of my skin and the status associated with it provided power, making my sense of privilege in school settings obvious. I feel confident that being one of four Latino students in an all-White school would have been very different (as would the meaning of a nickname like "Brown Girl/Morena"). Interestingly, my gender was not a source of power in my school and I was often sent to the principal's office for "unladylike behavior" such as playing football with the boys or questioning the way teachers spoke to some students (but perhaps my racial privilege allowed me to speak up or play with the boys).

For many, privilege is a self-perpetuating process. For example, families with high educational attainment tend to have jobs that pay well and have greater job security (e.g., physician, professor). This offers better housing, access to better schools, food stability, high quality health care, etc. Children growing up in these homes are likely to be healthy, do well in school and have high expectations for their future (Swartz, 2008). As such, they are likely to have high educational attainment and get better paying, more stable jobs. For instance, in the US, at least 47 percent of earnings by age 30 can be explained by parents' income (Guldi, Page, & Stevens, 2006). Subsequently, the children of the more affluent are likely to enjoy the same privilege that their parents did, providing intergenerational transmission of power. Thus, power works to maintain itself, if not accumulate more.

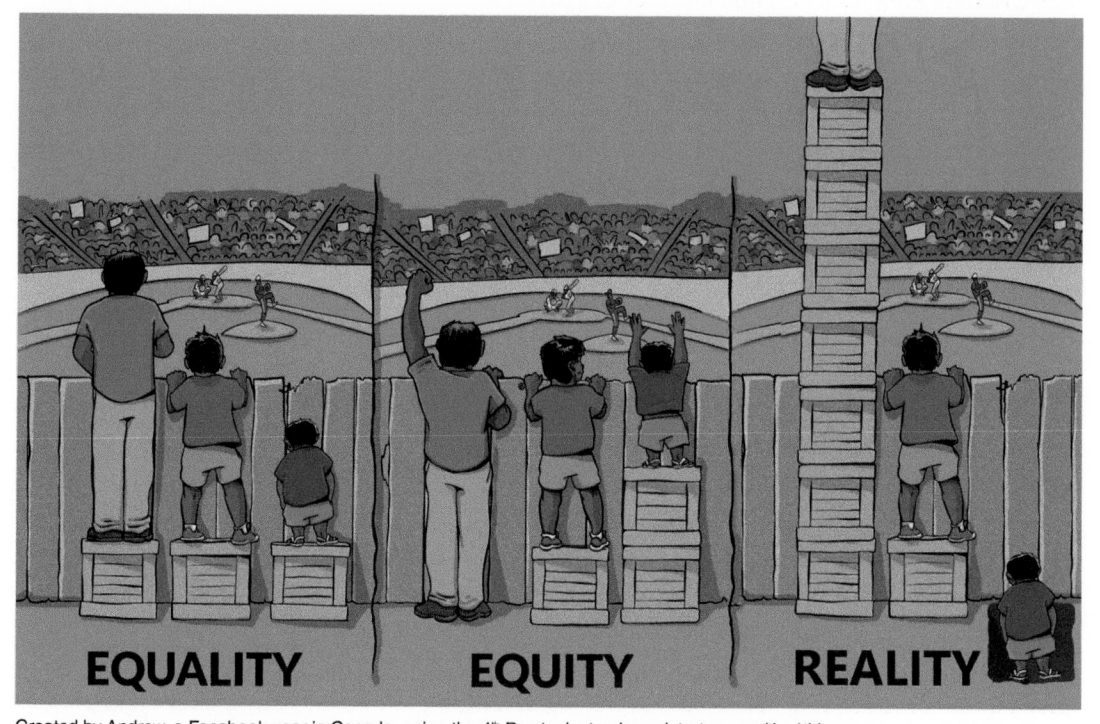

Created by Andrew, a Facebook user in Canada, using the 4th Box tool, storybasedstrategy.org/the4thbox

Zero-Sum (Finite) Versus Zero-Plus (Infinite) Power

As mentioned earlier, theorists have often questioned whether there is a finite (zero-sum) amount of power or if more can be generated and shared (zero-plus). Belief in either type comes with different goals for social justice, ranging from depowerment of some to creation of more power for others – or what Julian Rappaport (1987) described as "expanding resources." Zero-sum conceptualizations of power are predicated on conflictual characteristics of power with people fighting to keep or gain power (Culley & Hughey, 2008). The zero-plus ideas of power can be one-sided, in which those with less power need to be empowered, but those currently holding disproportionate amounts of power do not need to be depowered or even acknowledge their disproportionate privilege. Each conceptualization of power has varying approaches for promoting social justice and equitable distributions of power.

Empowerment

Empowerment, the increasing of power, is often described as a value, process, and theoretical model (Zimmerman, 2000; Zimmerman & Eisman, 2017). As mentioned in Chapter 3, social justice and equity are clear values in community psychology (CP) and changing power distributions is an essential process for promoting these goals. As a process, empowerment involves the "mechanisms by which people, organizations, and communities gain mastery over their lives" (Rappaport, 1984, cited in Weissberg, 1999, p. 17). As a theoretical model, the process and the outcome of empowerment are meaningful and are tied to the context and population being empowered (Zimmerman, 2000).

Empowerment is about obtaining, producing, or enabling power. This can happen at the individual, group, community, and social level. Maton (2008) describes it as "a group-based, participatory, developmental process through which marginalized or oppressed individuals and groups gain greater control over their lives and environment, acquire valued resources and basic rights, and achieve important life goals and reduced societal marginalization" (p. 5). This definition includes a process but also emphasizes outcomes – control over resources. Based on the work of Zimmerman (2000) and Speer and colleagues (Speer & Hughey, 1995; Speer, Hughey, Gensheimer, & Adams-Leavitt, 1995), we represent in Table 4.1 the various domains and dynamics of empowerment at four levels of analysis. Some of the outcomes are reinforcing of the processes, as better empowerment outcomes should generate more empowerment processes and vice versa.

The concept of empowerment has stimulated much discussion in CP, with two special issues of the *American Journal of Community Psychology* dedicated to it in 1994 (Serrano-García & Bond, 1994) and 1995 (Perkins & Zimmerman, 1995) and one in the *Journal of Community Psychology* in 2008 (Speer, Newbrough, & Lorion, 2008). Empowerment is not a stable or global state of affairs. As the vignette at the beginning of the chapter highlights, people can feel empowered in

Table 4.1 Empowerment processes and outcomes at multiple levels of analysis

Levels of Analysis	Processes	Outcomes
Individual	• Training in critical thinking • Participation in action groups • Mentoring experiences • Connecting with people in similar situations • Training in value-based practice	• Consciousness-raising • Participation in social action • Assertiveness • Expanded options in life • Sense of control • Mentoring others
Organizational	• Shared leadership • Training in group facilitation • Participation in decision making • Sense of common purpose	• Increased resources • Enhanced connections • Solidarity with other groups • Influences public opinion
Community	• Access to government • Participation in civic organizations • Political education • Target local issues	• Improved quality of life • Enhanced health and wellbeing • Democratic institutions • Improved access to services • Coalitions for wellbeing • Tolerance of diversity
Societal	• Struggles for democracy • Struggles for liberation • Solidarity across social groups • Resisting globalization • Political and economic literacy	• Redistributive policies • Support for disadvantaged people • Government accountability • Control of resources by poor • Progressive social policies • Resists economic neoliberalism

Source: Expanded from Lord and Hutchison (1993), Speer and Hughey (1995), and Zimmerman (2000).

some settings but not in others. Similarly, people may work to empower one group while oppressing others along the way. For example, in Bolivia, as part of the efforts to pay retribution to Indigenous people, who have historically been oppressed, land is being redistributed. However, much of this land being retitled is being seized from peasant communities and unions to be given to Indigenous people (Fontana, 2014). Thus, the empowerment of Indigenous Bolivians is resulting in the depowerment of peasants.

Empowerment theory has gained great support and is now a popular culture term used in conversations, marketing campaigns, and even product labels (e.g., empowerment perfume). Empowerment theory has also been greatly critiqued over the past 50 years. One important critique is that the theory has traditionally held a masculine focus on mastery, control, and power over traditionally feminine values of cooperation and communion (Riger, 1993) and at times, ignores the less vocal and disempowered (Serrano-García & Bond, 1994). These critiques have been further extended by French Canadian community psychologists through the lens of radical feminism (Nelson & Lavoie, 2010).

As empowerment is relational, focus on only individual and not social power runs the risk of perpetuating the status quo. In a review of publications on CP, Cattaneo, Calton, and Brodsky (2015) found that many interventions with empowerment aims tended to omit social relevance to people's lives and social power, thus potentially promoting good feelings but not actual change. As Brodsky and Cattaneo (2013) warn, "empowerment is not only experienced internally but also enacted socially, requiring a response from the social world" or else "we risk laying the blame for disempowerment at the feet of marginalized communities" (p. 337).

It is important to caution against assumptions that one can empower another. As community psychologists, we can help facilitate others to empower themselves through interventions we help design, create, or implement – but we do not empower others (Gruber & Trickett, 1987; Riger, 1993). Although Freire (1970) cautioned that only the disempowered can empower themselves, it is important to consider how those in power can play an important role as allies to marginalized groups who want to create change, as explained in Chapters 1 and 18.

As the term "empowerment" permeates popular culture and policy, its application is often antithetical to the spirit of empowerment. One clear example is the efforts of the US Child Protective Services to mandate empowerment training to women in order for them to regain custody of their children. As such, these mothers are legally required to attend an empowerment courses, which typically require that they do not have romantic relationships with men and become more financially autonomous, while demonstrating remorse and deference to the court system (Reich, 2005). Given the lack of choice of what is needed to better themselves or the power to decide if they wish to take the course, court-ordered empowerment is essentially a depowering process.

Fortunately, interventions to promote critical consciousness and cultivate skills and resources for having more power to, with, from, and within have led to a greater sense of empowerment for a variety of people and increased their health and wellbeing (e.g., Iftikhar, Khadim, Munir, & Amir, 2018; Sarkar, Dasgupta, Sinha, & Shanbabu, 2017; Tucker et al., 2017; Zimmerman et al., 2018), supporting the importance of issues of power in promoting social change and social justice.

Power is everywhere; it's in interpersonal relationships, families, organizations, corporations, neighborhoods, and countries. Power can be used for ethical or unethical purposes. It can promote wellbeing, but it can also perpetuate suffering (Hook, 2007). Thus, a dynamic conceptualization of power is needed, one that takes into account the multifaceted nature of identities and the changing nature of social settings. As community psychologists, we must perpetually consider our power when working with individuals and collectives, as well as these individuals' and groups' power in relation to other people (including us), contexts, and processes.

Empowerment and Resilience

Both empowerment and **resilience** – the ability to adapt well in the face of threat, hardship, tragedy, trauma, and other sources of stress (Rutter, 1993) – are strength-based approaches that community psychologists utilize in working with and for communities (Cowen, 1991). Recently, Anne Brodsky and Lauren Cattaneo (2013) crafted a conceptual model of how these two constructs can work in conjunction to support social justice and individual and collective wellbeing. To understand the Transconceptual Model of Empowerment and Resilience (TMER), an overview of the pieces are needed.

Resilience is a process of adaptation, coping, and growth that results in a change to the self, but not necessarily the surrounding environment. It is conceptualized to always occur within a context of risk, that is a setting or situation in which there are potentially dangerous power differentials, and it has five key components: awareness, attention, action, reflection and maintenance. People with conscious *awareness* are able to consider and question the dominant narratives around them or their situation and reinterpret what is observed and experienced. For instance, a homeless person might feel ignored and unworthy of help when people walk past him on the street without noticing him or actively denying requests for food and/or money. Awareness could be realizing that these interactions are wrong, hurtful, and could change. Another example of awareness is being conscious that these interactions are based on discriminatory beliefs, fears, or indifference and are not facts or true representations of one's worth. Further, awareness could involve questioning how some lose housing while others do not or how inequitably resources are distributed. *Intention* involves the identifying, setting, and working towards goals. The above mentioned homeless person could set goals for more stable housing such as enrolling in a non-profit or federal housing program, working with other precariously housed people to identify housing options, or gaining employment that involves housing. With awareness and intention, *action* is needed. This requires putting these goals into action and working toward futures that awareness allows one to see. *Reflection* is the continuous and iterative process of considering how awareness, intentions, and actions are working. It is noticing successes and considering things that might work better. In our example, how is the person needing housing considering his goals, what is needed, his success in meeting these goals, and the new goals and needs he can identify? Finally, *maintenance* is needed throughout to ensure survival. This involves flexibility, adaptation to change, and appreciation of incremental growth (Brodsky et al., 2011). See Fig. 4.2 for an illustration. Of course, resilience occurs as a response or adaptation to unequal power relations in social structures and interactions.

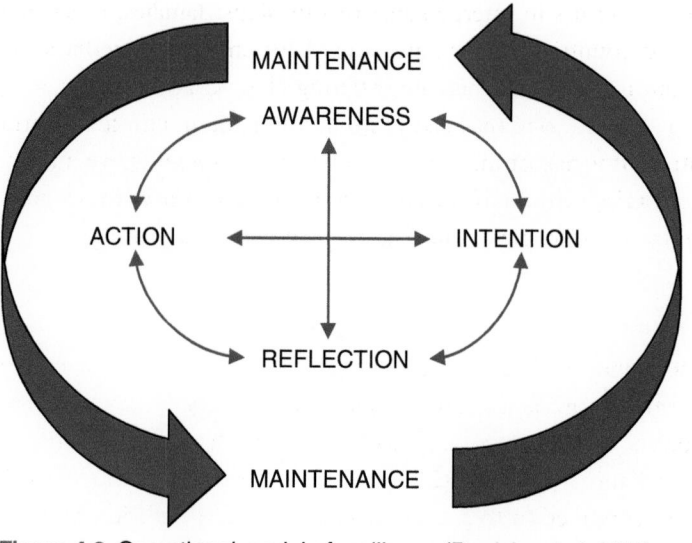

Figure 4.2 Operational model of resilience (Brodsky et al. 2011)

Transconceptual Model of Empowerment and Resilience

The Transconceptual Model of Empowerment and Resilience (TMER) integrates resiliency theory and empowerment theory by connecting their related and synergistic parts. As Fig. 4.3 shows, these are iterative processes that occur through social, collective, and individual processes. Resilience involves "internal local level goals that are aimed at intrapersonal actions and outcomes – adapting, withstanding, or resisting" (Brodsky & Cattaneo, 2013 p. 338). Resilience enables coping and quick recovery in the face of adversity, trauma, or other difficulties. Empowerment, as you have read in this chapter, is inherently social and multifaceted. Brodsky and Cattaneo noticed that empowerment and resilience in their own work shared many of the same components and put together a model that connected these theories explicitly. As such, the TMER attempts to identify the convergences and divergences of these two theories. One key component is risk. Risk is inherent in resilience, but not always a part of empowerment. Resilience is a response to threat, while empowerment might be used to overcome risk but can also be exercised when there is no threat or risk to power. Another way in which TMER differentiates resilience and empowerment is the magnitude of change needed. In this model, the higher the magnitude of change needed, the more important resilience is as a first step. Take our homeless example – it would likely be important for him to find stable housing for himself and perhaps his family (resilience – change to self) before he'd be able to work towards creating accessible housing options for others (empowerment – meaningful change to individuals' social systems). Further, when large changes are needed, empowerment efforts might not work without considering resilience. Getting groups of precariously housed people to work towards accessible housing might not be effective if the people themselves do not have goals, awareness, and intention to change their housing situation. Often movements towards empowerment start through the process of resilience.

Important to TMER is the appreciation that a focus solely on resilience can facilitate individual coping procedures or internal change processes that could lead to meaningful change but could also simply perpetuate the status quo. For instance, if an organization works only to house that

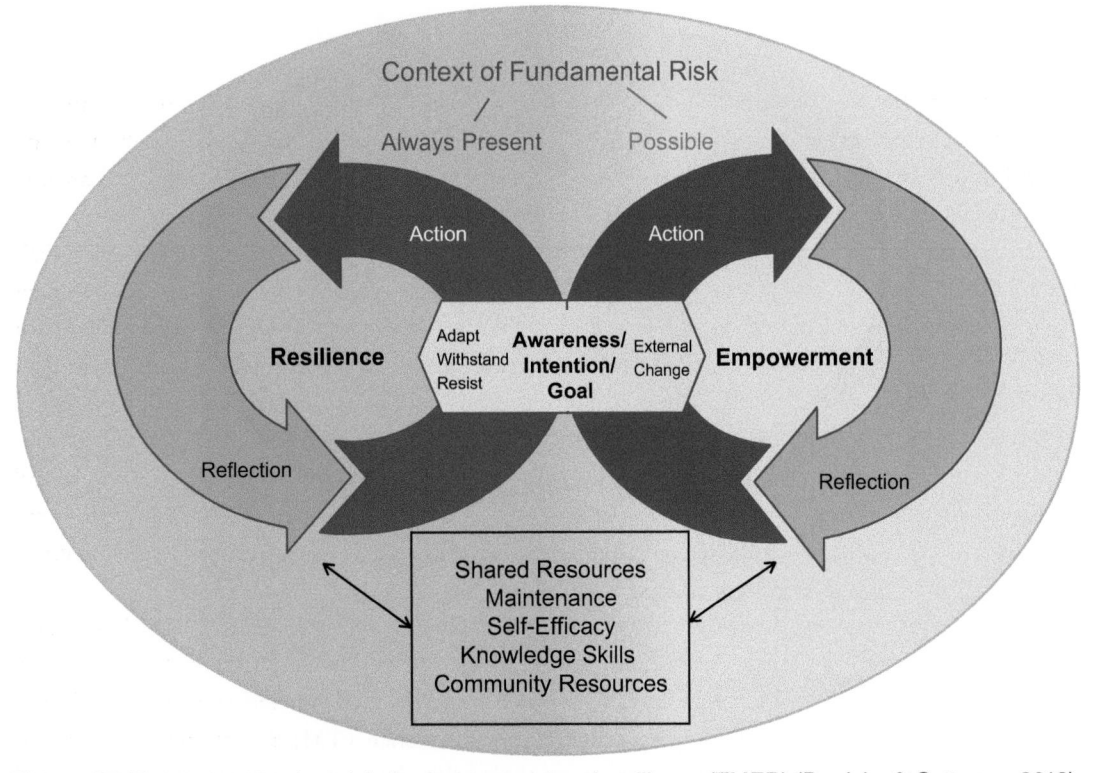

Figure 4.3 Transconceptual model of empowerment and resilience (TMER) (Brodsky & Cattaneo, 2013)
Copyright © 2013 John Wiley and Sons. Reproduced with permission.

one homeless man, and other individuals like him, they might claim success for helping these people adapt to a situation in which accessible housing is lacking, but they have not changed the status quo that caused the housing to be limited, too expensive, or unequally distributed. That is why we should consider resilience in conjunction with empowerment, which seeks to change power structures and allocations. This is differentiating between status quo and status quakes (Cattaneo et al., 2015).

TMER is a relatively new integration of two important theories for promoting wellbeing. It is focused on the connection between resilience and empowerment, which collectively are linked to a range of outcomes from parental empowerment in students' education (Kim & Bryan, 2017) to surviving intimate partner violence (Munoz, Brady, & Brown, 2017). The application of these theories through TMER in CP has been promising. For instance, discussions with Black men as part of the Black Lives Matter movement have found important ways in which resilience and empowerment work independently and together towards supporting change (Godsay & Brodsky, 2018). Similarly, research on social movements in Hong Kong has found differential connections between resilience and empowerment for different types of people (Chan, Cattaneo, Mak, & Lin, 2017). Thus, when we consider power and efforts towards empowerment, we should consider the role resilience plays in people's efforts to work towards such social chance.

Further, for individual and collective wellbeing, issues of power contribute to feelings of having a voice, the right for self-determination, the opportunity to contribute, and for those contributions to be appreciated by others. These components are part of what Prilleltensky (2014) describes as **mattering**.

Mattering

In order to be healthy, physically and psychologically, as an individual, collective, or community, we must feel that we matter. That is, that we are recognized for who we are, our abilities and contributions as well as feel that we have a meaningful impact on others and/or the world around us. Put simply, *mattering* means feeling valued and feeling like you add value.

Recognition is important for our wellbeing, as it demonstrates social power. For instance, feeling invisible, inconsequential, forgotten or neglected engenders feelings of powerlessness, whereas having a voice and being heard are essential to feeling empowered. Additionally important for mattering is that we have an *impact* – that we make meaningful and perceptible contributions to our lives and the lives of others. This could be part of interpersonal interactions or large political movements. As social creatures, these contributions should somehow be acknowledged or validated by others. When we are recognized and have an impact that is appreciated by others, we feel that we matter. These senses of meaning-making, mattering, and thriving (Prilleltensky, 2014) are essential for wellbeing and connect to issues of distributive and procedural justice described in Chapter 3. See Fig. 4.4 for a pictorial illustration.

Important to mattering is power. Power plays a fundamental role in how we see social problems and opportunities, how we are able to participate in change (or perpetuate the status quo), how others listen to (or silence) us, the impact of our voice/actions, and our persistence in the face of challenges. Power is exercised through social capital, which involves social patterns, connections, and opportunities that facilitate power over, within, to, from, and with. Importantly, social capital is a form of power that is focused on social connections.

Social Capital

The idea of capital is derived from economics and sociology and is focused on the resources and assets of individuals and collectives, be it material/physical (e.g., financial, possessions) or nonmaterial (e.g., psychological, educational, social). As Bradley and Corwyn (2002) note, capital connects social and material resources with the important dimension of social relationships. All forms of capital are important when considering power, but social capital is the one area that community psychologists focus on most. However, other types of capital can bolster social capital. **Financial capital** involves material resources and is often a combination of income and occupational status. Financial capital offers access to many material, educational, and health resources and is described by some as a "barometer of access to opportunities" (Bradley & Corwyn, 2002 p. 372). **Human capital** is based on "changes in persons that bring about skills and capabilities that make them able to act in new ways" (Coleman, 1988, p. 100). It includes such things as education, job training, and occupational status.

Social capital involves nonmaterial resources that are derived from social relationships, norms, and networks. As Coleman (1988) describes, "like other forms of capital, social capital is productive, making possible the achievement of certain ends that in its absence would not be possible" (p. 98). This could apply to hearing about a job through "weak ties," like your brother-in-law's friend's cousin (Granovetter, 1973), trusting the value of the diamond you bought at the jewelry

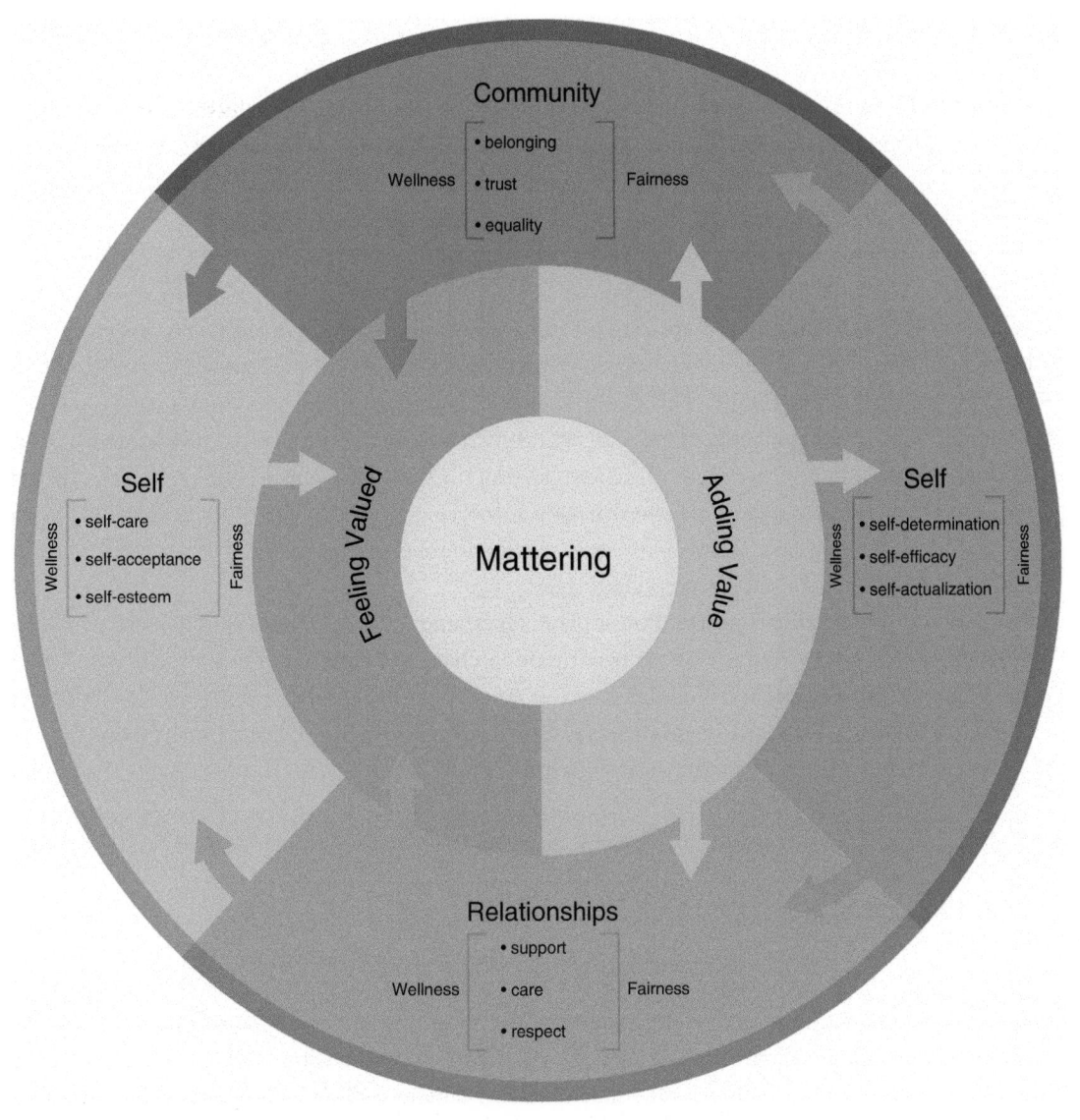

Figure 4.4 Representation of *Mattering* connections at the individual, relational, and community level
www.fshdsociety.org/wp-content/uploads/2018/06/2018-Connect_IsaacPrilleltensky.pdf

store belonging to a member of your synagogue, or feeling comfortable letting your children walk around the neighborhood without you or another adult (Coleman, 1988).

In his widely popular book *Bowling Alone: The Collapse and Revival of American Community*, Robert Putnam (2000b) distinguished between physical/financial, human and social capital: "Whereas physical capital refers to physical objects and human capital refers to properties of individuals, social capital refers to connections among individuals – social networks and the norms of reciprocity and trustworthiness that arise from them" (Putnam, 2000b, p. 19).

In our view, social capital includes collective resources consisting of civic participation, networks, norms of reciprocity, and organizations that foster (a) trust among citizens, and (b) actions to improve the common good. Fig. 4.5 shows the various dimensions of social capital

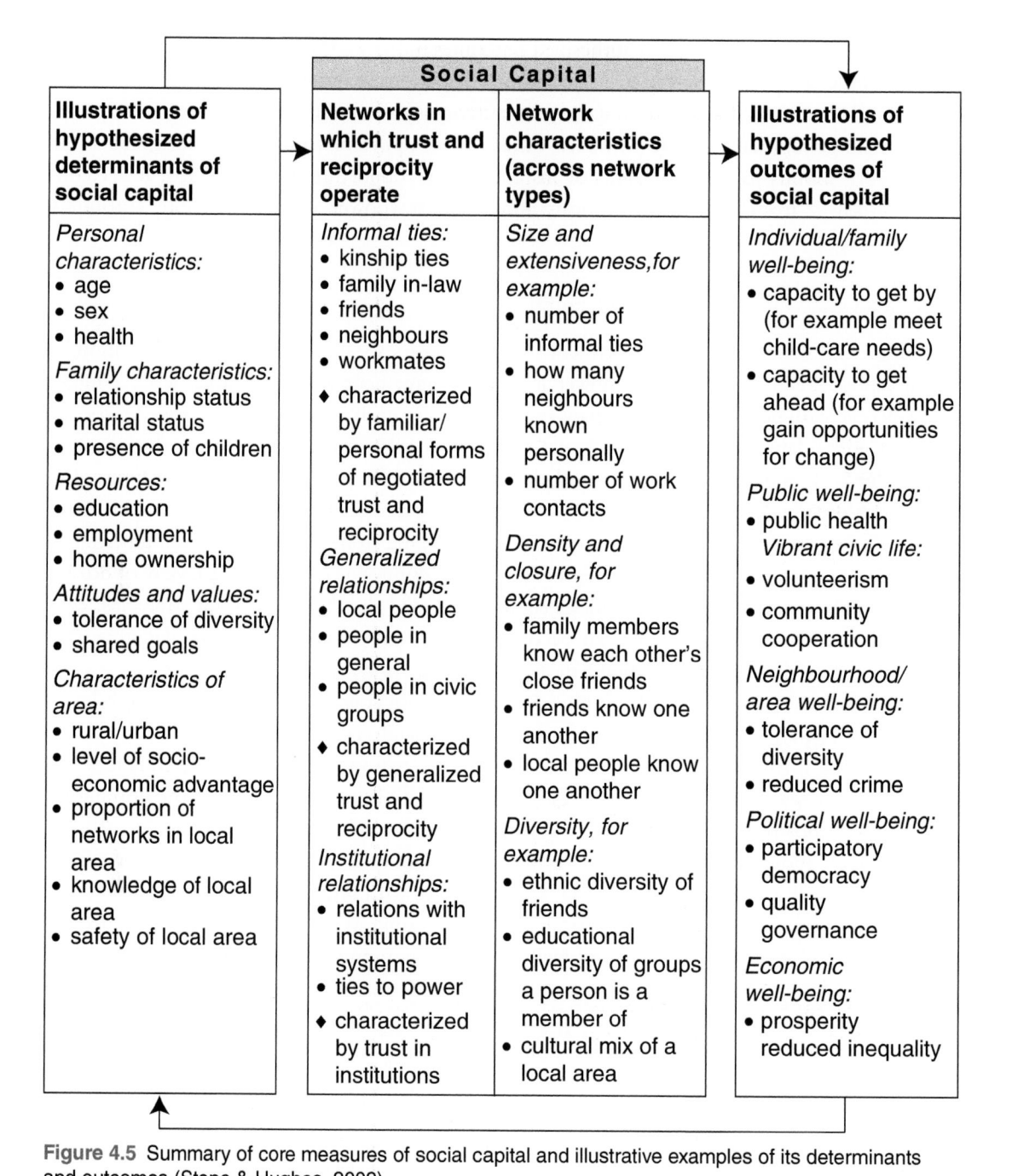

Figure 4.5 Summary of core measures of social capital and illustrative examples of its determinants and outcomes (Stone & Hughes, 2002)

Reproduced with permission from the Australian Institute of Family Studies.

identified by Stone and Hughes (2002) in their study of social capital in Australian families. As may be seen, social capital involves networks of trust and reciprocity that lead to positive outcomes at multiple levels of analysis, including individual, family, community, civic, political, and economic wellbeing. Fig. 4.5 summarizes the types and characteristics of networks. Density, size, and diversity are key factors in the quality of community connections. Another important feature of this figure is that the hypothesized outcomes influence the very determinants of social capital. Some of the outcomes, such as civic participation, may generate more social capital. Accordingly, we should see determinants and outcomes of social capital as exerting reciprocal and not unidirectional influence on each other. It is important to consider that more social capital corresponds to more power. For instance, more opportunities (power to), fewer constraints (power from), more connections and alliances (power with), and more autonomy (power from).

Individual and Community Social Capital

In considering social capital, it is worthwhile to consider individual social capital and community social capital. Let's consider social power for civic engagement at an individual level. I might know people with political power. Perhaps my son plays baseball with the mayor's son. Maybe my spouse went to law school with the district attorney. Possibly my job intersects with politicians and power brokers in my community regularly (e.g., I'm a realtor who sold them their house, I'm an interior designer who decorated their homes, I'm captain of the police, etc.). As such, I am likely to have high social capital for a variety of goals ranging from obtaining a building permit to remodel my house to proposing new legislation for my community. Based on a review of dozens of community organizing efforts, Smock (2004) concluded that "with the right strategies, even the most disenfranchised residents can become active participants in the public decisions that shape their lives" (p. 261), suggesting a measure of social capital for all.

At a community level, my community could have high social capital by having high levels of civic participation, community cohesion, and financial resources. Our community social capital, in the form of connections of trust and participation in public affairs, enhances our community's capacity to create structures of cohesion and support that benefit the population and produce positive health, welfare, educational, and social outcomes (Schneider, 2006). Vast research indicates that cohesive communities and civic participation in public affairs enhance the wellbeing of the population. Communities with higher participation in volunteer organizations, political parties, and local and professional associations fare much better in terms of health, education, crime, and wellbeing than communities with low rates of participation. This finding has been replicated at different times across various states, provinces and countries (DePiccoli, 2005; Kirst, Lazgare, Zhang, & O'Campo, 2015; McKenzie & Harpham, 2006; Putnam, 2000a, 2000b). For instance, Saegert and Winkel (1996) found that social capital increased empowerment and voting behavior at the group level. Kanacri et al. (2016) found connections between empathy, concerns about poverty, giving, and civic engagement. Orr (2007) summarized multiple social change efforts by stating that "effective community organizing can improve urban residents' quality of life" (p. 253), supporting the importance of community social capital.

Bridging and Bonding Capital

Some theorists consider social capital in terms of **bridging capital** and **bonding capital**. *Bridging capital* is the connections between people, groups, and communities. For example, recently a friend's toddler was diagnosed with a rare genetic condition. This friend asked me [Stephanie] if I knew anything about it. I had never heard of the condition, but as an academic, I know lots of people who do medical research. By asking friends, who then asked their friends, we were able to connect the toddler's parents to the physician that identified and named the disease within 48 hours. Through our social relationships, we were able to bridge these people. In CP, bridging capital is often used to discuss connections between groups.

Bonding capital involves more intimate social and emotional connections between people. These feelings engender social cohesion, support, connection, commitment, and belongingness. It is this type of social capital that explains the socioemotional feelings for **sense of community** (see Chapter 7). There is evidence that greater bonding capital in geographic communities is affected by civic engagement and predicts perceived collective efficacy (Collins, Neal, & Neal, 2014). In studies of natural disasters, bonding and bridging capital are key components of community resilience (Aldrich & Meyer, 2015).

Such things as country clubs, ethnic associations, farmers' associations and men's groups increase bonding. Coalitions, interfaith organizations and service groups can enhance bridging. However, risks are associated with how these forms of capital are used. For instance, if bonding overshadows the need for bridging (Schneider, 2006), that is, if every group in society was interested only in what is good for its own members, there would be little or no cooperation across groups (i.e., lots of bonding but little bridging). Bridging is a necessity of every society. It is a basic requirement of a respectful and inclusive society. However, there are examples of groups investing in bonding to prevent bridging (and subsequently changes in power). Classic examples include the Ku Klux Klan and movements that support ethnic cleansing.

Further, if bonding leads to preoccupation with one's own wellbeing and the neglect of others, we see a problem. The problem is even greater if social capital is used to promote unjust policies or discrimination. "Networks and the associated norms of reciprocity are generally good for those inside the network, but the external effects of social capital are by no means always positive" (Putnam, 2000b, p. 21). Proponents of mindsets such as NIMBY (not in my backyard) and coalitions of elite businesses exploit their power and connections to achieve goals that are in direct opposition to the values of CP:

> Social capital, in short, can be directed toward malevolent, antisocial purposes, just like any other form of capital ... Therefore it is important to ask how the positive consequences of social capital – mutual support, cooperation, trust, institutional effectiveness – can be maximized and the negative manifestations – sectarianism, ethnocentrism, corruption – minimized. (Putnam, 2000b, p. 22)

Another serious risk of the current discourse on social capital is its potential deflection of systemic sources of oppression, inequality, and domination. There is a distinct possibility that social capital may become the preferred tool of governments to work on social problems because it puts the burden of responsibility back onto the community (Blakeley, 2002; Perkins, Hughey, & Speer, 2002). We believe that communities should become involved in solving their own problems. But that is *part* of the solution, not the *whole* solution. No amount of talk about social support can negate the fact that inequality exists and that it is a major source of suffering for vulnerable populations. Social support can buffer some of the effects of inequality, but it would be unjust if it was used to support the same system that creates so much social fragmentation and isolation. Hence, we caution against social capital becoming the new slogan of governments. Furthermore, we call on people to create bonds of solidarity to enhance, not diminish, political action against injustice. We concur with Perkins et al. (2002) who claim that "excessive concern for social cohesion undermines the ability to confront or engage in necessary conflict and thus disempowers" (p. 33). In considering our three sample issues: housing, immigration, and climate change, connections between people and groups can help buffer the stress for people experiencing such things as relocation, new cultures, insecure housing, or extreme weather. However, social capital must be considered at the individual and community level as well as which components are based on emotional ties (bonding) and social connections (bridging). Further, how these ties contribute to social justice or injustice, equity or inequality, and wellbeing or poor physical, mental, and community health. Next, we connect power explicitly to wellbeing.

Power and Wellbeing

Prilleltensky (2012) defines wellbeing as a "positive state of affairs, brought about by the simultaneous and balanced satisfaction of diverse objective and subjective needs of individuals, relationships, organizations, and communities" (p. 2). Accordingly, various signs or indicators of wellbeing exist at these multiple levels or sites. At the individual level, wellbeing is manifested in terms of personal control, choice, self-esteem, competence, independence, political rights, and a positive identity (*power from*) (see Table 4.1). At the relational level, the individual is embedded in a network of positive and supportive relationships and can participate freely (that is *power to* and *power with*) in social, community, and political life. The person is an active member of the community. At the community and societal level, the individual is able to acquire such basic resources as employment, income, education, and housing. (See Chapter 3 for more discussion.) Thus, wellbeing is not a matter of individual health, but rather a transaction between individuals and their environments (Prilleltensky, Nelson, & Peirson, 2001) that involves objective (e.g., physical) and subjective (e.g., psychological and emotional) components (Prilleltensky, 2012). In its work with disadvantaged people, CP is not just concerned with liberation from oppression but also with the achievement of a state of personal, relational, and collective wellbeing. It treats wellbeing as part of fairness (Prilleltensky, 2012) so that in order to achieve equity, we must not seek the same for all, but ensure that all have what is needed (Frankfurt, 2015).

Recognizing Power as Privilege

Perhaps the largest social problem today is the complacency of so many people who enjoy many social and economic privileges. Many people have little awareness of the problems facing disadvantaged people and ignore their role in contributing directly (e.g., voting against policies, polluting, saying hateful things) and indirectly (e.g., not questioning where or how products are made, cheating on taxes, never using reusable bags) to these issues. As a consequence, advantaged people tend to go blithely along in their lives, without much concern about these issues. But, this is not just about "other people"; it is about all of us. Consciousness-raising, anger about social injustice, and a passion for social change are antidotes to this complacency.

We all enjoy privileges in our lives. However, most of us (authors included) do not question these sources of privilege and the ways they might oppress others. Are you using a computer for your schoolwork? Have you ever considered the people in the factory that made that computer and whether they enjoy a living wage or safe work conditions? Have you thought about the environmental consequence of the production of that computer and who will feel the consequence of that impact on the physical environment? The mere fact that you are being educated, reading this book and/or participating in a course demonstrates privileges that most of the world's population does not enjoy – those who do not have electricity, access to education, job prospects, or even adequate food. We are not advocating for the abandonment of your education or your computer, but that we all should consider the ways in which we are privileged and the consequences of that power on the wellbeing of others.

Inequality at a System Level

There are many dimensions of social issues and problems that can be traced to root causes of oppression and loss/lack of power. First, as we noted in Chapter 1, society tends to engage in "victim blaming" of disadvantaged people (Ryan, 1971). The social context in which the problems facing disadvantaged people arise and the issues of inequitable allocation of power are typically ignored, leaving expectations for individuals to "pull themselves up by their bootstraps." Framing problems in terms of individual-level difficulties leads to fragmented services for individuals, rather than efforts at collective action for social change. An example of victim blaming is to view homeless people as lazy, unmotivated, and deserving of their social condition. In the US, almost half of the homeless work (Culhane, 2010). Unfortunately, with the current US minimum wage rate, a person could work 40 hours a week for 52 weeks of the year and still be 25 percent below the federal poverty line for a family of three (Cauthen & Fass, 2008) and in many industrialized countries, 50 hours a week at minimum wage may not be enough to stay out of poverty (https://data.oecd.org). One of the consequences of victim blaming is for individuals to self-blame and *internalize oppression*. When this happens, people begin to accept and shape their own identity based on the stereotypes, flaws, and weakness that others attribute to them. As such, people tend to accept unjust treatment, as they increasingly view themselves as unworthy of equity. This feeling of powerlessness is the invisible form of power discussed earlier, as it involves historical and institutional issues of power that extend beyond direct interactions between individual people.

Internalized oppression is associated with a range of negative outcomes and reduction of protective factors. In addition to health issues and psychosocial problems in living (e.g., stress, food scarcity, poor health) (Prilleltensky, Nelson, & Peirson, 2001), disadvantaged people are often isolated from networks of support and corresponding social capital. People lack homes, immigrate to new countries, or struggle with mental health problems, and many others tend to be socially isolated. Disadvantaged people also experience feeling powerless. Powerlessness is not just a personal quality (e.g., feelings of helplessness and lack of control) but rather something that is experienced in the context of asymmetric relationships with other people and systems. Powerlessness is related to the discrimination that is experienced by groups and individuals who are held to single standards (i.e., those that assert the superiority of male, White, heterosexual, able-bodied people). Long-standing patterns of sexism, racism, heterosexism, ableism, and stigma serve to rationalize and perpetuate power inequalities at multiple levels of analysis.

Moreover, disadvantaged people have been, and continue to be, subjected to exclusion and segregation from a range of social and community settings. Women who experience the "glass ceiling" in career advancement and who are confined to low-paid "pink-collar" jobs or social assistance are but one example of how existing social conditions maintain inequality and social exclusion. Further, when women internalize that oppression, they behave in ways that can perpetuate that inequality. For instance, women in the workplace are less likely to speak up during meetings when they assume others will not view their contribution as helpful or smart. They will not apply for management jobs when they believe that they will not get it anyway, or as we have increasingly seen in news stories and lawsuits, women will silently endure sexual harassment and abuse in the workplace for fear that reporting will end their career and have no impact on the male perpetrator. Although experienced by individuals, perceptions of powerlessness are engendered through systemic levels of inequality (e.g., large disparities in the distribution of power across groups).

Community Psychology and Power Structures

Community psychologists have recently turned their attention toward better understanding and challenging community power structures (Christens, Inzeo, & Faust, 2014; Kivell, Evans, & Paterson, 2017; Neal & Neal, 2011). Community power structures are dynamic networks of institutions and those who occupy important institutional roles (e.g., mayor, corporate CEO, university president, foundation director, police chief), as well as those who play important roles brokering relations between these institutions (Mills, 1956; Neal & Neal, 2011). These power structures often wield power over the general social structure of a community and policy initiatives. For example, in many local communities, networks of real estate and development interests dominate urban planning, community development narratives, and decision-making. This structural view of power highlights the fact that power to affect local policy "derives from occupying an advantageous position within the pattern of relationships through which resources are exchanged" (Neal & Neal 2011, p. 163). Mapping and understanding community power structures helps researchers and community partners develop a localized theory of power that can inform grassroots action to build community power (Christens et al., 2014; Kivell et al., 2017).

Drawing across various theories and based on previous work (Prilleltensky, 2008b), ten complementary components of power are useful to consider in critical analyses, research, and in creating social change and interventions:

1 Power refers to the capacity and opportunity to fulfill or obstruct personal, relational or collective needs.
2 Power has psychological and political sources, manifestations and consequences.
3 We can distinguish between power to strive for wellbeing, power to oppress, and power to resist oppression and strive for liberation.

4 Power can be overt or covert, subtle or blatant, hidden or exposed.

5 The exercise of power can apply to self, others, and collectives.

6 Power affords people multiple identities as individuals seeking wellbeing, engaging in oppression, or resisting domination.

7 Whereas people may be oppressed in one context, at a particular time and place, they may act as oppressors at another time and place.

8 Because of structural factors such as social class, gender, ability and race, people may enjoy differential levels of power.

9 Degrees of power are also affected by personal and social constructs such as beauty, intelligence, and assertiveness, constructs that enjoy variable status within different cultures.

10 The exercise of power can reflect varying degrees of awareness with respect to the impact of one's actions.

Since CP is based on identifying power inequalities and working to redistribute power more equitably, understanding the role of power in social justice is essential, as are understanding depowerment, overpowerment, empowerment, and how these manifest in the ecology of life.

Social Justice Needs to Question How Power is Allocated

In thinking about power, one must consider that it is dynamic and contextual. It can include dyadic interactions, large corporations, government decision-making, or even global stereotypes about a group. Identifying power issues is largely dependent on the width and acuity of the lens used. Using the vignette at the start of the chapter as an example, the mother had *power to* provide for her children, prepare them for school, take them there, etc. Yet the immigration policies had *power over* her, where one traffic stop could separate her from her children forever. She also lacked *power from* being subjected to racism. That form of racism, commonplace for many immigrants, also takes power from participating as an equal at her children's school and in her community more generally. If internalized, such lack of power could result in stress, illness, and feeling powerless (i.e., further lessening power to). In considering power, we must look at interactions from many angles and always consider the context.

Chapter Summary

Power is foundational to all human interactions – from extreme caste systems to subtle interpersonal dynamics. Power is fluid, dynamic, and relational. As community-engaged researchers, we must always look for the ways in which power impacts us. From our power and privilege as researchers, to the ways the groups we work with have power to, others have power over, and structures keep power from. Our challenge is to constantly refocus our lens (from zoom to wide angle and everything in between). Throughout the book, we will draw attention to power, as power is fundamental to the work of community psychologists, and as more theories and methods are introduced, be sure to consider how they relate to power.

From Power to Politics

Mariolga Reyes Cruz, PhD[2], University of Puerto Rico

CP began "with a vision of what ought to be, a vision for a just and democratic society (a good society) that community psychologists would contribute to bring about by working for social justice" (Rappaport, 2005, p. 237). Consistent with this vision, community psychologists ally with people from marginalized communities and other segments of society to address the conditions that produce/reproduce social injustice (Prilleltensky, 2004). Thus, it is clear that for CP to engage in the pursuit of a just society we need to examine power in all its complexity (as this chapter shows: "power is everywhere"). The question remains, can we understand power without an understanding of politics?

This chapter demonstrates that power can be understood from many vantage points. Our ideas about and experience of power can frame what we may or may not do, individually and/or collectively, at different moments and contexts. But understanding how power manifests itself and how it can serve to address the needs of a particular group is not enough for a CP that aims for transformative social change (Sánchez, 2012).

Community psychologists work towards a more equitable distribution of resources by engaging in efforts that expand the opportunities for marginalized groups to participate in the decisions that affect their lives. This work is often done at invited, claimed, or created spaces in the local context (see Gaventa's power cube model described in this chapter). But entering "the game" and getting to play is not the same as changing the game itself (see Sánchez, 2012). After all, understanding, experiencing, and/or wielding power does not bring about transformative social change without mobilizing around a shared vision of what a just society should look like. Moreover, a focus on power without an attention to politics runs the risk of psychologizing a sociopolitical dynamic, hence depoliticizing power.

The Argentinian philosopher Enrique Dussel presents an alternative view of power that is particularly relevant to a critical CP. Historically, power has been defined and experienced as control, authority, and domination (as in the sociologist Max Weber's view for instance). But the exercise of control, authority, domination ("power over"), is not power itself but manifestations of the corruption of power. For Dussel (2008), power is manifested in "the 'will-to-live' of the members of a community" (p. 14). Power is always potential (see also Sánchez, 2012). As Hanna Arendt (1958/1998) argued, power is "not an unchangeable, measurable, and reliable entity like force or strength," power "springs up between men [*sic*] when they act together and vanishes the moment they disperse" (p. 200). Power as "the will-to-live" is manifested when we get together to do what we need to do to live and preserve life.

On September 20, 2017, two weeks after Hurricane Irma hit the archipelago of Puerto Rico[3], Hurricane María swept through the already battered land as a category 4 storm. The government had repeatedly warned the population to make the appropriate preparations including storing provisions for 72 hours. But no one could really be prepared for what followed, particularly the government, after a decade of economic depression and a longer trend of dismantling public institutions (Mazzei & Sosa Pascual, 2017; Wiscovithc & Sosa Pascual, 2018). While the islands were in darkness and silence (the electric grid and communications network were destroyed by the storms), our families in the diaspora watched in horror at the news that reached the continental US about the unfolding humanitarian crisis. As time passed, more people became overwhelmed by a sense of helplessness in the aftermath of the disaster (Jervis, 2018). However, as soon as people mobilized to attend shared needs, power emerged.

---

[2] Correspondence should be addressed to mreyescruz@gmail.com. Special thanks to Christopher Sonn for his comments on an earlier draft of this commentary.
[3] Puerto Rico is a territory of the US comprised of a "big island" (with 76 municipalities) and two smaller island-municipalities (Culebra and Vieques). The islands are inhabited by 3.3 million people who do not have the right to vote in US elections but whose destinies are in large part controlled by the US Congress. About 5.5 million Puerto Ricans live in the continental US where they can vote (Román, 2018).

In the early hours after Hurricane María left, before local or international help could figure out how to proceed, people took stock, looked for their neighbors, and got together to lend each other a hand, attending to personal and collective needs. Newspaper reports told stories about neighbors getting together to open roads, share their shelter and basic resources, and repair the electric grid in rural and urban areas. Mutual help centers sprang up across the territory, providing free food and a place for sharing information, resources, and support. Brigades of volunteers helped rebuild homes, restore small farms, offer basic medical care, and provide legal assistance and psychological support. The power to do something about the dire circumstances people were facing did not depend on neighbors "taking power" away from others, but on their capacity to join efforts to take care of each other.

Despite the dominant Western view that people can and should be independent and autonomous from one another, a person alone can rarely take care of oneself and all of their needs in order to sustain life. From the moment we are conceived, we are interconnected to others (some of these people are very well-known to us and countless others will remain in complete anonymity). For example, in order for you to quietly read this book, someone had to teach you how to read, someone had to write the book, the materials from which the book is made had to be produced by other people, someone else had to take care of printing and marketing, and, somehow you had to be involved with others in the basic exchanges necessary so that you could have access to the book you are reading now independently. If you do not grow your own food, someone has to do it and make it accessible nearby so you can purchase it. Infrastructure (e.g., ships, trucks, fuel, shops) must be in place for you to have a meal and read at night, to get the clothes you are wearing, and so on. These have all been made possible by others. In Puerto Rico after Hurricane María, people without a vegetable garden or cash did not have access to food or fuel. Thus, when we think of power as potential, as what emerges from a community's will-to-live, we can also have a sense of what happens when a community is unable to garner its power to attend to its common needs in, for instance, the aftermath of a devastating disaster or a school mass shooting.

Following Dussel's argument, a community's power can only be enacted through "an activity that organizes and promotes the production, reproduction, and enhancement of the lives of the members of that community" (2008, p. 14), that activity is *politics*. The objective of politics is the satisfaction of social demands raised by the people whose needs have not been met. When those needs are manifested as social problems, we need politics to resolve them. *Political power* is the "convergence of wills toward a common good" (Dussel, 2008, p. 15). This kind of power is always held by the community, even if it cannot be expressed. But in order for political power to be manifested, the community needs to find ways of reaching consensus towards the common good. In the example about people's responses to Hurricane María in Puerto Rico, a sense of empowerment made it possible for some people to get together and address immediate individual and collective needs. However, we should not confuse empowerment with political power. We can find ways to take care of one's own, even those in our communities, without attending to the common good. In Puerto Rico, for instance, while a resurgence of creativity and solidarity in response to the post-hurricane disaster is palpable, it has not led to a convergence of "word and deed" (Arendt, 1958/1998, p. 200) against the most draconian austerity plan in recent history (Stiglitz, 2017) – at least not yet. A chain of events is unfolding, accelerating a neoliberal agenda that will leave thousands of people without work, electricity, access to public schools and public higher education, health care, basic work protections, liveable wages, and retirement (Marxuach, 2018). This agenda is enforced by the corruption of power and politics manifested as authoritarianism, oppression, exploitation, and violence. But, as Dussel (2008) warns us, the political is corrupted

> the moment in which the political actor (the members of the political community, whether citizens or representatives) believes that power affirms their subjectivity or the institution in which they function ... as the *center or source* of political power ... Why? Because all exercises of power through any institution (from that of the president to the police) or through any political function (when, for example, citizens meet in open town councils or elect a representative) have as their primary and ultimate reference point the *power of the political community* ... The *corruption*, moreover, is double: it corrupts the governors who believe themselves to be the sovereign center of power, and it corrupts the political community that allows itself (consents) to become *servile* rather than be an *actor* in the constitution of the political. (pp. 3–4)

We are living at a crossroads. Around the globe, people are facing enormous challenges that seem well beyond their grasp. In the last decades, income inequality has grown considerably (Alvaredo, Chancel, Piketty, Saez, & Zucman, 2018). The gap between the very rich and everyone else has widened to inconceivable levels (Oxfam International, 2018; Stiglitz, 2011). The dominant neoliberal ideology is destroying the foundations for just and democratic societies, even in rich post-industrial countries (Sánchez, 2012). The idea of unlimited economic growth that has dominated economic thought, industry, and public policy globally has proven disastrous for the pursuit of the common good because the resources of the planet are indeed limited (see Natale, Di Martino, Procentese & Arcidiacono, 2016). It is precisely at this juncture that we need a conception of power grounded in politics.

Although speaking about social change in the pursuit of a good society may sound utopian for some, others would argue that we need utopias to guide our steps (Galeano, 2001). In Puerto Rico, like everywhere else, people are resisting injustice, dreaming collectively and publicly, acting together to bring about caring, more democratic societies (Klein, 2018). CP as social critique (Rappaport, 2005) has an important contribution to make in the pursuit of the good society by articulating complex, experiential understandings of *political power* that aim at transformational social change. In the struggles for social justice in the 21st century, critical community psychologists can connect the experience of empowerment at personal and community levels with the emergence of political power. We can tell the stories of people getting together to conjure political power in pursuit of the common good.

Key Terms

Bonding capital: Resources derived through intimate social and emotional connections between people.

Bridging capital: Resources derived from having connections to people, groups, and communities.

Depowerment: The reduction of power in relation to others; can range from a reduction of privilege to the magnification of perceptions of powerlessness.

Empowerment: A relational concept that emphasizes choice, control, and the ability to influence.

Financial capital: Material resources, often involving income and occupational status.

Globalization: Interaction and integration among the people, companies, and governments of different nations, including international trade and investment and information technology.

Human capital: Resources derived from skills and capabilities.

Internalized oppression: The acceptance and development of one's identity based on the stereotypes, flaws, and weakness that others attribute to them and others like them (most often based on race, ethnicity, gender, sexuality, physical and mental ability).

Mattering: Feeling valued and feeling like you add value. Key components include being recognized and having an impact.

Oppression: A state of domination where the oppressed suffer the consequences of deprivation, exclusion, discrimination, exploitation, control of culture, and sometimes even violence; while the sources of oppression are external, oppression can also be internalized into negative beliefs about oneself.

Overpowerment: The experience of a high level of privilege compared to others.

Power: The capacity and opportunity to influence the course of events in one's personal life or in the life of others in the community.

Privilege: Power of advantage given to some people and not to others.

Resilience: The ability to adapt well in the face of threat, hardship, tragedy, trauma, and other sources of stress.

Sense of community: The feeling derived from belonging to a particular group where the individual experiences bonds of affection, influence, companionship, and support.

Social capital: Collective and relational resources consisting of civic participation, networks, norms of reciprocity and organizations that foster trust among citizens and actions to enhance the common good.

Resources

Read more about non-violent protests for social change:

Mahatma Gandhi: www.biography.com/people/mahatma-gandhi-9305898

Archbishop Desmond Tutu: www.bbc.com/news/world-africa-10725711

Mkhuseli Khusta Jack: https://www.sahistory.org.za/people/mkhuseli-khusta-jack

Freedom Riders: www.smithsonianmag.com/history/the-freedom-riders-then-and-now-45351758/
www.pbs.org/wgbh/americanexperience/films/freedomriders/

Anti-Apartheid Movement: www.nonviolent-conflict.org/the-anti-apartheid-struggle-in-south-africa-1912-1992/

https://nvdatabase.swarthmore.edu/content/south-african-blacks-boycott-apartheid-port-elizabeth-1985-86

THINKING LIKE A SYSTEM
ECOLOGY AND COMPLEXITY
IN A GLOBALIZED WORLD

5

Warm-up Questions

Social workers and counselors often use "Ecomaps" when working with their clients to understand an individual's or family's relationships with people, groups, and organizations. Mapping out these relationships can help identify sources of both supports and challenges to facilitate the helping process. It is also just a simple tool for thinking about our social context. As a warm-up to this chapter, draw a diagram on a sheet of paper similar to Figure 5.1 and write your name in the large middle circle. Then in the remaining circles, list the other elements of your "ecosystem." You can add parts of your family and peer groups of course, but also pay attention to other aspects of your ecosystem that affect your wellbeing such as organizations (workplace, school, faith-based), your neighborhood or community, and broader factors such as economic, environmental, or political factors. When you have most of the circles filled, draw lines and arrows to show how these factors at different levels affect you and how these factors affect each other. Be sure to also note where you have an influence on these factors by drawing arrows from your circle outward.

After filling in the diagram, take a look at your picture. What stands out to you? What was challenging about this exercise? What factors contribute to your wellbeing? In what ways do these factors interact with each other? Which factors have the *most* influence on you and your wellbeing? Why? Where do you have control or influence over these factors? Where do you lack control or influence?

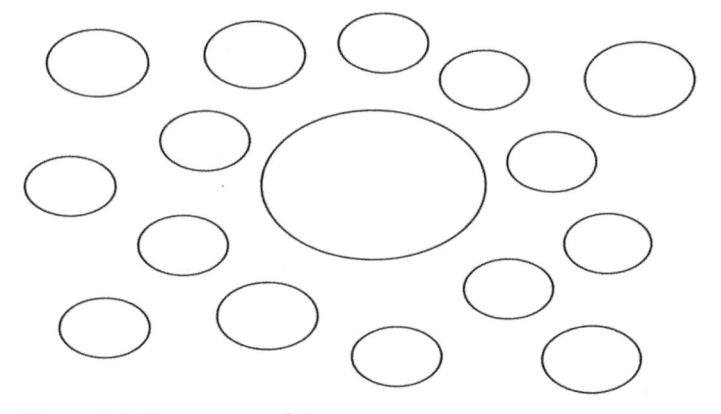

Figure 5.1 Ecomap template

Learning Objectives

In this chapter you will learn about

- The ecological model and systems theory
- The differences between simple, complicated, and complex problems
- Systems thinking and the ecological model for a deeper understanding of social systems and social problems
- How macro-level contextual phenomena such as globalization and neoliberalism influence health and wellbeing

Introduction to Systems Thinking

In Chapter 1, we introduced you to the idea that community psychology (CP) is primarily focused on the relationship between individuals and the multiple social **systems** in which they are embedded. These social systems range from the family system and peer groups, to social systems such as organizations, neighborhoods, and institutional systems, on out to the broader global economic, political, social, and environmental systems. In Chapter 3, we described the concept of "context" and the goal of community psychologists and social scientists to fully understand the social, economic, physical, cultural, and political conditions of a given community – the actual state of affairs in which people live. There is a strong belief in CP that we should never lose sight of the wider context when attempting to understand people and social processes (Kagan, 2007; Seidman, 1988). As Trickett (1996) reminded us, sometimes we can lose sight of these contextual elements as "context is the water in which we fish swim" (p. 226)[1]. Looking back at your ecomap from the opening exercise, what contextual elements did you miss? The ecological model, a contextual understanding, and **systems thinking** are central to the way the community psychologist thinks and acts on social issues.

Design theorists Horst Rittel and Melvin Webber (1973) introduced the term "wicked problem" in order to draw attention to the complexities of addressing social problems. They suggested that "one cannot understand the problem without knowing about its context" but they also cautioned that addressing wicked problems is not as easy as "first understand, then solve" (p. 162). Complexity can be wicked to understand, wicked to manage, wicked to tame. Given the wicked nature of the issues we are trying to understand and address in CP, it is nearly impossible (but not impossible!) to define social problems and their contexts and describe their full nature (see Box 5.1). Every complex problem can also be considered a symptom or a cause of another problem. For example, homelessness is a *symptom* of challenging economic conditions and housing policies, both a *symptom* and a *cause* of mental health issues and substance abuse, and a *cause* of stress and physical health problems. Most issues we address in CP are in reality a set of interlocking issues and constraints, which change over time, embedded in a dynamic social context. Furthermore, the many stakeholders involved in any social analysis or intervention will have various and

---

[1] See also the provocative 2005 "This is Water" Kenyon College commencement speech by David Foster Wallace: www.youtube.com/watch?v=8CrOL-ydFMI

changing interpretations about what might be a problem, what might be causing it, and how best to resolve it based upon their position, role, and experiences (Flaspohler et al., 2003).

Understanding the complex nature of social problems and solutions is a core challenge for community psychologists. We need to embrace complexity and recognize that these complex systems pervade every aspect of our lives and our communities (Louzao, 2014). This is why, in this complex, globalized world, it is critical to take an ecological systems perspective to understand the influence of broader cultural, political, and economic factors that shape people's ability to thrive. In this chapter, we explore the concept of "context" through a discussion of **systems theory** and the ecological model.

Box 5.1 What makes a problem complex?

What is different about these three challenges: (1) baking a cake; (2) sending a rocket to the moon; and (3) raising a child? In a 2002 paper, Glouberman and Zimmerman provide this example to help us understand the importance of approaching complex problems differently than how we approach simple and complicated problems.

> In simple problems like cooking by following a recipe, the recipe is essential. It is often tested to assure easy replication without the need for any particular expertise. Recipes produce standardized products and the best recipes give good results every time. Complicated problems, like sending a rocket to the moon, are different. Formulae or recipes are critical and necessary to resolve them but are often not sufficient. High levels of expertise in a variety of fields are necessary for success. Sending one rocket increases assurance that the next mission will be a success. In some critical ways, rockets are

similar to each other and because of this there can be a relatively high degree of certainty of outcome. Raising a child, on the other hand, is a complex problem. Here, formulae have a much more limited application. Raising one child provides experience but no assurance of success with the next. Although expertise can contribute to the process in valuable ways, it provides neither necessary nor sufficient conditions to assure success. To some extent this is because every child is unique and must be understood as an individual. As a result, there is always some uncertainty of the outcome. The complexity of the process and the lack of certainty do not lead us to the conclusion that it is impossible to raise a child. (p. vi)

Unlike simple and complicated problems, complex problems and complex systems carry with them large degrees of ambiguity and uncertainty (Wheatley, 1992).

Systems Theory and Systems Thinking

Systems theory comes primarily from the fields of physics and engineering. However, systems theory and systems thinking have important implications for CP and other social fields as varied as anthropology, education, political science, sociology, public health, and law. General Systems Theory emerged as a way to address the increasing complexity of social problems (Forrester, 1971,1994; Von Bertalanffy, 1968) with the understanding that all socioecological systems are marked by interconnectedness within dynamic, ever-changing processes of self-organization, growth, and adaptation. Social systems are considered open systems in that they are composed of interacting components with identifiable, permeable boundaries and are engaged in continuous exchange with other systems and their environment (Lauffer, 2010). Social problems have multiple sources that require a more complex understanding of the dynamic interrelationships within and between systems and the environment (Forrester, 1994).

A system is simply an interconnected set of elements that interact together and function as a whole. Some examples of social systems include a family, a neighborhood, an organization, a school district, a system of care for homeless youth, a coalition of organizations, a national health-care system, and capitalism (Foster-Fishman, Nowell, & Yang, 2007). Community psychologists and systems theorists highlight key aspects when thinking about social systems:

1 The elements and subcomponents of social systems are interrelated and involve interconnected parts (e.g., people, institutions, processes) in a functioning whole.
2 Social systems are open systems – they are always interacting with the environment, are subject to outside influences, and can affect other systems.
3 Social systems are dynamic and always changing.
4 Any level or unit within a system can be viewed as a system.
5 The properties of systems are emergent – they cannot be solely predicted from the properties of individual elements in themselves.
6 Social systems are different than natural systems in that they involve people and people have ideas, beliefs, assumptions, attitudes, and worldviews and these enter into systems as properties.
7 The actors in human systems do not necessarily have the same interests, so conflict and the exercise of power are inherent (Burton, 2003; Burton & Kagan, 2015; Foster-Fishman et al., 2007; Harrison, 2005; Kagan, Burton, Duckett, Lawthom, & Siddiquee, 2011).

Thus, systems *thinking* is a way of understanding the world based on the systems principles described above. It is a worldview as well as a process of organizing information in order to understand how systems function by examining interrelationships between parts, the root causes of targeted issues, and how parts of a system work to create a functioning whole (Checkland, 1999; Hodges, Ferreira, & Israel, 2012; McPhearson, 2013; Stroh, 2015; Trochim, Cabrera, Milstein, Gallagher, & Leischow, 2006). Systems thinking is fundamental to research, theory, and practice in CP because no social concern exists in isolation. Challenges related to housing and homelessness, immigration, and environmental sustainability are all parts of a larger system of interacting networks, and identifying those variables that are most crucial for understanding desired health, behavioral, and sustainability outcomes can be formidable (Stokols, 2018). CP is ultimately concerned about social justice and social change and these goals require a sophisticated understanding of the broader contexts that give rise to social problems (Seidman, 1988). Too often, well-meaning change agents are trapped into a narrow way of defining and responding to social issues as if they were merely complicated (Glouberman & Zimmerman, 2002). We can't understand or change a complex system by studying its parts only; we need to attend to the whole system, the parts, and the interaction between the parts. Furthermore, a central aspect of a systems approach is that we view a system with a specific problem focus or questions and attempt to identify the system attributes that are most relevant to making change.

Foster-Fishman and Watson (2012) offer a helpful "system cloverleaf" to help better understand the different parts that make up a system and identify targets for change (Figure 5.2). If we take our homelessness example, we can explore how the system cloverleaf can be used as a tool to examine system conditions and interactions that contribute to the problem of homelessness. For

Figure 5.2 The system cloverleaf

Source: Foster-Fishman, P., & Watson, E. (2017). Understanding and promoting systems change. In M. A. Bond, I. Serrano-García, C. B. Keys, & M. Shinn (Eds.), *APA handbook of community psychology: Methods for community research and action for diverse groups and issues* (pp. 255–74). Washington, DC: American Psychological Association.

example, regarding *mindsets*, what are the dominant assumptions about the causes of homelessness among people and organizations working on the issue? Regarding *regulations*, are there formal or informal policies or procedures getting in the way of addressing homelessness? Examining issues of *power* in a system might lead us to ask "To what extent do people experiencing or at risk of homelessness have a seat at the table to help local agencies design programs and other solutions?" An example of *interactions* across parts of the system might be when limited *resources* – such as lack of funding or information – constrain meaningful *connections* and collaboration across organizations, which limits their ability to work together to better integrate services and supports for people experiencing or at risk of homelessness. This systems cloverleaf framework helps us get beyond vague references to "the system" to do the deeper system analysis needed to better understand and change systems.

System theory and systems thinking provide the foundation for a better understanding of complex social problems and potential solutions. However, individuals are nested within a set of contexts, including families, organizations, systems, communities, and societies (Bronfenbrenner,

1979; Maton, 2000, 2008; Nelson & Prilleltensky, 2005). To promote this holistic understanding of individuals and their wellbeing, the discipline of CP has adopted ecological systems theory (EST) and the ecological metaphor to guide our thinking and action.

The Ecological Metaphor

What is the Ecological Metaphor?

Community psychologists James Kelly, Ed Trickett, and colleagues (Kelly, 1966; Trickett, Kelly, & Todd, 1972) introduced the metaphor of ecology to CP and defined it as the relationship between individuals and the multiple social systems in which they are embedded. Kelly argued that in studying the transactions between people and their environments, the metaphor of an ecosystem is more appropriate than the dominant mechanistic, reductionistic metaphor used in individual psychology to study basic human processes of learning, cognition, perception, and brain–behavior relations. An ecological perspective forces us to rethink typical psychological understandings of social problems – such as "antisocial behavior" and "juvenile delinquency" for example – as it shifts our problem framing from individual pathology to system dysfunction (Watts, 1992).

The ecological metaphor, which flows from the value of holism presented in Chapter 3 and systems theories presented above, suggests that communities are open systems with many different levels and connections. The perspective of ecological levels of analysis and the ecological metaphor in CP entails the argument, from a living systems standpoint, which itself is structured in interdependent fashion. The value of the ecological metaphor for CP lies in its ability to contextualize the issues and problems that face disadvantaged people over time and across multiple levels of analysis and to embrace the value of holism over reductionism. Whereas systems theory focuses on boundaries and interactions of elements within a system in which individuals are part, the ecological model rests on an evolutionary, dynamic, and adaptive view of human beings in continuous interaction with the proximal and distal elements of their environment.

The ecological metaphor in CP is based on ecological systems theory (EST), originally proposed by Bronfenbrenner (1977, 1979). Bronfenbrenner's initial articulation of EST identified four systems – the **microsystem**, **mesosystem**, **exosystem**, and **macrosystem** moving from smaller and closest to the individual to larger and more complex. The smaller systems nested within the larger systems, organized metaphorically like a Russian nesting doll around the individual (see Figure 5.3) (Bronfenbrenner, 1979). The *microsystem* consists of such people as the family and peer groups where individuals have direct social interactions with others. The *mesosystem* contains those situations in which two or more microsystems come together in some way, for example the relationship between an individual's peers and their family at a birthday party or a child's parents interacting with their child's school at a parent-teacher conference. Seidman (1983, 1988) considered the mesosystem to be the most complex unit of analysis in that it encompasses the arena of between–system social relations.

Exosystems include settings that influence the individual but in which the individual does not directly participate. For example, students and teachers do not generally play a role in, or have direct experiences of, education policy-making, but educational policies nonetheless influence their classroom and school experiences (Neal & Neal, 2013). Lastly, *macrosystems* include broad cultural influences or ideological patterns that characterize a given society or social group that have long-ranging consequences. The macrosystem is the most abstract and complex of

Figure 5.3 Matryoshka stacking nesting doll from Russia
Source: Igor Drondin from Pixabay.

Bronfenbrenner's four systems. These broader, interlocking social norms and forces are distal and hard to see (like the concept of "power," discussed in Chapter 4, or "**neoliberalism**," discussed later) but have a strong impact on human development and wellbeing.

The macrosystem shapes the patterns of social interactions at other system levels. For example, the dominant belief in some cultures that parents should be solely responsible for raising their children has an effect on how that society takes care of children who may not have adequate supports at home. Considering the power of the macrosystem helps us make sense of why a rich country like the US might tolerate a high child poverty rate while countries such as Finland, Denmark, and Sweden may not.[2]

Bronfenbrenner (1986) later introduced a fifth system – the **chronosystem** – reflecting change or continuity across time that influences each of the other systems (Figure 5.4). Transitions like a young person's move from high school to college or work are part of the chronosystem, as are historical events such as economic recessions, political revolutions, and wars. Just like your eco-map from the opening exercise, the whole ecosystem surrounding an individual is more than just a sum of its parts. The ecological underpinning of CP moves us beyond the consideration of context and its influence on people's lives, towards adopting a systems perspective in our work (Kagan et al., 2011). Failure to think systemically and practice ecologically reproduces the dominant culture's emphasis on individualism and encourages the tendency to engage in "victim-blaming."

Recently, Riemer and Harré (2017) joined other community psychologists to encourage the field to more strongly acknowledge that people are embedded not just in social systems, but also in non-human ecosystems that both impact human wellbeing and are impacted by human actions.

---

[2] According to the latest data available (OECD, 2019), Finland, Denmark, and Sweden had relative child poverty rates of less than 10 percent. Note however that this is only for Scandinavian-born children. These countries are much more willing to accept high poverty rates for immigrants. In the US, 22 percent of all children are living in relative poverty.

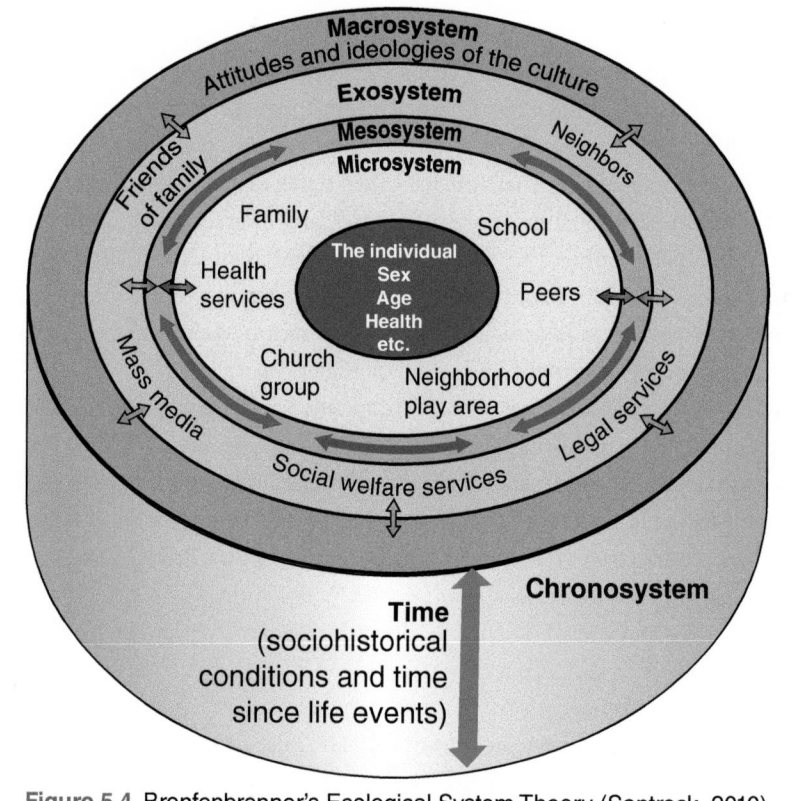

Figure 5.4 Bronfenbrenner's Ecological System Theory (Santrock, 2010)

Republished with permission of McGraw Hill Education, from Santrock, J. W. *Life-span development* (9th ed.), © 2010 McGraw Hill Education; permission conveyed through Copyright Clearance Center, Inc.

Human-caused climate change and its many current and anticipated negative impacts on the world's most vulnerable is a good example of that. Levine, Perkins, and Perkins (2005) for example, introduced a "biosphere," and Moskell and Allred (2013), based on the work of Van Voorhees and Perkins (2007), argued for a "geosphere" that forms an outer ring beyond the macro level of society. This is an emerging area for CP, as the natural environment and sustainability have not been very prevalent issues within the field. The focus has been on social ecology rather than on natural ecology and the transactions between human systems and the natural world (Bennet, 2005). Some suggest that CP currently has an "underdeveloped theory on the relationship between humans and the natural world" (Moskell & Allred, 2013, p. 2). Given that impacts on natural and human systems from global warming have already been observed (IPCC, 2018), and the increased urgency to study and prepare for the inevitable impacts of global climate change and related social and environmental problems, there is potential for CP to make significant contributions toward a more sustainable world (Riemer & Harré, 2017; Riemer & Reich, 2011; Stokols, 2018).

Ecological Principles

Kelly, with contributions by others, introduced four enduring ecological principles drawn from the study of biological communities and applied to human communities: interdependence, cycling of resources, adaptation, and succession (Kelly, 1966; Trickett, Kelly, & Todd, 1972; Trickett, 1984; Trickett, Barone, & Watts, 2000).

Interdependence

The principle of interdependence asserts that every event or phenomenon should be seen as part of a whole and only properly understood with reference to every other part of the larger system (Ife, 2002). The different parts of an ecosystem are interconnected and changes in any one part of the system will have ripple effects that impact other parts of the system. All of these levels are interconnected and the relationship between people and their contexts is one of bidirectional influence – an individual is subject to the influence of systems but can also be an originator of action on systems (Riger, 2001). From a sociopolitical perspective, interdependence is a necessary element of resource sharing, solidarity, and joint social action. As such, this principle serves as a mobilizing strategy for empowerment and social change (Watts, 1992).

In natural systems, it's easy to witness the interdependence of living things – plants thrive on the carbon dioxide emitted by animals while animals depend on the oxygen emitted by plants. So too can we see the interdependencies in social systems. For example, we know that in the US, African Americans account for a higher proportion of new HIV diagnoses and those living with HIV compared to other races/ethnicities (Centers for Disease Control and Prevention [CDC], 2017). We also know that mass imprisonment, as a result of the "war on drugs" is contributing to the transmission of HIV/AIDS and other blood-borne diseases. Research conducted in the US, where ethnic and racial minorities are many times more likely than Whites to be imprisoned for drug-related offenses, has found that disproportionate imprisonment rates are one of the key reasons for the markedly elevated rates of HIV infection among African Americans (Adimora et al., 2003; Johnson & Raphael, 2009). Add to that the fact that decreasing funding for public schools and increased spending for prisons leave poorly educated children to grow up financially strapped and more likely to commit drug-related offenses and we begin to understand what Michelle Fine (2000) refers to as the "unholy trinity" between public education, the criminal justice system, and the economy.

Actions affecting any point in a system will have ramifications throughout the system. In this example, we see the interdependence of public education, incarceration rates, structural racism, and inequities in HIV/AIDS transmission. Understanding and attending to the unintentional side effects of changes at any level of a system is an important implication of the principle of interdependence.

Cycling of Resources

This principle focuses on the identification, development, and allocation of resources within systems. In the natural world, larger animals feed on smaller ones and leave fertilizer for plants. It is the manner in which "energy, needed suppliers, or nutrients are generated and cycle through biological communities" (Trickett, 1984, p. 266). Under this principle, the outputs of one part of a system can also be seen as inputs into others (Hawe & Riley, 2005). In the social world, resources move into and around various social settings. These resources might include money, knowledge, professional expertise, leadership, settings, networks, and time (Hawe, 2017; Trickett, Kelly, & Vincent, 1985). One clear finding from the experience of deinstitutionalization – replacing isolated long-stay psychiatric hospitals with community mental health services – is that, with a few notable exceptions, resources were not reallocated from mental hospitals into community support and housing programs as was needed (Kiesler, 1992). Without adequate support following discharge, people with mental health problems experience a "revolving door" of readmission to, and discharge from, these institutions and a likely increase in levels of homelessness. The cycling of resources principle draws attention to potential untapped resources in a system.

We can see the principle of cycling of resources in the example of the war on drugs mentioned above. By isolating and punishing the drug users through incarceration, we take away the resources they need most: services and human connection. Understanding this, the Portuguese government in 2001 tried a radically different approach to get a handle on their drug problem – the government decriminalized the use and possession of heroin, cocaine, marijuana, LSD, and other illicit street drugs (Hari, 2015). They believed that focusing on treatment and prevention instead of jailing users would decrease the number of deaths as well as HIV infections. Since decriminalization, the rate of new HIV infections in Portugal has fallen precipitously and overdose deaths decreased from 80 the year that decriminalization was enacted to only 16 in 2012 (European Monitoring Centre for Drugs and Drug Addiction, 2015). Experts suggest the policy changes worked because users were more likely to seek out care when decriminalization reduced stigma and increased resources – plus services were provided, such as needle replacement, detox programs, therapeutic communities, and employment options for people who use drugs. The Portugal example shows that by decriminalizing drug use and providing supports and bonding opportunities (which were financed through the money saved on stopping the war on drugs) they were able to positively affect the problem (Hari, 2015).[3]

Adaptation

In natural systems, organisms respond in a variety of ways to cope with changing conditions and resources. In the social world, the principle of adaptation suggests that individuals and systems must cope with and adapt to changing conditions in an ecosystem. **Resilience** (introduced in Chapter 4) as a concept is usually focused on the individual – particularly children or youth in difficult circumstances – and described as "the process of adapting well in the face of adversity, trauma, tragedy, threats or significant sources of stress – such as family and relationship problems, serious health problems or workplace and financial stressors" (American Psychological Association [APA], 2018, para 4). However, in ecological systems theory, resilience extends beyond the individual to the capacity of the system to continually change and adapt in the face of disturbance, stress, or adversity (Norris, Stevens, Pfefferbaum, Wyche, & Pfefferbaum, 2008; see Chapter 4).

Resilience takes place at multiple levels involving individuals, organizations, communities, systems, and societies. Organizations are resilient and demonstrate adaptive capacity when they monitor, assess, and respond to internal and external changes (Connolly & York, 2003). Communities are resilient when they link adaptive capacities to a positive trajectory of functioning and adaptation after a disturbance (Chandra et al., 2010; Norris et al., 2008). Resilience is the ability of a system or community to survive disruption and to anticipate, adapt, and flourish in the face of change. For example, in Scot's home community of Miami, the coastal location, combined with a high groundwater table and complex canal water management system, makes it inherently vulnerable to rising sea levels and stronger hurricanes. Projected maximum sea level rises would inundate large sections of the area, with negative effects on people, property, and the local economy. One way that the community is responding to these new challenges is by developing and implementing climate-adaptive zoning and building codes, community resilience hubs, and permit process modifications to reduce risk and economic losses.

---

[3] Check out Johann Hari's 2015 TED Talk on this topic: www.ted.com/talks/johann_hari_everything_you_think_you_know_about_addiction_is_wrong

Succession

Succession is a fundamental concept in ecology and refers to the more or less predictable and orderly changes over time in the composition or structure of an ecological system. In the natural world, changes in the environment may create conditions more favorable to one species and inhospitable to others. Systems have somewhat natural cycles of renewal to establish new levels of homeostasis. As Trickett (1984) suggests, "its metaphorical value for human communities lies in its focus on understanding how historical factors have contributed to the current way the setting is and how this history provides a perspective for couching decisions about immediate action within a longer-range time frame" (p. 267).

In CP, the concept of succession means "taking the long view" in understanding historical swings of perspective and power that influence how social issues are framed and addressed (Levine & Levine, 1992; Tseng et al., 2002). For example, in the US – like in many democratic countries – political power regularly swings back and forth between parties promoting more liberal (Democrat) or conservative (Republican) policies. With conservatives holding power like we see in 2020 in the US, the political forces are swinging hard toward protectionism and nationalism with a renewed emphasis on personal responsibility and deregulation of markets.

With more liberal parties in power, national priorities may favor equity, sensible regulation of markets, and compassionate immigration policies. A long-term perspective requires our sustained involvement with and commitment to marginalized groups and communities even when the political climate may appear favorable to the cause. Taken together, these ecological principles provide guidance for how to take the environment into account when attempting to understand and intervene in social systems.

Why is the Ecological Metaphor Important?

A metaphor can be a tool to help us understand and make sense of the world. Community psychologists use an ecological metaphor because they believe that mainstream psychology has focused too much on individual psychological processes and neglected the important role that social systems play in human development. The ecological metaphor helps us frame problems and solutions at multiple levels of analysis. We know that social systems can have a profound impact on the wellbeing of people and communities. Community psychologists need to understand the harmful or oppressive qualities of human environments – those that block personal growth and create problems in living – and the positive qualities of environments that promote health, wellbeing, and competence (Cowen, 1994). We need to understand and promote the characteristics of communities that promote liberation and wellbeing.

It is also important to recognize that environments sometimes affect different individuals in distinct ways. This has been called **person–environment fit** (French, Rodgers, & Cobb, 1974). A certain quality of the environment provides a good fit (or has a positive impact) for only some individuals. An example of this is provided by Canadian community psychologist Pat O'Neill (1976) in a study of fourth-grade girls in conventional and open-space classrooms. Open-space classrooms are organized into large open areas with few partitions and teachers are flexible in their teaching approach. He found that students who were high in divergent thinking (creativity) had higher self-esteem in open classrooms than in conventional classrooms. Thus, open-space classrooms had a positive impact on self-esteem, but only for those children high in divergent thinking. O'Neill (2000) introduced the idea of **cognitive CP** as a way of highlighting the importance of both individual and environmental qualities and the interrelationship between the person and the environment. Think of what type of environment is a good fit for you. If you are a private person, a noisy university residence hall with several roommates is unlikely to be a setting in which you would be comfortable. In thinking through wellness and in designing programs and other interventions, the fit between individuals and their environments is important.

Community and environmental psychologists have been instrumental in developing ways of conceptualizing and assessing human environments (Linney, 2000; Moos, 2003; Shinn & Toohey, 2003). Community psychologist Jean Ann Linney (2000) offers three ways of thinking about and assessing environments: (1) participants' perceptions of the environment; (2) setting characteristics that are independent of the behavior of participants; and (3) transactional analyses of the dynamic relationship between behavior and context. We briefly consider each of these three approaches, which can be applied to both neighborhoods/communities and settings (e.g., schools, community organizations, workplaces).

Perceived Environments

Rudolf Moos (1994) and colleagues have emphasized the importance of the social climate or atmosphere of a setting. The key notion with this conceptualization of environments is the emphasis on people's perceptions of the environment. Most people can think of settings that they have experienced as oppressive and settings that were experienced as empowering. Moos has argued that there are three broad dimensions of different social environments: relationships, personal development, and systems maintenance and change.

We can apply each dimension to a familiar setting – a school. The relationship dimension is concerned with how supportive or cohesive the setting appears to be. Are the teachers caring and compassionate? The personal development dimension addresses the individual's need for self-determination. Does the school provide opportunities for autonomy, independence, and personal growth? The systems maintenance and change dimension is concerned with the balance between predictability and flexibility. Does the school provide clear expectations, yet at the same time, demonstrate openness to change and innovation? Too much predictability in a school can produce boredom and resentment because it may reflect rigid authoritarianism and resistance to change. Too much flexibility, on the other hand, can produce confusion due to continuous uncertainty and flux. Moos and colleagues have developed self-report questionnaires tapping these three broad dimensions and specific sub-dimensions to assess classrooms, families, community programs, groups, and work settings (Moos, 1994).

Objective Characteristics of Environments

A second approach to the assessment of environments is to examine characteristics of settings that are more objective and independent of the behavior of individuals who participate in those settings. Different types of measures (e.g., observational methods, demographic and social indicator data) are used to assess qualities of environments, such as the physical and architectural dimensions, policies and procedures, and environmental resources. One example of an observational method cited by Linney (2000) is the PASSING approach designed by Wolfensberger (1972) to assess the extent to which facilities for people with disabilities reflect the construct of normalization. Wolfensberger (1972) defined normalization as the "utilization of means which are as culturally normative as possible in order to establish and/or maintain behaviors and characteristics which are as culturally normative as possible" (p. 28). External observers spend several days observing these settings to come up with ratings on a number of different dimensions, including physical integration of the setting with the community, the promotion of resident autonomy, social integration within the neighborhood, and many more (Flynn & Lemay, 1999).

Rutter, Maughan, Mortimore, and Ouston (1979) used both observational and social indicator/demographic information in a study of 12 inner-city secondary schools in London, England. The major goal of the research was to identify characteristics of school atmosphere and to see whether those characteristics related to students' rates of delinquency, behavioral problems, academic achievement, and attendance over the three years they were enrolled in these schools. An important finding of the study was that the school atmosphere measures predicted outcomes over and above the characteristics of the students at the time they entered these schools. More recent research has also demonstrated that schooling quality has significant effects on student outcomes (Caldarella, Shatzer, Gray, Young, & Young, 2011; Konstantopolous & Borman, 2011; MacNeil, Prater, & Busch, 2009; Wang & Degol, 2016). Reflecting the ecological principle of interdependence, school climate does make a difference for students.

Viewing a setting such as a school through the lens of the principle of interdependence also forces us to look objectively at how policies affect the quality of schooling and outcomes for students. For example, in the US, we know that on average, levels of per-student spending in school systems are positively associated with higher student outcomes (Baker, 2016). School funding in the US comes from a combination of three sources: 45 percent local money, 45 percent from the state, and 10 percent from the federal level. The local contribution relies heavily on local property taxes and property values vary a lot from neighborhood to neighborhood, district to district. With that variation in values comes a variation in available tax revenues across neighborhoods and districts. This is exacerbated by the reality that families and businesses in more affluent areas are more able to donate money and other resources to their local schools. Add it all up and it means that schools and districts in poorer areas receive less money and are more likely to see lower outcomes for students. In his research on school funding fairness in the US, Baker (2016) concluded:

> While money alone may not be the answer, adequate and equitable distributions of financial inputs to schooling provide a necessary underlying condition for improving the adequacy and equity of outcomes. (p. 19)

In short, money matters.

Transactional Approaches

Linney (2000) describes transactional approaches as those that include both the behavior of individuals and characteristics of the environment. One transactional approach is the concept of **behavior settings** developed by Barker (1968). The two main components of a behavior setting are a standing or routine pattern of behavior and the physical and temporal aspects of the environment. There are implicit guidelines on how to behave in behavior settings. For example, a classroom science lesson and a gym period are different behavior settings, and the behavior of people in these settings can be better predicted on the basis of the setting than on the characteristics of the people in the setting.

One interesting extension of the behavior settings concept is Barker and Gump's (1964) theory of understaffing. They asserted that as the size of an organization increases the number of people available to staff the different behavior settings also increases. Furthermore, they hypothesized that, in small organizations, individuals would experience more invitations and pressure to take responsibility for staffing the different settings than they would in large organizations. In a study of high schools, they found support for this theory of understaffing. Students in smaller schools, including students with academic and social difficulties, were involved in a wider range of activities than students in larger schools. This approach to the understanding of environments has important implications for the CP value of participation and collaboration. Small, more intimate environments are apt to pull for more participation than larger, more impersonal environments. The downside to small settings, such as high schools, is that the number of activities in which students can participate is often restricted and the burden of responsibility is higher.

What Is the Value Base of the Ecological Metaphor?

The ecological perspective addresses the meta-value of holism. Western science and ways of thinking about the world have emphasized linear, simple, reductionist, and fragmented ways of understanding. In psychology, people are broken down into component parts (learning, perception, cognition) and are examined as isolated entities. The value of holism helps remind us that social problems must always be understood as manifestations of a wider system. The ecological perspective revives the emphasis on holistic thinking, feeling, and acting, which was evident in Gestalt psychology (Humphrey, 1924).

The holistic emphasis of the ecological perspective is also quite similar to the worldview of many Aboriginal people in Canada and around the world. Connors and Maidman (2001) assert that the roots of tribal culture lie in holistic thought, which involves "interdependence between the environment, people and the spirit" (p. 350). In the traditional worldview of Aboriginal people, there is a strong emphasis on the interconnection of people with their spiritual roots and the natural environments and on balance and harmony. Aboriginal holistic thinking also incorporates values (e.g., bravery, respect, cooperation) in the form of teachings, which guide community members, unlike Western science, which claims to be value neutral. The medicine wheel (see Figure 5.5 on p. 102) is a symbol of holism:

> This form of thought is often symbolized by the sacred circle or medicine wheel, which contains the teaching about the interconnection among all of Creation. The circle is a symbol that represents the knowledge offered by holistic world-views shared by Aboriginal people. From this perspective, elements that affect change in a person are simultaneously seen as impacting on the person's family, community, nation and surrounding environment. (Connors & Maidman, 2001, p. 350)

How Can the Ecological Metaphor Be Implemented?

Jim Kelly and Ed Trickett have expanded on the four principles of the ecological perspective and have outlined their implications for preventive intervention (Kelly, 1986), the training of community psychologists (Trickett, 1984), and the conduct of research (Trickett, 1984; Trickett et al., 1985). The major implication of the ecological metaphor for research is that research needs to be conducted in a much more collaborative and participatory manner than mainstream psychological research (Hawe, 2017; Trickett, 1984; Trickett et al., 1985; Ryerson Espino & Trickett, 2008). Since CP research is carried out in the community with community partners, it stands in contrast to the mechanistic approach of experimental psychology and other basic sciences that are conducted in laboratories, in which the variables under study are isolated from their normal

Figure 5.5 Medicine wheel
Source: Image by PublicDomainArchive from Pixabay.

environment and tightly controlled. Community members and settings are stakeholders in the research, who want to ensure that their needs are met. In community research, people are active participants in the research process, not passive subjects (see Chapter 13).

Moreover, community researchers are not exclusively detached, objective scientists. They are human beings with interests, agendas, values, and feelings (as described in Chapter 3). Community psychologists are passionately concerned about disadvantaged groups and oppressive social conditions; they want to change the world, to make communities more caring and just. We believe that it is important for community psychologists to write more about their experiences and describe their worldviews and standpoints in their research reports and writings.

What about implications for community intervention and practice? Trickett (1986) has identified several implications of the ecological metaphor for intervention. First and foremost, the spirit of the ecological approach to social change is distinctive. Not only are problems framed in terms of a systemic analysis described in the chapter, but the process of the intervention is one that is participatory and collaborative, ideally with multiple stakeholders engaged to represent the different system aspects and layers. Trickett (1986) captures this in the following passage:

> The spirit of ecologically-based consultation is to contribute to the resourcefulness of the host environment by building on locally identified concerns to create processes which aid in empowering the environment to solve its own problems and plan its own development. This spirit is concretized in the kinds of activities engaged in by the consultants, which further highlight the distinctiveness of the ecological metaphor. (p. 190)

In ecological intervention, community psychologists work *with* rather than *on* people.

A second implication for community intervention is that attempts to change one part of the system will have side effects on other systems and that these ripple effects will often not be anticipated. The ecological metaphor suggests that social change is not linear. Attempts to solve a problem may lead to new problems in another context (Sarason, 1978). The case of the war on drugs cited earlier is an example of this, as is the increased use of agricultural pesticides during the green revolution, which helped to reduce food insecurity for millions of people but had unintended negative effects on the environment and public health (Carson, 2002).

A third implication of the ecological perspective is that the intervention should not focus exclusively on the attainment of outcome goals for participants in a specific program. While it is important to see how individuals benefit from programs and other interventions, the ecological perspective draws attention to goals and at multiple levels of analysis – organizations, systems, neighborhoods, communities, and social policies. A successful ecological intervention builds the capacity of the setting to mobilize for future action and create other change efforts. The extent to which setting members participate in and take ownership for social action is also important. We will address other implications for social interventions and systems change in Chapters 9 and 10.

Fourth, there are implications of the ecological metaphor for the role and qualities of the interventionist. Since ecological intervention is flexible and improvisational in nature, researchers and consultants must be able to form constructive working relationships with different partners from the host setting. They must problem-solve, think on their feet, be patient and take time to get to know the setting and the people within it. They must not jump into offering solutions, but rather need to tolerate the ambiguities and frustrations that inevitably occur in any intervention, and help the setting to mobilize resources from within or to identify external resources. They must also be creative and attend to issues of entry and exit from the setting (Kelly, 1971).

A fifth implication of the ecological metaphor for community intervention is that the dimension of time is highlighted. The changing nature of ecosystems and human adaptation requires a long-term perspective. Contemporary social problems have both historical roots and future consequences. When community psychologists examine social issues and problems from an ecological perspective, they consider these issues and problems at multiple levels of analysis and over a long-term perspective.

Finally, it is important to consider both individual and setting characteristics in community intervention. For example, research by O'Neill (2000) and colleagues has shown that social change tends to occur when there are recent improvements in social conditions (an environmental characteristic) and when people have a sense of injustice and a belief in their personal power to effect change (individual characteristics).

What Are the Limitations of the Ecological Metaphor?

The ecological metaphor has value in providing a systemic and holistic perspective for the understanding of human experience and behavior and has led to the development of different ways of understanding and assessing human environments. To date, however, CP has tended to focus primarily on micro- and meso-levels, to the neglect of macro-level structures and interventions. While community psychologists often focus on risk and protective factors at multiple levels of analysis, they do not yet adequately address the macro or structural level of the ecology (Joffe & Albee, 1988; Prilleltensky & Nelson, 2009; Sarason, 1984). Inattention to the macro-level of analysis is not a limitation of the ecological perspective per se, but rather due to (1) the limited degree to which community psychologists have been trained to examine larger social systems and structures; and (2) how researchers are dependent on funding from government and foundation sources of funding and this can bend research interests in the direction of the interests of those offering grants (Heller, 2016; Pfeffer & Salancik, 2003; Sarason, 1976a).

One important limitation is that the ecological perspective does not specifically assist in tackling issues that are fundamental to social justice including equity, human rights, structural oppression, and discourses of power (Gridley & Turner, 2010; Ife, 2002). Watts (1992) proposed adding a sociopolitical perspective to our ecological understanding to focus our analysis "toward historically based patterns of control and domination and the systems that maintain it" (p. 125). Fundamental social justice principles such as class, gender, and race are often missing from an ecological analysis (Ife, 2002). This is why the ecological perspective needs to be complemented by a concern for social justice.

Community psychologists Neal and Neal (2013) offered a second limitation when they argue that conceptualizing ecological systems as nested masks the relationships between them. Instead, they suggest that ecological systems should be conceptualized as networked, where each system is defined in terms of the social relationships surrounding an individual, and where systems at different levels relate to one another in an overlapping but non-nested way. This alternative "networked" model defines ecological systems in terms of patterns of social interaction and represents a substantial reframing of ecological systems theory (Hawe, 2017).

A third limitation of ecological and systems perspectives is that in their emphasis on circular causality (the idea that everything is causally related to everything else), these perspectives do not take into account or highlight power differences within ecosystems. For example, the phenomena of child maltreatment and violence against women can be understood in terms of an ecological perspective, with multiple layers of influence. But it is also important to recognize that some players have more power than others in any ecosystem and that those individuals who abuse power must be accountable for their actions. Abused women and children are not architects of their abuse. There is a need to understand the implicit and explicit culture of institutions (Sarason, 1972), the ways in which policies differentially influence different cultural groups (Birman, Trickett, & Buchanan, 2005), and the degree to which the social norms of the broader culture – as reflected in institutions, systems, policies, and discourse – converge, diverge, or conflict with the hopes, beliefs, and traditions of various cultural groups (Tyler, Sussewell, & Williams-McCoy, 1985). A critical application of the ecological model is a politicized one (Prilleltensky & Nelson, 2009). This is why the ecological metaphor needs to also be complemented with an understanding of power (Trickett, 1994; see Chapter 4).

Lastly, while community psychologists have adopted the ecological metaphor and ecological principles as core concepts in the field, there has been limited focus on natural ecology, environmental issues, and the transactions between human systems and the natural world (Bennet, 2005). However, as Riemer and Harré (2017) point out in the 2017 edition of the *APA Handbook of Community Psychology*, there has been increasing coverage of environmental issues within CP. For example, the *American Journal of Community Psychology* published a special section on global climate change in 2011 (Riemer & Reich, 2011) and the Society for Community Research and Action (SCRA) Environment & Justice Interest Group was founded in 2009 and now publishes a quarterly column in *The Community Psychologist*. There is also an increasing number of environmentally focused CP conference presentations and posters as well as a keynote address on the topic at the SCRA Biennial Conference in Miami, Florida (Harré, 2013). This is a welcome development given the urgency of addressing global climate change and other environmental problems and the potential for CP to make significant contributions toward a more sustainable world (Riemer & Harré, 2017). However, while CP is increasingly targeting environmental ecological issues, immense political challenges exist as exhibited in the US government's deregulation of the energy industry, president Donald Trump's decision to remove the US from the Paris Climate Agreement, and the deletion of nearly all mentions of climate change and climate science from most official US government websites.

Complexity in a Globalized World

Imagine it is 20 years from now and you are asked by someone much younger to describe what it was like 20 years ago. How would you go about describing the current global, social, economic, and political context to someone who is too young to remember? What features of our current times would you highlight? Would you focus on the political or economic climate in your country or locality? Would you talk about the environmental challenges facing the world? Might you point out the numerous conflicts related to terrorism, tribal hostility, and war? Or would you highlight how migration, poverty, inequality, globalization, and natural disasters are affecting people around the world? How about the benefits and drawbacks of rapid changes associated with technological advances, social media, and information exchange? Where would you start?

A critical and thorough application of systems thinking and the ecological model helps remind us that we can't ignore the broader forces shaping human and community development and wellbeing around the world. Many of these forces involve complex power dynamics that are ambiguous and hard to see, but we ignore them at our peril. Ecologically speaking, we are referring to these mostly hidden forces as the *ideological macro-level* that encompasses and permeates the other levels (Nafstad, Blakar, Carlquist, Phelps, & Rand-Hendriksen, 2007).

Ideology, as we use it here, is a comprehensive set of beliefs and conscious and unconscious ideas that dominate society. They can serve to control the positive or negative ways in which individuals and groups adapt to and master their environments (Nafstad et al., 2007). Thus to end this chapter, we'd like to briefly introduce two late capitalist market ideology concepts that are gaining increasing attention in CP: neoliberalism and globalization. In our experience, most students have not been introduced to the concept of neoliberalism. Many, however, are at least familiar with the concept of globalization. Later in Chapter 15, we'll expand upon this short introduction to these concepts.

Neoliberalism

George Monbiot (2016) argues that the central ideology that dominates our lives and plays a critical determining factor in community wellbeing is mostly hidden from view. The neoliberal ideology has become so deeply embedded in our collective understanding that it is taken for granted, unexamined, and seemingly beyond question (Harvey, 2007). "So pervasive has neoliberalism become that we seldom even recognize it as an ideology" (Monbiot, 2016, para 3).

Neoliberalism is a theory of political economic practices based on the assumption that human wellbeing can best be advanced by maximizing individualism and entrepreneurial freedoms while promoting private property rights, individual liberty, unfettered markets, competition, and free trade (Harvey, 2007; Mahon 2008). Its moral underpinnings are individual liberty, competition, individual responsibility, and work ethic. Neoliberalism recasts the role of the government by shifting responsibility from the state to the market and from the collective to the individual (Taylor-Gooby, 2004). The dominant neoliberal narrative is about rugged individualism, and has led to policies that support the privatization of public goods – such as schools, parks, utilities, and prisons – the development of public–private partnerships, an increase in market-driven decisions, a diminished role for governments, and a reduction in government spending and budget deficits.

One risk of neoliberalism is that it profoundly changes the social contract between the individual and the community towards more extreme individualism (Nafstad et al., 2007; Nelson, 2013). Neoliberal political economic practices such as privatization of public goods also exacerbate inequality, spawning unprecedented concentrations of wealth in the hands of just a few people (Harvey, 2007).

Globalization

This neoliberal reality means that we now live in a world characterized by an increasingly pervasive globalized ideology of competition (Nafstad et al., 2007). As a contested term, "globalization" means different things to different people. It has economic, cultural, social, and health connotations. Moreover, globalization has been marked by "some remarkable successes, some disturbing failures and a collection of what might be called running sores" (Saul, 2005, p. 3). In his book *Globalization and its Discontents*, Stiglitz (2002) documents the many benefits derived from open communications between developed and developing nations. In some poor countries, irrigation projects doubled the incomes of farmers; HIV/AIDS projects prevented the spread of the disease; and literacy initiatives enhanced the education of children and women. When Jamaica opened the market to the import of US milk, local producers suffered, but many more children had access to cheaper milk. Similarly, in his book *The End of Poverty*, Columbia economist Jeffrey Sachs (2005) has shown that market-based changes in many poor countries have led to economic growth and reduction of poverty. Consider the case of China. In 1981, 64 percent of the population had incomes of less than a dollar a day, but by 2001, 17 percent of the population lived on less than a dollar a day. Thus, in only 20 years, poverty was dramatically reduced in China. However, it was accompanied with tremendous environmental degradation (Economy & Levi, 2014).

In spite of these positive impacts of globalization noted by Stiglitz and Sachs, globalization also has a dark side. For example, the World Bank and the International Monetary Fund (IMF) have pushed for an agenda that does not take into account the needs of the people in developing nations. Governed by the mantra that market liberalization should cure all countries of their economic woes, they proceeded to impose measures that were inadequate for the realities of many countries, because of either timing, pace and culture, or lack of infrastructure. The cure turned out to be worse than the disease in many cases. Stiglitz (2002) recounts the growing gap between poor and rich countries, the devastation of some local industries due to unfair competition with subsidized products in the US and the lack of investments in unstable economies. In essence, Stiglitz contends that the interests of developed nations superseded the concern for poor nations. While poor countries were expected to open their markets in return for financial aid, the rich nations continued to subsidize products, creating an unfair advantage in their favor. The narrow focus on monetary policies surpassed concerns for safety nets. The obsession with economic growth superseded concerns for human development. Imposed solutions were no solutions at all.

Economic exploitation and disenfranchisement of disadvantaged people are widespread in both developed and developing countries. More and more low-income people in Western countries are being forced into "McJobs" (i.e., low-paying jobs in the service sector), while individuals in developing countries, particularly women and young people, are paid a pittance in wages to make the athletic shoes, clothing, and other commercial products that are widely advertised and marketed in Western countries. Even in Western countries, inequality soars with 1 in 5 US children living in poverty (OECD, 2019) and 14 percent of Spain's and 18 percent of Greece's population being unemployed (Eurostat, 2019).

Corporate power and global capitalism are also bringing about sweeping changes in the natural environment (environmental degradation), working conditions (loss of power and rights of working people and unions), culture (a rapidly developing "monoculture"), and government policy (tax cuts and a diminished role for the state in addressing social inequalities, preserving the environment and ensuring the health of the population; Korten, 2015). With government cutbacks at national and state levels, infrastructures (schools, housing, social programs) at the community level are being diminished, and communities are increasingly being asked to "do more with less."

Chapter Summary

This chapter makes clear that CP is concerned with the role of social context in wellbeing, and that "context" encompasses all levels of the ecology. Community psychologists feel it is critical to take an ecological systems perspective to understand complexity and the influence of settings and broader cultural, political, and economic factors that shape people's ability to thrive. We emphasize the need to be keenly cognizant of macro-level power structures and ideologies because they limit the level of power and control regular citizens have over these forces that affect their lives (see Chapter 4). Many of the social problems with which CP is concerned have been exacerbated by neoliberal policies and globalization. Decisions are being moved further and further away from people, and this has deleterious effects on human and community wellbeing. CP, like much of the dominant culture, has largely acquiesced to, and been complacent with, some of the damaging aspects of neoliberalism and globalization. As the saying goes, "If you are not part of the solution, you are part of the problem." In Chapter 15, Tod Sloan, Fernando Lacerda, Mariah Kornbluh, and Susan Eckerle provide a closer look at globalization and neoliberal practices as it relates to poverty, social justice, and the promise of global CP.

Challenges and Possibilities for Ecological Systems Analysis in Practice

Christiane Sadeler, Executive Director of the Waterloo Region Crime Prevention Council,[4] Canada

PRACTITIONER COMMENTARY

It is an important, if not vital, skill for community psychologists to practice ecological thinking. In fact, it must become like an automatic muscle so that we can carry this broader context to all planning, delivery, and research efforts in which we are likely to participate. Through my many years of working collaboratively with diverse service providers, grassroots groups, law enforcement and justice services, and with all orders of government, I've developed a strong preference for community-based solutions and upstream prevention approaches that challenge us to think about complex problems in new ways.

As the chapter states, ecomaps are frequently used to broaden the problem definition in a way that goes beyond the individual and family to the communities and (political, social, economic) systems that surround them. I am not sure I would agree that it is an "easy" tool, but certainly a necessary one. Since all of us are born into a context over which we often have little control, one of the additional learning objectives, in my mind, ought to be understanding the impact of systems thinking with regards to the early years – the experience of children and how the systems around them shape their future health and wellbeing. For example, we know that those of us who are born into poverty – even if we manage to leave poverty behind – have significantly reduced positive health outcomes when compared to our peers. The first five years don't determine us but they significantly shape us. I suppose, my passion for prevention and upstream measures comes from the knowledge that ensuring all children have their basic and essential needs met (think Maslow!) is our best equalizing approach. Interestingly enough, this line of thinking doesn't allow for the notion that "every child is unique and an individual." While that is a beautiful sentiment, it is also the antithesis of complex systems thinking. This makes me wonder how much even those of us who are critical of the status quo are influenced by its ideological underpinnings. This is why the Upstream campaign that the Waterloo Region Crime Prevention Council (WRCPC) has launched makes critical consciousness and mindfulness central to the methodology.[5]

The admission that community psychologists are ultimately concerned with social justice is refreshing and ought to become part of our professional badge of honor. And yet, we are a long way away from this featuring in our CVs or LinkedIn account unless we live in the academic world. And this is, I suppose, where I had the most trouble with the chapter. Yes, ecological and systems thinking are by now well recognized mental models. We are in impressive company with the World Health Organization (WHO), the US Surgeon General, the United Nation's sustainable development efforts and there are, I suspect, no public health departments that would not speak loudly and proudly of the social determinants of health. And to be sure that is a significant gain we have made over time. It hasn't always been thus.

In my line of work, speaking of the "root conditions" of crime was seen as apologizing for harmful human behavior, thereby looking to avert consequences (e.g., incarceration). But even in the most ruggedly individualist areas of work (and I can't think of a better example than enforcement and justice) it has escaped no one that our jails are full of people sharing some of the same characteristics that are indeed indicative of social, economic, and system failures. Google "racialized justice" and you will see what I mean. And yet, such knowledge does not translate into in-the-field system change efforts. At best we have moved from blaming the individual to blaming the family, and tacitly acknowledging risks that put someone at great distance from opportunities for a healthy, fulfilling, and lawful life. How come? Why has the theory that moves

---

[4]   (WRCPC, www.preventingcrime.ca)

[5]   There is a quick TED style talk by our Knowledge Exchange and Research Coordinator David Siladi that explains this further (https://youtu.be/tBev0m1WDhk).

thinking from "individual pathology to system dysfunction" not translated into any significant policy efforts that set people up for success in the first place?

I propose the following barriers need to be overcome for system approaches to have a chance and I suggest that these barriers need to be built right into the ecological model.

1   *The complexity of ecological thinking is overwhelming.* For services that work in an environment of an erosion of resources, a systems level analysis can be paralyzing. Municipal governments feel they cannot control Federal ones. Communities feel they have no influence over their local government beyond elections. Neighborhoods feel their experiences do not feature in larger community efforts. And so on. And they all would be right. The testing grounds for that level of comprehensive integration are few and far between. The service world – which started in a charity model of "doing to or doing for the damaged individual" has not significantly changed over the decades. Reflections are shunned and even actively avoided and the drift towards the status quo remains strong. Why? The status quo mostly benefits those of us are charged with questioning it potentially more than we might like to admit.

2   *To overcome the above barrier, we adopted the notion of "nothing about us without us."*[6] This mostly remains at the level of tokenism such as described by Arnstein in 1969. Putting people affected by an issue at the same table as those in power to affect decisions is mostly not well executed, in as much as we have a tendency to ignore our own power. That is why we need to encourage trial and error moments. But, if in the time of the "fail fast and move on" mantra you are the most likely to get hurt, your creative contributions will be hindered by that fear. And rightly so. Those in power are least likely to be harmed, even at the planning tables.

3   *Power does corrupt.* More significantly it is seductive. Hegemony is alive and well and unless it plays the central role of the villain in our models, those models are incomplete. We defer to those in power for a very complex array of psychological but also real needs. Cops, courts, and corrections are part of a multi-billion-dollar machine that is in turn supported by a multi-billion-dollar virtual reality machine called "entertainment media" that have clouded thinking about ecological perspectives to an extent where, despite the evidence, funds flow to the places where they are least effective. The "unholy" trinity described in this chapter receives its daily blessings in news augmented by "law and order" movies where complexity is not tolerated and super heroes come to rescue us from super villains.

4   *We don't "take the long view."* Climate change is here because multi-generational decision-making is essentially absent from resource tables. Prevention isn't just the poorer cousin to intervention. It isn't even in the family. A return to Indigenous approaches might have a chance to get us beyond this barrier, but that is fraught with facing histories of trauma and colonization. I cannot see the powers-to-be engaging in that beyond the low level of polite land acknowledgements (see #3).

5   *The notion of "objectivity" clouds the issue.* What is real and relevant is always in the eye of the beholder. In that sense, community psychologists ought to be the most ardent practitioners of self-reflection. We need to witness each other and become each other's mirrors. And that is best accomplished in small circles of practice through which we establish survival mechanisms.

6   *Often our solutions of today turn into our issue for tomorrow* (see #4). While I would argue that the war on drugs was never an attempt to eradicate addiction in the first place, but rather an attempt at containing the racialized and the poor, it is indeed one of the best examples of how a "solution" can lead to more deaths than if the problem had stayed at status quo. The number of people who were killed as a result of the war on drugs in Mexico alone was approximately 150,000 by 2017 (Congressional Research Service, 2018).

---

6   The saying has its origins in Central European political traditions. The phrase in its English form came into use in disability activism during the 1990s but has since moved to other interest groups, identity groups, and populist movements. In 1998, James Charlton used the saying as the title for a book on disability rights. Disability rights activist David Werner used the same title for another book, also published in 1998.

7   *Apathy and the bystander effect are behaviors of learned helplessness that prevent any ground-swell in using system thinking in the advancement of social justice.* Mostly we run through our days breathlessly and numb to the larger realities in which we live and work. Many system mechanisms keep this distance alive (I would suggest to the pain of others) through such things as "accountability measures" which have social services staff count human interactions like widgets to prove effectiveness.

So what does it all mean? Have I become all doom and gloom? At first glance you might think so; but that is not actually the case. I just think that we ought to actively build the notion of the above barriers into the ecological and system analysis work so that we can practice overcoming them. And here are three tools for that:

1   *Reflection above analysis.* We need to define our role in the system change process. Am I a leader, an early adopter, an agitator, a supporter, or an opponent?

2   *Change is a spiral.* Yes, we seemingly go round and round in circles. And yet with every time we come across a problem, our thinking and actions change and advance. We don't get it right the first time. Human rights manifestos were not written and adopted in a day. The seemingly small actions matter when they can be seen as part of a holistic whole. There are no heroes here. We are but a blip in time and a (sometimes ill-fitting) puzzle piece. If that ego-vague or ego-void place in the universe doesn't fit you then you likely should not be in CP. The ecological model is the most ego-busting model that I know and that also applies to those who, well, apply it.

3   *Values ground the system analysis and help us to speak up when it is most needed (which is often when it is least wanted).* This is not a heady experience because it is about passionately advancing justice even when we are afraid. And in the current days, fears are rampant. Most systems need people to be ruled by fear, not by passion. Fear is the energy that drives the bounce back to status quo.

Enacting change is never as easy as the models that capture the change momentum. Community work is messy, unpredictable, and immensely complex. Maybe that is why models such as the ecological model are bound to be critiqued for their omissions. However, change is possible and its momentum is often fueled by stubborn attachment to values and principles of engagement. Here are five that I cling to at times like a life raft: accept uncertainty, acknowledge complexity, trust community, embrace possibility and, above all, proceed with humanity.

Key Terms

Behavior setting: A standing or routine pattern of behavior and the physical and temporal aspects of the environment.

Chronosystem: As an update to ecological systems theory, Bronfenbrenner later introduced the chronosystem to reflect change or continuity across time that influences each of the other systems.

Cognitive CP: A way of highlighting the importance of both individual and environmental qualities and the interrelationship between the person and the environment.

Ecological systems theory (EST): EST highlights the different environments that may influence our behavior in varying degrees throughout our lifespan. It helps us examine individuals' relationships within communities and the wider society. It identifies four systems – the microsystem, mesosystem, exosystem, and macrosystem – where the smaller systems are nested within the larger systems.

The ecological metaphor: A model adapted from the natural sciences that shows the relationship between individuals and the multiple social systems in which they are embedded. It is used to suggest that people must be understood in the context of the total environment.

Exosystems: Part of Bronfenbrenner's initial articulation of EST, the exosystem include settings that influence the individual but in which the individual does not directly participate.

Ideology: A comprehensive set of beliefs and conscious and unconscious ideas that dominate society that serve to control the positive or negative ways in which individuals and groups adapt to and master their environments.

Macrosystem: Part of Bronfenbrenner's initial articulation of EST, the macrosystem includes broad cultural influences or ideological patterns that characterize a given society or social group that have long-ranging consequences.

Mesosystem: Part of Bronfenbrenner's initial articulation of EST, the mesosystem contains those situations in which two or more microsystems come together in some way, for example the relationship between an individual's peers and their family at a birthday party or a child's parents interacting with their child's school at a parent-teacher conference.

Microsystem: Part of Bronfenbrenner's initial articulation of EST, the microsystem consists of the family and peer groups where individuals have direct social interactions with others.

Neoliberalism: An ideology and a theory of political economic practices based on the assumption that human wellbeing can best be advanced by maximizing individualism and entrepreneurial freedoms while promoting private property rights, individual liberty, unfettered markets, competition, and free trade.

Person–environment fit: The degree to which there is a match between a particular environment and a person's interests, preferences, knowledge, skills, abilities, personality traits, values, and goals.

System: An interconnected collection of parts that are coherently organized to function as a whole.

Systems theory: The interdisciplinary study of complex systems in nature, society, and science, and a framework by which one can investigate and/or describe any collection of parts that work together to produce some result.

Systems thinking: A way of understanding the world that helps us grasp its complexity. It is a process of organizing information in order to understand how systems function by examining interrelationships between parts, the root causes of targeted issues, and how parts of a system work to create a functioning whole.

Resources

The Systems Thinker: https://thesystemsthinker.com

ABLe Change Framework: www.ablechange.msu.edu/

Tom Wujec: Got a wicked problem? First, tell me how you make toast: www.youtube.com/watch?v=_vS_b7cJn2A

Peter Senge: Systems thinking for a better world – Aalto Systems Forum 2014: www.youtube.com/watch?v=0QtQqZ6Q5-o

RadioActive Episode 11: The road to you know where is paved with good intentions – Dr. Ed Trickett shares his nuanced way of understanding ecological theory and the ecology of our social world: www.mixcloud.com/natalie-kivell/radioactive-ep11-the-road-to-hell-is-paved-with-good-intentions-ecological-theory-w-ed-trickett/

PREVENTION, PROMOTION, AND SOCIAL CHANGE

6

Warm-up Questions

Before you begin reading this chapter, we invite you to reflect on the following questions:

1 Reflecting on your childhood, think of some stressful situations or contexts that threatened your sense of wellbeing. What were some of the resources or protective factors (personal qualities, relationships, situations) that helped you deal with those stressful situations?
2 How can a social problem like homelessness be prevented?
3 What does social change mean to you? What recent examples of social change can you think of?

Learning Objectives

The goal of this chapter is to provide you with an overview of three key concepts in community psychology (CP): prevention, promotion, and social change.

In this chapter you will learn about

- The three different approaches to prevention
- Applying these different approaches to the prevention of homelessness
- The importance, value base, and limitations of prevention and promotion
- The process of "framing the issue"
- The difference between ameliorative and transformative social change

Going Upstream

There is a popular parable in public health that tells of a group of villagers working in the fields by a river.[1] As they were working, someone suddenly noticed a baby floating downstream. A woman jumped in and rescued the baby, brought it to shore and cared for it. During the next several days,

---

[1] This story is also often called "The River Story" or "The Upstream Story." Some attribute it to the community organizer Saul Alinsky. Some people refer to it as a traditional story or simply as the "public health parable."

more babies were found floating downstream, and the villagers rescued them as well. Before long there was a flow of babies floating downstream. Soon the whole village was involved in the many tasks of rescue work: pulling these poor children out of the stream, ensuring they were properly fed, clothed, and housed, and integrating them into the life of the village. While not all the babies could be saved, the villagers felt they were doing well to save as many as they did.

Before long, however, the village became exhausted with all this rescue work. Some villagers suggested they go upstream to discover how all these babies were getting into the river in the first place. Had a mysterious illness stricken these poor children? Had the shoreline been made unsafe by an earthquake? Was some hateful person throwing them in deliberately? Was an even more exhausted village upstream abandoning them out of hopelessness?

A huge controversy erupted in the village. One group argued that every possible hand was needed to save the babies since they were barely keeping up with the current flow. The other group argued that if they found out how those babies were getting into the water further upstream, and they could repair the situation up there that would save *all* the babies and eliminate the need for those costly rescue operations downstream. "Don't you see," cried some, "if we find out how they're getting into the river, we can stop the problem and *no* babies will drown? By going upstream we can eliminate the cause of the problem!"

"Going upstream" is a fitting metaphor for prevention, promotion, and social change efforts in CP and in related disciplines. Like the villagers in the story, it is easy to be overwhelmed by the immediate and critical needs of people in crisis and we often feel compelled to focus our efforts on their care and treatment. At the same time, if we only focus on those suffering from a particular problem and fail to address the social conditions that led people to experience hardship in the first place, then we best prepare for a "game without end" (see Watzlawick, Beavin, & Jackson, 1967). We'd need to prepare for an endless flow of "babies in the river." This chapter looks at the CP concepts of prevention, promotion, and social change and utilizes the issues of homelessness and housing instability to elucidate how we apply these concepts to such critical social issues.

What are Prevention and Promotion?

Prevention

Prevention has its roots in the field of public health. At its core, *prevention* is keeping something that would have happened from happening (Shinn, Baumohl, & Hopper, 2001). The public health approach to prevention has been very successful in reducing the *incidence* (the number of new cases in a time period) of many medical diseases and harmful behaviors (i.e., smoking, substance abuse, teenage pregnancy), yet this approach is effective mostly with diseases and social issues that have an easily identifiable cause. The problem with prevention when applied to mental health and psychosocial problems is that many of these social issues are ambiguously defined, caused by multiple factors, difficult to assess, and challenging to solve using any one strategy (Albee, 1982; Shinn et al., 2001). Consistent with the ecological perspective described in Chapter 5, most psychosocial problems are determined by multiple influences, from the individual to the societal level.

A typology of preventative interventions suggests three approaches (Institute of Medicine [IOM], 1994; Mrazek & Haggerty, 1994). **Universal prevention** is available to the general public or a whole population group that has not been identified on the basis of individual risk. They are sometimes targeted at people in a particular stage of life (e.g., all newborn babies). **Selective prevention** is targeted at individuals or subgroups of the population who have significantly higher than average risk due to membership in a certain group (e.g., single mothers). Selective prevention interventions seek change such as reducing risks and enhancing strengths and typically feature actions targeted at or for individuals (Robinson, Brown, Beasley, & Jason, 2016). **Indicated prevention** is targeted at high-risk individuals who are identified as already having minimal, but detectable signs, symptoms or biological markers, indicating predisposition for the problem (e.g., children having disciplinary problems at school).

Universal, selective, and indicated approaches to prevention differ in two ways. First, they differ with respect to the timing of an intervention. Universal and selective approaches take place before a problem has occurred, but indicated approaches are used during the early stages of the problem. Second, they differ with respect to the population served. Everyone is served in a universal intervention; only those who are "at risk" are served in a selective intervention; and only those who are already showing signs of a problem are served in an indicated intervention. In this book, we use the term *prevention* to mean **primary prevention**, which includes both universal and selective (or high-risk) approaches. Primary prevention is a focus on preventing new cases of a given problem. Primary prevention strives to reduce the incidence or onset of a disorder in a population. Interventions that focus on identifying, targeting, and treating existing cases of a given problem are referred to as **secondary prevention**. Secondary prevention by definition is not really prevention, but rather early detection and intervention on problems that have already emerged (Mrazek & Haggerty, 1994). What can be prevented through secondary approaches, however, is the worsening of the problem or the emergence of other related problems.

Thinking about the practice of prevention as it relates to one of our exemplar social issues – homelessness and stable housing – helps illustrate how the different types of prevention can be applied to an issue that is of great concern to many researchers and practitioners of CP. Drawing on the definition of homelessness presented in Chapter 1, we consider people to be homeless if they live without conventional housing or are forced to take up residence in shelters (Shinn et al., 2001). People are "at risk" for homelessness when their current living situation has become insecure due to cost burdens and often combined with mental health or substance abuse issues. As we learned above, prevention efforts are successful if new cases of a problem do not occur. So how do we prevent people from becoming homeless? This is a complex issue with multiple causes and no easy solutions. To understand better the CP concept of prevention, let's explore some promising examples of universal, selective, and indicated approaches to the prevention of homelessness.

Universal Strategies for Preventing Homelessness

Universal preventive interventions are those that are available to the general public or a whole population group that has not been identified on the basis of individual risk. In order to truly prevent homelessness, a strong emphasis must be placed on addressing the role of social and economic deprivation – for most people, homelessness is a manifestation of extreme poverty (Interagency Council on the Homeless, 1994). This means framing contemporary homelessness as the product of conscious social and economic policy decisions (National Health Care for the Homeless Council, 2012; Shinn, 2007). Universal prevention solutions to the problem of homelessness entail: (a) social policies that make housing and comprehensive health care affordable and accessible to everyone, (b) adequate income through policies that establish a living wage for those able to work, and (c) appropriate unemployment benefits for those who cannot work (Shinn, 2007; US Interagency Council on Homelessness [USICH], 2010).

Selective Strategies for Preventing Homelessness

Selective prevention targets particular subgroups with elevated risk for developing a problem. Individuals are "at risk" of homelessness when their housing situation becomes insecure. Selected prevention strategies might target, for example, any of the following (Shinn et al., 2001):

- lower-income people
- families who have trouble affording housing
- poor people at particular life stages
- neighborhoods with large concentrations of homeless people.

The Community-Based Homelessness Prevention Program (CHPP) created six homeless prevention centers in areas of Philadelphia where a high rate of shelter use had been reported (Wong & Hillier, 2001). These centers targeted people who were at risk of becoming homeless due to recent loss of employment/income, or change in household composition. Participants received a range of services such as brief case management, referrals to educational and occupational training programs, and emergency rental assistance. The CHPP is a type of selective (primary) prevention effort as it aims to prevent homelessness by helping households deal with immediate needs while also addressing the complex factors that led to their precarious housing situation in the first place.

Indicated Strategies for Preventing Homelessness

Indicated preventive interventions are targeted at high-risk individuals. These are people identified through some form of screening as already showing signs or symptoms of the problem. Indicated prevention programs often use evidence such as eviction notices, utility shutoff notices, reports of domestic violence, or workplace disability claims to identify individuals and families in need of assistance. These programs typically offer some combination of cash grants or loans, counseling on budgeting and finances, legal services, mediation with landlords or mortgage holders, and other types of advocacy (Shinn, 2007; Shinn et al., 2001). In the case of individuals with severe mental illness and/or substance use disorder, indicated approaches that provide housing services under consumer control, combined with housing subsidies and money management services, have been shown to be helpful (Shinn et al., 2001). Table 6.1 presents the three prevention strategies and provides examples of each.

Table 6.1 Strategies for the prevention of homelessness

Strategy Type	Description	Examples
Universal	Broad-based policy actions aimed at creating conditions that promote housing stability	Policies for affordable and accessible housing and health care; living wages
Selective	Actions targeted at people who are at risk due to difficulty affording housing	Subsidized housing; neighborhood-based services and supports
Indicated	Actions targeted at people who are already showing evidence of housing instability	Cash grants/loans, financial counseling, legal services, mediation with landlords or mortgage holders, advocacy

Health Promotion

Complementary to prevention is the concept of **health promotion**. Where prevention, by definition, focuses on reducing problems, promotion can be defined as the enhancement of health and wellbeing in populations. In practice, health promotion and prevention are closely related. For example, efforts to promote healthy eating, physical activity, fitness, and abstinence from smoking can also prevent obesity, diabetes, and cardiovascular disease. Similarly, promoting healthy social skills in children can prevent school dropout, family conflict, and interpersonal violence.

There has been an increasing focus on the promotion of health and wellbeing (Cowen, 1994, 2000; Prilleltensky, Laurendeau, Chamberland, & Peirson, 2001). Health promotion approaches are often provided on a universal basis to all individuals in a particular geographical area (e.g., neighborhood, city, state, or province) or particular setting (e.g., school, workplace, public housing complex). Moreover, health promotion is more likely to focus on multiple ecological levels than on risk reduction, which is more often aimed at individuals.

Cowen (1996) identified four key characteristics of efforts to promote mental health or wellbeing: (1) They are proactive, seeking to promote mental health; (2) they focus on populations, not individuals; (3) they are multidimensional, focusing on "integrated sets of operations involving individuals, families, settings, community contexts and macro level societal structures and policies" (p. 246); and (4) they are ongoing, not a one-shot, time-limited intervention. See Box 6.1 for some of the ways that wellness can be promoted.

Box 6.1 Routes to Psychological Health and Wellbeing

Cowen (1994) argues that there are several key pathways towards mental health promotion:

1 **Attachment**. Infants and preschool children who form secure attachments to their parents and caregivers early in life fare well in later life. Home visitation programs that work with parents and their infants are one example of a strategy to promote attachments.

2 **Competencies**. The development of age-appropriate and culturally relevant competencies is another health promotion strategy. School-based social competence (e.g., social problem-solving skills, assertiveness, interpersonal skills) enhancement programs are one promising approach.

3 **Social environments**. Another pathway to the enhancement of health and wellbeing is to identify the characteristics of environments that are associated with health and then direct social environments towards those characteristics that have been shown to be important for wellbeing. Changing family, school, community, and larger social environments can be used to promote health.

4 **Empowerment**. Empowerment refers to perceived and actual control over one's life and empowering interventions are those that enhance participants' control over their lives. An empowerment approach stresses the importance of providing opportunities for people to exercise their self-determination and strengths, so that they are in control of the intervention.

5 **Resilience and resources to cope with stress**. The ability to cope effectively with stressful life events and conditions is another key pathway to health and wellbeing. Life stressors are often seen as presenting an opportunity for growth, if the person has the resources to manage the stressors.

Related to Cowen's inclusion of "social environments" as an important consideration for the promotion of mental health, many in the public health and mental health fields have increasingly focused their health promotion efforts on what has come to be known as the **social determinants of health**. These are the economic and social conditions and systems that influence the wellbeing of individuals, communities, and societies (Raphael, 2008; World Health Organization [WHO], 2008). Community psychologists understand that health and mental health start in our homes, schools, and communities and that the quality of these circumstances is shaped by the distribution of money, power, and resources at global, national, and local levels (Marmot, 2015a). We will expand on the concept of social determinants of health and mental health in the sections that follow.

The Importance of Prevention and Promotion

"An ounce of prevention is worth a pound of cure." "A stitch in time saves nine." These proverbs, much like the parable that opened this chapter, get to the heart of why prevention is important. Once problems occur, they are very difficult to treat. Often one problem cascades into another. Treatment methods can be helpful, but many people experience relapse or reoccurrence of problems. Moreover, even if treatments were 100 percent effective, there are not nearly enough trained mental health professionals to treat all those afflicted with mental health and psychosocial problems in living. The prevalence rates of psychosocial and mental health problems far outstrip available human resources. Albee (1990) stated that as "the history of public methods (that emphasize social change) has clearly established, no mass disease or disorder afflicting humankind has ever been eliminated by attempts at treating affected individuals" (p. 370).

Another argument for primary prevention and health promotion is that they can save money in the long run. Both institutional and community treatment services provided by professionals for health, mental health, and social problems are very costly. The costs of hospitalizing a person for one day is several hundred US dollars in most Western countries and it is not uncommon for therapists to charge more than $100 for an hour of therapy.

There is now good evidence that preschool prevention programs provide a solid economic and social return on the original financial investment in such programs (Belfield et al., 2015; Nelson, Prilleltensky, & Hasford, 2013). Research on the High/Scope Perry Preschool Program, a preschool educational program for economically disadvantaged children living in a community in Michigan in the US, found an annual return to society of $5.80 for every dollar invested (Heckman, Moon, Pinto, Savelyev, & Yavitz, 2010). In the UK, researchers found that from a societal perspective, the pay-off for certain mental health prevention and promotion efforts exceeds £10 for every £1 spent (Knapp, McDaid, & Parsonage, 2011). An ounce of prevention really is worth a pound of cure!

The principles of prevention and promotion can be applied at different ecological levels. Much of the early work of community psychologists in prevention was person-centered. It focused primarily on promoting the wellbeing and competence of individuals (Cowen, 1985). Some examples of person-centered approaches to homelessness prevention include providing financial counseling, foreclosure prevention assistance, and job skills training. Prevention programs can also target settings, such as schools, to promote relational wellbeing. An example of this type of prevention is changing the high school environments to better support youth who identify as lesbian, gay, bisexual, or transgender (LGBT)(Heck, Flentje, & Cochran, 2011). LGBT students often face harassment, both physical and verbal, which leads to high dropout rates and increased risk for homelessness. Finally, prevention and promotion can also be applied at the macro level. Macro-level prevention and promotion seek to promote collective wellbeing through changes in public policy (Albee, 1986). For example, in the US, the McKinney-Vento Homeless Education Assistance Improvements Act of 2001 established as policy that each state educational agency ensures that every homeless youth has equal access to the same free, appropriate public education, including a public preschool education, as provided to other children and youths.

The Value Base of Prevention and Promotion

Prevention and health promotion focus on the values of health and wellbeing. Many people think of health or mental health in negative terms, for example, as the absence of disorder. But a broader view of health can be framed in positive terms, as the presence of optimal social, emotional, and cognitive functioning within a health promoting and sustaining context. According to the Epp (1988) report *Mental Health for Canadians: Striking a Balance*:

> Mental health is the capacity of the individual, the group and the environment to inter-act with one another in ways that promote subjective well-being, the optimal development and use of mental abilities (cognitive, affective and relational), the achievement of individual and collective goals consistent with justice and the attainment and preservation of conditions of fundamental equality. (p. 7)

According to this definition, mental health is defined ecologically in terms of transactions between the individual and their environment, not just in terms of qualities of the individual. The value of health, which underlies the concepts of prevention and promotion, holds that health is a basic human right. Article 24 of the United Nations Convention on the Rights of the Child (United Nations, 1991), for instance, asserts "the right of the child to the enjoyment of highest attainable standard of health" (p. 11), while Article 19 of the convention asserts that children should be protected from harmful influences on their health: "State parties shall take appropriate legislative, administrative, social and educational measures to protect the child from all forms of physical or mental violence, injury or abuse, neglect or negligent treatment, maltreatment or exploitation, including sexual abuse" (p. 8). Albee (1986), Marmot (2015a) and Prilleltensky (2012) also place the value of justice squarely in the center of prevention and promotion arguing that wellbeing is not naturally distributed among people, but rather according to power dynamics, political disputes, and ethical considerations.

Development of Prevention and Promotion Efforts

The Division of Violence Prevention (DVP) at the Centers for Disease Control and Prevention (CDC) suggest a four-step public health approach to developing strategies for preventing problems (Mercy, Rosenberg, Powell, Broome, & Roper, 1993; Saul et al., 2008). Also referred to as the "prevention-intervention research cycle" (IOM, 1994; Mrazek & Haggerty, 1994), this model has emerged as the dominant framework for prevention and promotion research. This approach starts with the challenging first step of defining the problem we want to prevent (Kidder & Fine, 1986; Seidman, 1986; Seidman & Rappaport, 1986). This includes an accurate assessment of the causes of the problem and identifying the people, groups, and settings most affected by the problem. The second step involves determining the relevant risk and **protective factors** associated with the problem. The goal in this step is to understand the factors that are associated with heightened risk for the problem, as well as what buffers protect people from the problem. Using the insights from steps one and two, the third step involves the development and testing of interventions to increase protective factors and/or reduce risk factors. These interventions might take the form of programs, environmental changes, systems interventions, or new social policies (Bess, 2015; Saul et al., 2008). The final step involves implementing the interventions that have proven to be effective and ensuring their widespread adoption and use. There is the assumption that broad use of these effective strategies will result in population-level decreases in the problem. One major challenge in this area is that many communities do not benefit from evidence-based strategies due to a longstanding chasm between research and practice.

The CDC's Interactive Systems Framework for Dissemination and Implementation (ISF), released in 2008, was designed to help close this gap between research and practice. Many community psychologists are currently focused on this challenge of how best to support translation, capacity building, and effective delivery of evidence-based interventions in community settings (cf. Chinman et al., 2012; 2008; Flaspohler, Lesesne, Puddy, Smith, & Wandersman, 2012; Saul, 2008; Wandersman et al., 2008), as well as active participation of community residents in the planning and implementation of community-based promotion and prevention projects (Nelson, Amio, Prilleltensky, & Nickels, 2000; Nelson, Pancer, Hayward, & Kelly, 2004).

Implementing Prevention and Promotion

As we noted earlier, there are two interrelated approaches to implementing prevention and promotion: one focuses on risk reduction for mental health problems and the other on community-wide approaches to health promotion (Cowen, 1996, 2000; Biglan, 2015).

Risk Factors, Protective Factors, and High-Risk Approaches to Prevention

A substantial amount of research has confirmed that most psychosocial problems are associated with many different risk factors. A *risk factor* is any factor that is related to the occurrence of a problem (Luthar, Sawyer, & Brown, 2006). Risk factors are not only individual characteristics or attributes, but also the social and economic circumstances in which persons find themselves and the broader environment in which they live. These risks to mental health manifest themselves at all stages in life and are not static. They can change in relation to a developmental phase or a new stressor in one's life. Moreover, the effects of risk factors may be exponential. That is, most people can withstand one risk factor without being adversely affected, but when there is a "pile-up" of risk factors, the impacts may be particularly devastating (Putnam, 2016).

Some individuals, however, demonstrate resilience in that they are able to withstand exposure to many risk factors (Cowen, 2000; Luthar et al., 2006). Resilience is the process of adapting well in the face of stress or adversity and is not a fixed attribute of the individual (Masten, 2001; Rutter, 2012). Many individuals survive, and even thrive, in the face of adversity because they have protective factors, which are resources that help to offset or buffer risk factors and reduce vulnerability to environmental risks (e.g., coping skills, self-esteem, support systems). Albee (1982) views the incidence of mental health problems as an equation:

$$Incidence = \frac{\text{Risk Factors} = \text{Organic causes} + \text{Stress} + \text{Exploitation}}{\text{Protective Factors} = \text{Coping skills} + \text{Self} - \text{esteem} + \text{Support systems}}$$

As implied in this equation, risk and protective factors can occur at multiple levels of analysis (IOM, 1994; Luthar et al., 2006). For example, risk factors can occur at the individual (low self-esteem), family (marital discord or separation), and community (living in a violent community) levels of analysis. Similarly, protective factors can be individual (good coping skills), family-based (a warm and loving relationship with one parent), or community-based (opportunities for socialization, recreation, or skill development) in nature. The World Health Organization highlights the ecological nature of determinants of health and mental health and provides an illustrative set of factors at multiple levels that may threaten or protect health (Table 6.2).

The risk and protective factor formulation is based on the broader approach of social stress theory. Community psychologist Barbara Dohrenwend (1978) introduced *social stress theory* to CP as a framework for understanding both how social environments can have negative impacts on individuals and how social interventions can be designed to prevent social stressors or reduce the negative consequences of social stressors. A central thesis of social stress theory is that stressful life events and changes, particularly negative life events, create stress reactions in individuals and that the long-term consequences of these stress reactions can be negative, neutral, or positive; that is, stress presents an opportunity for growth as well as the potential for negative outcomes. Dohrenwend (1978) asserted that there are a variety of psychological and situational factors that can moderate the impacts of stressful life events. For example, a person with a good social support

Table 6.2 Ecological nature of health risk and protective factors

Ecological Level	Risk Factors	Protective Factors
Individual attributes	• Low self-esteem • Cognitive/emotional immaturity • Difficulties in communicating • Medical illness, substance use	• Self-esteem, confidence • Ability to solve problems and cope with stress • Communication skills • Physical health, fitness
Social circumstances	• Loneliness, bereavement • Neglect, family conflict • Exposure to violence/abuse • Low income and poverty • School failure • Work stress, unemployment	• Social support • Good parenting/family interactions • Physical security and safety • Economic security • School achievement • Job Satisfaction
Environmental factors	• Poor access to basic services • Injustice and discrimination • Social and gender inequalities • Exposure to war or disaster	• Equality of access to basic services • Social justice, tolerance, integration • Social and gender equality • Physical security and safety

Source: Based on World Health Organization, 2014.

network or good coping skills may adjust well to a stressful life event such as marital separation, whereas a person without such resources may fare worse. These moderating factors are what we mean by "protective factors" or "stress-meeting resources."

Identifying and understanding the sources of risk and prevention allows us to determine how to target and implement prevention efforts. For example, at the individual level, Rutter (1987) has proposed four mechanisms for how people can overcome adversity: (1) reducing risk impact; (2) interrupting negative chain reactions stemming from stressful life events; (3) enhancing self-esteem and self-efficacy; and (4) creating opportunities for personal growth. At the social and environmental levels, prevention and promotion is about tackling the social determinants of health – policies pertaining to basic rights and opportunities (e.g., food, education, employment, and energy), social surroundings (e.g., neighborhood characteristics and housing), and the nature of our social fabric (e.g., social connectedness, access to health care, and equal opportunity for political voice), all shaped by the distribution of money, power, and resources, both worldwide and within countries (Marmot, 2015a; WHO, 2014; 2008). Due to the dynamic and multi-layered nature of risks and protective factors, community psychologists believe that effective prevention and promotion efforts need to be multi-layered and multi-sectoral.

Since Dohrenwend's (1978) initial formulation, research in CP has led to a greater understanding of the role of particular life events, such as job loss (Dooley & Catalano, 2003) and divorce (Sandler, 2001), in the evolution of psychosocial problems. In particular, research has helped to clarify the ways in which stressful life events can have negative impacts on individuals.

Sometimes, stressful life events set in motion a variety of additional problems or ongoing life strains to which people must adapt. For example, unemployment leads to ongoing financial strains that impact one's marital, family, and social network relations as well as food and housing security. Thus, it is not just the stressful life event that is the problem, but all that ensues in the aftermath of that event. Research has clarified the role of individual and social mediating factors (e.g., coping skills, family socioeconomic status, community resources) that link stressful life events with negative outcomes for individuals. Community psychologists have used knowledge gained about mediating and moderating factors to design preventive interventions to reduce the negative impacts of stressful life events such as job loss (Price, Van Ryn, & Vinokur, 1992) and parental divorce (Sandler, 2001). For example, mentoring programs have been successfully used to both enhance the support and offset the stressors faced by children or youth lacking social support (DuBois et al., 2002; Dubois & Rhodes, 2006).

While many of the original prevention and promotion programs used the risk reduction or selective approach, focusing on individuals at risk, more recently there has been a greater emphasis on setting-wide and community-wide approaches to prevention. These environmental approaches to prevention focus not only on specific prevention programs but also more broadly on building the capacities of organizations and communities. A major focus of these interventions is developing partnerships or coalitions of various community stakeholders to plan, implement and evaluate the intervention (Foster-Fishman et al., 2006; Janzen, Nelson, Hausfather, & Ochocka, 2007; Kellam, 2012; Miller, Reed, & Francisco, 2013; Nelson, Pancer, et al., 2004). Comprehensive community-wide initiatives have been used to address a variety of issues, including substance abuse, HIV/AIDS, heart disease, immunization, teenage pregnancy, and violence (Christens & Inzeo, 2015; Roussos & Fawcett, 2000).

What are the Characteristics of Effective Prevention and Promotion Programming?

When community psychologists work with communities to design and implement prevention programs, we want to know that these efforts will make a difference. It's one thing to demonstrate effectiveness in a relatively controlled environment where the program model is closely adhered to and researchers can apply rigorous evaluation. It is more challenging, however, to know if that same program model will be effective when transferred to other settings and implemented by different people (not researchers) in variable contexts – the so-called "real world." Program implementation processes are affected by many contextual variables, aspects of the prevention delivery organization, program innovations, and the level of training and technical assistance provided to organizations implementing the program (Durlak & DuPre, 2008).

The importance of **fidelity** to the model is an ongoing issue within the field of CP, as researchers struggle to determine how much adaptation a tested prevention program can endure and still remain effective (Backer, 2002; Blakely et al., 1987). Fidelity is the extent to which the intervention corresponds to the originally intended program model. On one hand, it has been shown that programs are more effective when implemented with close correspondence to the original model (Durlak & DuPre, 2008). On the other hand, there is support within the field for recognizing that differing cultural, organizational, and community contexts warrant on-site modification of programs (Ringwalt et al., 2003). Then there are those in the middle who suggest that adaptation is acceptable up to a certain point, beyond which continued dilution would compromise the program's integrity and effectiveness. Durlak and DuPre (2008) found evidence in their review that indicators of both fidelity and adaptation were positively related to outcomes. They suggested that it is important to find the right mix of fidelity and adaptation to the cultural and community context. Hawe, Shiell, and Riley (2004) have made a distinction between the "form" and "function" of an intervention that might help with this debate. They believe that a program may have fidelity in terms of function (adherence to set of intervention principles), but be adaptable in terms of form (the particular ways that the program functions are delivered). For example, if a program has the principle of involving key stakeholders in the development of a program, this may be done in different ways, thus demonstrating fidelity to the function but adaptability in terms of the form.

Researchers have examined how the implementation of theoretically important program function components (i.e., active ingredients, core elements, key characteristics) relates to outcomes. Looking more generally at the characteristics of effective prevention programs targeting substance abuse, risky sexual behavior, school failure, and juvenile delinquency and violence, Nation and colleagues (2003) identified nine characteristics that were consistently associated with greater effectiveness of prevention programs. Effective programs: (1) were comprehensive, (2) utilized varied teaching methods, (3) provided sufficient dosage (intensity and duration of program), (4) were theory-driven, (5) provided opportunities for positive relationships, (6) were appropriately timed, (7) were socioculturally relevant, (8) included outcome evaluation, and (9) involved well-trained staff. Table 6.3 provides definitions of each of these nine characteristics.

Table 6.3 Definitions of the principles of effective programs (Nation et al., 2003)

Principle	Examples
Comprehensive	Multicomponent interventions that address critical domains (e.g., family, peers, community) that influence the development and perpetuation of the behaviors to be prevented
Varied teaching methods	Programs involve diverse teaching methods that focus on increasing awareness and understanding of the problem behaviors, and on acquiring or enhancing skills
Sufficient dosage	Programs provide enough intervention to produce the desired effects and provide follow-up as necessary to maintain effects
Theory driven	Programs have a theoretical justification, are based on accurate information, and are supported by empirical research
Positive relationships	Programs provide exposure to adults and peers in a way that promotes strong relationships and supports positive outcomes
Appropriately timed	Programs are initiated early enough to have an impact on the development of the problem behavior and are sensitive to the developmental needs of participants
Socioculturally relevant	Programs are tailored to the community and cultural norms of the participants and make efforts to include the target group in program planning and implementation
Outcome evaluation	Programs have clear goals and objectives and make an effort to systematically document their results relative to the goals
Well-trained staff	Program staff support the program and are provided with training regarding the implementation of the intervention

Source: Copyright © American Psychological Association. Reprinted with permission.

The Limits of Prevention and Promotion

Prevention is a core concept in the field of CP (Albee, 1986, 1996, 1998), although some in the field have long suggested it has outlived its usefulness (Rappaport, 1987, 1981). If we critically examine prevention, we have to acknowledge its limitations. These limitations include the challenge of **dissemination** and adoption, balancing rigor with community participation, and not losing focus on the social or structural sources of injustice. We review each of these limitations below.

The Challenge of Dissemination and Adoption

When prevention programs are found to be effective, there is a need to disseminate them widely, or bring them "to scale" so that they become institutionalized. However, despite research evidence, effective programs are often not widely adopted (Miller & Shinn, 2005). Transferring effective programs into community settings and maintaining them is a complicated, long-term process that requires attending to the successive, complex phases of program diffusion (Durlak & DuPre, 2008). As such, there are calls within the field to expand the scope of prevention research to include greater attention to strategies focused on the implementation process to provide an important foundation for improved success in taking effective programs and policies to scale (DuBois, 2017; Durlak & DuPre, 2008).

The Interactive Systems Framework for Dissemination and Implementation (ISF) is one example of a strategy developed by community psychologists and prevention researchers to help bridge research and practice by specifying the systems and processes required to support dissemination and implementation of evidence-based programs, processes, practices, and policies (see the two special issues of the *American Journal of Community Psychology* – Wandersman et al., 2008; Flaspohler et al., 2012). The framework draws attention to three systems: (1) the prevention synthesis and translation system (information on "best practices" from demonstration projects); (2) the prevention delivery system (the capacity of the local system to adopt the model program); and (3) the prevention support system (technical assistance to help the local community implement the prevention model). There is frequently a mismatch between what scientists design and what communities have the capacity to implement (Miller & Shinn, 2005). Durlak and DuPre (2008) found that several specific components of ISF were related to effective implementation (e.g., shared decision making at the local level, opportunities for training).

Balancing Rigor with Community Participation

Another criticism of prevention as it is currently practiced is that it is something that is done *by* professional "experts" *to* "at-risk" people. Professionally-driven approaches may not address what these so-called at-risk people need or want – they may be disempowering and create dependencies on service systems. Furthermore, they tend to focus on deficits rather than the strengths of community members. Rather than promoting "top-down" approaches to dissemination, Miller and Shinn (2005) have argued that prevention researchers should learn from communities instead of expecting communities to only learn from the wisdom of academics. They suggest that partnering with communities and learning about effective models and ideas that grow out of community experience would better serve the field.

The Better Beginnings, Better Futures project in Ontario, Canada is a successful example of this community partnership approach (Nelson et al., 2000; Nelson, Pancer, et al., 2004). We can locate, study, and help develop and test strategies for dissemination of successful homegrown programs that fit community capacities and values. Community inspired and designed prevention and promotion efforts can and do achieve favorable results despite having limited or no academic origins (DuBois, 2017). Furthermore, dissemination processes emphasized in the prevention–intervention research cycle model may result in overlooking, and thus under-investing in, a substantial number of promising strategies for prevention and promotion (Miller & Shinn, 2005).

Prevention programs that are community driven, with residents in low-income communities actively participating in the planning and implementation of prevention programs in their communities, are better aligned with the values of CP. These programs are not only driven by community members, but they are also designed to change or create settings in the community to foster the wellbeing of families and children. Moreover, Nelson et al. (2000) have proposed concrete steps for value-based partnerships in prevention programs, which include processes for inclusion, participation, and control by disadvantaged people in the design of prevention programs.

Consistent with the overarching approach of this book, Sandler (2007) takes the "bottom-up" approach one step further in arguing that community psychologists should identify issues of structural injustice in the dissemination of prevention programs. "Valorizing an increase in the power of communities versus the power of intervention scientists is not in itself a step toward social justice; doing so does not address the fundamental problem of the existing structural injustices manifest within communities" (Sandler, 2007, p. 276). For Sandler, the dissemination of effective prevention programs must address both structural injustices (sources of oppression) and wellbeing.

Focus on Social or Structural Injustices

While the direction towards more community-driven approaches is a positive one, prevention needs to move even further towards macro-level analyses and interventions. The "prevention science" approach tends to "medicalize" and "depoliticize" prevention. We are critical of this approach, not because we are against science, but because the particular form of science being promoted by the medical profession is very narrow in emphasis. Selective approaches to prevention, which predominate, are often carried out with low-income people because poverty, low social class, and unemployment are one set of major risk factors for many different mental health problems (Perry, 1996). Moreover, selective approaches typically address the bottom half of Albee's (1982) equation (i.e., promoting protective factors), rather than the top half of the equation (i.e., reducing stress or exploitation). Also, programs that promote protective factors tend to be person or family-centered, ignoring the larger social environment (Febbraro, 1994).

Albee (1986, 1996, 1998) has argued that prevention should be linked to social justice. A social justice approach to prevention strives to address the causes of the causes through social change efforts. Thus, prevention should not just be focused on changing individuals, families or communities, but on larger social structures in which people and settings are embedded. To translate this rhetoric into action, we believe that prevention should encompass not just programs but also social policies. Since economic inequality is a major structural cause of psychosocial problems (Cahill, 1983; Hertzman, 1999; Wilkinson, 1996), policies that strive to reduce this, such as those practiced in Western and Northern European countries, show the forms prevention can take at the macro level (Peters, Peters, Laurendeau, Chamberland, & Peirson, 2001). As we learned in Chapter 1, those countries with more generous social policies have significantly less people experiencing homelessness. Not only have countries like Sweden been successful in reducing the level of poverty and economic inequality in their society, but also the literacy and numeracy skills of children in the bottom economic quintile in Sweden are vastly better than those of children in the bottom economic quintiles in the US and Canada (Hertzman, 1999). These findings suggest a need for more emphasis on advocating for change in social and economic policies to promote social justice and wellbeing (Marmot, 2015a).

Prilleltensky (2012) places justice squarely in the center of wellbeing, arguing that wellbeing is not naturally distributed among people, but rather given to power dynamics, political disputes, and ethical considerations. Similarly, the WHO's Commission on the Social Determinants of Health (2008) overarching recommendations for promoting health and wellbeing include tackling the inequitable distribution of power, money, and resources. By ignoring the structural determinants of wellbeing we discount "those causes that are embedded within economic, class- and gender-based patterns of social relationships" (Labonte, 1994, p. 79). The North American Regional Council of the World Federation for Mental Health (1993, cited in Albee, 1998) had this to say:

> Poverty is the single most significant obstacle to positive mental health and quality of life in North America. We believe that the eradication of poverty is the first step in primary prevention of mental illness and related social problems. Canada and the United States must urgently confront poverty. (pp. 125–6)

This sentiment is supported by recent research on poverty and the developing brain. As it turns out, the conditions that attend poverty – what a National Scientific Council report summarized as "overcrowding, noise, substandard housing, separation from parent(s), exposure to violence, family turmoil" (National Scientific Council on the Developing Child, 2014, p.4), and other forms of extreme stress – can be toxic to the developing brain, just like drug or alcohol abuse.

Promoting wellbeing, therefore, requires more than just the prevention programs that focus on reduction of risk at the individual level, it requires political and societal organization to redistribute resources, promote democracy, and empower individuals (Schueller, 2009). Only a primary approach to prevention in the form of political action and social change can increase social equality and reduce the social conditions that lead to emotional distress (Albee, 1982; 1996; Biglan, 2015; Perry & Albee, 1994; Marmot, 2015a; Putnam, 2015).

Social Change

What is social change? This is a question with which community psychologists and other concerned citizens often wrestle. Think for a moment about your own beliefs about social change. What examples would you provide in response to the question "What is social change?" For example, concerning the issue of homelessness and stable housing, what changes related to this issue would you consider social change? Consider one solution that usually comes to mind when thinking about how to address this issue in urban settings: homeless shelters. Is the development of homeless shelters an attempt at social change? Or are shelters merely an attempt to care for those experiencing homelessness while leaving the causes of homelessness unaddressed?

While the concept of social change means different things to different people, in CP, social change generally refers to changes in the broader social systems, structures, institutions, culture, and overall social relationships in a system, community, or society. However, the term *social change* does not always connote the type of change that community psychologists would consider positive. For example, between 1933 and 1945 there were dramatic social changes to the social and cultural life in Nazi Germany, as the country was transformed into a fascist totalitarian state that controlled nearly all aspects of life. Racism and hatred for Jews were central features of the Nazi regime. While we must admit that this historical event is an example of social change, this form of change is certainly not consistent with CP's values and desire to work towards justice, equality, and wellbeing.

Seeking social change in the direction of justice, equality, and wellbeing begins with the recognition that something is fundamentally wrong or unfair (Jason, 2013). Taking action to promote social change means directing our focus upstream to the root causes of this unfairness. This requires a critical analysis of the issue to understand the root causes and the reasons why the problem exists in the first place. Then we can direct our research and action towards deeper levels of change. While Chapter 10 will focus on the concept of "social interventions" in more detail, here we will focus on defining the problem, consider types of change, and wrestle with the meaning of the word "transformation."

Problem Definition: Framing the Issue

Every effort to promote social change should begin with a process of critical analysis to define the issue – in partnership with those most affected by the problem – and together shape a more complex understanding of the challenges (Tseng et al., 2002). This deeper analysis and understanding of why some social problems exist is a process called *framing the issue*. Recall from chapter one that framing is the "central organizing idea or story line that provides meaning" (Gamson & Modigliani, 1987, p. 142) to "events related to an issue" (Pan & Kosicki, 1993, p. 56). How social issues are framed often dictates what interventions will be used to address them (Seidman, 1986; Seidman & Rappaport, 1986). Our social change efforts risk being constrained by our frames of reference – the ways in which we conceptualize problems (diagnostic framing) and solutions (prognostic framing) (Benford & Snow, 2000; Smail, 2001). For example, too often, social problems are defined in terms of individual difficulties or deficiencies. This framework leads to victim blaming and misguided solutions targeted at people experiencing the problem instead of the underlying causes (O'Neill 2005; Ryan, 1971).

Central to any critical analysis of social issues is an analysis of the underlying power dynamics – the focus of Chapter 4. However, as we learned in Chapter 5, most issues we are concerned about in CP can be classified as "wicked problems" that are inherently difficult to define or understand fully. But we need a place to start. Framing the issue – preferably by building a shared, although tentative, understanding of the problem with others – provides opportunities to discuss and lay out alternative understandings, competing interests, priorities, and constraints.

Types of Change

In CP, we believe that meaningful change in the direction of justice, equality, and wellbeing requires changes in the underlying social conditions that cause human suffering. To help us distinguish between change efforts that alter oppressive social conditions and those that merely make adjustments *within* oppressive systems, we make use of two complementary change typologies: (1) *First vs. second order change* (Watzlawick, Weakland, & Fisch, 1974); and (2) *ameliorative vs. transformative change* (Prilleltensky & Nelson, 2009). First-order change and amelioration are types of change efforts that strive to create change within a system, without altering its underlying values, assumptions, structures, and power arrangements (Jason, 2013; Prilleltensky & Nelson, 2009; Watzlawick et al., 1974). These types of changes are often referred to as "changes without a difference" or "changeless change" due to the fact that they create small changes within a system that still remains unchanged. First-order changes do not alter the fundamental social context that may lead to a problem's development and maintenance. Seidman (1988) refers to first-order, ameliorative change as "tuning," where the goal is to help a system function more effectively, efficiently, and harmoniously within existing structural arrangements. The basic structural arrangements contributing to the problem remain unaltered.

To be sure, ameliorative change is important and needed. Getting a homeless family space in a shelter makes a big difference to that family. However, without transformative changes, any ameliorative gains may be undermined in the long term. We can only fit so many families in shelters and a shelter is not a home. Ameliorative interventions are attractive because they reduce the severity of consequences from the most deeply rooted problems, however they risk hindering our quest to make needed fundamental changes (Jason, 2013; Seidman, 1988).

Our earlier discussion of homeless shelters provides a useful example of a first-order change. Homeless shelters respond to the problem of homelessness by attempting to improve the condition of people experiencing homelessness through providing a short-term place to sleep, shower, eat, and get access to needed medical and mental health services. We desperately want everyone to have a roof over their head and these other basic needs met. However, homeless shelters can never be a solution to the problem of homelessness; they can only respond to individuals who need assistance. Without addressing the systemic and structural injustices that contribute to housing insecurity and homelessness, the problem will persist.

So what would a second-order, transformative solution look like? Second-order change strives to change the system itself along with the underlying rules, assumptions, roles, and relationships governing the system's structure (Foster-Fishman & Behrens, 2007; Seidman, 1986; Watzlawick et al., 1974). Seeking second order change first requires a fundamentally different framing of the problem. A more critical analysis of housing insecurity and homelessness suggests that the problem results from differences in material living conditions that are shaped by public policies that are in turn shaped by economic and political structures and their justifying ideologies. This turns our attention and social change efforts toward fundamental changes in affordable housing and wage policies, access to education, health and mental health care, bank lending practices, income and wealth inequality, and the economic and political structures that maintain these injustices. For a more detailed look at the different ways in which housing insecurity and homelessness can be framed and the corresponding implications for social change efforts, refer to Table 6.4.

One simple way to elucidate the difference between first order (ameliorative) change and second order (transformative) change is to look back at the parable that opened the chapter. Doing the difficult and necessary work of pulling children from the river is first order change. Children are saved from drowning, and that's a very good thing, but the conditions that led them to fall in the river are left unchanged. More children are certain to fall in. By contrast, second order change forces us to examine the root causes of this terrible problem. By stepping away from the immediate crisis (leaving others to take care of the children of course) and simply asking "Why?" we may find that there is a low bridge crossing the river upstream that is missing guardrails. Children crossing the bridge with their parents are accidentally falling in because the bridge has been neglected and in need of major repairs. Furthermore, when we ask why the bridge is in such a bad state, we learn that funds allocated for regular bridge maintenance in this area of town have for years been diverted to other, more affluent neighborhoods. This decision to reallocate funds was made without knowledge of or input from the community most affected. Armed with this new understanding, we can work with others to not only get the bridge repaired immediately to prevent future accidents (also first order change), but to also work to address the structural sources of the problem: unjust systems and decision-making processes in local government. We need to change the rules of the game. This is second order change.

The complementary concepts of **amelioration/first order change** and **transformation/second-order change** are heuristics that provide useful models to support our sense-making about social change. However, some community psychologists have come to believe that the dichotomous portrayal of amelioration vs. transformation, or first vs. second order change does not accurately reflect the complex nature of social change or the fact that social transformation often stems from ameliorative action and the experience gained in ameliorative work (Burton, 2013; Kagan, Burton, Duckett, Lawthom, & Siddiquee, 2011; Kivell, 2016; Nelson, 2013; Prilleltensky, 2014; Walker, Burton, Akhurst, & Degirmencioglu, 2015). For example, Kagan et al. (2011) proposed a reconceptualization of the ameliorative–transformative distinction as two dimensions of change: scope and extent. *Scope* refers to spatial and temporal elements going from very local, short-term changes to broader, long-term changes. *Extent* refers to whether or not social relations are changed: is the change merely incremental in nature or does it re-write the rules of the situation? Putting these two dimensions together to analyze the scope and extent of change gives us a

Table 6.4 The importance of problem definition/framing – homelessness example

Diagnostic Framing of Homelessness	Key Concepts for Addressing Homelessness	Primary Approach for Addressing Homelessness	Practical Implications of the Approach
1. Homelessness results from genetic differences and biological dispositions	Identifying the genes and processes causing problems can reduce homelessness	Carry out more and better biomedical research	Medicalization of homelessness and endorsement of the societal status quo
2. Homelessness results from differences in access and quality of social services	Strengthening social services can reduce homelessness	Create more and better services in hospitals, clinics, and social service agencies	Focus limited to promoting the welfare of those already experiencing homelessness
3. Homelessness results from differences in important modifiable risk factors	Encouraging people to gain job skills, financial literacy, or mental health counseling can reduce homelessness	Develop and evaluate job training, financial literacy, and mental health programs	Programming that ignores the material basis of homelessness and endorses the societal status quo
4. Homelessness results from differences in material living conditions	Improving material living conditions can reduce homelessness	Conduct research and disseminate results of how differences in living conditions create homelessness	Assumption that governmental authorities are receptive to and will act upon research findings
5. Homelessness results from differences in material living conditions shaped by public policy	Advocating for public policy that reduces disadvantage can reduce homelessness	Analyze how public policy decisions impact housing stability and homelessness (i.e., policy analysis)	Assumption that governments will create or modify public policy on the basis of its effects upon housing stability and homelessness
6. Homelessness results from differences in material living conditions that are shaped by economic and political structures and their justifying ideologies	Homelessness can be reduced by influencing the societal structures that create and justify inequality and inadequate access to affordable housing	Analyze how the political economy of a nation creates inequalities and identify avenues for social and political action	Requirement that reducing homelessness requires building social and political movements that will shape public policy
7. Homelessness results from the power and influence of those who create and benefit from social inequalities	Increasing the power and influence of those who experience disadvantage and oppression can reduce homelessness	Critical analysis empowers the majority to gain understanding of and increase their influence and power	Requirement that these social and political movements recognize and shift imbalances of power within society

Source: Adapted from Raphael, 2012 (Table 1.1, p. 14). Printed by permission of Canadian Scholars' Press. Copyright © 2012 Dennis Raphael, the contributing authors, and Canadian Scholars' Press Inc. All rights reserved.

more nuanced perspective on social change. Another way to deepen our understanding of social change is to consider the different targets for social change at multiple ecological levels of analysis. We will break down the different levels that can be targeted for social change when we discuss social interventions in more detail in Chapter 10. Before we end this chapter, however, let's turn a critical eye toward the concept of transformation.

What is Transformation Really?

The term *transformation* is often used to denote just about any kind of major change in people, organizations, communities, and societies. We generally think of transformation as profound, fundamental change that alters the very nature of something (Gass, 2012). Something that is transformed can never go back to exactly what it was before. We suggest that in order for social change efforts to be transformational, they need to change the structures of society. Social change efforts are transformational only when they challenge and change entrenched, oppressive power structures. Transformative social change processes require recognition of power inequalities and structured disadvantage in our understanding of social problems and in our remedies for change (Barnett, 1997). Transformative social change is about working to bring about a radically better society by shifting the balance of power in political, economic, and social systems.

Shifting the balance of *political power* changes the level of decision-making authority of people and groups in both the private sphere and public affairs. Shifting the balance of *economic power* alters the distribution of resources and the workings of markets and corporations. Shifting the balance of *social power* means altering the status and position awarded to different social groups. These three systems of power combine to produce a *social order*, and transforming this social order is the ultimate task of transformative social change. Change of this nature is ultimately political in that transformative interventions involve strategic attempts to shift the relationships of power and the outcomes of those relationships (Gramsci, 1971). Political analysis and critique of the status quo are fundamental to this process. Along these lines, Prilleltensky (2008b) uses the concept of transformative psychopolitical validity to refer to changes that alter the balance of power to foster distributive and procedural justice. To assess whether a social change is transformative or not we have to ask who has the power? Has the power structure remained the same or has it been altered (Prilleltensky, 2014)? Table 6.5, adapted from the work of the people at the Social Justice Project and the Center for Transformative Change (www.transformativechange.org), offers a framework for thinking about the kind of change for which different forces in society are fighting. The spectrum runs left to right with the left side tending towards more democracy, equality, and justice and the right side tending towards more oppression, inequality, and authoritarianism.

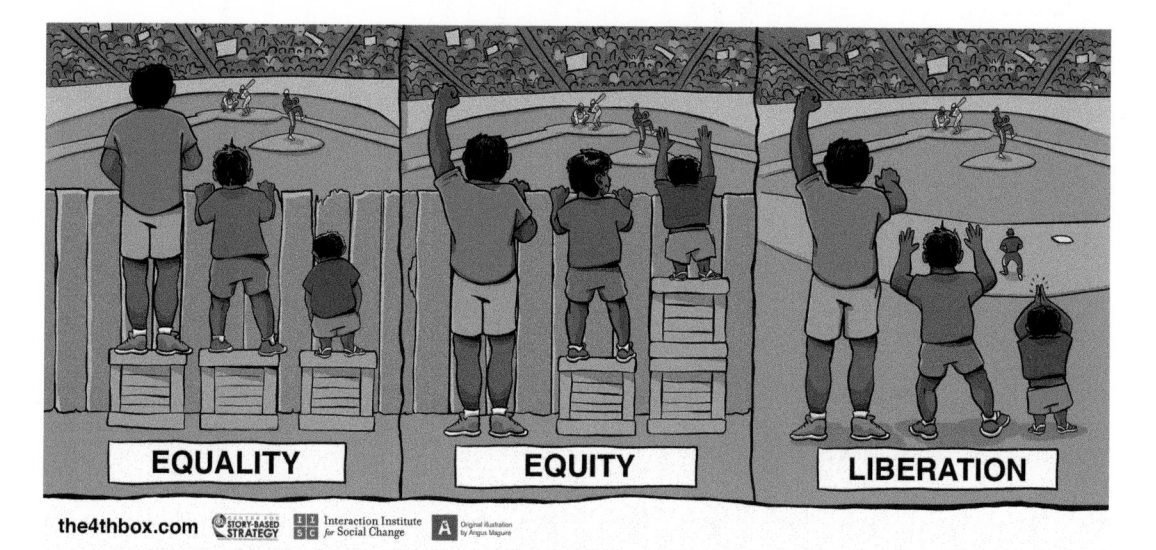

Transformative efforts can range in the type of social change they aim for
Source: Interaction Institute for Social Change interactioninstitute.org I Artist: Angus Maguire madewithangus.com.

Table 6.5 Spectrum of transformation

Societal Transformation Spectrum

Revolutionary	Radical	Systemic	Liberal	Neo-Liberal	Conservative	Reactionary
Seeks to replace the entire existing system with something completely new that represents the highest form of democracy, equality, and justice for all people	Seeks to replace whole parts of the existing system to gain higher levels of democracy, equality, and justice	Seeks to shift some institutionalized power (laws, control of resources, decision-making structures) and make living conditions better to gain greater democracy, equality, and justice in oppressed communities	Seeks to lessen the effects of system injustices through a reformist approach – keeps the system intact while making some adjustments primarily through the use of government resources and regulations	Seeks to consolidate wealth upwards through economic growth and expansion of trade, deregulation of the "free market," increased public resources directed to criminalization, and militarization, privatization of public services like schools and transportation	Seeks to oppose any and all progressive economic, social or political change through maintaining political, economic, & social structures that privilege Whites, men, heterosexuals, citizens, and other dominant groups	Seeks to centralize economic, social, and political power where patriarchy, White supremacy, and unbridled capitalism are unquestioned norms

< – – – – – – – – – – – TRANSFORMATION – – – – – – – – Amelioration – – – – – – – – TRANSFORMATION – – – – – – – – – – – >

< – – – – – – – INCREASING Social, Economic, & Political Power of Oppressed – – – – – – INCREASING Social, Economic, & Political Power of Privileged – – – – – – >

< – – – – – – INCREASING Democracy, Equality, & Justice – – – – – – INCREASING Oppression, Inequality, & Authoritarianism – – – – – – >

Source: Adapted from Social Justice Leadership and the Center for Transformative Change, http://hiddenleaf.org/wp-content/uploads/2010/06/Spectrum-of-Transformation-2010-copy.pdf.

Transformative change in many respects is a change process that is never really complete. Rather we should think about transform-"ing" (Weick, 1979) to emphasize the ongoing intentional process of radically changing oppressive social structures and the thinking that maintains them. The work of transformation unfolds over time; much of our old identities, practices, and power relations pass away and radically altered new ones emerge. Often, we do not even know what the resulting change will look like. Recent events in the struggle for marriage equality around the world are illustrative of this gradual unfolding and emergent nature of transformation. In nearly two dozen countries, gay marriage has gone from unthinkable to law of the land in just a couple of decades, as people's views changed over time and set the stage for a major societal shift in social power for gay men and women in these countries (see https://www.pewresearch.org/fact-tank/2019/10/29/global-snapshot-same-sex-marriage/). But despite these important successes there are still many who struggle every day for the right to define themselves, to access gender-appropriate healthcare, gain parental rights, and to live without harassment by other people, the police, or the government. Nearly 80 countries still criminalize consensual, adult, same-sex activity, or use other laws to marginalize and persecute lesbian, gay, bisexual and transgender (LGBT) people (Sexual Orientation Laws, 2016). Same sex marriage is an important social change, but it is not social equality; the struggle continues (Manning, 2015).

Chapter Summary

During the 1960s, a time of social change in the US, many of the founders of North American CP argued for the need to change oppressive social conditions in pursuit of social justice (Albee, 1986; Goldenberg, 1978; Rappaport, 1987). Social change emphasizes the importance of a vision and values of a more just and caring society (Prilleltensky, 2001) and recognizes the fact that many social problems, including health and mental health problems, are strongly related to socioeconomic inequalities and other imbalances of power (Dohrenwend & Dohrenwend, 1969). Changing oppressive social conditions and transforming power relations is the best form of prevention and promotion.

But transformative social change is very difficult to achieve because it threatens the power of dominant groups within society. Efforts to promote transformative change take time and in many cases may not be fully achievable. Each social problem is different and exists in a unique cultural and historical context. There is no recipe for transformation. We may never know if our research and action will produce the type of changes we seek. Furthermore, the most pressing social problems are globalized, complex, and interrelated, demanding that we pay close attention to the potential trade-offs when we work for social change. For example, do we risk harming the economy when we fight to protect the environment and address the power dynamics that contribute to global climate change? How are local communities affected when we work to change immigration policies to increase the power and wellbeing of immigrants?

Community psychologists have contributed to the development of social intervention strategies and participatory processes that we discuss in more detail in Chapter 10. However, the field of CP has not yet fully embraced the need for transformative social change in its research and practice. To do so, CP needs to adopt the value of social justice as a major principle, become more political and critically attentive to issues of power, engage in solidarity with oppressed groups and social movements, and utilize alternative research methods that are suited to the study and promotion of social change.

PRACTITIONER COMMENTARY

On Being a "Double-Agent" for Prevention, Promotion, and Social Change

Shauna Reddin, University of Prince Edward Island, Canada

This chapter really gets to the heart of what I believe to be the defining features of CP. Prevention, promotion, and transformative social change are the clearest expressions of the underlying values base and core beliefs of CP that set it apart from other forms of psychology. If we can collectively avoid or resolve many psychological problems that individuals face through community interventions that prevent illness or promote wellness, we should do so. It is both cost effective and more humane. Recognizing that prevention and promotion issues often go deep into the heart of social inequalities, the chapter then makes the call for CP to work towards transformative social change that will reduce or remove the inequalities that are the origins of most social issues. These are all very easy ideas to agree with, and the assumption I had as a student was that this would not be a hard sell in practice. My experience as a practitioner over the last ten years has been more nuanced.

I work in policy, planning, and program evaluation in a small jurisdiction. Prince Edward Island, Canada's smallest province, has responsibility for delivering public health care, education, and social services, but only has the population and tax base of a small city at around 155,000. In my career I have primarily focused on mental health and addictions, including embedding prevention, early intervention, and harm reduction[2] into the traditional treatment system. More recently, I have been working in education with a focus on mental health literacy and early intervention in schools. In my experience, there have been two critical realities that complicate the apparently straightforward goals of prevention and promotion when applied in a practice setting: developing strong relationships and establishing a shared vision.

Relationships are crucial to success in social interventions undertaken by community psychologists. When projects I have participated in have worked the best, it has been because of the relationships that exist to bridge gaps in the planning or program structure. When projects have failed it has most often been from a lack of buy-in from participating stakeholders, either explicitly or covertly, rather than a problem with the program's theory of change or evidence base. This is the most significant issue in my experience of transferring evidence-based programs or practices into the "real world" – it's full of people who may or may not want to play along or play nicely. Folks have their own agendas, and their jobs have limits to their scope and mandate. Risk aversion is a real thing – not wanting to rock the boat in favor of maintaining the safety and predictability of the dominant power systems. This is particularly acute when you take the prevention lens and focus on structural injustices, as that is when people can sometimes come face to face with their own privilege, or underlying stigma around recipients of health and social programs.

It is also really important to understand the layers to prevention when working in interdisciplinary and community-based spaces, and how they impact our shared vision of what the goals or choice of intervention approach to prevention and promotion truly are. If two colleagues are both in agreement that their role is preventative, but they do not define the level at which their prevention efforts are aimed, significant confusion and even conflict can arise. A nurse and a social worker may have very different understandings or beliefs around how "upstream" to go in identifying a prevention target; I once found myself in an argument with a school-based nurse over the importance of hand hygiene in schools as preventative of mental health issues. Add to this the enormous influence of branded approaches to both prevention and treatment with industries built around train-the-trainer workshops, licensing, and materials for purchase, which I have

---

[2] "Harm reduction refers to policies, programs and practices that aim to minimize negative health, social, and legal impacts associated with drug use, drug policies and drug laws. Harm reduction is grounded in justice and human rights – it focuses on positive change and on working with people without judgement, coercion, discrimination, or requiring that they stop using drugs as a precondition of support." Harm Reduction International (www.hri.global/what-is-harm-reduction)

seen in the form of branded programs to teach Social and Emotional Learning (SEL) in schools. There are many external influences on the choice of approach. Thus, shared vision and effective communication become key in successful prevention, intervention, and research.

Layering community participation and self-determination for the consumers or clients in a system or program adds both credibility and complexity to the work. This has been something I have wanted to do but have found very difficult to execute. Choosing a focus for preventative efforts can be overwhelming, as many clients have multiple risk factors that brought them to needing help, and those factors would require different approaches to influence. But as a mentor recently said when talking about the scope of prevention needs in the community, "The good news is that regardless of what issue you choose to bite off, you can be guaranteed lots to chew on."

A final reflection I'd like to bring to this chapter is the challenging real-world experience of balancing of first and second order change. The text does a very good job of clearly describing the differences in both approaches and potential impact, and suggests that this is not a simple dichotomy, but rather dimensions of the same work. I agree, but I also want to comment on the messy and very cloudy reality of this work as a person attempting to navigate it in practice. Pragmatically, most of the people reading this text are going to need to work for a living, and most jobs exist within institutions and organizations engaged in first order or ameliorative work. Even if you're lucky enough to land paid work that explicitly permits a focus on social justice and transformative change, like at a private foundation or a research grant, you may still find economic, social, and political pressure to focus on individually modifiable risk factors rather than issues of social justice. I have encountered significant issues of territoriality and protectionism over my career, across all levels. I have worked with both individuals and projects that have been held back by perceived or actual limits imposed by mandate or scope of funding. A colleague of mine who works in program development has expressed significant frustration with being told to "stay in your lane" by those higher up the ladder when she attempts to embed transformative approaches in her work.

To counter-balance this frustration, it has been absolutely crucial for me to find good people who are also doing this work to act as mirrors, life rafts, and cheerleaders. I think it's well acknowledged that clinical psychologists and other therapists require self-care and mentorship in order to do good work and not burn out. I would suggest that this work also requires this level of attention if it is going to be sustained. The process of prevention, promotion, and transformation is a marathon, not a sprint. Some days doing this work makes me feel like a double-agent, officially working on ameliorative system improvement projects to grease the wheels of a person-blaming machine, while subversively watching for like-minded folks to partner with in order to change the direction of that very machine towards structural and societal change. But other days I go to conferences about mental health literacy in schools or read a news release from government piloting a basic universal income project as a strategic response to high social service program costs and I feel less of an outsider and more an early adopter on a wave of really exciting change. As I read this chapter, written a decade after I graduated from a CP master's program, it makes me feel as though the field of CP continues to be a critically reflective discipline and is capturing the nuances and change processes under way in the field of prevention, promotion, and social change.

Key Terms

Amelioration/First order change: Change within a system, without altering its underlying values, assumptions, structures, and power arrangements.

Dissemination: The complex task of transferring effective prevention programs widely into community settings.

Fidelity: The extent to which the intervention corresponds to the originally intended program model.

Health promotion: Efforts to enhance the health and wellbeing in populations.

Indicated prevention: Interventions targeted at high-risk individuals who are identified as already having minimal, but detectable signs of the problem.

Primary prevention: A focus on preventing new cases of a given problem.

Protective factors: Situational factors that can moderate the impacts of stressful life events.

Secondary prevention: Interventions that focus on identifying, targeting, and treating existing cases of a given problem.

Selective prevention: Preventive interventions targeted at individuals or subgroups of the population who, due to membership in a certain group, have a significantly higher than average risk of developing problems.

Social determinants of health: The economic and social conditions and systems that influence the wellbeing of individuals, communities, and societies.

Transformation/Second order change: Changes to system itself along with the underlying rules, assumptions, roles, and relationships governing the system's structure.

Universal prevention: Preventive interventions targeting the general public or a whole population group that has not been identified on the basis of individual risk.

Resources

The Homeless Hub a national research institute devoted to homelessness in Canada: www.homelesshub.ca

The Roadmap for the Prevention of Youth Homelessness: www.homelesshub.ca/youthpreventionroadmap

Prevention Journals and Websites

Applied and Preventive Psychology: www.journals.elsevier.com/applied-and-preventive-psychology

Journal of Prevention and Intervention in the Community: www.tandfonline.com/loi/wpic20

Journal of Primary Prevention: https://link.springer.com/journal/10935

Prevention Science: https://link.springer.com/journal/11121

The Prevention Institute: www.preventioninstitute.org/

COMMUNITY, CONNECTION, AND PARTICIPATION

7

Warm-up Questions

As a warm-up to this chapter, make a list of all the things that make up the community where you currently live. List whichever aspects of the community that seem important to you – the people, places and spaces, the sights and sounds, the roads, rivers, and other physical features. Using this list, *draw* your version of your community on another piece of paper. You don't have to be able to draw well, in fact, use your non-dominant hand to worry less about the "art" and more about the activity itself. Use symbols and words to include everything on your list and anything else that comes to mind that you see, hear, and feel about your community.

Now take a moment to look at the representation of your community. What stands out? Which aspects of your community did you highlight? What things did you leave out? What are the positive aspects of community that you featured? Did you try to convey any negative aspects such as crime, traffic, or environmental hazards? How important is this community to you? Do you feel strongly connected to this community? Do you have good bonds with others there? Do you feel like you have a say about what goes on? Do people trust and help each other in your community? If you are reading this chapter for a class, try to share your pictures and stories with your classmates to explore the different characteristics you each highlighted and the varied perspectives on the communities in which you live.

Learning Objectives

In this chapter you will learn about

- The concepts of community, sense of community, inclusion, social capital, networks, civic participation, and community capacity

- How to apply these concepts to help make sense of the complexity of neighborhoods and communities

What is a Community?

In this chapter we explore five interconnected concepts utilized in the field of CP: **community**, **inclusion**, social capital, **social networks**, and **community capacity**. Community psychologists recognize the community as the fundamental context for human development and the setting within which social change can be accomplished (Kagan, Burton, Duckett, Lawthom, & Siddiquee, 2011; Wiesenfeld, 1996). The interest in communities is justified in a world where different groups intersect and often experience conflict over resources. We live in a world where communities of various identities share space, time, work, pasts, present, and futures. Each community has to value its own identity and diversity as well as the identities and diversity present in other groups. But communities differ not only among themselves but also within themselves. What, on the surface, may look similar may hide vast differences. For example, not all Indigenous people share the same culture (Dudgeon et al., 2002), and not all immigrants experience the same challenges. We can talk about a community of women, within which there are obviously multiple communities of Chicanas, Indigenous, African-American, privileged, poor, disabled, and able-bodied women, among others. Every time we invoke a group of people, there are going to be multiple identities within it (Brodsky, 2017; Brodsky, Loomis, & Marx, 2002; Serrano-García & Bond, 1994). Communities also, at times, define themselves in exclusive terms reminiscent of apartheid or in inclusive terms reminiscent of solidarity (Putnam, 2002). People exist in multiple communities that can be defined by geographic boundaries as well as shared interests, beliefs, and identities.

The concept of community is core to the discipline of CP. But what is a community? By 1955, sociologist Hillery had already identified 94 different definitions of the term. The term *community* has been used to refer to such diverse entities as neighborhoods, community groups, institutions, religious groups, work organizations, and professional organizations, and it has been used at different ecological levels ranging from small groups, such as family units, to nationalities (Dalton, Elias, & Wandersman, 2006). At its most basic level, the word community implies a group of people who have something in common. We can think of a *locational* community such as your neighborhood, village, city, or country; or we can think of a *relational* community such as a group of friends or your religious congregation (Bess, Fisher, Sonn, & Bishop, 2002; Heller, 1989; Krause & Montenegro, 2017; McMillan & Chavis, 1986). Members of a relational community may share a culture or a common interest where geographical proximity is less important. You are likely part of relational communities with people around the globe through ubiquitous online social networks such as Facebook, Twitter, Instagram, WhatsApp, and Snapchat (see Box 7.1). There are countless forces, dynamics, and places that bring people together. Some of us feel quite close to the community of community psychologists, while others feel close to the fans of a sports team or to members of a religious group. Some of us can feel close to these three groups at the same time. We can belong to multiple communities simultaneously. What communities do you belong to?

Figure 7.1 is a creative representation of Hyde Park, one of Chicago's most racially diverse neighborhoods and an important cultural and political hub of Chicago's African American community. Communities are dynamic, co-constructed, historically determined, and complex (Dutta, 2016; Wiesenfeld, 1996). Communities are both shaped by the actions and perceptions of their inhabitants and also shape those inhabitants' actions and perceptions. Likewise, Christens (2019) reminds us that communities are also affected by powerful outside forces such as history, local politics, the economy, and globalization.

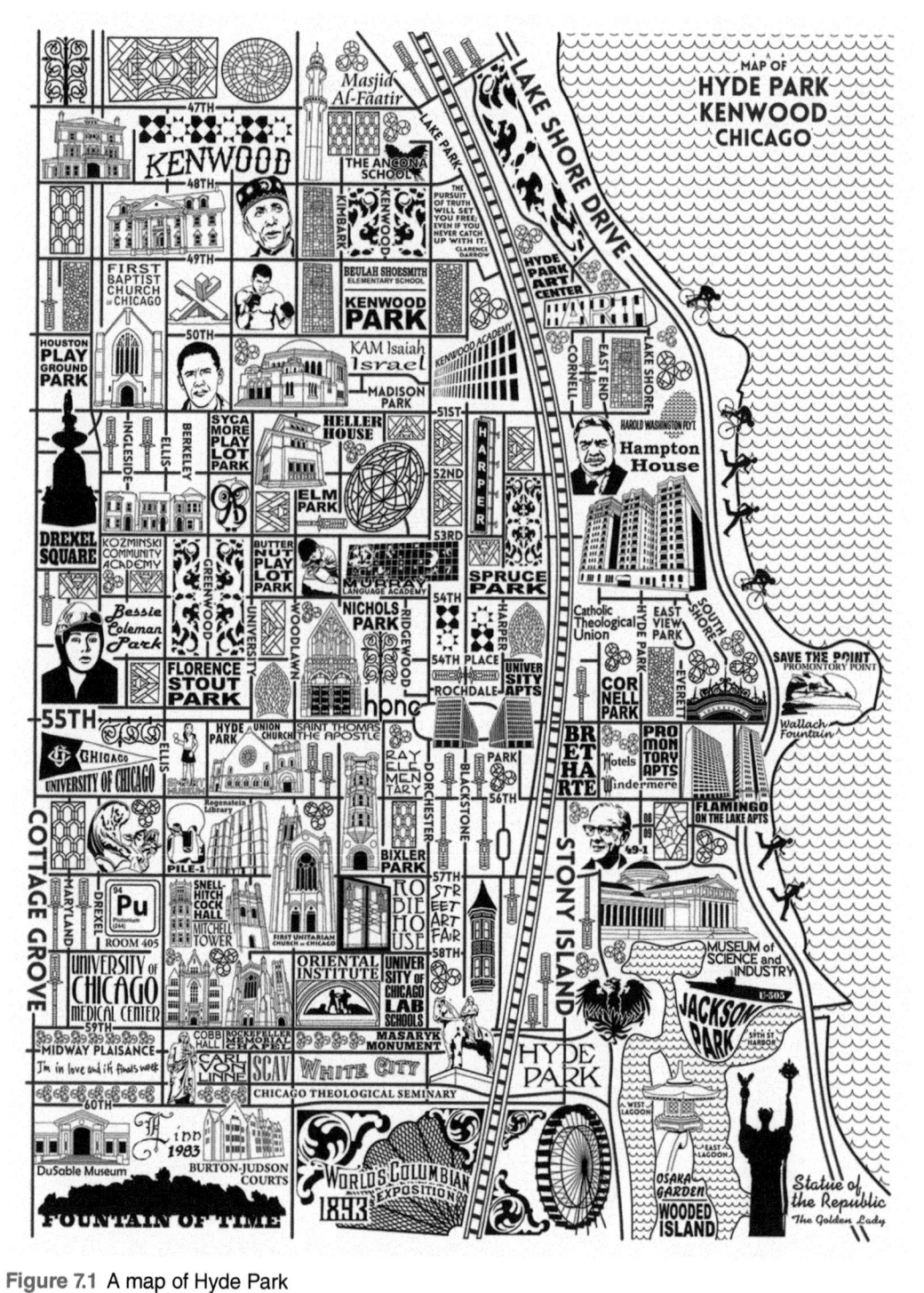

Figure 7.1 A map of Hyde Park

Most people experience both positive and negative sides of community. Positive aspects of community include **social support**, cohesion, sense of belonging, and working together to achieve common aims. Negative aspects of community include rigid norms, conformity, exclusion, segregation, and disrespect for diversity. Our challenge as community psychologists is to promote the growth-enhancing and social justice aspects of community while diminishing the negative potential. We want to use community and power to promote social justice and not to stifle creativity or perpetuate the status quo.

In this book, we describe how community psychologists seek to promote the balance between the forces of community and power (see Chapter 4) and between community and diversity. We also acknowledge that psychological empowerment and empowering processes are not enough without social justice and a redistribution of resources (Sandler, 2007). At the same time, achieving power without positive social connections and support, within and across groups, may lead to untoward effects (Alsop, Bertelsen, & Holland, 2006). Without empowerment, we risk maintaining the status quo, and, without community, we risk treating people as objects. In this chapter we explore community, connection, and participation through a focus on the interconnected concepts of **sense of community**, inclusion, social capital, social networks, and community capacity.

Sense of Community

The concept of a psychological sense of community was introduced by community psychologist Seymour Sarason (1974). In his view, sense of community captured something very basic about being human: our need for affiliation in times of sorrow, our need for sharing in times of joy, and our need to be with people at all other times. He defined sense of community as:

> the sense that one belongs in and is meaningfully a part of a larger collectivity; the sense that although there may be conflict between the needs of the individual and the collectivity, or among different groups in the collectivity, these conflicts must be resolved in a way that does not destroy the psychological sense of community; the sense that there is a network of and structure of relationships that strengthens rather than dilutes feelings of loneliness. (Sarason, 1988, p. 41)

Sarason astutely observed a decline in support in traditional communities and an increased alienation on the part of people in Western countries. He argued that most people yearn to be connected to others through relationships that give expression to their needs for intimacy, diversity, usefulness, and belonging, but that these types of connection are too often lacking. Also, often lacking are adequate social structures that would offer citizens opportunities to participate and take action that might remedy their sense of alienation (Heller, 1989). Communities help to fill human needs for support and connection. Isolation and psychosocial problems in living are likely to follow when these needs are not met. Relational communities also provide "mediating structures" (Berger & Neuhaus, 1977) in that they serve to connect individuals to the larger society while providing a source for the satisfaction of personal needs through social attachments. Sarason argued that the overarching mission of CP should be to create a psychological sense of community.

Since Sarason's (1974) coinage of the term, many have tried to operationalize and distil the meaning of sense of community, all in an effort to understand the positive or negative effects of this phenomenon. McMillan and Chavis (1986) are credited with formulating an enduring, yet often contested, conceptualization of SOC. According to them, the concept consists of four domains: (1) membership; (2) influence; (3) integration and fulfilment of needs; and (4) shared emotional connection. *Membership* is the notion that there are clear boundaries between those who are or are not part of the community. *Influence* describes the ways in which members influence and are influenced by the community. *Integration and fulfillment of needs* are demonstrated by shared values within the community and the sharing of resources and satisfying of needs (whether emotional or material). *Shared emotional connection* offers positive contact between members, opportunities to share experiences, methods for honoring members, and a sense of investment by members in the community as a whole.

These four domains of sense of community sparked a great deal of interest and research in the field of CP. Special issues of the *Journal of Community Psychology* in 1986 and 1996, and a book on the subject (Fisher, Sonn & Bishop, 2002) summarize very well the early progress in this area. Wilkinson (2007) later conceptualized psychological sense of community, attraction, and neighboring as parts of **social cohesion**. Based on a study of 20 rural communities in Canada, he found that their levels of social cohesion vary depending on linguistic, geographic, historic, and cultural variables. Over the last four decades, the concept of a sense of community has generated a great deal of research and theorizing in the field across a variety of contexts, such as residential blocks, schools, neighborhoods, workplaces, or online social networks (c.f. Chavis & Pretty, 1999; Fisher et al., 2002; Hughey, Speer, & Peterson, 1999; Long & Perkins, 2007; McMillan & Chavis, 1986; Nowell & Boyd, 2014; Peterson, Speer, & McMillan, 2008; Reich, 2010; See Box 7.1).

Box 7.1 Are Online Communities Really Communities?

Six Degrees, Friendster, and Myspace introduced the world to online social networking and quickly gained popularity among teenagers and young adults. Myspace was the largest social networking site in the world from 2005 to 2008 until Facebook expanded to include non-university student users and offered features that improved the social networking experience. Now there are many social media platforms that each have millions of active users including YouTube, Instagram, WhatsApp, LinkedIn, Twitter, Reddit, Snapchat, WeChat, and Pinterest.

Groups within these online social networking platforms seem to have many of the characteristics of offline communities, but what makes online groups and sites communities? Some have proposed that greater online access and interactions can lead to networked individualism that allows people to "remain connected, but as individuals rather than being rooted in the home bases of work unit and household. Individuals switch rapidly between their social networks" (Wellman, 2002, p. 15) rather than remain in a group or community. Some studies have found evidence that many of the individual feelings, commitment, and perceptions are similar in online and offline groups (e.g., Baym, 2007; Blanchard, 2007; Nip, 2004).

Reich (2010) utilized focus groups and surveys with youth to explore whether typical uses of social networking sites such as Facebook and Myspace by early and late adolescents support sense of community or whether these sites are simply populated by people networking with other individuals. She found little support for membership in general or any of the specific membership characteristics of sense of community identified by McMillan and Chavis (1986). Teens' networks were large and expansive with little evidence of overlap or boundaries. She did find that these sites support a feeling of shared emotional connection, however investment in the sites' continuation and existence was low. In the end, her study found little support for these sites engendering a strong sense of community. For Reich, social networking sites appear to be prominent aspects of adolescents' lives but their typical uses of these sites do not seem to be communities. Rather, they appear to simply be a way for individuals to be networked with other individuals online.

However, online spaces that have more exclusive membership and shared purpose tend to have characteristics that resemble physical communities. For instance, guilds on World of Warcraft (a massive multi-player online role playing game; MMORPG) and fan groups on virtual worlds for children such as Club Penguin and Webkinz have clear methods of communication, identification of who is a member or not, and high levels of emotional and instrumental sharing and supporting (e.g., Williams et al., 2006; Reich, Black, & Korobkova, 2014). While typical uses of Facebook or YouTube may not reflect community membership for most people, dedicated subgroups on these platforms seem to connect well to our conceptualizations of communities (e.g., Yilmaz, 2016; Reich et al., 2014).

Additionally, online spaces may offer a key platform for civic engagement for young people who have been historically silenced within offline spaces. In a meta-analysis of 36 studies examining the association between social networking sites (i.e., Facebook and Twitter) and political activity, 82 percent of the studies indicated a positive correlation between participating online and engaging in social action (i.e., demonstrations and rallies), especially among youth and younger adult populations (15–30 years; Boulianne, 2015). Smith (2013) found that eight in ten adolescents use some social networking site and that this online engagement is strongly associated with engaging in political activity when compared with non-users.

Various conceptions of community and sense of community are related to the values of caring, compassion, and support for community infrastructures. Moreover, community and sense of community can be conceptualized at multiple ecological levels of analysis. In shifting away from clinical psychology, early community psychologists recognized that distressed individuals need more than caring and compassionate therapists; they need caring and compassionate relationships and communities (See Box 7.2). At the level of the individual, the concept of social support highlights the importance of relationships and the different types of support that stem from supportive relationships, including emotional support, guidance, and tangible and financial support and socialization. Many community psychologists have contributed greatly to the development of the concept of social support, research on social support, and the development of social support interventions (Barrera, 1986; Cohen, Underwood, & Gottlieb, 2000; Gottlieb, 1981). As an alternative or complement to professional treatment, community psychologists have helped to conceptualize, design, and evaluate individual-level support interventions, using non-professional and volunteer helpers. Meso-level interventions to promote relational wellbeing include professionally led support groups and self-help/mutual aid groups and organizations that are formed by, and for, people who share a common problem or concern (Cohen et al., 2000; Humphreys, 1997).

Box 7.2 Austin's Community First! Villages for Ending Homelessness

"Housing will never cure homelessness, but community will." This is the idea behind Community First! in Austin, Texas where they focus on the stabilizing power of social connection. *Community First! Village* emerged out of founder Alan Graham's volunteer work through Mobile Loaves & Fishes. Alan and friends from St. John Neumann Catholic Church fed homeless people out of the back of a pickup truck. As they spent nights on the streets and developed relationships with homeless people, they started asking: "What is it that you desire?" What they heard, was that people were looking for community (Kimble, 2018) https://mlf.org/community-first/.

What are the Limitations of Sense of Community?

As Bess et al. (2002) have noted, Puddifoot (1996) highlighted two significant problems in the way researchers have defined community. First, community is defined too broadly as a catchall term to refer to such diverse entities as neighborhoods, community groups, institutions, religious groups, work organizations, and professional organizations. Given this broad use, *community* risks losing its specific meaning and conceptual utility. Secondly, he contends that the practice of referring to communities by type may lead to an artificial polarization. The primary example of this is the common practice of referring to two qualitatively distinct, yet often related, types of community – relational and locational. Chipuer and Pretty (1999) also observe the inconsistent usage of community and sense of community in the literature. They point out that terms such as neighboring, social cohesion, and community identity are sometimes used synonymously with sense of community and sometimes as related terms.

Another concern with community and sense of community is that most definitions stress similarity among the members of a community as a necessary condition for group identity and cohesion. As Wiesenfeld (1996) noted, this tendency toward homogeneity enhances similarities, conceals differences, and does not reflect the complexity and dynamic, historically determined nature of community processes. Townley, Kloos, Green, and Franco (2011) identified a "core values conflict" (p. 69) in CP between the defined homogeneity of a sense of community and the heterogeneity inherent in the value of diversity. CP researchers Neal and Neal (2014) and Stivala, Robins, Kashima, and Kirley (2016) utilized agent-based simulation models to demonstrate that it is unlikely for a high-level of diversity and sense of community to be observed together. These papers and others renewed a debate in the field about the tension between diversity and sense of community and led to a special section of the *American Journal of Community Psychology* on this topic (Neal, 2017).

Ann Brodsky (2017) and colleagues (Brodsky et al., 2002) take a different view and argue that sense of community can be experienced as positive or negative, and that we can experience **multiple psychological senses of community (MPSOC)** because none of us are members of only one community (Brodsky, 2009; Brodsky et al., 2002; Brodsky & Marx, 2001; Hughey & Speer, 2002; Wiesenfeld, 1996). They suggest that even if sense of community and diversity are conflictual, "the ability to form MPSOC in the multiplicity of settings where some aspect of our identity defines us as 'us' creates an intricate web of bridging and bonding relationships which actually strengthen ties between communities, rather than weakening them" (Brodsky, 2017, p. 271).

Lastly, the field of CP may have, over the years, evoked the concept of community as a value against which the worth of any work in the field is measured and, as such, protected the very concept of community from any form of meaningful critical reading (Christens & Speer, 2006; Coimbra et al., 2012; Collins, 2010; Dutta, 2016, 2018: Evans, Duckett, Lawthom, & Kivell, 2016; Seedat & Lazarus, 2011; Townley et al., 2011). Community is an elastic, social, political, and theoretical construct that holds a variety of contradictory meanings (Collins, 2010). Our tendency to romanticize the idea of community to mean everything good, risks minimizing the fact that community can also be used to exclude, oppress, and preserve inequity (Sampson, 2012). For example, members of racially exclusive resident associations may feel a sense of community and work well together, but do so against the common good more broadly by being unwelcoming to families of color (Warren, Thompson, & Saegert, 2001). Tight-knit local communities can often create barriers to wall in the "good" and exclude the "bad" (Hillier, 2002). Sense of community is an important and useful tool in CP, but we must also acknowledge that many people are excluded from or discriminated against in communities by virtue of their gender, sexual orientation, ethno-racial background, abilities, age, or other characteristics. This forces us to think more about the concept of inclusion.

Inclusion

As Western societies have become more culturally diverse and CP has become a more diverse body of people, there has been greater attention to diversity and the promotion of inclusion in CP theory, research, practice, and training. In the 1990s and early 2000s, feminist, critical, and community psychologists, such as Ingrid Huygens, Irma Serrano-García, Meg Bond and Rod Watts, began to draw attention to how racism, sexism, classism, ableism, and heterosexism are forms of sociopolitical oppression and elaborated on the need for interventions that strive to eliminate such oppression and promote inclusion (Huygens, 1996a, b; Trickett et al., 1994; Watts, 1992; Watts, Williams, & Jagers 2003).

What is Inclusion?

The term "inclusion" has its roots in the field of disabilities (Oliver & Barnes, 1998; see also Chapter 19). In particular, parents and advocates of individuals with developmental disabilities have promoted the idea and practice of inclusion and community because of widespread practices of segregation and exclusion of adults and children with developmental disabilities (Merrells, Buchanan, & Waters, 2019; O'Brien & O'Brien, 1996; Schwartz, 1997).

Historically, people with developmental disabilities have been labeled by professionals (with psychologists playing a lead role in this) with such pejorative terms as "mental defectives," "feeble-minded," "idiots" and "morons." The stigma and shame that families with a child with a developmental disability experience and that which those children experience themselves, have persisted. Today, many people with developmental disabilities are surrounded by a "sea of services," in institutions, special schools, special classes within schools, and special living facilities (McKnight, 1995). Parents and advocates have contested this approach and reclaimed language with terms like "inclusion," "mainstreaming," and "community integration." The language of inclusion suggests that the community, not people with disabilities, needs to change; communities and community members need to become more welcoming and hospitable to people with disabilities (O'Brien & O'Brien, 1996; Salzer & Baron, 2014; Schwartz, 1997).

The principle of inclusion goes beyond people with disabilities; it applies to a variety of groups that have been subjected to social exclusion. Inclusion is an organizing principle that applies more broadly to people who have been discriminated against and oppressed by virtue of specific characteristics such as gender, sexual orientation, ethno-racial background, economic resources, abilities, age, etc. Sexism, heterosexism, racism, ableism, and ageism are all forms of social exclusion. Inclusion is an antidote to exclusion and can be conceptualized at different ecological levels of analysis. At the individual level, inclusion entails the recovery of a positive personal and political identity – the development of a personal story of empowerment. At the relational level, inclusion means welcoming communities and supportive relationships. At the societal level, inclusion is concerned with the promotion of equity and access to valued social resources that have historically been denied to oppressed people.

Community psychologist Meg Bond (1999) has argued that inclusion entails both a culture of connection and the legitimization of varied perspectives. The notion of connection, which has been emphasized by feminist writers as important for women's growth and empowerment (Jordan, Kaplan, Miller, Stiver, & Surrey, 1991), focuses on interdependence, team work, relationships, and sense of community. Connection stands as an alternative to the emphasis on individualism that is widespread in the Western world. The idea of varied perspectives suggests that, in any setting, there are multiple perspectives that reflect people's unique circumstances and experiences. It has been observed that disadvantaged people understand the idea of multiple perspectives very well because they learn the norms and perspectives of their own group and they also have to learn the norms and perspectives of the dominant group in order to cope with and survive that reality (Bond, 1999). In other words, disadvantaged people live in multiple worlds and have to bridge these worlds every day of their lives.

On the other hand, advantaged people have more trouble understanding multiple perspectives. Advantaged people are often oblivious to the life experiences and circumstances of disadvantaged groups because they do not have to cope with those realities or be accountable to disadvantaged people (Jost & Major, 2001). Moreover, legitimization of these varied perspectives counters the belief that there is one true, external reality and one single standard against which everyone should be judged.

Bond and Mulvey (2000) have made a distinction between representation and perspective that is important for the principle of inclusion. *Representation* refers to the participation and inclusion of disadvantaged groups (e.g., the representation of women in CP), while *perspective* refers to the unique and varied perspectives of disadvantaged groups (e.g., the inclusion of feminist perspectives that challenge male domination). Representation is a necessary but insufficient condition for inclusion; the incorporation of perspectives that are critical of the status quo is needed as well. Together, representation and perspective enhance the voices of disadvantaged people, providing them with opportunities to name their experiences rather than being silenced and suffering in that silence (Reinharz, 1994).

The principle of inclusion is closely tied to that of accountability and commitment. Bond (1999) has argued that forces supporting exclusion are lack of accountability and differential privilege. When dominant groups are not accountable for their impact on subordinate groups, exclusion and oppression of the subordinate group occur. In contrast, inclusion is promoted when dominant groups become aware of their relative power and privilege and are accountable for their impact on the subordinate group. But inclusion has been difficult to promote because dominant groups have historically held on to their power and privilege.

Why is Inclusion Important?

Failure to promote inclusion leads to conflict in communities and leaves the door open for oppression to occur. Sexism, heterosexism, racism, and ableism are all forms of exclusion that have psychological and political dimensions (Prilleltensky & Gonick, 1996; Shakespeare, 2006; Watts et al., 2003). Moreover, these different forms of exclusion sometimes intersect, such that some disadvantaged people experience double or triple jeopardy. For example, Black feminists have written about how Black women have to overcome both White and male supremacy and, in some cases, heterosexual supremacy (Collins, 1991; hooks, 2002). Our invited contributors go into much more depth and specificity about some of the problems facing women, minorities, people who have experienced unemployment, poor people, gay, lesbian, bisexual and transgendered people, and people with physical and mental health disabilities later in this book. The concept of social capital can assist us in developing a deeper understanding of the complex nature of inclusion and relational connectedness in and across communities.

Social Capital

In responding to the tension between diversity and sense of community noted above, Townley et al. (2011) suggest that community psychologists not ask about diversity's relationship with sense of community narrowly, and instead start asking about diversity's relationship with a much bigger and more inclusive construct, social capital. As introduced in Chapter 4, social capital refers broadly to the qualities, social ties, and capabilities of communities that are related to the wellbeing of individuals and collectives. While capital is usually thought of in terms of economic assets, Bourdieu (1986) believed that economic, cultural, and social capital together form the foundation of social life and dictate one's position within the social order. Bourdieu's concept of *cultural capital* refers to the collection of resources such as skills, tastes, posture, clothing, mannerisms, material belongings, and qualifications that one acquires through being part of a particular social class. Certain forms of cultural capital are valued over others, and can help or hinder one's social mobility just as much as income or wealth.

Putnam (1995, 2000a, b) drew heavily from Coleman (1988) arguing that communities can also have *social capital*, including a range of community organizations and networks, civic participation, community identity, and norms of trust and mutual support. Social capital refers to a specific type of resource (social relationships) that facilitates action and social support. In this section we discuss how stronger social ties within and among communities are a prerequisite for civic participation, community development, and social action aimed at the promotion of social justice and collective wellbeing.

While sense of community attracted a lot of attention within CP, allied terms such as **"community cohesion"** and "social capital" gained currency in other disciplines such as sociology, community development, and political science. The concept of social capital contends that different forms of social association (features of social organization, bridging and bonding social ties, see Bourdieu 1986; Coleman, 1988; Putnam, 1993) constitute a resource that can be conceptualized as capital that can be utilized to facilitate cooperation and coordination for mutual benefit (Peterson & Zimmerman, 2004).

The main difference between sense of community and social capital arguably lies in the level of analysis. Whereas sense of community is a psychological construct that is experienced by individuals and typically measured and discussed in aggregate at the group or neighborhood level, social capital is a collective resource, a common good, a feature of communities, rather than the property of an individual (Bourdieu, 1986; Warren et al., 2001). Social capital is understood as a property of social networks with members both benefitting and contributing in an effort to achieve personal and collective goals (Saegert & Carpiano, 2017).

Research on social capital in CP and related disciplines provides several important insights about social connections. The first is the distinction between different forms of social capital, namely *bonding* and *bridging* social capital (Szreter & Woolcock, 2004; Warren et al., 2001) first highlighted in Chapter 4. Bonding social capital refers to trusting and co-operative relations between members of a community or network who see themselves as being similar in some identified ways. **Bridging social capital**, by contrast, comprises "relations of respect and mutuality between people who know they are not alike in some sociodemographic (or social identity) sense (differing by age, ethnic group for example)" (Szreter & Woolcock, 2004, pp. 654–5).

Szreter and Woolcock (2004) also identified **linking social capital** as a type of bridging capital, which connects regular citizens with those in power. For example, how well local community members know of and have access to local decision-makers such as city council members is a form of linking social capital. Scholars have defined this type of capital as embodying norms of respect and networks of trusting relationships between people who are interacting across explicit, formal, or institutionalized power or authority levels in society (Szreter & Woolcock, 2004).

Much like the sense of community and diversity tension described earlier, there is a similar tension between these types of social capital. The more intense a community's inwardly focused

Figure 7.2 Flooding in New Orleans
Source: FEMA/Alamy Stock Photo.

bonding relationships, the more potential for insularity. While bonding social capital facilitates the cultivation of a strong internal SOC, it potentially limits members' ability to interact with and access resources in other communities through bridging relationships (Neal, 2015).

For example, sociologists Elliott, Haney, and Sams-Abiodun (2010) compared post-disaster outcomes for residents of two U.S. communities in New Orleans, the Lower Ninth Ward, a poor, majority African American community, and Lakeview, a more affluent, majority White community. They found that while Ninth Ward residents relied on bonding social capital for strong informal support during Hurricane Katrina, they received less support overall. The authors concluded that a lack of bridging social capital to people outside the affected area and ties with individuals with more resources resulted in less support and reduced resilience for Ninth Ward residents compared with those in Lakeview. Kaniasty and Norris (1995, 2004) refer to this as the "rule of relative advantage" (1995, p. 451) because one's community and political connections, along with social class determine the availability and accessibility of resources. Hughey and Speer (2002) have suggested that "navigating [this] tension between internal cohesion and external relationships ... is the central challenge of community psychology" (p. 76).

Saegert and Carpiano (2017) identify three main applications of social capital in CP. The first is that social capital, much like social support, is a resource that can be a protective factor against harm or contribute to resilience. The second strand positions social capital as an aspect of empowerment which highlights the purposive nature of social relationships, its key role in how power relations are maintained and transmitted, and the importance of resources within social networks (Bourdieu & Wacquant, 1992; Christens, 2012, 2019). This speaks to the potential of communities to improve the wellbeing of their members through the synergy of associations, mutual trust, sense of community, and collective action (Hooghe, 2003; McKenzie & Harpham, 2006; Putnam, 2000b). Ginwright (2007) introduced the idea of **critical social capital** to describe the development of leadership and political consciousness in marginalized groups as a way to shape political identities and take action to improve social and material conditions in Black communities. In CP, we see social capital as a resource inherent in particular social relationships in communities that can be mobilized for action to achieve individual and collective ends. A third application sees social capital as a component of social regularities in social settings manifested in norms, interactional patterns, routines and practices, and social networks, each of which can mutually influence the others (Seidman, 2012).

Citizen Participation

One community process that both depends on and contributes to SOC, inclusion, and social capital is **citizen participation**. This is defined as "a process in which individuals take part in decision making in the institutions, programs, and environments that affect them" (Heller, Price, Reinhartz, Riger, & Wandersman 1984, p. 339). Reid (2000) suggests that "the participating community" (p. 3) is an ideal type of community with democratic and shared leadership, in addition to well-informed citizens who are encouraged to participate meaningfully in the community. However, civic participation is not the same as volunteering or community service. Participation is about engaging with others in ways that influence decisions in groups, neighborhoods, communities, or society (Dalton, Elias, & Wandersman, 2006). Examples include serving on a community change coalition, attending and speaking at school board meetings, meeting with government officials to advocate change, hosting or attending town halls to deliberate about common hopes and concerns, and engaging in community organizing, protests, or rallies.

Civic participation by residents in communities provides opportunities for individuals to build relationships of trust and reciprocity with others, allows for individuals to experience higher levels of **collective efficacy**, encourages collective **community building** processes, helps leverage greater access to resources and increases political influence through collective political power (Collins, Neal, & Neal, 2014; Foster-Fishman, Pierce, & Van Egeren, 2009; Hyman, 2002; Pancer, 2015; Ohmer 2007; Speer & Hughey, 1995; Wandersman & Florin, 2000). Pancer's (2015) research on civic engagement of youth demonstrated the benefits of participation on their own wellbeing as well as the ways in which their level of civic involvement was influenced by the different systems and environments in which they live. When residents young and old have opportunities, and realize they have influence in communities, this contributes to their confidence and feeling of self-worth, enhances their ability to express and advocate for themselves, and builds community.

Meaningful civic participation and engagement with others in communities can also help foster inclusion and connect people across differences (Ponce & Rowe, 2018). Madyaningrum and Sonn (2011) found that participation in a community arts project fostered individual and social awareness about different groups within the broader community. Their case study of a community arts project in a regional town in Victoria, Australia showed how participation helped challenge social representations attached to particular social identities and contribute to the transformation of unequal power relationships.

While participation may be a valuable opportunity for everyone, it is not evenly available across the population in communities. Scholars have noted the existence of a "participation paradox" in that vulnerable citizens who most need the material and social benefits resulting from civic participation are the least able to do so due to the overwhelming demands of economic survival (Verba & Nie, 1972). It is hard to engage fully in community life when you have to work multiple jobs to make ends meet. Poverty and exclusion create a sort of vicious cycle: the lower the economic and social capital people possess, the less the participation; the less the participation, the lower the economic and social capital. Furthermore, high levels of wealth inequality allow the rich to manipulate the rules of the game, to influence elections and political mobilization, and establish barriers and incentives that systematically include some voices while leaving other voices out of the decision-making process (Gaventa, 2016; see also Chapter 4).

Collective efficacy

Based on Bandura's (1997) social cognitive theory, collective efficacy is about common beliefs in the capacity to take coordinated action and emphasizes residents' shared sense of active engagement on issues that affect their lives (Sampson, Morenoff, & Earls, 1999). While civic participation is the behavioral manifestation of **community empowerment**, collective efficacy captures the community's perceptions of social cohesion and their collective capability for action. Collective efficacy can serve as a "collective gauge of a community's or neighborhood's emotional disposition toward collective action to address community issues" (Christens, 2019, p. 139).

Research on collective efficacy has demonstrated strong links to civic participation behaviors and to indicators of community wellbeing. Communities with higher levels of collective efficacy experience lower rates of violence and enjoy more civic participation (Foster-Fishman, Cantillon, Pierce, & Van Egeren, 2007; Sampson, Raudenbush, & Earls, 1997). CP researchers have found that when residents feel connected to their neighbors and believe that by working together, change is feasible and they are more likely to be active, engaged citizens. For example, in Chicago, Sampson (2012) found that neighborhoods with high collective efficacy had lower levels of violence and better health indicators such as birth weight and infant mortality. Shared expectations of action and mutual trust also tend to reinforce each other. Foster-Fishman and colleagues found that when people thought their neighbors would be engaged, individuals were more likely themselves to be active in their neighborhoods and communities (Foster-Fishman, Pierce, & Van Egeren, 2009; Foster-Fishman et al., 2007).

In marginalized communities and poor ethnic enclaves, however, civic participation, collective efficacy, and strong social bonds and organizations *within* communities may be insufficient to build the necessary connections *across* communities and to more powerful actors and institutions in order to change the relationships and gain access to outside resources (Bourdieu, 1986; Gibbs, Campbell, Akintola, & Colvin, 2015; Roy, Hughes, & Yoshikawa, 2013). Building "bridging" social capital across communities and with financial and public institutions can help bring greater resources and opportunities into vulnerable communities and build the trust and cooperation necessary to act and exercise social power through their relationships (Christens, 2012; Portes, 1998; Warren et al., 2001).

What are the Limitations of Social Capital?

While social capital provides a conceptual tool for better understanding the social fabric at the heart of communities (Saegert & Carpiano, 2017), some have suggested there is a dark side. A counter literature argues that all capital is inherently social and that to label one aspect of everyday life in this way serves to undermine this crucial insight and depoliticize the contribution of social analysis (Atkinson et al., 2017; Fine, 2010). And much like the critiques of sense of community above, the networks of social association referenced by social capital underwrite as much exclusion as inclusion (Portes, 2014). A review of social capital and mental health literature found that the closed internally cohesive conditions necessary for bonding social capital to flourish also caused exclusionary practices towards outside groups. This has the potential to exacerbate existing tensions within communities (Almedom, 2005; Kirkby-Geddes, King, & Bravington, 2013).

In addition, Warren et al. (2001) emphasize that the main problem for poor communities may not be a lack of social capital, but that their social assets, such as strong neighborhood bonds, have greater obstacles to overcome and are constantly under assault. Social capital can only bring limited benefits to marginalized people and groups because access to economic or cultural capital is often cut off by the larger society (Saegert & Carpiano, 2017). For example, the social capital of wealthier communities is reinforced by the fact that they have greater financial and human capital resources, and their schools and other institutions are stronger. Warren et al. (2001) provide this example of the differences in how Parent-Teacher Associations (PTA) in US schools can make change depending on access to financial capital:

> PTA members in an affluent community can discuss the latest curriculum innovations with schoolteachers. PTA members in an inner-city school can work together too. But instead of using their social capital to advance pedagogy at the school, they must discuss how to get an unresponsive central bureaucracy to fix the ceiling that has been falling down in the school auditorium for the last ten years. (p. 3)

In a similar vein, Jennings (2007) suggests that the assumption that social capital is what is missing in poor neighborhoods is problematic because it ignores structural inequality in these communities. He dismisses the notion that social capital can be analyzed in the absence of a framework of power and racial analysis. He refers to this as a "de-racialization of social capital" (p. 91) when researchers overlook racial and ethnic differences. Jennings notes how the language and use of social capital has been adopted by privileged groups as a way to preserve their position and that these groups have often resisted self-help initiatives in Black communities. He sees this perspective as problematic, as it simply assumes inner-city, low-income, and minority communities have higher levels of apathy and less civic engagement.

Lastly, Christens (2012) argues much of the research on social capital lacks attention to psychology and the self and collective efficacy that can be developed by those who become empowered to act and exercise social power through their social relationships. He highlights the work of Ginwright (2007) who makes connections between the development of leadership capabilities and political consciousness and the relational contexts in which individuals are embedded. Ginwright's conception of *critical social capital*, centers on the "connections to small community-based organizations in Black communities that foster political consciousness and prepare Black youth to address issues in their communities" (p. 404).

In summary, social capital refers to the collective resources of civic participation, collective efficacy, networks, norms of reciprocity, and organizations that foster (a) trust among citizens, and (b) actions to improve the common good. However, like SOC, its use has been critiqued and a critical lens should be used in viewing its role in supporting communities. In considering social capital as the relationships between and among individuals, it is important for community psychologists to consider the social networks that people inhabit.

Social Networks

Seidman's (1988) work on social regularities encouraged community psychologists to examine social relations and temporal patterns that link micro and macro level phenomena within a setting, or "those patterned social processes that across time determine setting – and individual-level outcomes" (Seidman, 2012, p. 5). Sarason (1976b) similarly argued that CP should focus on individuals in the context of social networks and that what is important is not our current connections but rather the "connections potentially available to us" (p. 322). A social network perspective offers windows into the complex relational ties that exist between people within and across organizations and communities (Christens, 2012) and understanding relationships and networks is vital to CP's goal to enact social change to enhance wellbeing (Neal & Christens, 2014). The breadth of an individual's connections and potential connections enables one to tap a greater variety of resources for adaptation and wellbeing. In light of our discussion on social capital, these ties provide bridging, bonding, and social capital. In considering social power globally (Chapter 4), social networks illuminate visible and invisible powers, bearing in mind who is connected and who is not.

Closely intertwined with social capital theory, the study of social networks in the social sciences contributes to our ability to conceptualize and examine social relationships and relational structures (Borgatti, Mehra, Brass, & Labianca, 2009; Granovetter, 1973; Wasserman & Faust, 1994). "The volume of social capital possessed by a given agent ... depends on the size of the network of connections that he can effectively mobilize" (Bourdieu 1986, p. 249). Given CP's longstanding focus on the interplay between individuals and their social context, a network perspective and the use of network analysis strategies in research and action makes sense. As Neal and Neal (2017) point out, many theories and frameworks used in CP, such as empowerment (Zimmerman, 2000), social regularities (Tseng & Seidman, 2007), and ecological systems theory (Bronfenbrenner, 1977, 1979; Kelly, 1966), can be explored using a network approach. In this section, we highlight some of the key concepts in the study of social networks and provide some examples of how **social network analysis (SNA)** is used in CP.

A social network is simply a set of relationships within a social context. These relational ties can be among individual people, groups, organizations, or systems (or some combination) and are often referred to as *actors* or *nodes* in a network. The *ties* are the direct connections between two nodes that capture the relationship; for example, connections among a group of friends. *Density* captures the overall level of connectedness in a network by measuring the proportion of all the ties in a network that have actually formed relative to all that could possibly form. Fig. 7.3 shows the difference between a dense and a sparse network. Dense social ties are thus not always predictive of better outcomes, however. As Granovetter (1973) argued, less intimate connections between people and groups based on infrequent social interaction may nonetheless be critical for acquiring social resources such as job referrals because they integrate the community by bringing together otherwise disconnected subgroups (e.g., bridging capital). Researchers use social network analysis to measure the entire system or structure of relationships and often represent these networks visually. Common measures used to understand relationships in social networks include frequency of interactions, communication, levels of trust, or information and resource exchange.

Drawing on social network theory, Neal (2015) highlights two concepts that are useful to understanding social networks. *Homophily* refers to the tendency for social relationships (i.e., ties) to form between people with something in common more often than between people who do not. This facilitates social relationship development because it allows individuals to connect

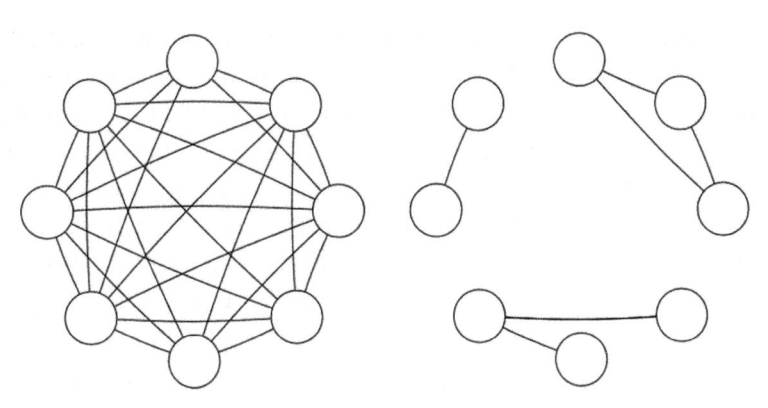

Figure 7.3 Examples of two social networks

around similar interests, whether it's tastes in movies, political leanings, or sharing a similar country of origin. *Proximity* refers to the tendency for relationships to form between people, groups, and organizations who are located nearby more often than with those farther away. Decades of research have demonstrated that homophily and proximity shape the formation of community social networks and recent research suggests that these forces play a role in the development of social ties online (Neal, 2015; Huang, Shen, & Contractor, 2013).

Neal and Christens (2014) suggest three ways social network perspectives offer promise for studying organizational, neighborhood, and community phenomena. First, relational and network perspectives show how relationships serve as links between different levels of analysis. This aids community psychologists in exploring transactions between individuals, settings, and larger social systems. Second, relational and social network perspectives offer sophisticated methods for understanding relationships, contexts, and settings. Third, they suggest that relational and social network perspectives can enrich CP theory and research. For example, Neal and Neal (2011) add to our understanding of power by suggesting that social power is based on an individual's or an organization's structural position within a social network of relationships. In social network terminology, this aspect of social power is captured by the concept of *betweenness,* which measures how many people a person is connecting indirectly through their own direct links (Wasserman & Faust, 1994). Similarly, Burt's (1992) concept of structural holes demonstrates that certain actors in some networks have greater power when their own interpersonal ties span gaps between clusters of densely connected individuals. Gergen (2009) argues that this new vocabulary is needed for psychology to move beyond our traditional conceptions of self and community to understand relationships and networks as primary. A social network perspective offers a window into the complex arrangements of relational ties that exist between people, organizations, and systems within and across various settings.

SNA is a methodology that has been utilized in CP in a variety of distinct settings, such as schools, churches, and coalitions. Freedman and Bess (2011) utilized SNA to examine the "forming" stage of an emergent and locally-based coalition focused on promoting food security. A few years later, a special issue of the *American Journal of Community Psychology* on networks (Neal & Christens, 2014) provided a sampling of the ways network and relational perspectives are being utilized in the field. Papers in this issue explored how individual relationships could provide a more holistic understanding of a setting (e.g., Alia, Freedman, Brandt, & Browne, 2014; Jason, Light, Stevens, & Beers, 2014; Langhout, Collins, & Ellison, 2014; Neal, 2014a) and Christens, Inzeo, and Faust (2014) demonstrated how relationships operate across multiple ecological systems to channel power in community organizing. Other papers highlighted how exploring organizational relationships and networks advance theory and research on larger social systems like coalitions (e.g., Cardazone, Sy, Chik, & Corlew, 2014; Evans, Kivell, Haarlammert, Malhotra, & Rosen, 2014; Neal 2014).

CP researchers in Miami have also applied a social network perspective to the problem of youth homelessness (Paterson, McInerney, & Evans, 2019). In order to map the network of formal and informal resources for homeless youth and determine the level of systems integration, the team worked with community partners to conduct a social network analysis of organizations considered part of the Youth Homelessness Initiative (YHI) in Miami-Dade County. Forty-four organizations were asked about their inter-organizational connections and frequency of communication with other organizations in the system. These data were analyzed and a social network map was created to understand the most central organizations, **network density**, and overall level of system integration (Fig. 7.4). In the network graphic, the ties are lighter or darker based on

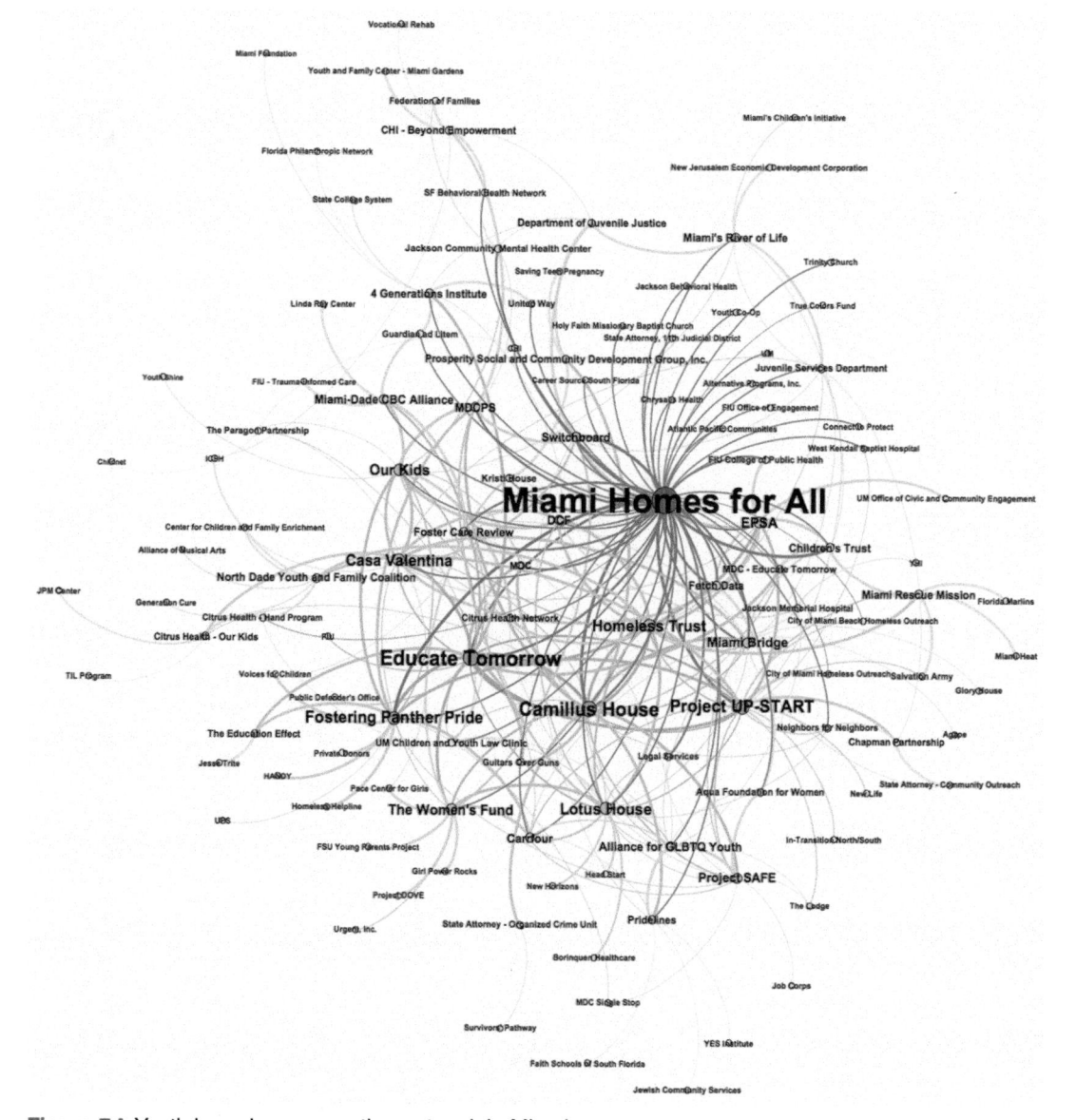

Figure 7.4 Youth homeless prevention network in Miami

Paterson, McInerney, and Evans (2019). *Using social network analysis as a tool in action research* (unpublished manuscript). University of Miami, Miami, FL.

frequency of communication. The darker lines represent the most frequent communication relationships, whereas the very light lines show relationships that are very infrequent. Overall network density was calculated as .021 indicating that only 2 percent of all the possible connections that could be made between organizations are being made in this network. Organizations in the network were not very well connected to each other and that was getting in the way of their ability to work together toward shared goals. Findings were shared with the steering committee of the YHI to serve the broader objectives of creating a stronger network of resources for homeless youth in Miami-Dade County, informing policy advocacy, and putting in place a clear strategy for strengthening the overall network and system of care.

We find much in common between sense of community, social capital, and social networks and with other relational concepts such as social support, neighboring, community cohesion, collective efficacy, community capacity, and citizen participation. In essence, they all deal with the intersection of people, organizations, wellbeing, and community, as well as the power to work together for shared goals. CP researchers have examined the social, cognitive, and affective impacts of interpersonal relationships, relationships between individuals and their environments, and between organizations in systems using several of these conceptual tools. We end this chapter by briefly discussing a concept that is directly related to the presence of strong social capital in communities: community capacity.

Community Capacity

Fawcett et al. (1995) defined community capacity as "the community's ability to pursue its chosen purposes and course of action both now and in the future" (p. 682). They suggested it is influenced by a variety of personal, group, and environmental factors, such as relationships with, and support and other resources from, all relevant sectors and agencies within the community, including educational, health, religious, and business organizations. Chaskin (2001) offers a definitional framework for community capacity based on the literature and research on comprehensive community initiative. He defines community capacity as:

> the interaction of human capital, organizational resources, and social capital existing within a given community that can be leveraged to solve collective problems and improve or maintain the well-being of a given community. It may operate through informal social processes and/or organized effort. (p. 295)

Community capacity, thus, is the combined influence of a community's commitment, resources, and skills that can be deployed to build on community strengths and address community problems and opportunities. *Commitment* is the collective will to act, based on a shared awareness of problems, opportunities, and possible solutions. *Resources* are the financial, natural, and human assets and methods to deploy them intelligently and fairly. *Skills* are all the assets, talents, and expertise of individuals, organizations, and networks that can be marshaled to address problems and seize opportunities (The Aspen Institute, 1996).

One dimension of community capacity touched on in the previous section is the existence of inter-organizational networks that are characterized by reciprocal links, frequent supportive interactions, overlap with other networks, the ability to form new associations, and cooperative decision-making processes (Goodman et al., 1998). Strong social bonds and effective organizations *within communities* provide the foundation as "strong community institutions, like churches, schools and PTAs, fraternal orders, and small-business associations, are essential to integrating individuals into society" (pp. 8–9). In his groundbreaking research on neighborhoods in Chicago, Sampson (2012) found that the density of nonprofit organizations has a notable positive effect on neighborhoods regardless of racial segregation, poverty, or other social conditions that make life in these settings so difficult. "It is the totality of the institutional infrastructure that seems to matter in producing healthy communities" (Sampson, 2012 p. 209). Similarly, Ginwright (2007) suggests that community institutions such as schools, churches, and youth programs that are located in Black communities contribute to the development and maintenance of critical social capital for Black youth and their communities. The combination of individual leadership, organizational capacity, social capital, and networks contributes to a community's capacity to access resources and solve collective problems.

Communities have the capacity to take action on issues of shared concern if four conditions are met: (1) the institutional and social relations are in place to reach all community members; (2) the institutions are accountable to their constituents (members, consumers, citizens); (3) the institutions, collectively and individually, have the ability to mobilize resources to respond to changing conditions; and (4) there is an enabling system (Chavis, Florin, & Felix, 1992) in place to develop and maintain community development and problem-solving initiatives (Chavis, Speer, Resnick, & Zippay, 1993). In order to make progress on the social problems facing communities, they must develop the collective skills and efficacy to design and deploy strategic activity as means to achieve long-term outcomes (Ospina et al., 2012). The development of community capacity and social capital through community development and social policy formulation is important for the promotion of collective wellbeing. Box 7.3 highlights one comprehensive effort to build community capacity for action on a particularly important environmental issue: climate change and extreme weather events.

Chapter Summary

This chapter explored the notion of "community" through a discussion of concepts community psychologists have employed as heuristics and research tools. Rapid change, high mobility, environmental degradation, globalization, and racial, ideological, and ethnic conflict tear at the fabric of community. Research tells us that factors such as social connectedness, social cohesion, trust, community bonds, and civic participation facilitate social interaction and information exchange and that cohesive communities achieve better rates of health, education, tolerance, and safety than fragmented ones. And yet, while the reported positive outcomes are many, it's important to remember that sense of community and group unity can be used to exclude others. It is equally important to keep in mind that the call for community may be used to deflect responsibility from governments from investing adequately in public resources (Blakeley, 2002). Whereas bridging and bonding are desirable qualities of healthy communities, they can restrict opportunities for challenging power structures and for engaging in productive conflict. Although sense of community, social capital, and strong social networks can contribute to health and welfare, it can also depoliticize issues of wellbeing and oppression (Perkins, Hughey & Speer, 2002).

Box 7.3 Miami's Community Resilience Hubs

Miami is among the most weather and climate vulnerable areas of the world. At the same time, the extent of income and wealth inequality in Miami-Dade County is breathtaking. In 2016, *Bloomberg* ranked Miami number one for the largest wealth gap of any major US city (Teproff, 2016). In Miami, 70 percent of residents live in liquid asset poverty; 67 percent of households are one emergency away from falling into debt or losing a home; and 59 percent of County residents have insufficient funds to survive three months after a natural disaster without aid. These two features of vulnerability (weather/climate and social) converge in ways that highlight the reality that lower-income communities disproportionately shoulder the burden of the negative effects of climate change and severe weather events like hurricanes. In the lead-up to hurricane Irma in 2017, the *Guardian* reported that in the lower income neighborhood of Liberty City, only about one in five homes were boarded up or showed other signs of storm protection. By contrast, virtually every property in Miami Beach was replete with sandbags, storm shutters and hurricane-resistant glass (Pilkington, 2017).

Grounded in this understanding that communities of color and lower income communities suffer disproportionate impacts of severe weather events and climate change because they generally have less access to resources to respond and recover, the Communities Building Resilience (CBR) Initiative in Miami seeks to create Community Resilience Hubs in five local neighborhoods. *Community Resilience Hubs* are community-serving facilities augmented to support residents and coordinate resource distribution and services before, during, or after a natural hazard event. They are efforts to increase a community's adaptive capacity and resilience by providing residents with community capacity and access to resources through sites they identify as well-trusted and well-utilized in their community (e.g., community centers, faith-based organizations, recreation centers). They provide trusted locations for residents to gather and gain access to resources year-round while also providing opportunities for local governments and organizational partners to coordinate adaptation, housing improvements, community-building, communication, and civic participation and advocacy efforts through one neighborhood hub (Baja, 2018).

The goal of the CBR Initiative in Miami is to enhance community capacity, social networks, and civic infrastructure through resilience hub activity so that communities can better prepare for, and will be better able to withstand and recover quickly from, a major storm and the effects of sea level rise. In addition to hosting supplies, communications, and resources in the event of an emergency, they serve community members year-round as a center for community-building and community revitalization. Through the hubs, they hope to enable, catalyze, and support community leadership at the local and state levels in order to achieve effective policies and improved government responsiveness to communities' climate-related needs.

All communities are inherently political (Collins, 2010). In other words, our understanding of communities and social connectedness needs to be balanced with an equal understanding of power, rights, and social justice. As Watts (2017) reminds us, "communities and their social and power relations are quite complicated – and dynamic" (p. 282). A community orientation needs to be balanced with an empowerment orientation concerned with the dynamics of power that enable and catalyze effective social action toward liberation and justice (Christens, 2012; Collins, 2010; see also Chapter 4). In describing a "Third Position," Bob Newbrough (1995) outlined a synthesis of the individual and the collective that adds in the principle of equality to balance the three concepts through a dynamic process of justice towards the "Just Community." As we have discussed in earlier chapters, and will return to in the chapters to come, effective action toward liberation and justice requires shifting power relationships within and across communities.

The Resilient Belmont Cragin Community Collaborative (RBCCC)

Judith A. Kent, *National Louis University, Chicago, USA;*

Suzette Fromm Reed, *National Louis University, Chicago, USA;*

James Rudyk, Jr., *Northwest Side Housing Center, Chicago, USA;*

Audrey Stillerman, *Community Wellness Center, Office of Community Engagement and Neighborhood Health Partnerships, Chicago, University of Illinois Hospital and Health Sciences System, USA*

PRACTITIONER COMMENTARY

We didn't realize that we were engaged in the work of CP. We've been practitioners for some years now, and through our university partnership, we are learning to apply the language and the tools of the discipline. We have taken the CP perspective on such concepts as sense of community, social capital, and community capacity. We've applied theory to our practice of inclusion, citizen participation, and the building of social networks and bonding–bridging ties as we work for a better Belmont Cragin. James Rudyk, Jr. makes this consideration in connection with his role as executive director of the Northwest Side Housing Center in the community and with his focus on community organizing and development. A partnership with Dr. Audrey Stillerman, an integrative family physician dedicated to the co-creation with community members of strategies for prevention and healing, led to the partnership with Suzette Fromm Reed and Judith Kent, research consultants from National Louis University. All members of the Resilient Belmont Cragin Community Collaborative (RBCCC), this team has bonded and developed a sustainable relationship based on our shared passion for utilizing Adverse Childhood Experiences (ACEs) as a frame for addressing community issues.

Driven by an understanding of the complexity of our neighborhood, Chicago-based RBCCC built a model of community development that moves beyond a traditional, single-issue, top-down approach to a more all-inclusive, integrative approach involving multiple issues and led by a wide range of stakeholders. Community members, leaders, and advocates created the multi-faceted model in Belmont Cragin, one of Chicago's 77 neighborhoods; ours is a multi-cultural, multi-ethnic, predominantly Latino community that includes White ethnics and Middle Easterners.

In 2014, staff of Northwest Side Housing Center (NWSHC), a key agency in Belmont Cragin, realized the need to embrace complex neighborhood issues in order to successfully address resident housing issues of predatory lending and foreclosures. We also needed to address youth development, public education, health, aging in place, and local small business development. Through a partnership with and grant funding from Local Initiative Support Corporation (LISC) Chicago in 2015, NWSHC initiated a comprehensive community planning process that engaged over 600 residents over 6 months. A clear demonstration of citizen participation, our community created its first-ever, resident-led and -driven community development plan, *The Belmont Cragin Quality of Life Plan: United, Vibrant, and Diverse.* This effort deepened our social networks as community members began to contribute to a better Belmont Cragin with personal and collective benefit.

In 2015, through our Quality of Life Planning efforts and in collaboration with a local high school, we initiated a partnership with Chicago Public Schools and the PCC Community Wellness Center to open a Federally Qualified Health Center at the high school. Partners together explored resources to support the community. Our focus became the impact of ACEs on health, education, and other life outcomes; we considered how best to foster resilience and healing. Our bonding work with Steinmetz youth and parents, expanding to bridging endeavors with healthcare providers, coalesced in December 2016 when, with the support of City of Chicago health center start-up funding, PCC engaged national experts to train community members on childhood trauma and resilience.

In continued community collaboration on the Quality of Life plan, residents identified four issues as community priorities: affordable housing, quality public education, employment and local business development, and access to health resources. Bonding ties were strengthened by ongoing community engagement and the intentional, collective approach to social change through the adversity–resilience–healing frame. Not only did a context for community issues and solutions emerge, but it also sparked a passion among the residents. Shared emotional connection and influence, belonging, and support within an inclusive neighborhood has continued to deepen the sense of community within Belmont Cragin as well as a sense of commitment to working collectively for our common purpose. One example is a group of immigrant mothers who have come together across school, ethnicity, and language boundaries to work with Chicago Public Schools, Chicago Park District, and the City of Chicago to secure 66 million dollars for a new elementary school and community center for their children. This collective of parent leaders were empowered to effect positive change through their increased sense of belonging and mutual support.

Embodying the community's commitment to creating conditions for a thriving, self-healing community, the RBCCC was then formed at the end of 2016. An integral step to building a community resilient to both personal trauma and other, larger community-wide trauma was the creation of the linkages among diverse, multiple stakeholders in the Belmont Cragin social network which resulted in bridging social capital. During the initial three-year Quality of Life planning period, the community sustained our grassroots initiative, and stakeholder engagement grew to over 1,000 residents by 2018.

The RBCCC is a cohesive network of multiple organizations and community members operating under the community-identified adversity–resilience–healing frame. It prioritizes strengthening collaboration at the community level, moving beyond the individually-focused work of each partner organization. Co-creating and disseminating a common language of our frame has laid the foundation for a trauma-informed, healing-centered culture across members and member institutions; three wards of the City of Chicago, one district of the Chicago Police Department, six public health and healthcare organizations, seven social services agencies, and three institutions of elementary, secondary, and post-secondary education are part of the RBCCC.

As members of the RBCCC, we prioritize genuine stakeholder collaboration through shared leadership with residents. This approach places all of us at the table, ensuring that we are embedded in diverse efforts in the neighborhood. We know, and realize with humility, that none of us can build a flourishing community alone, that we must be in relationship with others to meet our goals. Successful RBCCC partnerships have emerged from building meaningful internal and external relationships, those within and beyond Belmont Cragin. These first-degree internal and external partners have shared our extensive external networks locally, regionally, and nationally to create second-degree, external relationships with global experts and practitioners undertaking trauma and resilience in their communities.

Our partnerships have emboldened us to step outside of our comfort zone, to push boundaries, and to be innovative to advance this work through a common vision of a thriving community and the common language of ACEs and community resilience. RBCCC stakeholders can best see, understand, and articulate their role in their own spheres of influence and how that fits into larger plans and actions around healing and thriving. Through continuous co-creating and collaborative implementation of incremental steps toward this shared vision and intentional building of community, our work has steadily grown over a short period of time.

With all relationships and partnerships comes tension. Each RBCCC member and partner agency experiences the need to balance the high time and funding demands within their own settings with additional commitments to partners. While bonding within the community creates internal cohesion, tension can occur in bridging as trust is built with external partnerships. There has been tension between the Chicago Police Department (CPD) and our community because of both the national sociopolitical climate around policing and the perceived lack of historical positive community involvement by the CPD. Active relationship building with CPD officers, including having the CPD host meetings and provide trainings for their staff, has reduced tension. Further tensions exist among community needs, policies, and procedures in a local funding system that is not designed for collaboration. For example, obtaining ethics approval for data collection from our large, chaotic, urban school system to evaluate program effectiveness, a funder requirement, was difficult.

Belmont Cragin has met the challenge between internal cohesion and external relationships to experience continued growth of social capital and sense of community. Thirty community stakeholders attended *On the Table,* a city-wide civic engagement event with the president of the Chicago Community Trust. The RBCCC's hosting of funders' events and fundraising activities has resulted in more than $300,000 for resilience work in the neighborhood.

The neighborhood regularly hosts formal presentations on ACEs and resilience, self-care, and healing followed by community planned, supported, and co-led conversations, which enhances social capital and sense of community. More than 75 parents and community residents and 150 staff from various neighborhood schools have participated. Additionally, twelve individuals from five stakeholder organizations, have completed train-the-trainer's workshops designed to empower residents to lead trainings on ACEs, resilience in the face of childhood trauma, and community healing from trauma. The spring 2019 establishment of an RBCCC steering committee of research, health, and policy experts to support resident-led initiatives serves to ensure that the major influencing voice is that of the people who live and raise their families in Belmont Cragin.

Resident-organized neighborhood celebrations, information and education events that sustain community engagement have contributed to resilience and positive change. For example, Resilience Week in summer 2019 was a multiple-event initiative based on the themes of physical and emotional wellbeing, fitness and nutrition, housing and financial stability, and education. Community residents led celebrations and workshops during this important demonstration of shared purpose and positive change.

Sustainability has proven to be a characteristic of the Belmont Cragin community and the RBCCC. The common language and shared vision of the resident-identified adversity–resilience–healing frame along with resident interviews, focus groups, and community-wide summits attest to RBCCC's commitment to attending to community voice and engagement. In June 2019, the community organized a follow up to *The Belmont Cragin Quality of Life Plan: United, Vibrant, and Diverse* with a 200-person community summit to discuss community vision and how residents want to be involved in ongoing community initiatives. We remain committed to community voice, citizen participation, and sustainability as Belmont Cragin moves ahead in the planning for our future.

The RBCCC network and system has resulted in positive community change across social issues including physical and emotional wellbeing, financial stability, and education. Moving forward, we aim to change the community narrative to one which celebrates and leverages our assets, ownership and agency and returns power to the people. Further, the RBCCC strives to prevent pervasive intergenerational, unresolved childhood trauma by strengthening our sense of community safety and connection, the foundation for resilience and thriving. Our long-term, systems-level goal is to dismantle the structures perpetuating health disparities and unequal distribution of resources in all low-income communities of color, resulting in transformative change in Belmont Cragin and beyond.

Key Terms

Bridging social capital: Relations of respect and mutuality between people who know they are not alike in some sociodemographic sense (differing by age or ethnic group for example).

Citizen participation: A process in which individuals take part in decision making in the institutions, programs, and environments that affect them.

Collective efficacy: A group's shared or common beliefs in its capacity to take coordinated and interdependent action on issues that affect their lives.

Community: The interrelationships and connections of people and settings, including the concepts of sense of community, social support, community capacity, and social capital.

Community building: Attempts to build community capacity and engage residents of communities in solving shared problems.

Community capacity: The interaction of human capital, organizational resources, and social capital existing within a given community that can be leveraged to solve collective problems and improve or maintain the wellbeing of a given community.

Community cohesion: Similar to sense of community, community cohesion refers to the aspect of togetherness and bonding exhibited by members of a community.

Community empowerment: Bottom-up approaches to community change that shift the balance of power to engage community members as agents of community change.

Critical social capital: The development of leadership and political consciousness in marginalized groups as a way to shape political identities and take action to social and material conditions in communities.

Inclusion: With roots in the disability studies, inclusion is concerned with the promotion of equity and access to valued social resources that have historically been denied to oppressed people.

Linking social capital: A form of bridging capital, which connects regular citizens with those in power.

Multiple psychological sense of community (MPSOC): The proposition that we are members of multiple communities and are not limited to experiencing just one SOC.

Network density: The overall level of connectedness in a network which is understood by measuring the proportion of all the ties in a network that have actually formed relative to all that could possibly form.

Sense of community: The sense that one belongs in and is meaningfully a part of a larger collectivity. The concept consists of four domains: (1) membership; (2) influence; (3) integration and fulfilment of needs; and (4) shared emotional connection.

Social cohesion: Refers to the patterns of social interactions and values emerging from social relationships, such as trust and norms or reciprocity.

Social networks: A set of relationships within a social context. These relational ties can be among individual people, groups, organizations, or systems (or some combination).

Social network analysis (SNA): A methodology for measuring the entire system or structure of relationships across a system.

Social support: Positive benefits that stem from social relationships, including emotional support, guidance, tangible and financial support, and socialization.

Resources

Community First! Village: https://mlf.org/community-first/

Lawrence Community Works – a good example of an initiative that takes a Network-Centric Approach to community building: www.lawrencecommunityworks.org/site/

Plastrik, P., & Taylor, M. (2006). NET GAINS: A Handbook for Network Builders Seeking Social Change: http://networkimpact.org/downloads/NetGainsHandbookVersion1.pdf

Understanding community collaborations through social network analysis: www.mdrc.org/chicago-community-networks-study/introduction-social-network-analysis

Katcher, R. (2010). Unstill waters: The fluid role of networks in social movements. Nonprofit Quarterly, Summer, 52–9: https://nonprofitquarterly.org/unstill-waters-the-fluid-role-of-networks-in-social-movements/

COMMUNITY PSYCHOLOGY INTERVENTIONS

II

Introduction to Part II

In Part II of the book, we explore what community psychologists can do to promote liberation and wellbeing through social, community, organizational, small group, and individual interventions. To suggest useful and meaningful action, we have to know the level of analysis and the target of interventions. We begin with the big picture and work our way down to the smallest unit of analysis – the individual. The four chapters emphasize that we have to target multiple levels of intervention in our efforts to promote liberation and wellbeing. Even if we are limited in our ability to act on multiple domains, we have to ensure that our actions promote synergy across domains.

Chapter 8 provides an overview of the philosophy, roles and skills of community psychologists as change agents. Unlike professional schools that propose rigid distinctions among the personal, the professional, and the political, we argue that such distinctions are untenable and even incongruent with the values of community psychology.

In order to exert a positive influence, community psychologists can act as insiders or outsiders. Insiders work in organizations and push for beneficial changes there. Outsiders put pressure on organizations from the periphery. There is plenty to change in society and its institutions to justify effective roles as either insiders or outsiders, but whatever role is chosen, it's important to consider the scope and extent of the desired change as captured in the distinction between first-order or ameliorative and second-order or transformative change (Burton, Kagan, Duckett, & Siddiquee 2011; Prilleltensky & Nelson 2009; Watzlawick, Weakland, & Fisch 1974). As discussed in Chapter 6, amelioration refers to changes that provide support to people within the current system structure (e.g., job counseling for recent immigrants) but do not challenge power imbalances or fundamental structures of injustice and inequality, whereas transformation refers to structural changes that go to the root of the problem (e.g., changing immigration laws that prevent new-comers from obtaining jobs). It may not always be easy to determine if our interventions actually have transformative potential and it may not always be possible or desirable to engage in trans-formative work. However, it's important to be reflective about this distinction and not to delude ourselves into thinking that we are making fundamental changes when we are not.

To promote liberation and wellbeing, either as an insider or an outsider, a community psycholo-gist requires a set of skills. Chapter 8 introduces individual skills (e.g., effective communication, leadership), group skills (e.g., facilitation, conflict resolution) and community skills (e.g., advocacy, partnership building). These skills can be applied in a variety of settings. To put the skills in con-text, we introduce a cycle of praxis consisting of vision, needs, cultural context, and action.

Chapter 9 is about social interventions that operate at the community or societal level. We question the values and assumptions of social interventions, and we critique their limitations. But, shortcomings notwithstanding, there is little doubt that social interventions have the power to influence millions of people through the actions of governments and social movements. The chapter is divided into two main sections: what community psychologists can do in government and what they can do in social movements (SMOs) and non-government organizations (NGOs). Within government, community psychologists can, for example, promote legislation, policies, and programs that invest in human development. In the second part of Chapter 9, we identify roles for community psychologists within SMOs and NGOs (e.g., coalition builders, activists). These roles help in recruitment, public education campaigns, protests, strategic planning, and political efficacy overall. The chapter offers a wide-ranging menu of options for community psychologists to act as agents of change in society at large.

Chapter 10 deals with interventions at the organizational and community levels. We believe this level of involvement and intervention by community psychologists is important because most community change happens in, and through, organizations and inter-organizational collabora-tions. We ask what community psychologists can do to build organizational capacity to make these settings empowering for the members and effective at promoting change in the community. Organizations that do not promote the wellbeing of workers cannot be effective in promoting the wellbeing of citizens. We review the characteristics of empowered and empowering organizations and identify roles for community psychologists that will enable them to bring about the desired qualities. At the inter-organizational level, we look at the role of collaborations, partnerships, and networks in addressing complex social problems and creating collective impact. We will review the role of community psychologists as conveners, facilitators, managers, collaborators, and partners.

The final chapter of this section, Chapter 11, addresses the dynamics involved in small group and individual interventions. In keeping with the theme of accountability, we discuss the struggle with the tension between ameliorative and transformative work. Is it fair to expect people who suffer exploita-tion and oppression to become activists when they are hurting? Is it fair not to expect them to do this and treat them only as victims? We offer some paths towards resolution of these dilemmas. In doing so, we articulate the skills that a community psychologist would want to rely on in individual and small group work. Our framework for this chapter combines the qualities introduced in Chapter 10 with stages of change. We believe that people don't jump towards personal or social change. People require a warm-up period prior to committing to any kind of lasting change. Therefore, we strongly suggest being in tune with people's readiness for change. Once a change has been accomplished, we must endeavor to make it sustainable and to disseminate it to other communities of interest.

AN OVERVIEW OF COMMUNITY PSYCHOLOGY INTERVENTIONS

8

Warm-up Questions

In the field of education, much has been written about school improvement, school change and educational reform. Based on your extensive experience in schools as a student, make a short list of a few ways that schools and education could be improved. After you have made this list, try to cast aside all your assumptions about schools and education and think again, a little harder this time, about how schools and education could be radically transformed. Make a short list of some more fundamental changes in education.

1   Compare the two lists. How do they differ?

2   How hard was it to make the second list? Why?

Learning Objectives

The core concepts and framework that we introduce in this chapter serve as a foundation for the remaining chapters in this section, in which we go into more depth about interventions at the social (Chapter 9), organizational and community (Chapter 10), small group, and individual (Chapter 11) levels of analysis.

In this chapter you will learn about

- The community psychologist as an agent of social change
- The goals, framing, and process of community psychology (CP) interventions
- Different settings for CP interventions

The Community Psychologist as an Agent of Social Change: Connecting the Personal, Political, and Professional

In this section, we discuss the role of the community psychologist as an agent of social change. However clear we are as community psychologists about our values, the world of action is one that is complicated and rife with conflicts, contradictions, and ethical dilemmas. When we try to change the status quo, we inevitably run up against many obstacles and much resistance, including our own blind spots and weaknesses. Creating social change is a struggle. Our values are constantly challenged in the intervention work that we do. Sometimes we experience value conflicts and have to decide which values are most important in a particular context. At other times, we have to choose between many different ways of implementing our values.

In addition, for us to change and to help others to change, we need to understand how social influences prevent us from transforming our attitudes and behavior. In particular, we need to understand our relationship to our own power and privilege. Many theories claim that society influences us. We claim that society does not just influence us; society is in us. It is not just a matter of society shaping our ways; we embody society within ourselves. Therefore, it is very hard to be critical of society when we are it, and it is very hard to be critical of ourselves when society doesn't want us to be critical of the status quo. We are part of the status quo; we are the very society we wish to criticize.

The Making of a Community Psychologist

We believe that being a community psychologist is a question of identity, a definition of who we are and who we want to be, independent of where we work or study or what our official title is. Each community psychologist is a whole person. As whole people, our personal, political, and professional selves are intertwined. One cannot be a community psychologist in one's public life at work and then go home to one's private life and "turn off" the values that inform one's work as a community psychologist. Rather the personal and political, the private and public, and the professional and citizen parts of the community psychologist come together through a journey of "conscientization" – the process of gaining awareness of the conditions that oppress people – and **"praxis"** – critical "reflection and action upon the world to transform it" (Freire, 1970, p. 33).

Moreover, each community psychologist has a unique personal journey that brought them to the field. As Ira Goldenberg (1978) observed some time ago:

> Social interventionists are not born, they are made.... The making of a social interventionist can best be understood in terms of a process through which certain classes of events become the experiential ground for subsequent social actions which, if not defined as "deviant," are acknowledged to fall outside the mainstream of expected or anticipated behavior. The process itself, which is rarely smooth or predictable, is punctuated by specific circumstances which are no less socially salient than they are personally significant. (pp. 29 and 34)

Like Goldenberg (1978) and others (e.g., Langhout, 2015; Reyes Cruz & Sonn, 2011; Sloan, 2000), we believe that community psychologists need to be reflexively aware of their values, experiences, and power, and to relate their personal biographies. Our values and social analyses are not fixed entities, but rather constantly emerging perspectives on both where we are currently and where we want to be. **Reflexivity** is an important antidote to arrogance, dogma and believing that we have the right answer. The point is that personal, political, and professional growth is an ongoing process, not an end state.

Reflexivity and accountability are necessary to unpack personal privilege. An example that illustrates this point is male privilege. All of us authors grew up in sexist, patriarchal societies, in which many privileges were, and still are, bestowed upon the male members of our team, simply by virtue of our gender. In 2015, for example male professors in the US earned on average $18,300 more compared to their female colleagues (or put another way, women made approximately 84 percent of what men earned) (Hatch, 2017). Finally, we want to make clear that connecting the personal and political comes through our relationships with others. It is important to build a support network and sense of community and to have places where we can be nurtured, sustained, and challenged in our growth as community psychologists. Community psychologists need a peer group of like-minded people from CP, other academic disciplines, and the community, committed to social justice and social change. Moreover, we need to be genuinely supportive of one another and appreciative of our strengths. There is a danger that conscientization can be stifled if the group climate is one of competition, evaluation, and constantly calling each other out, focusing on who is the most "pure" or righteous in the enactment of their values.

Can I Make a Living Disrupting the Status Quo? Community Psychologists as Insiders and Outsiders

If CP is more of a social movement than a profession (Rappaport, 1981), we must ask how community psychologists are going to make a living. Who is going to hire and pay them to disrupt the status quo? Not surprisingly, community psychologists find employment based on their professional credentials rather than their values or political beliefs. Most often doctoral-level community psychologists are hired to work in university, research, or government policy settings, and masters-level and doctoral-level community psychologists work in a variety of human service settings, including health, education, mental health, child welfare and children's mental health, counseling, and others. Because of their broad training in research and action, graduates of CP have little problem finding job opportunities that require the skill-set that they have acquired through their graduate training (O'Donnell & Ferrari, 2000; Johnson-Hakim & Boal, 2017).

While community settings may hire community psychologists, they will nevertheless resist efforts by community psychologists and others to change the status quo. In a previous publication, Isaac and Geoff identified some ways in which community psychologists working as insiders or consultants in a variety of these settings can challenge the status quo and strive to shift the paradigm of practice (Prilleltensky & Nelson, 2002). Scot and colleagues have also written about how community psychologists can work with their organizations to promote critical community practice (Evans, Kivell, Haarlammert, Malhotra, & Rosen, 2014; Evans, Hanlin, & Prilleltensky, 2007; see Chapter 10). Community psychologists as leaders, program managers, teachers/professors, and researchers can work within their organizations and institutions to promote more just organizations and **transformative** practice. There are always dangers and concerns about "rocking the boat," but many settings provide at least some latitude for change. A good role for the community psychologist here is that of a critical friend: somebody who can challenge you and provide constructive feedback because you trust that your friend has your best interests at heart (Evans, 2015).

Community psychologists can also work outside the system for social change. Those who work independently, or for one setting, can be hired to work as external evaluators, consultants, or researchers for another setting. They can often have considerable influence in working for social change in these outsider roles (Evans, 2015; Evans & Kivell, 2015). There are also situations in which community psychologists are not invited by a setting but work as unsolicited interventionists. In other words, the community psychologist approaches a setting or community to partner on some project or intervention. Finally, community psychologists can work in their private lives as change agents. As citizens, they can join and participate in a variety of social change organizations and activities.

The Community Psychologist as a Professional

While community psychologists work collaboratively with community groups and de-emphasize the "expert" role, they are trained professionals who have a set of core competencies and skills (Dalton & Wolfe, 2012; Nelson, Poland, Murray, & Maticka-Tyndale, 2004). Through formal training, community psychologists learn not just to integrate values and experience, but action, research, and theory as well. In this section, we focus on intervention or praxis skills, realizing that these are interrelated with research skills.

Over the last several decades a significant effort has been put towards the identification of core competencies for CP practice, both to inform educational programs and to communicate to potential employers the kind of skills and training they can expect from hiring a community psychologist. Thomas, Neill and Robertson (1997), for example, made a distinction between core or foundational knowledge, skills and competencies, and skills for professional praxis. Similar lists of competencies were developed by Nelson and Prilleltensky (2010) and Dalton and Wolfe (2012). Building upon this earlier work, the Council of Education Programs of the Society for Community Research and Action generated a list that is available on their website (www.communitypsychology.com/competencies-for-community-psychology-practice/). All of these lists overlap significantly, demonstrating the shared understanding in the field. In Table 8.1, we list the main competencies and skills associated with the two broad domains of intervention identified by Thomas et al. (1997).

Table 8.1 Domains, competencies, and skills for CP intervention

Domains	Competencies	Skills
Core/foundational	Assumptions	Understand the central role of power in the social world; frame problems in terms of power inequities; challenge victim-blaming assumption; focus on strengths
	Values	Clarify the vision and values on which interventions are based; advocate for values that promote liberation from oppression; and personal, relational, and collective wellbeing
	Principles and theories	Understand and apply CP concepts and theories (e.g., prevention, empowerment, sense of community); use ecological and systems approaches to intervention focusing on group, organizational, community, and social change, rather than individualistic approaches
Professional praxis	Personal effectiveness	Personal reflection and conscientization; communication skills (basic attending and influencing, assertiveness, leadership, setting boundaries)
	Partnership and collaboration	Consultation; group process facilitation; organization development; community development; partnering with diverse stakeholders, including disadvantaged people; team-building
	Technical competencies	Project management; grant-writing; oral and written communication skills

The core knowledge and foundations of community intervention refer to the basic assumptions, values, concepts, and theories of CP that we presented in Chapters 1 and 3, while the competencies and skills of professional praxis, identified by Thomas et al. (1997) include (a) personal-effectiveness skills (e.g., communication and interpersonal skills), (b) collaboration skills (e.g., consultation, networking, partnering), and (c) technical skills (e.g., skills in grant-writing, research, evaluation). This latter set of competencies and skills cannot easily be learned in the classroom. Supervised community service learning and practicum placements in community settings are necessary to provide trainees with real-life experiences in community intervention (Bennett & Hallman, 1987; Evans, Nelson, & Loomis, 2009).

In this section, we have discussed a number of issues relating to the community psychologist as an agent of social change. Becoming a community psychologist involves more than acquiring professional credentials. It is a process of identity development in which the community psychologist develops a self-critical awareness in the context of their life experiences in the larger social and political milieu. This identity development involves connecting the personal, political, and professional parts of oneself. We noted different ways in which community psychologists can function as insiders and outsiders, disrupting the status quo and creating social change. While few settings will employ people as social change agents, we discussed some possibilities that permit community psychologists to make a living and bring about change. Finally, we provided an overview of some of the core competencies and skills that characterize community psychologists as professionals.

The Focus of Community Psychology Interventions

Aims of Community Psychology interventions

In this section we examine the focus of CP interventions. The aim of any CP intervention is to change circumstances for the purpose of improving the wellbeing of individuals, groups, and communities (Nelson & Prilleltensky, 2010). Prilleltensky (2012) defined wellbeing as "a positive state of affairs, brought about by the simultaneous and balanced satisfaction of diverse objective and subjective needs of individuals, relationships, organizations, and communities" (p.2). *Objective needs* refer to material and physical needs required for survival and thriving (e.g., food and shelter) while *subjective needs* include the emotional and psychological nutrients required for flourishing, such as having a sense of control and being valued by others (Diener, Lucas, Schimmack, & Helliwell, 2009; Prilleltensky 2012). According to Prilleltensky, wellbeing is related to justice and is best considered a continuum ranging from suffering at the lowest level, to confronting unjust conditions, to coping, and, at the most optimal level, thriving. Thriving is both the process of striving to achieve one's full potential and the state of being fulfilled, such as when an individual experiences full life satisfaction (Buettner, 2010; Prilleltensky, 2012). Or, in reference to the capability approach introduced in Chapter 4, people thrive when they experience real opportunities to do and be what they have reason to value (Munger, MacLeod, & Loomis, 2016). As Holzkamp (1983), Sen (1999b), Nussbaum (2003), Wilkinson and Pickett (2009), Prilleltensky (2012), and others have argued, distributive and procedural justice provide the optimal conditions under which people and communities thrive. Following the discussion in Chapter 6, under sub-optimal conditions of justice, people's wellbeing is compromised. Many people and communities will try to cope with these sub-optimal conditions by finding ways to optimize their wellbeing within the given conditions (e.g., by dealing with the negative emotions the conditions evoke or by gaining more access to power). In the worst case of persisting conditions of injustice, people experience significant suffering.

Thus, as community psychologists, our interventions can be aimed at raising critical consciousness among oppressed groups under persistent conditions of injustice, and promoting their empowerment to resist their oppression; we can support people and communities to cope with the sub-optimal conditions of justice; or we can work alongside communities and their allies in their fight for creating optimal conditions of justice. While all of these interventions are important, there is an inherent danger to settle on helping people to cope with sub-optimal conditions rather than trying to change them. That is, the support provided to affected communities, while well intended, could actually hurt them in the long-term by strengthening the status quo. On the other hand, it can be challenging for individuals and communities to fight an unjust system when they struggle to meet their basic needs or have deeply internalized oppression and feel hopeless. Under these circumstances it may be important to first address these immediate needs before broader collective change can be targeted. But, this should always be considered as a step towards more significant transformations. Ultimately, our interventions should aim at shifting the balance of political, economic, and social power toward optimal conditions of justice. Thus, how we frame issues, and how that guides our overall strategic approach, is important.

Framing the Issue

As discussed in Chapters 1 and 6, how social issues are **framed** often dictates what interventions will be used to address those issues (see also Seidman & Rappaport, 1986). The distinction between **ameliorative** and transformative approaches discussed in Chapter 6 is useful here. Ameliorative interventions tend to frame issues as problems and as technical matters that can be resolved through rational empirical problem-solving (Sarason, 1978; Nelson & Prilleltensky, 2010). The contributions of higher-level ecological factors and structures and power dynamics are often ignored or minimized in this formulation. For example, macro-level health promotion interventions may aim to change social norms and practices regarding eating, drinking, smoking, and exercise to prevent heart disease or other health problems. Issues of power and exploitation, such as the role of tobacco companies in promoting nicotine addiction, or the fast food industry (McDonald's, Coca Cola) in promoting an unhealthy diet as well as how the stress of inequality and poverty contribute to people engaging in these behaviors, are seldom addressed. In addition, individuals and communities affected by these health issues are often perceived as people at risk who need to be educated or guided rather than as partners in advocating for changes to the system that puts profit before people.

Transformative interventions, on the other hand, frame issues in terms of oppression and inequities in power, and emphasize the strengths of people rather than their deficiencies (although an increasing number of ameliorative approaches are also strength-based). While research and problem-solving are used to address the issue, the overall focus is on liberation from oppression and changing the social systems that give rise to unhealthy conditions and behaviors. Gender, race, and class are examined as intersections of oppression, and vulnerable groups are engaged in a process of consciousness-raising about themselves and their political reality. The larger macro context of global capitalism is seen as overarching specific risk and protective factors at the micro and meso levels of analysis. The social determinants of health are examined to understand the "causes of the causes" and address them at their root.

Both ameliorative and transformative approaches may examine issues and problems in terms of an ecological perspective that is attuned to multiple levels of analysis. However, more often than not, ameliorative interventions are targeted at the personal and relational levels. Prevention programs that strive to enhance competence and build social support are examples. When the macro level is addressed in ameliorative interventions, power dynamics at that level are often insufficiently considered or completely ignored, such as the contributions of large food, tobacco, and pharma companies and their lobby groups.

In transformative interventions, issues and problems are examined in terms of power dynamics that are conceptualized as occurring at multiple levels of analysis. In transformative interventions, a systems approach to social change is taken (Christens, Hanlin, & Speer, 2007; Foster-Fishman, Nowell, & Yang, 2007; Foster-Fishman & Watson, 2017). Intervention occurs at all levels of analysis, but there is concerted effort to change power relationships and to alter the fundamental nature of the system. The collective level of analysis is in the foreground, even for interventions at the personal and relational levels. An example of this is a smoking prevention program that Isaac developed with the Latin American community in Kitchener-Waterloo, Canada, in which children and parents engaged in social action against cigarette companies (Prilleltensky, Nelson, & Sanchez Valdes, 2000).

Also, in transformative approaches there tends to be a more explicit consideration of how values inform the choices of specific interventions. While both approaches are linked to values of holism, health, and caring and compassion, in transformative interventions greater emphasis is placed on the values of self-determination, participation, social justice, respect for diversity, and accountability to oppressed groups.

Intervention process

While we agree with Rappaport (1981) that there are multiple valid solutions to complex social issues, we believe there are certain approaches and processes that are more conducive to resulting in transformative changes. Ameliorative interventions tend to use an "expert-driven" and professional approach (Nelson, Amio, Prilleltensky, & Nickels, 2000). These interventions are often also service-oriented, helping a client to find solutions to a specific issue. The community psychologist uses their knowledge of risk and protective factors and program models to design the intervention. Often standardized intervention methods and tools are used. If theory is applied, it is primarily in the context of evidence-based practice, that is, the application of empirically-validated interventions, or in the context of theories of change related to program evaluations. A positive development over the last couple of decades is that strength-based and collaborative approaches are increasingly being used in the context of ameliorative approaches. While this raises the chances of moving toward transformative change, the scope and extent of these interventions are still mostly incremental and locally oriented, rather than aiming at broader shifts in political, economic, and social power.

Table 8.2 Cycle of praxis

Dimensions	State of Affairs	Subject of Study	Outcome
Vision and values	What should be the ideal vision? What values should guide our vision?	Social organizations that promote a balance among values for personal, relational, and collective wellbeing	Vision of justice, wellbeing and empowerment for oppressed communities
Cultural and social context	What is the actual state of affairs?	Psychology of individual and collective, as well as economy, history, society, and culture	Identification of prevailing norms and social conditions oppressing minorities
Needs	How is the state of affairs perceived and experienced?	Grounded theory and lived experience	Identification of needs of oppressed groups
Action	What can be done to change undesirable state of affairs?	Theories of personal and social change	Personal and social change strategies

Source: From Prilleltensky and Nelson (2002).

Approaches most conducive to promoting transformative change acknowledge the complexity of getting at the root cause of social issues. They are conducted in solidarity with marginalized communities, focused on collective action that challenge the status quo of existing power structures, and are emerging and engaging in a cycle of action and reflection. Prilleltensky and Nelson (2002) suggest that to guide the process of transformative change, one has to be clear about values, social and cultural context, people's needs, and strategic action. This requires a back and forth between the application of values, action, critical reflection (including the use of theory), and learning, which is commonly referred to as "praxis," as popularized in the context of critical pedagogy, especially by Paulo Freire (2006).

The cycle of praxis described in Table 8.2 was introduced by Prilleltensky and Nelson (2002) as a way to capture this constant cycle of reflection and action. Each one of the four elements of praxis in this table addresses a specific set of questions and has a concrete outcome. When the outcomes of the four components come together, they create a powerful synergy. This is what we are after when we participate in efforts to create transformative social change. The cycle of praxis can be applied not only to social change but also to processes of organizational and community renewal as well.

While social change organizations can be effective in seeking transformation, sometimes they can perpetuate injustice within them, as we will see in Chapter 10. Group members can have different views, styles, and backgrounds. This can create strain, tension, and sometimes internecine conflict. In our experience, it is not important that coalition members agree on everything. What is important is that members strive to find common ground to advocate on those issues on which there is agreement. To guard against our personal tendencies to monopolize agendas or neglect others' contributions, we recommend looking at the tools for social change in Box 8.1.

Box 8.1 Tools for Working for Social Change

1 Practice noticing who's in the room at meetings – how many men, how many women, how many White people, how many people of color. Is the majority heterosexual, what are people's class backgrounds? Don't assume you know people. Work at being more aware.

2 Count how many times you speak and keep track of how long you speak. Count how many times other people speak and keep track of how long they speak.

3 Be conscious of how often you are actively listening to what other people are saying as opposed to just waiting your turn and/or thinking about what you'll say next.

4 Practice supporting people by asking them to expand on ideas and get more in-depth information before you decide to support the idea or not.

5 Think about whose work and contribution to the group gets recognized. Practice recognizing people for the work they do and try to do it more often.

6 Work against creating an internal organizing culture that is alienating for some people. Developing respect and solidarity across race, class, gender and sexuality is complex and difficult, but absolutely critical.

7 Be aware of how often you ask people to do something as opposed to asking other people what needs to be done.

8 Remember that social change is a process and that our individual transformation and liberation is intimately connected with social transformation and liberation. Life is profoundly complex and there are many contradictions.

Source: Courtesy of Professor Douglass St. Christian, Department of Anthropology, University of Western Ontario, Canada.

Roles for Community Psychologists

Since ameliorative interventions frame issues and problems typically as technical matters that can be resolved through rational and empirical problem-solving, the role of the community psychologist is to lend their professional expertise to the community to solve problems. The roles of program developer and program evaluator are emphasized. The professional expertise of the community psychologist is in the foreground, while the political role of the community psychologist is in the background. Goldenberg (1978) argues that the roles of social technician and social reformer characterize the ameliorative approach. Social technicians and reformers work with those who hold power; they identify with and accept the goals of existing settings; they emphasize adaptation to social conditions; and they do not believe that transformative change, as we have discussed it in this and previous chapters, is needed.

Since transformative interventions frame issues and problems in terms of oppression and inequities in power that require resistance and liberating solutions, the role of community psychologists is to work in solidarity with oppressed groups to challenge the status quo and create social change. Social and political action is emphasized, along with program development and evaluation. The political role of the community psychologist shares the foreground with the professional role. In contrast to the previously mentioned roles of social technician and social reformer, Goldenberg (1978) argues that **social interventionists** work with oppressed groups; they do not identify with or accept the goals of existing settings; they emphasize conscientization; and they believe that fundamental social change is needed.

As we have discussed, the aim of CP interventions is to improve wellbeing at multiple levels. Wellbeing can be conceptualized along a continuum from suffering to thriving. What level of wellbeing we are aiming at has a lot to do with the way we frame the issue and the processes we engage to create change. The distinction between ameliorative and transformative interventions provides a way to capture some of these differences. Currently, many CP interventions tend to be more ameliorative in nature, leading several community psychologists to call for a more critical CP (Angelique & Kyle, 2002; Evans, Duckett, Lawthom, & Kivell, 2017; Kagan et al., 2011; Prilleltensky & Nelson, 2002; Reyes Crus & Sonn, 2011). Our point here is not to suggest that ameliorative interventions are not worthwhile; they are useful and important. Rather, what we are suggesting is that greater emphasis needs to be placed on transformative interventions. Unless we challenge unjust social conditions and power inequities, we will be forever engaged in ameliorative interventions. While we have emphasized the contrast between ameliorative and transformative approaches in this chapter, in practice it is possible to blend the two. To conclude and build upon the definition by Nelson and Riemer (2014), a **(critical) community psychology intervention** can then be defined as an intentional process put in place to positively affect the wellbeing of individuals, groups, and/or the broader population by promoting changes toward optimal conditions of justice.

Settings for Interventions

Across the world, community psychologists work in a variety of settings. In our view, there are three main settings in which we can practice the trade of CP: (1) human services; (2) **alternative settings**; and (3) settings for social change. But there is one more setting where our professional skills and our lives intertwine – home.

Community Psychology Begins at Home

By 'home' we mean the place where we live, study, train, work, and play. In other words, it is not just what we do from 9 to 5, or what we do when we wear the official community psychologist hat. It is what we do all the time. Since values and social ethics inform all aspects of our human experience, not just our professional work, community psychologists try to promote these values in all spheres of life. The values we presented in Chapters 1 and 3 apply to relationships with our family, peers, co-workers, fellow students, and community members. It would be inconsistent with the value of accountability to witness injustice at home and remain silent, just as it would be absurd to behave compassionately towards community members but despotically towards family members.

This does not mean that we have to behave like formal professionals all the time and that we have to treat our friends and relatives as if they were in need of help. Not at all – it simply means that we try to incorporate our values at home as much as at work. We do this naturally because it is part of who we want to become, not because we are supposed to wear a community psychologist badge all the time.

This natural integration of values into our lives makes our profession exciting. It affords us an opportunity to become more integrated human beings, trying to do what is beneficial for us, our partners, relatives, friends, and our communities at the same time. In the university setting, for example, CP faculty members can promote wellbeing among the students by making sure courses are accessible, financial stress is reduced by providing teaching and research assistantships or scholarships, and by jointly advocating for needed structural changes in the university (e.g., increasing the number of faculty members from Black, Indigenous, and other racialized groups).

Table 8.3 Settings, examples, and roles for community interventions

Settings	Examples	Roles
Human services	Community mental health agencies Independent living centers Department of community services Department of public health School board Child and family services	Program developer Program manager Program evaluator Human resources manager Health promoter Unit manager
Alternative settings	Women's shelters Community economic development corporation Resource center for people with HIV/AIDS Self-help group run by community members Immigrant and refugee advocacy center	Social advocate Team leader Community developer Group facilitator Board member
Social change settings	Public interest research group Social policy institute Trade and labor unions Political parties	Researcher Public speaker Policy developer Writer

Human Services

"Human services" is a generic term for organizations providing health, mental health, disability, housing, community, and child and family services, among others. These organizations can be part of government, funded by government, or funded by charities or private agencies. Some human-service agencies receive funding from a combination of sources – government, charities, and foundations. In Table 8.3 we see some examples of the various settings, along with possible roles for community psychologists.

Examples of human services include community mental health centers, children's mental health services, counseling agencies, alcoholism and substance abuse treatment facilities, child welfare agencies, community-based correctional services, and services for people with disabilities. These services are typically staffed by psychologists, social workers, and a variety of other health and social service professionals and afford community psychologists an opportunity to redefine ways of helping.

Community psychologists can promote change as insiders or outsiders. In either case, chances are that some resistance will be encountered from management and workers alike. Sometimes the resistance derives from diverse strategies; sometimes it derives from divergent values. If the former is the case, a partnership for change is possible. If the latter is the case, we may have to reconsider our ability to work with organizations that do not share our vision and values. To guard against unpleasant surprises, Cherniss (1993) pointed out that before considering an intervention in a human service organization, it is important to consider such questions as:

- Whose interests will be served?
- Is there value congruence between the change agent and those with whom they will be consulting?
- What form will the intervention take (e.g., action research, consultation, skills training)?
- What previous interventions have been tried and with what success?

Along with our colleagues Leslea Peirson and Judy Gould, we [Isaac and Geoff] consulted with a children's mental health agency in a review of its mandate. A value-based approach was used as the foundation for organizational change (Peirson, Prilleltensky, Nelson, & Gould, 1997; Prilleltensky, Peirson, Gould, & Nelson, 1997). As consultants, we negotiated with the agency to have an advisory committee with representation from management, staff, board members, parent consumers, service providers from other agencies, and members of the community at large. The primary guiding values of the mandate review were self-determination (what stakeholders want), collaboration (participation of stakeholders), and distributive justice (how stakeholders believe the agency should allocate scarce resources). Focus groups and survey questionnaires were used to gather data regarding the agency's values and vision, needs, resources, and mission from a wide range of stakeholders, including young people involved with the agency, non-referred young people, parent consumers, non-referred parents, agency workers and board members, school personnel, and other service-providers. This approach was designed to be highly inclusive in gaining input on stakeholders' views about what the mandate of the agency should be.

When we were first interviewed for the job of the mandate review, we explicitly acknowledged our bias in favor of prevention, and staff were concerned that we would impose our agenda on them. We indicated that while we were biased towards prevention, decisions about prevention versus treatment would be made by them, not us. In the end, the staff also wanted more prevention! We had an initial disagreement on strategies for children's mental health, but not on values. We asked agency staff and other service providers how they would allocate the budget of the agency to different service areas. Respondents indicated that 39 percent of the budget should be devoted to prevention and consultation programs. While the agency did provide some prevention programs at the time of the review, these findings suggested that it should increase its commitment to prevention. In our follow-up with the agency, we found that several of the final recommendations and directions were being implemented by the agency. Another interesting finding emerged from this change process. When young people were asked what mattered to them, they stressed the importance of employment opportunities; making sure parents, teachers and service providers listen to and understand them; youth support groups for different problems; and prevention programs. In other words, the young people wanted community change and community-oriented intervention approaches, not traditional clinical services. For us, these findings underscored the value of involving the young people themselves in the process of change. Other examples of transformative work in the human service sector can be found throughout the book (e.g., the shifts in mental health work discussed in Chapter 1 and Chapter 20).

Alternative Settings

Alternative settings are voluntary associations that are created and controlled by people who share a problem or an oppressive condition. Within alternative settings there is a strong emphasis on creating a supportive community, non-hierarchical structures, holistic approaches to health, consensual decision-making, and horizontal organizational structures that promote participation and power-sharing, building on the strengths of diverse people who do not "fit" into existing programs and advocacy for social change. Such settings are formed as an alternative to mainstream organizations that are not based on these same values and which often blame the victims for not adjusting to existing social conditions (Reinharz, 1984). Community psychologists can assist in the creation of such settings, as well as with ongoing consultation.

Self-help/mutual aid organization (also referred to as peer support) is an example of an alternative setting (Humphreys & Rappaport, 1994; Nelson, Kloos, & Ornelas, 2014; see also Chapter 20). Self-help/mutual aid groups have several characteristics. They are small groups in which people who share a common problem, experience, or concern come together to both provide and receive support. Members are equals, and the groups are voluntary and not for profit. There is a wide variety of such groups and organizations including the following: loss-transition groups (e.g., bereavement groups, separation/divorce support groups); groups for people who do not have a problem themselves but who have a family member with a problem (e.g., parent support groups, Al-Anon and Alateen); stress, coping, and support groups (e.g., AA, psychiatric survivor groups); and consciousness-raising and advocacy groups (e.g., Mothers against Drunk Driving, women's groups). There is a large range of different types of self-help groups available to people and their popularity has increased in recent decades. There are several thousand mental health self-help groups in Australia, the UK, and the US, for example. In the US, these are utilized by over 2 million adults annually (Markowitz, 2015). Increasingly, self-help/mutual aid groups also take place in online settings (Barak, Boniel-Nissim, & Suler, 2008). By hosting self-help/mutual aid groups online, participants are given more flexibility and can protect their identity if they wish (Chambers, Canvin, Baldwin, & Sinclair, 2017).

How should professionals relate to self-help groups? When self-help group members are asked this question, they basically state that they want professionals to be "on tap but not on top" (Constantino & Nelson, 1995). In other words, self-helpers want professionals to practice good partnership, emphasizing respect, collaboration, equality, and appreciation for the knowledge and experience of self-helpers. One vehicle through which professional and self-help collaboration has occurred is through self-help clearinghouses and resource centers (Brown & Rogers, 2014; Madara, 1990). Self-help resource centers are organizations that promote the self-help concept through information and referral, education, networking, consultation, and research. Community psychologists can assist self-helpers through research and evaluation, consultation and advocacy. However, it is crucial that community psychologists act in an empowering manner rather than in a way that promotes professional dominance and consumer dependency (see Box 8.2. as an example).

Box 8.2 Community Psychologists Help in Alternative Setting

Our colleagues Mary Sehl (1987) and Ed Bennett used a community development approach to create an 80-unit housing cooperative with affordable rents for new Canadians. Sand Hills Cooperative Homes became a springboard for a variety of other community-based initiatives. For example, Isaac became involved with Latin American families in the Sand Hills project, and together they formed the Latin American Educational Group. Using a participatory action research approach, the group identified the need to promote the Spanish language skills of children and prevent smoking (Prilleltensky, 1993). Heritage language classes were created, as well as a smoking prevention program with a community action component which addressed the role of cigarette companies in promoting youth addiction to tobacco (Prilleltensky, Nelson, & Sanchez Valdes, 2000; Prilleltensky, Nelson, & Peirson, 2001).

Settings for Social Change

Of all the settings where community psychologists can practice their trade, this is perhaps the most neglected and, at the same time, the most important area. On the continuum of transformation, this is the end where most profound change may be accomplished. Community psychologists have an opportunity to participate in social movements as organizers, consultants, researchers, and as citizens exercising their democratic rights to have a voice (Maton, 2000). There are social change and **social movement organizations**, described in Chapter 10, which have great potential to go beyond amelioration and towards transformation.

There are a number of social movement organizations (SMOs) with which community psychologists could ally themselves. In their influential article on this topic McCarthy and Zald (1977) describe an SMO as "a complex, or formal organization which identifies its preferences with a social movement or a counter-movement and attempts to implement those goals" (p. 1218). These include anti-poverty movements (see Chapter 14), feminist movement organizations (see Chapter 16), gay and transgender movement organizations (see Chapter 18), among many others. These organizations are often coalitions of groups and individuals who view themselves as a part of broader movements for social change. The guiding vision is one of a society free of racism, sexism, heterosexism, poverty, violence, and environmental degradation; a society which celebrates diversity, shares the wealth and practices equality, peace, sustainability, and preservation of the natural environment.

Some social movements begin with efforts by alternative settings. Some of the social issues identified in Chapter 1, such as discrimination, racism, powerlessness, stigma, and others, have been picked up by groups that have grown into social movements. Some psychiatric survivor self-help organizations have been vocal in protesting against psychiatry and for the civil and social rights of people who have experienced mental health problems (see Chapter 20). Self-help organizations for people with disabilities have actively lobbied for resources and for the rights of citizens with disabilities (see Chapter 19). The Independent Living Centres (ILCs) movement in the US and Canada is a good example of advocacy by people with disabilities. ILCs are cross-disability, consumer-driven, and community-based self-help organizations that have a sociopolitical analysis of disability. ILC advocates have pushed for a new paradigm approach to disability policy and practice, emphasizing consumer control, housing, employment, mutual support, and civil rights (Lord & Hutchison, 2007). Similarly, rape crisis centers have been a focal point for feminists organizing for social change (Campbell, Baker, & Mazurek, 1998), and social enterprises such as co-ops have provided alternatives for profit-oriented businesses (Weber & Geobey, 2012).

In this section we reviewed settings for interventions. Unlike other professions that advocate a separation between personal and professional life, in CP we are pleased to combine our professional values with our personal lives. Hence, the practice of CP begins at home. Home means the places where we live, work, study, socialize, and play. We can wear the official community psychologist hat in diverse settings, including human services, alternative settings, and social change organizations.

Chapter Summary

The aim of this chapter was to provide an overview of CP interventions. The next three chapters expand on social, community, organizational, small group, and individual interventions. As community psychologists we blend the personal, the political, and the professional. This amalgam of roles enables us to be as influential as we can in our personal, civic and occupational lives and promote conditions for people to thrive. To be as useful as we can, we need to develop technical skills, aptitudes for collaboration, and personal effectiveness skills. These skills may be used for amelioration, transformation, or a combination of the two. Whereas amelioration refers to interventions designed to promote wellbeing, transformation refers to interventions aimed at changing power relations in society that underpin many of the barriers to wellbeing in the first place. The last section of the chapter dealt with four settings for interventions: home, human services, alternative settings, and social change.

Key Terms

Alternative settings: Settings that are designed to be alternative to, and are often in opposition to, mainstream or traditional settings (e.g., an alternative school).

Ameliorative: An approach to intervention that focuses on improvement, rather than fundamental change, of underlying assumptions, values, and power structures, also known as first-order change.

Critical community psychology intervention: An intentional process put in place to positively affect the wellbeing of individuals, groups, and/or the broader population by promoting changes toward optimal conditions of justice.

Framing: Reframing how social issues are conceptualized or understood; transformative interventions involve reframing the way issues are typically understood.

Praxis: The integration of theory and practice in social intervention; it includes attention to cultural context, vision, action and needs.

Reflexivity: The subjectivity and social location of community psychologists in their roles as social interventionists, including the privileges that they enjoy.

Social interventionist: One who engages in transformative social change, as contrasted with social technician and social reformer roles.

Social movement organization: An organization that is specifically dedicated to transformative social change.

Transformative: An approach to intervention that focuses on fundamental change of underlying assumptions, values, and power structures; also known as second-order change.

Resources

Websites in Community Psychology

Mark Burton and Carolyn Kagan maintain the website for CP in the UK. The website contains very useful information: www.compsy.org.uk. Click on the general leaflet about CP at Manchester Metropolitan University. The leaflet provides an excellent overview of roles and skills for CP interventions.

The Consortium for the Advancement of Social and Emotional Learning is supported by the work of many community psychologists working in schools. Roles and skills for work in this field are covered: www.casel.org.

Many of the skills covered in this chapter relate to working with others in groups and communities. An excellent overview of community collaboration: www.communitycollaboration.net

The Community Toolbox, developed and maintained by the Center for Community Health and Development at the University of Kansas, provides excellent resources, examples, and tools for interventions at multiple ecological levels: http://ctb.ku.edu/en/default.aspx

Relevant Journals

- Journal featuring CP practice internationally, *Global Journal of Community Psychology Practice*: www.gjcpp.org/en/
- Journal devoted to theory and research on social action called *Mobilization*: www.mobilization.sdsu.edu/index.html
- *Journal for Social Action in Counseling and Psychology*: www.psysr.org/jsacp/

Books

Bond, M. A., Serrano García, I., and Keys, C. B. (Eds.). (2017). *APA handbook of community psychology* (Vol 1 & 2). Washington, DC: American Psychological Association.

Prilleltensky, I. & Nelson, G. (2002). *Doing psychology critically: Making a difference in diverse settings*. London: Red Globe Press.

Scott, V.C. & Wolfe, S.M. (2015). *Community Psychology: Foundations for Practice*. Thousands Oak, CA: Sage.

SOCIAL INTERVENTIONS

9

Warm-up Questions

Picture a delicious apple pie. Now imagine that whole pie represents 100 percent of the wealth owned by residents of the US. If you split the population of the US into five equal groups with the top wealth holders in the top 20 percent, the next highest wealth holders in the second 20 percent and so on, how much of the overall pie do you think each of the five groups hold? Start with the top 20 percent of wealth holders – how big is their slice of pie? What about the bottom 20 percent? Draw it out on a piece of paper if that helps you visualize it.

Getty Images/iStockphoto

Once you have a picture of what you *believe* the distribution of wealth in the US looks like, think about what you think the distribution of wealth *should* be. How are these pictures different? Michael Norton and Dan Ariely (2011) surveyed US citizens about the distribution of wealth and discovered two things. First, people dramatically *underestimated* the current level of wealth inequality (check out this video infographic to see how accurate your estimate is – www.youtube.com/watch?reload=9&v=QPKKQnijnsM&feature=youtu.be). Second, all demographic groups – even those not usually keen on wealth redistribution – desired a far more equal distribution of wealth than the status quo.

If you buy into community psychology's concern for social justice, what is a more just distribution of wealth? If you believe that wealth should be distributed more equitably, how do you propose we make it so? What would be the best way to challenge the system and create something new? Sadly, since Norton and Ariely's publication in 2011, the gap between the rich and the poor has become even wider. This has led some to worry that "if wealth inequality in the United States continues to soar at its current rate, the top 10 percent of Americans could own 100 percent of the nation's net worth by 2052" (Johnson, 2019).

Learning Objectives

In this chapter you will learn about

- What social interventions are
- Why social interventions are important
- The value base of social interventions
- How social interventions promote wellbeing and liberation
- The strengths and limitations of social interventions

The Social Determinants of Wellbeing

Meet Richard Wilkinson, world-renowned health scientist based in the UK. Through the publication of *Unhealthy Societies: The Afflictions of Inequality* (1996), Wilkinson changed the way many people think about health and wellbeing. He reported in this book, and subsequent works with Kate Pickett (2009; 2017, 2019; Pickett & Wilkinson, 2015), the results of comparative studies on health, inequality, and longevity. Main conclusion: unless we change the social environment in which people live, and reduce levels of wealth and income inequalities, our chances of improving health and wellbeing are minimal (see also Gray, 2001). Based on his studies, Wilkinson regrets the current state of affairs in the helping professions.

Sometimes it is a matter of providing screening and early treatment, other times of trying to change some aspect of lifestyle, but always it is a matter of providing some service or intervention. This applies not just to health, but also to studies of a wide range of social, psychological, developmental, and educational problems. What happens is that the original source of the problem in society is left unchanged (and probably unknown) while expensive new services are proposed to cater for the individuals most affected. Each new problem leads to a demand for additional resources for services to try to put right the damage which continues to be done. Because the underlying flaw in the system is not put right, it gives rise to a continuous flow, both of people who have suffered as a result, and of demands for special services to meet their needs.

The US Institute of Medicine concurs. In a study by this institute at the beginning of the century, the research committee recommends the endorsement of a "social environmental approach to health and health intervention" (Smedley & Syme, 2000, p. 3). The co-chairs of the committee reported that

> societal-level phenomena are critical determinants of health ... Stress, insufficient financial and social supports, poor diet, environmental exposures, community factors and characteristics, and many other health risks may be addressed by one-to-one intervention efforts, but such efforts do little to address the broader social and economic forces that influence these risks. (Smedley & Syme, 2000, p. 3)

Their point is that "fixing individuals" without "fixing societies" is obviously not enough. Make no mistake; this situation applies not only to health but also to psychosocial problems, discrimination, exclusion, and marginality. We cannot eliminate racism by eliminating one racist at a time when the cultural norms uphold discrimination.

As discussed in Chapter 6, it is not enough to change "downstream" individual-level factors such as lifestyle factors. We also have to change "upstream" societal-level factors such as public policies. As Nosrati and Marmot (2019) observe, "the 'causes of the causes' of ill health do not operate in isolation from one another and they tend to be mutually shaped at the intersection of powerful political and economic forces" (p. 377). Hence, social and economic policy and practice may be the major route to improving overall wellbeing (House, Schoeni, Kaplan, & Pollack, 2008; Wilkinson & Pickett, 2017). There are beneficial health effects of certain educational, income-support, civil rights, employment, welfare, and housing policies. In the education arena, for example, early childhood interventions and policies promote advanced education. The longer people stay in school, the healthier they become. In the civil rights arena, immediately following the implementation of the policy in the sixties, there was a remarkable improvement in the cardio-vascular health of African American women (Kaplan, Ranjit, & Burgard, 2008).

While we applaud the change in focus from the personal to the collective, we question whether the new focus will lead to transformational or merely ameliorative changes in society. Are more social services the answer to oppression and discrimination? Will more Band-Aid solutions reduce the effects of economic insecurity? We think not. Though necessary, it is insufficient to shift focus from the personal to the social level. Once we work at the social level, we have to make sure that we will try to transform systems of oppression and inequality. We do not want to perfect systems that ultimately contribute to oppression and ill-health.

In this chapter, we explore **social interventions (SIs)** and discuss their implications for second-order change and for transformation. In the next chapter, we discuss community and organizational interventions. Here we concentrate on large-scale interventions driven by either governments or **social movement organizations (SMOs)** and **non-governmental organizations (NGOs)**.

What Are Social Interventions?

Social interventions are intentional processes designed to affect the wellbeing of the population through changes in systems, values, policies, programs, distribution of resources, power differentials, and cultural norms (Bennett & Hallman 1987; Hawe, Shiell, & Riley, 2009; Maton, 2000; Seidman, 1988). By intentional processes we mean interventions that are methodically planned and carefully executed. To achieve wellbeing at the personal, relational, and collective domains, we have to attend to the various components provided in the definition above. To alter values without altering policies and programs is ineffectual. Re-writing policies without allocating more resources to the poor is merely window-dressing.

Our definition, we agree, sets a very high standard for what constitutes a valid SI. We expect this to change values, programs, policies, and power relations. This is, indeed, a tall order. But, we argue, if we want to achieve transformation, as expressed in Chapters 6 and 8, then we must make an effort to go beyond the current state of affairs. We approach this task with conviction but also with great humility. We acknowledge that others before us have tried and understood the enormity of the task. This is not a deterrent, but rather a call to humility.

In general terms, SIs can be driven by government or by NGOs. Within government, community psychologists can work as "insiders," trying to implement policies and programs that liberate people from oppressive forces (including government itself). Outside government, community psychologists can work in or alongside SMOs (e.g., Anti-nuclear Movement, Extinction Rebellion, #blacklivesmatter) and NGOs (e.g., Greenpeace, Oxfam, Amnesty International, The Children's Defense Fund).

In the Belly of the Beast

To the average citizen, governments look like huge and amorphous structures that have a life of their own. Yet they consist of real people sitting in offices, making decisions that affect the lives of thousands and sometimes millions of people. Change in government policies is never quick, but community psychologists have an opportunity to influence policy directions by being inside the "belly of the beast" (Jason, 2013; Maton, 2017; Maton, Humphreys, Jason, & Shinn, 2016; Phillips, 2000). Through the collection of taxes, governments have enormous resources at their disposal. How to use the money is a question of intense debate within government and across the political divide.

From the outside, government may seem ugly, "political" and contentious. In fact, it often is. But if we don't become involved, who will? If we resign ourselves to the exclusive role of outsiders, we will never have direct access to decision-making power or influence. This is a definite risk. Many people are put off by the idea of politics. The media have managed to equate politics with corruption and waste. But the fact is that politics is the vehicle for the transformation or preservation of just or unjust policies. As Margiola Reyes Cruz reminds us in her commentary in Chapter 4, it is political power that holds the most potential for transformative change. It is possible that well-intentioned people may wish to pursue other avenues for social change, but it is essential to realize the strengths and limitations of each approach. Community psychologists understand that we need both bottom-up organizing and government support for major social changes to happen (Christens, 2019).

Governments are not monolithic entities. That is, not all parts of governments follow the same policy, and not all members of a particular ministry agree on policies and priorities. The challenge for community psychologists is to insert themselves in places where change can be promoted and to find sufficient supports within and outside government for their work. True, the work is hard, but the rewards can be enormous. Changing policies that will improve the wellbeing of millions of people can be very satisfying. Imagine if you were instrumental in implementing a more progressive taxation system, redistributing wealth from the top 10 percent of the population to the bottom 30 percent (George, 2002). Or if you were able to secure unemployment insurance for people made redundant due to plant transfers to developing countries. Or what if you participated in legislation to extend medical insurance to the entire population? For example, the Affordable Care Act enacted in the US in 2010 halved the number of citizens without health insurance, with estimates ranging from 20 to 24 million additional people covered during 2016. Those would be pretty major achievements.

Challenging the Status Quo

Often, governments are at fault for failing to provide adequate resources for disadvantaged communities. When policies and practices discriminate, or fail to protect those with less power, it is time to challenge the status quo. In this chapter we will review SIs that vary in the degree to which they challenge the structures of power. Some social movements, such as the civil rights movement in the US and the anti-apartheid movement in South Africa challenged power structures and sought to change the distribution of rights among Black and White people (Freeman, 1999; Seedat, Duncan, & Lazarus, 2001). Other SIs target local government and are satisfied with less ambitious aims, such as better services or public transport (Orr, 2007; Smock, 2004; Speer & Hughey, 1995). Yet other efforts, such as community **coalitions**, seek to promote health, prevent HIV/AIDS, reduce violence, or to improve systems (Bess, 2015; Christens et al., 2016; Emshoff et al., 2007; Foster-Fishman & Watson 2012, 2017; Freedman, Ketcham, & Bess, 2011).

Either from the inside or from the outside, the principle to remember is that we are there to link the immediate concerns of citizens with larger structures of inequality. We should not deny the immediate needs of abused children or rape victims. They must be carefully looked after. But if we want to prevent future instances of rape and child abuse, we have to look upstream. We should keep one eye on the river and one eye on the bridge.

The Value-base of Social Interventions

We have to distinguish between the overall values we wish to promote and the particular values we need to advance in a concrete situation. The values expressed in Chapters 1 and 3 call for the promotion of personal, relational, and collective wellbeing. Our aim is to balance values of self-determination, caring and compassion, and respect for diversity with principles of social justice and sense of community. As John Ralston Saul (2014) observed, the merit of values is judged by their relative contribution to an overall state of wellbeing, achieved through tension and balance among complementary principles.

For a first step, this seems enough. We keep in mind the complementary set of values – not a single value, but a set of values – discussed in Chapter 3. But this is only the first step. Next, we have to ascertain what values are neglected in a particular social context and devise strategies to bring them from the background to the foreground. We agree that sense of community is a desirable aim for human societies, but if it turns into pressure to conform, the overall wellbeing of the individual is bound to suffer. We also agree that social justice must be fought for when it is absent; its pursuit, however, should not detract from caring about the partners with whom we collaborate.

Value-driven processes are goals in themselves. Because of that, we have to concern ourselves with the value of accountability. How can we make changes in societies and how can we be held accountable for our actions? As noted in Chapter 3, without accountability, all the other values remain theoretical. Goethe (1906) put it well: "knowing is not enough; we must apply. Willing is not enough; we must do" (p. 130).

The Importance of Social Interventions

Social interventions are important for seveal reasons.The first and obvious one is that without SIs we can forget about the promotion of wellbeing and liberation. If we were living in an ideal society, devoid of conflict and blessed with plenty, we may not need to worry about liberation and struggles. But that is not the case; the scale of disparity and suffering is immense. In formulating a new global agenda for health equity and sustainable development in 2015, the General Assembly of the United Nations adopted the development agenda: "Transforming our world: the 2030 Agenda for Sustainable Development" (United Nations, 2015b). In this report, they describe why we need bold action on the 17 Sustainable Development Goals (https://sustaina bledevelopment.un.org/sdgs):

> We are meeting at a time of immense challenges to sustainable development. Billions of our citizens continue to live in poverty and are denied a life of dignity. There are rising inequalities within and among countries. There are enormous disparities of opportunity, wealth and power. Gender inequality remains a key challenge. Unemployment, particularly youth unemployment, is a major concern. Global health threats, more frequent and intense natural disasters, spiralling conflict, violent extremism, terrorism and related humanitarian crises and forced displacement of people threaten to reverse much of the development progress made in recent decades. Natural resource depletion and adverse impacts of environmental degradation, including desertification, drought, land degradation, freshwater scarcity and loss of biodiversity, add to and exacerbate the list of challenges which humanity faces. Climate change is one of the greatest challenges of our time and its adverse impacts undermine the ability of all countries to achieve sustainable development. Increases in global temperature, sea level rise, ocean acidification and other climate change impacts are seriously affecting coastal areas and low-lying coastal countries, including many least developed countries and small island developing States. The survival of many societies, and of the biological support systems of the planet, is at risk. (p. 5)

The second reason is that we need SIs because individual and programmatic approaches are not adequate to address the range of problems that we collectively face (Evans, Kivell, Haarlammert, Malhotra, & Rosen, 2014; Maton, 2000). As noted elsewhere in the book, individual interventions are prone to blame victims, to be ineffectual, to stigmatize, and to deflect attention from structural predicaments (see, in particular, Chapters 5 & 6). Social interventions are also important because they address power differences and their impact on health and wellbeing (see Chapter 4). Social interventions aim to help people not only cope with the stresses of society, but to transform oppressive systems and structures (Evans, Duckett, Lawthom, & Kivell, 2017). SIs are our main vehicle for the promotion of transformational or second-order change.

In this review we concentrate primarily on SIs that are, or have the potential to become, transformative. We review the actions of governments, NGOs and SMOs and the roles of community psychologists within these settings. In the next chapter we consider the case of citizen participation in community development, organizations, partnerships, and coalitions.

The Role of Community Psychologists Working in Government

For radicals and activists, this question in the title doesn't make sense. After all, isn't government the main culprit of many of our social ills? This is only partly true. Although it is fashionable to blame governments for most of our problems, we have to remember that they are the custodians of public resources. Of course, some do a better job than others at safeguarding our natural resources and protecting public institutions, but that doesn't make government antithetical to the idea of wellbeing; it only makes some of its policies antithetical to it (Chomsky, 2000).

Let's consider first some of the more **ameliorative interventions** of governments. In some countries, Departments of Health make sure the water is potable and that every child is vaccinated. They also promote healthy eating and exercise (Marmot & Wilkinson, 2005; Smedley & Syme, 2000).

Departments of Education provide free education and literacy training. Ministries of Transport make sure that cars do not emit illegal levels of pollutants and that most regions have access to adequate public transportation. These are some of the bread-and-butter activities of governments and they rarely challenge the societal status quo; they don't question the power structures. Although in wealthy countries we take these activities for granted, poor governments struggle to provide any kinds of water and transportation at all (Collier, 2007).

Some governments, however, engage in more than amelioration. Rich and poor countries alike can create profound changes in the wellbeing of the population. Some can even contribute to the liberation of oppressed groups within them. But national governments, especially in the Southern hemisphere, are subject to regulations imposed by the International Monetary Fund (IMF) and by the World Bank that interfere with their ability to improve quality of life. Many would argue that large multi-national corporations and the non-democratic international trade organizations that protect their business interests are restricting the good that governments can do for its citizens. In countries of the Northern hemisphere, corporations put pressure on governments to cut taxes and reduce public spending.

One way to understand the influence of corporations and the IMF on governments is *globalization* (Gamble, 2001; Klein, 2007; Pilger, 2002; see also Chapters 5 and 15). Fighting globalization has become an important role for governments bent on protecting the sovereignty of their countries. The pervasive influence of corporate power in government exists throughout the world, so much so that we now have a word for it – **corporatocracy**: a system of government that serves the interests of corporations (Perkins, 2005, 2016; Sachs, 2011). Understanding the influence corporations and international trade organizations have on democracy and how people mobilize to resist corporatocracy is a major growing edge for CP.

In poor or rich countries, community psychologists can combat the negative aspects of globalization and corporatocracy and assist in the promotion of **human development**. They can work in any one of the following state, provincial, or federal ministries: human services, community services, child and family services, health, urban planning, multiculturalism, care of the elderly, disabilities, and others.

Key roles for community psychologists working in any of these government departments are **program developer** and **program evaluators**. Governments develop multiple projects in the fields of health, education, community development, mental health, recreation, multiculturalism, urban planning, and others. Program developers work with various levels of government to implement new initiatives. In Ontario, Canada, for instance, a government officer worked with several communities to implement the Better Beginnings, Better Futures Program, an early intervention and prevention project (Nelson, Pancer, Hayward, & Kelly, 2004; Pancer, Nelson, Hasford, & Loomis, 2013; Worton et al., 2018). This officer collaborated with various communities and teams of researchers in implementing the initiative. Starting in the early 1990s, the government officer wanted community members to be well represented in the planning and execution of the program. In order to ensure resident participation in the various stages of the program, she instituted a procedure whereby all committees should consist of at least 51 percent of local residents. This enabled a great deal of resident participation throughout the many sites of the project in Ontario. Although seemingly a simple intervention, the psychologist opened the door for community members to gain meaningful participation (Pancer & Cameron, 1994). Consistent with the values of CP expressed in Chapter 3, this community psychologist made a difference from within government.

As community psychologists, our skills in collaboration and partnership creation can make a positive contribution to programs, as can our knowledge on what works, what doesn't, and how to evaluate programs (Chinman et al., 2008; Cook, 2015; Macnaughton et al., 2015; Nelson, et al., 2014; Scott et al., 2019). Government interventions such as Better Beginnings, Better Futures and similar projects require resident participation, collaboration across sectors, value-based partnerships and a social change agenda that goes beyond amelioration. By engaging community members in the process of human development, community psychologists can play a role in the empowerment of disadvantaged groups.

Another important role for community psychologists within government is that of **health promoter**. Community psychologists can work with community groups to examine local conditions that lead to poor health and design collaborative strategies to improve the built environment and access to affordable, healthy food. The media have been used successfully in various countries to improve health and prevent the risks of cardiovascular disease and lung cancer (McAlister, 2000). In addition, community psychologists in government can work with various human service organizations to increase the support they give to people with severe mental health problems (see Chapter 20).

Promoting Equality

Based on international comparisons, Wilkinson and Pickett (Wilkinson 1996; Pickett & Wilkinson, 2015) arrived at the conclusion that countries with a smaller gap between a rich and poor produce healthier outcomes for their citizens than countries with a large gap. Because of more egalitarian income distribution, the life expectancy of Japanese people dramatically increased by 7.5 years for men and 8 years for women in the 21 years from 1965 to 1986. Japanese people experience the highest life expectancy in the world, almost 80 years, in large part because in that period of time they became the advanced society with the narrowest gap in income differences. Communities with higher levels of social cohesion and narrow gaps between rich and poor produce better health outcomes than wealthier societies with higher levels of social disintegration. We have known for a long time that poverty is a powerful predictor of poor health (Marmot & Wilkinson, 1999), but now there is strong evidence that equality and social cohesion are also powerful determinants of wellbeing.

As Wilkinson observed, social cohesion is mediated by commitment to positive social structures, which, in turn, is related to social justice. Individuals contribute to collective wellbeing when they feel that the collective works for them as well. Social cohesion and coherence are "closely related to social justice" (Wilkinson, 1996, p. 221). The discussion on housing policy and attitudes toward homelessness in Chapter 1 is a good example of that.

The job of promoting equality is particularly challenging for community psychologists. It is challenging because most societal structures reflect and reproduce inequality (Korten, 2015; Ryan, 1994). As *policy developers*, community psychologists have a chance to influence, to some extent, policies, programs and practices that affect inequality. Based on research, information provided by social planners, government priorities, and values, policy developers create new laws and programs that can affect the lives of millions of people. This type of work is very well suited for community psychologists, as it integrates knowledge of research, community needs, and interventions (Macnaughton et al., 2015; Maton, 2017; Maton, Humphreys, Jason, & Shinn, 2017; Phillips, 2000). The work of Hiro Yoshikawa and colleagues (Britto, Yoshikawa, & Boller, 2011; Yoshikawa et al., 2013) on early childhood development (ECD) is an example of research and policy recommendations that can influence inequality in education in order to affect both early and later human development, in cognitive, health, and socioemotional domains. Many of their policy recommendations deal with closing the gap between rich and poor children.

Overcoming inequality in schooling is a major arena of intervention for community psychologists. Rhona Weinstein (2002), recipient of the 2001 award for contributions to theory and research in CP from SCRA, outlined possibilities for action for community psychologists at research and policy levels. Education, for Weinstein, is a basic human right of which many minority children are deprived due to discriminating policies and practices in schools and communities. In a famous 1954 case in the US (Brown vs Board of Education), Kenneth Clark, a former president of the American Psychological Association, submitted evidence regarding the deleterious effects of segregation on the mental health of Black children (Clark, 1974). That evidence was highly influential in promoting racial integration in schools. If full equality in education were achieved in most countries, a truly transformational leap could take place in the world. In the US however, the current trend toward privatization of public schools puts the delivery of education services into the hands of private, for-profit corporations. Many believe that privatization weakens public schools and sacrifices the rights and opportunities of the majority for the presumed advantage of a small percentage of students (House, 2018; Ravitch, 2013).

Another potentially **transformative intervention** is the development of policies that redistribute wealth and income. Community psychologists can develop policies for demonstrating the positive effects of equality on wellbeing, as shown by Pickett and Wilkinson (2015), and try to develop policies to implement progressive tax laws that redistribute wealth from the richest echelons of society to those in need, such as single parents without supports (George, 2002). Alternatively, they can develop policies that challenge exclusion and discrimination.

As *action researchers*, community psychologists can influence policy processes through the dissemination of relevant data. Community psychologists can contribute to the policy process using action research, the ecological framework, and social justice values (Maton, Humphreys, Jason, & Shinn, 2017). Research conducted on the benefits of the Pathways to Housing program model of Housing First in New York City drew attention in the US and internationally because research findings showed that a majority of individuals with serious mental illness who were chronically homeless were able to successfully become stably housed (Tsemberis, 1999; Tsemberis & Eisenberg, 2000). These findings helped to convince Health Canada to fund the At Home/Chez Soi project through the Mental Health Commission of Canada to implement in five Canadian Cities (Keller et al., 2013). The model has been adopted across western Europe (Aubry, Bernad, & Greenwood, 2018; Greenwood, Stefancic, Tsemberis, & Busch-Geertsma, 2013) and Australia (Johnson, Parkinson, & Parsell, 2012).

Community psychologists can work alongside community groups to both expose injustice and learn about what works (see Chapters 12 and 13). Critical social psychologist Michelle Fine has had a long career of partnering with youth and communities to expose and challenge inequities in, and privatization of, public education through participatory action research to try to effect policy change (Cammarota & Fine, 2008; Fine, Burns, Torre, & Payne, 2008; Fine et al., 2004). She is the founder of the Public Science Project (http://publicscienceproject.org/) that partners with communities to design, conduct, and support research and practice aimed at interrupting injustice.

Psychologists with a social, community, and developmental orientation have secured influential positions as advisors to legislators and policy makers. In a few cases, psychologists have successfully run for public positions (see Lorion, Iscoe, DeLeon, & VandenBos, 1996). Community psychologist

Debra Starnes served as city councilwoman in Atlanta for several terms (Starnes, 2004). In accepting the award for Distinguished Contribution to Practice in Community Psychology from SCRA in 2004, she urged community psychologists to get in the policy arena:

> Governing bodies need your values, your education, your tenacity and endurance … your ability to inquire and interpret and your sense of fairness and justice – and we need these things at the decision-makers' level, where decisions are made daily, that affect people's lives. (p. 6)

To strengthen the connection between CP and public policy we recommend more training programs such as the one developed at the Florida Mental Health Institute (Weinberg, 2001), continued leadership by the Public Policy Committee of the Society for Community Research and Action (www.scra27.org/what-we-do/policy/), and more policy-oriented research (Maton, 2017; Maton, Humphreys, Jason, & Shinn, 2017; Nelson, 2013).

Protecting National Resources and the Public Sector

We move now from the national to the international scene. Whereas in the past powerful countries invaded territories and dispossessed people of their resources by brute force, in the present, international lending agencies pressure poor countries to open their markets to foreign competition (Gamble, 2001). Whereas in the past, raw materials and slave labor were extracted from colonies, nowadays economic empires expect the poor to buy their products (Korten, 2015). In many instances, as in the case of Haiti (Aristide, 2000), countries became poor precisely because of a history of colonization, oppression, and dependency. Forceful contact with colonizers not only depleted environmental resources but also tarnished social traditions of native groups. In the case of Indigenous Australians this resulted in economic deprivation, psychosocial problems and health outcomes comparable to so-called Third World countries (see Chapter 15).

As poor countries depend – often because of histories of colonization – on foreign loans, lending institutions like the International Monetary Fund (IMF) dictate terms and conditions that demand cuts to social services, health care, and public education (Gamble, 2001). Economic growth and efficiency, touted as the only way to prosperity, require the privatization of public utilities and services, resulting in massive unemployment of public sector workers and restricted access to health, education (Korten, 2015; Shaoul, 2001), and sometimes even water, as in the case of Ghana.

The case of rice producers in Haiti illustrates the dynamics of globalization quite well. Governments are forced to open markets and lift restrictions on imports; local producers have to compete with cheaper foreign products that are either subsidized or produced with more efficient equipment. Once the local competition is eliminated, prices go up and fewer people have access to them (Aristide, 2000; Korten, 2015; Weisbrot, 1999).

The public sector often comes under attack by policies of privatization. In the field of education, for instance, soon after hurricane Katrina hit New Orleans in 2005, there was a concerted effort by promoters of free market capitalism to replace the public school system with vouchers and charter schools (Klein, 2007). Similar school privatization efforts are underway in Puerto Rico after hurricane Maria, sparking island-wide protests (Klein, 2018). The belief that competition will offer poor students better choices resulted in the flight of good teachers, principals, and students from poor schools to magnet and charter schools, lowering even further the quality of education in disadvantaged communities. As Hargreaves and Fink (2006) observe:

> Schools and school leaders are on an uphill slope. Injustice is everywhere. When American schools were segregated by race, governments introduced busing and integration, only to see wealthy whites take flight to protected enclaves in the suburbs. Because people in many countries have historically separated themselves into different communities by class or race, turning their local schools into segregated institutions, some reformers suggested market choice and magnet school and charter school options so that minorities and the poor wouldn't be confined only to what their own neighbourhoods could offer. However, market and magnet school strategies ended up exaggerating the injustices even further as the affluent parental "tourists" exercised their right to choose, while "vagabond" parents with few financial or social resources were left even further behind. (p. 148)

As if promoting equality at the national and global level was not difficult enough, imagine how hard it would be to challenge global policies. Psychologists working in government have limited opportunities to resist globalization. If they live in rich countries, most of their governments espouse globalization because they want access to new markets. If they live in poor countries, their governments have limited options for resisting globalization. Opposing globalization is something that may be easier to do from outside government. In the next section of this chapter we explore some opportunities to use psychological research and action in solidarity work at the national and international levels (see, for example, the work of Psychologists for Social Responsibility at www.psysr.org and the Society for the Study of Peace, Conflict, and Violence at https://peacepsychology.org/).

It is challenging for community psychologists to fight global economic trends. One way they can do this is by linking with external groups to put pressure on government to be accountable to the people. Using our knowledge and skills of empowerment, citizen participation, and social change, community psychologists can open doors to citizens to enter the halls of power and learn the rules of the game. In one telling case, residents of Better Beginnings, Better Futures communities organized themselves, with the help of government psychologists, to fight budget cuts in their funding. The programs withstood various changes in governments and several ministers with shifting political agendas.

Strengths and Limitations of Government Social Interventions

The resources held by governments enable them to create profound change: sometimes positive sometimes negative. The benefits, which can be classified into four categories, speak to the issue of sustainability (Fullan, 2005; Hargreaves & Fink, 2006):

1 *Breadth*. Government action on health, education, transportation, housing, and human rights can reach far and wide and touch almost every citizen of the country. New laws banning smoking or discrimination against same-sex couples affect everybody in urban and rural regions. This benefit may be regarded as wide horizontal impact.

2 *Depth*. Changes promoted by governments affect not only vast geographical regions but within each location they affect human beings deeply. Each individual is affected by human rights legislation or a progressive taxation system. Government interventions have the potential to lift children and families out of poverty and to prevent epidemics by massive immunization campaigns.

3 *Length*. Once a change is written into the law, interventions can last a long time. New educational policies can last decades, as can mental health initiatives such as deinstitutionalization. The longevity of the changes can have profound impacts on people's lives.

4 *Sustainability*. Once a commitment is made, resources are likely to be made available until a change in power takes place.

Some of the weaknesses of government action can be gleaned from preceding discussions. In brief, they are:

1 *Ameliorative*. The first risk of government action pertains to its ameliorative nature. Almost by definition, governments do not want to alter power structures. This would constitute self-depowerment, a noble aim but not one characteristic of people in office. As a result, we risk interventions that primarily engage in bandaid approaches (Taylor, 1996).

2 *Conservative*. In a similar vein, many policies concentrate on changing individuals and not the social environment. Even with the best of intentions, governments often end up blaming the victim (Ryan, 1971). Too often, rather than opposing globalization and other elite-driven programs designed to reshape the world to meet corporate needs, governments serve the same interests, perhaps reducing corporate damage but never threatening corporate power. Too often, government dampens popular support for change by supplying the appearance of justice rather than the reality (Fox, 1999).

3 *Regressive*. In some instances, governments are not only conservative, they are outright regressive. Austerity measures in the UK are a case in point. Since 2010 in the UK, the Conservative government has initiated more than 30 billion pounds in cuts to welfare payments, housing subsidies, and social services leading one United Nations expert to suggest that efforts by the government to pare state spending were "entrenching high levels of poverty and inflicting unnecessary misery in one of the richest countries in the world" (Kingsley, 2018, para 2). Researchers estimate that up to 900,000 more people could fall into poverty in the UK due to Brexit (Britain's move to leave the European Union) (Joseph Rowntree Foundation, 2018). The decimation of the public service and safety nets has also happened in developing countries resulting in disproportionately negative impacts on children and women (Ortiz & Cummins, 2013). Even when government administrations do make some positive changes, these gains can be reversed by the next administration. The Obama administration in the US was able to open up access to health care for millions through the Affordable Care Act only to see efforts to dismantle these benefits come during the Trump administration. Sadly, even when government-targeted policy-level changes are championed by community psychologists, they do not do enough to directly challenge neoliberalism (Nelson, 2013).

Dilemmas Faced by Community Psychologists Working in Government

Governments change, and with them their philosophy and pilots. The crew does not get to choose the pilot. If the pilot's philosophy is congruent with the crew's, there will be a smooth ride, but if it differs, it is usually the crew who have to change their views. We know a few psychologists who started their jobs under one government and were compelled to resign when governments changed. They found it nearly impossible to work with people whose philosophies were antithetical to their views of health and wellbeing. From being supporters of consumers and enablers of community action one day, they were expected to cut services and impose top-down managerial styles the next. To survive under adverse circumstances workers need the support of their peers and superiors. The dilemma of working for someone whose ideology you do not share is a difficult one. Not all psychologists can afford to resign and look for another job, especially when governments are cutting down funding for social services.

Another serious dilemma is what Prilleltensky, Walsh-Bowers, and Rossiter (1999) called "systemic entanglements" (p. 329). This is a situation in which psychologists have to be accountable to several "masters." Community psychologists working with local government offices in community development settings present a case in point. I [Scot] worked with a team of students to help document the community engagement process during the formative stage of a public housing redevelopment project in Miami (Kesten, Perez, Marques, Evans, & Sulma, 2017). Although officially under contract with the county community development office, over time, the team found ourselves accountable to four different groups: (1) the public housing office; (2) public housing residents; (3) a multi-university research consortium; and (4) our own discipline of CP. Each group was attending to and serving interests that were at times compatible but in other circumstances conflictual. The team found this challenging to navigate. One necessary capacity of the community psychologist working in communities is the ability to recognize when an accountability gap exists in community interventions and to remain accountable to the vulnerable group while balancing professional integrity (O'Neill, 1989). Although our team espoused the value of

---

Box 9.1 Towards Transformative Social Interventions

In his commentary in the second edition of this text, Dennis Fox offered these additional critiques of the idea of community psychologists working in the "belly of the beast":

> Emphasizing the kinds of social change possible within traditional governments and advanced by traditionally pragmatic policy-oriented NGOs can lead to an unnecessarily restricted vision of what transformative change might mean. For example, ... the "insider" goals identified as transformative (progressive taxation, universal health insurance and the like) are designed to make our current system more bearable (more fair and less destructive), not to replace the system with a fundamentally better one. If accomplished, these changes would ease injustice and make life measurably better – people might be "happier," as this chapter's preliminary exercise suggests – but they would also leave intact the underlying system of corporate and state power.
>
> An additional problem with government work is that emphasizing program evaluation and similar roles as key to instigating change leads to an exaggerated belief that injustice exists because of bad data rather than elite power. Demonstrating to authorities, for example, that inequality leads to ill health is unlikely to persuade them to create an egalitarian society. Although more data always seem useful, the lack of data is rarely the most crucial barrier to resolving our most serious societal problems (Fox, 1991).
>
> If CP is – or is trying to be – a psychology of liberation, then we have to acknowledge government as a central source of injustice. Governments do react to pressure for change, but rarely generate their own. It's our job to help create that pressure. Thus, social movement organizations of the kind this chapter describes are the most important element in building strains to the boiling point, at which time government is more likely to respond regardless of whether its agencies are filled with do-gooders or automatons. Our dilemma is how to practice this kind of from-the-bottom politics effectively and honestly, without overwhelming our audience, burning ourselves out or accepting invitations to become rock-no-boat insiders beholden to governments or large non-governmental funding sources.

accountability to the most vulnerable group, in this situation we felt like we wandered into messy terrain. Being able to resolve these tensions is not always easy. Clarity of roles, expectations, and accountabilities, as well as a degree of autonomy, are vital. But, this requires cooperative partners, which one cannot always take for granted.

When the community psychologist believes in resident participation in community decisions but others are less than enthusiastic, conflicts arise. Siding with one community group over others can jeopardize professional relationships and antagonize your peers – not a cheap price to pay for your values. We always recommend engaging in reflective practice and working with a group of supporters in peer supervision, either inside or outside the organization. Situations such as those just described require support and understanding by people who know your work (Rossiter, Prilleltensky, & Walsh-Bowers, 2000; Rossiter, Walsh-Bowers & Prilleltensky, 2002). While not always an antidote to potential conflict, we can always benefit from ongoing reflection on the nature of our practice and using the experience of challenging community research and action to gain a deeper shared understanding of the community, society, and social change and our own roles in maintaining or challenging the status quo (Evans, Kivell, Haarlammert, Malhotra, & Rosen 2014).

The Role of Community Psychologists in Social Movements and Non-Government Organizations

In general, social movements and social movement organizations (SMOs) tend to be more transformative than non-government organizations (NGOs; Chetkovich & Kunreuther, 2006; McAdam, 1999; Piven & Cloward, 1978). Yet many social movements collaborate with NGOs and vice versa. Sometimes NGOs are part of networks that support social movements. A social movement is "an organized set of people vested in making a change in their situation pursuing a common political agenda through collective action" (Batliwala, 2008, p. 3). Social movements share the following three features (Hall, 1995):

1 *Social change*: social movements promote or resist some kind of social change in order to uphold an explicit set of values.
2 *People power*: people come together to promote or resist the change.
3 *Collective action*: people undertake collective actions such as sit-ins, strikes, marches, media campaigns, protests, and others.

NGOs are dedicated to fostering a particular cause for the improvement of human and/or environmental wellbeing. Some, but not all, NGOs try to advance the three features of social movements (Chetkovich & Kunreuther 2006; Evans, 2012; Evans, Hanlin, & Prilleltensky, 2007). Others can be very conservative. Here we concern ourselves primarily with NGOs that support social movements in line with the goals and values of CP, as explained in Chapter 3. Examples of social movements include the women's movement, Black Lives Matter, the human rights movement, and the environmental movement, which are supported, respectively, by NGOs such as the National Organization for Women and The National Association for the Advancement of Colored People (NAACP) in the US, Amnesty International, and Greenpeace. In contrast to these movements, which are in line with the values of CP, some movements – such as the men's rights and White supremacy movements – oppose the principles of liberation and wellbeing that we espouse and uphold instead patriarchal institutions (Green, 1999; Tarrow, 1998).

As "outsiders," social movements have fewer resources than governments do. In fact, the very essence of social movements is often predicated on getting more resources. We explore below some of the processes leading to the emergence of social movements and some of the strategies used to obtain more material or symbolic resources (Bourdieu, 1998). Depending on context, strategy, traditions, and leadership, movements may use more or less contentious strategies to get their points across (Della Porta & Diani, 1999; Katsiaficas, 1997; Tarrow, 1998).

Roots of Social Movements

Based on the work of social movement scholars and activists (Bourdieu, 1998; Della Porta & Diani, 1999; Freeman & Johnson, 1999; Gerlach, 1999; Hall, 1995; Kahn, 1982; Katsiaficas, 1997; Stout, 1996; Tarrow, 1998), we identify the following roots of social movements.

Suffering and Deprivation

People are driven to action when some of their basic human rights are denied (Hall, 1995; Tarrow, 1998). We can think of suffering and deprivation as the opposite of wellbeing and liberation. Manifestations of suffering are present at the collective, relational and personal domains. Concrete examples of suffering derive from the lives of poor people. At the collective level, poor people in the Southern hemisphere suffer from two sets of devastating experiences: (1) *insecurity, chaos, violence*; and (2) *economic exploitation*. Narayan and colleagues (Narayan, Patel, Schafft, Rademacher, & Koch-Schulte, 2000) interviewed thousands of people who commented on the fear of living with uncertainty, deprivation, and lack of protection.

In the struggle for survival, the social relations of the poor also suffer. Suffering at the relational level is marked by *heightened fragmentation* and *exclusion*, and by fractious social relations. The personal dimension of suffering in poverty is characterized by powerlessness, limitations, and restricted opportunities in life; physical weakness; shame and feelings of inferiority; and gender and age discrimination. Impotence in the light of ominous societal forces such as crime and economic displacement fuels the sense of powerlessness. This type of suffering engenders justified rage and indignation in many poor people. When the suffering is tied to an assessment of the power differentials leading to it, consciousness-raising takes place.

Consciousness-raising

Suffering in itself is not enough to generate action. People have to connect their plight to external factors. Otherwise, fatalism and internalized oppression ensue (Moane, 1999). Bombarded with messages of incompetence, many poor people believe they are to blame for their misfortune (Stout, 1996). Connections between personal suffering and external roots of oppression and exploitation are the beginning of consciousness-raising (Cerullo & Wiesenfeld, 2001; McLaren & Lankshear, 1994). It is only when people begin to unveil the societal causes of oppression that a new awareness ensues. Although this is only the first step in bringing about change, it is highly liberating because people discover that they are not to blame for their suffering and that they have the capacity to challenge the status quo (Cerullo & Wiesenfeld, 2001; Collins, 2008; Freire, 1970; Hirsch, 1999).

Congealing Events

Although discrimination and exclusion may be the daily bread of many people, changes in consciousness often do not take place until there is a crisis or a catalytic event that puts suffering in sharp relief. Such was the case when Rosa Parks occupied a "White" seat in a bus in Montgomery,

Alabama, on 7 December, 1955. This was a catalytic event triggering the bus boycott and the formation of the Montgomery Improvement Association, which was very influential in the civil rights movement (Freeman & Johnson, 1999). In another example, the repression of the Chinese government and their attempt to take more and more control of Hong Kong is an ongoing *crisis*. But, the protests of 2019 were triggered by a specific *catalytic* event – opposition to the introduction of the Fugitive Offenders amendment bill proposed by the Hong Kong government (see www.scmp.com/topics/hong-kong-protests).

Political Opportunities

Despite the presence of the three conditions listed previously, efforts to create a movement may be thwarted by political repression. If the regime does not permit freedom of expression or association, organizers will encounter barriers (Hall, 1995; Tarrow, 1998). The regime has to be democratic enough to enable people to organize without fear of repression or violations of human rights. At the same time, the political climate has to be such that popular support will be gained for the emerging movement.

Preparing for Action

The next step in the formation of social movements is the progression from consciousness to action. Collective action requires coordination and sophisticated levels of organization, communication, and strategies, as well as a collective identity, shared framing of the problem and vision, and a movement culture (Taylor & Whittier, 1992). In this section we review some of the necessary factors in the transition from awareness to preparation for action.

Multiple Sources of Support

Some scholars argue that the presence of diverse organizations within the movement is a vital condition for action. If some organizations face difficulties, others assume the leadership and continue the preparation. In fact, not all organizations need to have precisely the same ideology; it is enough to have an agreement on broad issues.

Gerlach (1999) studied the structure of social movements and concluded that there are two main characteristics that make them resilient. The first one is the fact that they consist of multiple groups that serve different and complementary functions. The second feature is that these diverse groups share symbolic and concrete resources. They have common reading materials, invite the same speakers to talk to their groups and often have overlapping memberships.

People with serious mental health problems have been subjected to oppressive treatments by "well-meaning" helpers (Whitaker, 2002; see also Chapter 20). Their oppressive experiences congealed into a large social movement to reclaim their rights and ability to participate in their treatment (Chamberlin, 1990; Nelson, Lord, & Ochocka, 2001). Psychologists played a role in the anti-psychiatry movement and in the consumer/survivor movement. The history of these movements shows that they rely on various groups and that they share members and an ideology.

Congruence of Interests

While disagreements across organizations are common and expected, it is important to emphasize common interests and goals. For a social movement to engage in action, partners have to agree on certain actions that will advance the overall wellbeing of the affected population. "Purists" remain isolated and fail to collaborate because they expect everyone else to think exactly like them. Diversity within movements has to be accepted and managed carefully (Della Porta & Diani, 1999). Social movement theorists contend that the development of a collective identity is one of the most central tasks facing a movement (Gamson, 1992; Melucci, 1989; Taylor & Whittier, 1992). To develop a collective identity, a group must define itself as a group, develop shared views of the social environment, a shared understanding of power, shared goals, and shared opinions about the possibilities and limits of collective action.

Communications Network

One of the factors that ensures collective action is disseminating information to as many people as possible about a particular concern. Newsletters, websites, public rallies, media campaigns, all are important in letting people know that there is an injustice that must be addressed (Freeman, 1999). The role of *networker* is an important one for community psychologists (Foster-Fishman, Berkowitz, Lounsbury, Jacobson, & Allen, 2001). Social media has increasingly become an effective tool for social mobilization and education. Examples such as Arab Spring, #blacklivesmatter, the Spanish Indignados Movement, Occupy Wall Street, Greta Thunberg's #FridaysForFuture, and the North Dakota access pipeline protests show that social media really has transformed how participants in these movements communicate and plays a central role in shaping the decisions that individuals make regarding whether to attend protests, the logistics of the events, and the likelihood of success (Tufekci & Wilson, 2012). The Black Lives Matter movement is a prime example of social media users on Twitter, Facebook, and other platforms collecting and organizing in powerful ways (Kidd & McIntosh, 2016).

Organizational Effectiveness

Organize, organize and organize! This is the lesson we derive from organizers such as Si Kahn (1982), Saul Alinsky (1971), and Jane McAlevey (2016). Each organization within the social movement has to perfect the art of internal and external effectiveness. This requires a delicate balance between attending to the needs of their members and completing tasks. Two threats assail organizational effectiveness. One is the lack of attention to members' needs for personal attention (Speer, Hughey, Gensheimer, & Adams-Leavitt, 1995). The other is the lack of attention to task orientation. We have to be good at both. Without attending to members' voices we neglect relational and personal wellness. Without attending to specific tasks we neglect the aims of the movement.

As *organizational leaders*, community psychologists can help in devising a strategic direction; establishing democratic decision-making processes; inspiring members; monitoring the implementation of actions and taking the pulse of the membership to know whether people are, overall, satisfied with the work, or feeling disaffected or burnt out. In essence, the leader has to keep an eye on the internal health of the organization and the external effectiveness of its actions (Bond, 1999; Maton, 2008; Maton & Salem, 1995).

Resource Mobilization

Resource mobilization refers to the infusion of human, intellectual, organizational, and material resources into emerging movements (McCarthy & Zald, 1977). "According to this model, strain leads to discontent, from which grievances result, yet the movement will remain dormant until resources are infused" (Hall, 1995, p. 6). Jenkins (1999) compared three movements launched by

Californian farm workers since World War II and came to the conclusion that the one that succeeded, the United Farm Workers, did so because of the mobilization of essential resources. "The crucial ingredients for the UFW's success were the mobilization strategy adopted by the union organizers and major changes in national politics that enabled the UFW to mobilize sufficient external resources to compensate for the powerlessness of farmworkers" (Jenkins, 1999, p. 278).

Collective Action Strategies

When discontent has matured into organization and when frustration has turned into motivation for change, it is time for action. A number of strategic actions have proven efficient in the past.

Recruitment – Numbers Count

Every social change organizations needs volunteers and paid staff to spread the message of change, to talk to new recruits, mail information, talk to the media, go to protests, learn about issues, and write briefs. Strategic recruiters go to places where discontent is latent or manifest and where large numbers of sympathizers may be found. Faith and religious organizations often offer support for social justice causes (Hall, 1995; Speer & Hughey, 1995).

Media Campaigns

The role of the media cannot be underestimated. As French sociologist Pierre Bourdieu (1998) noted:

> [T]he media are, overall, a factor of depoliticization, which naturally acts more strongly on the most depoliticized section of the public ... Television (much more than the newspapers) offers an increasingly depoliticized, aseptic, bland view of the world and it is increasingly dragging down the newspapers in its slide into demagogy and subordination to commercial values. (pp. 73–4)

The challenge to counteract this trend has to be taken seriously by psychologists interested in social change. Effective social movements nurture writers who can express the movement's views in mainstream and alternative media.

The skills of community psychologists as *researchers and writers* cannot be underestimated in media campaigns. In Chapter 19 you will see how community psychologists helped to mobilize people with disabilities in letter-writing campaigns. Social movements require up-to-date information to educate their own members and the public about issues of concern. Information on the source, scope and effects of pollution or discriminatory policies and practices can be vital for strategic actions such as recruitment or media campaigns.

Increasingly grassroots organizations wish to evaluate the effectiveness of their actions. Programs and actions may be measured against values and/or outcomes. Community psychologists can help organizations to find out whether their efforts are congruent with their own values and with predicted or desirable effects. As *program evaluators*, community psychologists can contribute to the improvement of campaigns and collective action.

Writers can express information about current social issues and the values of movements in impassioned ways. The Society for Community Research and Action has been active in support of social change by writing and disseminating Policy Position Statements (http://scra27.org/what-we-do/policy/policy-position-statements/). These statements are intended to communicate our discipline's perspective on pressing social issues and matters of public health and wellbeing. The goal is to provide clear, succinct summaries of scientific research and accumulated knowledge from practice accompanied by recommendations to policy makers and the general public. For example, a 2018 policy statement published on the website highlighted the empirical literature to describe the negative effects of deportation and forced separation on individuals, families, and the broader community in the US (SCRA, 2018). The authors argued that

> Federal immigration policies should keep families together through comprehensive immigration reform that ends the threat of deportation and bolsters hardship exemptions for all family members. Local communities should prioritize safety and inclusion for all families, regardless of immigration status, by developing programs to foster support networks, sense of belonging, mental health/healing, building community, and collective political action, as these types of programs foster hope and wellness for children and families. (p. 4)

In addition to writers and researchers, social movements need eloquent *speakers*. Movements need articulate representatives who can speak with confidence in front of a TV camera or a city council. While in graduate school, CP students often make presentations to colleagues in class and at conferences. These experiences strengthen their public-speaking skills and their ability to debate issues. These competencies cannot be underestimated, particularly when working with marginalized people who often feel intimidated by audiences (Stout, 1996). For example, Scot and a team of graduate students worked with grassroots youth organizers in Miami to make statements at local public school board meetings arguing for more mental health supports and against increased policing in schools.

Coalitions

As indicated by Gerlach (1999; see the section 'Multiple Sources of Support', discussed previously), effective social movements are most resilient when they share the load. In the case of the Pro-Choice movement in the US, for instance, Staggenborg (1999) found that more progress was achieved by the work of coalitions than by the work of individual organizations. Furthermore, she found that established organizations with paid staff were more efficient in their coalition work than informal groups staffed mainly by volunteers. Similar findings were reported in a special section of the *American Journal of Community Psychology* dealing with community coalition building (Wolff, 2001). In fighting poverty, Narayan, Patel, et al. (2000) report that "coalitions representing poor people's organizations are needed to ensure that the voices of the poor are heard and reflected in decision making at the local, national and global levels" (p. 265). The Mobilizing Against Nestle example in Box 9.2 illustrates the importance of coalitions and their mobilization for social change.

As *coalition builders* community psychologists can help in the identification of shared values, goals, and missions (Evans, 2015; Nelson, 1994). Applying principles of collaboration, community psychologists can bridge differences and create bonds of commonality where shared values exist. Building value-based partnerships for solidarity is a task that calls for many community psychological skills. To promote the values of caring and compassion, health, self-determination, power sharing, human diversity, and social justice, we need to engage with partners in four skilful tasks: building relationships and trust among partners, establishing clear agreements and norms of reciprocity, sharing power and resources, and challenging ourselves to make sure that we do not perpetuate, consciously or unconsciously, oppressive practices (Nelson, Prilleltensky, & MacGillivary, 2001; Wolff et al., 2017).

Box 9.2 Mobilizing Against Nestlé: The Infant Formula Action Coalition (INFACT)

Psychologist David Hallman and the United Church of Canada mobilized their resources to stop Nestlé from distributing infant formula in developing countries. David Hallman (1987) described his role working for the United Church of Canada on the boycott of the Nestlé corporation. Nestlé was the major marketer of infant formula, developed in the 1800s by Henri Nestlé, to women in developing nations. Advertising in hospitals and free samples were provided to new mothers, with infant formula as a symbol of Western affluence and progress. By the time the free samples were exhausted, mothers' breast milk had dried up and they were forced to use formula. This resulted in increased rates of infant malnutrition and mortality brought about by poor conditions for the use of formula in developing countries, including lack of clean water, lack of refrigeration, mothers diluting formula because they found it expensive, and difficulty sterilizing bottles and teats. All of these conditions can increase infants' exposure to sources of infection.

As these problems became evident to health care workers, a coalition of community groups across the world was formed in 1977 to oppose the promotion of formula. The Infant Formula Action Coalition (INFACT), which consisted of religious organizations, health care organizations, women's groups, nurses, the La Leche league, and others, decided to conduct an international boycott of Nestlé products. The United Church of Canada donated David Hallman's time to work with INFACT and the boycott committee. In 1984, three years after the boycott started, Nestlé met with INFACT representatives and resolved all issues, thus ending the boycott. This social intervention illustrates the importance of coalitions and their mobilization for social change. What is remarkable about this intervention is that there was an organized worldwide outcry and opposition to a major international corporation which had a successful impact that has benefited babies throughout developing countries. And a community psychologist was behind it!

Lobbying and Political Influence

In discussing the human development successes that the state of Kerala, India achieved, Franke and Chasin (2000) concluded that "Kerala's quality-of-life achievements result from redistribution. But why has redistribution occurred in Kerala?" (p. 24). According to the authors, the answer lies in the century-long history of popular movements in the state. "These movements have gone through many stages, from caste improvement associations to trade unions and peasant associations to Communist parties to the Kerala People's Science Movement" (Franke & Chasin, 2000, p. 24). These social movements have forced the government to listen to the concerns of the poor and have lobbied successfully for the introduction of poverty alleviation measures. The importance of social movements in reducing poverty cannot be underestimated. The case of Kerala demonstrates that governments can respond to social movements and coalitions. Through participatory democracy and civic associations, citizens created enough pressure on government to institute land reform and other distributive policies that enhanced the wellbeing of the poor.

Protest and Non-violent Civil Disobedience

Sometimes the only way to get attention is to engage in contentious actions such as disruption of meetings, occupation of premises, road blockades, marches, or civil disobedience. These forms of mass mobilization aim to create change by amassing individuals around issues. This approach assumes that visible, non-violent public actions by large numbers of people can generate enough power to compel concessions from established institutions (Checkoway, 1995). Compelling research by Erica Chenoweth and Maria Stephan (2011) confirms that civil disobedience is the most powerful way of shaping global politics. They found that non-violent resistance presents fewer obstacles to moral and physical involvement and commitment, and that higher levels of participation contribute to enhanced resilience and greater opportunities for tactical innovation and civic disruption.

During the civil rights movement in the US, Martin Luther King, Jr. involved people in local demonstrations in an attempt to force issues for national legislation. King believed in the value of a "non-violent campaign" and its power to move progress. In his famous *Letter from a Birmingham Jail* (1963) he outlined the four basic steps of non-violent protest: "collection of the facts to determine whether injustices exist; negotiation; self-purification; and direct action" (p. 2). He goes on to explain that the purpose of direct action was to create a crisis situation out of which negotiation could emerge:

> Nonviolent direct action seeks to create such a crisis and foster such a tension that a community which has constantly refused to negotiate is forced to confront the issue. It seeks to so dramatize the issue that it can no longer be ignored. (p. 4)

As we are compiling this third edition, people in all parts of the world are mobilizing to force action on pressing issues. In West Virginia, US for example, public school teachers' demonstrations led to a bill that moved to raise state employees' pay by 5 percent. The demonstrations shut down schools for nine days, with teachers vowing not to return until they received better pay and working conditions. Ultimately, state lawmakers gave in. There have been similar teacher protests and strikes in Los Angeles, Denver, Oakland, Raleigh, North Carolina, and Puerto Rico.

Extinction Rebellion (https://rebellion.earth) is an international movement that started in London and aims to use non-violent civil disobedience to avert a climate breakdown. They promote mass "above the ground" civil disobedience – in full public view. In one of their early actions, they blockaded streets of London for more than a week, with more than 1,000 arrests. Soon after, the UK government adopted a climate emergency resolution.

In 2019, mass uprisings in Africa have succeeded in toppling dictators. Algeria succeeded in pressuring Abdelaziz Bouteflika to resign after 20 years as president. Just a few days later, protesters in Sudan were celebrating the ouster of Omar al-Bashir, Sudan's president of 30 years, after a three-month-long uprising against his regime. These are just a few examples of how when people come together to resist oppression and promote justice, change can happen. Community psychologists can contribute to these collective actions as *community researchers, planners of action,* and *organizational leaders.*

Strengths and Limitations of Social Movement Organizations and Non-government Organizations

Social movements may not have the resources governments do, but they have people power and the potential to create consciousness to change government itself. Anti-colonial movements, labor movements, human rights movements, the women's movement – all have had an enduring impact (Brazier, 1999).

Strengths

Some of the clear strengths of movements are as follows:

Transformative

Movements seek radically to alter oppressive power structures. Anti-apartheid movements in South Africa and civil rights movements in the US managed to transform the way millions of people are treated in law and in front of each other (Freeman, 1999; Seedat et al., 2001). However, Nelson Mandela, Martin Luther King Jr. and their followers fought intentionally for a peaceful multi-racial democratic and just society rather than just against apartheid or oppression. Transformation requires a "radical imagination": a vision of something better, not just the absence of the problematic conditions (Khasnabish & Haiven, 2012).

Participatory

Unlike government interventions, which can be top-down, social movements recruit, rely on, and reach out to people who are disenfranchised and oppressed and their allies. Poor and disadvantaged people have an opportunity to participate in creating their own destiny. In Latin America, community psychologists collaborate with social change movements in enhancing community participation (Cerullo & Wiesenfeld, 2001; Reich, Riemer, Prilleltensky, & Montero, 2007; Rosa, 1997).

Integrative

Social movements, at their best, promote not only social change but also meaning in life (Matustik, 1998). The women's movement promoted not only changes in policies, which are crucial on their own right, but also changes in personal philosophy (hooks, 2000b). Such collective action fostered a new way of life, a new way of relating and a new way of being in the world. Women in the movement were concerned not only with changing governments and corporations but also with transforming sexual and family relationships. It was about a philosophy of life as much as anything else. The same can be said of the work of activists in El Salvador, who fought not only the government but also forms of oppression at every level in the community. The outcome of this was devotion to a cause and a passion for meaning in life (Rosa, 1997).

Limitations

But with strengths come weaknesses. We consider a few below.

Unaccountable

Due to the informal structure of some social movements, some people allow themselves liberties that would not be tolerated in more formal structures. Katsiaficas (1997), for instance, noted the aggression displayed by some youngsters in the youth movement in Europe in the 1970s and 1980s. Similarly, some may be turned off by anti-fascist action (more popularly known as "antifa") and their use of violence and intimidation as a tactic to attack conservatives and nationalists in Australia, Europe, and the US. While aggression can be a necessary part of social mobilization, many worry that use of violence can work against their ultimate cause.

Contradictory

In her work with the Piedmont Peace Project, Stout (1996) reported the inconsistent behavior of some of her peers. While highly concerned about social justice on the outside, some neglected basic values on the inside. Contradictions are pervasive and must be carefully monitored. Means of accountability articulated in Chapter 3 may be brought to bear on these two points.

Transitory

Some movements, such as the student movement in France in 1968, do not manage to survive the initial stages of formation. Following the student uprising, some gains were achieved and some changes were made to educational policy. However, as Tarrow (1998) pointed out, the movement did not last long. Associated with this risk is the threat of cooptation (Salem, Foster-Fishman, & Goodkind, 2002).

Insular and Self-defeating

Some movements become so focused on the rights of their own members that they become insular and fail to establish bonds of solidarity with others who are also oppressed (Benhabib, 1996). Worse still, some can become self-defeating, engaging in internal fights that detract from the cause of solidarity (Della Porta & Diani, 1999; Tarrow, 1998). The concept of intersectionality (Crenshaw, 1989, 1990; see Chapter 21) challenges this tendency to separate people and problems on the basis of factors like race, gender, sexuality, or class. Instead, it pushes us to examine the ways that social and policy issues are simultaneously about multiple, intersecting systems of oppression and develop to build a strong web of diverse organizations and activists working together (Kunreuther & Thomas-Breitfeld, 2015).

Indifferent to Diversity

While solidarity with other oppressed groups is healthy, indifference to their unique circumstances is not. Assuming that one type of oppression is similar to the next violates the principle of diversity and diminishes self-determination.

Dilemmas Faced by Community Psychologists Working in Social Movement Organizations and Non-government Organizations

First and foremost, income is an issue. It is hard to get well-paid jobs in SMOs and NGOs. Jobs are scarce and they are often only temporary when tied to particular, time-bound campaigns. Without a guaranteed source of income, it is hard to make a living from activism. Many community psychologists volunteer their time to work for a variety of causes.

A second dilemma pertains to expectations and task orientation. Social movements consist of people from diverse backgrounds, some of whom may not be used to efficient ways of working. Adjusting to the norms of an SMO is a challenge for people who are used to being very efficient with the use of their time.

Similar to dilemmas presented in government positions, value clashes can also occur in SMOs and NGOs. We have to make choices about whether to confront peers or let go of minor misdemeanors. But what to do when basic norms and values are violated? What if we risk internal solidarity by pointing out the unethical behavior of a well-respected leader? These are not easy situations. Linda Stout (1996) faced many risks when she confronted her board members in the Piedmont Peace Project. She challenged them to renounce their homophobic tendencies. It was not easy for her, but she decided that certain values cannot be compromised. She took a risk and stood by her convictions.

As a young person, Isaac took some risks by the mere act of reading progressive literature. Once he had to go to the youth movement to burn some books because they heard that the police might raid the center. He did not endure any pain or suffering, but many of his friends and relatives did. Proceeding with caution was a must then and it is a must today. In some parts of the world, transformative activity can cost you your life.

There are no set answers for these dilemmas. What we can recommend, as we have in the past, is to unite with like-minded people in sharing ethical dilemmas and searching for solutions (Prilleltensky, Sanchez Valdes, Walsh-Bowers, & Rossiter, 2002; Prilleltensky, Walsh-Bowers, & Rossiter, 1999; Rossiter et al., 2000, 2002).

Chapter Summary

Community psychologists have opportunities to promote social change as insiders working within government and as outsiders working in SMOs and NGOs. In both settings there are ample opportunities to promote wellbeing and liberation. While governments tend to concentrate on ameliorative functions such as risk reduction and social aid, social movements seek to change structures of inequality. The former engage in policy development, legislation, and funding of new programs, the latter in collective action such as protests and civil disobedience. In both instances it is possible to pursue wellbeing and liberation. Government work is not antithetical to emancipation. Under pressure from women's movements, a sea change in levels of human development took place in Kerala.

While some social movements proliferate, others dwindle. On the one hand we witness youthful and courageous opposition to globalization, and on the other we face massive apathy to poverty and victimization. Some governments dismantle the public sector at the same time as they tout prevention and promotion. Contradictions abound within governments, social movements, and within our own lives. Our challenge is to keep our values front and center and to create opportunities for transformation where amelioration reigns. But over and above these challenges, the biggest challenge for community psychologists is simply to get there, to be part of social movements, to document their work, to assist them, and to reach a new level of congruence between our philosophy and our actions. The most significant role community psychologists can play may be "entering into alliances with community-based groups engaged in campaigns against some form of injustice[,] ... sharing one's resources and expertise and accepting their leadership" (Steinitz & Mishler, 2009, p. 407).

Key Terms

Ameliorative interventions: Purposeful activities designed to alleviate the results of living in unjust and prejudicial societies.

Coalition: A group of groups dedicated to achieving social, economic, or health goals for a particular sector of the population.

Corporatocracy: A system of government that serves the interests of corporations.

Health promoter: Person assigned the role of improving an aspect of the population's health.

Human development: Refers to comprehensive improvement in the education, health, housing, social, and economic conditions of a population.

Non-governmental organizations (NGOs): Non-profit, citizen-based organizations dedicated to fostering a particular cause for the improvement of human and/or environmental wellbeing.

Program developer: Person collaborating with others in developing a governmental or non-governmental project.

Program evaluator: Person in an organization tasked with assessing the efficiency and effectiveness of social interventions.

Resource mobilization: Infusion of material, intellectual, and human resources into social change efforts.

Social interventions (SIs): Intentional processes designed to affect the wellbeing of the population through changes in values, policies, programs, distribution of resources, power differentials, and cultural norms.

Social movement organizations (SMOs): Organizations dedicated to challenge the status quo and to transform conditions that have an impact on human and/or environmental wellbeing.

Transformative interventions: Intentional processes designed to alter the conditions that lead to suffering.

Resources

Check out Erica Chenowith's TEDx talk, "The success of nonviolent civil resistance": www.youtube.com/watch?v=bGBamfWasNQ

Five classic resistance texts:

de Beauvoir, S. (1989). *The second sex*. New York: Vintage Books.

Galeano, E. (1973). *Open veins of Latin America*. New York: Monthly Review Press.

Freire, P. (2006). *Pedagogy of the oppressed (30th anniversary ed.)*. New York: Continuum.

Fanon, F. (1991). *The wretched of the Earth*. New York: Grove Weidenfeld.

Baran, P., & Sweezy, P. (1996). *Monopoly capital*. New York: Monthly Review Press.

Watch the documentary "Unnatural causes: Is inequality making us sick?" (2008), produced by California Newsreel: www.unnaturalcauses.org

Mobilization is an academic journal devoted to theory and research on social action: www.mobilization.sdsu.edu/index.html

Read the recent report on inequality in health called "Closing the gap in a generation: Health equity through action on the social determinants of health by the World Health Organization (WHO)": http://whqlibdoc.who.int/publications/2008/9789241563703_eng.pdf

ORGANIZATIONAL AND COMMUNITY INTERVENTIONS 10

Warm-up Questions

All of us interact with organizations in some way just about every day. We work in organizations, we go to school in organizations, we purchase goods or services from organizations, and we organize, play, create, volunteer, and worship in organizations. Think about an organization you are a part of; one that is an important part of your life currently. What have you noticed about this organization? Is the mission or purpose of the organization clear? Would you say that the organization is structured well and effective at getting things done and achieving its goals? How about the people in the organization, are they happy and cared for? What is it like to work in, or be a part of this organization? Are organizational policies and practices fair and equitable? Is it a diverse organization or is it dominated by one group? Do all members have a say in organizational decisions or just a few at the top? How does the organization handle conflict? What challenges does the organization face? What pressures from the outside world affect the organization's ability to thrive? What changes would you make in the organization if you could?

Learning Objectives

In this chapter you will learn about

- The role of organizations in community and social change
- Organizational and community interventions and why they are important
- How organizational and community interventions promote wellbeing and liberation
- The roles for community psychologists in organizational and community settings
- The strengths and limitations of organizational and community interventions

Introduction to Organizational and Community Interventions

We focus here on organizational and **community interventions** because most efforts for liberation and wellbeing in communities take place in, or through, some type of formally organized entity such as community-based organizations, coalitions, or networks. To enable community change, first we have to build strong organizations and coalitions. Organizations possess human and material resources that are crucial for initiating and invigorating ameliorative and transformative interventions. But, we should not take it for granted that these organizations are sufficiently equipped for social change or that they will examine critically their own role in promoting suffering and oppression, either in their own workers or in the communities they serve. Some scholars have worried that community-based organizations, and the funding apparatus that supports them, are so focused on professionalized, ameliorative services that they actually maintain or even strengthen social inequality (Evans, Hanlin, & Prilleltensky, 2007; INCITE! Women of Color Against Violence, 2007; Kivel, 2007).

Community psychologists are keen to understand how people organize themselves in formal or informal organizations and coalitions in order to create positive change in the world. Because we understand how the health of community organizations and the wellbeing of communities are interconnected, we cannot think about community change without considering **organizational capacity**. Similarly, we cannot think about organizational capacity, without asking: "Capacity to *ameliorate* problems or capacity to *transform* conditions that create problems?" While community-based organizations provide a variety of functions – from service provision and programming to advocacy, community-building, and social action – we focus here on the transformative potential of these organizations (for a discussion of transformative vs. ameliorative change see Chapters 6 and 8).

The focus of Chapter 9 was on larger social movement organizations and non-governmental organizations with a broader, sometimes global mandate, but here we turn our gaze to those community-based organizations working for change in neighborhoods and communities. We start with a brief introduction to community-based, civil society organizations and how they can be both empowering for their members and empowered to work for social justice. We'll then discuss **organizational interventions** and the role of community psychologists as change agents in these settings. From there we'll move to the interorganizational level and consider the importance of coalitions and networks. Lastly, we'll discuss the different types of community interventions and the role of community psychologists in promoting community change.

Civil Society Organizations

The term **civil society sector** refers in general to nonprofit, charitable, and non-governmental organizations, institutions, and voluntary associations that are neither part of the government nor for-profit business. Also referred to as the "third sector," this set of institutions covers a broad swath of entities such as hospitals, universities, social clubs, professional organizations, day care centers, grassroots development organizations, health clinics, environmental groups, family counseling agencies, self-help groups, religious congregations, sports clubs, job training centers, human rights organizations, community associations, soup kitchens, homeless shelters, and more (Salamon, 2010).

Salamon (2010) offered an operational definition for Non-Profit Institutions (NPIs) that can be used to distinguish the type of sector an organization belongs to and to compare organizations across countries. His use of the term "institution" here is meant to encompass everything from small grassroots organizations to larger universities and hospitals. Salamon (2010) recommended five defining characteristics. First, they are *organizations,* which "have some structure and regularity to their operations, whether or not they are formally constituted or legally registered" (p. 177). Second, they are *private* and separate from the state even though they may receive government support. Third, they are *not profit-distributing.* Unlike for-profit businesses, they do not distribute any profits generated to their owners, members, or stockholders. These non-governmental entities produce goods and services that provide benefits to the broader community, and do not seek to benefit only their members. Fourth, they are *self-governing,* meaning they have mechanisms for internal governance and are fundamentally in control of their own affairs. Fifth, they are *non-compulsory* in that "membership or participation in them is contingent on an individual's choice or consent, rather than being legally required, or otherwise compulsory" (p. 178). Here is how Salamon (2010) summarizes the large group of organizations that this definition covers:

> The result is a quite broad definition of the nonprofit sector, encompassing informal organizations (organizations that are not registered and/or non-observed or that are staffed entirely by volunteers) as well as formal organizations (those that are registered or otherwise visible to statistical authorities); religious as well as secular organizations; primarily member-serving organizations such as professional associations, labor unions, and business associations as well as primarily *public-serving* organizations; organizations with paid staff and those staffed entirely by volunteers; and organizations performing essentially *expressive* functions – such as advocacy, cultural expression, community organizing, environmental protection, human rights, religion, representation of interests, and political expression – as well as those performing essentially *service* functions – such as the provision of health, education, or welfare services. (pp. 178–9)

In the US, where there were approximately 1.56 million nonprofits registered with the Internal Revenue Service (IRS) in 2015, we use the term **human service organizations** to refer to those non-governmental, community-based organizations that operate exclusively for service provision, community building, or advocacy purposes. *Human services groups* such as food banks, homeless shelters, youth services, sports organizations, and family or legal services composed over one-third of all of these public charities (35.2 percent) in the US in 2015 (McKeever, 2019). In addition to being an enormous economic force in communities, human service organizations can play a critical role in bringing people together to influence government and do what governments can or will not do (Hall, 2013).

As we saw in Chapter 8, community psychology (CP) begins at home, where we live, where we work, where we volunteer. It would be unpsychological for us to expect to contribute to others' wellbeing and liberation when we suffer from oppression and indifference in our own backyard. It would be equally unpsychological for us to promote wellbeing in the community at large when we ignore the plight of those next to us at work. Therefore, we deal in this chapter with interventions that promote the wellbeing of workers in organizations and of citizens in communities. We look at organizational development as an end in itself, designed to improve the life of workers, and as a means to an end – the promotion of wellbeing and liberation in disadvantaged communities. These organizational aims are congruent with the principles and values of CP around the globe (Reich, Riemer, Prilleltensky, & Montero, 2007).

What Are Organizational Interventions?

Inasmuch as community psychologists strive to promote liberation and wellbeing in marginalized groups, we are interested in organizational interventions to build sufficient capacity to foster these two goals. Communities depend on organizations for their improvement, while organizations justify their existence by assisting communities. Organizations are the primary vehicle through which we direct our work with communities and community change almost always occurs through the efforts of people organized in either formal or informal organizations (Christens, 2019). For us, organizational interventions are systematic methods of enhancing an institution's capacity to promote the personal, relational, and collective wellbeing of their workers and community stakeholders. Working in community-based, human service organizations requires us to attend, simultaneously, to internal organizational issues while also keeping the focus on community action for social change.

The broader field of organizational development has focused on the concept of organizational capacity – the ability of organizations to "do things" – and the process of capacity building in organizations. For instance, Doherty and Mayer (2003) describe organizational capacity as "the combined influence of an organization's abilities to govern and manage itself, to develop assets and resources, to forge the right community linkages, and to deliver valued services – all combining to meaningfully address its mission" (p. 2). Organizational capacity building then, is the process of identifying what organizational capacities need strengthening and applying targeted strategies most likely to build those capacities (Evans, Raymond, & Perkins, 2014). While the concept of organizational capacity is useful in many ways, community psychologists prefer to frame these capacities as organizational empowerment and the development of empowering organizations.

Organizational Empowerment (OE)

Swift and Levin (1987), Gerschick, Israel, and Checkoway (1990), and Zimmerman (2000) made the distinction between *empowering* organizations (those that produce empowerment for its members) and *empowered* organizations (those that are empowered to influence the larger system). Some organizations do a good job at empowering their own members but don't always engage in political action or systems change. Others manage to focus more attention on issues of power, oppression, and disadvantage. Maton and Salem (1995) characterized empowering organizations as settings that enable workers, service recipients, and community stakeholders to experience greater self-determination (personal wellbeing), social support (relational wellbeing), and awareness of political forces impinging on their lives (collective wellbeing).

Peterson and Zimmerman (2004) further developed a theory of empowered organizations by making the distinction between intraorganizational, interorganizational, and extraorganizational empowerment. **Intraorganizational empowerment** includes characteristics that we normally associate with organizational capacity and empowering organizations: the quality of the internal structure and functioning of organizations. **Interorganizational empowerment** refers to the relationships, transactions, and collaboration across organizations. **Extraorganizational empowerment** refers to an organization's ability to affect broader systems. Influencing policy and practice, creating alternative settings, and deploying organizational resources in the community would be considered extraorganizational outcomes of an empowered organization.

If we start with the premise that we want strong, empowered organizations that are transformative and "capable of mounting and sustaining challenges to unjust systems" (Christens, 2019, p. 92), then we need to first understand what type of extraorganizational practices build power and work toward systemic changes that promote community, reduce inequality, and enhance wellbeing (Christens, 2019, Evans et al., 2011). To that end, we start with a discussion on extraorganizational empowerment to set the vision for empowered and transformative community organizational practice, followed by a discussion of interorganizational empowerment and the importance of interorganizational collaboration, and finally turn the gaze inward to outline the intraorganizational conditions required for transformative practice in community settings.

Extraorganizational Empowerment

At the extraorganizational level, human service organizations risk contributing to the maintenance or strengthening of social inequality by explicitly and implicitly reinforcing and perpetuating certain ideas through the services they provide. For example, the mere existence of homeless shelters, food kitchens, and the various systems and networks that interact with and depend on these services "reinforce the idea that shelters are the appropriate solution to homelessness – as opposed to, say, homeless people organizing themselves, or transforming an economic system that produces far more empty homes than there are homeless people to fill them" (West, 2018, p. 20). It is easy to see how organizations can get stuck addressing the symptoms of a broken system and actually become part of the problem. This forces some consideration of the tension between the provision of services and promoting social change.

Services or Social Change?

Community wellbeing is predicated on emancipation from oppressive forces. Therefore, as community psychologists, we are not content to improve narrow aspects of health, such as better hygiene or diet awareness, when systemic conditions of inequality perpetuate hunger. Similarly, we are not satisfied to improve charity services when the conditions that lead to charity in the first place continue unabated. In the language of Chapters 6 and 8, we seek to develop community interventions that go beyond amelioration and move towards transformation. This is not an "either/or." We do not advocate the elimination of social supports because they do not eliminate economic exploitation. Services are very much needed. What we do advocate for is the pairing and integration of ameliorative and transformative thinking and action (Martin, 2007; Prilleltensky & Nelson, 2002).

Much of what is classed as human service work tends to focus on helping people cope with and rise above the toxic aspects of society while leaving oppressive systems, structures, and the ideologies that maintain them unchanged and undiscussed (Albee, 1986; Gil, 1998; Ife, 2002). Too often organizations neglect an analysis of the broader systemic sources of the problems of the lives of their clients, or have insufficient institutional capacity to address them. In his essay, "Social Services or Social Change?" Kivel (2009) levied a similar critique, arguing that social services do little to address the root causes of inequality and oppression and instead serve to maintain the status quo. Some commentators suggest that transformative change by community-based human service organizations is impossible because they are often too overwhelmed by the intense need in communities and constrained by the political and policy stances of their donors (Bess, Prilleltensky, Perkins, & Collins, 2009; Harvey, 2010; Kunreuther, 2002).

Community-based organization practitioners face competing principles, ideologies, and interests while trying to tackle social problems in social contexts that are dynamic and complex. In responding to the problems and needs of the community, organizations are often faced with difficult choices. On the one hand, they can choose to work for the betterment of human relations, chiefly by providing *services*, supports, and access to resources. On the other hand, organizations can choose to work for the betterment of human relations *politically*, by engaging in advocacy and social action, to affect the allocation of power and resources. However, in some countries, such as the US and Canada, non-profit organizations can risk their charitable, tax-exempt status if they engage in too much advocacy or back political candidates. Thus, for a variety of reasons, community-based human service organizations generally choose to focus on services and leave the riskier work of social action to others. As a result, there exists a forced separation of concern for what is political, long range, and large scale, from attention to service activities which must occur every day, over and over again if people are to survive (Withorn, 1984). Services then, are thought to exist to address individual needs, while **community organizing** groups and movements concern themselves with large-scale community and societal changes. Service work and political activity are viewed as separate in purpose and function:

> The purpose of organizing is to alter community environments and contexts so they are more responsive to the needs and values of people, whereas the purpose of service provision is to accommodate individuals to better function in and adapt to the circumstances they are confronting. (Christens & Speer, 2015, p. 214)

Unfortunately, this separation has become institutionalized into the very fabric of community practice.

We recommend intervening in communities in such a way that they receive services and resources and increase their political awareness and capacity for mobilization at the same time. Hence, we put emphasis here on strategies that ameliorate and, concurrently, have the potential to transform. Good ameliorative work depends on a broader political vision – or it degenerates into charity that only enhances the power of the service provider and the existing social order. Furthermore, the best transformative practice is informed by an awareness of everyday needs in order to maintain its legitimacy. In other words, good services must be politicized and good politics must value and push for services as one aspect of a broad social agenda (Withorn, 1984).

> We need to provide services for those most in need, for those trying to survive, for those barely making it. We also need to work for social change so that we create a society in which our institutions and organizations are equitable and just, and all people are safe, adequately fed and sheltered, well-educated, afforded safe and decent jobs, and empowered to participate in the decisions that affect their lives. (Kivel, 2009, p. 130)

Although these strategies are not the norm but rather the exception in many organizations, efforts in the not-for-profit and community organizing sectors illustrate work that increasingly seeks to blend services with social change (Chetkovich & Kunreuther, 2006; Evans et al., 2007; Minkoff, 2002; Orr, 2007; Smock, 2004). This logic is consistent with critical approaches to social work (Carniol, 2010; Fook, 2012; Gil, 1998; Mullaly, 2002; Pease & Fook, 1999) and empowerment perspectives (Gutiérrez, 1990), which propose that realizing social justice goals of community practice requires simultaneous attention to individual needs and critical action to address root causes of individual and social problems.

Gates (2014) offers three lessons related to the benefits of integrating services and social change. First, services directed at meeting basic needs can enhance individual capacity for leadership. Providing relief creates more space in an individual's life to consider taking on a more active role (see also the discussion of this in Chapter 11). Second, services build trust between organizations and vulnerable populations and provides a foundation for future work together. Third, services can be provided in ways that support overall organizing goals. With the right background and training, service providers can help individuals see their problems as part of a larger political and social struggle.

Since 1999, the Building Movement Project (www.buildingmovement.org) has been examining how community-based organizations can better blend services and social change. Over the years, they have compiled numerous case studies of organizations finding creative ways to integrate services and social change into their missions, goals, organizational cultures, and practices. One case study that illustrates how organizations can effectively blend these approaches features the St. John's Well Child and Family Center in Los Angeles, California that aims to address the extreme poverty and health inequities experienced by many South Los Angeles residents (Kunruether & Bartow, 2010; see Box 10.1). The St. John's case study revealed four lessons for organizations wanting to be effective at blending services and social change:

1 Make staffing decisions that support engagement in both service and social change.
2 Break down internal "silos" between direct service activities and advocacy work.
3 Assemble a board that shares your vision for social change.
4 Partner with funders that support policy change as well as delivery of direct services. (pp. 6–8)

They also made use of strategic partnerships with other service providers, organizers, and advocates to effect larger social change. Services and social change may exist in uneasy tension with one another, but it can be done!

Box 10.1 St. John's Well Child and Family Center

Founded in 1964, the St. John's Well Child and Family Center (https://www.wellchild.org) delivers high-quality primary and preventive medical, dental, and mental health services to uninsured, underserved, and economically disadvantaged persons in Los Angeles. Through their health clinics, they serve patients through community outreach and health education, childhood development assessments and support, case management, and health insurance enrollment. In addition to these services, they also collaborate with others to develop systems, organizations, and programs to advance equity and fairness and to empower and address the needs of all community members, especially the most vulnerable and disadvantaged members.

St. John's approach is to continually search out the root causes of the problems facing their patients. For example, as they continued to diagnose hundreds of cases of lead poisoning among children, St. John's and Esperanza started to map the buildings where these families were living. They then joined forces with the organizing and advocacy group Strategic Actions for a Just Economy (SAJE). SAJE brought significant community and tenant organizing expertise to the table, including a recent campaign in which they succeeded in extracting major concessions from developers that were displacing hundreds of low-income residents in downtown Los Angeles. The three organizations formed the *Healthy Neighborhoods, Same Neighbors Collaborative*, a targeted effort to address the negative health outcomes associated with sub-standard housing in South Los Angeles. St. John's and Esperanza identified the root cause of the housing-related health problems experienced by the clinic's patients, while SAJE added a new dimension by holding tenants' clinics to inform residents of their rights and support their efforts to organize for better living conditions. (Kunruether & Bartow, 2010, p. 4)

In reflecting on the importance of this work, one of the doctor's at St. John's summarized well the importance of both services and social change: "You can't expect us in good conscience to treat these kids and send them back to the same slum housing conditions that made them sick in the first place. We have to do something about it" (Kunruether & Bartow, 2010, p. 3).

Critical Community Practice

While many organizations see the value in pursuing a broader social change agenda, the current economic, and sociopolitical environment creates a heightened sense of urgency for services and immediate relief. Uncovering and examining the root causes of the issues that create a demand for direct services is important to transformative change, but it is often a slow and deliberative process. The pull toward reactive, ameliorative services that address important human needs is strong. Many human service organizations are grappling with how to keep their staff and constituents focused on the big picture (e.g., race equity, economic justice, etc.) when so many are struggling to meet their basic needs (Building Movement Project, 2010). Immediate needs often present themselves as a crisis, and we have a tendency to want to respond to the crisis with action, sometimes neglecting the source (recall the "upstream" analogy from Chapter 6). Furthermore, a focus on reactive, individual services can be an impediment to building power for more transformative social change (Kivel, 2009). It is important to recognize the very real challenges inherent in attempting to both heal the wounds of the suffering and challenge the systems that cause the suffering in the first place. In this context, it is necessary to place a stronger emphasis on the organizations and interorganizational networks that can effectively challenge elite interests, domination, and oligarchy (Christens, 2019). A commitment to critical, transformative community practice is needed and community psychologists can be committed partners in the process.

Critical community practice is "action based on critical theorizing, reflection, and a clear commitment to working for social justice through empowering and transformative practice" (Henderson, 2007, p. 1). This approach to practice works under the assumption that social transformation is possible when people have a voice, power, and access to resources (Prilleltensky & Nelson, 2002). Ife (1997) traces models of critical community practice in the US back to Jane Addams and many who came after who saw social work as "an essentially critical practice to bring about a better, fairer, and more just society rather than merely providing professional interventions to individuals and families" (p. 178).

Butcher, Banks, Henderson, and Robertson (2007) build on the work of Ife (1997, 2002), Brechin (2000), and Barnett (1997) to base their model of critical community practice on four interlocking concepts: critical consciousness, critical theorizing, critical action, and critical reflection. *Critical consciousness* comprises the assumptions, value commitments, dispositions, and mindsets that necessitate enhancement of creative and analytical skills in organizations. Critical consciousness consists of two key components: a critique of social conditions that lead to suffering and an awareness that people can change these conditions (Freire, 1970, 1973; Prilleltensky, 2012; Pees, Shoop, & Ziegenfuss, 2009). *Critical theorizing* is about praxis: putting forward practical models with a critical–theoretical base to better understand the current situation and to suggest alternative futures and strategies for change (Sonn & Quayle, 2014). During the course of efforts to achieve transformative changes, we gain new insights to inform both theory and practice (Christens, 2019). Critical action refers to coordinated action by organizations, practitioners, community members, and policy makers, through social movement building and collective, transformative action. Through transformative practice, power dynamics and oppressive systems, rather than individuals, represent the target of intervention for producing community change in communities (Rappaport, 1977; Prilleltensky & Nelson, 2002; Evans et al., 2007). Finally, *critical reflection* prompts community practitioners to engage in active, ongoing, public, collective reflection upon practice and to reflect upon the social and political context in which practice is embedded (Dokecki, 1992; Newbrough, 1995).

Critical community practice requires that community-based organizations and practitioners participate in ongoing reflections on their ideologies and practices, to use their practical experiences to inform a shared understanding of the community, society, and social change, and to use practice as a measure to evaluate theory and vice-versa (Evans, 2015). While not meant to be a limiting prescription for organizational practice in communities, the model of critical community practice is a useful orientation towards transformative community interventions and an overarching framework through which these ideas can be organized (Evans, Kivell, Haarlammert, Malhotra, & Rosen, 2014; Hook, Mkhize, Kiguwa, & Collins, 2004).

Interorganizational Empowerment

While building strong organizations is important, it is insufficient to the task of transformative social change. Collaborative efforts are one way to combat the increasing fragmentation and services focus that comes with the ever-increasing number of nonprofit organizations mentioned above. Community based organizations too often operate using an isolated approach oriented toward crafting the right solution within a single organization, with the hope that the most effective organizations will build enough power to extend their impact more widely (Kania & Kramer, 2011). As such, organizations focus on internal capacity-building and try to invent independent solutions to major social problems, often working at odds or competing with each other and increasing the resources required to make meaningful progress (Frumkin, 2002). But, it is becoming clearer that empowered organizations "work with and through other organizations – and they have much more impact than if they acted alone" (Crutchfield & Grant, 2007, p. 108). Networks, coalitions, alliances, and other forms of interorganizational collaboration are seen as more effective strategies for building power to affect the broader systems and policy changes needed to reduce suffering and promote liberation and wellbeing. We'll expand on coalition-building in the section below on community interventions.

Intraorganizational Empowerment

In order for community-based organizations to engage in transformative practice alone or as part of interorganizational collaborations, a degree of organizational capacity and empowering conditions needs to be in place. Building on his earlier work on empowering community settings, Maton (2008), Fedi, Mannarini, & Maton (2009) identified six distinct features: (1) group-based belief system that inspires strength-based change; (2) core activities that are engaging and meaningful; (3) relational environments that foster a sense of community within and beyond the setting; (4) opportunity role structure for people to express their views and talents; (5) visionary and committed leadership; and (6) organizational learning where diversity is valued and conflict resolution praised. According to Maton (2008), empowering settings with these characteristics lead to empowered citizens, empowered members, and potential engagement in social change.

In addition to being empowering for its members, and developing the requisite leadership, management, and technical capacities to get things done, organizations as open systems need to build **adaptive capacity** in order to handle complexity and respond to internal and external changes (Connolly & York, 2003; Evans & Kivell, 2015; Schneider & Somers, 2006). In short, community-based organizations and coalitions need to become **learning organizations**. A learning organization is one that supports systems thinking and constantly evaluates and adjusts its operations in line with its values, goals, and changing contexts (Senge, 1990; Senge & Scharmer, 2001). An organization with a culture of learning is one that "supports and encourages the collective discovery, sharing and application of knowledge" (Gill, 2009, p. 49). Building a learning culture in organizations requires the creation of organizational enabling structures that support systems thinking, dialogue, reflective practice, and continuous learning at the systems level (Evans & Kivell, 2015; Marsick, 2000; see Box 10.2).

Box 10.2 The Transformation Team (T-team)

What practical steps can organizations take to become learning organizations? The transformation team (T-team) is one way for community-based organizations to put reflection and learning into action. *T-teams* are small groups in organizations that meet regularly and provide a protected space for dialogue, opportunities for members to increase their understanding of organizational issues and reflect on organizational practice, and support to examine shared mental models assumptions (Evans et al., 2007). Through their work with various organizations, Evans and Kivell (2015) were able to identify eight necessary ingredients for successful organizational learning through T-teams: (1) organizational readiness; (2) leadership buy-in and participation; (3) T-team purpose and structure; (4) attention to inclusion and diffusion; (5) balance of learning and action; (6) dialogue; (7) linking organizational development to critical community practice; and (8) the role of the **critical friend**.

Natalie Kivell consulted with The Helping House (THH) in Kitchener-Waterloo, Ontario to create an internal T-team to guide an organizational visioning and organizational change process. THH serves the local community through programs ranging from a homeless shelter for men to community centers and a food distribution program helping over 42,000 adults, families, and children every year. As the T-team at THH reflected on their emerging vision statement, a dialogue began between two contrasting themes:

"having needs met" and "thriving." The question arose as to whether it was enough to provide for those who are suffering, versus the importance of providing conditions through which people could thrive in the community. This turned into a deep reflection on their shared understanding of power and privilege in communities. This moment in particular created a dramatic shift in the T-team's conceptualization of the organization and how it needed to frame its work moving forward. The executive director remarked that the reflection and learning practices started by the T-team are so deeply built into the organizational culture that staff at all levels now ask themselves at every turn: "How does this decision ensure that people in our organization and our community will belong and thrive?"

Roles of Community Psychologists Working in Organizations

We identify two potential roles for community psychologists working in organizations. The first is the promotion of empowering practices within the organization. The second is the pursuit of empowered outcomes in the community served by the organization. These roles may be fulfilled either as **internal** or **external agents of change**. To be effective, community psychologists require certain skills. The skills we present extend the **emotional competencies** of effective leaders documented by Goleman (1998) described in the following pages. Whereas Goleman's skills of emotional intelligence apply primarily to organizational efficacy, we discuss the implications of such skills for transformational work. Finally, based on the work of Prochaska and colleagues on processes of change, we describe the steps necessary to succeed in organizational development (Prochaska, Norcross, & DiClemente 1994; Weick & Quinn, 1999).

Promote an Empowering and Empowered Organization

Some values, such as self-determination and participation, can be promoted in organizational interventions, but in very different degrees. The literature on employee involvement and participation demonstrates that organizations vary greatly in the degree of autonomy they grant to their workers and volunteers. Most business organizations tend to limit employee input to suggestions for problem-solving activities (Fullan, 2008; Klein, Ralls, Smith Major, & Douglas, 2000; Sisodia, Wolfe, & Sheth, 2007), whereas human services and alternative settings usually afford workers and volunteers more voice and choice (Cherniss, 2002; Cherniss & Deegan, 2000; Lord & Hutchison, 2007; Maton & Salem, 1995; Nelson, Lord & Ochocka, 2001). This may reflect the fact that the latter "focuses on empowerment and well-being" and the former on "productivity and profitability" (Shinn & Perkins, 2000, p. 635). It should be noted, however, that within each type of organization, business, public sector, or human services, there is also great variability in the amount of control and participation given to workers (Ashkanasy & Dorris, 2017; Edmonson, 2012; Kegan & Lahey 2016).

Interventions to enhance worker participation often take place in small groups like T-teams (Box 10.2) where colleagues can reflect on organizational culture and practices and discuss ways to improve productivity or service delivery. Similar initiatives have been called Total Quality

Management (TQM) or Quality of Working Life (QWL). In essence, groups are formed to analyze processes and outcomes of work and ways to enhance effectiveness and satisfaction. The nature of the groups varies greatly, with some being initiated by management, some by external **consultants** and some by union–management committees (Johnson & Johnson, 2000; Klein et al., 2000). Interventions to enhance participation like T-teams are intended to be more transformational, creating enduring changes to organizational culture, whereas other attempts can be surface-level and tokenistic.

Although it is hard to generalize because of the variability in teams and forms of worker participation, several reviews documented positive effects for both productivity and worker satisfaction (Driskell, Salas, & Driskell, 2018; Johnson & Johnson, 2000; Klein et al., 2000; Lacerenza, Marlow, Tannenbaum, & Salas, 2018; Shinn & Perkins, 2000; Weick & Quinn, 1999). Reviewers seem to agree that the overall impact on productivity and worker satisfaction depends on the duration, intensity and actual – as opposed to perceived – control over jobs. When these conditions are present and long lasting, organizations improve their services and workers feel better about their jobs. When interventions are short-lived and half-hearted, positive results fade quickly (Fullan, 2006, 2008).

Reducing stress and burnout in the workplace is an aim of many managers, consultants, and workers themselves. Strategies to alleviate stress include participation in decision-making, structural innovations, ergonomic approaches, role-based interventions, social support, and provision of information. In a comprehensive review of the literature, Beehr and O'Driscoll (2002) found that most interventions had only modest effects on stress reduction. Some of the most promising strategies included worker participation in decision-making and role clarification. Role ambiguity, role conflict, and role overload are three serious causes of strain. Making sure that workers know what is expected of them, that they do not have unrealistic caseloads, and that they have management support for their duties are useful ways of decreasing strain (Beehr & O'Driscoll, 2002).

Role ambiguity is very common in human service organizations. In several of our studies, workers in clinics and human service organizations reported dilemmas related to caseloads, territoriality, diffused responsibility, and lack of support by supervisors and management (Evans et al., 2007; Evans et al., 2011; Prilleltensky, Sanchez Valdes, Walsh-Bowers, & Rossiter, 2002; Prilleltensky, Walsh-Bowers, & Rossiter, 1999). Participants reported that peer support, management backing, and the creation of a safe space for sharing dilemmas were essential components of effectiveness, satisfaction, and sometimes even "emotional survival" (Ashkanasy & Dorris, 2017; Edmonson, 2012). Social support in the workplace has long been recognized as an important correlate of worker wellbeing (Chapman & Sisodia, 2015; Marek, Schaufeli, & Maslach, 2017; Shinn & Perkins, 2000; Stansfeld, 1999; Worline & Dutton, 2017).

Transformational interventions that enhance the wellbeing of workers can be found in both the human and business sectors (Quinn, 2015). In the human services sector, including health, mental health, disabilities, education, and employment organizations, transformational workplaces tend to have horizontal structures with minimal hierarchies. In addition, they tend to make decisions by consensus and to flatten power differentials within the organization (Reinharz, 1984; Riger, 2000). Many feminist organizations were created with visions of equality and mutual accountability (Angelique & Mulvey, 2012; hooks, 2000c). Self-help organizations often espouse egalitarian structures as well, as do alternative settings that are value based, mission oriented and human focused (Cherniss & Deegan, 2000). In reviewing the creation of alternative settings in human services, Cherniss and Deegan noted that "the self-development of the staff and the health of the organization were considered to be two of the most important priorities" (2000, p. 374). The Maven Leadership Collective featured in Box 10.3 focuses on supporting the wellbeing of leaders in diverse organizations.

Box 10.3 "Put your Oxygen Mask on First"

When you fly on an airplane, the flight attendant instructs you to, in the event of an emergency, put your oxygen mask on first, before helping others. Why is this an important rule for ensuring survival? Because if you run out of oxygen, you can't help anyone else with their oxygen mask. The Maven Leadership Collective in Miami, Florida uses this metaphor as a reminder that if we don't take care of ourselves as we go about the difficult work of helping others, we can experience burnout, stress, fatigue, reduced mental effectiveness, and other health problems. Maven is a nonprofit organization that invests in creative social impact leaders who are queer and trans people of color and allies to build communities that thrive even in the face of crisis, transition, and tragedy. Their mission is to make leadership in community organizations more diverse and the organizations more sustainable. Maven's governance structure reflects this mission as it is 100 percent people of color, 70 percent queer, 50 percent female, and 50 percent under the age of 35. With numerous activities that focus on self-care and model wellness for their teams, the founders believe community leadership begins with our own self-care so that we may better serve others. For example, their "Maven Moves" program is a free community yoga series for all levels that celebrates all bodies (https://www.mavenleadership.org).

Internal and External Agents of Change

Community psychologists can help organizations and communities from the inside or the outside. Graduating community psychologists often get jobs as program planners, grant writers, managers in human services, program evaluators, or directors of community services or government departments. Other community psychologists open their own consulting firms and work for other organizations on contract (Viola & McMahon, 2011). Alternatively, consultants get government grants to help community organizations deliver a service or evaluate their programs.

As either internal or external agents of change, community psychologists can exert more or less control over the process of change. Depending on the level of control exercised, Dimock (1992) identified six possible roles for agents of change. In decreasing order of control, they are as follows:

- *Director:* manager or administrator who makes decisions and gives instructions in order to control the intervention
- *Expert:* system analyst or organizational consultant who diagnoses problems and uses knowledge to tell others what to do
- *Consultant:* community developer and consultant who makes suggestions and whose influence derives from respect and trust

- *Resource:* group trainer or resource provider who helps groups to collect data and provides training in planning skills
- *Evaluation or research collaborator:* consultant or collaborator who designs and implements program and organizational evaluation and research with organizational partners
- *Facilitator:* process consultant, helper, or group observer who assists with group processes
- *Collaborator:* staff, board, or community member who is interested in change and joins groups or teams planning and carrying out interventions.

Bond (1999) and Evans (2015) urge community psychologists working within organizations to consider taking on a gently disruptive role to help organizations develop a more critical approach to practice. Bond (1999) coined the concept *connected-disruption* to describe the need to be able to point to unjust practices and still remain engaged with most people in order for them to listen to us. Evans (2015) uses the concept of *critical friend* to highlight this tricky practice of critique in the context of trust and mutual respect. Acting as problematizing agents, community psychologists can challenge assumptions, disrupt problematic patterns and practices, and disturb complacency. To be effective, this must be preconditioned by strong relationships, connection, and honoring individual humanity (Bond, 2007).

As internal or external agents of change, community psychologists can fulfil any one of these roles (see Table 10.1). We caution, however, against the adoption of director or expert roles, as they tend to alienate partners. However, it is possible to be a manager or executive director, but still work in a very collaborative manner; the position does not have to dictate the intervention style. We favor intervention styles that are collaborative and that share control across levels of the organization and the community, not only because they are in line with our values but also because they are more effective (Bond, 2007; Dimock, 1992; Ife, 2002; Johnson & Johnson, 2000; Klein et al., 2000; Prilleltensky & Nelson, 2002; Shinn & Perkins, 2000).

Emotional Competencies and Their Transformational Potential

To be effective as internal or external agents of change, community psychologists require a set of skills. In Chapter 8, we highlighted some of the skills expected from a practicing community psychologist. In this section we want to emphasize some of the interpersonal and emotional competencies required to interact with people in organizations and communities. Goleman (1998) integrated a great deal of research concerning the personal and interpersonal skills that predict satisfaction in families, work, school, and communities. He called this set of skills "emotional intelligence."

Table 10.1 Internal and external agents of change in organizations

Internal Agents of Change	External Agents of Change
Managers	Organizational consultant
Executive director	Member of the community
Administrator	Conflict resolution mediator
Staff member	Trainer
Member of the board	Program evaluator

Goleman's work provides a valuable foundation for understanding what is required to become an effective change maker. However, his contributions do not emphasize the same value base or transformational goals that we deem important for CP. Goleman neither necessarily critiques the exploitive nature of the corporations he studied, nor does he emphasize the need to use emotional intelligence to overcome oppression and injustice. Hence, we present here the main emotional competencies identified by Goleman (1998) and their transformational potential. We agree with Goleman that these skills are vital for communicating effectively with others and exerting influence in respectful ways. He is very clear that change needs to take into account how other people feel about it. In our view, Goleman's main contribution is to personal and relational wellbeing. We are interested in distilling the implications of his theory for collective wellbeing as well.

In a review of studies of work organizations, Cherniss and Adler (2000) found that individuals who excel at their jobs also have many of the skills that characterize emotional intelligence. Goleman's emotional competencies concentrate on the values of caring, compassion, and collaboration at the interpersonal level. We see in them potential to contribute to social justice and accountability at the collective level. If Goleman highlighted personal and interpersonal intelligence, we want to develop the concept of collective intelligence, or the ability of the individual to think about the wellbeing of the collective, and the capacity of the collective to act on behalf of the individual. As community psychologists, it is our job to find ways to promote collective intelligence, not just interpersonal skills.

Steps for Organizational Change

Building organizational capacities for transformative practice often requires an intentional process of organizational change. Prochaska and colleagues postulated a theory of change that has been successfully used and applied to individuals and organizations (Prochaska et al., 1994; Weick & Quinn, 1999). The theory describes predictable and necessary stages of change. In Chapter 8, we apply this theory of change to individuals, but here we apply it to organizational work. For each one of the steps we describe key questions for planning and implementation. These questions should help community psychologists trying to produce change and recruit support for it.

The first two stages of change relate to **pre-contemplation** and **contemplation**. In pre-contemplation it is possible that nobody, except perhaps you, or a few silent others, are aware that something needs to be done about an unsatisfactory situation. In which case, somebody needs to raise consciousness about the problem. In contemplation, you are already planting the seed to move the process forward. Discontent may turn into positive action. But as Bond (1999) and Evans (2015) stress, for others to listen to you, you need to stay connected while creating a minor (or major) disturbance to the status quo.

The third step, *preparation*, involves the planning and design of innovations or alterations to the current system of work, service delivery, or communication patterns, whatever the case might be. During the *action* phase, it is very important to make sure that all stakeholders affected by the new system of work are involved, which, to reiterate, not only is it in line with our values but is also the most efficacious way of going about change because it creates ownership, commitment and accountability (Dimock, 1992; Goleman, 1998; Johnson & Johnson, 2000).

Once the action has been initiated, it is crucial to put in place systems for monitoring accurate implementation of the intended changes. The sustainability and dissemination of innovations depend on a careful plan for making the innovation or new program an integral part of the institution (Dalton, Elias, & Wandersman, 2006). In the absence of *maintenance* and monitoring systems, change is likely to be weak and short-lived. Although parts of the next step, *evaluation*, cannot be undertaken until changes have been introduced into the system, some aspects of the evaluation can be undertaken during the implementation phase itself. This will enable a formative assessment of how things are going. By observing the change process itself, we are able to feed back useful information that can improve and refine the innovation while it is being introduced. We call this process *action research* (Reason & Bradbury, 2001) and you will learn more about it in Chapters 12 and 13.

Strengths and Limitations of Organizational Interventions

The strengths of organizational interventions derive primarily from their *potential to affect the lives of thousands or millions of people*. Organizations affect our lives in multiple ways. The sooner we make workplaces, schools, civic institutions, and government departments more participatory, value-based, and transformational, the sooner we will be able to improve the lives of workers and communities alike. As social change happens in, through, and because of organizations, the potential to use organizations to produce larger changes is significant. Given that community psychologists work or volunteer in organizations, they have many opportunities to make a change. This potential notwithstanding, we realize that change is a hard and humbling enterprise.

We have to be conscious of traps and threats. *Complacency and resistance* are major barriers to change. Swimming against the tide can be emotionally draining and potentially risky. Challengers of the status quo risk exclusion, marginalization, labeling, and potential unemployment. The forces of resistance are almost always stronger than the forces of change (Beehr & O'Driscoll, 2002; Dimock, 1992; Hahn, 1994; Klein et al., 2000; Weick & Quinn, 1999).

The ubiquitous risk of cosmetic changes is called *tokenism*. It is a technique used to introduce small changes that create the appearance of change but in fact help to prevent transformations. Sullivan (1984) calls this phenomenon *dislocation*, by which he means "a process whereby something new is brought into a cultural system and has the ability to mute the partial critical insight of that cultural system" (p. 165). Changes of a minor nature are introduced into organizations with the purpose of creating an aura of innovation, changes that invariably delay attention to more structural issues.

An exclusive *inward focus* is another potential deviation that needs to be monitored. McAdam (1999) uses the concept of **oligarchization** to characterize the tendency of organizations to focus more on the maintenance of the organization itself rather than community goals. Additionally, because nonprofit community organizations cannot survive if they do not respond to the demands of their external environments, this creates a *resource dependency* that makes organizations subject to the demands of the external entities like funders that provide their needed resources (Pfeffer & Salancik, 2003). Some organizations invest in development only to advance the *interests of upper management or privileged stakeholders* (Alvesson & Willmott, 1992; Baritz, 1974; Hollway, 1991; Lawthom, 1999). Business and human service organizations alike have also been criticized for starting *half-hearted initiatives* that create expectations of improvement but amount only to passing fads that strengthen the status quo (Prilleltensky, 1994; Prilleltensky & Nelson, 2002).

If the primary purpose of community organizations is to build power to promote wellbeing and social justice in communities, what interventions strategies are most likely to achieve those goals? We move now from the internal capacities of effective organizations to discuss the various interventions that organizations and coalitions use to foster positive change.

Community Empowerment

In the previous sections, we have discussed the limitations of service provision and ameliorative approaches often used by organizations in communities. What are other forms of community intervention that are more likely to contribute to community empowerment and systems change? Community interventions are efforts by organized groups and agencies to enhance the wellbeing of community members marginalized by social practices of exclusion, cultural norms of discrimination, and economic policies of injustice and inequality (Ife, 2002; Mullaly, 2002; Orr, 2007; Smock, 2004). While there are a variety of ways to intervene in communities, including targeted or community-wide interventions designed and implemented by professionals, commensurate with CP's commitment to empowering and transformative processes, we focus on three overlapping community empowerment strategies that aim to build social power through ongoing empowerment processes: community-building, coalition-building, and community organizing. We ground the discussion of these three strategies in the theory of community empowerment.

In his 2019 book entitled *Community Power and Empowerment*, Christens (2019) asks a critical question: "How do community groups develop and exercise social power to foster the conditions for greater pluralism and flourishing?" (p. 124). He goes on to propose a framework for *community empowerment* that should seek to accomplish five goals: it should (1) be understood as inextricably linked to individual and organizational empowerment processes; (2) be distinguished from other closely related processes such as community program delivery; (3) draw on understanding of community and social power from community organizing and social movements; (4) mine ideas and practices from the fields of community development and public health; and (5) emphasize the links between power and empowerment (see Chapter 4). An emphasis on social power as the primary outcome of community interventions helps to keep the emphasis on transformational change (Prilleltensky, 2008b).

Community Building

Community-building interventions intend to mobilize and build the "community" attributes of the place by ensuring resident engagement in and ownership of the work, forging connections among stakeholders, and strengthening civic capacity and voice (Kubisch, Auspos, Brown, & Dewar, 2010). Community building is about increasing the capacity of a community through developing individual leaders, increasing organizational capacity, increasing social capital and sense of community among residents, and increasing civic capacity across the neighborhood's individuals and organizations. Chaskin (2001) offers a definitional framework for community capacity based on the literature and case studies from a comprehensive community initiative. He defines community capacity as the interaction of human capital, organizational resources, and social capital existing within a given community that can be leveraged to solve collective problems and improve or maintain the well-being of a given community. It may operate through informal social processes and/or organized effort. (p. 295)

Asset-based community development (Kretzmann & McKnight, 1993) is one approach that engages residents in a process of mapping the capacities of the residents, organizations, local culture, and physical features of an area then working to connect, organize, and orchestrate instrumental links among them to build local knowledge, investment, creativity, hope, and control. The purpose of community capacity building is to create opportunities for people in a community to work together, develop a vision and strategies for the future, make collaborative decisions, and take collective action while building the individual skills and capabilities of a range of participants and organizations within the community (The Aspen Institute 1996). Because of the difficult nature of community change, community capacity building requires simultaneous attention to strengthening individuals, formal organizations, and the relational networks tying them to each other and to the broader systems of which they are a part (Chaskin, 2001).

Christens (2019), however, worries that community-building approaches too often focus on the delivery of distinct programs or projects and dilute the social power-building aims of community empowerment. This tendency arises partly because the sorts of organizations that drive community-building efforts on the ground are primarily development- or service-oriented nonprofits rather than social movement or advocacy organizations. His concern highlights the importance of intentionally framing community-building efforts more explicitly with reference to the systemic conditions, higher-order actors, and processes that promote or constrain communities' ability to effect change (Chaskin & Karlstrom, 2012).

Coalition Building

Coalitions, networks, neighborhood alliances, and other forms of interorganizational collaboration are seen as effective strategies for building community power to effect the broader systems and policy changes needed to benefit marginalized communities. Bringing together organizations and groups with similar missions, goals, and concerns makes better use of limited resources and increases the chances that a shared agenda can be achieved (Evans, Raymond, & Perkins, 2014). Building the capacity of coalitions in communities requires a focus on the relationships between organizations and the creation of a shared purpose, shared objectives, and collective power. Coalition building is about the creation and maintenance of shared spaces that provide the opportunity for a variety of community organizational actors to coordinate resources and action (Foster-Fishman, Salem, Allen, & Fahrbach, 2001; Kubisch et al., 2010). Community coalitions are an outcome of community building and have the potential to contribute to greater community and systems capacity through building stronger social and interorganizational networks (Bess, 2015; Butterfoss & Kegler 2009).

Building coalitions requires a focus on the relationships and coordinated activities across organizations that are needed to develop a shared purpose and effectively build and exercise power (Christens, 2019; Peterson & Zimmerman, 2004). The perception of shared goals in particular has been cited as important in galvanizing initial participation (Knoke & Wood 1981; Norris 2001) and contributing to the coalition's capacity for systems change (Nowell 2009). Ensuring that all actors agree about the core purpose of the work is critical to creating and maintaining focus. Developing a common vision and plan of action is one of the most time-consuming and complicated tasks a community collaborative undertakes. It is also one of the most essential. Too often, the goals sought by collaborative community change initiatives are defined too broadly or abstractly at the outset, either for political reasons or resulting from the absence of good theory or solid evidence about what produces community change (Kubisch et al., 2010). Just as organizations need a level of capacity to get things done, so do interorganizational collaborations.

Goodman et al. (1998) define **collaborative capacity** as the conditions needed for coalitions to collaborate effectively and build sustainable community change. Foster-Fishman, Salem, et al. (2001) conducted a review of the literature and developed an integrated model for building collaborative capacity. The model posits that coalitions need collaborative capacity at four critical levels: within members (skills and knowledge); within their relationships (good interpersonal relations); within their organizational structures (operational capacity); and within the programs they sponsor (the design and implementation of effective community-based programs). Similarly, Zakocs and Edwards (2006) reviewed the literature on coalitions and identified cohesion, membership diversity, and formalization of rules/procedures as factors that were associated with coalition effectiveness.

Collaboration across organizations is difficult and necessary. One of the most important things a community psychologist can do is to join with these groups as action researchers, consultants, evaluators, and partners to help groups figure out how to work better together toward shared goals. See for example the work of community psychologists Penny Foster-Fishman and Erin Watson supporting collaborative systems change efforts using their ABLe Change Framework (Foster-Fishman & Watson, 2012; http://www.ablechange.msu.edu/). Foster-Fishman and Watson developed the ABLe Change Framework ("Above and Below the Line") to provide coalitions with the conceptual and practical tools needed to effectively design and implement systems change initiatives. Their attention to building capacity for process considerations – what they call "Below the Line" – targets the implementation processes and collaborative capacities needed to achieve desired the "Above the Line" systems change outcomes. These capacities reflect the skills and knowledge "that system actors need to effectively respond to the shifting demands of the Above the Line work" (Foster-Fishman & Watson, 2012, p. 508).

Comprehensive Community Initiatives (CCIs)

Comprehensive community initiatives (CCIs) is an umbrella term for place-based, collaborative approaches that all share a common commitment to human and community development that is comprehensive, locally-based, centered on citizen participation, involves public-private partnerships, and collaboration of multiple agencies (Chaskin & Karlstrom, 2012; Fulbright-Anderson, 2006). CCIs seek to promote positive change in individual, family, and community circumstances in marginalized neighborhoods by applying the principles of comprehensiveness and community building to improve physical, social, and economic conditions. One fairly recent parallel model emerging out of the principles and practices of CCIs is **collective impact**.

Collective Impact

Collective impact is defined by Kania and Kramer (2011) as "the commitment of a group of important actors from different sectors to a common agenda for solving a specific social problem" (p. 36). Kania and Kramer suggest that successful collective impact efforts share five features: (1)

a common agenda; (2) shared measurement (see also the reference to collective impact evaluations in Chapter 13); (3) mutually reinforcing activities; (4) continuous communication between stakeholders; and (5) backbone support. Proponents of collective impact asserts that when these five conditions are present, collaborative initiatives can gain momentum and achieve large-scale systems change (Kania, Hanleybrown, & Juster, 2014). Similar to the research on collaboration, the collective impact model stresses the important role of the lead agency or "backbone" organization in guiding and supporting collective action (Hanleybrown, Kania, & Kramer, 2012; Turner, Merchant, Kania, & Martin, 2012; Varda, 2018).

One example of a collective impact approach is the Promise Neighborhoods initiative supported by the US Department of Education. This effort bought together nonprofit agencies, schools, government, business, families, students, and other partners to create aligned supports from cradle to career to work toward desired results that cover the cradle-to-career continuum, from ensuring that children enter kindergarten ready to succeed in school to increasing high school graduation rates to getting more parents involved in supporting student learning. The Indianola, Mississippi Promise Community initiative documented a relative 76 percent improvement in the percentage of kindergartners arriving at school grade-ready (McAfee, Blackwell, & Bell, 2015).

While collective impact has found its way into the vernacular of many community initiatives and grantmaking agencies, it is not without its critics. One central critique of the impact model is that it ignores decades of research on collaboration, CCIs, and community organizing (Cabaj & Weaver, 2016; Christens & Inzeo, 2015; Kubisch et al., 2010; McAfee et al., 2015; Wolff, 2016; Wolff et al., 2017). Critics also have concerns over its "grasstops" approach; professionals, organizational staff, and community gatekeepers dominate the agenda-setting process and implementation and are not always committed to resident leadership and ownership (Christens, 2019). This results in a lack of grassroots community involvement and what Vu Le (2015) pointedly refers to as "trickle-down community engagement ... when we bypass the people who are most affected by issues, engage and fund larger organizations to tackle these issues, and hope that miraculously the people most affected will help out in the effort, usually for free" (p. 4).

Coalitions dominated by government agency staff and power figures from large organizations may limit the involvement of marginalized groups by the sheer numbers of those with power (Chavis, 2001). Himmelman (1996) describes efforts that are driven from the grasstops or outside the community as *collaborative betterment*, where the approach reflects similar processes generally used by organizations. He contrasts betterment approaches with *collaborative empowerment* endeavors that are led from within the community and geared toward building community capacity rather than only focused on specific outcomes (e.g., educational or health outcomes). Building resident power refers to having residents, primarily those from low-income neighborhoods, recognized as individuals who can and should influence local decisions and who play an active role in making change happen (Zimmerman, 2000). To their credit, the originators of the collective impact model have addressed some of these critiques in recent updates to the framework. In 2015, Kania and Kramer's fourth article in the Collective Impact series focused on the importance of equity and argued that inclusion in the change process of the people most affected by an issue is imperative. Authentic and inclusive community engagement is, without a doubt, a condition for transformational impact.

Community Organizing

A weakness in most community-based coalitions, collaborations, and partnerships is the absence of community organizing (Wolff et al., 2017). Community organizing initiatives engage residents in sustained efforts to collectively investigate and address mutual concerns through the exercise of power and collective mobilization (Christens & Inzeo, 2015; Christens & Speer, 2015). Community organizing engages individuals and organizations to participate in addressing problems and concerns collectively, through the exercise of power leveraged through the coordinated mobilization of these individuals and groups (Speer, Tesdahl, & Ayers, 2014). This approach to community intervention prioritizes leadership by people who are most affected by the issues of concern, rather than by those who are professionally or politically involved in working on those issues, and seeks to alter the relations of power between the groups that have traditionally controlled decisions and the residents of marginalized communities (see Box 10.4).

Box 10.4 Pacific Institute of Community Organizations (PICO)/Faith in Action

Community psychologist Paul Speer and his colleagues spent years studying an organization that is trying to make change rather than simply cure, an organization that pursues social change (Speer, 2002; Speer & Hughey, 1995; Speer, Hughey, Gensheimer, & Adams-Leavitt, 1995). Pacific Institute of Community Organizations (PICO – now named Faith in Action, https://faithin-action.org/) was a community-organizing network with affiliates in 25 cities across the US. PICO helped to organize communities to demand more resources for children, families, crime prevention, poor neighborhoods, and people with addictions and other social problems. This organization was very clear on the need to transcend therapeutic models and to use community power to access more resources. Three principles supported PICO's organizing efforts:

- Empowerment can only be realized through organizing.
- Social power is built on the strength of interpersonal relationships.
- Individual empowerment must be grounded in a dialectic of action and reflection.

PICO was successful in empowering its members and in getting results. Like other empowering organizations, this one allowed members to rotate in their roles and to engage in a variety of tasks. Some of the jobs done by members and volunteers included getting information from public officials, asking politicians difficult questions, mobilizing communities for rallies, arranging transportation, arranging media coverage, facilitating meetings, and so on. Some of the results included better resources for communities and increased awareness of the political dynamics oppressing the poor and the disenfranchised. In one campaign PICO obtained from the city council and private corporations $9 million for substance abuse treatment and prevention. Now under their new name, Faith and Action continues to engage thousands of people through federations and sustain long-term campaigns to bring about systematic change at all levels.

To build collective power, community-organizing initiatives engage local residents through one-to-one meetings in which residents listen to each other's hopes and concerns for their community. The themes from these meetings and additional data collection inform strategic selection of specific issues that the initiative seeks to address through public actions (Christens et al., 2016; Speer & Hughey, 1995). Through collective reflection, they learn to think systemically about social problems and solutions and critically analyze issues, contexts, and strategies for building power and taking collective action (Christens, Inzeo, & Faust, 2014).

Ginwright (2010) provides an example of young people involved in organizing for immigrant rights in Milwaukee, Wisconsin. Students United for Immigrant Rights (SUFRIR) is the youth arm of Milwaukee-based Voces de la Frontera. Voces de la Frontera is a membership-based community organization led by low-wage workers, immigrants, and youth working to protect and expand civil rights and workers' rights through leadership development, community organizing, and empowerment (https://vdlf.org). Students from local high schools did a close analysis of the Development, Relief, and Education for Alien Minors (DREAM) Act and led informational meetings, marches, dialogue sessions, and school walkouts about immigrant rights. Through strategic efforts to build collective power, Voces and SUFRIR's statewide organizing campaign won in-state tuition at public colleges for Wisconsin immigrant students in 2009. This was one of the most important pro-immigrant state level victories in the US that year. Voces also built new alliances statewide with diverse constituencies like dairy farmers and law enforcement to support restoring access to driver licenses for Wisconsin immigrants. After these wins, SUFRIR formally merged with the Black student organization Students United in the Struggle (SUITS) and together formed Youth Empowered in the Struggle (YES), and remained the student arm of Voces de la Frontera. YES fights for quality public schools, for dignity for Black and Brown students, and for immigrant, worker, and student rights.

Christens and Inzeo (2015) highlight three distinctions between community organizing and other approaches to community change: (1) deep resident engagement; (2) analysis of power; and (3) capacity to address conflict. While community coalitions and collective impact efforts primarily bring together established organizational leaders and decision-makers, community organizing initiatives develop nonprofessional resident leaders as their primary drivers of change. As illuminated in the SUFRIR example above, people closest to the problem should be part of the solution to that problem (Stahlhut 2003). Grassroots community organizing initiatives can be viewed as empowerment processes (Christens, 2019; Christens et al., 2014), building individual and community capacity and fostering what McAdam (1999) refers to as *cognitive liberation* – collective optimism about the capacity to change social and neighborhood conditions (Ginwright, 2007).

In addition to deep resident engagement, community organizing involves a critical analysis of power. Unlike other community interventions, power is a central concern in grassroots community organizing models and organizers understand that most problems people face result from a lack of power (Christens & Inzeo, 2015; McAlevey, 2016). Groups work together to identify powerful stakeholders in a community, determine the basis of their power, and document who their allies and opponents are in order to develop strategies for action. Community organizers ask questions such as: How do the current arrangements of power in this community contribute to the problems that we seek to address? Which people or entities hold the power to make (or block) meaningful changes in community systems (e.g., education and transportation)? What are the relationships between powerful actors in this community? The process of answering these questions is often referred to as **power mapping** (Christens & Inzeo, 2015; Noy, 2008).

Lastly, community organizing approaches differ from other forms of community intervention in willingness to utilize and capacity to address conflict. While it may be possible, and even preferable, to seek collaborative solutions to community change, it is more common to encounter resistance to changes from those whose resources or relative power would be reduced in the process. Conflict approaches utilize oppositional tactics to bring about desired ends. Examples include marches, sit-ins, strikes, and mass protests called "actions." The rationale for using a conflict strategy is the understanding that powerful people and institutions will not work to reduce injustice unless direct pressure is applied (Chaskin, Brown, Venkatesh, & Vidal, 2001). Community organizing groups are prepared for forms of mobilization that engage conflict as well as collaboration (Christens & Inzeo, 2015; Speer & Christens, 2014).

Christens (2019) provides a useful concept map to highlight the various interrelated pathways through which community empowerment approaches benefit participants in empowerment process as well as the broader community (Fig. 10.1). Participant pathways refer to the benefits accrued to residents who are participating and leading change. Ecological pathways lead to improved community wellbeing through successful changes to policies, systems, and environments. Finally, pluralist pathways demonstrate the benefits of living in a community with a more egalitarian power structure. Christens acknowledges that this framework can appear overly simplistic and linear and doesn't fully capture the bidirectional influences and feedback loops operating in each of the pathways. However, the concept map provides a holistic perspective on the interconnected aspects of community empowerment.

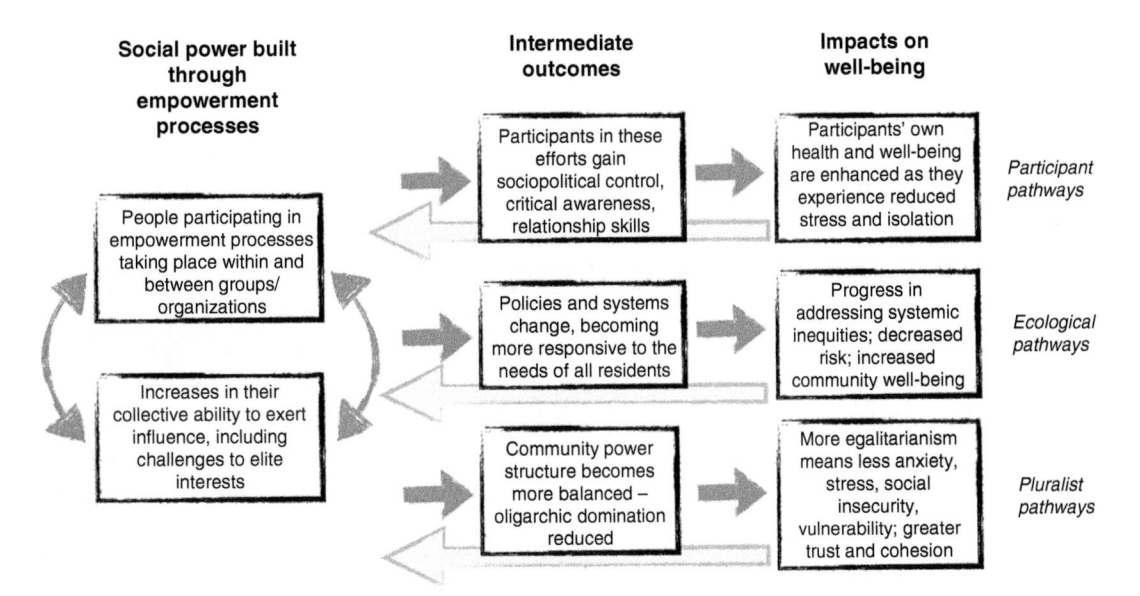

Figure 10.1 Empowerment process and outcomes

Source: From Christens, 2019, p. 159. Copyright © Oxford University Press 2019; reproduced with permission.

The Roles of Community Psychologists Working in Communities

The skills and processes required for organizational change noted above apply to community change as well. In many cases, community psychologists represent one organization in working with another. Neighborhood centers, schools, community mental health clinics, and universities all interact with each other and with government in starting new programs or policies. But, if the skills are similar, the contexts are different. We are moving from one level of analysis to another, a larger one. Interorganizational work is becoming prevalent in CP, and for good reasons. No one organization has the power to enhance community wellbeing on its own. As discussed above, inter-agency coalitions can mobilize multiple partners for interventions with synergistic outcomes (Foster-Fishman, Salem, et al., 2001; Wolff, 2001). Given the promise of partnerships for community change, we chose to concentrate a part of this chapter on the role of **partnership maker**. The creation of coalitions is really a prelude to community change. Hence, we also discuss the role of **change maker**. Finally, we discuss the role of **knowledge maker**, which should always accompany intervention efforts.

Partnership Maker

To make a change in a community you need allies and partners. We describe below eight steps in the creation and actualization of partnerships for change. In each step the community psychologist assumes a particular role. They wear different hats depending on the phase, but always keep all the hats in their bag, just in case, for partnerships are very dynamic and boundaries across phases often blur. Still, it is useful to identify the primary role in each step. Based on our previous work and reports of other community psychologists we identify eight main roles for the seven main tasks of partnership building (Elias, 1994; Foster-Fishman, Berkowitz, et al., 2001; Nelson et al. 2000; Nelson, Prilleltensky & MacGillivary, 2001; Prilleltensky, 2001; Prilleltensky, Peirson, Gould, & Nelson, 1997; Wolff, 2001).

- *Inclusive host:* Whether you are initiating the partnership yourself, or you have been invited to one, you need to behave like an inclusive host. Power differentials are always at play in partnerships, primarily when community members with little or no formal education join the group. We think it is very important to contribute to a climate of respect and mutual support.
- *Visionary:* Once we are comfortable with each other, the business of change begins. We caution against skipping this stage. As a collective, partners need to establish a common vision for the project. Our role is to help in visioning outcomes and processes for the collaborative work.
- *Asset seeker:* This is an important role for two reasons. First, in line with the values of self-determination, collaboration, and respect for diversity, we want to afford everyone an opportunity to express her or his views about what needs to be done. Each person has the right to express an opinion, regardless of expert status. Second, and just as importantly, valuable knowledge emerges from everyone in the partnership: citizens, professionals, and volunteers alike. We will never know what material or conceptual assets people bring unless we look for them.
- *Listener and sense maker:* To define the problem cooperatively we need to listen carefully to what all the partners are saying. Next, we need to formulate the problem in light of previous research and local knowledge.

- *Unique solution finder*: At this stage we wear the doer hat. The time has come to take action, and to find a solution that is uniquely suited to this context. We have to be able to read the context and assess the group's readiness for action.
- *Evaluator*: Throughout the planning and implementation, we study the work of the partnership. We engage partners in evaluating the process and the outcomes of the work.
- *Implementer*: This is a crucial role. After gathering information, engaging partners, and evaluating solutions, the time has come to implement sustainable changes.
- *Trendsetter*: It is not enough to have an excellent pilot project that gets forgotten soon after it was born. We have to ensure that partners adopt the innovation and disseminate it widely. We have to create enduring trends, not just passing fads.

Change Maker

How do we make sure that partnerships do not end up reproducing the status quo? After all, collaboration is a powerful tool used by protectors of the status quo. Business elites and conservative groups strike alliances to repel threats to the dominant social order (Barlow & Campbell, 1995; McQuaig, 1998). The risk of dislocation, reviewed in the context of organizations, applies equally to partnerships and coalitions. It is entirely possible that coalitions for health, safety, and prevention divert attention from political reform. Hence, we make a distinction between partnership maker and change maker. For us, change makers have to elicit in themselves and others the transformational potential of emotional competencies. This involves asking hard questions: Whose interests does the coalition represent? Whose power will be enhanced? Whose values will be upheld? Whose lives will be improved by the intervention? (Lord & Church, 1998).

The emotional competencies for transformation reviewed earlier are a resource for community change. They just need to be focused on how the interventions will improve the lives of those with less power, less access to services, and less influence. Organizations such as PICO and SUFRIR strive to keep a focus on social change, as do consumer/survivor organizations struggling to change not only psychiatry but also society's perceptions of people with mental health problems (see Chapter 21). We want to make sure that our interventions transcend amelioration and move towards transformation. This is where some of the principles and practices of critical community practice can guide us.

Knowledge Maker

Community psychologists have much to learn from successful and failed interventions. Each intervention consists of mini cycles of interventions. By studying the enabling and inhibiting factors each step of the way, they can improve the next cycle, and the one after that. We call this a formative evaluation. At the end of a project or a major initiative, it is time to take stock of what has been accomplished, what has been learned, and what could be done differently in the future. We call this summative or outcome evaluations (see also the discussion of different types of evaluation in Chapter 13). An action research or developmental evaluation approach that promotes learning by all stakeholders, throughout the whole process, ensures that important lessons are not lost along the way (Elias, 1994; Evans, Rosen, Kesten, & Moore, 2014; Preskill & Gopal, 2014; Reason & Bradbury, 2001; see also Chapters 12 and 13). Part of the community psychologist's job is to nurture a culture of learning.

Strengths and Limitations of Community Interventions

The strengths and limitations of community interventions can be gleaned from a review on citizen participation and community organizations. Wandersman and Florin (2000) report that the main effects of citizen participation are related to physical and environmental conditions of the community, levels of crime, provision of social services, interpersonal relationships, sense of community, satisfaction with place of residence, personal efficacy, and psychological empowerment. Although these are positive and encouraging findings, their review does not reveal outcomes associated with increased political activity or direct social action. Most effects appear to be associated with ameliorative – as opposed to transformative – actions. Herein lay the main benefits and shortcomings of community interventions.

There is little doubt that community interventions can improve quality of life. Tangible outcomes in the form of reduced crime, abuse, and violence, improved health, and cohesion and urban civility make a difference in the daily lives of community members (McNeely, 1999; Power, 1996). However, Paul Speer (Speer et al., 2014) worries that in this current neoliberal global context, community interventions have too easily gravitated toward safer forms of community work, such as consensus, collaborative, and community-building approaches, to the exclusion of approaches that directly challenge injustice (DeFilippis, 2008; DeFilippis, Fisher, & Shragge, 2006). Our challenge then, is to blend the pursuit of short-term care and compassion with the long-term struggle for justice. For it is only when justice prevails that political, economic, and social resources can be distributed fairly and equitably.

Dilemmas Faced by Community Psychologists Working in Organizations and Communities

Once you are trained to identify injustice at the interpersonal, organizational, community, and societal levels, it is hard to keep it a secret. Once you associate with people who share your passion for making a difference, it is hard to ignore norms of oppression. "What's the problem?" you may ask. The problem is that many others may not share your passion or convictions. When opposition mounts, you face a tough choice: struggle and resist, or acquiesce. As Bond (2007) claimed, it is hard to remain connected with the people who perpetuate injustice. The dilemma is how far you can challenge the system before you begin paying a price in the form of exclusion, labeling, and disconnection. The opposite dilemma is no less pressing: how to live in harmony with your values if you do not enact resistance (Langhout, 2015, 2016)?

The foregoing dilemmas refer to taking action. A further quandary is what type of action to take. What to do when we are aware that, despite much rhetoric, we are stuck in ameliorative mode? We are encouraged to see the field of CP wrestling with these dilemmas and looking for ways to (re)commit our community research and action to the work of decolonization, liberation, and social transformation (Montero, 2007). Dutta, Sonn, and Lykes (2016) suggest that if we are to make good on our commitment to transformative rather than ameliorative social change, "it is imperative to build on and develop new approaches to interrogate, confront, resist, and address structural violence through our research and practice, which include documenting critique and excavating radical possibilities" (p. 352).

Chapter Summary

In this chapter we considered how community psychologists could make a difference in organizations and communities. Our discussion was grounded in empowering processes and organizational, interorganizational, and community empowerment. We drew a distinction between interventions in organizations and communities that ameliorate conditions of suffering and disadvantage and those that seek to make more profound transformations. This tension between amelioration and transformation pervades CP as the themes throughout this book testify. We featured community interventions that have the highest potential to: (1) engage those most affected by the issues; and (2) build community power. We should also mention that in addition to the community intervention concepts and practices featured here, there is a wealth of additional scholarship in CP related to community-level, systems interventions that we were not able to include (e.g., Behrens & Foster-Fishman, 2007; Hawe, Shiell, & Riley, 2009; Lawlor & Neal, 2016; Schensul & Trickett, 2009; Trickett et al., 2011, to name just a few).

Much of the work of community psychologists happens in organizations and communities. The severity, scale, and complexity of social problems in communities demand a persistent focus on the promotion of social justice, accountability, and meaningful participation and empowerment. These efforts require skills and competencies that can be strategically applied at different stages of organizational and community interventions. Utilizing empowering approaches, grounded in the experiences of those most affected by oppressive social conditions, increases the likelihood of success in these interventions. We described some of the roles community psychologists can play as internal or external agents of change in organizations. At the community level, we identified three primary roles for community psychologists: partnership maker, change maker, and knowledge maker. Most of the skills and steps discussed in the organizational context may be applied in the community context and vice versa. What is your role in organizational and community change?

Key Terms

Adaptive capacity: An organization's ability to handle complexity and respond to internal and external changes.

Change maker: A skilled promoter of interventions that will improve the lives of those with less power, less access to services, and less influence.

Civil society sector: This term refers in general to nonprofit, charitable, and non-governmental organizations, institutions, and voluntary associations that are neither part of the government nor for-profit business.

Collaborative capacity: The capacities needed for coalitions to collaborate effectively and build sustainable community change.

Collective impact: The commitment of a group of important actors from different sectors to a common agenda for collaboratively solving a specific social problem.

Community interventions: Efforts by organized groups and agencies to enhance the wellbeing of community members marginalized by social practices of exclusion, discrimination, and injustice.

Community organizing: Engaging residents in sustained efforts to collectively investigate and address mutual concerns through the exercise of power and collective mobilization.

Consultant: A person who works with an organization or community and assists them in achieving their goals.

Contemplation: The early phase in a change process in which people realize that something needs to change.

Critical community practice: Action based on critical theorizing, reflection, and a clear commitment to working for social justice through empowering and transformative practice.

Critical friend: A person who joins with community partners to gently critique practices in order to illuminate relations of power and shape action to better achieve mutually agreed social justice objectives.

Emotional competencies: Set of skills required to handle self and others in a respectful and efficient manner consistent with a set of cogent values.

Extraorganizational empowerment: An organization's ability to affect broader systems, influence policy and practice, create alternative settings, and deploy organizational resources in the community.

External agent of change: The role assumed by community psychologists or others who wish to push for changes from outside an organization or community.

Human service organization: In the US, this term refers to those non-governmental, community-based organizations that operate exclusively for service provision, community building, or advocacy purposes.

Internal agent of change: The role assumed by community psychologists or others who wish to change a practice from within an organization.

Interorganizational empowerment: Refers to the quality of relationships, transactions, and collaboration across organizations.

Intraorganizational empowerment: The quality of the internal structure and functioning of organizations.

Knowledge maker: A skilled researcher and/or evaluator who engages in action research and evaluation to promote learning by all stakeholders.

Learning organization: An organization that supports systems thinking and constantly evaluates and adjusts its operations in line with its values, goals, and changing contexts.

Oligarchization: The tendency of organizations to focus more on the maintenance of the organization itself rather than community goals.

Organizational capacity: The combined influence of an organization's abilities to govern and manage itself, to develop assets and resources, to forge the right community linkages, and to meaningfully address its mission.

Organizational interventions: Systematic methods of enhancing an institution's capacity to promote the personal, relational, and collective wellbeing of their workers and community stakeholders.

Partnership Maker: A skilled facilitator of the creation and actualization of partnerships for change.

Power mapping: The community organizing process of identifying powerful stakeholders in a community to determine the basis of their power and to document who their allies and opponents are in order to develop strategies for action.

Pre-contemplation: State of affairs in which people do not realize the need to change a practice or a situation.

Resources

- Promise Neighborhoods initiative supported by the US Department of Education: www2. ed.gov/programs/promiseneighborhoods/index.html)
- The Collective Impact Forum website features information and case studies on collective impact approaches to community change: www.collectiveimpactforum.org/what-collective-impact
- You studied in this chapter some of Faith in Action's interventions and strategies: https:// faithinaction.org/
- A group of community psychologists has developed a web-based community toolbox that contains user-friendly guidelines for community development: http://ctb.ukans.edu
- The building movement project aims to synergize the work of grassroots organizations into a national social movement: www.buildingmovement.org
- Organizing for power has resources for organizers, activists, students, journalists, or anyone trying to learn about creating positive social change: http://organizingforpower.org

INDIVIDUAL AND SMALL GROUP INTERVENTIONS

Warm-up Questions

As community psychologists who work across ecological levels – from trying to provide care and support for people who have experienced extreme suffering to affecting policy and economic conditions – we are often faced with the question of which level we should intervene at and where to target our limited resources (including our time). As discussed in Chapter 2, in certain parts of the world community psychology (CP) emerged from clinical psychologists who felt that just working at the individual level is not sufficient. Meanwhile, in other parts of the world CP developed from social movements trying to raise critical consciousness toward transformative political changes. You may have been pondering this question yourself. Thus, as a warm-up exercise for this chapter, we would like you, in groups of three to four, to reflect on and discuss the following scenario and how you, as community psychologists, would approach the situation that Manuel was faced with as a student.

When I [Manuel] was a student in Berlin wanting to become a child and youth clinician, I did a one-year clinical internship in a progressive youth prison in Berlin, Germany. The prison was, and still is, exemplary in regard to its emphasis on re-integration of youth rather than on punishment. The prison had a school, multiple training workshops on site for a variety of jobs, and a process by which the youth work progressively toward leaving prison (e.g., starting with supervised visits outside of the prison and ending with working outside the prison during the day and just returning at night). Many of the youth had experienced various traumas and hardships during their lives and seemed to be profiting from the clinical support they received from my internship supervisor, a very talented clinical therapist.

One of the youth I worked with was Ali, a refugee from Libya. His parents sent him to Germany on his own when he was just 16 to prevent him from having to join Hamas, a militant group fighting a civil war in Libya. During his young life, he had already experienced extreme trauma, including witnessing the beheading of his uncle and brother. When he first came to Germany, it took a very long time to get his application for asylum processed. While he was waiting, he was not able to work or go to school. Being bored and surrounded by the relative wealth and consumerism that exists in Germany, while having very little that could earn him the respect of others, he got involved in an armed robbery, which brought him into the prison. In my role as a clinical intern, I supported Ali and helped him navigate the steps toward freedom and societal integration. Ali was very bright and eager to learn and get an education. When I ended my internship, he just got permission to study in a school with a very good reputation. His goal was to make a lot of money so that he could buy nice furniture for an apartment. We spent a lot of time talking about life goals as well as his challenging past. At the end of my internship, I was confused about my own future direction. While I believe I was able to make a difference in the life of Ali and set him up on a good path forward, I felt myself questioning my career path as a clinical psychologist. I knew there were many more refugees like Ali and other people struggling in German society and maybe it would make more sense to work on the root causes of some of the issues they were facing, such as improving the asylum approval process or changing our consumerist orientation as a society. But, if I started to work on those issues instead, who would have helped Ali? Ali's needs at that time were to be able to function in this new society that provided him with refuge. What are your thoughts on this? What advice would you have given me if I would have approached you back then to help me with my struggles? Discuss this first as a small group and then share your thoughts with the whole class.

Learning Objectives

In this chapter you will learn about

- Individual and small group interventions and why they are important
- The value base of individual and small group interventions
- How individual and small group interventions promote wellbeing and liberation
- The role of community psychologists in promoting individual and small group interventions
- The limitations and dilemmas individual and small group interventions pose for community psychologists

The Role of Small Group and Individual Interventions in Community Psychology

Is it fair to expect community members wounded by interpersonal and social oppression to change society while they are hurting? At what point do we expect people who have been damaged emotionally and socially to turn their attention to the plight of others? If we expect them to do so too soon they may not be ready or it may not even be fair. After all, they may need some time and space to nurse their wounds and recover, spiritually and psychologically, from experiences of subjugation and minimization just like Ali in the example above. On the other hand, if we don't connect their plight to the plight of others, in some form of solidarity, we may end up isolating them and their source of discomfort even further. There seems to be a unique paradox at play here. Without some kind of individual attention and space, individuals may not process their own sources of suffering and alienation; but with too much space and individual attention they may not connect their own suffering to the suffering of others, or join hands with others to overcome the forces pressing them down. The paradox may be resolvable if we time individual and small group interventions right and if we connect them to larger efforts at social transformation. As discussed in the opening chapter to this section (Chapter 8), individual wellbeing is linked to conditions of justice. Individual and group interventions can move individuals along the wellbeing spectrum by reducing suffering and raising critical consciousness; but, true individual, relational, and community thriving requires optimal conditions of social justice and thus, collective actions and social transformation (Prilleltensky, 2012).

It is entirely possible that citizens experiencing **psychosocial emergencies** (e.g., abuse, depression, homelessness, crime) may be depleted and unable to turn their attention to the psychopolitical sources of personal, relational, and collective suffering. Some of them may justifiably want to focus on the pain of abuse, depression, or eviction. Some of them want food and basic health care for their children now. They cannot wait until a radical social transformation takes place. And they are right. So we, community psychologists and community workers of all stripes, rally behind their cause to demand psychosocial emergency help now. But, our political awareness tells us that something must be done to stop these tragedies from happening in the first place. As discussed in Chapter 6, we need to move "upstream." Something tells us that it's not fair that some live in opulence and others in destitution. But the unceasing demand for services and emergency supplies barely leaves time for transformative work. So we face a serious dilemma: When do we stop looking at the individual emergencies in order to put out the fire that is causing so many burns in the first place? It may seem out of place to worry about politics when children cannot eat now. It may seem utopian to think of a better society when homeless families are on the streets now. But if we fail to dream and we fail to put out the fire, more and more casualties will continue to require our immediate attention and nobody will have the foresight to think about the future, or the other children who will become homeless and hungry if we don't act now.

In the context of this dilemma, we explore the role of individual and small group interventions. Our premise is that individual and small group interventions must be connected to the large socioeconomic spheres that dictate so much of what transpires at the local and micro levels of experience and analysis. Hence, we are in favor of providing psychosocial emergency services, provided they are accompanied and paralleled by efforts at social transformation. Otherwise, however well-intentioned they might be, individual and small group interventions strengthen the **status quo** by giving the message that what ought to change is primarily psychological and not sociological. By the same token, we oppose societal interventions that neglect the psychological needs of individual members and force social changes without community consultation (Aldarondo, 2007; Lord & Hutchison, 2007; Quiñones Rosado, 2007; Toporek, Gerstein, Fouad, Roysircar-Sodowsky, & Israel, 2005). A good recent example of this balancing act between addressing individual psychological needs while working with the community in doing so is the "Promoting Community Conversations About Research to End Suicide" program described by Trout, McEachern, Mullany, White and Wexler (2018). This program addresses the needs of Indigenous youth in Alaska who are struggling with suicidal thoughts. This program is a community health intervention that draws on networks of Indigenous health educators "who host learning circles in which research evidence is used to spark conversations and empower community members to consider individual and collective action to support vulnerable people and create health-promoting conditions that reduce suicide risk" (Trout et al., 2018, p.396).

Think of yourself as a practicing community psychologist. You are under pressure to look after psychosocial emergencies such as abuse, neglect, and teenage pregnancy, but you know that you cannot expend all your energies treating the casualties of social decay. If you do, you'll have no time or stamina to prevent them in the first place. Well, most of us community psychologists feel that way. In this chapter we review the benefits of individual and small group interventions but we caution against glorification of their virtues, lest we forget that psychosocial emergency treatments have their limitations. Not surprisingly, their usefulness is a question of timing, balance and context.

Hitherto we have turned our attention to interventions with people who require some form of help. But this is only one way of using individual and small group interventions. These strategies may also be used with people who do not necessarily hurt but can, and want to, fight injustice and promote optimal conditions of justice. The foci may change, but some of the tools are the same. In both instances we need to be good listeners, good communicators, and good challengers of the status quo. This preamble alerts us to the many uses of individual and group interventions. They can be used in supporting the unwell, but also in channeling the transformational energies of the well-enough. Let's see how we can do this in our work and personal lives.

What Are Individual and Small Group Interventions?

Situations requiring individual and small group interventions are as diverse as the sources of oppression and suffering. Our holistic notions of health and wellbeing as linked to conditions of justice require that we intervene at the personal, relational, and collective levels. Problems of abuse, homelessness, and discrimination have multiple sources and multiple manifestations. While the problems go beyond any one individual's scope of action, the repercussions are often felt deeply at the personal level (Goodman et al., 2007; McWhirter, 1994; Perilla, Lavizzo, & Ibáñez 2007; Williams, 2014). To help individuals cope with problems in living and to strengthen their personal resources we devise individual and small group interventions. These interventions identify people's assets and build on their **resilience**. However, these strategies are not meant exclusively for people experiencing psychosocial challenges, for they can also be used to generate social change with people who are fortunate not to experience severe challenges.

For us, then, individual and small group interventions are paths and strategies towards coping and social transformation at the same time. Interventions of this kind may occur in mental health centers, community centers, adult education programs, and schools, as part of a prevention program, or as a component of mutual help projects. Furthermore, they may be directed by community, clinical, school or organizational psychologists, natural helpers, mentors, lay people, or community workers. The crucial component for us is that people working with individuals and small groups follow the values and principles of CP articulated in earlier chapters. This means constant attention to the balance among values for personal, relational, and collective wellbeing. This type of work requires the skillful combination of compassion and empathy with the ability to challenge preconceived notions of community members. All of it in such a way that trust may be built between the helper and the community member (Corey & Corey, 2003).

We want to be clear though that some mental health problems require the specialized treatment of clinical psychologists or counselors. However, there are many issues in life that may be addressed with the help of natural helpers in the community such as youth leaders, pastors, mentors, friends, teachers, and relatives. Hence, personal and small group work happens in parenting groups, counseling sessions, mutual help associations, and so on (Gitterman & Shulman, 2005; Miller, Blau, Christopher, & Jordan, 2012).

Chapter 1 outlined two key goals of CP: wellbeing and liberation. Driven by these goals and by the values expressed in Chapter 3, the task is to develop skills that can put these visions into action. The remainder of the chapter deals with that challenge.

Values Supporting Work with Individuals and Small Groups

While all the values articulated in Chapters 2 and 3 play a role in wellbeing and liberation, the need for some values may be more pressing for some people than for others. People's needs, in turn, are greatly determined by the context of their lives. Hence, we cannot predetermine what combination of values will be most helpful to a woman before we know her situation. Victims of abuse, during a certain phase of their recovery, may need more compassion than assertiveness and self-determination. They may not have the emotional wherewithal to deal with the abuser or with the system that often re-victimizes them. But, after a certain period of mourning, reflection or participation in self-help groups, victims may be ready to fight the system and help others who have been equally victimized. As discussed in Chapter 4, empowerment is closely linked to mentoring relationships and participation in action groups. Connecting with others in similar situations is a source of support and growth; it's comforting and energizing at the same time (Alsop, Bertelsen, & Holland, 2006; Bryan, & Arkowitz, 2015; Lord & Hutchison 2007).

The question we have to ask ourselves is what does this person need right now? As we progress in our work, we have to ask ourselves how their needs have changed over the course of our relationship. These are questions we cannot answer for ourselves. Our partners in the helping relationship have a big say in what they need. We accompany them on their journey, but we don't necessarily tell them where to travel, even if at times we may suggest a different route (Kamya, 2007).

The Importance of Individual and Small Group Interventions

This question has a three-part answer. They are important because they enhance personal, relational, and collective wellbeing. As may be seen in Table 11.1, the effects of individual and small group interventions may be felt at all these levels. Whereas some individual interventions may concentrate on the emotional wellbeing of the person in front of us, others can target relational or societal domains, such as norms of aggression or social capital (Aldarondo, 2007; Maya Jariego, 2017; Sandler, 2007; Toporek, Gerstein, Fouad, Roysircar-Sodowsky, & Israel, 2005).

At the personal level, research has documented some of the beneficial effects of counseling and therapy. Positive outcomes include better coping, higher sense of control, improved life satisfaction, renewed appreciation for one's voice, enhanced self-concept, as well as other positive effects (Feltham, Hanley & Winter, 2017; Joyce, Wolfaardt, Sribney, & Aylwin, 2006). These positive outcomes concern primarily a person's wellbeing. Equally beneficial outcomes include liberation from oppressive psychological, social, or political forces (Prochaska, Norcross, & DiClemente, 1994). Emancipatory outcomes at the personal level include overcoming internalized oppression, personal de-blaming, empowerment and making the connection between personal suffering and political circumstances (Green, 2007; McWhirter & McWhirter, 2007). Personal wellbeing is closely tied to political wellbeing (Goodman et al., 2007; McGillivray & Clarke, 2006; Prilleltensky, 2012; Prilleltensky & Nelson, 2002).

Table 11.1 Potential contributions of individual and small group interventions

Concerns	Domains		
	Personal	Relational	Collective
Wellbeing	• Effective coping • Resilience • Better quality of life • Voice and choice • Dignity and self-respect • Respect • Sense of control	• Supportive relationships • Caring and compassion • Participation in decisions affecting one's life • Respect for diversity in relationships • Better parenting	• Enhanced social capital • Higher educational outcomes • Reduced prevalence of mental health problems • Economic productivity • Sense of community • Improved safety
Liberation from oppressive forces	• Overcome internalized oppression • Personal de-blaming • Personal empowerment • Expression of anger • Protest against personal and social injustice • Clear connections between personal and social injustice	• Support people to leave abusive relationships • Prevent emotional abuse in family, school, and work • Join with others in struggle for liberation • Accountability in relationships • Relationships based on "power with" instead of "power over"	• Group action against patriarchy and other forms of domination • Links with other solidarity groups • More leaders in social movements • Citizens with political consciousness • Education about sources of injustice

Working with individuals or small groups can also have positive effects in the relational domain. They can improve relationships, balance power dynamics, and increase participation in decisions affecting one's life and others. The benefits of individual and small group work can radiate outwards and create positive ripple effects. If I learn in a group how to identify my own biases and how to communicate with others better, those who surround me at work and at home will benefit from my participation in such groups (Barrera, 2000; Cohen, Underwood, & Gottlieb, 2000; DiAngelo, 2018; Maton, 2008).

At the collective level, this kind of work can strengthen social capital, reduce the prevalence of mental health problems, improve community safety and even generate social action to challenge oppressive norms (Putnam, 2000b). We are reminded of Margaret Mead's "never doubt that a small group of people can change the world. Indeed, it is the only thing that ever has." Research demonstrates that empowerment is a very relational construct (Christens, 2012). Few are the people who empower themselves without joining groups or getting support from others (Alsop et al., 2006; Lord & Hutchison 2007).

In addition to these beneficial outcomes, let's not forget that all our work in organizations, communities, and social movements reviewed in earlier chapters rely heavily on our ability to work with people – another useful legacy of clinical and counseling psychology. There is, in fact, a great deal of correlation between our ability to listen empathically and to be a small group facilitator and our ability to be effective in any kind of organization. As Goleman (1998) noted, there is a core set of **emotional intelligence** skills that are transferable from setting to setting.

Promotion of Wellbeing and Liberation

Individual and small group interventions can, and often do, go together. A common intervention in community psychological work is home visiting. In many early intervention programs, parents work with a nurse, a psychologist, a community worker, or a volunteer. Mothers are often given advice on how to stimulate their infants and what to expect from them at different developmental phases (Reich, Penner, & Duncan, 2011). Often these mothers also attend parenting groups where they share experiences and learn from each other.

Prochaska and colleagues observed that people move through different phases when they get ready to make changes in their lives (Krebs, Norcross, Nicholson, & Prochaska 2018; Prochaska et al., 1994; see also Chapter 10). Although more recent research shows that people do not necessarily move sequentially from one stage to another, there is evidence that a certain amount of readiness is needed to engage in behavioral changes and move to action (Adams & White, 2005; Breda & Riemer, 2012; Brug et al., 2005; DiClemente, Nidecker, & Bellack, 2008). The heuristic value of the Prochaska model lies in identifying certain prerequisites for affective, behavioral and cognitive change. In this chapter we apply these phases to individual and small group work. Our dual emphasis is on how people work to alter circumstances oppressing them and create changes to give up some of their power and privilege. Whereas the former concentrates on forms of empowerment, the latter deals with forms of **depowerment** (see Chapter 4). In this section we deal with both kinds of change.

During the various phases of change there are certain jobs that need to be done. In this section we describe the tasks community members embark on. In the next section, we focus on what we, as community psychologists, need to do to enable community members to be effective change agents.

Helping encounters come in many forms. In some instances, service providers and service recipients are paired because of a third-party order. Such is the case when a court mandates a young person to see a probation officer or when a school principal sends a child to a counselor. In other cases, help is voluntarily sought from a social worker or a psychologist. In yet others, it happens because the community psychologist is part of a project and people trust her and come to her with their personal issues.

Pre-Contemplation

During pre-contemplation some people are in denial. Our role as agents of change is to begin exploring what some of the challenges affecting them in life are. Some may feel uneasy or unhappy but may be unable to articulate the source of oppression or concern. Some others may completely deny the mere existence of an issue. A milestone is achieved when they can verbalize what is bothering them and what may be the source of the problem. Whereas some people may be the subject of oppressive relationships or discriminatory practices, others may be exerting too much power over others, causing themselves and others pain and suffering. But being the complex beings that we are, most of us are somewhere in between these two poles of oppressed or oppressors. In fact, most of us experience some of both (Goodman, 2001). In some realms of our lives, we suffer some form of minimization and exclusion; in others we do the same to other people. This requires that we, as helpers, view our clients and ourselves as potentially inflicting pain on others, directly or indirectly, wittingly or unwittingly, consciously or unconsciously. This interpretation rejects simple categorizations of people as either oppressors or oppressed. In pursuing wellbeing and liberation, we think that lasting changes come about when individuals reflect on their dual roles in life as contributors to wellbeing and possible oppression at the same time.

Table 11.2 Steps for interventions with individuals and small groups

Steps	Work with Individuals	Work with Small Groups
Pre-contemplation	• Explore sources of oppression and suffering • Explore need for accountability	• Review reasons for coming together • Legitimize group's existence
Contemplation	• Refine and define areas of work • Think about personal, relational, and collective changes	• Refine and define areas of work • Establish principles for working together • Validate misgivings and hesitations
Preparation	• Choose specific goals and areas of change • Warm up to idea of doing things differently	• Devise plan for achieving personal and group goals • Have timelines for preparation phase
Action	• Experiment with actions to overcome oppression • In cases of over-empowerment, explore ways of sharing power and increasing accountability	• Balance attention to participatory processes with concrete actions • Decide ahead of time on schedule but remain open to changes as group evolves
Maintenance	• Put in place systems of sustainability that will reinforce personal empowerment or depowerment, as the case might be	• Develop norms and procedures to sustain and institutionalize change either in people's behaviors or in social changes pursued
Evaluation	• Evaluate process and outcomes of change, not only at the end of a trial period but throughout work phase as well	• Group conducts formative and summative evaluations of the work
Follow-up	• Put procedures in place for individual to check with self and others to see if changes are maintained	• Institutionalize procedures to help group members to remain accountable to each other

In group work, the beginning stages also require that the group review its origins and aims (Dimock, 1987; Johnson & Johnson, 2000). In cases where the group is mandated, as in patients in psychiatric hospitals or young people in court-ordered treatment, there may be animosity towards the leader or other members of the group. Hence, we think it's important to spend some time clarifying feelings and legitimizing the group's existence, if such can be accomplished.

Contemplation

Whether it is in individual or small group work, we recommend that people spend some time during the contemplation phase defining the problem. It is all too possible and common to jump into action before knowing what the problem is. Ideological influences are such in our society that people can seriously misjudge the source of their suffering. A common misattribution is to impute to oneself blame for things beyond one's control. Unemployed people blame themselves for losing their jobs and victims of spouse abuse blame themselves for not doing the right things. Advice programs, widely prevalent in North America, oversimplify problems and hosts are quick to diagnose a mental disorder. Contemplation requires that we explore carefully what we need to change and where we should channel our energies. Beware of actions that precede contemplation.

Group work also requires some contemplation with respect to values and working principles. Do we have a leader? Do we make decisions by consensus? Do we rotate in our roles? Starting a process with only an implicit understanding of how it "should" work can have significant consequences at later stages (Munger & Riemer, 2012). People come to the table with varied experiences and expectations. The sooner we clarify them openly the better off we are. It is at this stage that misgivings and hesitations need to be aired. Otherwise they can fester like wounds, create resistance and undermine ownership (Nelson, Prilleltensky & MacGillivary, 2001).

Preparation

The preparation phase is very important. Eager clinicians send their clients to do something different, only to find out later that they were not ready for it. After all, change is hard. Habitual modes of relating to others and thinking about ourselves are profoundly engrained in our individual and collective psyche. Imagery, visualization, concrete plans, and achievable goals can all help in moving forward.

Action

Action, then, is only one more element in the equation, albeit an important one. People need a great deal of support to experiment with new ways of being and relating to the world. Some mechanisms for the promotion of resilience include person-centered changes such as enhanced self-esteem, while others entail environmental modifications. Action must take into account research on resilience, for it elucidates naturally occurring mechanisms (including those in people's community context) that can be incorporated into helping processes, especially when dealing with forms of oppression (Atallah, Contreras Painemal, Albornoz, Salgado & Pilquil Lizama, 2018; Runswick-Cole & Goodley, 2013).

Groups can act as powerful resources in introducing new behaviors in their members or getting rid of undesirable ones (Johnson & Johnson, 2000). The literature on mutual help and organizing confirms that empowerment often grows out of social support and solidarity (Christens, 2012; Gitterman & Shulman, 2005; Speer & Hughey, 1995). But, groups can be powerful in multiple ways, not all of them positive. Norms of conformity can suppress creativity, and power dynamics can further oppress vulnerable members. Hence, attention to process is crucial throughout the life of the group (Johnson & Johnson, 2000; Munger & Riemer, 2012).

Maintenance

If you have ever tried to change something, you know how difficult it can be to sustain the new behavior. If you tried to stop smoking or to lose weight, you probably know that starting is not as hard as keeping it up. This is why the stage of maintenance is so crucial (Prochaska et al., 1994). Planning for change without planning for maintenance is likely a recipe for failure. Imagine you decided to start exercising every other day for 30 minutes. You made a plan that read like "exercise for 30 minutes Monday, Wednesday, and Friday" but you did not plan exactly what time. What if somebody invites you to go out for a drink instead or if you just have too much to study? You may have had a good beginning, but you did not have a contingency plan or a maintenance plan. Groups can be powerful in creating norms of accountability. Alcoholics Anonymous creates pacts among its members that serve to maintain the gains newly acquired. Attending the meetings and sharing the personal odyssey towards sobriety helps people with addictions to keep the risk at bay.

Evaluation

Evaluation should not be relegated to the end of the change process. Nothing is more disappointing for group members or facilitators than to realize at the end that you had missed the ball from the beginning, that you didn't notice some people were disengaged, that therapy or other activities weren't working, that there wasn't ownership of the process. To prevent this, it's important to build in reflective practice structured moments where people can express their feelings about how things are going, either in group or individual quests for change (Patterson & Welfel, 2000). This requires the creation of a truly safe space where discontent may be expressed and achievements may be celebrated. Role modeling is crucial for formative evaluations to work. The message from the facilitator of change ought to be that mistakes happen, things can go wrong and it is better to express discomfort as is felt. A skilled facilitator balances opportunities for process reflections with concrete actions and achievements.

Follow-up

Part of maintenance and evaluation is follow-up. Setting dates for reviewing new practices, assigning roles for championing new procedures, animating processes that keep an innovation alive are all parts of follow-up. Institutionalizing innovations is the culmination of change.

The Roles of Community Psychologists Working in Individual and Small Group Interventions

In a nutshell, the role of a community psychologist is to enable and support the progression from pre-contemplation to maintenance and follow-up. But, for this to occur, certain skills and roles have to be developed. Tables 11.3 and 11.4 describe eight roles that should be present every step of the way. While the discrete learning of these roles is vital, it is their integration that is crucial for success in facilitating change in individuals and small groups (Prilleltensky & Prilleltensky, 2006). What is expected of a skilled facilitator is to invoke the most appropriate role at the most opportune time. Based on the first edition of this book, Prilleltensky and Prilleltensky (2006) elaborated affective, behavioral, and cognitive (ABC) strategies to reinforce the eight roles presented as follows. To engage people in processes of change, we need to involve their emotions, their actions, and their thoughts. ABC strategies help us to be very specific in our roles.

The eight roles we recommend can be summarized in the acronym I VALUE IT, which stands for:

Inclusive host
Visionary
Asset seeker
Listener and sense maker
Unique solution finder
Evaluator
Implementer
Trendsetter

In the next sections we describe these roles. Tables 11.3 and 11.4 present concrete ways to exercise these roles.

Table 11.3 ABC – I VALUE IT: Roles and strategies for personal wellbeing in work with individuals

| Role | Strategy | | |
	Affective	Behavioral	Cognitive
Inclusive host	Make person feel safe and welcome to explore sensitive issues and ways of thriving	Help person experiment with new modes of behavior, including asking for help or admitting insecurity	Encourage exploration of meanings associated with issues
Visionary: Process	Ask what processes or ways of working would make person feel comfortable	Find out what behaviors person expects from self and from you in the process	Articulate goals and objectives for process of working together
Visionary: Outcome	Explore what feelings would person like to have or experience as result of work	Inquire what new behaviors would person like to see in self and others	Help visualize better state of affairs and personal role in it
Asset seeker	Affirm person's unique feelings and abilities	Recognize previous ways of coping and thriving that can be built upon	Identify meaning and meaning making ways that help integrate experiences into life narrative
Listener and sense maker	Collaborate in exploring full range of feelings	Explore how own behavior impacts self and others, and how others' behaviors impact self	Make connections between feelings, behaviors, thoughts and meanings associated with them
Unique solution finder	Overcome emotional barriers in enacting new behaviors and reward and celebrate new behaviors	Articulate plan of action and break new behaviors into small chunks	Use cognitive strategies such as reframing and challenging cognitive errors
Evaluator: Past efforts	Explore feelings associated with past efforts at change or thriving	Evaluate past behaviors and their successes	Examine interpretation of past efforts
Evaluator: Present efforts	Explore feelings associated with current efforts	Evaluate present behaviors and their successes	Examine interpretation of current efforts
Evaluator: Future efforts	Anticipate feelings associated with future efforts	Identify what behaviors have to occur to explore future actions	Plan evaluation of future actions and explore associated meanings
Implementer	Explore feelings associated with making new behavior or perceptions part of life	Create a plan to make new behavior or perceptions part of life and for handling barriers	Develop cognitive strategies for making changes integral part of your life and for anticipating barriers
Trendsetter	Explore feelings associated with taking risks and becoming a leader	Explore steps needed to disseminate changes in other parts of your life or with other significant others	Work on self-perceptions of leadership qualities and opportunities

Source: From Prilleltensky & Prilleltensky, 2006; reproduced with permission from John Wiley & Sons.

Table 11.4 ABC – I VALUE IT: Roles and strategies for personal wellbeing in work with groups

Strategy			
Roles	**Affective**	**Behavioral**	**Cognitive**
Inclusive host	Create safe environment for people to express views and emotions	Structure time and space where safe and fun dialogue can occur	Promote sharing of personal narratives and interpretations of events and beliefs
Visionary: Process	Foster feelings of affiliation and solidarity in group work	Engage people in activities to devise a vision for working together	Address basic assumptions about working in groups
Visionary: Outcome	Make the vision alive and foster ownership of it throughout the organization or community	Involve people in the development of a vision for team, unit, organization, or community	Analyze gap between actual and desire state of affairs
Asset seeker	Make sure you recognize and affirm people's strengths	Help people develop inventories of own strengths	Reframe life experiences and ways of coping as strengths
Listener and sense maker	Establish processes for people to feel heard and valued	Structure opportunities for people to speak, learn, and problem solve together	Learn how to listen to each other and problem solve in teams
Unique solution finder	Small wins keep people engaged and energized	Assign specific actions in line with goals and objectives	Identify what values, beliefs, and assumptions either promote or inhibit new actions
Evaluator: Past efforts	Make it safe to explore past failures and successes	Get people involved in evaluation criteria that is meaningful to them	Analyze links between sites, signs, sources and strategies of wellbeing
Evaluator: Present efforts	Reward people for sharing sources of stress	Use empowerment-based evaluation and appreciative inquiry to evaluate efforts	If change is needed, create cognitive dissonance between aspirations and actual actions
Evaluator: Future efforts	Build trust by showing your own personal commitment to act	Institutionalize mechanisms to monitor wellbeing of staff and community members	Create narrative of ongoing growth and development
Implementer	Celebrate attempts to implement new behaviors and attitudes into life of organization or community	Build structures that support new behaviors and attitudes and foster sustainability	Tell stories of success and how they have helped other people improve wellbeing
Trendsetter	Generate enthusiasm among peers about being leaders in a field	Have a participatory plan for disseminating lessons learned	Spread the message across organizations and communities in compelling ways

Source: From Prilleltensky & Prilleltensky, 2006; reproduced with permission from John Wiley & Sons.

Inclusive Host

The role of inclusive host calls for the creation of a welcoming atmosphere. In such a climate people feel safe to explore sources of oppression, avenues for empowerment, vulnerabilities, as well as personal and social privilege. An inclusive host makes space for all guests to feel at home. In a non-judgmental atmosphere people begin to consider aspects of their lives they didn't feel comfortable to explore before. This is the case in individual and small group interventions alike, although it is somewhat harder to achieve in the latter because of the gaze of multiple spectators.

An inclusive host strives to make all members of the group as accepting as possible. This requires a "reading" of where people are at during the conversation. Skillful facilitators have a finger on the pulse of the group at all times. This is quite a sophisticated ability, as it requires identification of people's moods as individuals and as a group. Some of the questions inclusive hosts ask themselves are shown in Table 11.5.

Once people feel comfortable and ready to do some individual or group work, it is important to help them envision a better, yet realistic, state of affairs. When people grow up in violent homes sometimes they come to believe that this is the way things are supposed to be. Their world of possibilities may be constrained by multiple factors including socialization, family experiences, community narratives, and deprecating messages about one's group or personal abilities.

Visionary

It is the role of the visionary to expand the realm of possibilities and establish values and principles to guide the work. Hence, in our role as visionaries we fulfil the dual task of aspiring to a better state of affairs and creating norms that will help us work together at the same time. In short, we envision the end and the means to achieve it. But, we don't envision it by ourselves. We most definitely include the group and our associates in making the decision. Hence, we need to become visionaries of a good process and a good outcome, as seen in Tables 11.3 and 11.4.

In individual work there are only two people (the person seeking help and the helper/therapist) making decisions about personal growth, coping strategies or social activism. In group situations, the process of crafting a vision and choosing values that guide the collaboration can be fairly involved. Some questions a visionary can ask him or herself at this stage can be seen in Table 11.5.

Asset Seeker

As asset seekers it is our job to identify sources of resilience, strength, and ingenuity in the people we work with (Prilleltensky & Prilleltensky, 2006). This is what is commonly referred to as a **strength-based approach** (McCammon, 2012; Saleebey, 2002). In individual encounters it is important to validate what the person in front of us is already doing well to cope with a problem or to fight injustice. Disenfranchised community members are used to hearing about their deficits, when in fact many of them have remarkable talent in coping with adverse circumstances. Within group settings it is vital not to leave anyone behind in our search for assets and strengths. People have experiential or academic knowledge they wish to have validated. To make sure we are effective in our search for assets we can ask the questions shown in Table 11.5.

Table 11.5 Questions community psychologists can ask themselves in each role

Role	Questions
Inclusive host	1 Is everyone feeling comfortable? 2 Is someone dominating the discussion in the group? 3 Are there some people who feel afraid to speak? 4 Have I made an effort to hear from all the people in the group? 5 Are people leaving the meeting enthusiastic or disappointed?
Visionary	1 Have all people expressed their aspirations? 2 Are we able to think of alternative ways of being? 3 Have we established a process that is democratic and inclusive? 4 Have we had time to think about the norms that we all want to follow? 5 Is there collective ownership for the values and vision we have created?
Asset seeker	1 Have I asked people how they cope with this difficult situation? 2 Have we discussed what each of us can contribute to the process? 3 Are we able to combine our strengths in a synergistic way? 4 Have I offered my input as an equal member of the group? 5 Have we explored different types of knowledge and wisdom that can help us in our collaborative work?
Listener and sense maker	1 Have I listened without interruptions to what people have to say about their issues? 2 Have I thought about it in ecological terms? 3 Have I expressed disagreement or alternative conceptualizations in a respectful way? 4 Have I thought about the influence of power inequality in this person's life? 5 Has the group agreed on the definition of the problem and possible solutions?
Unique solution finder	1 Have I considered with the group the risks and benefits of every course of action? 2 Have I consulted colleagues and the literature on the merits of various alternatives? 3 Is our work balancing attention to process with attention to outcomes? 4 Is the preferred action in accord with our values? 5 Do we have a contingency plan in case this strategy doesn't work?
Evaluator	1 Have we created a space to reflect on how we're feeling about our work together? 2 What have we done to evaluate our intervention? 3 Are people feeling safe enough to express disapproval? 4 Am I open to challenges and criticism? 5 Have we practiced how to give feedback in respectful and useful ways?
Implementer	1 Have I tried to be an inclusive host, asset seeker, good listener and solution finder? 2 Have I tried to identify with my partners the most suitable solution for the long term? 3 Have I made a mental list of the important considerations at play? 4 Have I considered the power differentials at play that might interfere with our goals? 5 Have I considered enabling and inhibiting factors that will impact our plan of action?
Trendsetter	1 What have we done to make sure that the changes we plan for are maintained? 2 How do we change the system, not just perceptions, in order to institutionalize innovations? 3 What group norms can we establish to help members sustain new behaviors? 4 How can we disseminate knowledge gained in one setting to others? 5 What do we know from the literature about institutionalizing innovations?

Listener and Sense Maker

A listener's main job is to attend carefully to what people are saying about their lives, challenges, struggles, and aspirations. We cannot emphasize enough the importance of letting people speak and explain in their own terms what they are experiencing and hoping and feeling. It is not uncommon for eager helpers to rush to give advice before they have listened carefully. Each of us brings to the table multiple assumptions that can lead to unwarranted conclusions about other people's lives. It is best not to presume anything about people's lives or views before we check it out with them (Green, 2007; Prilleltensky, 2009).

Once we have a good grasp of the issues and challenges ahead, we begin to conceptualize the problem and isolate the main factors causing and perpetuating suffering, injustice, and oppression in personal, communal, and social lives. As community psychologists, we always have our antenna up for signals of oppression and exclusion. Power differentials and inequality figure prominently in the lives of people we work with (Bond, 2016; Quiñones Rosado, 2007; Vera & Speight, 2007). Unlike other professionals in the helping fields, we do not necessarily concentrate on intrapsychic dynamics, although they may be an important part of the puzzle. For us, internal psychological processes are just one more element to consider. Ecologically speaking, we conceptualize problems in terms of micro, meso, and macro spheres. As noted in Chapter 1, holistic thinking is the perfect antidote against reductionism in the formulation of problems.

As we come to our own conclusions about a problem in living or a challenge to work on, we have to recognize that our views may differ from the group or the individual(s) we are working with. We have to consider the possibility that our conceptualization may be wrong or that it may take more dialogue for people to reach consensus on causes and possible solutions. Conflict is expected and unavoidable. The very way we deal with that may be therapeutic and growth enhancing.

To remind ourselves of the various tasks involved in being a good listener and sense maker, we can use the questions shown in Table 11.5.

Unique Solution Finder

Based on the vision, the assets, and the particular circumstances affecting a person or group, we craft together with them unique solutions. We call upon our previous knowledge, research, and experience to inform decisions uniquely suited to the plight of this person or collective. If a group wishes to use a confrontational technique with the city hall, and you know that this strategy will alienate potential allies, as a unique solution finder you want to discuss the merits of other options. If a victim of spousal abuse wishes to return to the marriage, and you know from her past experience and other research that this will probably not work out, as a unique solution finder you want to raise the possibility that this may not be the best way to proceed. In either case, our alternatives have to be accepted by the people we work with. There is no point in forcing our views upon others who are not ready to listen.

Our ability to identify transformational actions while keeping everyone effectively engaged at the same time is essential. We discussed in the previous chapter the set of emotional intelligence skills that can help us in organizational and community settings. These competencies come in handy when working with individuals and small groups. Questions that sharpen our skills as unique solution finders can be seen in Table 11.5.

Evaluator

As seen in Tables 11.3 and 11.4, it is recommended to evaluate previous, current, and future efforts. Empowerment-based evaluations and appreciative-inquiry methods make it safe for individuals and groups to explore what is going well, what needs changing and what can be done better in the future. To be an effective evaluator we have to build on the previous roles of listener and asset seeker. We need to celebrate prior achievements, however small, and make it safe for people to reflect critically on their own actions. Evaluating our actions is part of becoming a reflective practitioner and a learning organization. Some questions we find useful for the evaluator role are shown in Table 11.5.

Implementer

The main role of the implementer is to synthesize all the previous roles and to create structures that enable the adoption of new behaviors, policies, and practices. It is not enough to hope that individuals will stick to a plan. Incentives, supports, and rewards are required to sustain efforts at change. A skillful implementer takes the pulse of the individual or group often and decides what the best course of action is and how this decision will affect future accomplishments. In a sense, we are integrating all the skills when we assume the role of implementer. This is the meta-role community psychologists assume. The questions Prilleltensky and Prilleltensky (2006, p. 93) propose are used as a guide to becoming a proficient implementer and integrator of skills are shown in Table 11.5.

Trendsetter

Perhaps the toughest part of the job is to make changes last, both in our personal and institutional lives. This is why we have to pay particular attention to our role as trendsetters. To achieve a change is admirable, but to make it into a new trend is even more remarkable (Mayer & Davidson II 2000; Prochaska et al., 1994). This role supports maintenance and follow-up as described in Table 11.2. When starting new programs in the community so much effort goes into project development, recruitment, and evaluation that sustainability is often not a priority. By the time funding runs out in a few years, there are rarely plans for the continuation of the initiative.

Long-term planning applies to individual, group, or community change alike. The first priority is to institutionalize the innovation at the personal and local levels. Once that has been accomplished, it's important to take the message to other communities and groups (Mayer & Davidson II, 2000). In Chapter 15 we can see how Indigenous groups in New Zealand, in collaboration with treaty workers, strive to educate the entire population about Maori rights. Treaty workers have a systematic way of working with organizations so that education and affirmative actions may be institutionalized in government and private settings alike. It is not enough to raise the consciousness of a few people about the rights of Indigenous people – their plan of action includes a strategy for disseminating knowledge about past wrongs and possible ways of addressing them. This is an example of trend setting. The essence of trend setting is going beyond the initial goal.

What can be done to make trend setting a priority? Some questions community psychologists can ask can be seen in Table 11.5.

Trend setting is not only very challenging but is also very exciting. Community members like being part of something new and transformative. Motivation increases when people realize that their contributions may transcend the local level. Think of environmental trends such as recycling and composting and you can appreciate how much rarer they were 30 or 40 years ago than they are today. At first environmentalists encountered much more opposition than they face today when trying to institute earth-friendly policies and practices. The same may be said of civil rights activists who fought an uphill battle to obtain basic human rights. While their struggle is far from over, new trends, such as affirmative action and disability rights legislation, make it easier for people of color and people with disabilities to participate in society. However, those changes cannot be taken for granted as there are always interest groups who try to reverse new progressive trends as seen in recent political movements across the globe (e.g., in the US, Brazil, Poland, Hungary, Italy, etc.).

Strengths and Limitations of Individual and Small Group Interventions

We started this chapter with the concept of psychosocial emergencies. These are wounds that require urgent treatment. Abuse, neglect, violence, addictions, depression, and homelessness, all require immediate attention. And, when properly given and carefully applied, sensitive one-on-one and small group interventions can help. People recover hope, feel empowered, join others in fighting inequality, and enjoy the benefits of mutual support.

Research demonstrates that individual and small group interventions can help at the universal, selective, and indicated levels (if you need a refresher on these concepts see Chapter 6). At the universal level, schools that smooth the transition from elementary to high school by grouping children in small clusters and restructuring the school environment deliver positive outcomes. In the School Transition Environment Project (STEP) in the US, the school was reorganized so that Grade 9 students remained with the same group of students in the same part of the building for most of the day; they had a small group of teachers, and the class teachers handled many of the guidance-related issues for these students. Effectively this intervention created a smaller, more supportive environment within the context of a larger, more impersonal school. Compared with students in a control group, the students who participated in this new arrangement reported more positive attitudes towards school, had fewer absences, and had better marks (Felner & Adan, 1988). This is a universal intervention in that all school children in the US participate in the program. They all receive individual guidance and they all work in small groups. Such a program has proved to be effective in enhancing academic performance and satisfaction with school overall.

At the selective level, families at risk for abuse or neglect, or children at risk for educational underachievement benefit from individual and small group interventions with parents and children alike. Geoff Nelson and colleagues conducted two meta-analyses to find out whether programs such as home visitation and family preservation achieve reductions in abuse, and whether early intervention programs have lasting effects on children's educational wellbeing (MacLeod &

Nelson, 2000; Nelson, Westhues, & MacLeod, 2003). In both instances, Nelson and colleagues found that individual and small group interventions work. Some work better than others and some achieve longer-lasting results than others, but in general these analyses support the implementation of individual interventions with parents to prevent abuse and with children to enhance educational outcomes. Parents feel better about their children, obtain better employment and improve rearing knowledge and techniques. Children, in turn, become better learners and experience higher family and social wellbeing.

Sensitive home visitors help parents to remove blame and feelings of inadequacy. Trained group facilitators also help children of divorced parents to remove blame and feelings of inadequacy. Social support groups help people with addictions, mental health problems, physical disabilities, and other afflictions to overcome exclusion, marginality, and depression (Chinman et al., 2014; Levy, 1988).

At the indicated level, individual and small group interventions are also effective in coping with adversities such as ill-health and serious mental health problems. In Chapter 20 we can see how people with psychiatric conditions benefit from mutual help and empowering approaches.

At all levels, through a process of personal affirmation and safe exploration, individuals and groups achieve higher levels of wellbeing. In the best possible world, the newly gained confidence and psychological health would be invested in helping others achieve higher levels of wellbeing and collective liberation. But, often this is not the case. Self-actualization can easily turn into selfish actualization, a trend that has been inadvertently supported by traditional therapeutic approaches that reinforce individualism (Prilleltensky, 1994).

At present, most preventive interventions are person-centered or small-group-centered. This flies in the face of ecological formulations of problems. If problems reside in systems as much as in individuals, how come most of our psychological interventions put the onus of change on the victim and not on the system? Furthermore, most interventions wish to fix the person damaged and not the powerful ones inflicting the damage. These are inherent risks of individual and small group interventions. On one hand they are helpful, but on the other hand they divert attention from meso and macro sources of conflict.

A final caveat to keep in mind: the vast majority of individual and small group interventions are most likely ameliorative in nature. They soothe wounds and react to pain, but do not confront their origins. In a sense, they follow the medical model of "wait and they shall show up in your clinic" (Albee, 1990; Vera & Speight, 2007).

Dilemmas Faced by Community Psychologists Working with Individuals and Small Groups

What right do we have to convince people to work for social change, to oppose convention, to rebel? If we are clear about our values, we are bound to share them with the people we work with. If we have an agenda for change, we will want to propagate it. Who is to say that our values will not seep into the work we do with individuals and small groups. That would not be a dilemma if people invited and allowed us to work for social change, but what about groups who think we can help them with addictions and we end up talking about how corporations exploit children and poor people and entice them to smoke? Aren't we politicizing the helping process? The answer is we most definitely are. The dilemma lies not in pretending we are apolitical when in fact we are not, but in introducing agendas community partners may not be ready for, or interested in. After all, community psychologists are well known for working on health- and welfare-related issues but not on radical transformation.

In our view, the ethical way to proceed is to share our convictions, our analyses, and our strategies with people we work with. It is up to the partners to decide whether health can be isolated from corporate greed or not and whether they see any connection between eating disorders and the fashion industry. If our partners refuse to make the connections, or if they oppose our agenda, which is entirely possible, the collaboration may not work, in which case we gracefully exit the scene. We cannot be all things to all people.

It is also important not to psychologize everything and think that people who exploit others are simply misguided or psychologically unhealthy. That may very well be true. But, we must keep in mind that certain groups may expressly reject our values and wish us away. How wonderful it would be if we could easily tell who is misguided and who is a genuine despot. Until there is a quick procedure for such diagnosis, we are stuck with disclosing our values and seeing how far we can go with them.

Chapter Summary

This chapter merely touched upon ways of working with individuals and groups. Due to space considerations we could not expand on specific interviewing skills or group facilitation. Fortunately, there are excellent resources for learning the craft of interview and group processes (see Resources section below). In this chapter we chose to discuss the more likely roles of community psychologists and the likely stages people go through in their efforts to make personal or social change.

Prochaska's stages of change model provides a useful framework for conceptualizing discernable steps that effective self-changers go through, from pre-contemplation to maintenance and follow-up (Prochaska et al., 1994). There is merit in following their wisdom. Each phase builds on previous ones and skipping any may cause unnecessary regressions. Action without contemplation may be misguided and contemplation without action may be frustrating. Each phase includes specific tasks, which are enabled by a set of skills and roles.

We recommended the use of eight roles, applicable to work with both individuals and small groups: inclusive host, visionary, asset seeker, listener and sense maker, unique solution finder, evaluator, implementer, and trendsetter. Mastery of individual skills is important, but their integration and activation at appropriate times is vital.

The dilemmas we posed at the beginning and the end of the chapter are not easily resolvable. How do we allocate our time between psychosocial emergencies and long-term transformative social changes? How can we tell if people who reject our values are simply misguided or genuinely disinterested in the wellbeing and liberation of others? For how long do we try to persuade others before we decide they need to be disempowered instead of empowered? When do we tell ourselves we have too much power and we need to find ways of giving it up? Answers will perpetually vary across contexts. But, until all contexts look the same and before we can safely tell friend from foe, there is one simple answer: we struggle with each and every one of these dilemmas. At best, we will find colleagues to help us resolve them. At worst, we will pretend they don't exist.

Key terms

Depowerment: The process whereby powerful people and groups relinquish some of their power in order to bring about a more equitable state of affairs among people and groups.

Emotional intelligence: A set of personal and interpersonal skills that enable individuals to prosper and operate efficiently in social and organizational settings.

Psychosocial emergency: Situations that require immediate attention such as child abuse, neglect, or domestic violence.

Resilience: The process of using individual, group, and community assets to adapt well when faced with adversity, trauma, tragedy, and other sources of significant stress.

Strength-based approaches: Emphasize individual's and group's assets by identifying sources of resilience, strength, and ingenuity in the people and groups we are working with as community psychologists.

Resources

Working with Individuals

Aldarondo, E. (Ed.). (2007). *Advancing social justice through clinical practice*. London, England: Lawrence Erlbaum.

Corey, M., & Corey, G. (2003). *Becoming a helper*. Pacific Grove, CA: Brooks/Coles.

McWhirter, E. H. (1994). *Counseling for empowerment*. Alexandrian, VA: American Counseling Association.

Toporek, R., Gerstein, L., Fouad, N., Roysircar-Sodowsky, G., & Israel, T. (Eds.). (2005). *Handbook for social justice in counseling psychology: Leadership, vision, and action*. London: SAGE Publications.

Working with Groups

Dimock, H. (1987). *Groups: Leadership and group development*. New York: Pfeiffer.

Johnson, D., & Johnson, F. (2000). *Joining together: Group theory and group skills*. London, England: Allyn and Bacon.

Holman, P., Devane, T., & Cady, S. (2007). *The change handbook: Group methods for shaping the future* (2nd ed.). San Francisco: Berrett-Koehler Publishers.

Scott, V. C., & Wolfe, S.M. (2015). *Community psychology: Foundations for practice*. Thousands Oak, CA: Sage.

There are also a variety of relevant chapters in M. A. Bond, I. Serrano-García, C. B. Keys, & M. Shinn (Eds.), *APA handbook of community psychology: Methods for community research and action for diverse groups and issues*. Washington, DC: American Psychological Association.

COMMUNITY-ENGAGED RESEARCH

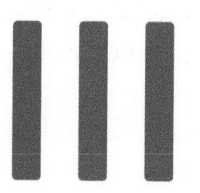

Introduction to Part III

> To be committed to an empowerment social agenda and to be consistent with that agenda in one's approach to social science theory, research and action is to be committed to identifying, facilitating, or creating contexts in which heretofore silent and isolated people, those who are "outsiders" in various settings, organizations, and communities, gain understanding, voice, and influence over decisions that affect their lives. (Rappaport, 1990, p. 52)

> To empower a community, we must become a community, supporting and challenging each other as we implement culturally competent, power- and race-sensitive inquiry. (Chávez, Duran, Baker, Avila, & Wallerstein, 2008, p. 103)

Research is a tool that can be used both as a process of empowerment and transformation and as a form of social control. For example, research has been used both to empower Indigenous communities to fight their colonial past and racist present as well as to justify colonization of Indigenous land by White settlers. In collaboration with oppressed people, other allies, and those with more power and privilege, community psychology research aims to construct knowledge that challenges the status quo and promotes liberation and wellbeing for all (Nelson & Prilleltensky, 2010; Prilleltensky, 2008b; Tebes, 2017).

In many cases, research is not the value-free endeavor of pursuing objective knowledge as it is often portrayed in psychology textbooks, but rather a political process ridden with issues of power and personal agendas (Prilleltensky, 2008). This starts with who is framing the research, who is getting to determine the research agenda, who controls the funding, who poses the research questions, who gets invited to be part of the research team, how the researchers relate to the participants, what methods are being used, how data are interpreted, and who is being informed about the research findings. Research is also used by dominant groups to exert invisible power (see Chapter 4) by influencing the way we think about certain groups, such as research that claims to demonstrate that certain racial or ethnic groups are less intelligent than the dominant group (see the book *The Bell Curve* written by psychologists Hernstein and Murray in 1994 as a classic example of that).

Many authors have pointed out that what is considered best practice in research is a social construction that is strongly influenced by the researchers' specific sociocultural and historical contexts, including the specific dominant research paradigms (Mertens, 2009; Tebes, 2017). For example, for a long time only lab-based research studies were considered acceptable in psychology, while today many researchers and research users have raised questions about the applicability of that type of research in addressing some of our most pressing social issues. This insight has led to a liberation process of scientific methodology itself and to the empowerment of those who advocated for methods that were not considered acceptable by the mainstream scientific community.

With that new freedom, however, also comes an increased responsibility to be conscious and intentional in the way we frame and conduct our research. Our goal with the two chapters in this part of the book is to provide you with useful information that will guide you in making decisions about your research questions and methods. It is our hope that at the end of this section you will feel that research can be meaningful, aligned with your values, and fun – just like the students who participated in our research methods courses or worked with us on research projects.

Chapter 12 presents background consideration regarding the general sociocultural and historical context of research and discusses the general nature of research and its purpose in society in regard to different types of human knowledge interests. We introduce a definition of community-engaged research and clarify some key research terminology. In Chapter 13, we review key aspects of each step in the research cycle from initially engaging with community partners about the research to mobilizing the generated knowledge for positive changes.

FRAMING COMMUNITY-ENGAGED RESEARCH

12

Warm-up Questions

In Box 12.1, we describe two different studies that focus on the same issue (body weight and shape preoccupation) with the same type of participant (young female dancers) in the context of co-educational dance studios. Read through the brief descriptions and then discuss the following questions in pairs.

1 What is your general reaction reading about each study? Which one do you feel more aligned with and why?

2 What do you see as key differences in the framing and research approach of these two studies?

3 Which study would you judge as more rigorous and trustworthy and why?

4 What type of knowledge is each study generating as a result of the research process and how is that knowledge used?

5 What assumptions about the world and how knowledge is created do each of the researchers seem to hold?

Box 12.1 Two Approaches to the Same Research Problem

Body weight and shape preoccupation (BWSP) is an important issue in many of our societies with significant medical, social, and psychological consequences, especially for adolescents and women. As such, it has also been the subject of many research studies. How this issue is framed and studied can differ quite significantly, however. Here we present an example of two studies that researched BWSP with the same type of participants in a very similar context but with two very different approaches and framing.

Study 1: Garner & Garfinkel (1980)

In this study, the authors wanted to understand the sociocultural factors that may influence the development of anorexia nervosa (referred to anorexia from here on), a medical terminol-ogy for BWSP that is considered pathological. The authors operated under the assumption that sociocultural factors, such as the expectation for women to be thin, communicated in magazines and other media creates pressure for girls to take action to meet these cultural expectations, such as excessive dieting. For this study, the researchers hypothesized "that subcultures in which pressures to be slim and diet are augmented give rise to a greater expression of the disorder in vulnerable adolescents" (p. 648).

To test their hypothesis they surveyed a population of professional dance (N=183) and modeling (N=56) students, who, according to the authors, must focus increased attention and control over their body shapes. Height and weight data and questionnaire data using a standard scale to assess the symptoms of anorexia were obtained from the participants. The same data were also collected from comparison samples of "normal female university students" (N=58), patients with anorexia (N=68), and music students (N=35).

The results indicated that anorexia and excessive dieting concerns were overrepresented in the dance and modeling students. In addition, within the dance group sample, those from the most competitive environments had the greatest frequency of anorexia. Garner and Garfinkel conclude that both pressures to be slim and achievement expectations in this sub-culture are risk factors in the development of anorexia. They discuss these findings in the context of other factors that contribute to the development of anorexia as a multi-determined disorder.

Study 2: Piran (2001)

Piran was also interested in the issue of BWSP among adolescent girls in the context of a dance studio. However, she did not want to frame it as a medical pathology determined by a "pressure for thinness" (p. 14) but rather hoped to explore the issue together with the girls in the context of a **participatory action research (PAR)** project without many preconceived notions about the nature of the issue. Her starting point was that the girls in this studio desired some changes and she saw her primary role as that of a facilitator of that change and only secondary as a researcher.

The initial phase of this research was focused on rapport building between her and the community of dancers. Piran spent a significant amount of time meeting all members of the co-educational dance school, especially the students who were between the ages ten and eighteen. In these meetings they explored the issues at hand and decided on goals and ways of working together as well as examining issues of compatibility. The rapport building with all stakeholders in the school, including the administration, allowed for the system to respect the students' knowledge construction and activism that resulted from this PAR project.

Initially, the girls and adolescent women expressed their extreme preoccupation with body shape, strong denigration of mature women's bodies, and a determination to control and manage their bodies. But, over the course of regular focus group meetings, the dancers started to examine shared adverse social conditions and started to protest their adverse experiences in the school. More and more they developed a hope that these conditions could be better understood and possibly changed. This process can be described as consciousness-raising. Each focus group started with a descriptive stage, followed by an interpretative critical stage, and, when relevant, an action-oriented phase.

Together, through these regular focus groups, the dancers developed a critical understanding of some of the environmental conditions that affected their BWSP. This included, among others, lack of privacy and feelings that their bodies were public, the use of bodies of women and minority groups as a way of expressing prejudicial attitudes, and social construction of femininity and masculinity and what it means to be strong, especially in the relationship to the male dancers in the studio. Another major issue was the way the male dancers treated the female dancers and put them down to compensate for their own shortcomings.

With each of these critical understandings, the participants took actions to create changes, such as challenging the male dancers and asking for more privacy from the staff in the school. Thus, when the project concluded, the girls and adolescent women had made significant changes to the environment that had oppressed them and, in the process, became empowered, which also shifted the way they felt about themselves and their bodies.

Learning Objectives

Research is both a rewarding and challenging process that sometimes can be hard to understand. There are so many different **research approaches**, designs, and methods and so many choices to make along the way even when studying the same issue, just as in the two example studies in Box 12.1. It is easy to feel incompetent and, thus, just stick with the methods we already know or not engage in research at all. But, research is a critical tool for social action and transformative change and our community partners are looking to us for some methodological expertise. Thus, we hope that with this and the next chapter, we can provide you with a better understanding of **community-engaged research**, its purpose, and its context.

Paying attention to context is an important principle of community psychology (CP) and research is no exception. Our worldviews, our values, our understanding of knowledge and how it is obtained, and our ethical principles all influence the type of **research questions** we ask and the methodological approaches to those questions. Thus, it is useful to provide some clarification of what the different philosophical paradigms underlying different research approaches are and to discuss those that are reflected in the way we conceptualized this and the next chapter. In addition, it is beneficial to have some shared understanding of some of the key terms used in these two chapters.

In this chapter you will learn about

- Philosophical considerations related to social science research, including key research paradigms
- The definition and purpose of community-engaged research
- The meanings of some key terms related to research

The Importance of Context and Challenging Assumptions

Research does not occur isolated from the "real world" but is done in specific sociocultural and historical contexts and is influenced by the ideas and norms that dominate researchers' scholarly and social environments (Tebes, 2017). In many cases, however, research methods are presented to students as "givens" and the paradigms from which the methods are derived and the philosophical assumptions that underlie those paradigms are typically unexamined and unchallenged. You may have experienced that in your undergraduate courses.

Thus, we will begin this chapter by exploring some of these fundamental questions about research and explain how this and the next chapter are positioned within that inquiry. We will then provide some thoughts regarding defining community-engaged research, as we understand it, for the purpose of this book. We will conclude the chapter by clarifying some core components of research, such as research approach, design, and methods.

Reflections on Research Paradigms

In his 1962 book, *The Structure of Scientific Revolutions*, philosopher Thomas Kuhn challenged the prevailing belief that science progresses through the slow and steady accumulation of "facts." Rather, he asserted that science progresses through the development of new paradigms. A paradigm is a set of beliefs, a worldview, a set of assumptions about the world and one's place in it. A paradigm also represents a consensus among a scientific community at a given time related to preferred and commonly accepted theories and methodologies (Chilisa & Kawulich, 2012; Lincoln, Lynham, & Guba, 2017). A dominant paradigm is one whose basic assumptions are so taken for granted by most people that to challenge them may be considered heresy. People believe that "this is the way the world is!" Once upon a time, it was widely believed that the sun and stars revolved around the Earth and that the Earth was flat. When the inconsistencies or problems of the dominant paradigm become evident, challenges were mounted and alternative paradigms began to emerge. At some point, old paradigms are abandoned and a new one is embraced. Such paradigm shifts are often met with skepticism and resistance because they challenge people's basic assumptions about the world.

This understanding of paradigms and paradigm shift was important in the evolution of social science as it identified science and the scientific process as social constructs that can be challenged and changed by social actors, both from within and outside of the scientific community. It also revealed the hidden power dynamics embedded in the scientific process and the role that science has played in strengthening the position of the dominant societal groups and oppressing groups at the margins, such as Indigenous groups, people with mental health challenges, racialized minorities, people dealing with poverty, and so on (Tebes, 2017). With this understanding in place, some researchers began to actively challenge the dominant positivistic paradigm and propose a variety of alternatives. This led to a period of great debate and conflict within the scientific community between the 1970s and the 1990s, often referred to as the "paradigm wars" (Cameron & Miller, 2007). While it goes beyond the scope of this chapter to discuss the different paradigms that emerged during that time in detail, it is useful to provide a brief overview. Considering some key paradigmatic questions is helpful for this purpose. To give you a fair warning, we will be using some big philosophical words in this section. Thus, get comfortable. Perhaps pour yourself a cup of tea/coffee, grab some nice chocolate, and play some relaxing music in the background.

Paradigmatic Questions

With respect to science and research, Lincoln et al. (2017) see paradigms as representing a philosophy of science that addresses several questions organized in four broad categories: **ontology**, **epistemology**, **axiology** (or ethics), and **methodology**.

1 *The question of ontology*: Questions of ontology relate to the researcher's underlying belief system about the nature of being and existence. What is the form and nature of reality? Is reality something tangible that exists "out there" and is it independent of you as the researcher? Or, are there multiple realities that are constructed and interpreted in the minds of researchers and other stakeholders in the research? These philosophical assumptions about the nature of reality are critical in the way we select our research approach, our methodologies, and make sense of our research data. Many Indigenous people, for example, believe that they have deep connections with the living and the non-living, with land, with earth, with animals, and with other beings (Chilisa & Kawulich, 2012). With this worldview then, it makes sense to use methods that are reflective of this relational understanding, such as storytelling and sharing circles.

2 *The question of epistemology*: In research, epistemological questions are about what the nature of knowledge is, how we come to know something, and how knowledge relates to the researcher as well as others. How do we know what we know? What is the relationship between me, as the researcher, and what can be known? Is it possible for researchers to find an objective truth that is independent of the observer? What forms of knowledge and types of human knowledge interests exist? What is the purpose of knowledge? What constitutes valid knowledge? Do we rely on intuitive knowledge such as beliefs, faith, and intuition, for example, or empirical knowledge that is derived from the systematic gathering of data based on sensory experiences? The issue of the objectivity and subjectivity of the researcher is important with respect to the question of epistemology and central to the issues discussed in this chapter.

3 *The question of axiology*: Axiology refers to the ethical question pertinent to research. That is, how do we act ethically as researchers or, put in simpler terms, what is right and wrong behavior in the context of research generally and a certain study context specifically? What values and principles guide our research? What are the participants' rights? Who is benefitting from our research? Does the research have the potential to cause harm? Whose voices are being amplified and who has control over the research agenda? How will the research partners work together and how will conflict be addressed (Lincoln et al., 2017)?

4 *The question of methodology*: Methodology is an umbrella term used for research approaches, design, methods, and procedures. Research methodology is about "the logic and flow of the systematic processes followed in conducting a research project, so as to gain knowledge about a research problem" (Kivunja & Kuyini 2017, p. 28). How can researchers go about finding out whatever they believe can be known? What tools can and should be used in the research to advance knowledge and promote change? One's assumptions about ontology and epistemology and one's values and ethics influence the choices we make about methodology. For example, if we value self-determination and empowerment, we will provide decision-making power to community stakeholders related to several or all aspects of the research cycle. If we have strict beliefs about the importance of an objective stance of the researcher, however, we will be less likely to involve members of the focus community in the decision-making process or limit their role to providing research data that we collect.

Major Research Paradigms

There are multiple ways in which the most prominent **research paradigms** in social science research have been organized (e.g., Chilisa, 2011; Lincoln et al., 2017; Nelson & Prilleltensky, 2010; Ponterotto, 2005). In Table 12.1 we present an overview based on Chilisa (2011) and Chilisa and Kawulich (2012) and the authors above, which differentiates between the positivist/post-positivist, constructivist/interpretative, transformative/emancipatory, and postcolonial/Indigenous research paradigms along core aspects of these paradigms, which relate to the questions discussed above. Key points of differentiation include the degree to which the need for **objectivism** is emphasized versus a value for subjective experiences and knowledge, whether generalization of knowledge or recognition of context-dependency is prioritized, how much values are seen as important in the context of research, how the relationship with research participants is set up, and which types of designs (e.g., experimental vs. descriptive) and data collection methods (e.g., focus groups vs. survey) are seen as most appropriate. We will briefly review each paradigm. This review draws primarily from three sources: Chilisa and Kawulich (2012), Lincoln et al. (2017), and Nelson and Prilleltensky (2010). The first three major paradigms described below are present in all three sources with slightly different terminology. Lincoln et al. (2017) have also added a participatory paradigm (which we reference in the Beyond the Major Paradigms section) while Chilisa and Kawulich (2012) included the postcolonial/Indigenous paradigm, which we include in our description of paradigms below.

Positivist/Post-Positivist Paradigm

Positivism dominated the natural and social sciences (including psychology) until other paradigms emerged in the second half of the 20th Century. Today, most researchers who subscribe to this paradigm ground their work within the ontology and epistemology of the updated

Table 12.1 Comparison of selected paradigms

	Positivist/ Post-Positivist Paradigm	Constructivist/ Interpretative Paradigm	Transformative/ Emancipatory Paradigm	Postcolonial/ Indigenous Research Paradigm
Primary knowledge interest	Instrumental knowledge	Practical knowledge	Emancipatory knowledge	Decolonizing and Indigenous as well as emancipatory knowledge
Primary reason for doing the research	To discover laws that are generalizable and universal	To understand and describe human experience and meaning-making	To understand structures of power and oppression and empower people to create transformative changes	To challenge deficit thinking and pathological descriptions of the former colonized communities and reconstruct a body of knowledge that carries hope and promotes transformation and social change among the historically oppressed
Philosophical underpinnings	Informed mainly by realism, idealism, and critical realism	Informed by hermeneutics and phenomenology	Informed by critical theory, postcolonial discourses, feminist theories, race-specific theories, and neo-Marxist theories	Informed by Indigenous knowledge systems, critical theory, postcolonial discourses, feminist theories, critical race-specific theories, and neo-Marxist theories
Place of values in the research process	Science is value free, and values have no place except when choosing a topic	Values are an integral part of social life; no group's values are wrong, only different	The science is grounded in values and the researchers are clearly positioning themselves with specific values. Research is done to promote transformative change for wellbeing and social justice.	All research must be guided by a relational accountability that promotes respectful representation, reciprocity, and rights of the researched
Nature of knowledge	Objective	Subjective; idiographic	Dialectical understanding aimed at critical praxis	Knowledge is relational
What counts as truth	Based on precise observation and measurement that is verifiable	Truth is relative to the people who participate in the study and their cultural, societal, and historical context	Informed by critical theory that unveils illusions and illuminates systems of power and oppression	Informed by the set of multiple relations that one has with the universe

Table 12.1 (continued)

	Positivist/ Post-Positivist Paradigm	Constructivist/ Interpretative Paradigm	Transformative/ Emancipatory Paradigm	Postcolonial/ Indigenous Research Paradigm
Methodology	Quantitative; correlational; quasi-experimental; experimental; causal comparative; survey	Qualitative; phenomenology; ethnographic; symbolic interaction; naturalistic	Combination of quantitative and qualitative action research; participatory action research	Participatory, liberating, and transformative research approaches and methodologies that draw from Indigenous knowledge systems
Techniques of gathering data	Mainly questionnaires, observations, tests and experiments	Mainly interviews, participant observation, pictures, photographs, diaries and documents	A combination of techniques in the other three paradigms	Techniques based on philosophic sagacity, ethno philosophy, language frameworks, Indigenous knowledge systems, and talk stories and talk circles

Adapted from Chilisa, 2011, and inspired by Chilisa and Kawulich, 2012; Lincoln et al., 2017; and Nelson and Prilleltensky, 2010.

post-positivist version, which is based on *critical realism*. Most psychology programs teach and conduct research using methodologies derived from this paradigm.

Ontology. Traditional positivism (also referred to as logical positivism) holds that there is one single objective reality driven by universal laws. It was assumed that this reality exists independent of the observer and can be apprehended through systematic scientific processes. The goal of science then is to discover these universal laws that correspond to the true nature of reality. An example of a positivistic law is B. F. Skinner's law of positive reinforcement, that any consequence that follows a behavior that leads to a subsequent increase in the frequency of that behavior is a positive reinforcer. In the post-positivist turn during the mid-20th century, this view was modified to what is commonly referred to as *critical realism*, which maintains that there is a single objective truth but recognizes that we can only imperfectly and probabilistically apprehend that truth. That is, the researcher can only discover reality within a certain realm of probability.

Epistemology. Within the positivistic paradigm knowledge is viewed as facts that can be empirically tested, confirmed, or disconfirmed, and are relatively stable and generalizable across specific historical-cultural contexts. Positivism subscribes to the dualistic position that the researcher and the research object (the participants and topic of study) are independent. The mind of the knower (the researcher) and what can be known (external reality) are separate from one another. To understand reality then, research must be objective and value free, so that the biases of the researcher do not interfere with understanding the phenomenon of interest. Thus, the epistemology underlying positivism/post-positivism is objectivism. Various methodological safeguards need to be put in place to control extraneous variables and reduce biases. Positivism further assumes that reality can be broken down (reduced) into component parts and causal mechanisms can be determined. Researchers develop a language of terms, concepts, and theories that are believed to correspond to external reality. Theoretical constructs are operationalized or grounded in observable events and behaviors.

Post-positivism shifts this paradigm away from the position of dualism. The mutual influence of the researcher and the researched is acknowledged. Knowledge is viewed as theories about reality that can be confirmed or disconfirmed (falsified). That is, critical realism recognizes that observations may involve error and that theories can be modified based on new empirical evidence. It is understood that observations are influenced by the observer's biases and worldview and that the mere process of observing could influence what is seen. Post-positivists still believe, though, that objectivity can be achieved by safeguarding against these individual biases using multiple measures and observations and triangulating the data to gain a clearer understanding of what is happening in reality. Further, replication by others is highly valued to confirm the observed findings.

Axiology. "Facts" and "values" are viewed as distinctly different and separate in positivism. Research should be "value neutral" in pursuit of the truth about the nature of reality. Post-positivism, on the other hand, acknowledges that the values of the researcher do enter the research process. As was noted in the previous paragraph, the goal is to reduce the impact of value biases by introducing a number of methodological safeguards. However, post-positivist researchers believe that they can use research findings to advocate for social change and many community psychologists are using post-positivist methodology for that purpose.

Methodology. Quantitative and laboratory methods, adopted from the natural sciences, are the primary tools used in post-positivist research. There is an emphasis on the development of reliable and valid scales to measure theoretical constructs (e.g., questionnaires that assess sense of community or empowerment). Moreover, hypotheses about the nature of reality are tested and verified (or falsified) through experimental and correlational research. While positivism has emphasized experimental laboratory methods, post-positivism utilizes more field research in naturalistic settings. Community surveys and program evaluation using experimental and quasi-experimental designs, which we describe in the next chapter, are typical of post-positivist community research. There is also an emphasis on using multiple research methods. Qualitative methods are used by post-positivist researchers for exploratory research of relatively under-researched phenomena (e.g., to develop new hypotheses), in the development of new measures, and to triangulate or interpret quantitative findings (determining the consistency of findings using multiple methods). Qualitative methods are seen as particularly useful for the exploratory or discovery phases of research to generate hypotheses that can be tested.

The first example study in Box 12.1 by Garner and Garfinkel (1980) is an example of study conducted within the post-positivist framework. The authors assume there is an objective reality that can be approximated with inferences drawn from a research sample. The issue of interest is framed using medical terms. The research participants are passive in the research process and are involved primarily to provide data points for the statistical analysis.

Constructivist/Interpretative Paradigm

The constructivist/interpretative paradigm has relatively recently emerged as an alternative human sciences paradigm of inquiry in the social sciences. This shift in thinking was primarily driven by feminist researchers, who challenged the existing approach to science, because it imposed the male-dominated view of reality as the universal one. Many researchers in CP feel aligned with the epistemology and methodology of this paradigm but may not always fully agree with the relativism of its ontology (Tebes, 2017).

Ontology. The constructivist paradigm is in dialectical opposition to the dominant positivist/post-positivist paradigm. In comparison with post-positivism, constructivism is more phenomenological, interpretive, relational, holistic, and humanistic. The focus is more on language, communication, subjective human experience, and the meaning that people make of their experiences in their historical, social, cultural, and political contexts.

Constructivists believe that reality is socially constructed and that there are as many intangible realities as there are people who are mentally constructing them based on their experiences in their respective contexts. In other words, in a social and community context, individuals make meaning of their experiences. Thus, reality is not some absolute, universal truth that can only be understood by scientists; rather, reality is dependent on the individuals and groups who hold such constructions, with no one construction being more or less "real" or "true" than another. Reality is relative to the people who participate in the study and their cultural, societal, and historical context, which is commonly referred to as *relativism*.

Epistemology. In contrast to the position of dualism in the positivist paradigm, the researcher and the research object are assumed to be interrelated rather than separate. Moreover, research is subjective, value-laden, and inductive. Since reality consists of multiple social constructions, the researcher and the participants co-construct or create the findings. Language does not correspond to any external reality independent of the observer, but rather reflects the mental constructions of individuals, which is the basic tenet of constructivism. While some statements about reality may be universally endorsed, most are understood as culturally bound and historically and context dependent.

Axiology. Values are an inextricable part of the research, as the researcher and the research participants bring their values into the research process. However, the assumptions of relativism and constructivism renders it impossible to prescribe one set of values over another. Thus, the research is value-bound or influenced, rather than value-driven. Given the potential vulnerability that exists when people share their lived experience, the researcher has a great responsibility to develop trust with the participants and follow careful ethical procedures. Also, there is a responsibility to ensure that the voices of the participants are represented as accurately as possible and that the sharing of these voices with the public does not cause harm to the participants and their communities (e.g., by perpetuating certain stereotypes about that community).

Methodology. The main purpose of interpretative research is to understand people's lived experiences and how they make meaning of them. Social constructions are generated through dialogue, reflection, and a close working relationship between the researcher and participants. Primarily qualitative methods are used to elicit and understand people's constructions and participatory processes are used to arrive at a consensus on the findings and their meaning. Qualitative methods are used to understand the values, interests, and meanings that underlie language, discourses, and texts. Relatively open-ended questions are used to solicit participants' accounts of their lived experience and their interpretation of that. Thus, the primary data in qualitative analysis are people's words, not numbers or statistics. Increasingly, artistic methods such as photos, drawings, or collective murals are used as well, often in combination with focus groups and interview or other language-based data (Wilson & Flicker, 2014). Some constructivists also use quantitative methods in their research.

While the raw data are representative of the perspective of the participants, the analysis and interpretation are mostly done by the researchers. In addition, the way the questions are asked during an interview or focus group can also influence the way the participants' experiences are captured. That is why researchers often bring their interpretations back to the participants to verify that the researchers are capturing the participants' constructions of the issue under study accurately (often referred to as member check). Further, following the feminist standpoint theory, it is important that the researchers reflect on and describe their assumptions about reality, their values, ideological biases, their relationships with the participants, and their connection to the research topic. For example, Manuel, Scot, Geoff, and Isaac will likely interpret interviews with women about their experience in higher education somewhat differently to Stephanie who shares this experience with the participants. This explicit description of one's standpoint allows the user of the research findings to put those into the context of the researchers' background and values.

Transformative/Emancipatory Paradigm

The transformative or emancipatory paradigm (sometimes also referred to as the critical paradigm) has its roots in Marxism, German **critical theory** and contemporary forces for social justice and social change, including participatory action research, feminism, as well as critical race, critical disability, and queer theory. It is well aligned with the CP values we discussed in Chapter 2, especially the focus on social justice and transformative change.

Ontology. This paradigm assumes that there is an external reality but that this reality is layered. On the one hand there is the surface reality, which is visible and can directly be experienced. On the other hand, there are deep structures that are unobservable but significantly impact our lives. Unlike positivism, the *transformative paradigm* holds that reality is constituted of institutional and social structures that have been historically shaped by social, political, cultural, economic, ethnoracial, and gender factors. This paradigm also assumes that there are social inequalities that are contested and that there are conflicts between dominant and subordinate groups. The term "transformative paradigm" emerged from a family of research approaches with a common theme of emancipating marginalized communities from the oppressive structures that create inequalities and limit people's agency, causing harm to their wellbeing (Mertens, 2009). The idea is that researchers and communities work together towards transformations through collective action.

Epistemology. Given the emancipatory focus of this paradigm, the purpose of knowledge is then to provide the understanding and insights needed to create the desired transformation. Teo (1999) identified three functions of critical knowledge. First, *deconstruction* can be used to critique mainstream theories and research (e.g., see Fox, Prilleltensky, & Austin, 2009, for critiques of various sub-fields of psychology). Critical analyses are particularly attuned to issues of values, power, structures, and personal agency. Second, *reconstruction* can be used to reframe psychological issues through an analysis of power. For example, the Brazilian educator Paulo Freire reframed the purpose of learning from one of conforming with societal expectations to a process of becoming increasingly conscious of the deeper structures in society that maintain the status quo and keep marginalized groups in their place. Third, *construction* is the development of new critical theories that take into account issues of oppression and power and are grounded in a different way of framing social issues.

The epistemology of the transformative paradigm shares a lot in common with the one of the constructivist paradigm. The researcher and the research object are assumed to be interrelated and research is value-laden. Research findings are mediated through the values of the researcher and the participants. The importance of the researcher working and being in solidarity with research participants who are oppressed and disadvantaged is emphasized. Reflexivity is another important concept for the critical paradigm as part of a social constructionist epistemology (Alvesson & Sköldberg, 2000; Mertens, 2009). Since the values of the researcher shape the research, it is important for researchers to be self-reflectively aware of their values and position in society.

Axiology. Research conducted from the standpoint of the transformative paradigm is value-driven (Prilleltensky & Nelson, 2002). Researchers and participants begin with a moral and political position that underlies the entire research enterprise. Moreover, the transformative paradigm emphasizes the values that we identified in Chapter 3, including self-determination, social justice, respect for diversity, inclusion, and accountability to oppressed groups.

Methodology. There is an emphasis on dialogue and dialectical processes. Research is reflexive and transformative; findings are always a work in progress that is subject to new insights and critiques as the research process unfolds. Highly participatory and social-action-oriented approaches are used towards the goal of emancipation of oppressed groups (Lykes, 2017; Tebes, 2017). Inclusion of the voices of disadvantaged people and democratization and demystification of the research process are emphasized in the transformative paradigm. The practical purpose of research is contributing to emancipation and transformation and the specific **research objectives** and questions (grounded in the needs of the community) are what drive the choice of the **research design** and methods. Thus, both quantitative and qualitative methods are used, depending on the research question. For example, a community survey may be used to demonstrate the prevalence of suicidal thoughts among transgender people, while a focus group may be used to gain collective understanding of the sociohistorical root structures of the internalized and direct oppression these communities experience.

The second example in Box 12.1 by Piran (2001) is a good example of a study conducted within the transformative paradigm. The goal is not to identify general laws about a medical condition but instead get a sense of the way the young women in a dancing school understand their environment. There is a clear focus on creating positive change within the context of the study. Piran is using participatory action research methods to engage the dance students and the whole school environment in a critical consciousness and collective change process.

Postcolonial/Indigenous Research Paradigm

Chilisa (2005, 2011) and Wilson (2008) have discussed another paradigm, which is grounded in Indigenous worldviews and ways of knowing with a strong emphasis on the relational nature of the world and knowledge. This paradigm includes postcolonial Indigenous research conducted in former colonized societies in Africa, Asia, Latin America, and with Indigenous peoples in Australia, Canada, the US, and other parts of the world (Chilisa & Kawulich, 2012). Reyes Cruz and Sonn (2011) and Dutta (2018) have encouraged community psychologists to reconsider some of our core concepts, such as "culture" and "community," from a decolonizing perspective and there is an increasing number of community psychologists who frame their research within this paradigm.

Ontology. Key to the Indigenous ontology is the idea of unity of all things and the belief that human beings are deeply interconnected with the living and the non-living, with the land, the earth, with animals, and other beings (Chilisa, 2011). Indigenous' understanding of concepts such as "community" and individuals' relationship to communities can only be fully comprehended with that deeply ecological perspective of organically interconnected webs of relationships (Dutta, 2018; Fettes, 1998).

Another important aspect of an Indigenous ontology is the deeply spiritual view of the world, which makes it quite different from most Western research paradigms, which come from the tradition of the enlightenment movement, which intentionally de-emphasized the role of religion and spirituality in making sense of the world through science.

Epistemology. Related to the description above, knowledge is seen as fundamentally relational (Chilisa & Kawulich, 2012). Among Indigenous people knowledge is shared primarily through storytelling. As Wilson (2008) explains:

> The major difference between those dominant paradigms and an Indigenous paradigm is that those dominant paradigms build on the fundamental belief that knowledge is an individual entity: the researcher is an individual in search of knowledge, knowledge is something that is gained and therefore knowledge may be owned by an individual. An Indigenous paradigm comes from the fundamental belief that knowledge is relational. Knowledge is shared with all of creation. (p. 56)

Axiology. The postcolonial Indigenous paradigm is grounded in a strong value for social justice and the wellbeing of all of creation. It emphasizes respect for marginalized communities' belief systems and a relationship between the researcher and the participants that is grounded in equality and mutual trust (Chilisa & Kawulich, 2012). Working with Indigenous communities requires a respect for the elders and time for relationship building. In addition, it is important to come with an understanding of how colonization has created a collective trauma that has deeply impacted Indigenous communities to this day. This includes a recognition of the jurisdiction of Indigenous peoples over their culture, heritage, knowledge, and political and intellectual domains (Indigenous Peoples' Health Research Centre, 2004). This implies that research agreements need to be negotiated and formalized with the authorities of an Indigenous community before any research is conducted with their people. Ownership, control, access, and possession of all data and information obtained through the research must be guaranteed to the Indigenous Peoples. It is also important that the research benefits the community and does not cause any further harm.

Methodology. Indigenous methods are often based on traditional ways of creating and sharing knowledge in Indigenous communities that are reflective of the relational ontology and epistemology such as storytelling, healing methods, sharing circles and songs (Chilisa, 2011; Chilisa & Kawulich, 2012).

Beyond the Major Paradigms

These paradigm wars of the 20th century have more or less been replaced by a "paradigmatic soup" (Buchanan & Bryman, 2007), where the distinctive boundaries between different paradigms have become blurry. Increasingly, scholars are looking for commonalities and connections across different paradigms (e.g., Gioia & Pitre, 1990; Tebes, 2017).

What has emerged is a **methodological pluralism** and **pragmatism** in how research is approached in the applied social sciences. *Pragmatism* focuses on the practical implications and outcomes of the research, with a strong emphasis on using research to solving practical issues of importance to communities. Within this approach, methodological choices are made primarily based on which design and methods will most likely provide the needed answers to the research questions and meet the research objectives and less based on ontological and epistemological considerations (Johnson & Onwuegbuzie, 2004; Tebes, 2017). This approach to science is well aligned with the action-oriented applied research of CP, which is driven by the practical research questions that are relevant to the community partners we are working with and the communities they represent (Tebes, 2017).

In addition, most paradigms share in common an epistemological understanding that the view of our world is constructed and depends on the perspective of the observer (Tebes, 2017). This is true, independent of the ontological belief of whether a reality exists independent of people's construction of it. Thus, research needs to find ways of "bridging the divide between each of our individually constructed knowledge claims" (Tebes, 2017, p. 29).

This methodological liberation movement, however, also puts a bigger burden on the researcher to be conscious and intentional about the different methodological choices they make and how they approach the research process. While these choices may no longer be nicely wrapped in one paradigmatic package, a conscientious researcher nevertheless still has to grapple with ontological, epistemological, ethical, and methodological questions.

This diversion from paradigmatic fundamentalism, however, also opens up the research process to input from the community and other stakeholders (Tebes, 2017). Scientific paradigms are often foreign to people outside of academia, who are much more driven by the pragmatic and action-oriented questions that affect their own wellbeing as well as those of others.

This evolution in the debate on paradigms, which is well aligned with CP research, was one motivation for us to structure the research chapters in this edition a little bit differently. It was our goal to present the many choices a researcher and a research team has to make in a pragmatic and value-based, rather than paradigmatic, way. It is important to note, however, that there are still many pockets of scientific inquiry that operate within specific paradigms, whether consciously or not. Many traditional psychology departments, for example, are still dominated by the (post-) positivist paradigm. For instance, inferential statistics is predicated on its ability to infer to other populations, based on a discoverable truth, which is inherently objectivistic. Thus, it is useful to be knowledgeable about what a paradigm is and how it changes. This will help us to recognize when one has been trapped within a specific paradigm and offers ways to break free from the paradigmatic chains.

Additionally, it has been argued that methodological pluralism grounded in pragmatism is itself a scientific paradigm with a set of epistemological and methodological choices (Johnson & Onwuegbuzie, 2004). Similarly, Guba and Lincoln (2005), in an updated version of their classic chapter on paradigms, felt compelled to add the *participatory paradigm* to their typology. This new paradigm, besides its strong emphasis on stakeholder and community participation in the research process, shares a lot in common with what we have described above as well as with the other paradigms introduced in this chapter. In a way, using a research paradigm framework is like a lens that allows the researcher to more clearly see the mental models and social structures they have been operating within, and thus, liberates them to consciously change them. Thus, the conscious reflection about ontology, epistemology, axiology, and methodology represents a form of empowerment for the researcher. Maybe you will experience that as you read through this and the next chapter.

With this reflection in mind, it is important to note that this chapter is based on some core beliefs and values that relate to the four core aspects of research paradigms discussed above. We agree, for example, with constructivism and Tebes' (2017) idea of perspectivism, that while there is likely an objective reality that exists independent of the researcher, the real essence of the object cannot be known. Reality as it presents itself to us, as researchers, is constructed, which is especially relevant in the applied social sciences, such as CP. The subject and the object are dependent and cannot be separated when we are trying to make sense of the world. That is, all knowledge of reality is dependent on the view and limitation of the individual observer, in what Tebes (2017) refers to as *perspectival reality*. This also implies that there are multiple realities, which may be shared among multiple people.

Whose version of reality dominates is, in itself, an issue of power and privilege. The way we understand reality is a social process situated in a specific sociopolitical and cultural context and moment in history. This implies that the scientific process is best understood as a conversation rather than a search for an objective truth (Tolan, Chertok, Keys, & Jason, 1990). That is, "the purpose of community psychology research is to construct knowledge as shared understanding" (Tolan et al., 1990, p. 7; see also Tebes, 2017).

We agree with the transformational/critical paradigm that this shared understanding should provide communities, especially marginalized communities, with a deeper understanding of the individual, relational, and societal conditions that either promote liberation and wellbeing or perpetuate oppression and suffering (Prilleltensky, 2008b, 2012). Ideally, the generated research knowledge should also provide guidance on how to engage in action that will contribute to transformations leading to less suffering and more thriving.

We also believe that the core CP values and principles introduced in Chapters 1 and 3 should guide our research. This includes an ecological perspective, self-determination and participation (empowerment), community and inclusion, social justice and accountability to oppressed groups, and reflexivity (Nelson & Prilleltensky, 2010; Tebes, 2017).

Finally, we embrace the idea of *methodological pluralism* where the choice of design, methods, and procedures is driven by the research purpose and questions as well as considerations of usefulness, credibility, ethics, power, and feasibility (see discussion on design decisions in the next chapter).

Such beliefs and values are reflected in the way we present the concepts in this and the next chapter. However, it is also important to recognize that there are some people who will disagree with our take on this topic. Thus, this chapter's structure is a reflection of our own background and journey as researchers (see the Preface for information about our journeys).

Purpose of Knowledge in Society

As we will discuss below, a key purpose of research is to generate knowledge. Knowledge itself, however, is a complex and much-discussed phenomenon. With the postmodern turn in philosophy of science and an increasing diversity of voices in the research arena, there is now an increasing recognition that knowledge is not a unified entity but that there are multiple claims to representing reality and multiple ways of knowing (Lincoln et al., 2017; Tebes, 2017). There is a close relationship between knowledge and power, as eloquently explicated by the French philosopher Michel Foucault (e.g., 1983) and discussed in Chapter 4. Who defines what counts as knowledge, controls knowledge production, and gains access to it becomes even more important in what many contemporary observers have described as the "knowledge economy." That is, an economy where the manual labor is mostly done by machines and robots (or by underpaid workers in countries with less strict labor laws) and the majority of "meaningful" jobs rely heavily on advanced knowledge in certain areas and increasingly also across areas (Hirsch-Kreinsen, Jacobson, Laestadius, & Smith, 2005). Instead of being outside of societal power struggles, researchers are deeply embedded in them. Thus, as a community psychologist, it is important to critically reflect on these power dynamics and how we, as researchers, are implicated by that. We will elaborate on these aspects of power in relationship to research throughout the next chapter.

Thus, before we try to define research, it is useful to reflect on the purpose of knowledge relative to our human interests in society and differentiate between different types of knowledge. For this purpose, it can be helpful to refer to the typology of knowledge from the early work of the German philosopher Jürgen Habermas (1971). Habermas described three primary areas of cognitive interests in which humans generate knowledge. These knowledge interests are technical, practical, and emancipatory. *Technical* interests relate to our desire to control our environment and make predictions of what outcomes certain actions will result in. This is mostly of interest in the context of manipulating the material world (e.g., getting from A to B by pedaling on a bike) but can also include the management of people if one considers them as part of the material world and in a functional way (e.g., if I provide people experiencing homelessness and severe mental health issues with unconditional housing and support services, it will result in increased likelihood of stable housing for them and improved quality of life). The knowledge needed to satisfy this human interest is facts and causal explanations, commonly referred to as instrumental knowledge. Experimental and quasi-experimental designs and observational methods (empirical-analytical methods) are the preferred research methods for generating this type of knowledge, from a post-positivism paradigm (William, 1999; Shadish, Cook, & Campbell, 2002). Community psychologists are frequently involved in outcome studies and evaluations of social interventions and prevention programs, which often seek to generate instrumental knowledge and utilize these types of research methods (Miller, 2017).

The second type of knowledge interest is *practical* and relates to the need to understand and interpret the actions, thoughts, emotions, and intentionality of other people and the social norms that guide people. This is part of our social interaction and communication. This interest requires knowledge that facilitates mutual understanding of meaning making; that is, knowledge of how certain people or groups experience the world around them and make meaning of it and how that guides their action (e.g., how do refugees experience immigrating to a country that has a very different culture compared to their home country and how does that experience guide their actions in their new country?). Hermeneutic methods that rely on the interpretation of communicative data (e.g., written diary entries or qualitative interviews) are the typical methods used to generate this type of knowledge through scientific inquiry (Denzin & Lincoln, 2017; William, 1999). Many community psychologists use these methods, for example, to give voice to the often ignored or silenced experiences of marginalized communities (Brodsky, Mannarini, Buckingham, & Scheibler, 2017; Tebes, 2017).

Finally, the third knowledge interest, *emancipatory*, drives self-reflection and critical consciousness (see Chapter 4 for a discussion of critical consciousness). It requires a deep knowledge of those institutional and environmental forces that affect a person's life and limit their agency (including hidden and invisible forms of power). It also involves a critical reflection on one's own positionality and complicity in enabling these conditions to continue (for a great example of this, see the book *White Fragility* by Robin DiAngelo, 2018). If, for example, a company is producing their product in an environmentally harmful way but is marketing the product to consumers as environmentally friendly (i.e., greenwashing) and I buy it, then I continue to contribute to the destruction of the environment. This type of knowledge is emancipatory because it leads to insights into the correct reasons for one's problems, resulting in a perspective transformation, which in turn enables actions for transformative social change. With my understanding of the company's practice of greenwashing, for example, I may advocate for laws that require all companies to clearly note the true environmental costs of their product as assessed by an independent third-party agency. The methods of choice may be grounded in critical social sciences (e.g., feminist theory, critical race theory, queer theory, critical disability), such as participatory action research as well as Indigenous methods (Mertens, 2009; Lykes, 2017; Tebes, 2017; William, 1999). It may not be surprising that many community psychologists are drawn to these types of research given their interest in creating meaningful social change (Tebes, 2017; Nelson & Prilleltensky, 2010).

With this basic understanding of the purpose of knowledge relative to human interests in society, we are now ready to move towards a definition of community-engaged research.

Definition of Community-engaged Research

We will provide the definition of community-engaged research in two parts. We will first review a more general understanding of research and then define the community-engaged aspect of it.

General Understanding of Research

A common basic understanding of scientific research is "the systematic investigation into and study of materials and sources in order to establish facts and reach new conclusions" (Lexico, n.d.). While the specific wording of this definition may be contested, there are three critical aspects of research embedded in this definition that are generally agreed upon: (1) generation of knowledge; (2) use of data sources; and (3) using a systematic process.

Generation of Knowledge

First, the primary goal of research is to *generate knowledge* that is trustworthy and provides society or specific stakeholders with a deeper understanding of a relevant phenomenon, including how to create transformative social change. A group of researchers, for example, may want to produce reliable knowledge about the reasons for why rates of drug use have significantly increased in certain communities. Policy makers and non-governmental organizations (NGOs) can then rely on that knowledge in shaping evidence-based policies, allocating funding, or developing prevention programs. CP researchers often have secondary goals for their research such as creating an empowering process for research participants, supporting the development of research competencies among community partners, or creating social change.

In the previous section, we discussed three different types of knowledge, which often requires different types of methodologies. An understanding that different research methodologies contribute to different types of knowledge, each with differing ability in meeting different human knowledge interests, may liberate the researcher from having to prescribe to just one type of research methodology (e.g., hermeneutics). Instead, the specific knowledge interests, research objectives and questions, values, and contexts will drive the choice of research methods.

Community psychologists generally embrace diversity in methods ranging from art-based Indigenous methods to randomized controlled experiments (Jason, Keys, Suarez-Balcazar, Taylor, & Davis, 2004; Tebes, 2017). In many cases, those methods are combined to meet multiple knowledge interests with a strong emphasis on emancipatory knowledge for social transformation.

Data Sources

Research processes involve specific *data sources*, which can be either material (e.g., hair samples) or non-material sources (e.g., observations of people, interviews, and surveys). The latter often depend on different forms of human communication (e.g., verbal, written, arts-based). The choice of data to be gathered depends, among other things, on the type of knowledge to be produced (as discussed above), the research questions, the specific context and community of interest (e.g., art-based methods are often used with youth because they are more engaging and require less verbal or written skills; Wilson & Flicker, 2014), the resources for data collection, and in many cases, a personal preference by the researcher or other stakeholders for certain types of data. The latter can be influenced by the specific research paradigm with which a researcher feels aligned (Chilisa & Kawulich, 2012; Tebes, 2017).

Systematic Process

Research is a *systematic process* of gathering, processing, analyzing, and interpreting those data sources. That is, the researchers use specific and explicit methodological procedures that are well-justified based on agreed upon criteria of excellence, the research problems and questions, the specific research context, values, and ethical principles. These procedures should be well documented so that others can judge the trustworthiness and ethical soundness of the research findings (Jason et al., 2014).

It is important to note that the above definition of research represents an understanding of research in the context of non-Indigenous science whose basic principles were significantly shaped during the Enlightenment period in Europe in the 18th century. The Enlightenment movement placed a strong emphasis on reason as the primary source of authority and legitimacy. This understanding of scientific research is also based on a Western worldview that tends to see the world as divided in individual components and as a machine that can be systematically studied so that it can be controlled (Koger & Du Nann Winter, 2010). Early science was mostly focused on natural phenomena, which significantly shaped the way scientific inquiry has been conceptualized. This influenced the way human psychological and sociocultural phenomena have been studied. The experimental design, for example, is still often considered the preferred scientific method. This form of scientific knowledge construction, however, has been criticized for its role in colonization and oppression (Chilisa, 2011). Also, some scholars have emphasized that Indigenous ways of knowledge are more holistic and representative of the human experience because they account for spiritual aspects and the wisdom of the elders that is grounded in centuries of experiential knowledge and transferred from generation to generation (Chilisa, 2011; see also Chapter 15). At a time when the application of science has resulted in the destruction of the world that sustains us as human beings (and many other life forms), it seems appropriate and timely to critically reflect on the value of these alternative ways of knowing. For the purpose of this chapter, however, we will ground our discussion in the non-Indigenous ways of inquiry, as the large majority of CP research is based upon them. For information about research from an Indigenous way of knowing, please consult the recommended resources at the end of the chapter.

Community-engaged Research

Community-engaged research is a specific approach to research that has the same key characteristics as described above but with the explicit purpose of addressing an issue that impedes the wellbeing of certain communities. In addition, the expectation is that the research is conducted collaboratively with members of the communities affected by that issue as well as other key stakeholders such as NGOs and governmental organizations working with the affected community (Lykes, 2017). The US Centers for Disease Control and Prevention (CDCP), for example, defined community-engaged research as "the process of working collaboratively with groups of people affiliated by geographic proximity, special interests, or similar situations with respect to issues affecting their well-being" (Centers for Disease Control and Prevention (CDCP) 2011). Similarly, the W.K. Kellogg Foundation's Community Health Scholars Program (2001) defines community-based participatory research (CBPR) in the health field as "a collaborative approach to research that equitably involves all partners in the research process and recognizes the unique strengths that each brings. CBPR begins with a research topic of importance to the community with the aim of combining knowledge and action for social change to improve community health and eliminate health disparities" (p. 2, quoted in Minkler & Wallerstein, 2008). CBPR is one of the most prominent branches of community-engaged research, especially in the health field. Another important branch is generally referred to as *participatory action research*, which emerged from applications of Kurt Lewin's action research in North America and Europe and the liberation movement in Latina America, Asia, and Africa (Lykes, 2017; Wallerstein & Duran, 2008). All of these community-engaged approaches emphasize the application of research for the purpose of addressing issues identified by communities (primarily those marginalized in society) and the importance of participation and engagement of community stakeholders throughout the research process, building upon the strengths and assets they can contribute. This approach to research is well aligned with CP's core values such as participation, wellbeing, self-determination, social justice, and empowerment. In fact, most research by community psychologists can be classified as community-engaged research, with some degrees of variation (Tebes, 2017). That is the reason we are featuring this approach in the next chapter. Before we discuss the research process in the next section, it is useful to clarify a few key terms.

Key Research Terms

When thinking about research, it is useful to differentiate between research methodology, approach, objectives, questions, design, and data collection methods. The term *methodology* was already introduced earlier as a key aspect of research paradigms. It is an umbrella term used for decisions regarding research approach, design, methods, and procedures, which are informed by the ontological, epistemological, and ethical orientation of the researcher. For the purpose of this chapter, the *research approach* refers to the research paradigm or tradition researchers use to frame their research and judge its quality (e.g., applied mixed-method social science research), how they relate to the community of interest for their research and conduct the research process (e.g., community-based participatory research), and how they structure and engage with their research team and partners (e.g., inclusion of community researchers and consensus decision-making; use of an advisory board with a quorum of 50 percent community members). A researcher's approach is often relatively consistent across different research projects.

Research teams and key stakeholders often have multiple *research objectives* including personal (e.g., completing a thesis), practical (e.g., providing evaluation data for a community program or policy, impacting policy), and intellectual goals (e.g., developing theory) (Maxwell, 2012). *Research questions* are typically derived from the objectives in combination with a comprehensive literature review assessing the state of the current research and theory related to the phenomenon of interest and, in many cases, in consultation with key stakeholders (e.g., representatives from partner organizations or funders). While the objectives are kept more general, the research questions need to be relatively specific to ensure that the research process can actually provide concrete answers to the questions. The research questions should drive decisions about the design (see discussion on design decisions in Chapter 13). The *research design* (sometimes also referred to as the research methodology) is the roadmap for the research and includes the type of study approach/design (e.g., descriptive, experimental, quasi-experimental, or action-research; cross-sectional vs. longitudinal; single-level vs. multi-level), data collection methods (e.g., survey, interviews), participants and sampling, procedures, and analysis plan. The purpose of the design is to have a detailed plan that, if successfully executed, will result in satisfactory and credible answers to the identified research questions.

While this description is likely a review for many of our readers, it is nevertheless important to specifically name these different components of research because all too often they are not explicitly considered or are confused with each other (e.g., referring to a community-engaged research approach as a research design). With the definition of community-engaged research in place and the clarification of these key terms, we are now ready to discuss the research process in more detail in Chapter 13.

Chapter Summary

In this chapter, we laid the groundwork for thinking about community-engaged research. We discussed the broader sociocultural and political contexts of research, which include thinking about research paradigms. These involve beliefs about that nature of being and existence (ontology), the nature and way of knowing (epistemology), the question of ethics (axiology) and methodology, which inform the overall research approach, design, and data collection methods. We also reviewed different types of knowledge, including technical (instrumental questions), practical (questions regarding intersubjective meaning-making), and emancipatory (questions of how to create transformative change) knowledge. See Box 12.2 for a definition of community-engaged research, based on our discussion. We concluded the chapter by clarifying the terms research methodology, approach, design, objectives, and questions.

Box 12.2 A Definition of Community-engaged Research

We can define community-engaged research as a collaborative and systematic investigation into and study of materials and sources in order to generate new knowledge that advances the wellbeing of individuals, groups, and communities and equitably involves all partners in the research process building upon their strengths.

Key Terms

Axiology: Ethical question pertinent to research and the role values play in the research.

Constructivism: The belief that reality is socially constructed and that there are as many realities as there are people constructing them. This belief rejects the idea that there is a universal reality that exists independently of the observers and their sociocultural historical context.

Critical theory: A term used as a general umbrella term as well as a term for a specific school of thought. As an umbrella term, it is a general reference to theoretical frameworks in the social and human sciences (e.g., critical race, critical disability, queer, and feminist theory) that include a critique of the oppression and exploitation in a society with an impetus of creating transformative change. This includes a theory of capitalism, often grounded within Marxism, to make sense of sociohistorical and economic processes and developments that influence most aspects of our lives. As a more specific term, it is used to describe a school of thought referred to as the Frankfurt School developed primarily by scholars associated with the Institut für Sozialforschung (Institute for Social Studies) in Frankfurt, Germany.

Epistemology: A researcher's understanding of the nature of knowledge, how they come to know something, and their relationship as a researcher as well as those of others to that knowledge.

Indigenous methods: Research methods based on the belief that people are interconnected with other living and non-living beings, the land, and the earth as well as traditional ways of creating and sharing knowledge in Indigenous communities such as storytelling, healing methods, sharing circles and songs.

Methodology: The research approach, design, methods, and procedures used for a research project.

Methodological pluralism: The belief that different types of quantitative and qualitative methods are appropriate in conducting research. The specific choice of method should be determined based on its appropriateness and effectiveness in answering the research questions.

Objectivism: Within the research context, objectivism refers to the belief that the existence and nature of things in the world are independent of the person observing them and that those things can, in theory, be directly observed.

Ontology: A researcher's underlying belief system about the nature of being and existence.

Participatory action research (PAR): A research approach of working collaboratively with communities in making research-related decisions and co-creating knowledge related to an issue of interest that leads to action and transformative change regarding the issue. PAR typically follows a cycle of research, action, and reflection. It is also often used as an umbrella term that relates to a variety of critical research approaches such as feminist and queer research, critical disability and critical race theory research, and postcolonial and Indigenous research.

Positivism: Holds that there is one single objective reality driven by universal laws. It is assumed that this reality exists independent of the observer and can be apprehended through systematic scientific processes.

Post-positivism: An adaption of positivism grounded in critical realism, which maintains that there is a single objective truth but recognizes that researchers can only imperfectly and probabilistically apprehend that truth. Knowledge is viewed as theories about reality that can be confirmed or disconfirmed (falsified).

Pragmatism: A practical and outcome-oriented approach to research emphasising the primacy of the research objectives and questions in determining the research methodology and featuring methodological pluralism.

Research approach: The research tradition researchers use to frame their research and judge its quality, how they relate to the community of interest for their research and conduct the research process, and how they structure and engage with their research team and partners.

Research design: The roadmap for the research including the type of design, data collection methods, participants and sampling, procedures, and analysis plan.

Research objective: The personal, practical, and intellectual goals for a research study.

Research paradigm: A set of beliefs, a worldview, a set of assumptions about the world and one's place in it. A paradigm also represents a consensus among a scientific community at a given time related to preferred and commonly accepted theories and methodologies.

Research questions: Specific questions which are supposed to be answered through the research process and whose answers will further the research objectives.

Transformative paradigm: Emerged from a family of research approaches (feminism, critical race theory, queer theory, etc.) with a common theme of emancipating marginalized communities from the oppressive structures that create inequalities and limit people's agency, causing harm to their wellbeing. The idea is that researchers and communities work together towards transformations through collective action.

Resources

Books

The following books provide a lot of information regarding the context of research including CP research:

Alasuutari, P., Bickman, L., & Brannan, J. (2008). *The SAGE Handbook of Social Research Methods.* London: SAGE Publications.

Bond, M.A., Serrano-García, I., Keys, C.B., & Shinn, M. (Eds.), *APA handbook of community psychology: Methods for community research and action for diverse groups and issues.* Washington, DC: American Psychological Association.

Chilisa, B. (2011). *Indigenous research methodologies.* Thousand Oaks, CA: SAGE Publications.

Denzin, N. & Lincoln, Y. S. (2017). *The SAGE handbook of qualitative research* (5th ed.). Thousand Oaks, CA: SAGE Publications.

Jason, L. A., & Glenwick, D. S. (Eds.). (2016). *Handbook of methodological approaches to community-based research: Qualitative, quantitative, and mixed methods.* New York: Oxford University Press.

Patton, M. Q. (2014). *Qualitative research & evaluation methods: Integrating theory and practice.* SAGE Publications.

Wilson, S. (2009). *Research is ceremony: Indigenous research methods.* Black Point, NS: Fernwood Publishing.

Articles and Book Chapters

Campbell, R., & Wasco, S. M. (2000). Feminist approaches to social science: Epistemological and methodological tenets. *American Journal of Community Psychology, 28*(6), 773–91.

Gioia, D. A., & Pitre, E. (1990). Multiparadigm perspectives on theory building. *Academy of Management Review, 15*(4), 584–602.

Kidd, S., Davidson, L., Frederick, T., & Kral, M. J. (2018). Reflecting on participatory, action-oriented research methods in community psychology: Progress, problems, and paths forward. *American Journal of Community Psychology, 61*(1–2), 76–87.

Kivunja, C., & Kuyini, A. B. (2017). Understanding and applying research paradigms in educational contexts. *International Journal of Higher Education, 6*(5), 26.

Ponterotto, J. G. (2005). Qualitative research in counseling psychology: A primer on research paradigms and philosophy of science. *Journal of Counseling Psychology, 52*(2), 126–36.

Prilleltensky, I. (2003). Understanding, resisting, and overcoming oppression: Toward psychopolitical validity. *American Journal of Community Psychology, 31*(1–2), 195– 201.

Reyes Cruz, M., & Sonn, C. C. (2011). (De)colonizing culture in community psychology: Reflections from critical social science. *American Journal of Community Psychology, 47*(1–2), 203–14.

Tebes, J. K. (2017). Foundations for a philosophy of science of community psychology: Perspectivism, pragmatism, feminism, and critical theory. In M. A. Bond, I. Serrano-García, C. Keys, & M. Shinn, *APA handbook of community psychology: Methods for community research and action for diverse groups and issues.* Washington, DC: American Psychological Association.

THE RESEARCH CYCLE

13

Warm-up Questions

In Part II, we spoke to the importance of being consistent with our community psychology (CP) values when we design interventions to support individuals, organizations, and communities in promoting positive changes towards generalized wellbeing. The same is true when planning, designing, and implementing research studies as community psychologists.

Imagine you are being asked to develop and implement a research study to better understand the vulnerability of people who experience homelessness in the face of the unfolding climate crisis. Where would you start? What key steps would you take? What are important considerations in the research process to ensure it is aligned with CP values? Get together as a group of 3–4 people to discuss these questions and plan this hypothetical research challenge. Keep your notes and compare them to the key aspect of **community-engaged research** introduced in this chapter.

Learning Objectives

The goal of this chapter is to familiarize you with the process of conducting community-engaged research from beginning to end. While you likely have been exposed to certain aspects of conducting research more generally, there are specific considerations when conducting community-engaged research from a CP framework. This includes considerations such as meaningful participation of key community **stakeholders**, power sharing, working with marginalized communities, and matching **research designs** with community needs and the complexities of social issues.

In this chapter you will learn about

- Key phases of the community-engaged research process
- Considerations of approach, design, and methods for research in CP
- Issues of power in conducting community-engaged research
- Challenges and benefits of community-engaged research

Overview of the Research Cycle

It is useful to conceptualize the action-oriented community-engaged research process as a cycle with multiple key steps or phases, as can be seen in Fig. 13.1 (Buettgen et al., 2012;

Figure 13.1 Cycle of community-engaged research

Mertens, 2009; Janzen, Ochocka, & Stobbe, 2016; Travers et al., 2013). The research cycle begins with the *initial engagement and focusing of the research*, which ensures a shared understanding and agreement among the key stakeholders prior to conducting the research. This includes gathering information about the issue at hand (e.g., the vulnerability of people experiencing homelessness as weather patterns change as part of global climate change) and collaboratively defining the problem, objectives, and research questions (e.g., understand the expected climate change-related weather changes and how people experiencing homelessness in specific regions typically respond to challenging weather as well as what local resources are available to them). With this information in place, the best possible *research design* for answering the research questions in the specific research **context** can be determined. Then, the *research team*, who will carry out the research as planned, is composed and this team will follow specific procedures for *recruiting participants and collecting the data*. Once data have been gathered *the analysis* of those data can begin. The research team then engages, often in close collaboration with key stakeholders, in the *interpretation* of the results from the analysis, reflecting on their implications for theory and practice, and *mobilizing the knowledge* to inform actions (policy change, change in organizational strategy, etc.) and future research. Conceptualizing the research process as a cycle symbolizes that the research process is not linear and straightforward but often requires a back-and-forth between phases (e.g., collect more data after the initial analysis). The symbol of a cycle is also well aligned with Indigenous and participatory action research approaches and represents clear links with community needs and stakeholder participation (Mertens, 2009). As such, the research process is not seen as separate from the specific context of the research inquiry but embedded in it and typically involves a longer-term commitment and immersion of the researcher in the issues, needs, and context of disadvantaged people and other community members (Janzen et al., 2016; Jason, Keys, Suarez-Balcazar, Taylor, & Davis 2004). Opportunities for meaningful participation by key stakeholders can be (and most often should be) provided at each step of this research process; but, often community stakeholders do not want to participate in all aspects of the research (e.g., coding of qualitative data). We will now discuss each of these steps in the research cycle in more detail. First, though, please read the case study in Box 13.1 as we will refer to this study throughout the remainder of the chapter.

Box 13.1 Case Study: Homelessness and Vulnerability to Climate Change

For the purpose of illustrating key concepts in this chapter we are using a community-engaged research study that relates to two of our three exemplary issues: environment and homelessness. The main *research objective* of this study was to explore the vulnerability of people experiencing homelessness to global climate change in the urban areas of Waterloo region. Waterloo region is located in Southern Ontario, Canada, and includes three medium-size cities (Waterloo, Kitchener, and Cambridge) that are all connected to each other. Vulnerability is defined by the Intergovernmental Panel on Climate Change (IPCC) as "the degree to which a system [including people] is susceptible to, or unable to cope with, adverse effects of climate change, including climate variability and extremes" (Intergovernmental Panel on Climate Change (IPCC) 2007 p. 6). People experiencing homelessness are one of several marginalized groups that are especially vulnerable to climate change because of their higher exposure to extreme weather (e.g., snow, rain, extreme heat) and their reduced ability to cope with the negative impacts of that exposure (e.g., existing health issues, no place to get dry). In addition, we wanted to inform the strategic planning of the regional government and local non-governmental organizations (NGOs) related to climate change adaptation, and contribute to the scholarly development of the research team members (Klein & Riemer, 2011; Wandel et al., 2010). The study was co-led by Johanna Wandel, a human geographer at the University of Waterloo, and Manuel Riemer in close partnership with two of their students, the regional government, several community organizations, and three **peer researchers** with experience of homelessness. We used a community-engaged **research approach** with a community advisory group and the involvement of community members with experience of homelessness. The two main students involved were full members of the research team and developed their own thesis projects from this study. The study employed a mixed-method cross-sectional *research design* with a secondary analysis of regional climate change modeling data, and 48 interviews with individuals who have experience with absolute homelessness in the main urban areas in Waterloo region. More details of this study, its approach, and its design will be presented throughout the chapter. The community report of the study is available on the companion website for this book.

I. Initial Engagement and Focusing

Community-engaged research typically begins with engaging key community stakeholders as potential partners in the research as well as informants about the focus and framing of the research. The initial phase addresses important questions related to who is driving the research and who should be involved in the research partnership. Together, the key partners then decide on the exact focus of the research and how to frame it. In traditional research, this step is often a lot simpler as the research is driven by the university-based investigator(s) and the focus is based on their intellectual curiosity and/or gaps identified in the existing literature. With community-engaged research anchored in CP values, things are a little bit more complicated and involved.

Engaging with Community in Research

Participation and Community Control

In the traditional approach to research, the researchers are the primary ones who determine what their research objectives and questions are. They are in control of the research agenda, manage the research process, and own the data (Nelson & Prilleltensky, 2010). Community-engaged research, however, emphasizes community engagement and action outcomes in identifying, researching, and offering solutions to the challenges facing communities, especially those at the margin of society (Travers et al., 2013). Key stakeholders participate as research partners and have a certain level of control over major decisions regarding the research agenda and approach. Research is conducted with communities and not just about them; thus following the slogan of the disability movement for self-determination in North-America: "Nothing about us without us." Arnstein's "ladder of citizen participation" (Arnstein, 1969; 2004) provides a good framework for thinking about stakeholder participation in research. In her typology of participation, Arnstein describes eight rungs on the ladder ranging from manipulation to community control. Often citizen engagement processes such as informing, consultation, and placation, for example, result in tokenism. That is, while citizens (or representatives of the researched community) may be able to receive information and have their voices heard through some consultation process, they lack power to insure that the decision-makers (e.g., the researchers) will actually incorporate their input. Only if the citizens (or community representatives) hold some or all power in the decision-making process (community control), will they experience true participation. A more recent typology of engagement specifically related to youth can be found in Wong, Zimmerman, and Parker (2010).

Thus, as a community psychologist engaging in research, one of the first questions you will have to ask yourself is: How do you relate to the community you are doing research with and what is your role as a researcher? As community psychologists we are doing research *with*, rather than on communities. Stoecker (2003) has suggested three possible roles for researchers. First, there is the role of *initiator*, who begins an inquiry for personal, practical, and/or intellectual reasons and then invites community stakeholders as partners in their research journey. The second role of researchers is that of a *consultant*. By consultant, Stoecker (2003) means that the professional is the person who does the research, which is a different definition of consultancy from that typically used in CP. Stoecker suggests that a community can commission a professional to do the research but needs to put in place accountability mechanisms and ensure that the community remains the "owner" of the research. The third role is *collaborator*, in which the research is neither community driven nor researcher driven, but rather some blend of the two. Community psychologists take on all three types of roles depending on the specific context and need as well as the specific skills of the researcher.

In the illustrative case study introduced in Box 13.1, the members of the research team were motivated by the desire to address the vulnerability to global climate change by marginalized groups and try to identify preventative adaptive strategies to reduce existing vulnerability. Additionally, two of the researchers were on the tenure track for their respective professor positions and needed to obtain grant funding and publish journal articles and their students needed to develop their research theses. Thus, initiation was for practical and personal reasons. The government partners and community organizations who joined the research project, however, had also independently identified the vulnerability of people experiencing homelessness as a key issue they needed to better understand in the regional context. Thus, their engagement with the research team was a rather straightforward process and they helped frame and focus the research from there on.

Creating Optimal Conditions for Engagement

Regardless of the role of the researcher relative to the community stakeholders, it is important to create optimal conditions for their engagement in the research process. This includes developing clear collaborative structures and procedures and being upfront about the different stakeholders' expectations regarding the research (Kirst, Altenberg, & Balian, 2011; Munger & Riemer, 2012). One way of doing this is setting up a written **memorandum of understanding** (see details and examples in the Community Toolbox at https://ctb.ku.edu/en/table-of-contents/structure/organizational-structure/understanding-writing-contracts-memoranda-agreement/mainexample as well as the companion website for this book). An awareness of the power dynamics and power differentials when creating diverse research collaborations including community stakeholders is also critical. For this purpose, a reflection on the three forms of social power, as discussed by Gaventa (1980) and Culley and Hughey (2008) (see also Chapter 4), and how they apply in the research context is useful. Deciding who participates in a meeting (hidden power), for example, is a form of power that often is held by the university-based principal investigator.

While community-engaged researchers are generally aware that collaborations that include a diverse group of stakeholders (e.g., professionals from multiple sectors, members from different cultural groups, key decision-makers, members from the focus community) are advantageous for having important perspectives represented, there is a tendency to work with the people we already know or who are similar to ourselves (Munger & Riemer, 2012). This is likely related to the fact that creating a strong sense of community tends to be more challenging within diverse groups, as discussed in Chapter 7 (see also Neal & Neal, 2013). Thus, it is helpful to conduct a systematic stakeholder analysis to determine what type of roles, groups, and perspectives should be included and who could represent those within the collaborative partnership (Munger & Riemer, 2012; Sofaer, 2000; Stoecker, 2013). This also includes consideration regarding what types of skills, resources, expertise, and connections may be needed. Chapter 7 in *The Community Toolbox* (Center for Community Health and Development (CCHD) 2017c) provides a good overview of stakeholder involvement and analysis. Once key stakeholders are identified, it is important to stay committed to creating the conditions that will enable them to join the collaboration. Members of certain groups may be hesitant to be involved in research either because of bad experiences with researchers and research in the past, because they are not sure how they can contribute, or because they are not convinced that they can justify investing the necessary time and effort. Simply sending out an invitation will likely not be sufficient in these cases. Conducting research that addresses issues of importance to community stakeholders and is meaningful to them goes a long way in that regard. Once the collaboration is formed, it is important to pay attention to group dynamics throughout the research phases (Munger & Riemer, 2012; Sofaer, 2000).

Framing and Focusing the Research

While it is ideal to collaborate with diverse stakeholders prior to framing and focusing the research with specific objectives and research questions and applying for funding, it is not always feasible. In our case study, we had researchers from two relevant academic disciplines and two government representatives involved in framing the objectives for the research study prior to applying for funding. However, we did not get people with experience of homelessness and representatives of community organizations involved until we had the funding secured. The decision to focus on homelessness and vulnerability to climate change in our region was driven by the intellectual interest of the lead researchers and their students, a gap identified in the literature, and a need identified by the government representative responsible for issues related to homelessness in our region. Once the people with lived experience, representatives from community organizations, and other key stakeholders joined us (after we received funding), we further refined the specific objectives and research questions based on everybody's input. In many cases, the involvement of stakeholders and the framing of the research is an iterative process.

An important step in framing the issue and settling on research objectives is identifying the needs of the community. Ideally, the research focus results directly from a specific need identified by the community with which the researcher is working. Even if other factors determined the initial research focus (e.g., the intellectual interests of the researcher or an identified gap in the literature), the research should at least be aligned with priorities for, and the needs of, the community you are working with. Whenever possible, a systematic needs assessment with community surveys, focus groups, and town hall meetings can be very helpful in that context (Ross & Jaafar, 2006; see also Box 13.2). A comprehensive literature review is also needed in order to identify what knowledge regarding the focus issue already exists and what knowledge gaps still need to be addressed. A literature review is also helpful for identifying methodological approaches to researching the focus issue as well as experts that could be consulted. Related to the discussion in Chapter 12, the group needs to decide what type of knowledge they would like to generate and for what purpose (e.g., influencing policy). Furthermore, it is useful to have a **theoretical framework** that guides the formulation of research questions, the development of survey or interview questions, and the interpretation of the results.

In our case study, for example, our work was inspired by the 2007 IPCC report on the impacts of climate change and guided by the climate change vulnerability model developed by Smit and Wandel (2006). Based on that framework, we identified the need to understand the expected exposure of people experiencing homelessness due to extreme weather as well as their capacity to cope with the consequences of the exposure. Our community stakeholders, including those with lived experience of homelessness, made it very clear that there needed to be a clear path of how the research would lead to action benefiting the community, including informing the strategic planning for climate change adaptation in the region. Based on these considerations, we settled on the following three core objectives: (1) To explore the vulnerability of people experiencing homelessness to global climate change in the urban areas of Waterloo region; (2) To identify future changes in the target group's vulnerability given what we know from climate and air quality science; and (3) To implement an effective knowledge transfer and community engagement process for the dissemination of the research findings.

II. Design

The research design, as mentioned in Chapter 12, is the methodological strategy that is supposed to produce, in the best way possible, the evidence and data needed to address the identified research objectives and provide adequate answers for the specific research questions (Bickman & Rog, 2008).

In our case study, the research team needed climate modeling data that would identify the future risk of exposure to extreme weather as well as data about how people experiencing homelessness in Waterloo region currently experience and cope with extreme weather, which we obtained through qualitative interviews. In addition, information about the available network of services available to people experiencing homelessness was needed, which we got through a review of different documents provided by our project partners as well as through their expertise of working in this area. Together, these data provided what the research team and their partners required to determine the future vulnerability to climate change in the region for this specific population. That is, the research problem and questions should drive the design choices, not the other way around. It is important to note, however, that those researchers who work from specific **research paradigms** in a more purist way may reject specific designs and methods because they do not fit with the ontological and epistemological tenets of that paradigm. A follower of the constructivist paradigm is unlikely to endorse the idea of using an experimental design with quantitative questionnaires as the data collection method. As discussed in Chapter 12, however, we took a more practical stance and emphasized the importance of matching designs with specific research objectives and questions.

In applied community-engaged research, the design decisions are seldom straightforward. There are many different options available and many questions that need to be answered before the research collaborative can settle on a specific design. We agree with Bradbury and Reason (2008) that the purpose here "is not with getting the labels of criteria 'very right' but with drawing attention to important choices that an action researcher must make and thus with extending a useful conversation about getting valuable work done well" (p. 229). This is a conversation that, ideally, involves key stakeholders such as the members of the research team, the focus community, and the group of knowledge users. This will increase credibility and usefulness of the study for the community and other knowledge users. The job of the lead researchers here is to be the experts who can present the relevant options in an accessible way including the benefits and disadvantages of specific designs and methods.

There are quite a few types of designs available and these have been organized in different ways into typologies. It is beyond the scope of this chapter to adequately discuss them all. Good overviews and reviews can be found in Alasuutari, Bickman, and Brannan (2008), Bickman and Rog (2008), Denzin and Lincoln (2017), Jason and Glenwick (2016), Patton (2014), and Shadish, Cook, and Campbell (2002). There are some general considerations that are worth discussing in the context of a CP textbook, however. We will present the considerations in three major parts. The first part reviews considerations related to ensuring that the research design matches the objectives of the study. We will use the three types of knowledge interests (technical, practical, and emancipatory) introduced in Chapter 12 to organize that part. The second part discusses considerations specifically related to CP, such as its applied nature, considerations of context, a focus on relationships, promoting change, and respect for diversity. The third part then presents some additional, more general considerations of research design applied to community-engaged research. These include utility, credibility, ethics, power, and feasibility.

Matching Design with Research Objectives

An important function of the research design, as mentioned, is to ensure that the research objectives are met and adequate answers for the research questions are generated. While objectives and questions are specific to each research study, they are typically related to generating different types of knowledge. Thus, in the following we will discuss what types of designs are good matches for the three major types of knowledge we identified in Chapter 12: technical, practical, and emancipatory knowledge.

Technical Knowledge

Technical knowledge interests typically relate to questions of instrumentality, prediction, and manipulation, especially in the natural science area (William, 1999). Thus, research questions based on this interest typically ask questions about the distribution or relationships of specific variables. This includes questions of causality, associations, and distribution. We will first discuss questions of causality and then questions related to the latter two.

Causality. An example of a question of causality relevant to CP would be whether a prevention program has a positive effect on the desired outcomes or to what degree certain social determinants of health are related to the wellbeing of specific marginalized groups. While definitions of what constitutes a cause and effect can differ, it is generally understood that for a factor A (e.g., a program) to be considered the cause of an effect on B (e.g., improved wellbeing in participants) three conditions need to be met simultaneously: (1) A and B need to be related in that if A changes, B also changes (which in statistical terms is assessed through covariation); (2) A needs to precede B in time; and (3) there is no reasonable third factor that could explain the relationship between A and B (Shadish et al., 2002).

The effect of an intervention or cause is often expressed through a counterfactual analysis: what happened to a group with the intervention in place and what would have happened if they did not get exposed to the intervention (Shadish et al., 2002). It is called a counterfactual conditional because in reality it is not possible to measure the same group simultaneously with the intervention in place and without the intervention. That is why designs, such as experiments and quasi-experiments, have been developed to approximate this counterfactual analysis. By either having a valid comparison group that closely resembles the experimental group that receives the intervention or by studying the same group before and after they receive the intervention and ruling out alternative explanations for changes, one can establish conditions that are similar to the counterfactual conditional and, thus, estimate an effect. A strong research design includes both a valid comparison group and multiple pre- and post-intervention assessments. It is important to note that this type of logic is linked to the post-positivist paradigm and the idea of objectivism and would not fit with the tenets of constructivism (see Chapter 12).

Experiments use a random process for assigning who gets the cause (program) or not. In such a design, each unit (e.g., person, program, classroom) has an equal chance of getting assigned to the cause. Quasi-experiments typically do not include a random-assignment process to the intervention and comparison group(s) while "true" experiments do. Correctly executed random assignment is the most reliable strategy for generating an initial comparison group that is most similar to the intervention group, which is why experiments are considered the most trust-worthy design for establishing cause and effect (Bickman & Rog, 2008; Shadish et al., 2002). However, there can be practical, epistemological, and/or ethical reasons why an experiment may not be the best methodological choice, as discussed earlier. Quite a few community psychologists also have concerns about using experiments and quasi-experiments because of their historical association with logical positivism, a research paradigm that for a long time dominated the social sciences (see discussion of paradigms in Chapter 12), as well as issues of not considering people's preferences, individual differences, or artificiality of context (Bickman & Reich, 2015). Shinn (2016), however, argued that traditional research approaches such as social experiments "can contribute to system change that promotes empowerment, social justice, and liberation from oppression" (p. 1). This is especially important because experiments remain influential in policy circles. Ultimately, an experiment is a methodological tool that can be used to cause harm or be used to create positive social change. Working closely with community partners in determining whether an experimental design is the right choice and how to best implement it, is a good way of avoiding negative consequences of social experiments and maximizing their benefits. There are many different types of experiments and quasi-experimental designs available that fit specific purposes, types of phenomena, and contextual conditions (see Shadish et al., 2002, for a good introduction and review). For an example of an experimental study that had significant policy impact on homelessness across the world, see Box 13.2.

Box 13.2 Example of Experimental Research Study with Positive Impact on Homelessness

An example of an experimental quantitative study creating technical knowledge is the evaluation of a supported housing intervention for homeless people conducted by Sam Tsemberis and colleagues (Tsemberis, Gulcur, & Nakae, 2004). As an example of post-positivist research, this study assumed that there is an external reality, homelessness, and that interventions can be causally related to improvement in that reality.

Tsemberis and colleagues evaluated the Pathways to Supported Housing program for homeless people with a history of mental illness and substance use in New York City. Pathways is based on the principle of consumer choice over where and with whom they live and the principle of Housing First that consumers should not have to meet requirements of participation in treatment or sobriety to receive housing. Over 200 participants were randomly assigned to the Pathways program, in which they received rent supplements to access housing, or to the typical services (usually emergency services, such as shelters) available to this population and were followed up on every 6 months over a 2-year period. The Pathways group obtained housing earlier, remained stably housed for longer and reported more choice than those receiving standard services. The two groups did not differ in terms of psychiatric symptoms or substance use.

Since this initial experiment, other research studies have replicated similar positive findings in multiple countries, including the At Home/Chez Soi research demonstration project, which examined Housing First as a means of ending homelessness for people living with mental illness in Canada. The project followed more than 2,000 participants for two years, and was the world's largest trial of Housing First, with demonstration sites in Vancouver, Winnipeg, Toronto, Montréal, and Moncton (Aubry, Nelson, & Tsemberis, 2015). As a result of the positive findings and the active knowledge mobilization by the researchers, the Housing First model has now been widely adopted as a key strategy to reduce homelessness in many countries in North America and Europe.

Associations and Distribution. Descriptive and correlational analyses of observational data, such as community surveys, are typically understood as supporting technical knowledge. *Descriptive analyses* try to establish the current status and distribution of a variable or phenomenon (e.g., the percentage of recent immigrants to a country who experienced a decline of their health since living in their host country). Typical analyses include frequencies, averages, range, percentages, odds and other indicators of a sample distribution. *Correlational analyses* explore the relationships between two or more variables. Most applications in CP are regression-based analyses such as multiple regression, multi-level modeling, and structural equation modeling. Multi-level models are especially useful for community psychologists because one can explore the simultaneous and interactive effects of variables across multiple ecological levels (e.g., individuals nested in family units and neighborhoods; see below) as well as the patterns of change over time (Raudenbush & Bryk, 2002). Structural equation models are used in CP because they allow for modeling complex mediation and moderation effects (Luke, 2005). Mediation analysis explores the indirect effect of variable A on B through one or more other variables (e.g., the indirect positive effect of studying on test results by feeling prepared and reducing test anxiety). Moderation (also called interaction effects), on the other hand, describes the relationship between two variables A and B depending on the values of a third variable C (e.g., the strength of the correlation between poverty and the performance on a test depending on whether the person is being racialized).

While these analyses of observational data are valuable and produce interesting insights, they are only as good as the data being collected. Poorly worded survey questions, for example, can be interpreted differently by different social or cultural groups and can produce unintended systematic differences in the sample data, and, therefore in the findings. Methodological approaches to prevent these types of issues, such as cognitive interviewing (Willis & Artino, 2013) and item response theory (Embretson & Reise, 2011), exist, but are currently rarely utilized in CP (for an example using these methods, see Riemer et al., 2012).

Similarly, a sample that mostly includes representatives of a certain group (e.g., White university students) and lacks representation from other, especially minority and marginalized, groups (e.g., older low-income adults or racialized individuals) could be significantly biased toward the dominant group and may limit the ability to explore how intersecting identities impact the issue of interest. Stratified random sampling ensures that a meaningful representation of these groups is included in the sample by oversampling from specific populations (Bickman & Rog, 2008).

By the nature of their marginalization, certain groups are much more difficult to reach, however, such as men who have sex with men, people dealing with AIDS/HIV or drug addictions, sex workers, and people experiencing homelessness. Respondent-driven sampling (RDS) is a sampling technique that was specifically developed to survey these hard-to-reach populations (Sabin & Johnston, 2014). Similar to snowball sampling (where participants help identify other potential participants), RDS starts with a few individuals (the "seeds") from the target population, who then recruit more respondents, who, in turn, will recruit further respondents. RDS provides the analytical tools to accurately interpret data that have been collected this way without biasing the results. For example, Bauer, Scheim, Pyne, Travers, and Hammond (2015) describe how they used the results of their RDS survey to identify intervenable factors associated with suicide risk in transgender persons. These findings were considered credible by researchers, policy-makers, and practitioners alike and resulted in significant policy and practice changes.

Practical Knowledge

Practical knowledge interests are about understanding and interpreting the actions, thoughts, emotions, and intentionality of people and the social norms that guide humans, that is human social interaction and communication (William, 1999). Thus, it is not surprising that **interpretative methods** such as qualitative interviews, focus groups, and arts-based methods such as Photovoice, collaging, and digital storytelling are the most popular among researchers who pursue these types of knowledge interests (Denzin & Lincoln, 2017). One strength of these methods is their ability to capture the lived experience of people, and, thus, bring previously hidden and marginalized voices to the forefront. For that reason, participating in a study using one of these interpretative methods can often be an empowering experience (Ross, 2017). In addition, these methods provide an opportunity to capture the experience and meaning-making of participants in their specific cultural-historical and sociopolitical context. For example, in our case study we explored the experience of dealing with extreme weather among people experiencing homelessness in Waterloo region, in Ontario, Canada. The sociopolitical context of Canada, the specific climate in the region, the geographical mix of three different cities with their own history, the availability of affordable housing, shelters, social services, and specific programs, all played a role in assessing the vulnerability of people experiencing homelessness in Waterloo region and understanding the experience with extreme weather.

A variety of sampling strategies exists to generate qualitative samples ranging from those that seek broad representation of the target community to those that seek out members with specific characteristics, such as key informants or exemplars. A great overview of different sampling strategies for qualitative research can be found in Patton (2014). There are also different ways of generating, analyzing, and interpreting qualitative data. In phenomenological research, for example, the researchers often collect a relatively small sample (often less than ten participants) with whom they conduct in-depth interviews with a few open-ended questions in order to understand the participants' lived experience of a particular situation or phenomenon (e.g., being stigmatized due to their immigration status) (Dowling & Cooney, 2012). While phenomenological research is mostly descriptive in nature, Grounded Theory is an approach to inductively generate theories based on the interpretation of qualitative data (e.g., a theory of how stigmatization generates poor health outcomes among marginalized communities). For this purpose, the researchers go through cycles of data collection, analysis, and interpretation until a point of theoretical saturation has been reached (Chun Tie, Birks, & Francis, 2019). Discourse analysis is another interpretive approach specifically for the analysis of written, vocal, or sign language use (Wodak & Meyer, 2015). The conversations and discussions about undocumented immigrants from Central and South America in the US on social media is one example that could be analyzed using this type of analysis. Other common qualitative methodologies include ethnography (see below), content analysis (a general approach to extracting specific themes within qualitative data), and narrative analysis (capturing narrative life stories of participants). Accessible and comprehensive overviews of interpretative and qualitative methods can be found in Denzin and Lincoln (2017) and Patton (2014).

Emancipatory Knowledge

Emancipatory knowledge (also referred to as transformative knowledge) interests seek to gain a deeper understanding of those institutional and environmental forces that affect a person's life and limit their agency and capacity to control the factors that affect their wellbeing (including hidden and invisible forms of power). This critical consciousness forms the basis for an empowerment process of taking action to change oppressive factors in the ecological layers of people's lives (see Chapter 4). In many cases, the research itself is an integral part of the action toward transformative social change and the change process is the focus of the research. In this process, knowledge is being co-created between the university-trained researchers and the researchers and participants from the community, in most cases marginalized and disadvantaged communities. Generating emancipatory knowledge often requires breaking with mainstream approaches, challenging language and concepts commonly used in academic theories as well as everyday life, and amplifying the voices of those who are commonly silenced in society.

Research that seeks to generate this type of knowledge is typically grounded in critical theory and encompasses participatory action research, feminist and queer research, critical disability and critical race theory, and postcolonial and Indigenous research (Denzin & Lincoln, 2017; Lykes, 2017; Kemmis, 2008; Kidd, Davidson, Frederick, & Kral, 2018; Minkler & Wallerstein 2008; Mertens, 2009). Broadly speaking, critical theory is an umbrella term in social and political science that refers to a range of theories and theoretical frameworks that are critical of the societal status quo and seek to transform society rather than just understanding and explaining it (Seidman, 2017).

Campbell and Wasco (2000), for instance, have identified four themes that characterize feminist research methods. First, feminist research expands the range of methods. Feminists have pioneered the use of qualitative methods (Campbell & Wasco, 2000; McHugh, 2014) and they have developed new methods, such as concept mapping. Second, feminist research connects women through "openness, trust, caring, engagement, reciprocal relationships and solidarity among women" (Prilleltensky & Nelson, 2002, p. 298). Third, feminist research strives to reduce power differences in the research relationship by engaging participants as co-researchers and co-analysts in the research process. Fourth, the emotionality of science is recognized in feminist research. Emotion and subjectivity are treated as important sources of data in feminist research (Campbell & Wasco, 2000; McHugh, 2014).

Critical race methodology emphasizes the importance of generating counter-narratives by offering space "to conduct and present research grounded in the experiences and knowledge of people of color" (Solórzano & Yosso, 2002, p. 23; see also Donnor & Ladson-Billings, 2017). Indigenous research, which is grounded in oral traditions of sharing knowledge, also emphasizes the importance of using stories as a way to make sense of the natural and social world (Kovach, 2010; Kovach, 2017). Interpersonal dialogue is important in this story capturing and sharing process. Queer theory "challenges the normative social ordering of identities and subjectivities along the heterosexual/homosexual binary as well as the privileging of heterosexuality as 'natural' and homosexuality as its deviant and abhorrent 'other'" (Browne & Nash, 2016, p.5). As such, it has a strong emphasis on analyzing and deconstructing the dominant discourse related to sexuality, sexual health, and gender identity. Similarly, critical disability research tries to shift the focus of traditional disability research focused on fixing deficits within the person to a strength- and empowerment-based approach focused on changing disabling societal conditions and infrastructure (Buettgen et al., 2012). Additionally, there are theories that focus on the intersection of these critical lenses, such as Chicana critical race theory (Delgado & Stefancic, 1998).

Participatory action research is an umbrella term that relates to many of these approaches (Bywater, 2014; Kidd et al., 2018; Kral & Allen, 2016). It has its roots in participatory research that emerged from work with oppressed people in developing countries, particularly Latin America (e.g., Fals Borda 1987; Freire, 1970), on the one hand, and in action research that was first introduced in North America over 60 years ago by Kurt Lewin (1946), on the other hand. Levin proposed cycles of problem definition, fact finding, goal setting, action, and evaluation to simultaneously solve problems and generate new knowledge (Nelson & Prilleltensky, 2010).

Given the strong emphasis on subjective experiences, giving voice to marginalized people, and sharing stories across these different but related research traditions based in critical theory and/or Indigenous knowledge, most research designs use qualitative and art-based methods such as interviews, focus groups, sharing circles, photovoice, and digital storytelling. These designs also typically involve engaging smaller research samples to allow for participation and co-creation of knowledge. In addition, the emphasis on action and social change as part of the research process requires a long-term commitment and engagement with the communities with whom the researcher is working. Engaging in this type of research also involves a critical reflection on one's own positionality in society and complicity in enabling oppressive societal conditions to continue.

It is important to note that many CP research studies do not seek to generate just one type of knowledge but multiple types and will blend approaches and use mixed-methods. Also, many emancipatory elements such as working with marginalized communities and an emphasis on participation, action, and critical reflection have now been adopted more broadly as reflected in the way we have conceptualized and written this chapter.

Specific Design Consideration for Community Psychology

Our values and principles in CP lead us to focus on specific types of research problems. These tend to be of an applied nature, emphasize the importance of context and relationships, include an interest in change and development, and value and respect diversity. We will now briefly discuss designs, methods, and types of analyses that are well suited to capture these aspects.

Applied

Most CP research deals with applied research questions. Even if the questions are theoretical in nature, they still typically relate to applied problems (e.g., processes of developing resilience and empowerment). Thus, a lot of CP research is conducted in applied contexts outside of university settings and with participants who are not university students in an introductory psychology course. Thus, in CP, designs and methods that are strong in external and ecological validity are often preferred over those that are strong in internal validity but lack external validity (Lykes, 2017; Tebes, 2017). A lot of applied research in CP can best be classified as program evaluation, which has been defined as

> the systematic collection of information about the activities, characteristics and results of programs to make judgments about the program, improve or further program effectiveness, inform decisions about future programming, and/or increase understanding. (Patton, 2008, p. 39)

As Patton's definition suggests, program evaluation research is used to inform decision-making on how a program can be improved or become more efficient (formative or developmental evaluation) or whether a program should be continued (summative evaluation). Similarly, policy evaluation is asking questions related to the content, implementation, and impact of social policies (National Centre for Injury Prevention and Control, n.d.).

While the research approach and methods of evaluations are often very similar to the ones described in this chapter, a distinctive feature is that there is typically not an expectation that this type of research produces knowledge that is transferable beyond the specific program or policy being evaluated. A program evaluation, for example, may ask if a specific program in Waterloo region intended to reach people experiencing homelessness during instances of extreme weather is effective in preventing health risks.

However, since the publication of the first edition of Carol Weiss's *Evaluation Research: Methods of Assessing Program Effectiveness* in 1972, there has been considerable growth in the field of evaluation research and the boundaries between applied research more generally and evaluation research have become somewhat blurry. There are many examples of program and policy evaluation studies published in CP journals and books (e.g., the special issues in the *Global Journal of Community Psychology* on CP and public policy by Perkins, García-Ramírez, Menezes, Serrano-García, & Stromopolis, 2016; see also Miller, 2017 for a review).

At the beginning of the evaluation research journey there was a strong emphasis on the separation between the evaluator (i.e., the researcher) and those who are developing, implementing, and using the program (or policy) in order to ensure the independence and objectivity of the evaluator. Over the last several decades, however, there has been a significant shift towards approaches that are aligned with community-engaged research principles such as stakeholder (Pancer, 1997), empowerment (Fetterman & Wandersman, 2005), and developmental (Dozois, Blanchet-Cohen, & Langlois 2010) approaches to evaluation. These types of evaluation resemble, in many ways, the research cycle described in this chapter.

Many different types of evaluations and evaluation designs are available (Patton, 2014). The choice depends on the nature of the program and policy, the stage of development the program is in, the size and duration of the program (e.g., a small single site one-time program or an ongoing large-scale multi-site program), the evaluation questions of the program developers, funders and other stakeholders, and other factors such as the resources available for the evaluation. Thus, just like community-engaged research more generally, the evaluation design is driven by the needs and questions of the key stakeholders and the specific context. Box 13.3 provides a brief overview of some of the most common types of program evaluation.

Box 13.3 Program Evaluation Types

Needs assessment: A needs assessment is a systematic process for identifying perceived and unperceived community needs and gaps between existing and desired resources and conditions (Centers for Disease Control and Prevention (CDC) 2013). Often a combination of different methods such as community surveys, focus groups, key informant interviews, Photovoice, and geographic information systems (GIS) are used to get a comprehensive picture of what the needs, existing resources, and gaps are. This information can then be used to inform new programs and initiatives.

Evaluability assessment: Evaluability assessment seeks to determine whether a program or intervention is ready to be evaluated, especially in regard to its effectiveness in reaching expected outcomes. A program must meet three criteria to be evaluated: (1) clear, specific and measurable outcome goals; (2) clearly articulated program components; and (3) a rationale that links the goals and program components. It is common for program constituents to have difficulty articulating the logic and the outcome goals of the program in question. The rationale that links program

activities and outcomes is the program's theory of change (Chen, 2005). The program's theory can be implicit and unique to the program, or it can be one that is explicitly drawn from the research literature. A logic model that either graphically (typically with a flow chart) or in table format explicitly links program activities with ultimate outcomes through a chain of intermediate steps is a good way to discern the implicit or explicit program theory with the key stakeholders (Frechtling, 2007). A good logic model is very helpful in guiding the measurement framework for the evaluation. Frechtling (2007) provides a great introduction on logic models and The Community Toolbox has a useful section on developing a logic model and theory of change including several good examples (Center for Community Health and Development (CCHD) 2017b, Chapter 2, Section 1).

Process/Implementation evaluation: Process evaluation involves an evaluation of the implementation of the program components as compared to program outcome goals. Typically, process evaluation is concerned with providing information on the program components, whether they were implemented as intended, the frequency or intensity with which they are provided and how satisfied consumers (e.g., the student in a mentoring program) and program implementers (e.g., the mentors) are with them (Pancer, 1997; Patton, 2014). In the context of formative evaluations during early stages of the program, process evaluations are used to inform the development of the program so that it can be adjusted to ensure better efficiency and effectiveness. Within summative evaluations, process evaluation (typically referred to as implementation evaluation in that context) is used to determine if the program was implemented as intended (Chen, 2005). This is important in case the measured outcomes are not as positive or strong as the program developers had hoped for.

Impact/Outcome evaluation: Outcome or impact evaluation is concerned with evaluating the extent to which the expected changes occurred as a result of the program or intervention (Chen, 2005; Patton, 2014; Posavac & Carey, 2007). That is, the evaluator is trying to generate instrumental knowledge in the form of causal relationships (program A is causing a measurable effect in a measurable indicator of an expected outcome B). For example, an outcome evaluation may ask if a program to reduce health risk for people experiencing homelessness in a specific region during extreme weather events is effective in reducing instances of respiratory illnesses among this population. Research designs to establish causal relationships, such as experiments and quasi-experiments are, thus, typically considered the strongest for this type of evaluation (Rossi, Lipsey, & Henry, 2018). Non-experimental qualitative approaches, however, are also increasingly popular as are mixed-method evaluations (Patton, 2014).

Collective impact evaluation: There is an increasing realization among change makers that many of today's complex social issues cannot be meaningfully changed by a single program, policy, or intervention. Instead, multiple activities, programs, and initiatives that mutually reinforce each other are needed to actually create meaningful transformative change (Kania & Kramer, 2011). This approach requires a coordinated collaborative effort of multiple sectors, organiza-

tions, and individuals, which Kania and Kramer (2011) have coined as "collective impact." It typically includes a group of organizations and individuals who are coordinated and supported by a backbone organization as well as a shared measurement framework. This framework provides the basis for a shared learning process, which is commonly referred to as collective impact evaluation (Parkhurst & Preskill, 2014). These types of evaluations attempt to assess the change-making process as a whole, including its context, the quality and effectiveness of the collective initiative, the ways in which influential systems are changing, and the extent to which progress regarding the agreed upon target outcomes is made (Parkhurst & Preskill, 2014). The evaluation of the Vibrant Communities – Cities Reducing Poverty collective impact initiative of the Tamarack Institute in Canada is a great and often referenced example of such an evaluation (Vasey, 2018).

Cost-Benefit Analysis: The focus of cost-effectiveness and cost–benefits evaluation is on efficiency (the relationship between effectiveness in achieving outcomes to effort expended to achieve outcomes). This type of evaluation seeks to answer the following questions: Does the program achieve its goals at a reasonable cost? Are there less costly ways of achieving the same or better outcomes? Cost-effectiveness and cost–benefits evaluation are done in the context of an outcome evaluation with some type of control or comparison group, or a time-series design. In addition to gathering data relevant to outcomes, the evaluator must determine the costs of the program (e.g., personnel, facilities, materials, equipment) and other services used by the consumer in order to have a fairly comprehensive comparison of costs across the different programs being compared (Rossi et al., 2018; Yates, 1998). While cost-effectiveness compares the effectiveness to the costs of different program options, cost–benefits analysis tries to quantify the benefits to participants in terms of monetary values (benefits could include employment income and savings in human service expenditures).

Contextual

In CP, we recognize that context matters and, in fact, we are often interested in understanding specifically how the context interacts with the individual in producing certain outcomes, such as the impact of certain community characteristics on wellbeing and empowerment (Tebes, 2017). Thus, it is important to use designs and methods that take context into consideration (Fowler & Todd, 2017). Many qualitative methods provide an opportunity to probe key informants for contextual information and understand how contextual factors influence individuals, which is why they are a popular approach to understanding context (Brodsky, Mannarini, Buckingham, & Scheibler, 2017; Maxwell, 2012). During ethnographic studies, for example, the researcher immerses themselves in the real-life environment of their participants, often over an extended period of time, to fully understand the culture and other aspects of the participants' context (Naidoo, 2012).

Multilevel modeling enables researchers to model nested ecological quantitative data, such as surveys with students who are nested in classrooms and schools, and investigate the simultaneous and relative impact of factors at each of these levels (e.g., impact of a students' immigration status, the teachers' cultural competence, and school climate on students' experiences of bullying) (Fowler & Todd, 2017; Raudenbush & Bryk, 2002). As an example, Christens and Speer (2011) used multilevel modeling to explore the contextual influences on participation among people involved in congregation-based community organizing. Their three-level model included participation in meetings over time at Level 1, characteristics of the individual participants at Level 2, and neighborhood characteristics at Level 3. The analysis allowed them to explore the influence of each level simultaneously, including the interaction of factors across levels.

Geographic information systems (GIS) provide a visual representation of how certain characteristics (e.g., individual income and immigration status) are distributed geographically, which can be very eye-opening, especially when studied over time. Perkins, Larsen, and Brown (2009), for example, used GIS for a longitudinal evaluation of the community-wide impact of a neighborhood revitalization project. Using GIS, the authors were able to study to what degree the redevelopment of a brownfield had spill-over effects on other parts of the community, such as the perception of the neighborhood and private investments in houses in the surrounding neighborhoods. Ideally, a design that explores contextual factors includes data from a variety of contexts (e.g., multiple neighborhoods) and uses analytical techniques that allow for the systematic analysis of contextual factors. In another application, Townley, Pearson, Lehrwyn, Prophet, and Trauernicht (2016) combined GIS with participatory mapping to examine the activity spaces of homeless youth and how those relate to sense of community and wellbeing.

Relational

Whether it is social support, acts of interpersonal racism, development of community within a classroom, or a collaborative network of community agencies, a lot of phenomena community psychologists and their community partners are interested in are relational (Neal & Christens, 2014). There are many different aspects of relationships that can be studied such as the strengths and quality of the relationship and the type of interactions between two or more agents. Often relational phenomena are actually not researched as relationships but simply as one person's perception and reflection on a relationship. Generating relational data is challenging because it requires that you have data from all sides of a relationship. That is, for a couple, one would need data from two people while for a network of ten agencies one would need data from each agency about their relationship with each of the other nine agencies. Social network analysis takes advantage of network and graph theory in generating both descriptive statistics for whole networks and sub-parts of the network (including dyadic relationships), as well as a visual representation of these relationships (Wasserman & Faust, 1994). For example, Long, Harré, and Atkinson (2013) used social network analysis to investigate how a recycling intervention in a New Zealand high school community created a behavioral impact across the networks of friends within this school. They found that changes in recycling behavior were clearly influenced by the students' close social networks. For example, the degree of change in an individual's pro-environmental behavior across time was predicted by friends' prior behavior.

Systems, such as organizations, contain a variety of complex and dynamic relationships (Foster-Fishman & Watson, 2017; see also Chapter 5). Mixed-method case studies are a popular way of understanding some of the complex relationships within a system. For example, Dittmer (2019) looked at how the students in a small value-based school interacted with the system of actors (e.g., teachers and the principal) and structures in the school in creating agency for social justice, action and world citizenship. Systems dynamic modeling is another mixed-method approach to investigate the relational dynamics in complex systems (Foster-Fishman, Nowell, & Yang, 2007). Here, the team first generates a model of a system based on a specific focus problem (e.g., teacher burnout in a school). Typically, this will include a causal loop diagram, which represents the relationship of different parts of the system as interconnected balancing and reinforcing feedback loops. For example, more teachers in a school will reduce the workload of teachers, which can reduce their exhaustion and thus their burnout. But, adding more teachers drains the financial resources of the school, which may have other negative consequences that can affect burnout, such as outdated educational technology. Generating the system model is typically a very collaborative process that includes multiple and diverse key stakeholders. The system designer can then input this model, plus existing qualitative and quantitative data, to make predictions of how the system will likely behave if certain interventions are introduced into the system (e.g., hiring more teachers). This is especially helpful in anticipating unintended consequences.

Developmental/Change

Many CP researchers are interested in studying change and developmental processes, such as the impact of a prevention program (Fowler & Todd, 2017). While it is possible to reflect on changes and developments retrospectively, it has also been shown that a person's recall of the past is prone to memory issues and that the view of the past is influenced by our current perceptions and state of being, especially in trying to recall past emotions (Aaker, Drolet, & Griffin, 2008). While in some cases that may not be an issue, in other situations it may be better to have a longitudinal design with multiple waves of data collection to check in with participants at different time points. Growth-curve modeling (Raudenbush & Bryk, 2002) and time-series analysis (Wei, 2013) are two prominent ways of analyzing such longitudinal data and looking for patterns of change.

Participatory action research studies, which are especially focused on co-creating real changes with participants – such as their empowerment – during the course of the study, will often have ongoing data collection, such as reflective journals or minutes from group meetings in order to capture the process of consciousness raising, action, and reflection (Lykes, 2017; Piran, 2001).

Respect for Diversity

Considerations of diversity are also important for CP research and design planning. A small survey sample, for example, will provide the researcher with a very limited ability to explore interaction/moderation effects based on group differences. As will be discussed in Chapter 18, for instance, there is an increasing awareness of and sensitivity related to a person's gender identity. Thus, it is now relatively common to include more than just "male" and "female" as answer options in the demographic section of a survey (e.g., trans-male, trans-female, non-binary). In the analyses then, however, many of these additional options will often be collapsed into one "other" or "gender-queer" category, because the survey sample is too small to have enough representation in each of these categories, which affects the statically power of commonly used statistical tests. The experience of a trans student in a classroom, however, may be very different from that of a non-binary student. Qualitative methods often provide the ability to explore the impact of diverse backgrounds in a more nuanced way. However, qualitative samples are often relatively small and there is a danger that the experience of a small number of people is taken to represent that of a whole group. Also, the diversity in the sample may not always play out within distinct variables but are intertwined in what has been referred to as intersectionality (see Introduction to Part IV and several chapters in Part IV which reference this concept). For quantitative data, one can use profile analysis, a person-centered approach, to explore how the intersection of multiple predictor variables relate to a specific outcome variable by creating individual profiles that several people share in common (Howard & Hoffman, 2018). For example, Hardy and colleagues (in preparation) used profile analysis to explore the social wellbeing with cisgender LGBQ ($n = 406$) and transgender ($n = 110$) participants from a sample of LGBTQ individuals who completed an online survey as part of the Outlook Study. Four distinct social wellbeing profiles were identified for LGBQ participants, and three profiles were identified for the transgender participants, with varying levels of social wellbeing represented. These profiles mapped individuals across six relevant factors: discrimination, sense of safety, outness, social support, sense of belonging, and community acceptance. Profile analyses like these can help to better tailor services to specific characteristics of people rather than assuming everybody who identifies as LGBTQ has the same needs related to social wellbeing.

Additional Design Considerations

Besides the matching of design to specific research objectives and research problems, there are also other more general factors that should be considered when making design decisions. These questions can be organized into five major categories: utility, credibility, ethics, power, and feasibility. Table 13.2 provides some specific questions relevant to these and the earlier design considerations.

Utility

Three key factors in the utilization of research knowledge are (1) how well the research products meet the needs of specific knowledge users; (2) how credible the research findings are perceived; and (3) the quality and amount of the effort sharing the research products with key knowledge users (Landry, Amara, & Lamari, 2001). Involving key knowledge users early on and throughout the research cycle is a useful approach that contributes to all three factors. In our case study, we involved decision-makers from the regional government and community organizations in deciding on the specific research questions and the design. This early involvement by these key stakeholders led to a situation where our findings met specific pre-determined needs of these knowledge users and the study results had credibility for them because they had influence over the way the data were collected.

Credibility

Credibility of the research design and methodology strongly relates to how trustworthy and valid the research findings are to key audiences. Credibility among the academic community is often related to tradition and common practices within a specific discipline as well as established criteria of excellence (Tebes, 2017; Tolan, Keys, Chertok, & Jason, 1990; see also discussion of paradigms in Chapter 12). Credibility with other knowledge users and stakeholders may be influenced by psychological, sociopolitical, and cultural factors. For example, a lot of non-academic people in Western societies associate numbers with rigorous science while they discount qualitative data as too subjective. In certain communities, on the other hand, qualitative data are much more relatable and in line with their cultural practice and beliefs, and, thus, may be seen as more credible. For this reason, it is useful to not make these decisions in isolation but together as a group and in consultation with different stakeholders. Another key factor in establishing credibility is to ensure the best match between the nature of the research questions and the design, as discussed above.

Ethics

Ethical considerations play a role throughout the research cycle but they are also important to consider in design decisions. For example, a mental health provider may not be willing or able to assign their clients to a no-treatment control condition because of ethical concerns. In many countries researchers have to get approval for their research design and procedures from an institutional ethics review committee to ensure compliance with agreed upon ethics for research. Key ethical considerations in regard to the design typically include the level of potential risks and burden certain designs and methods expose the participants to, whether the perspective of the participants will be adequately captured, confidentiality of the participants, lack of coercion, fairness in allocation of potential benefits (e.g., access to treatment) and selection into the study, and how the research findings may perpetuate certain stereotypes about the focus community (see also discussion on this in the data collection section). Reflecting on issues of power is also an important ethical consideration, which will be addressed in the next section.

Power

According to Prilleltensky (2008b), power can be understood as "the capacity and opportunity to fulfill or obstruct personal, relational, or collective needs" (p. 119). This duality of using power to fulfill or obstruct needs also applies to research design and methods as some can be quite empowering to certain communities while others can feel very disempowering. When working with marginalized people such as racialized communities, for example, it is important to consider that members of these communities often experience being silenced and not being heard in mainstream society. Thus, a methodology that brings their voices to the forefront and makes them heard can be an empowering experience. A grounded theory approach with qualitative interviews, for instance, may be a good methodology for that purpose.

While power is ubiquitous and linked to many aspects of CP research, it is not always clear and straightforward which methodologies and designs promote wellbeing and empowerment and which perpetuate oppression. Thus, it is important to reflect regularly on one's research practices and their effects in regard to issues of power, oppression, and promotion of wellbeing. Prilleltensky (2003, 2008b) introduced the framework of psycho-political validity as a guide for assessing the degree to which power is being considered in CP action and research.

Feasibility

Feasibility is about the ability to actually successfully carry out the study as planned. This depends on a variety of factors that can be organized into two major categories: resources and acceptability. Unfortunately, a lot of research designs that capture complex community phenomena adequately can be relatively resource intensive. The two major types of resources in the context of research studies are human and financial resources, which are, of course, related (e.g., highly skilled staff tend to be very expensive). Early and careful planning and budgeting for needed resources are important to avoid issues later on. When using peer researchers, for example, it is important to ensure that you have sufficient funding to adequately pay them for their work in order to avoid exploitation (Guta et al., 2014).

Feasibility is also dependent on the acceptability of the research design, methods, and procedures. Acceptability is important in regard to both community partners and potential participants. If, for example, the elders of an Indigenous community reject a quantitative survey as culturally inappropriate because they associate that with exploitative research in the past, then the design is not feasible because you will not get access to that community. Consulting early on and frequently with representatives of key stakeholders and conducting pilot studies are two good strategies to assess acceptability.

Concluding Thoughts About Design

These design considerations are not meant to discourage you from engaging in this type of research, but instead encourage you to be realistic in planning the study. If, for example, you realize that you will not be able to obtain the resources for adequately answering your original research questions, you want to either simplify the research questions or choose another research problem to focus on. Given the complexity of the design decisions, it is important to allow sufficient time for this and ensure the needed expertise is available within the team to make informed decisions. Once the design decisions have been made, it is useful to create a project plan that can guide the implementation of the research design.

Table 13.1 Key decision factors for CP research design

Decision Factor	Key Questions

Research Objectives	• What type of knowledge are you trying to generate?
	   ■ Technical (instrumental) knowledge (e.g., questions of causality, association, and distribution)
	   ■ Practical knowledge (e.g., understanding how people make meaning of their lived experience; giving people voice)
	   ■ Emancipatory knowledge (e.g., understanding systems of power and oppression; creating transformative change)

CP-Specific	*Applied* • What is the intended application of the research? • Is the study a form of program evaluation? *Context* • Are you trying to study the context at multiple nested levels of analysis simultaneously (if so, consider multilevel modeling)? • Are you trying to understand how characteristics in specific geographical areas affect people (if so, consider GIS)? • Can the impact of the contextual factors be understood through the experience of individual participants (if so, consider qualitative interviews and focus groups or mixed-methods case studies)? • Is it important to study the context in-depth and over time by emerging oneself into the community (if so, consider ethnographic research)? *Relational* • Are you trying to understand the network constellations of individuals or organizations (if so, consider social network analysis)?

Table 13.1 (continued)

Decision Factor	Key Questions
	● Are you trying to understand complex systems, system dynamics, and change (if so, consider case studies or systems dynamic modeling)
	Development/Change
	● Are you interested in studying developments of quantifiable factors over time (if so, consider growth curve modeling or time series analysis)?
	● Would you like to co-create real changes with participants – such as their empowerment – during the course of the study (if so, consider participatory action research)?
	Respect for Diversity
	● Are you trying to feature the lived experience of one or two groups that are often not featured in research (if so, consider using qualitative research and art-based methods)?
	● Would you like to understand the intersection of multiple predictor variables related to a specific outcome variable by creating individual profiles that several people share in common (if so, consider profile analysis)?
Usefulness	● What is the intended impact of the research?
	● What type of knowledge is needed?
	● Who are the potential knowledge users?
	● How can knowledge users be involved in the research process?
	● What makes this research applicable and relevant in the specific practical context of the knowledge users?
	● How complex will the findings be? Can they be easily communicated to a lay audience?
	● What are the best ways of mobilizing the knowledge?
Credibility	● What are the prevalent criteria of research excellence used by the target audience?
	● What type of design does the research team find defensible given the research problem and questions, ethical issues, and the available resources?
	● How well is the design matched with the phenomenon under study?
	● What types of values does the research approach align with?
Ethics	● Does the design align with ethical principles of interacting with the target community?
	● Are there any general ethical challenges (e.g., lack of confidentiality, coercion, conflict of interests)?
	● Do the results from this research present ethical challenges (e.g., cause harm to specific groups)?
	● Are the risks and potential burdens the study presents justified by the potential benefits?
Power	● What power dynamics in the psychology and politics of wellness, oppression, and liberation, at the personal, relational, and collective domains, affect the phenomena of interest?
	● What is the potential of the research to promote personal, relational, and collective wellness by reducing power inequalities and increasing political action?
	● To what degree does the research design perpetuate past and current power inequalities and oppression?
Feasibility	● What is the timeline?
	● What financial resources are needed and available?
	● What human resources are needed and available?
	● What specific requirements and limits does the specific research context present (e.g., the potential to provide the needed sample size)?
	● How acceptable is the design to the community partners and the participants?
	● How demanding is the research design in regard to the expertise, skills, and time needed to carry it out?
	● What is the motivation of the target community to participate in the study?

III. Research Team

Once the research partnership is established, the research has been framed, and design decisions have been made (and funding secured) it is time to develop the core research team that will carry out the research. Teamwork is a critical component of most modern work places and research is no exception. Developing a good team can be challenging, though, and teams often struggle with power dynamics and conflict. In many cases, applied community research requires interdisciplinary and diverse teams. This can include peer researchers from the community and other team members with less research experience and different perspectives and interests. As mentioned previously, increasing diversity can create challenges with engendering a strong sense of community among the team (Neal & Neal, 2013) and it can easily lead to power imbalances. Thus, it is important to be very intentional in the development of a team and pay close attention to issues of power.

Roles

Typical roles in a research team may include one or two principal investigators, university-based co-investigators, community-based co-investigators, a project manager, student research assistants, and other research staff, which can include peer researchers (see below). The actual number of team members can vary widely, ranging from a study carried out by a single researcher to large research teams spread across multiple cities or even countries.

Peer researchers "are members of a research project's target population who are trained to participate as co-researchers" (Flicker, Roche, & Guta, 2010, p.4). In some studies, peer researchers partner in all aspects of the research while, in others they are involved in only certain aspects, such as participant recruitment, data collection, and/or interpretation of the data. Involving community members, especially those who are marginalized, in the research process can be an empowering experience that builds capacity (Guta, Flicker, & Roche, 2013). In addition, their participation frequently contributes to higher quality data and a more appropriate and acceptable approach for the study (Buettgen et al., 2012). The different levels of training and experience with conducting research, the closeness to the focus issue (especially if it is related to a traumatic experience in the past), and the existing relationship to members of the target community, can also lead to specific ethical challenges and power dynamics when working with peer researchers (see Flicker et al., 2010, for an overview). Thus, it is important to be very intentional when engaging peer researchers and provide the appropriate conditions to ensure that their engagement in the research is a mutually beneficial experience.

Power Issues in Teams

Power across team members may differ based on the type of role (e.g., principal investigator vs. project manager), status (e.g., professor vs. student), experience and training (e.g., university-trained vs. no formal training), connection to the target community (e.g., insider vs. outsider), staff status (e.g., paid staff vs. volunteer), and other factors (e.g., being marginalized in society). Each of these potential power differentials can contribute to power struggles, which, in turn, have been shown to harm the ability of teams to function and perform and to negatively affect the wellbeing of individual team members (Greer, Van Bunderen, & Yu, 2017). Ways to reduce the likelihood of such power struggles are to create structures and processes that distribute power and reduce power differentials, develop a strong sense of community and good communication among the team, and be conscious and reflective (Munger & Riemer, 2012). Specific structures include a memorandum of understanding (MOU; also called terms of reference) that clearly identifies mutually agreed upon roles and responsibilities as well as decision-making and conflict resolution processes; publication agreements that identify up front planned publications and how decisions regarding authorship will be handled (see example on companion website); a communication plan that details responsibilities for frequency and mode of communication; and a clear project plan that details tasks, responsibilities, and deadlines. Tools, such as the power cube introduced in Chapter 4, can be used to facilitate reflections on issues of power as a team. Team outings and shared meals can foster a strong sense of community. Being conscious and intentional about issues of power does not necessarily mean that all members of the team will have the same decision-making power. It is probably not fair if a student, who is only a member of the team for a year and has minor responsibilities, has the same decision-making power as an investigator, who is working on the project throughout its full life-cycle and has significantly more responsibilities. But, meaningful involvement of all team members is aligned with our values of inclusion, respect for diversity, wellbeing, and addressing issues of power.

In our case study, for example, we [Manuel and his collaborators] hired three peer researchers with lived experience of homelessness. We consulted with our community partners who work with people experiencing homelessness about the recruitment and appropriate conditions for the hiring (e.g., the level of pay). Our initial planning of the research included partners from local government agencies and community organizations, several university-based researchers, and the peer researchers. The former three groups had significantly more knowledge and experience with the research process and also enjoyed a higher level of social status in society more generally, together resulting in an important power differential. If left unaddressed, this could have easily led to meetings where the latter three groups dominate the discussion while the peer researchers remained silent.

In order to prevent this situation, a student member of the research team and I [Manuel] met with the three peer researchers one hour before the start of the first meeting. We went over the research process, the topics for that meeting, and how they can contribute to the discussion for each of the topics. As a result, the three peer researchers actively participated in the discussion and felt very comfortable making their voice heard during the meeting. This, in turn, led to very valuable information and insights shared by the three peer researchers and, thus, a better research study.

Besides the initial planning and decision-making about the design and procedures, the peer researchers also played a critical role in the recruitment of participants, conducted interviews in pairs with a student-researcher, and contributed to the interpretation of the results. In the recruitment process, the peer researchers' insights about where and how to best recruit participants and their existing relationships with many people experiencing homelessness in our region resulted in a very high participation rate for a population that is normally hard to reach. In the interviews, the peer researchers were able to pick up on subtle cues and important information that would have otherwise been missed by the university-based researchers. During the interpretation stage, the peer researchers helped by putting the findings into context and making sense of specific results. Two of them also chose to contribute to the community report resulting from the study and were listed as co-authors (Wandel et al., 2010).

Prior to the start of the interviews, we provided the peer researchers with training on the research process and procedures, qualitative interviewing, and important ethical considerations. For example, it is critical that any form of potential coercion is avoided in the recruitment process. People who know the peer researchers from before may feel obligated to participate when asked by their peers. This potential ethical issue can be attenuated by having the peer researcher be involved in the recruitment, but have the consenting process be done by a university-based researcher (Flicker et al., 2010). As this example demonstrates, there are many advantages to involving community members and peer researchers in a research team. But, when doing so, it is also pertinent to invest great effort into creating the right conditions for their involvement. During the course of the project, we regularly reflected on potential and actual power dynamics in our team and best practices of partnering with peer researchers.

IV. Participant Recruitment and Data Collection

Once the research methodology and plan are settled and the needed financial and human resources have been secured, the study can be conducted. This includes following specific procedures for recruiting participants, carrying out the data collection and/or obtaining the secondary/archival data, and then the analysis and interpretation of the data. The specifics of these steps depend on the methodological choices and consideration during the planning phase and go beyond the scope of this chapter. There are, however, some general considerations for how these steps are carried out in the context of community-engaged research worth mentioning. In this section we discuss issues related to participant recruitment and data collection. They relate to ethics, power, and reflection, which are all interconnected.

Ethics

Unique ethical issues will emerge in community-engaged research projects that can be avoided if teams broaden their bandwidth on how they conceptualize ethical risks in their studies. Consider the following examples that might make an institutional review board (IRB), which is responsible for ensuring that researchers comply with set ethical principles in their studies and avoid unnecessary risks, nervous: the close involvement of community members as fellow researchers on projects, involving paid peer researchers in a study of opioid use among drug users, or paying sex workers an unusually high (i.e., equitable) honorarium for their participation in a project. As a result, IRBs may over scrutinize community-engaged projects. This can make community members on the team feel considerably disempowered when "control" of the project shifts from the team (albeit temporarily) to the IRBs at the lead investigators' universities (Travers et al., 2013).

In addition, unique and emerging ethical issues that go beyond what is traditionally considered in reviews by IRBs commonly present themselves in community-engaged research (Flicker, Travers, Guta, McDonald, & Meagher, 2007). IRBs typically operate in a traditional biomedical framework where *risk to individuals* is assessed, but *risks to communities* are ignored (Flicker et al., 2007). Let us illustrate with an example. A group of researchers may find in a study of HIV risk behaviors in HIV-positive gay men that gay men of color may be having more unprotected sex compared to White gay men. While the IRB may have adequately assessed risk to individual study participants in their review of this study, they would have likely missed the risk of stigmatizing HIV-positive gay men of color. This can occur if such results were released publicly without any attention to context or the fact that a community that already experiences significant social marginalization could face further exclusion as a result. Thus, it is our responsibility as researchers to ensure that risks to communities are kept to a reasonable minimum.

Power

We have already emphasized the role of power in other aspects of the research cycle and this phase is no exception (Ochocka, Janzen, & Nelson, 2002). Again, considering the three forms of power introduced in Chapter 4 is useful in this context. The first form of power (*superior bargaining resources/visible*), for example, is reflected in control over decision making related to the human and financial resources of the study. In most research studies, the grant budget for funded research is provided to the university of the principal investigator, potentially giving this investigator most of the power in regard to the resources. Of course, this power can be shared with other investigators and community partners through governing committees and boards, as well as transferring funds to research partners (Curwood, Munger, Mitchell, Mackeigan, & Farrar, 2011).

Other aspects of this first form of power are differentials in the research team in regard to experience, knowledge, and skills related to research. Overcoming these differentials often requires extra efforts such as training and mentoring for non-university or more junior members of the team. Existing power differences in society due to ascription of status and different forms of discrimination (e.g., racialization, gender) also play a role, both in regard to the relationships of the researchers amongst each other but also between the researchers and the research participants (Chávez, Duran, Baker, Avila, & Wallerstein 2008). A member of an Indigenous community, for example, may be very hesitant to be open and honest in their responses in an interview with a White researcher, because of the historical and ongoing colonization and exploitation of Indigenous people by White Europeans and the questionable role researchers played in that. Therefore, extra steps may be necessary to ensure the quality of research sample and data.

The second form of power (*control of participation and debate/hidden*) is also present throughout this phase. We already addressed some issues related to participation above. Other issues related to recruitment of participants, for example, relate to how participants are invited and by whom. For instance, a lot of surveys are conducted online these days. This may exclude people who do not feel comfortable with this type of technology or don't have easy access (e.g., people experiencing homelessness). For our study with people experiencing homelessness, we relied heavily on our peer researchers and community partners for recruitment. However, we realized later that our recruitment process did not provide easy access to recent immigrants to Canada because they were underrepresented in the shelter system and were not well connected to networks of our peer researchers. Other issues related to this second form of power are connected to who sets the agenda for meetings, who chairs the meetings, who decides which questions get included in a survey or interview protocol, and who conducts the interviews. In all of these cases, it is important to bring this more hidden form of power to the forefront and then act upon that awareness. A team may still decide to let the principal investigator chair their meetings, but at least they had a chance to make that decision consciously rather than just accept it as a given.

The third form of power (*shaping interest/invisible*) plays out in different ways during this phase. For example, in an interview with a Black participant, a White interviewer may ask questions in ways that reflect certain stereotypes they have about Black people. On the other side, due to internalized racism, a Black participant may underreport the strengths that exists in their community and that they hold personally (Chávez et al., 2008). Even relatively neutral looking survey questions can contain item bias, that is, the questions are interpreted differently or answered differently for participants from different racial groups or communities (Iwata, Turner, & Lloyd, 2002). An important factor in this context is the question of whether the researcher is an outsider or insider, that is, whether they are part of the focus community or not (Chávez et al. 2008). An insider researcher can draw upon their lived experience and relate to the participant in a more direct way compared to an outsider. The insider's own internalized oppression or privilege, however, can affect how they see the community. For example, they may not be able to identify community assets because they undervalue community resources (Chávez et al., 2008). Thus, in many instances it is useful to have both insiders and outsiders on the research team. In our case study, interviews were conducted by a team of university-based researchers and a peer researcher. This combination turned out to be invaluable as both were able to relate to the participants in different ways, providing a more comprehensive picture of the participants' lived experience of dealing with extreme weather.

Reflection

Paying attention to the three aspects above requires ongoing reflection both as an individual researcher but also as a team. As an individual, it is important to reflect on how one's positionality in society generally, and within the research team specifically, may affect interactions with others on the team as well as with participants. For example, a White researcher may feel personally attacked if in an interview a participant of color comments negatively about their experience with White people. This could easily lead to being defensive and to interpret the comment in a different way than it may have been intended. Reflective journaling throughout the research process can be a useful tool to reflect on one's "presuppositions, choices, experiences, and actions during the research process" (Mruck & Breuer, 2003, p. 3). The notes from these reflective journal entries also will help with transparency about the research process and can aid with the analysis and write-up of the research (Ortlipp, 2008).

Similarly, it is useful to build in regular times for reflection as a team. This could be a section at the beginning or end of a team meeting, a full meeting devoted to reflection, or a team retreat. Reflection can be related to the team itself (e.g., power dynamics) or the research process and interaction with research participants. Janzen and Ochaka (under review) developed a community-based research excellence tool that can be used as a guide for these reflections within a team.

V. Analysis and Interpretation

Once the data are collected and processed, it is time for the data analysis, followed by the interpretation of the results. In certain cases, there is also a back and forth between data collection, analysis, and interpretation. A grounded theory approach, for example, may require additional collection of qualitative interviews if a new theme emerges from the analysis that needs to be further explored with additional data (Chun Tie et al., 2019). The specifics of the data analysis depend on the general methodological orientation, the research design, and the data collection methods. As mentioned earlier, it goes beyond the scope of this chapter to discuss those specifics in detail. Thus, we will focus on more general considerations again.

While community partners tend to be less involved in the nitty-gritty of the data analysis process, they are likely to want to be involved in the interpretation and then the knowledge mobilization of the findings and there are good reasons to make a significant effort to involve them (Cashman et al., 2008; Travers et al., 2013). Involving community partners in the interpretation of the results helps with a deeper and better understanding of the context and the meaning of the findings, increasing acceptance of the validity and relevance of the findings, developing and/or recommending clear action steps that are grounded in the findings and will work for the community and policy makers, and with mobilizing the knowledge within the networks of community partners; whether these are organizations representing or working with the community or other relevant actors within the community.

Cashman et al. (2008) have identified a few lessons learned in regard to the collaborative analysis and interpretation process. First, it is important to clarify the respective roles of the university-based researchers and the community partners collaboratively upfront. Ideally, the community partners should have the opportunity to be involved as much or as little as makes sense to them and the university-based partners. Second, the strength and prior experience each person brings to the table needs to be identified and an investment needs to be made to develop capacities where they are needed. Next, it is important to be aware that data analysis and interpretation are an iterative process that may require regular meetings and a significant amount of work between those meetings for further analyses that will aid the interpretation of findings and expand them as needed. Collaborative analysis and interpretation can take significantly more time than non-collaborative processes, often several months more. There are no shortcuts if all partners are to be involved in an equitable manner. When mixed methods are used, the process can be further lengthened because the different data types may need to be triangulated and/or sequenced, where one depends on the completion of the other. Thus, it is important to realistically plan for that in the timeline and ensure the commitment of all parties involved. Also, it is often recommendable to simplify the data and results to aid understanding. Visual aids such as concept maps, infographics, and easy to interpret statistical graphs are often very useful for that purpose. The work of Edward Tufte provides a lot of good examples and tips of how to present complex data in a way that is easily interpretable for lay people (www.edwardtufte.com/tufte/). However, in doing this, it is important to not oversimplify complex relationships or speak down to community partners. If this data visualization is done well during the interpretation process, it will significantly help with the knowledge mobilization process as well. In our case study, we met with our peer researchers to share the results of the qualitative analysis of the interviews with people experiencing homelessness. We had a good discussion about the meaning of those findings and then we provided the peer researchers with a high-end digital camera to capture images in our region that represent findings and quotes they felt were important. Those images were then later shared in reports and presentations to support those findings (see example). Once there is a shared understanding of the findings, it is time to share those with your key audiences and mobilize the knowledge you generated for social change and promotion of wellbeing.

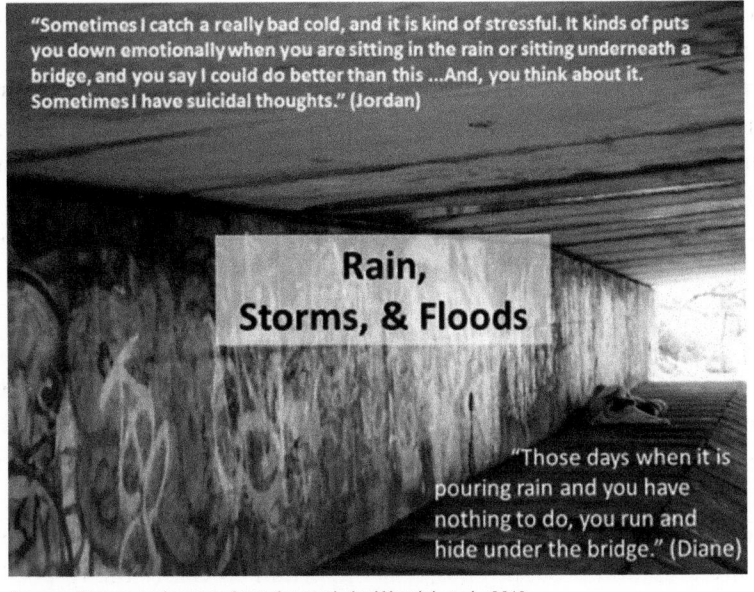

"Sometimes I catch a really bad cold, and it is kind of stressful. It kinds of puts you down emotionally when you are sitting in the rain or sitting underneath a bridge, and you say I could do better than this ...And, you think about it. Sometimes I have suicidal thoughts." (Jordan)

Rain, Storms, & Floods

"Those days when it is pouring rain and you have nothing to do, you run and hide under the bridge." (Diane)

Source: Picture and quotes from the study by Wandel et al., 2010.

VI. Knowledge Mobilization

Most CP researchers are hoping for their research to contribute to social change and positive policies that will increase social justice and the flourishing of individuals and communities. Most likely this is what motivates you as well. Thus, it is important to mobilize the knowledge generated through research beyond the typical scholarly outlets such as academic journals (Worton et al., 2018).

Knowledge mobilization (also referred to as knowledge transfer and exchange [KTE] or knowledge dissemination) "is a process of exchange between researchers and knowledge users designed to make relevant research information available and accessible to stakeholders for use in decision-making about practices, programs and policies" (Institute for Work & Health, n.d.). In addition, knowledge mobilization can include concrete actions that community-based researchers engage in alongside their community partners in regard to creating change, such as advocacy, program development, and community mobilization (Worton et al., 2018).

For example, motivated by the community report for our case study on homelessness and global climate change, several groups came together to discuss the development of a climate change adaption plan that would reduce the vulnerability of people experiencing homelessness and other vulnerable groups in our region. We also facilitated a scenario-planning session with key stakeholders that incorporated the data from our study. Scenario thinking is a facilitation technique designed to collaboratively anticipate multiple possible future scenarios (e.g., different combinations of a changing homelessness population, global climate change, and investment in community support structures such as affordable housing), which can then aid in planning community and resource development (Holman, Devane, & Cady, 2007). In addition, our community partner from the regional government indicated that seniors are another potentially vulnerable group and that it would be useful to conduct similar research with them. This motivated us to submit another funding application focused on seniors and heatwaves, which was funded by the Social Science and Humanities Research Council of Canada (Eady, Dreyer, Hey, Riemer, & Wilson, under review).

Generally, there are three models of knowledge transfer discussed in the literature (Reardon, Lavis, & Gibson, 2006). In the first case, the producer of the knowledge (i.e., the research team) plans and implements strategies to push knowledge toward specific knowledge users (e.g., academic, practitioners, organizational leaders, policy-makers) who the producers and/or their community partners have identified as relevant. In the second case, the knowledge users "plan and implement strategies to pull knowledge from sources they identify as producing research useful to their own decision-making" (Reardon et al., 2006, p. 1). The third case involves relationship building between knowledge producers and users and active exchange between them. In this process researchers help the knowledge users to build capacity for using the research knowledge and the knowledge users guide the researchers in producing relevant research findings. Ideally, researchers take this integrated approach to knowledge mobilization. That is, they involve community stakeholders, including key knowledge users, early on in the process. The more they are involved throughout the process, the more likely the research findings will be relevant to them and the better understanding of the meaning and implications of the findings they will have.

Independent of the type of knowledge transfer, it is important to prepare the findings in an accessible and suitable format for different types of knowledge users (Worton et al., 2018). For an academic audience, we would likely write a scholarly article with technical language and a lot of detailed information about our methods and research approach, while for a community audience, a community report with less emphasis on method and more accessible language would be a better way to go. For policy-makers, it is often better to have very short 2–4 page policy briefs or fact sheets. The challenge in this process is to distill the information about the research into the most relevant information and present it in an engaging way without losing critical substance and complexity. Working in a team of university-based researchers and community partners on the knowledge mobilization products will aid with addressing this challenge. Creativity is encouraged in this context. Knowledge mobilization strategies can include theatre, film, interactive websites, visual graphics (especially infographics), photo exhibitions, spoken word texts, a variety of social media, and others. The graphic novella produced by Gemma Sou (2019) that focused on the recovery from Hurricane Maria in Puerto Rico, is a good example of a creative knowledge mobilization output (https://www.hcri.manchester.ac.uk/research/projects/after-maria/). In some cases, comprehensive workshops and toolkits are developed, which provide practical instructions and tools for how to apply the findings and lessons learned from the research (the Community Toolbox [https://ctb.ku.edu/en] and The Better Beginning, Better Futures Toolkit and Videos [http://bbbf.ca] are good examples of that; see also Worton et al., 2018).

John Lavis (referenced in Reardon et al., 2006) has proposed five principles that should guide knowledge mobilization to maximize uptake. These include:

1 What (is the message)?
2 To whom (audience)?
3 By whom (messenger)?
4 How (transfer method)?
5 With what expected impact (evaluation)?

Reardon et al. (2006) have developed a worksheet that helps researchers to plan knowledge mobilization strategies along these five principles. The Community Toolbox also provides a lot of useful information regarding different knowledge mobilization methods (Center for Community Health and Development (CCHD) 2017a). Worton et al. (2018) provide a description of a comprehensive knowledge mobilization strategy for an early childhood prevention program.

Chapter Summary

In this chapter we used the symbol of a cycle to review the key steps in the process of carrying out a community-engaged research study from the initial engagement with community stakeholders to mobilizing the generated knowledge for creating positive (ideally transformative) change for wellbeing. Key steps in this cycle are the initial engagement with community stakeholders and the focusing of the research, making design decisions, gathering the research team, recruiting participants, collecting data, analyzing and interpreting the data, and then finally mobilizing it. Throughout each of these steps, we discussed issues that are specifically relevant for conducting research in a community-engaged way, including issues pertaining to participation, ethics, and power. At the core of this cycle are design decisions, which are influenced by ensuring a good match of the design with the research objectives, the nature of CP values and principles, and other considerations such as utility, credibility, and feasibility. The discussions in this chapter are intended to present a general roadmap of issues to consider when going through the research cycle using a community-engaged approach with a CP framing. The details need to be filled in through a deeper dive into the relevant literature and, most of all, by gaining experience through practice. Engaging in community-engaged research with an openness for being wrong, failing, and learning from others and by being humble and patient, is the best way of building proficiency in conducting this type of research.

In this and the previous chapter we covered a lot of topics related to community-engaged research from a CP perspective. This collection of topics may leave you with the impression that doing community-engaged and transformative research within a CP framework can be a challenging task and, therefore, you may be worried about engaging in this type of research. We would be dishonest if we denied the complexity and challenges of conducting research that aligns with our CP values. However, it is also important to note that this approach to research is incredibly rewarding. For one, feelings of cognitive dissonance are significantly reduced when our research approach is aligned with our values. Second, when our research is set up to contribute to social change, our social change work as a private person and our work as a researcher are not competing with each other. In addition, through community-engaged research we are often developing long-lasting positive relationships and friendships with community partners. Finally, the positive impact of this type of research on the wellbeing of individuals and communities is often much more tangible and immediate – and there is a high level of personal satisfaction with being involved in something meaningful that matters to people. All of this makes it very worthwhile to face the challenges we described in this chapter, even in the context of a master's thesis, doctoral dissertation, or research career.

Research in Service of Community

Rich Janzen, Centre for Community-Based Research, Waterloo, ON, Canada

Many of the points made in this chapter resonate with me as a community-based researcher. In response, I want to share a brief story about a series of connected research projects conducted at the Centre for Community Based Research (CCBR). CCBR is a non-profit organization – a social enterprise with no core funding – where I have worked for over 20 years. Located in Waterloo, Ontario, Canada, its mission is to build more responsive and supportive communities, especially for those with limited power and opportunity. I chose a series of projects because my experience has been that a single project rarely achieves the wellness and liberation that we hope for (such is the humility of being a community-based researcher). My intention is that this example will enliven the theory outlined in this chapter (see also Ochocka & Janzen, 2014). This story highlights my conviction (Janzen et al., 2016; Neufeldt & Janzen, under review; Ochocka & Janzen 2008) that community-based research be as *community-driven, participatory,* and *action-orientated* as possible (these hallmarks draw on rich research traditions from Indigenous communities, the global South, and the global North respectively), and that research functions not only to produce knowledge, but also to mobilize both knowledge and people into active service of society.

I frame my story through the four phases of research that has guided CCBR for nearly 40 years (see Figure 13.2). These phases are similar to those mentioned in this chapter. However, they foreground the importance of a pre-planning phase, which we call "laying the foundation," in which a stakeholder steering committee is formed, the assumptions of research are discussed (covering such topics as those outlined in this chapter), and a shared understanding of the local context is highlighted. These steps help stakeholders to collaboratively determine the specific purpose of their research. The four phases also foreground that community-based research is more than a technical exercise. Much like the project of democracy itself, community-based research is also a relational exercise with ongoing negotiation among those involved – producing not final solutions but a "constantly upsetting imbalance between values and action" (Sarason, 1978, p. 379).

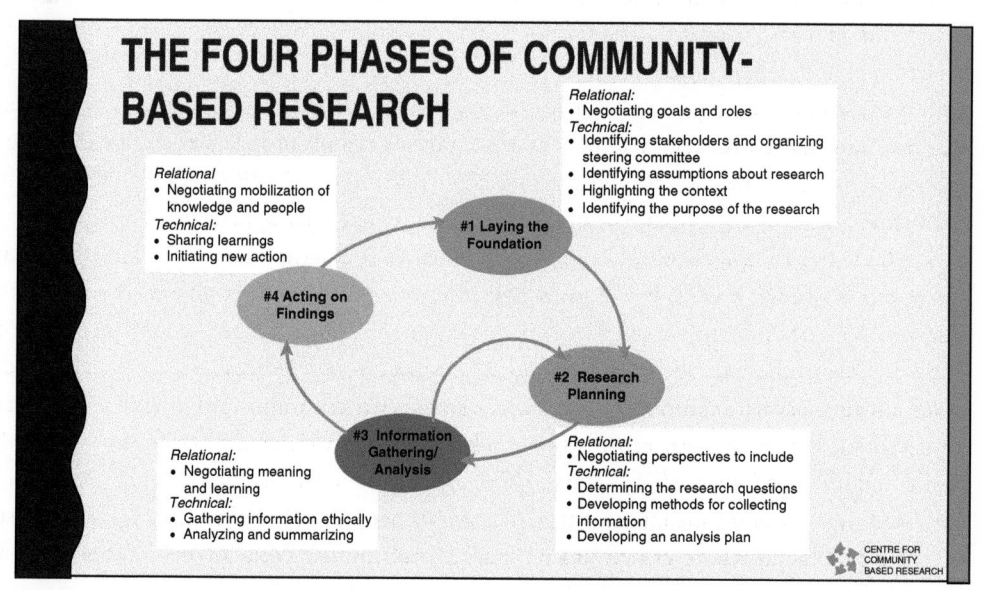

Figure 13.2 The four phases of community-based research

Source: Janzen, Ochocka, and Stobbe (2016). Towards a theory of change for community-based research projects. *Engaged Scholar Journal: Community-engaged Research, Teaching, and Learning, 2*(2), 44–64.

Between 2002 and 2010, CCBR participated in a series of five successive research and action projects to address immigrant unemployment and underemployment within Waterloo, Ontario. Each project engaged stakeholders to plan, act and reflect together. At the end of each project, the next set of actions was determined collectively by those involved in the previous projects. Altogether, there were about 350 people participating from 6 different stakeholder groups including immigrant/refugee newcomers, employers/business leaders, local government, academic institutions, community-based organizations, and non-governmental funders.

The first project was local consciousness-raising action research entitled "Voices for Change." This project was initiated by CCBR following some success we had provincially with immigrant employment research, including changing provincial legislation. Phase 1 began by talking with a small number of local players who eventually became the project steering committee guiding each step of the research. With some we had previously collaborated (newcomers, immigrant service providers, local government), while others we had not (business, academics, politicians). Our pitch was to use research as a way to highlight the underutilization of immigrant skills as a community-wide concern (not simply an immigrant special interest) under the banner of "Immigrant skills: we need them, we have them, let's use them." We talked about how the research should end with a call for constructive action, an idea that resonated strongly with newcomers and service providers who were growing impatient with simply pointing out barriers to newcomer employment.

When planning our methodology (Phase 2), the CCBR team recommended that a multi-staged, mixed-method approach was best suited to the purpose of the research. We would begin with a labor market analysis of local skill gaps ("we need them"), before conducting a survey of underutilized local immigrant skills ("we have them"), and we would end with interviews, case studies, and a document review about how to better utilize the skills of immigrants ("let's use them"). Through these discussions, and with the support of a sympathetic civil servant, we wrote a funding proposal to a federal government department (Canadian Heritage) and received a grant.

The information gathering and analysis (Phase 3) went largely as planned with the steering committee playing an active role in providing input to the CCBR-based research team. For example, one early challenge was how best to assess current skill gaps with a workforce planning board representative providing valuable advice. The steering committee also played a role in interpreting research findings across the various methods and in articulating them as part of a local community narrative. A great deal of attention was placed into acting on the findings (Phase 4). This phase was seen as an opportunity to stimulate greater community engagement on immigrant employment issues. First, the CCBR research team wrote and distributed a magazine-style report summarizing the research in a publicly digestible format and ending with "calls for change" directed at senior levels of government, employers and regulatory bodies. Second, the CCBR team and the steering committee organized a community forum that received considerable media attention in which findings were presented and discussed, and where local dignitaries and other forum participants physically signed large posters of the "calls for change." Third, we sent the report and signatures to the various provincial stakeholders responsible for implementing the calls for change (we did this same process simultaneously in two other communities to augment the "voices for change" provincially).

Shortly after completing this project, we were approached by our local United Way. They wanted to do some follow-up to leverage the momentum created. We decided to organize an exploratory meeting with a larger group of stakeholders than in the first project (about 20 people representing all 6 stakeholder groups mentioned above). At this meeting CCBR and the United Way floated the idea to organize an event that would focus on identifying local strategies to promote immigrant employment (in complement to actions identified in the first project that were directed at external players). The response to the idea was very favorable but some (notably business leaders) thought the project as presented was too small. What was needed they said was a much more ambitious "Immigrant Skills Summit" complete with a series of pre-summit task groups that would identify detailed local actions. While CCBR was invited to lead this project, the United Way resources were not enough for this larger vision and so we issued a call for Summit sponsors. Eventually 16 local sponsors stepped forward to cover project costs, which also served to deepen local engagement. As a community-based researcher, I would name this type of research as community needs and resource assessment for the purpose of creating a community action plan. In terms of methods, two focus groups were held for each of the five pre-Summit task groups resulting in discussion papers presented at the Summit. The Summit itself was attended by over 100 cross-sectoral community leaders that ended with a community-wide call to establish a new initiative called WRIEN (pronounced "Ryan" – Waterloo Region Immigrant Employment Network).

Given its broad-based community involvement, the Summit was a watershed event in creating a welcoming community for newcomers to Waterloo. It was also the catalyst for the next three projects (projects 3–5) that I will only briefly describe. The third project was immediately launched after the Summit. CCBR and the local Chamber of Commerce were asked (via Summit action steps) to co-lead what could be described as a "feasibility study" to determine the detailed operations of WRIEN and negotiate its new collaborative structure. The action phase of this project included writing funding proposals for a three-year WRIEN start-up period (in total almost $1million in local funds were secured). Once WRIEN was established under the leadership of the local Chamber of Commerce, a fourth project shifted the research from helping to create a community intervention to evaluating this intervention. A three-year developmental evaluation of WRIEN was launched under the leadership of CCBR, guided by a steering committee and including six mixed-methods and annual community forums. The evaluation enabled community stakeholders to continue to have ongoing input into directing this new comprehensive community initiative (Janzen, Seskar-Hencic, et al. 2012). Finally, a fifth project responded to a funding call from the federal government to establish a Local Immigration Partnership (LIP). A LIP would expand the local cross-sectoral collaboration beyond employment to address other issues of newcomer settlement and belonging. The WRIEN experience had readied the community to quickly respond to this call (only two other communities in Ontario were able to respond within the two-week timeline). At a meeting convened by WRIEN, the regional government was asked to lead the LIP application with CCBR subcontracted to conduct a series of community consultation focus groups and forums and to develop a LIP action plan (Janzen, Walton-Roberts, & Ochocka, 2012). The Waterloo Region Immigration Partnership was officially launched in 2010 under the three pillars of Settle, Work, and Belong. To this day it continues to engage diverse stakeholders in building strategies to welcome and include newcomers in community life.

As I reflect on this series of five projects, I realize that there was no master plan for this research to unfold. Yes, each project represented one complete cycle of the four-phase community-based research process. But it was at the end of each cycle that stakeholders decided what should happen next. Each project was a different type of research with its distinct purpose and type and degree of stakeholder involvement. Each project had its uniquely formed research team that included a combination of professional researchers, newcomers and students (including a number of CP students). Each project had its own funding model that was creatively pursued. Each project was initiated by different players (both researchers and non-researchers) with leadership and involvement in the project then negotiated (Ochocka, Janzen, & Nelson, 2002; Ochocka, Moorlag, & Janzen, 2010). In short, the focus was on using research to advance a larger community goal.

When talking about community-based research I like to use the analogy of the old Apollo space rockets. Each rocket had three fuel cells that successively fell away once the fuel was spent. It also had a small capsule on top that housed the astronauts. A community-based research project is like a fuel cell, not the capsule. It is valuable but not the main thing. Its role is to help propel something more important than itself, sometimes using multiple projects to advance a community's agenda. From this perspective, community-based research is not so much about researchers trying to engage community members in their research as it is collectively asking how research can be of service to community (Janzen & Ochocka, under review; Janzen et al., 2017; Janzen, Nguyen, Stobbe, & Araujo, 2015). CP students and graduates can lead this kind of research whether they work in academic or community settings.

Key Terms

Community control: Key stakeholders participate as research partners and have a certain level of control over major decisions regarding the research agenda and approach. Research is conducted with communities and not just about them.

Community-engaged research: A collaborative and systematic investigation into and study of materials and sources in order to generate new knowledge that advances the wellbeing of individuals, groups, and communities and equitably involves all partners in the research process building upon their strengths.

Context: Factors in a person's environment that influence their lived experience and wellbeing such as friends, family, school, work, communities, and the cultural, political, and economic factors.

Ethics: Key considerations about the impact of the research on participants such as the level of potential risks and burden certain designs and methods expose the participants to, whether the perspective of the participants will be adequately captured, confidentiality of the participants, lack of coercion, fairness in allocation of potential benefits (e.g., access to treatment) and selection into the study, and how the way research findings are shared may cause harm to the focus community.

Data collection methods: Research tools for systematic data collection from participants such as surveys, interviews, and focus groups.

Interpretative methods: Qualitative methods such as interviews, focus groups, Photovoice, collaging, and digital storytelling are used to capture the experience and meaning-making of participants. These qualitative data are then analyzed and interpreted by the researchers to capture the common experiences of the participants in a systematic and abstracted way.

Knowledge mobilization: "A process of exchange between researchers and knowledge users designed to make relevant research information available and accessible to stakeholders for use in decision-making about practices, programs and policies" (Institute for Work & Health, n.d.). It is often also referred to as knowledge transfer, dissemination, or translation.

Memorandum of understanding: A written agreement among a research collaborative or team detailing the way they want to work together, such as key responsibilities and roles, rules for decision-making and conflict resolution, and data ownership and publication guidelines. Sometimes also referred to as terms of reference.

Peer researcher: Members of the target population with lived experience of the issue of interest who are trained to participate as co-researchers.

Program evaluation: Applied social research used to inform decision making on how a program can be improved or become more efficient (formative or developmental evaluation) or whether a program should be continued (summative evaluation).

Stakeholders: Individuals, groups, and organizations which potentially have an interest (a stake) in the research because of the way they are affected by the issue of interest and/or the research or the way they are contributing to it. This can include members of the target population, funders, service organizations, government officials, community advocates, among others.

Theoretical framework: A conceptual structure of concepts, definitions, and theories related to the phenomenon or issue of interest grounded in a review of the theoretical and empirical work from existing literature. The theoretical framework introduces and describes the theory that explains why the research problem under study exists and also guides the framing of research objectives and questions, design choices, and the analysis and interpretation of the data.

Resources

General Resources on Methodology

Alasuutari, P., Bickman, L., & Brannan, J. (2008). *The SAGE handbook of social research methods.* London: SAGE Publications.

Bickman, L., & Rog, D. J. (Eds.). (2008). *The SAGE handbook of applied social research methods* (2nd ed). Los Angeles: SAGE Publications.

Browne, K., & Nash, C. J. (Eds.). (2016). *Queer methods and methodologies: Intersecting queer theories and social science research.* Burlington, VT: Ashgate.

Chilisa, B. (2011). *Indigenous research methodologies.* Thousand Oaks, CA: SAGE Publications.

Denzin, N., & Lincoln, Y. S. (2017). *The SAGE handbook of qualitative research* (5th ed.). Los Angeles: SAGE Publications.

Minkler, M., & Wallerstein, N. (Eds.). (2008). *Community-based participatory research for health: From process to outcomes* (2nd ed.). San Francisco, CA: Jossey-Bass.

Patton, M. Q. (2014). *Qualitative research & evaluation methods: Integrating theory and practice.* Thousand Oaks, CA: SAGE Publications.

Rossi, P., Lipsey, M., & Henry, G. (2018). *Evaluation* (8th ed.). Los Angeles: SAGE Publications.

Shadish, W. R., Cook, T. D., & Campbell, D. T. (2002). *Experimental and quasi-experimental designs for generalized causal inference.* Boston, MA: Houghton Mifflin Company.

Solórzano, D. G., & Yosso, T. J. (2002). Critical race methodology: Counter-storytelling as an analytical framework for education research. *Qualitative Inquiry, 8*(1), 23.

Wilson, S. (2009). *Research is ceremony: Indigenous research methods.* Black Point, NS: Fernwood Publishing.

Community Psychology and Research

Bond, M.A., Serrano-García, I., Keys, C.B., & Shinn, M. (Eds.), *APA handbook of community psychology: Methods for community research and action for diverse groups and issues.* Washington, DC: American Psychological Association.

Brodsky, A. E., Mannarini, T., Buckingham, S. L., & Scheibler, J. E. (2017). Kindred spirits in scientific revolution: Qualitative methods in community psychology. In M. A. Bond, I. Serrano-García, C. Keys, & M. Shinn (Eds.), *APA handbook of community psychology: Methods for community research and action for diverse groups and issues* (pp. 75–90). Washington, DC: American Psychological Association.

Lykes, B. M. (2017). Community-based and participatory action research: Community psychology collaborations within and across borders. In M. A. Bond, I. Serrano-García, C. B. Keys, & M. Shinn (Eds.), *APA handbook of community psychology: Methods for community research and action for diverse groups and issues* (pp. 43–58). Washington, DC, US: American Psychological Association.

Jason, L. A., & Glenwick, D. S. (Eds.). (2016). *Handbook of methodological approaches to community-based research: Qualitative, quantitative, and mixed methods.* New York: Oxford University Press.

Kidd, S., Davidson, L., Frederick, T., & Kral, M. J. (2018). Reflecting on participatory, action-oriented research methods in community psychology: Progress, problems, and paths forward. *American Journal of Community Psychology, 61*(1–2), 76–87.

Tebes, J. K. (2017). Foundations for a philosophy of science of community psychology: Perspectivism, pragmatism, feminism, and critical theory. In M. A. Bond, I. Serrano-García, C. Keys, & M. Shinn (Eds.), *APA handbook of community psychology: Methods for community research and action for diverse groups and issues* (pp.21–40). Washington, DC: American Psychological Association.

ISSUES IN COMMUNITY PSYCHOLOGY

Introduction to Part IV

This first half of the book (Parts I–III) is designed to introduce readers to foundational theories in community psychology (CP), some of the myriad methods, interventions, and questions we approach as community psychologists, and the values and vision that drive the work we do with communities. However, it is just an introduction, not a comprehensive review. As such, we hope that this is just a starting point for your learning about the field. We provided suggestions for future reading in each chapter and encourage you to delve deeper into the many concepts and practices described.

In an effort to make ideas more concrete, this newest edition selected three target topics – global climate change, housing instability, and immigration – to use as examples. Our hope was to highlight the multifaceted nature of these social challenges by describing them from different vantage points in community work. We also asked practitioners to contribute their thoughts at the end of many of the chapters. However, there are many other areas and topics that community psychologists target than those described in each chapter or by each practitioner. In our effort to provide consistency, we did not highlight the diversity of topics and settings in which our field works. To bring awareness to a few more salient topics, the second half of the book is dedicated to other areas that are of high importance to community psychologists. Of course, these are just global introductions that, given space constraints, cannot delve too deeply into these significant issues. Further, other important topics are not addressed.

Targeted Topics

In Chapter 14, Tod Sloan, Fernando Lacerda, Mariah Kornbluah, and Susan Eckerle Curwood introduce issues of globalization, poverty, social justice, and community psychology. These authors help contextualize how capitalism and growing global economies contribute to economic and social inequality. Importantly, they highlight the importance of a community perspective for understanding the causes of poverty and the ways to work towards social justice and transformative change.

In Chapter 15, Pat Dugeon, Mareva Glover, and Ingrid Huygens introduce readers to issues of colonization and Indigenous rights. They connect colonization and racism and then describe how decolonization is needed to establish Indigenous rights and sovereignty. Using Australia and New Zealand as examples, they highlight effective and ineffective work towards social justice and articulate how community psychologists can support decolonization.

Focusing on issues of gender in Chapter 16, Heather Gridley, Colleen Turner, Ronelle Carolissen, Sherine Van Wyk, and Monica Madyaningrum provide a brief overview of gender inequality and examine how community psychology could contribute to gender equity. They focus on how CP's core values and vision should lead towards ameliorative or, optimally, transformative research and practice that promote collective wellbeing for women.

In Chapter 17, Leslea Pearson, Glynis Clacherty, and Melissa Whitson focus on issues affecting families and their wellbeing. Although the authors touch upon issues of poverty and disadvantage, they caution against victim-blaming and argue for the need for a social justice and family wellbeing perspective to community work.

Lauren Munro and Robb Travers focus on lesbian, gay, bisexual, transgender, and queer (LGBTQ) issues in CP in Chapter 18. The two authors question heteronormative standards and position LGBTQ issues within a context of power relations and forms of oppression. They define relevant terms and describe settings, issues, and practices where community psychologists work towards social justice for sexual and gender minorities.

In Chapter 19, Thilo Kroll and Glen White describe ableism, physical disability, and community living. Focusing specifically on differing physical ability, the authors describe the important, and often unique, challenges of housing and community integration due to ableism and the role CP can and does play in supporting autonomous and integrated living.

Drawing on the experiences of psychiatric consumers/survivors, in Chapter 20, Bret Kloos describes some community-based challenges that arise from mental health problems as well as the community contexts and supports that promote healthful living, inclusion, and self-determination. He then goes on to offer resources for defining and viewing what is "supportive."

In Chapter 21, Ciann Wilson, Natasha Afua Darko, Amandeep Kaur Singh, and Brianna Hunt introduce readers to issues of race and racism. They describe global racism, theories addressing racism, and specific types of racial discrimination. They then connect awareness of race, critical race theory, and intersectionality to community psychology, articulating how social justice and transformation must center on people of color's lived experiences.

Intersectionality

As the chapter overviews demonstrate, and you will see when you read them, there are many overlaps in these social issues. For instance, globalization disproportionately affects those with fewer resources, which tend to be women and children, especially non-White women and children and those with differing abilities. Social issues are complex. In order to simplify issues for readers, we focused on specific aspects in isolation. However, community psychologists must consider the ecology of inequality in order to work towards social justice.

Intersectionality acknowledges that social categories and systems of oppression are inseparable (Hancock, 2016). The concept of intersectionality was popularized by a group of Black feminists who stated "We ... find it difficult to separate race from class from sex oppression because in our lives they are most often experienced simultaneously" (Combahee River Collective, 1977/1995, cited in Cole 2009, p. 234). They and others note how the focus on one element (e.g., race) runs the risk of minimizing the importance of other elements (e.g., gender, class) (Cole, 2009; King, 1988; Hancock, 2016). For instance, one could focus on issues of being Black in the US or being a woman in the US, but neither will capture what it is like to be a Black woman in the US. As Shields (2008) argues, "Intersectionality first and foremost reflects the reality of lives. The facts of our lives reveal that there is no single identity category that satisfactorily describes how we respond to our social environment or are responded to by others" (p. 304). As researchers and practitioners, who are members of various groups, and engaging with others who also are members of various groups, we must consider how our own intersectionality influences our values, vision, and practices as well as how we work with and conceptualize societal change and justice.

In this book we tried to highlight some of the framing, methods, practices, and theories that community psychologists utilize. However, we inevitably simplified issues by not adequately addressing issues of intersectionality. Further, even our three sample topics overlapped in important ways. For instance, global climate change is resulting in many areas becoming less habitable (e.g., land erosion, pollution, drought, armed conflict over diminishing resources), displacing many people, which leads to housing instability or migration. Importantly, climate refugees are typically those with the fewest resources who often experience high levels of discrimination in their home countries and their receiving countries. We have tried to stress the importance of an ecological perspective and this is especially true when considering the overlapping nature of inequality and nested systems of oppression. While limited, there is utility to considering global issues from each of these categories and/or identity groups.

GLOBALIZATION, POVERTY, AND SOCIAL JUSTICE

Tod Sloan, Fernando Lacerda, Mariah Kornbluh, and Susan Eckerle

Warm-up Questions

Over a billion people on the planet live in households that survive on the equivalent of a few dollars a day. Obviously, prices of goods in very poor regions may be quite different, but it is still worth reflecting in response to the following questions:

1 If you had to devote that few dollars toward the purchase of food to survive, what would you be able to buy?
2 What do you imagine you would be feeling if you really could not afford to obtain even the basic things you need? How would you feel when you perceive the very wealthy people around you enjoying themselves?
3 How do you explain the giant gap between the wealthy and the poor in societies around the world?

Learning Objectives

In this chapter you will learn about

- The relationship between the rise of corporate globalization, global poverty, and economic justice
- Global poverty origins, causes, and effects
- Community psychology research and action on poverty
- The detrimental effects of capitalism, consumerism, and globalization
- The opportunities for a global community psychology

Global Poverty: Basic Facts

In this chapter, we examine the relationship between the rise of **corporate globalization** and global poverty and economic injustice. After briefly reviewing the history of capitalist industrialization and its effects on what became known as the Third World (now termed the Global South), we discuss some of the ways in which the spread of capitalist **consumerism** is disrupting both the material and social wellbeing of the vast majority on the planet. Our primary aim is to highlight the crucial roles that communities and citizens can play in determining the outcomes of the political struggles for global social and economic justice.

We often find ourselves wondering why, in a world where billions of dollars are spent on weapons and war, space exploration, cosmetics, sports, and popular music, societies cannot manage to shift resources to solve the problem of global poverty? It is hard to imagine a more urgent task than this.

The problem can be illustrated with some basic data: While the world would need to invest US$265 billion annually for the next 15 years in order to eradicate hunger (FAO, IFAD, and WFD 2015), the world military expenditure in 2014 alone was US$1719 billion (SIPRI, 2015). The value of what the US alone spent militarily between 2009–14, more than four trillion dollars,

---

Box 14.1 Current Data on Global Poverty

From the World Bank, the major organization tracking global poverty:

The number of people living in extreme poverty globally remains unacceptably high and there are concerns about achieving the goal of ending poverty by 2030.

- According to the most recent estimates, in 2015, 10 percent of the world's population lived at or below $1.90 a day. That's down from 36 percent in 1990.
- In 2015, 736 million people lived on less than $1.90 a day, compared with 1.85 billion in 1990.
- More than half of the extreme poor live in Sub-Saharan Africa, with 2 million alone living in Nairobi's informal settlements and slums (Amnesty International Publications, 2009). In fact, the number of poor in the region increased by 9 million, with 413 million people living on less than US$1.90 a day in 2015, more than all the other regions combined. If the trend continues, by 2030, nearly 9 out of 10 extreme poor will be in Sub-Saharan Africa.
- The majority of the global poor live in rural areas, are poorly educated, employed in the agricultural sector, and are under 18 years of age.
- The share of poor according to a multidimensional definition that includes consumption, education, and access to basic utilities is approximately 50 percent higher than when relying solely on monetary poverty.

Source: www.worldbank.org/en/topic/poverty/overview
(retrieved June 11, 2018)

A crowded part of Kibera, one of Nairobi's largest slums

John Warburton-Lee Photography / Alamy Stock Photo

would have been more than enough to eradicate hunger in the world. See Box 14.1 for current data on global poverty.

A third of humanity scrapes by on an income equivalent to a few dollars a day or less. Such poverty is not just a lack of money. Poverty is a *lived experience* associated with hunger, illness, inadequate housing, illiteracy, human rights abuses, and social marginalization (Narayan, Chambers, Shah, & Petesch, 2000a). Technological and socioeconomic developments over the past 50 years have improved the situation of some social classes in particular parts of the world, but rapid population growth, continuing violent conflict, and epidemic diseases in poorer countries have basically negated progress overall. Poverty is not due to there not being enough to go around – it stems from societal and institutional arrangements that do not give priority to distributing resources in a manner that meets the basic human needs of everyone.

Poverty can be tied to key concepts of power and control within community psychology (CP) (Christens, 2019; see also Chapter 4). Those in positions of power are often the ones determining how resources ought to be allocated (e.g., lobbyists pushing for tax reform to benefit their personal investments, US involvement in certain international trade deals that do not address poor working conditions present in other participating countries, etc.). These individuals can then ensure resources are distributed in a manner that maintains existing power structures and benefits their corporate interests. Notably, individuals in poverty are often not at the decision-making table to ensure resources are distributed in an equitable and transparent manner. Community psychologists work to unmask these power structures, and push for both *procedural* (i.e., ensuring individuals from historically silenced groups are brought into the decision-making process) and *distributive* justice (i.e., to ensure equity in resource distribution; Prilleltensky, 2012).

Poverty and its Causes and Effects: Thinking Ecologically about Poverty

In order to address poverty, one must not only have an idea of what poverty *is*, but also of what *causes* it. Interventions that attempt to attack the root causes of poverty are inextricably interwoven with beliefs about poverty causation (see also "Problem Definition," in Chapter 6).

The broadest grouping of theories about the causes of poverty divides them into two categories: internal and external. *Internal* theories of causation place the responsibility for poverty with the individual experiencing it, typically arguing that poverty is the result of poor choices, a poor work ethic, or a maladaptive "culture of poverty." These theories often perpetuate existing social structures. This phenomenon is known as **system justification theory** (Jost & Banaji, 1994), in which the existing social arrangements that condition poverty are legitimized and instead, poverty is seen as an individual choice (e.g., someone being homeless because they choose to not work hard enough, a tribe in Sub-Saharan Africa suffering from poverty because they refuse to assimilate into modern society). William Ryan (1971) describes this psychological process as "victim blaming." This **ideology** maintains the status quo, diverting our attention towards individual differences rather than systemic root causes.

External theories of causation include social, economic, or political factors such as discrimination, job scarcity, or the lack of opportunities for participation in the political system. External theories provide a lens for identifying leverage points for systemic change efforts. For instance, tying homelessness to a lack of affordable housing highlights potential intervention points (e.g., providing affordable housing to those in poverty, raising the minimum wage, etc.).

A dialectical standpoint seems to be a good theory to explain poverty and its subjective consequences. Liberation psychologist, Ignacio Martín-Baró, in his studies that addressed fatalism, avoided psychological and economical reductionisms highlighting that

> fatalism is a behavioral pattern that the social order prevailing in Latin America encourages and reinforces in certain strata of the population. The rationality of the established system denies the people of these strata the satisfaction of their most basic needs, while at the same time permitting the dominant elites to wallow in luxury. (Martín-Baró, 1986/1996, p. 213)

Ideas regarding the causation of poverty ultimately determine both the social policies that can garner support, and also the types of programs and interventions that are designed and utilized by poverty reduction actors in both governmental and non-governmental spheres. A number of studies have investigated the relationship between theories of causation and governmental intervention in social welfare, showing internal attribution for poverty to be correlated with low support for government provision of social welfare programs, while external attribution is attributed with high support for government-provided welfare (Appelbaum, 2001; Bullock, Williams, & Limbert, 2003; Evans, Kelley, & Kolosi, 1992; Lofters, Slater, Kirst, Shankardass, & Quiñones, 2014; Shirazi & Biel, 2005).

From a CP perspective, the differing notions of poverty causation might be organized according to an ecological framework. The notion of ecological levels of analysis situates individual wellbeing within a nested set of contexts and affirms the interdependency of individuals and their familial, organizational, cultural, and social environments (see Chapter 5). An ecological lens encourages us not only to consider the state of people who are experiencing poverty, but also to examine the ways in which community or societal systems either assist people in exiting poverty or, conversely, place barriers in the way of that exit. Poverty can be viewed as related to characteristics of the individual, characteristics of the microsystem (locality or subculture), organizational practices, and/or characteristics of macrosystems. An ecological lens allows us to view poverty as a complex issue that is affected by all of these levels simultaneously.

Poverty reduction interventions can also be focused at different ecological levels, attempting to impact individuals and families, communities, or systems. Interventions may also differ in their intentions. Some are intended to ameliorate the negative effects of poverty, some are intended to move people out of poverty, and some are intended to prevent people from entering into poverty in the first place. *Effect amelioration* refers to strategies that alleviate some of the symptoms of poverty, and may provide people with a better standard of living, but without reducing the depth of their poverty. These strategies might include provision of services such as food, emergency shelter, or health care. While such services are helpful in providing immediate relief (i.e., first order change), they do not address the underlying causes of poverty.

Poverty reduction activities are interventions that reduce either the number of people in poverty or the depth of poverty that people experience. Interventions that reduce depth of poverty result in increased income or reduced need for expenditures, but without the addition of other interventions, are unlikely to enable people to exit poverty. Examples include reduced-cost goods or services, such as rental assistance programs or reduced-fare transit passes, policies that reduce the tax burden placed on people with low incomes, or programs that work to increase the uptake of subsidies among an eligible population. Interventions that reduce the number of people in poverty often work in the areas of education, employment, asset development, and may include microenterprise development programs (Schreiner & Woller, 2003), community loan funds (Murray & Rosenberg, 2006), or living wage policies (Luce, 2012). For instance, the Women's Microfinance Initiative provides small loans for women in East Africa to begin or expand their small business (https://wmionline.org/). A multi-site study of six microcredit initiatives found modestly positive effects (Banerjee, Karlan, & Zinman, 2015).

Anti-poverty interventions may focus at the level of prevention, seeking to ensure that people do not fall into poverty in the first place. These interventions may include equity-focused social policies targeting an entire population, such as universal health care, public education, or guaranteed basic minimum income policies (see Box 14.2). They may also include targeted

---

Box 14.2 What Is a Guaranteed Basic Minimum Income?

Everline lives in a rural village in Siaya County, Kenya, and never thought she'd own her own home. Then in 2013, she said in an interview, "My life changed." She was a guinea pig in Give-Directly's three-year-old experiment in poverty reduction, based on a simple idea: Just give cash to the poor. With $1,000, the rough equivalent to a year's income, the 36-year-old mother chose to buy two goats, 20 sheets of iron, blankets and a mattress — and also paid workers to build her a house. It's now her "proudest achievement." (Mayol, 2016, para 1)

GiveDirectly (www.givedirectly.org) is testing the idea of a universal basic income by providing regular payments to thousands of poor households in East Africa for over ten years. A basic income is a government ensured guarantee that would provide all people a basic income floor – an income that is enough to live on and that is provided irrespective of work simply because the recipient is a member of that community. It is provided to everyone, regardless of need, forever.

People from across the political spectrum from Dr. Martin Luther King Jr., to the conservative economists Milton Friedman and F. A. Hayek have expressed interest in the idea of a guaranteed Basic Minimum Income – also referred to as Basic Income, Basic Income Guarantee, and Universal Basic Income (UBI) – as well as Stephen Hawking and modern-day tech entrepreneurs Elon Musk and Mark Zuckerberg. Andrew Yang, an entrepreneur running for the Democratic nomination for the 2020 US presidential election, also supports UBI and his plan gives every US resident $1,000 a month.

Arguments for a basic income guarantee suggest it is the moral thing to do, and replacing various existing government programs with a basic income is more efficient. The modern labor market is very different than it was just a decade ago; long-term employment and consistent income is less guaranteed and robotics and automation is eliminating the need for some jobs. Proponents suggest that UBI could be a powerful way to enable civic engagement and could have a strong positive effect on democratic participation and social cohesion (Bregman, 2017; Santens, 2017).

Conservative critics argue that people will just spend the free money on drugs and alcohol and will stop working. Progressive critics worry about its limited ability to move people above the relative poverty line and potentially obscures how the power and influence of the corporate sector skews the distribution of the social determinants of health to threaten wellbeing (Navarro, 2009; Raphael, Bryant, & Mendly-Zambo, 2018). However, UBI differs from existing social welfare programs in the US and Canada in that it is both universal and has no work requirement. It is, therefore, believed to be very simple and easy to administer. It helps the working poor, single parents, and the homeless, without placing anyone under the management of a caseworker.

The advantages of the basic income structure are that it is universal – all members of society receive it, and the benefit remains in place as income fluctuates, maintaining the economic security of the benefit for precarious workers. It also restores progressivity to the tax system, under which marginal tax rates rise as income increases, rather than the other way around, as is currently the case in the US (Ikebe, 2016). A recent evaluation of a Partial Basic Income experiment in Finland returned some promising preliminary results (Kangas, Jauhiainen, Simanainen, & Ylikännö, 2019).

interventions aimed at those particularly deemed to be "at risk," such as single mothers or recent immigrants.

Finally, it is important to highlight that structural change is necessary to overcome poverty. If basic minimum income policies are not conjugated with policies toward real income distribution, they can be used as tools for political patronage through subjective co-optation (Euzébios Filho, 2016). Again, the ideas of Martín-Baró (1986/1996) on how to break away with fatalism can be enlightening: "Ultimately, overcoming the fatalismo of the poor majorities in Latin America demands a revolutionary change, a change in political and economic structures ... Only revolutionary practice will enable Latin American peoples to break the inflexibility of social structures that rigidly serve the interests of the few" (p. 220).

Community Psychology Research and Action on Poverty

Poverty reduction is highly congruent with the values of CP as a field that seeks to address social inequality, increase inclusion and empowerment of traditionally disadvantaged groups, and promote social justice. Yet in practice, at least in the English-speaking world, issues of poverty reduction have not been as prominent in the field. Poverty is frequently cited in the CP literature as a root cause of many different social problems, including homelessness, substance misuse, interpersonal violence, and mental illnesses. Community psychologists engage in a great deal of research and action on social issues that are determined by poverty. However, an examination of articles published in the *American Journal of Community Psychology* and the *Journal of Community Psychology* between 1999 and 2015 found relatively few articles that describe research or action directed towards the problem of poverty itself. Of those articles that did address poverty directly, the majority were concerned with ameliorative interventions, aimed at improving quality of life without addressing underlying power relationships or structural issues. Prilleltensky (2001) stressed the importance that the field of CP be critically reflexive, not only towards community partners, but towards our own practices as well. In particular, he notes the need for interventions focused on addressing issues of poverty and global inequity in order to promote collective wellness.

There are some examples in the fairly recent CP literature that do deal with poverty as a problem in its own right and go beyond ameliorative measures to propose new ways of working. Messinger's (2006) first-person account of evaluation of an anti-poverty program in the rural American south makes recommendations for the creation of more socially just planning processes through attention to power dynamics and the voices of economically and socially oppressed groups. McNeely's (1999) analysis of successful poverty reduction efforts across five traditions of community work extrapolates key components including meaningful resident involvement, asset-based approaches, and consciously changing institutional barriers to engagement. Caughy, O'Campo, and Brodsky (1999) call for researchers, planners, and policy makers to go beyond a focus on individuals to target structural issues including increasing poverty, the growing gap between the rich and poor, and the erosion of public social supports. Sadly, these and other excellent works that promote transformative social change to achieve poverty reduction, are often the exception rather than the rule.

Critical Community Psychology and Global Poverty

Our interest in critical CP, which is dedicated to social transformation, stems in part from our hopes that major groups of community psychologists, as well as other professionals, will reorient their work radically to contribute to the sociopolitical changes that would address the needs of the poorest people on the planet (Carr & Sloan, 2004). Community psychologists in the Global North have understandably tended to do work that might gradually improve local or regional family wellbeing, schools, social services, and neighborhoods. Yet, unless we significantly transform the underlying political and economic processes affecting all of these institutions at the global level, we are simply part of the problem; we are stabilizing systems that rely on the functioning of the larger system that reproduces inequality and destroys the natural environment. Patrick O'Neill (2005), in his Presidential Address to the Canadian Psychological Association, noted that "even in community psychology, theories about settings too often become translated into research on individual differences" (p. 13), and pointed specifically to poverty as an area in which, by focusing on individual-level rather than systems-level research, we "run the risk of advancing agendas antithetical to social change" (p. 13). To attend more directly to social justice and to engage in more transformative interventions, CP can better frame the problem of poverty in the context of **globalization** and **capitalism**. But the road will be long and hard. Fortunately many lessons about how to do this can be learned from community psychologists in the Global South as well as global social movements in general.

The example set by psychologists in Latin America is notable. Their interest in sociopolitical change guided the first efforts in community-level work. In order to challenge repressive governments, many psychologists started to criticize the social irresponsibility of psychological knowledge and practice (Andery, 1984/2001; Lacerda Jr., 2010). Inspired by social movements and grassroots community work carried out by clergy, educators, and social workers, these psychologists started to work in partnership with social movements and/or within poor communities with a clear focus on producing social and political change (Martín-Baró, 1986/1996; Lane, 1996; Góis, 2003; Góis, 2005; Flores, 2009; Freitas, 2000; Lacerda Jr., 2013; Dobles, 2015). Most of what is presented in this chapter is foundational knowledge for understanding how psychologists and others can follow in their footsteps and effectively fight contemporary poverty and social injustice.

Historical Context: What Are the Origins of Contemporary Poverty?

World history is usually taught in a manner that fails to convey the grand sweep of events, inventions, migrations, and social movements that led to the current global situation. Community psychologists and feminist researchers have stressed the need for decolonizing research methodologies. Pivotal to these efforts is the re-telling of history from the perspectives of those who have been historically silenced (Fine, 2006; Martín-Baró, 1986/1996; Sonn, Stevens, & Duncan, 2013). These narratives disrupt our taken-for-granted understandings of the world, and mainstream conceptions of history. Inherent in understanding these histories is an exploration of power. In the context of global poverty, terms such as globalization, capitalism, consumerism, and **modernization** need to be critically analyzed.

If one can manage to stand back a little from the biographies of kings and chronicles of war, what stands out is the enormity of the social and political changes associated with the rise of modern science and advancement in technologies. Just 500 years ago, the vast majority of the world's population lived in agrarian communities. Lives were simple, but most ways of life were self-sufficient and sustainable. When we look at surviving examples of self-sufficient life among Indigenous peoples, others may think of them as poor, but that is a judgment imposed from an external point of view. Now, roughly 75 percent of humanity is urbanized, separated from agricultural processes and embedded in interdependent systems of production, energy, transportation, and commerce. On average, urban lives are much longer and less physically challenging than pre-modern agrarian lives, but they are probably more stressful at psychological and social levels (Sloan, 1996). Modern life-styles are also not sustainable in terms of their impact on natural environments.

Science and Modernity

Most historical accounts seem to concur with the idea that the magnitude of the changes that occurred over the past 500 years was indeed unprecedented. While explanations of the rise of modernity differ, certain factors are always acknowledged. Applications of the scientific method led to increased human control over natural and physical processes. All technologies, from weapons and transportation to medicine and farming equipment, benefited from the application of scientific reasoning. As a consequence, the power of superstition, magic, and religious authorities over human knowledge was reduced. The economies and militaries of countries with advanced science and technology became more powerful. Europeans used this power to colonize other regions of the world beginning in the 1600s. This was rationalized as a "civilizing" process, but massacres, slavery, and economic exploitation were routine practices of colonizing powers.

Modern scientific rationality was thus preceded by the victory of the conquering power of the *conquistadores*: the domination and colonization of American Indigenous peoples preceded the great advancements in science. Violence, racism, exploitation, and domination were the precondition of European science and economic development (Dussel, 1992).

Industrialization and Imperialism

Philosophers of the 18th century Enlightenment period proposed rational ways of governing societies and, leaning on ideas such as democracy and equality, the rising commercial classes in Europe gradually displaced medieval nobilities to establish modern nation-states. The Industrial Revolution and the associated need for raw materials and new markets led to a second wave of colonization and conquest in the 1800s, known as the *era of* imperialism. During this period, the industrializing European powers consolidated at least a degree of control over most of the territory on Earth. Capital quickly accumulated in European and US banks (see Box 14.3). This was reinvested in further industrial development, increasing the need for even more resources from the colonies. Labor, minerals, lumber, food, and other raw materials were extracted on terms that were not favorable to progress in the colonies. In fact, centuries-old forms of agrarian subsistence were disrupted as colonial economies were organized for resource extraction rather than to meet local needs. In the process, the foundation for what was to become "Third World poverty" was laid. Previously autonomous communities became dependent on powerful webs of international commerce. Sustainable ways of life were replaced by labor-intensive systems of production serving the desires of distant populations for tea, coffee, cotton, silk, gold, silver, tobacco, hardwoods, fruit, and so on.

Modernization

The world wars of the first half of the 20th century accelerated industrialization in Europe, Japan, and the US, but weakened European colonial powers in a manner that provided openings for a wave of independence movements for the colonies in the Global South. Real competition and the ideological divide between capitalist and socialist/communist economies in the Cold War led to further conflicts in the second half of the 20th century – Korea, Vietnam, Angola, Central America and Afghanistan, for example. Resources sorely needed for schools, housing, sanitation, and other basic needs were diverted into weapons stockpiles. Decolonization was primarily accomplished by elites and the middle classes in the Southern hemisphere, often on the basis of political rhetoric about meeting the needs of the poor (Fanon, 1963). Indeed, poverty was a striking feature of the Third World as the colonizing powers gave up political control.

But, as seen above, the effects of capitalist industrialization were, and continue to be, harsh. As feudal rural arrangements collapsed, poverty spread and urban centers expanded as workers flowed into slums. Meanwhile, the drive for access to raw materials and bigger markets for industrial products fueled further European and American imperialism. When the former European colonies gained their independence in the post-World War II era, most of them had not developed significant industry of their own. They had been used, and continue to be used, by the colonizing powers as sources for raw materials, cheap labor, and agricultural products. The newly independent countries of the Third World were encouraged and helped to "modernize." The effect of modernization in practice, however, was the reordering of society in ways that increased the efficiency of capitalist production and the accumulation of wealth by the powerful classes in the global financial centers.

The thrill of independence for the colonies was quickly displaced by new forms of exploitation in a process that came to be known as *underdevelopment*. Goods and raw materials were bought cheaply in the peripheral societies and sold at high prices from the core, enriching middlemen and investors and leaving little local capital for development of the periphery. Elites in Third World countries had a share in profits but tended to keep their wealth in banks outside their own countries in order to avoid the wild economic swings of currencies in developing economies. Gradually, most Third World countries were encumbered with incredible debts incurred in hopes that development would follow. In some cases, interest payments alone consume up to a third or more of a country's gross domestic product. Research indicates that many loans were given with full knowledge that they would not be paid back, simply because Western corporations would profit from the business (Klein, 2007).

The solution proposed by the Western economic powers and the Western-trained elites of the Third World was known as *modernization*. Bundled in this concept were a number of processes experienced by Europe and the US over a span of two centuries: industrialization, urbanization, public education, literacy and democratization. None of these processes is inherently problematic (Sloan, 1996), but development was extremely uneven and often created new problems. Eventually, the framework of global geopolitics changed when the 1989 collapse of the Soviet Union left Western elites thinking that countries that hold democratic elections and foster market economies and free trade had undoubtedly discovered the best form of government and economy.

To summarize, as we try to account for contemporary global poverty, we need to see that modernization according to capitalist models left Third World countries only partly developed, with vast sectors of their populations stranded between previously self-sufficient agrarian lifestyles and unattainable middle-class urban lifestyles. Rampant unemployment, 40 percent to 70 percent of populations living below official poverty lines, high infant mortality, dislocation and social exclusion, government and police corruption, massive foreign debt – all these indicators of suffering in the Global South are fairly well known. Governments in these regions have had little room for action in response to poverty. They came increasingly under the control of the financial institutions of the world's economic powers such as the International Monetary Fund and the World Bank. This was the general scenario that gave rise to all the positive press about globalization and also to the resistance against it.

Globalization

The term *globalization* achieved its current popularity in the 1990s as a way of describing the process that is supposed to bring the benefits of science, democracy, free trade, international finance, communications systems, and corporation-controlled capitalism to the entire world. (See Box 14.3 for a review of the meaning of capitalism.) Some argue, however, that globalization is merely a euphemism for a later phase of capitalist modernization and exploitation. Quite a few individuals and groups are not convinced that this is the only possible path, and, ironically, one of their biggest concerns also happens to be democracy, or the lack of it, for example, in international trade negotiations. The dramatic turn-of-the-century protests in Seattle, Washington, Prague, and Québec against global financial and trade organizations, such as the International Monetary Fund (IMF), the World Bank, and the World Trade Organization (WTO), were only the tip of the iceberg of a broad social movement that aims to construct a different sort of global political and

---

Box 14.3 What Is Capitalism Anyway?

The term *capitalism* refers to an economic system and associated way of producing goods. In capitalist economies, the means of production (factories, offices, tools, materials) are privately owned. Therefore, profits from the sale of products are accumulated by individual owners or groups of owners and investors (corporations). Profits result when goods can be sold for more than the associated costs of materials, labor, transportation, energy, and equipment. In this process, "capital" (accumulated wealth in the form of money or assets) becomes the basis for other investment, either directly or through the banking system. Thus, workers are usually not in a position to earn enough to participate much in the accumulation of capital (except perhaps through pension plans over which they have little control). Instead, they compete with each other on the labor market, selling their time and skills for the best wages. The "reserve army" of the unemployed serve to keep wages low, since "there is always someone else who will take your job." The result is a fairly important divide between those who own and direct the productive system ("capitalists") and those who do the work, whether they are salaried managers or workers. This persistent divide is noted in Marxist sociology by the term class society.

The raw effects of capitalist economies in modern class society have been softened to some extent by labor unions and state welfare systems. Unions first formed to protect the interests of groups of workers in collective bargaining with the owners of the means of production. Government welfare systems emerged later as "**safety nets**" to ensure the basic health of the unemployed labor pool and the unemployable, particularly when the capitalist economic system is undergoing one of its occasional recessions. Unions and welfare systems are under attack in the era of globalization and neoliberalism for various reasons, in particular, because the ideologies of individualism and capitalism go hand in hand. Individuals are supposed to compete to survive in the free market. Collective bargaining by unions and taxes to support non-workers are perceived as brakes on businesses that might produce more jobs and better wages if left unhampered by constraints on individual competition.

The combination of modern science and technology with capital accumulation and investment led to the achievements of the Industrial Revolution in Europe and the US. Production systems became more effective and efficient. Marx himself was impressed by this and assumed that agrarian societies would have to move through a capitalist phase of industrialization before moving on to socialist and communist economies in which workers would benefit from direct control and ownership over the means of production.

economic order (Hawken, 2007; Korten, 2001; Steger, 2013). We will delve further into the debates about globalization later in this chapter.

In summary, understanding the origins of modern poverty is critical to informing the work of community psychologists invested in global social justice efforts. Arguably, exploring this history furthers our understanding of the conditions that perpetuate existing power dynamics and feelings of powerlessness. Community psychologists stress that understanding power must move beyond an individual level of analysis, and incorporate components of structural, social, political, and economic control that must be tracked over time (Neal & Neal, 2011; Prilleltensky, Nelson, & Peirson 2001).

In these processes, it is critical to involve diverse stakeholders and community members from historically exploited groups in the exploration and deconstruction of dominant world history narratives. Julian Rappaport (1995) stresses that narrative theory (which highlights the importance of storytelling and qualitative data collection in making sense of time, process, and history) will enhance our understanding of data and information, as well as increase citizen collaboration.

Ideology: A Key Concept for Understanding Consumerism

At the outset of this chapter, we asked how it is that the world has not yet solved the problem of global poverty. One can also ask, in light of what the world has experienced as a result of exploitation built into capitalist economics, why it is that so many people believe that it is a good system and blame themselves for their own difficulties in making ends meet? One answer to this question points to the power of the phenomena associated with ideology. *Ideology refers to a system of ideas and practices that sustain social relations of domination and oppression* (Thompson, 1984). It is essential to understand that we are not using this term in the more common, neutral sense used to denote any system of ideas, but rather in what is known as a "critical" sense. The Marxist notion of "false consciousness" (a tendency to see the unjust status quo as natural or given) is related to what we have in mind, but that implies a mostly cognitive process, as if changing ideology might simply involve more education. Ideological processes are always sustained not only by cognitive, but also by emotional, behavioral, and institutional practices (Sloan, 1996; Thompson, 1984). A critical notion of ideology would always attend to the interaction of these different aspects of structures of social injustice.

The power of ideology is not only its support for current power relations and structures. Ideological representations are powerful because their content corresponds to appearance of dominant patterns of social relations. Ideology portrays precisely what the human world is today, at least in surface appearance (Iasi, 2011). In order to make headway in the eradication of global poverty, it is essential to analyze a central ideological structure involved in corporate globalization: *consumerism*. Consumerism can be defined as the ideological process that orients much of life around earning money in order to purchase and make use of goods that are not actually necessary for survival and health.

At the behavioral level, consumerism entails that people purchase items that they do not really need. Note that they do not actually need to use any of the products they buy – the system simply requires that purchases be made. At the emotional level, making a purchase feels good thanks to an elaborate system of lifestyle advertising and status symbol construction. At the cognitive level, consumerism is justified as the driving force of economic growth, as evidenced by concerns about indicators of low "consumer confidence." Finally, at the institutional level, banks support consumerism through credit card offers and stores support consumerism by extending their hours of operation and redesigning malls as places to spend leisure time. In turn, many politicians promise to work for policies that favor economic growth, reduce taxes, increase salaries and maximize disposable income for consumer purchases.

We must now add the fact that in order to engage in the direct behavioral component of consumerism, people must be willing to work longer hours than necessary to earn the extra money needed to buy products that are not essential to survival. The entire advertising industry serves to make people feel they must have products that they objectively do not need in order to live comfortably. Accordingly, advertisements increasingly focus on identity and status issues that will be resolved if one owns or is seen using a product. Participation in consumerism does not feel like direct oppression or exploitation, but it is a form of domination nonetheless.

Arguably, consumerism has played a major role in destroying the fabric of community in Western society (Sloan, 1996) and is beginning to undermine community in the rest of the world. This is particularly visible in the isolated lifestyles of the new middle classes in the Global South in contrast to the more collective forms of life among the working classes there. People increasingly shift their free time into using cars, smart phones, entertainment products, and toys. In general, these are used either privately or in small groups (watching TV, videogames, social media). Dialogue, communication, social life, creative action – all key components of a thriving community – tend to be displaced by shopping and isolated entertainment.

The mainstream news media do not do much to raise awareness of the global impact of consumerism or of the political and economic forces that maintain the divide between the wealthy and rest of us. The news media pretend to offer a range of opinion, but actually exclude reasonable ideas and proposals that would disrupt current arrangements of wealth and privilege. The same media also tend to exclude minority parties from political debates – so the public only gets to hear major candidates leaning toward the middle ground of public opinion. A complicated process, labeled "**manufacturing consent**" by Herman and Chomsky (2002), seals off the ideological structure of corporate capitalist consumerism from effective criticism, and we all pay the price (see the companion website for links to Chomsky's video on this topic). The process of manufacturing consent involves collaboration between the institutions, political parties, think-tanks, and corporations that benefit from existing social arrangements and is designed to dull people's critical faculties and enhance their belief that things need to be the way they are.

Meanwhile, the resources that would be devoted in a rationally organized society towards the eradication of poverty are squandered. Instead of meaningfully employing the world's labor energies in the production and equitable distribution of sufficient food, shelter, transportation, schools, health clinics, recreation centers, and so forth, we have millions occupied in the production of unneeded products and other millions standing around as retail clerks waiting on consumers.

Many have implicated capitalism, neoliberal economics, and consumerism in creating the global climate crisis and preventing any real solutions from gaining traction (Benson & Craig, 2014; Klein, 2015; Koch, 2011). This is due to the fact that economic development has been conceptualized and institutionalized as a process of infinite expansion (Foster, 2015). We will need to reevaluate our relationship to ownership, work, and capital if we are to avoid ecosystem collapse and the accompanying social impacts of climate change. The various components of the ideological structure of capitalism and consumerism are going to be very hard to unravel and replace with a more sustainable economic system.

Globalization and Its Effects

As a description of what has happened since the fall of the Berlin Wall in 1989, the buzzword *globalization,* is useful only to a certain extent. First introduced in Chapter 5, the concept of globalization, at the most general level, simply means the spread of a local practice or product to the rest of the world. From this point of view, globalization actually started hundreds of years ago with the spice trade (Steger, 2013).

A second common use of the term *globalization* is slightly more specific, but still too broad in its scope for our purposes. Here, globalization is defined as both a process, and a result of that process. The primary drivers of such processes are all events, forces, and changes that are transnational, transcultural, and transborder. These include flows of capital, ownership and trade, telecommunications, transportation, political and military alliances, migration, and international organizations. Marsella (1998) notes that the results are greater interdependence, shifting personal, and collective identities and lifestyles, awareness of global conditions, increased linkages and chain reactions, and new levels and forms of control (i.e., trade, communications, finance). Marsella was one of the first psychologists to draw attention to the importance of these different forms of globalization:

> Human survival and well-being [are] now embedded in an entangled web of global economic, political, social and environmental events and forces! ... The scale, complexity and impact of these events and forces constitute a formidable challenge for psychology as a science and profession. They demand a major disciplinary response, including a rethinking of psychology's assumptions, methods and interventions and a rethinking of psychology's roles in understanding and resolving the challenges now before us. (Marsella, 1998, p. 1282)

Friedman's (2000) popular account of globalization, *The Lexus and the Olive Tree,* captures these dynamic processes and helps reduce the vagueness of the concept of globalization by focusing on the globalization of electronic communications, democratic practices, and financial systems. Even though Friedman supports globalization, he raises a few concerns about its consequences. However, he believes that the solution is simply more globalization (for example, better communications systems, better representative democracies, and more transparent financial systems).

A fast-growing group of concerned citizens and non-governmental organizations (NGOs) around the world do not agree that the kinks in globalization will simply work themselves out eventually through more globalization. They point out that the core capitalist economic practices driving globalization are inherently problematic. If these practices are continued, the global situation will only become worse. This core structure of globalization has driven workers, students, human rights activists, and environmentalists into the streets in protest of *corporate globalization* (Anderson & Cavanagh, 2000; Barker, 1999; Steger, 2013). It is essential to keep in mind that contemporary protests are not about the more general versions of globalization. Very few people have problems with improved communications and cross-cultural exchange, for example. When political leaders argue in favor of globalization, however, they are primarily referring to the expansion of capitalist market economies and "free trade." In order to avoid saying this overtly, they often speak of spreading "democracy," when they really intend to pressure governments to open their markets to foreign products.

Corporate globalization has been facilitated by financial policies of the IMF and the World Bank known as **"structural adjustment."** These policies require debt-ridden countries seeking loans to slash government spending on education and health, privatize government-owned enterprises, shift economies towards production of exports, and open themselves to flows of external capital. The extent to which the structural adjustment strategy is helping economies is hotly debated. While conservatives argue that it is just a matter of allowing free markets enough time to stimulate economic growth, progressives claim that corporate-led globalization concentrates wealth and power in the hands of a few and leads to further impoverishment for the masses of humanity. For instance, national markets have become increasingly volatile and democratic processes are quashed by transnational corporate decisions (see "Power Cube" in Chapter 4). Government subsidies for basic needs, such as water and electricity, are removed as structural adjustment requires that these essential services be privatized. Jobs are lost as companies relocate to employ workers who will accept lower wages often in countries with weak labor rights. Communities are disrupted as workers migrate in hopes of finding employment. Women and the rural poor are especially affected (Stromquist, 1998). Environmental protections are weakened as countries compete for foreign investment by promising limited regulation.

It is crucial to recognize the deep connection between globalization and the political economic ideology known as *neoliberalism* (introduced in Chapter 5). At the turn of the 21st century, neoliberalism made one famous historian critical of capitalism to argue that "Whatever limitations persist to its practice, neo-liberalism as a set of principles rules undivided across the globe: the most successful ideology in world history" (Anderson, 2000, p. 13).

Neoliberal policies and practices are designed to weaken progressive political organizing, and also to eliminate or, at least reduce, public investments that might reduce exploitation or social inequalities. Neoliberalism is grounded on the following principles: (1) that human beings are necessarily atomized, competitive, possessive, and selfish; (2) that society is merely an instrument that every individual can use to satisfy their selfish ends; (3) that social inequality is the natural consequence of individual differences and stems social life-producing dynamic movements; and (4) that freedom is always at stake when individuals or institutions try to control or regulate market forces (Anderson, 2000; Netto & Braz, 2006). These principles are antithetical to the values and vision of CP as described in Chapter 3 and throughout the book. Many of the social problems targeted by CP have been exacerbated by neoliberal policies (Nelson, 2013).

The main targets of neoliberal doctrine are the democratic functions and public services created during the era of the Welfare State, i.e., the social mechanisms created by governments to mitigate the consequences of social inequality, unemployment, and discrimination. However, after several decades of neoliberal doctrine, social safety nets in nation-states around the world have been reduced and some of the most savage modes of associated poverty have returned. The euphemistic term "austerity" is used to describe such government and public expenditure reduction strategies that are imposed by national and international financial powers. These measures are often described as common sense attempts to reduce public debt, but end up unfairly burdening those at the bottom of the economic ladder who rely most on government services (Blyth, 2013). For those people, austerity often means unemployment, loss of pensions, higher costs for utilities, decreased access to education and health care, malnutrition, greater inequality, and greater levels of poverty and precarity.

Box 14.4 Draft of a Global Program

1 Level labor, environmental, social, and human rights conditions upward.
2 Democratize institutions at every level from local to global.
3 Make decisions as close as possible to those they affect.
4 Equalize global wealth and power.
5 Convert the global economy to environmental sustainability.
6 Create prosperity by meeting human and environmental needs.
7 Protect against global boom and bust.

Source: Brecher, Costello, and Smith (2000). *Globalization from below: The power of solidarity* (pp. 68–9). Boston, MA: South End Press.

What are the alternatives to corporate globalization? Citing the major problems we have listed that tend to be associated with "globalization from above," Brecher, Costello and Smith (2000) propose a "globalization from below" that would take into account the interests of the great majority of the world's people (see Box 14.4).

The data are fairly convincing that the basic operating principle of corporate capitalism (the maximization of profits to enrich investors) runs counter to the interests of the vast majority of humanity (Kovel, 2007). A significantly different system for meeting human needs must be developed. This must be addressed by community psychologists and citizens in the 21st century.

One Specific Effect of Globalization: Uprisings and Insurgencies

A review of the state of affairs in the world shows that where there is oppression and exploitation, one can also find resistance and revolt. After the turn of the century and the world economic crisis in 2008, new social movements are responding to the contradictions of capitalism and globalization. General strikes and demonstrations by the *indignados* (the enraged ones) in Spain and other European countries, massive student demonstrations in Chile and Quebec, the Arab Spring, the Occupy movement in the US, and the "June Journeys" in Brazil in 2013 are clear examples that deep dissatisfaction with the neoliberal capitalist order is a worldwide phenomenon. See Box 14.5 for an interesting analysis of the June Journeys, also known as the Brazilian Autumn.

Box 14.5 June Journeys in Brazil

In an environment of passivity and acceptance of the "changing without rupture" strategy – that is, neoliberal measures (elimination of laws regulating finance capital, decreasing worker's rights, cuts in social spending) – implemented by Lula da Silva and Dilma Rousseff governments in Brazil, an increase of less than US$0.10 in the price of public transportation sparked demonstrations throughout the country that were only strengthened by the violent repressions perpetrated by police. These actions paved the way for the emergence of many questions about the contradictions of Brazilian society. For the first time, a social movement without any clear leadership (no political party, and no specific social movement) won a victory through demonstrations. After the "June Journeys," conservative sections of Brazilian society learned that the streets can also be a place of effective struggle and, from 2015 onwards, started organizing demonstrations advocating the return of military dictatorship. While the political implications of the riots and demonstrations are not yet clear, it is impossible to not ask: Can community psychologists play a meaningful role in uprisings like these?

These events are closely related to the global crisis of financial capital in 2008, and subsequent austerity measures that aimed to reduce social rights and amplify current patterns of exploitation (Solty, 2013). It is important not to forget that, before the recent struggles, during the last three decades of the twentieth century, Latin America was the main stage of several struggles led by peasants, Indigenous people, workers, and students. Against the neoliberal offensive, people's movements overthrew presidents, reversed privatization processes and prevented political coups. These popular movements in Latin America must be understood if one wants to understand the election or radicalization of governments such as Chavez in Venezuela, Morales in Bolivia, and Correa in Ecuador, which, for the first time in decades in Latin America (with the exception of the Cuban people), challenged interests of US imperialism. Such governments have been flawed, and, under external and internal pressure, have frequently fallen into autocratic modes that alienate their middle classes and multinational corporations. However, the attempts to forge an alternate path are nevertheless notable.

Revolts are part of the same global system: capitalism. While the simultaneous existence of a huge mass of wealth held by elites with billions of individuals facing poverty and misery always created revolts in human history, it is important to note that one can describe the current crisis as a structural (Mészáros, 2009) or organic (Solty, 2013) crisis, because it is woven into every sphere of social life on the planet. The current crisis is not only related to financial systems, but to the very process of production and reproduction of human life. Thus, the solution to environmental, political, social, and economic contradictions cannot be only local, but must be global (Mészáros, 2009).

While the present-day situation is marked by a succession of waves of global social struggles led by women, LGBT populations, and thousands of workers all over the world, there is currently no alternative project strong enough to confront corporate globalization. According to Solty (2013) the current situation can be understood as a transition period characterized by: the loss of consensus and divisions within the ruling classes, weakening in the hegemony of traditional ideologies over those who are dominated; and intensification of social movements, but without seriously threatening the existence of capitalism. During the transition, the old world is shaking, but the new is undefined. In this situation, the building of an active, positive, comprehensive, and feasible "utopia" is one of the most important challenges for anti-capitalist movements. It is here that ideology becomes important.

The Promise of Global Community Psychology

Given that we are addressing the issue of global poverty from the perspective of CP, it is important to note that changes in the field of CP itself will need to occur before it is up to the challenge. A leader in international psychology, Anthony Marsella (1998) boldly proposed an expanded vision for CP that would take into account the effects of globalization on personal and community wellbeing. This would be a "global community psychology." As we reviewed the effects of globalization and neoliberal ideology, the urgent need for such an approach became clear. Globalization may have some positive effects in some sectors, such as improved health and material standards of living, new meanings for life and freedom from oppressive traditions, but these changes, combined with negative effects, can be very disruptive if individuals are not supported by community structures that help them negotiate change. Changes associated with globalization can increase uncertainty and fear. Among groups with less support, these can lead to greater incidence of serious mental illness. Economic disruption can produce increased drug abuse, prostitution, and crime. Rapid social change produces societal stress and confusion, which is linked directly to the marginalization of certain groups, identity confusion, emotional distress, and behavioral problems. CP must address both the material and psychocultural aspects of social change if it is to be effective.

Participatory Democracy

One of the more obvious solutions to the decline of community brought about by consumerist individualism is the reconstruction of forms of community in direct response to the pressures that undermine community life (Freire, 1970). Community investment can foster growth in both individual and collective capital (Flora, 2004). In these efforts, community members begin to see themselves as vital members of the community, and as empowered agents of social change (Wandersman, & Florin, 2000). Relationships that form across community members and groups increase individual social capital, as well as the larger community's network of engaged citizens (see Chaper 7). Among the promising possibilities are the following, each of which strengthens local ties: food cooperatives; community gardens; systems for sharing tools and bartering skills in neighborhoods (see Box 14.6); agricultural, craft and manufacturing cooperatives; and co-housing projects that provide common spaces for intergenerational and mixed-income interaction. Each of

---

Box 14.6 Local Exchange Trading Systems

In cities such as Ithaca, New York, communities have devised their own currencies, called "time dollars" or "green dollars," to reduce dependency on working for cash. These systems usually involve a directory of members offering skills or products to other members. Time dollars are exchanged, or a tally is kept of each member's credits, for helping to paint a house, baking a cake, fixing a bike, having a guitar lesson or a massage, and so on. The benefits are numerous. People get to know each other and pick up skills. They don't have to spend time at their traditional job just to earn money to pay for a service (see www.ithacahours.com).

Underpinning these projects are the processes of citizen participation that can envision and organize them. Democracy must be deepened across all spheres of life in which decisions are made that affect the quality of people's lives. Democracy means much more than simply voting for or against a representative or a proposal. It is also an open process in which all those who have a stake in the outcome have a chance to reflect and develop an opinion, on the basis of adequate information, and move towards consensus on best outcomes with others who are also affected. The culture of deep democracy has not been well developed in advanced industrial society, so this is going to take a lot of practice.

A particular role for community psychologists in this connection should be to insist that in order to realize the promise of deep democracy, the values that inform participatory decision making must be implemented as fully as possible. Think of your own frustrations in meetings at work or school in which a group was trying to make a difficult decision. There is hope. Expert facilitators of group process point to the following values as central to effective decision making and offer methods for realizing them (Kaner, 2014):

- Full participation: Participants feel free to express opinions that diverge from the trend of the discussion.
- Mutual understanding: Participants work to comprehend fully the positions and ideas of others.
- Inclusive solutions: Decisions take into account and synthesize various proposals rather than excluding alternatives.
- Shared responsibility: Participants who have worked on a solution feel they have a stake in making it work.

these addresses one of the components of the problem – there will be no single solution, just a range of alternative ways of living that gradually emerge and become integrated with each other.

Community psychologists can be allies, resources, and students of community reconstruction efforts such as these. Langhout (2015) and Evans (2015) describe this role as a (critical) friend that embraces moments of conflict as opportunities for growth. In these efforts, community psychologists can pose critical questions such as: What are community members/groups missing from these efforts, and why? How will the community ensure an equitable and inclusive decision-making structure? How will we push towards eradicating root causes of inequity and combat the negative impacts of globalism?

When these core values guide group process, not only do groups become more effective, their members learn more and develop leadership skills that transfer to other spheres of life. Community psychologists can be trained to serve as facilitators for all sorts of community dialogues and deliberative processes that are occurring in relation to envisioning post-consumerist societies. Community psychologists can also play an important role in studying and accompanying exemplary community projects in **participatory democracy**. The documentation of these exemplars can be widely shared and emulated in other settings to facilitate social change (e.g., Barker, 1999; Watkins & Shulman, 2008).

Linking the Global and the Local

The ideals of participatory democracy are difficult enough to achieve in local settings. They are even more complicated when national governments and international organizations interact with local communities affected by multinational trade. The challenge is to preserve the advantages of a global economy and market without harming community, environmental, and human resources. This can only be done by attending to issues of human rights and social justice at each of the interdependent levels that affect collective, relational, and personal wellbeing (Edwards & Gaventa, 2001; Hawken, 2007). International organizations, both governmental and non-governmental, national organizations, community-based organizations, and citizens all need to be linked in new forms of networks and partnerships if the material and social needs of the world's poor are to be adequately addressed. Community psychologists occupy a crucial position at one of the main points of intersection of these various levels. The possibilities for action and related research are many, but all these possibilities require a fundamental shift in attitudes about citizenship and the professional roles of psychologists.

A first step in moving towards roles as citizen-professionals is to think through the issues involved in working in solidarity with oppressed groups (Montero, 1998; Nelson, Prilleltensky, & MacGillivary, 2001). In particular, issues arising from the perceived power of the expert need to be addressed. As discussed in Chapter 3, values and vision must be explicit when working with communities. This mode of practice will need to be continuously reworked, both at the professional and the personal levels, in order to achieve depowerment of the privileged participants within a project while simultaneously empowering and uplifting members of the disadvantaged group.

Important lessons can be learned from the advocates of community participation in development planning. A mode of empowerment that has been practiced extensively in Third World rural development projects is known as **participatory rural appraisal (PRA)**. This practice involves assembling knowledgeable members of a community to discuss needs and priorities for development. PRA has increased community input into planning, but recently serious questions have been raised. Cooke and Kothari (2001) are concerned that such practices may mask the fact that the important decisions about funding and projects are still made far from the communities that are affected by them. Participation may simply be a form of window dressing to make projects appealing to donors and reduce obstacles to implementation (see Chapter 4's three dimensions of power). In some cases, participation has been advocated in order to disconnect development projects from radical political movements. If participants can feel a part of incremental change in concrete projects to improve housing, for example, they are less likely to push for changes in the political order. Cooke and Kothari also advocate extensive participatory action research (Fals Borda, 2003; see also Chapter 12) in order to determine the sorts of things that are happening under the rubric of participation. It is not a matter of avoiding future participation, but of ensuring that it is meaningful, effective, and equitable.

Participatory solutions to poverty have been developed along other lines as well. Communities in India and Brazil have had considerable success with a process known as participatory budgeting (Fung & Wright, 2003). In Kerala, India and Curitiba, Brazil, for example, a portion of the city budget is set aside for citizens themselves to allocate after reviewing the city's needs. In Guelph, Ontario, an organization called the Neighbourhood Support Coalition uses participatory budgeting to determine the allocation of public and private funds (Pinnington, Lerner, & Schugurensky, 2009). Such forms of direct democratic planning are likely to spread, especially as cities attempt to tap citizen's visions for the future.

More direct political action is possible as well and has often led to significant improvement in conditions. Barker (1999) documents how global political and economic realities can be addressed at the margins of power in remote local settings. These accounts also reveal the degree to which all situations are now penetrated by globalization and, therefore, need to be addressed globally as well as locally. The Students Against Sweatshops movement is an impressive example of how local action can have a major impact on conditions far away (https://usas.org/).

Dozens of international NGOs and thousands of local non-profit organizations are working to transform the global economy in ways that would decrease exploitation and inequality (see Chapter 9). It is worth noting that the hopes resting with this "third sector" (after government and the market), also called civil society, can only be realized if NGOs themselves operate in ways that prefigure the sort of deep democracy that will need to characterize social relations in a more equitable society. NGOs often duplicate the authoritarian bureaucracies of the corporate and government structures they are attempting to transform (Ahn, 2007; INCITE! Women of Color against Violence, 2007). They do this partly in the name of efficiency and to please donors, but in the long run, opportunities to practice full participation in decision making are being bypassed. Tools of evaluation, participatory research, and critical inquiry can be utilized to challenge organizations to reflect upon their practices in relation to their larger mission (Mertens, 2009; Wandersman et al., 2005).

With these principles and practices in mind, groups can be mobilized into ever wider coalitions that organize strikes and boycotts, insist on major roles in the deliberations of world financial and trade organizations, shift government investments toward the needs of the poor, reduce the power of corporate decisions to affect communities in negative ways – the possibilities are endless.

Protecting Basic Human Rights

There is a critical link between human rights work and poverty eradication (Van Genugten & Perez-Bustillo, 2001). Nobel prize laureate Amartya Sen (1999b) has argued that economic development cannot proceed unless it is accompanied by civil liberties, such as freedom of assembly and speech. Governments that protect human rights are ensuring that the fruits of economic development will be enjoyed more widely and reducing the possibility that corruption will interfere with the efforts of individuals and businesses that obey the law. The protection of human rights also means that community organizers and labor leaders can represent their constituencies without fear of reprisals from paramilitary groups or company thugs. Poor people's movements towards inclusion in civil society depend on protected spaces for meeting and protest. In recent surveys of the poorest (Narayan et al., 2000), it was discovered that abuses of basic human rights by police and bureaucrats ranked as high among their concerns as improved economic possibilities.

The United Nations has approved various human rights documents that have been ratified by most countries, but these have been difficult to enforce. Nations tend to hide behind principles of sovereignty and are reluctant to allow international inspectors into prisons where political prisoners are being held. Progress in this area of global governance will be critical to the advancement of the world's poor. The recent establishment of the International Criminal Court is a good step, since it will bring those responsible for genocide and state-sponsored violence to justice. Nevertheless, human rights violations are still daily occurrences affecting many of the world's citizens, especially activists.

The abuse of human rights in relation to global poverty highlights the ongoing relationship between neoliberal policies, and the psychological health and wellness of under-served individuals and communities. As community psychologists continue to push for human rights, a core value within the field, we must continue to examine the root causes (i.e., poverty, neoliberalism) that create the conditions which can lead to the abuse of human beings.

Connections to Social Movements

Social movement implies organization of people. This organization achieves relative levels of formalization and stability. The actions of social movements can never be reduced to a single activity, but have social goals that can vary from specific to universal ones. Central to these social movements is a critical awareness of the structural sources of suffering and a rejection of systemic injustice. This process is referred to as **conscientization** (Freire, 1970) or critical reflection (Watts, Diemer, & Voight, 2011). Critical reflection in combination with sociopolitical support from peers, family, and community can serve as a key facilitator towards mobilizing historically silenced groups towards social action (Diemer & Li, 2011). The participants who energize social movements are individuals who express identities, needs, demands, and/or class positions. This means that social movements always express contradictions between different levels of social structure: production and consumption; politics and economy; state and market (Montaño & Duriguetto, 2011).

One important issue is that insurgent social movements have always challenged science and the professions. Marvakis (2011) documents how the modern social sciences emerged in opposition to the perspective of progressive social movements. The social sciences, on one side, tried to contribute to the governance necessary for the constitution of nation-states; on the other side, social sciences tended to legitimize the status quo, and that was done by explaining society from a different perspective than that of people who were challenging major spheres of society, i.e., social movements.

Social movements never were hostage to social sciences and any technologies of governance. Social movements have helped to change the face of social sciences. The insurgent potential of social movements opened space for silenced and oppressed voices like those of women, workers, and so on. These movements have been reflected in academic programs. For example, Parker (2007) presents many examples of how social movements are connected to the state of affairs in psychology: the Russian Revolution paved the way for historical-cultural psychology; feminist waves opened spaces for questioning many of the fundamental theses of positivism; anti-imperialist struggles are related to decolonial theory; and the aftermaths of the 1968 student and worker struggles are deeply related to critical psychology.

A way to sustain and empower Critical CP is to understand it as critical social science developed from the standpoint of social movements. This is especially important if the progressive political efforts that seek deep social changes in our society – the insurgent forces that tackle oppressive forces and exploitation – are sources for critical projects that aim to mobilize psychology against the dominant order. Martín-Baró (1980/2015) presented this idea clearly:

> Many of the current frameworks in psychology coincide with the social system in crisis. It is necessary to transform these ideal and practical frameworks from the standpoint of the people and their representative organizations. In a revolutionary society it is clear that real personal development and liberation are not possible without social development and liberation. In this sense, liberation (and de-alienation) of the individual demands liberation (and de-alienation) of society. (p. 488)

Chapter Summary

In summary, community psychologists confronting global poverty should expect to work as interdisciplinary participants in a broad social movement (Hawken, 2007; Montero, 1998). They will need to know as much about issues in global governance as about local practices. They need to be ready to catalyze change where it is ready to happen and to build the bases for change where it will be a long time coming. They will benefit from extended fieldwork in particular regions as well as from experience inside bureaucratic organizations such as the United Nations or development agencies and foundations. Students aiming for careers in global CP should, therefore, consider starting with international service organizations such as the Peace Corps or its equivalents (mostly for language learning and cultural understanding) and then enroll in graduate programs that allow for practical internships, fieldwork, and participatory action research with international organizations working on poverty, community development, and human rights.

There is no right way to go about this work. Each person will have their own contribution to make. This work is complicated and scenarios are complex. We can never know enough to be sure that what we are doing will work. The best corrective for this is to be deeply committed to working with others who share the goal of eradicating poverty. Only solutions that are imagined and realized collectively will endure. The fact that the beginning of the 21st century found the Earth with one clear superpower, both militarily and economically, points to the possibility for a new global order (Hardt & Negri, 2000). Will it be characterized by neo-feudal relations, with special enclaves for the rich protected from the hungry masses by armed guards, or by a new level of civilization, where differences are resolved peacefully and the world's resources are shared equitably? Our hope is that each of us will find ways to ensure that our work and our lives contribute to a global flourishing of social justice.

Key Terms

Capitalism: An economic system in which the means of production are privately owned and operated for profit.

Class society: The basic social and economic structure of a capitalist economy in which wealth, capital and power are concentrated in the hands of a small elite class, leaving those at the bottom of the class society with minimal resources and power.

Conscientization: The process of developing a critical awareness of one's social reality through reflection and action.

Consumerism: The process that orients a large part of life activity around earning money in order to purchase unnecessary goods.

Corporate globalization: The process by which transnational corporations are able to enhance profits and accumulate wealth, facilitated by government policies and international trade agreements.

Globalization: Events, forces and changes that are transnational, transcultural, and transborder in nature and which result in enhanced global interdependence (for example telecommunications, trade).

Ideology: Refers to a system of ideas and practices that sustain social relations of domination and oppression.

Imperialism: The control of land and raw materials and the subjugation of people by foreign powers.

Manufacturing consent: A process of promoting acquiescence to, and compliance with, existing social and power arrangements that is promoted through the media and social institutions.

Modernization: The processes of industrialization, urbanization, public education, literacy, and democratization.

Participatory budgeting: A democratic process in which community members decide how to spend part of a public budget.

Participatory democracy: An open process in which all those who have a stake in the outcome have a chance to reflect carefully and develop an opinion, on the basis of adequate information, and move towards consensus on best outcomes with others who may be affected by the decision.

Participatory rural appraisal (PRA): The practice of assembling knowledgeable members of a community to discuss needs and establish priorities for development.

Safety net: Systems that are set in place by governments to protect people from extreme poverty (i.e., systems of the welfare state that provide employment, financial support, housing, health, social services, and education).

Structural adjustment: Policies of the international financial organizations that require debt-ridden countries seeking loans to slash government spending on education and health, privatize government-owned enterprises, shift economies towards production of exports, and open themselves to flows of external capital.

System justification theory: The process by which existing social arrangements are legitimized, even at the expense of personal or group interest.

Resources

Basic Facts and News

United Nations Development Program – for current data on world poverty: www.undp.org

World Bank – data and information on development projects: www.worldbank.org

Essential Action – fact sheets and reports on corporations: www.essential.org

OneWorld – news on the general global situation: www.oneworld.net

Canadian Social Research – dozens of helpful links on globalization: www.canadiansocialresearch.net/global.htm

Inequality.org – a website full of basic tables and articles on the unequal distribution of wealth, primarily in the US: https://inequality.org/

Third World Network – news on international development (economics, environment, social) from the perspective of developing countries: www.twn.my

Yes! Magazine – a journal of positive futures, inspiring stories of progressive change and insightful essays: www.yesmagazine.org

Short video on global wealth inequality: http://therules.org/campaign/inequality-video/

Short video that explains Austerity: www.youtube.com/watch?v=go2bVGi0ReE

Oxfam International – a non-profit group that provides data on global poverty: www.oxfam.org

Policy Analysis

The Global Economy Project of the Institute for Policy Studies – excellent summaries of complex economic and political issues: www.ips-dc.org

The Center for Economic and Policy Research – in-depth research papers: www.cepr.net

International Forum on Globalization – an alliance of sixty activists, economists, and researchers propose innovative solutions: www.ifg.org

Alliance for Responsible Trade – alternatives to the Free Trade Area of the Americas: www.art-us.org

Grassroots Economic Organizing Newsletter – information on networks of worker cooperatives: www.geonewsletter.org

Program on Corporations, Law and Democracy – research on corporate responsibility: www.poclad.org

CorpWatch – information on corporate power and resistance to corporate globalization: www.corpwatch.org

The Co-Intelligence Institute – catalogues methods for practicing deep democracy in various settings: www.co-intelligence.org

Jacobin Magazine – critical perspectives on politics, economics, and culture: www.jacobinmag.com

Organized Resistance

Mobilization for Global Justice – central organizers at Seattle, DC, and Quebec protests – www. globalizethis.org

Convergence des Luttes Anti-Capitalistes/Anti-Capitalist Convergence – decentralized "affinity groups" working to challenge corporate globalization. Various websites – start at www. abolishthebank.org/

Global Exchange – creative projects confronting oppression and inequality: www.globalexchange. org

Students against Sweatshops – over 200 campuses organizing to improve labor conditions: https://usas.org/

Polaris Institute – a Canadian organization devoted to providing citizens with the tools and information to fight for democratic social change. Great accessible, educational materials here: www.polarisinstitute.org

Bretton Woods Watch – watchdog over the World Bank and the International Monetary Fund: www.brettonwoodsproject.org/

National Council on Dialogue and Deliberation and the Canadian Council for Dialogue and Deliberation – foster training in public dialogue methods: www.ncdd.org and www.c2d2.ca

Basic Minimum Income

www.usbig.net/whatisbig.php

www.givedirectly.org

http://basicincome.org

COLONIZATION

15

Pat Dudgeon, Marewa Glover, and Ingrid Huygens

Warm-up Questions

Before you begin reading this chapter, we invite you to reflect on the following questions:

1 What cultural groups exist in your country or region?

2 What cultural group(s) are you part of?

3 What do you know about the other cultural groups?

4 Would your life be different if you were part of any of the other group(s)? If so, how?

5 How would you notice if your cultural group was being treated unfairly?

6 If you woke up tomorrow to find that Indigenous people in your country freely determined their political authority and freely pursued their economic, social, and cultural development, would your country or region change? If so, in what ways?

Learning Objectives

In this chapter an Australian Aboriginal woman, a Māori woman, and a Pākehā (White) New Zealander draw on their life experiences and work as community psychologists to discuss colonization, racism, and decolonization. Concepts essential to the pursuit of wellbeing and liberation for communities affected by colonization, such as self-determination (tino rangatiratanga) and social justice, are explained and discussed. Case stories describe practical mechanisms for decolonization in Australia and New Zealand. The authors discuss emerging issues and suggest ways in which community psychologists can support decolonization and Indigenous self-determination.

In this chapter, you will learn about

- How community psychology (CP) has developed within a colonial, racist context
- How decolonization efforts have unfolded in two societies shaped by colonization
- The urgency of self-determination and social justice for Indigenous peoples
- Ways in which community psychologists can support decolonization

Colonization

Colonization is a broad term to describe the processes by which European nations exerted influence and control over other nations around the world from the 1500s onwards. The growth of European capitalism depended upon systematic exploitation of environmental and human resources in other lands, and was generally accompanied by political and cultural pressures upon other nations. By the 19th century, two-thirds of the world was colonized by European nations. It has become clear that colonization followed standard processes whereby control – over spirituality, land, law, language and education, health and family structures, and finally culture itself – passed from the **Indigenous** people to the colonizers (Nairn, 1990). The outcome for Indigenous populations around the world has been poor health, social disruption, low educational achievement, and suppression of culture, language, and spirit (Paradies, 2016; Wirihana & Smith, 2014).

Racism

Colonization is underpinned by racism, where people from one cultural group consider themselves superior to people from other cultural groups. As discussed in more detail in Chapter 21, racism is enacted and experienced at a personal level, at an institutional level, and more broadly at the societal level, as follows:

- Personal racism, where an individual's negative stereotypes and attitudes towards other racial groups cause him/her to discriminate against those groups.
- Institutionalized or structural racism, where organizations' policies and practices prevent members of oppressed groups from accessing resources and power.
- Ethnocentrism or **cultural racism**, where the values, beliefs, and ideas embedded in social representations endorse the superiority of one group over the other (Howitt & Owusu-Bempah, 1994; Jones, 1997).

Racism "creates an atmosphere in which a group finds itself in a devalued position" and this in turn leads to personal racism so that "those who are assumed to be inferior are treated differently and less favorably in multiple ways" (Australian Psychological Society, 1997, p. 10). Europeans have downplayed the role of disease, violence, and treachery in the processes of colonization and instead have attributed their cultural and economic dominance in other lands to their cultural "superiority" (Dudgeon, Wright, Paradies, Garvey, & Walker, 2014).

Through a combination of these forms of racism, European colonists ensured that their own ethnic group was the primary beneficiary of colonial capitalism, leading to their culture becoming dominant in Australia, New Zealand, the US, Canada, and elsewhere. The originating European colonial culture, along with the resulting colonies, are often collectively referred to as "Western."

Western science was used to construct the notion of race, which was used to construct the notion of the "inferior" aboriginal (Dudgeon, Wright, et al., 2014). Thus, racism and colonization have been supported by Western scientific theories of human evolution, eugenics, biological inferiority, and cultural deficit models.

European Ethnocentrism and Assumed Universality

Western science went beyond cultural racism to assume universality for its worldviews. During colonization, the European scientific paradigm was introduced as the only valid system of knowledge. Howitt and Owusu-Bempah (1994) describe the orientation of European social sciences as more than ethnocentric or culturally racist. They propose the term *Eurocentric* to capture the universality assumed by European worldviews. Thus, colonization is deeply intertwined with European worldviews, for example, viewing nature as a mechanistic system that can be exploited by humans, supporting a belief in human dominance over nature. The colonizing culture's institutions, which uphold and promote European worldviews, intentionally replace Indigenous systems and come to dominate colonial society.

Decolonization

Decolonization is a term for processes that address the impacts of colonial capitalism, racism, and Eurocentrism on a society. Decolonization can occur at structural and institutional levels in society, such as establishing Indigenous governments and institutions. Decolonization can also occur at the psychological level, whereby people become aware of the processes and outcomes of oppression, and their own part in it. This "consciousness-raising" element of decolonization is common across other civil and feminist rights movements and is similar to "liberation of consciousness" (Ivey, Ivey, & Simek-Morgan, 1993), "conscientization" (Freire, 1970) and liberation psychology (Watkins & Shulman, 2008). Both Indigenous and colonizer people have a part to play in these processes of psychological decolonization.

Decolonization supports Indigenous people to understand how they, as members of a racial group, are being systematically oppressed by the dominant culture. This enables them to take action towards social transformation. Facilitating an understanding of oppression and affirming the legitimacy of a people's ancestral culture encourages **cultural renewal** (Dudgeon & Walker, 2015). Decolonization helps members of colonizer groups understand and acknowledge their personal participation in the structural and cultural racism that maintains their group's economic and cultural dominance (Nairn, 2000). Decolonization is a process of exposing the ways in which power enables or inhibits people so they may join others in collective work for change (see Chapter 4).

Decolonization processes involving Indigenous and colonizer peoples are being undertaken all around the world. Community psychologists such as Dutta (2018), Boonzaier & van Niekerk (2019), and Reyes Cruz and Sonn (2011) have provided roadmaps for decolonizing CP itself. To help understand these processes of decolonization, examples are given from Australia and New Zealand.

Decolonizing Australia and New Zealand

Colonization and Change in Australia

To understand the contemporary culture(s) of Indigenous Australians and New Zealanders, both pre-contact and contact history need to be considered. The Indigenous people of Australia consist of two different cultural groups: mainland Aboriginal and Torres Strait Islander people. Aboriginal people have been in Australia for at least 65,000 years (Clarkson et al., 2017). As at 2016, the population of Indigenous Australian people was about 798,000 or 3.3 percent of the total population (Australian Bureau of Statistics, 2016). For Aboriginal people, land was not only a source of sustenance but also the materialization of their ancestors' journeys from the time of creation. Land was not owned, but one belonged to certain areas. Groups and individuals had rights and obligations to their "country." Obligations included looking after the country, maintaining sacred sites and performing ceremonies to ensure the country's wellbeing. Attachment to land is very powerful for Aboriginal people today. Even for those not living in places of origin, there are still spiritual, psychological, and familial bonds (for a brief history of the impact of colonization in Australia, see Dudgeon, Wright, et al., 2014).

Deeply entrenched settler cultural myths about (1) Australia as *terra nullius* (empty land); (2) Aboriginal people bowing submissively to white *settlers* (who began mass settlement in 1788); and (3) Aboriginal people inevitably *dying off*, still inform many people's understanding of Australian history. These myths and this historical perspective function to legitimize colonization and naturalize White interests. Over the past three decades, an emerging history has challenged such Eurocentric narratives by revealing Indigenous' Australian experiences of **genocide**, denial of human rights, alienation from land, and **assimilation** into European social models (Dudgeon, Wright, et al., 2014).

On the 13 February 2008, the then Prime Minister of Australia, Kevin Rudd, formally apologized to Australian Indigenous people for past mistreatment, particularly to those who are known as the Stolen Generations (children removed from their parents to force assimilation). This represents a profound move for Australia towards decolonization and **reconciliation**, which is the process of establishing justice and equality for Aboriginal and Torres Strait Islander peoples.

Cultural renaissance has emerged as a key goal for Indigenous people – celebrating survival, taking pride and joy in culture and identity, and revitalizing language and cultural practices. Since citizenship for Indigenous Australians was secured in a 1967 Referendum, social and political change has been considerable. In 2007, the Council of Australian Governments committed to "closing the gap" between the Indigenous and non-Indigenous Australian life expectancy, which has become known as the Close the Gap campaign. This was built on the 2005 Social Justice report released by the Aboriginal and Torres Strait Islander Social Justice Commissioner. The report urged all Australian governments to commit to achieving health equality for Indigenous people within 25 years. More recently, a resurgence in the Aboriginal civil rights movement led to the Freedom Summit gathering of leaders in Alice Springs in September 2015 and the revival of the National Freedom Movement. In November 2015, a Sovereign Union Gathering of Nations was held at Old Parliament House in Canberra.

In this wider context of change, constructions of mental health informed by Indigenous people have begun to emerge. There has been a move away from the disease model towards a focus on wellness, holistic health, and culturally informed and appropriate approaches (Hunter, 1997, Gee, Dudgeon, Schultz, Hart, & Kelly, 2014). An increasing number of Indigenous mental health professionals have begun to participate, reclaiming the authority to speak for, contextualize, and determine Indigenous mental health. Training courses for Indigenous people and mental health professionals assisted a shift in the conceptualization of mental health. Just like in other areas of mental health (see Chapter 1) terms such as "self-determination," "quality of life," and "wellbeing" entered the vocabulary of mental health professionals working in Indigenous settings

(Hunter, 1997). The Australian Indigenous mental health movement in the last decade has achieved substantial changes at various levels and in particular by the Australian Indigenous Psychology Association (AIPA) which formed in 2008. It is also worth noting that during this same year on the 3rd of July, 400 Aboriginal men attended a male health summit and released the landmark Inteyerrkwe Statement (Aboriginal Male Health Summit, 2008) that apologized to all Aboriginal women for any hurt caused.

One central aim of AIPA is closing the mental health gap and restoring the social and emotional wellbeing of Indigenous people across the nation. Some of the key educational achievements have been the training of significant numbers of mental health practitioners and psychologists of all ethnicities and lobbying for culturally safe mental health services for all Aboriginal and Torres Strait Islander people.

In 2013, the Australian Indigenous Psychology Education Project (AIPEP) commenced the work of achieving both representative equality within the discipline (at least 500 more Indigenous psychologists were needed as of 2015) and transforming pedagogical practices within spaces which train the mental health workforce in order to build cultural awareness and empower Aboriginal students and workers. The AIPEP is committed to removing the numerous barriers to education that have resulted in poor retention rates and the subsequent under-representation of Aboriginal people in the mental health workforce.

The Indigenous mental health movement also created the 2015 Gayaa Dhuwi (Proud Spirit) Declaration that builds on the 2010 Wharerata Declaration that was developed by the Wharerata Group of mental health leaders from Samoa, New Zealand, Australia, Canada, and the US. The Gayaa Dhuwi Declaration requires the Australian government to support:

1 building access to cultural healers and cultural healing;
2 the development of Aboriginal and Torres Strait Islander values-based social and emotional wellbeing and mental health outcome measures in combination with clinical outcome measures;
3 developing, and resourcing the implementation of policies to ensure that Aboriginal and Torres Strait Islander people are trained, employed, empowered and valued to work (and, where appropriate, lead) across the mental health system;
4 developing, and resourcing the implementation of policies to ensure the Australian mental health system supports Aboriginal and Torres Strait Islander leaders to practice culturally informed concepts of leadership within that system, within their communities, and among their constituents (Dudgeon, Calma, Brideson, & Holland, 2016).

Colonization and Change in New Zealand

Māori tribes migrated from Eastern Polynesia between AD 1200 and 1400 (Anderson, Binney, & Harris, 2015). In ancient Māori society each iwi (tribe) was a nation unto itself (Te Awekotuku, 1991) holding political authority as *tangata whenua* (people of the land) in their region. Colonization began in earnest in 1840, after The Treaty of Waitangi was signed by over 500 tribal leaders. The Treaty allowed for the establishment of a settler government, guaranteed that iwi would maintain their *tino rangatiratanga* (sovereignty) and guaranteed protection over property rights and *taonga* (cultural and social properties) (Durie, 1996). The Treaty promised that Māori would have equal citizenship rights to settlers, implying equal opportunity and access as well as spiritual and cultural freedom.

In contravention of the Treaty, White settlers established a national government excluding Māori and used the British army to force land sales and seize land. Overt legislation and policy destroyed the economic base and undermined the Māori spirit and culture. For example, the Tohunga Suppression Act of 1907 forbade the role of *tohunga* (people with superior knowledge particularly in spiritual matters) and enabled Christianity to supplant the ancestral gods or spiritual guardians (Roberts, Norman, Minhinnick, Wihongi, & Kirkwood, 1995). Following the Māori rural to urban shift in the 1950s and 1960s, tribal structures were discouraged on the grounds that they obstructed assimilation. As at 2017, Māori numbered over 730,000 in New Zealand (15 percent). Māori people are over-represented among the unemployed, the poor, the ill, and imprisoned (for a Māori account of the impact of colonization see Walker, 1990; for a **Pākehā** [White settler] perspective see Nairn, Pega, McCreanor, Rankine, & Barnes, 2006, especially pp. 285–6 and O'Malley, 2016).

The Māori renaissance and decolonization processes have seen past damage documented and acknowledged. Māori knowledge that has been submerged, hidden, or driven underground is being revived (Smith, 1999). Debate around Treaty interpretation is ongoing, but the process of token reparation is underway. Principles of partnership, protection, and equity have been drawn from the Treaty and promoted as essential to the relationship between Crown agencies and Māori. Three developments have accelerated the move towards Māori sovereignty (Durie, 1996):

- The worldwide move by Indigenous people towards **self-determination (tino rangatiratanga)** and greater autonomy.
- New Zealand's reaffirmed commitment to the Treaty of Waitangi in the 1980s and the subsequent inclusion of the Treaty in government obligations and legislation.
- Recognition, by 1980, that Māori worldviews and Māori understandings of knowledge were themselves distinctive.

Increased levels of awareness and debate of Māori rights have created a context for most professional associations (including the New Zealand Psychological Society) to include in their ethical guidelines the rights of Māori people to culturally appropriate service. In addition, many public services have attempted some form of organizational change to provide for Māori aspirations and needs.

Founding Concepts for Self-determination and Decolonization

The following concepts have their base in the activism of Indigenous groups and their supporters, rather than in Western academia.

Indigenous Authority and Self-determination – *Tino Rangatiratanga*

Change efforts in New Zealand have clustered around the central concept of *tino rangatiratanga,* the "unqualified authority" of the Indigenous people. This authority guaranteed in the Treaty of Waitangi that Māori tribes have self-determined political power to define and resource their priorities and that the Māori tribes are not just another minority group with special needs.

International law grants Indigenous peoples the full right to self-determination shared by all other peoples of the world, including all rights to decolonization and permanent sovereignty, as expressed in UN General Assembly Resolution 1514 (XV) of 1960. Although both New Zealand and Australia initially voted against the UN Declaration of the Rights of Indigenous Peoples (along with Canada and the US), they finally endorsed it in 2009. A key principle of the Declaration is self-determination and the fundamental right to the highest attainable wellbeing possible. The Declaration is also central to a significant 2014 Closing the Gap paper by Dudgeon, Walker, et al. (2014), which locates the comprehensive right to self-determination as the foundation of Aboriginal Australians' social and emotional wellbeing. Research across the disciplines, both in Australia and other neo-colonial cultures, has also found that self-determination is central to the reclamation of Indigenous wellbeing (Mazel, 2018; O'Sullivan, 2017). Box 15.1 provides an example of how Māori people are exercising self-determination through political participation.

Box 15.1 Decolonizing Politics

One way Māori people are resisting further acts of colonization and driving decolonization is via a greater involvement in politics. In contrast to Māori having disproportionately lower health and employment status and lower income and educational achievement, Māori are now proportionately over-represented in parliament. The 2017 parliamentary election resulted in the largest number of members with Māori ancestry (29 out of 120; 24 percent) an increase from 13 percent in 1996. Whilst their views are diverse as they sit in political parties across the ideological spectrum, Māori now have greater access to decision-makers, increasing their social power. The Māori public consequently expect a proportionately greater focus on reducing the inequity between Māori and European and Asian New Zealanders. Previous Māori politicians set a high bar directly condemning racism. For example, Dame Turia, who was a co-leader of the Māori Party (an Indigenous-rights political party) frequently and publicly raised Māori awareness of the colonizing intent of proposed laws.

Turia reframed the Foreshore and Seabed Act 2004, which vested ownership of the New Zealand foreshore and seabed in the state, as an outright confiscation of Māori land. In a speech to the New Zealand Psychological Society Conference in 2000, entitled "Colonization and trauma" Turia called the invasion suffered by many Māori during the 19th century land wars a "holocaust" that, like other holocausts, had resulted in disorder, specifically Post-Colonial Traumatic Stress Disorder (Selby, 2005). She questioned if the society of psychologists were acknowledging and correctly treating the "trauma of colonization" when they worked with Māori clients. In her call for New Zealand to "move on to the healing of relationships and reconciliation" (p. 68), Turia concluded that Māori needed to have "control over the healing process. To construct a framework where we are able to exercise power over our process of recovery ... We must learn to trust again, to love, to believe in our own abilities, to have our truths told and voices heard, to reclaim who we are." (p.68)

"True" Histories for Colonized and Colonizer

The retelling of history is another founding concept of decolonization, reconciliation, and anti-racism work in Australia and New Zealand. While moving towards self-determination, Indigenous people need to focus on appreciating themselves, prior to colonization, and understanding what happened during the time of colonization. Rethinking history is an important part of the process, as Smith (1999) states:

> Coming to know the past has been part of the critical pedagogy of decolonization. To hold alternative histories is to hold alternative knowledges. The pedagogical implication of this access to alternative knowledges is that they can form the basis of

alternative ways of doing things. Transforming our colonial views of our own history (as written by the West), however, requires us to revisit site by site, our history under Western eyes ... Telling our stories from the past, reclaiming the past, giving testimony to the injustices of the past are all strategies that are commonly employed by Indigenous peoples struggling for justice. (pp. 34–5)

For non-Indigenous groups, decolonization needs to include learning about, and responding to the real history of colonization. In Aotearoa New Zealand an education campaign about the Treaty of Waitangi facilitated by Pākehā educators was aimed at Pākehā communities and organizations (Huygens, 2011). Learning about the agreements made in the Treaty, and subsequent breaches by the government, has helped Pākehā understand the impact of colonization on Māori communities. For example:

"What I was taught at school and via media was seriously skewed! I feel as though I can actually engage in a conversation about Te Tiriti [the Treaty] now and be confident about it."

"An increased knowledge of the 'big picture' has created an empathy. The historical perspective has allowed me to truly look at it from a Māori world view." (Tangata Tiriti – Treaty People, 2016)

Māori community psychologist Rata and colleagues (Rata, Liu, & Hanke, 2008), found that reconciliation depended on Pākehā completing both cognitive and emotional work before a relationship of trust was possible (see Box 15.2).

These approaches of retelling history and engagement with understanding are forms of restorative practice that can be undertaken by non-Indigenous community psychologists. The revised edition of *Professional Practice of Psychology in Aotearoa New Zealand* (Waitoki, Feather, Robertson, & Rucklidge, 2016) now begins with specific encouragement to non-Māori psychologists to

---

Box 15.2 Social and Emotional Wellbeing

The emergence of a powerful new Indigenous mental health paradigm within psychology is also contributing to the de-colonization of the discipline and the creation of exciting new ways of thinking about Indigenous wellbeing and Indigenous CP as a distinct science and theory. Social and Emotional Wellbeing (SEWB) is a holistic paradigm, which recognizes the dynamic balance between a number of determinants that have been identified as central to health, namely physical, emotional, social, cultural, spiritual, and mental wellbeing (Dudgeon, Milroy, & Walker, 2014). This dynamic and holistic paradigm was taken up by the Aboriginal and Torres Strait Islander Emotional and Social Well Being (Mental Health) Framework

(2001) that in turn was informed by the landmark National Ways Forward Report (Swan & Raphael, 1995). Moreover, the holistic SEWB paradigm situates wellbeing as a connection to family and the larger community and therefore recognizes that the mental health of an individual is a whole of community achievement. This new Indigenous paradigm (or conceptual framework) is presented in an important text, *Working Together: Aboriginal and Torres Strait Islander Mental Health and Wellbeing Principles and Practice* (Dudgeon, Milroy, & Walker, 2014), as a de-colonizing transformation of CP which, in the focus on community driven understandings of wellbeing, is also in accord with the principles of self-determination.

critically understand the impact of the Western universalist heritage, colonization, and assimilation. Instead, when working with Māori clients, psychologists are urged to remember the intentions in Te Tiriti, and to be guided by Māori relational ethics, and holistic Māori models of wellbeing (Huygens & Nairn, 2016).

Social Justice in the Process of Colonization

Social justice is a core concept in any process to redress colonial injustice. There cannot be any reconciliation or decolonization to a position of injustice, that is, to accept and collaborate in an ongoing state of inequality, oppression, marginalization, poverty and powerlessness (Dudgeon & Pickett, 2000). As Michael Dodson, former Aboriginal and Torres Strait Islander Social Justice Commissioner (Council for Reconciliation, 1995) said:

> Social justice must always be considered from a perspective that is grounded in the daily lives of Indigenous Australians. Social justice is what faces you in the morning. It is awaking in a house with an adequate water supply, cooking facilities and sanitation. It is the ability to nourish your children and send them to a school where their education not only equips them for employment but also reinforces their knowledge and appreciation of their cultural inheritance. It is the prospect of genuine employment and good health; a life of choices and opportunities, free from discrimination. (p. 22)

Social justice means that the history of our nations is recognized and, within this, the political and cultural oppression of Indigenous people is acknowledged.

The Council for Reconciliation (1995) endorses the following principles in the achievement of social justice for Indigenous Australians:

- Equality not just before the law, but in the processes of living together at all levels.
- Respect for differences, without imposition and interference.
- The right to live as the cultural group chooses.
- Control of Indigenous destinies and over social processes insofar as Indigenous people wish to engage in them.
- Empowerment and self-determination and the resources to put this into effect.

In New Zealand, a process for redress for injustice is provided by the Waitangi Tribunal. The Tribunal hears any claim by a Māori group (including land claims) that some action of the Crown has been prejudicial to them and is in conflict with the principles of the Treaty (Temm, 1990).

Addressing Structural and Institutional Racism

In New Zealand, there has been a focus on structural and institutional racism rather than on personal racism or prejudice. As Pākehā Treaty worker Humphries puts it:

> Overt personal racism is well understood. Despite its potential for hurt, this is not the form of racism that undermines the very essence of Māori existence. Rather, it is the denial of difference in ways of being human – imposed by Pākehā over and at the expense of those Māori. (Kirton, 1997, p. 1)

Exposing structural racism usually involves analyzing an institution's power structures and attending to which cultural group is making the decisions. Comparing an institution's intentions (such as "education for all") with its outcomes (Māori student achievement falling behind other groups and Māori students dropping out) reveals social injustice. Placing the responsibility for the disparity on the institution itself ("Education system fails Māori") helps to highlight how our institutions benefit the cultural group who designed them and imposed them on Indigenous people.

Emerging Concepts and Issues

The concepts and themes in decolonization work by Indigenous people have remained constant, since most features of colonization have continued. However, the exploitation of Indigenous resources and denial of the legitimacy of Indigenous worldviews have taken new forms.

Continuing Colonization

"We are still being colonized (and know it) and ... we are still searching for justice" (Smith, 1999, p. 34). Just as legislation in the past was used to suppress Māori cultural practices, new regulatory proposals continue the attempt to erode Indigenous beliefs. Often significant social or public health campaigns are mounted in lieu of, or to continue to lobby for, new laws. One example is the campaign in New Zealand to stamp out bed-sharing. For several decades Māori have suffered tragically higher rates of Sudden Infant Death Syndrome (SIDS) than non-Māori. This is partly explained by the disproportionately high rates of smoking among Māori women while they are pregnant (estimated to be about 34 percent) and infant exposure to secondhand smoke. Traditionally Māori mothers kept their infant next to them at night, which had the benefit of supporting breastfeeding. This has been targeted as a modifiable risk factor for SIDS and two decades of public health campaigning and lobbying has been aimed at eliminating the practice. Unfortunately, reducing smoking while pregnant or reducing some of the wider social determinants of smoking, poverty, and deprivation have not been addressed or, as in the case of smoking cessation support for pregnant Māori women, have only sporadically been attempted. Māori health professionals responded by developing woven flax bassinets (wahakura) – a good example of the use of traditional knowledge and practices to solve a contemporary problem. A Pākehā version (putting a mattress in a plastic box), was then produced and has won more funding and support than the wahakura from the Pākehā dominated health services. It is the many small, often subtle, decisions made in institutions like this where racial superiority of the colonizer and racial inferiority of Indigenous people is acted out.

At the other end of life, there has been a call in New Zealand to normalize post-mortems, a practice that offends Māori beliefs and protocols regarding how to tend to a tūpāpaku (corpse) (Selket, Glover, & Palmer, 2015). Once death occurs the tūpāpaku becomes tapu (sacred). Autopsy can disrupt the wairua (spirit) of the deceased causing it to become lost. Appropriate rituals and practices must be followed to ensure smooth passage to the after-life and protection of the living. The pursuit to extend the use of foreign and highly invasive investigative post-mortem, even when alternative procedures exist (explained in Selket et al., 2015) is another example of elevating the colonizer's practices despite the spiritual damage that could ensue for Māori.

The commercialization and commodification of culture is another ongoing colonizing practice, whereby the Indigenous culture becomes an exotic commodity to sell and Indigenous activities are practiced on terms controlled by the colonizing culture, such as for tourism (Nairn, 1990).

The New Assimilationists

When collaborating with Indigenous people to establish Indigenous paradigms, non-Indigenous professionals need to avoid engaging in disempowering practices. Their well-intended help and theories are sometimes elevated as "the Indigenous Way." Despite appearing positive and supportive to the Indigenous community, it may be a new form of assimilation whereby Indigenous people serve as a means to fulfill the non-Indigenous person's intellectual, emotional, and political needs. As Cram (1995) says, "many Pākehā researchers have built their careers on the back of Māori – their research satisfying the criteria set by Pākehā institutions but offering nothing back to the Māori community in return" (p. 7).

Endorsing the Unique Status of Indigenous People

As a result of colonial capitalism's disruption to population groups over the past 500 years, including the proliferation of economic refugees, colonial societies are composed of many cultural groups. However, the racism of Eurocentric societies creates a sense of competition for "cultural space." This situation is often used and manipulated by dominant as well as minority cultural groups to deny Indigenous rights. Typical arguments are that "multiculturalism leaves no room for biculturalism (or Indigenous rights)" and that "Indigenous people are just another minority group." In decolonization work, it is crucial to endorse Indigenous peoples' unique status while recognizing the complex histories and rightful claims of numerous cultural groups.

Individuality and Collectivity in Framing Human Rights and Responsibilities

In working towards social justice, a focus on both collective and individual rights is important. Although people are unique individuals, their humanity depends on their social and cultural context. Western democracy reinforces the notion that human rights are held by individuals and that one's political power is derived from individual citizenship granted by a nation state. Indigenous and tribal peoples are struggling to retain a basis for their rights as collectives, as well as to retain a non-derivative notion of political authority – the notion that their political authority is collectively self-determined. For example, the Western process for obtaining informed consent to participate in research is highly individualized. Some information, such as genetic information is collective. Mead (1995) asserts that where the outcomes of research affect families and communities, they should have a role in determining consent.

The Role of Community Psychology(ists) in Decolonization

Psychology as a discipline and practice has emerged and grown within a global colonial framework and has played a role in legitimizing European dominance. Many authors, such as Prilleltensky and Fox (1997), Dudgeon and Pickett (2000) and Black and Huygens (2016) describe psychology as an example of a practice grounded in Eurocentric culture that purports to be objective and apolitical.

Two fundamental assumptions underlying the discipline have particularly excluded Indigenous people and Indigenous realities. These are the assumptions of **universal applicability** and a preoccupation with individualism. Although CP endeavors to resist these assumptions with a much greater focus on cultural, historical, and political contexts, the image of humankind may still be homogenized and the particular experiences and aspirations of Indigenous peoples may still be silenced.

Community psychologists can progress the decolonization of psychology and minimize a colonizing psychology's harmful impact at a number of levels. Below we suggest ways in which psychology can be decolonized at a fundamental theoretical level, at the levels of individual and community practice, and within the broader political arena.

Deconstructing and Critiquing Dominance and Injustice

A range of critical perspectives and approaches provide critiques and alternatives to the approaches used in dominant mainstream psychology. Among these are critical psychology, CP, narrative and discursive psychology, feminist psychology, liberation psychology, and emerging "Indigenous psychology" (Levy, 2007; Watkins & Shulman, 2008). Dudgeon and Pickett (2000) propose that these approaches can be inclusive of Indigenous realities and endorse Indigenous rights, because they challenge the dominant mainstream, work towards social change, and value the marginalized in their own cultural and political right.

Practice Implications for Community Psychologists

Community psychologists should be aware of how sociopolitical systems and histories affect the cultural groups they work with (Sue & Sue, 1990), employing an ethic of practicing in the presence of history (Tamasese, 1993). Community psychologists need to be aware of their own assumptions, values, and biases, including unconscious biases, and have the critical awareness to acknowledge that they have grown up in a racist society. Project Implicit has free online tests people can take to test their level of implicit bias (www.projectimplicit.net).

Similarly, Indigenous people need to be supported to identify positively with their own culture. For example, to support decolonization Māori researchers need to "have some form of historical and critical analysis of the role of research in the Indigenous world" (Smith, 1999, p. 5). One strategy would be to develop kaupapa Māori (approach grounded in Māori knowledge) training in CP and delivered in Māori training settings. Bridging courses for Māori community psychologists trained in Western CP to upgrade understanding and proficiency in kaupapa Māori CP would be beneficial. This would also support a much needed increase in the involvement of Māori in CP (Milne, 2005, cited in Herbert & Morrison, 2007).

Affirming Indigenous Authority, Expertise, and Self-determination

Dudgeon and Pickett (2000) urge that community psychologists prepare to engage with the Indigenous client and community as novices on cultural matters, with a willingness to take and heed advice. Mechanisms need to be developed for collaboration and direction from the client groups, so that Indigenous people themselves direct the engagement, whether in interaction between a community psychologist and a client or in establishing services and developing policy. For example, the Nursing Council of New Zealand (1996) developed a **cultural safety** approach whereby culturally safe service is defined by those who receive the service. In this way, Indigenous consumers and communities monitor the training and practice of non-Indigenous practitioners (Ramsden, 1991; Wepa, 2015). Similarly in the justice area, community psychologists did not become experts in Māori CP, but rather learned to recognize the limits of their own expertise and to refer appropriately (Glover & Robertson, 1997; McFarlane-Nathan, 1996; Roger & White, 1997). Treatment programs and health interventions developed by Māori community psychologists, recognizing Māori values and tikanga – the Māori way of doing things – and using Māori metaphors (Herbert & Morrison, 2007) are becoming more common as more Māori community psychologists graduate at PhD level. Within Western Australia, Indigenous mental health advocacy has been successful in changing the Mental Health Act such that the 2014 act requires that:

> A mental health service must provide treatment and care to people of Aboriginal or Torres Strait Islander descent that is appropriate to, and consistent with, their cultural and spiritual beliefs and practices and having regard to the views of their families and communities. (Department of Health, 2015, p. 2)

This act builds on the sustained work of the Indigenous mental health movement in providing culturally safe services and reforming the mental health system in general in order to address the specific cultural needs of Indigenous peoples.

Listening, Protesting, and Advocating

Indigenous people and their allies have used a variety of strategies and tools to facilitate change. Advocacy groups have formed and reformed to organize rallies, marches, petitions, sit-ins, and land occupations. Arts, crafts, song, dance, storytelling and theatre have been utilized to educate and motivate change. Political lobbying, upskilling, and infiltrating "the system" to work from within are popular modern-day tactics, as is the use of social media to educate and engage more Indigenous people and allies in action. Whether tribal elders meet with government officials to negotiate across the boardroom table or Māori protestors cut down flagpoles or behead statues of colonizers, all of these actions are being utilized as social change avenues. They have succeeded in gaining attention for desperate and urgent injustices, such as Black deaths in custody. Community psychologists can make an important contribution by aligning themselves with Indigenous goals and becoming advocates for change.

Chapter Summary

This chapter has defined what colonization is and how racism provides a rationale for it while also being a key strategy used in the colonizing process. European ethnocentrism and the claimed universal applicability of European thinking are other central constructs that are explained. The process of decolonization is described using examples from Australia and New Zealand. Finally, the role community psychologists can play is discussed. Although there are promising examples of CP used in the service of Indigenous rights, it remains to be seen whether the decolonizing approaches described in this chapter become part of a CP agenda for wellbeing and liberation.

We conclude with the words of Aboriginal Elder Richard Wilkes (2000) to community psychologists in Australia:

> Reconciliation cannot take place until the mean spiritedness of the nation is itself healed ... All healers know that it is no good just treating the symptoms. Together we must deal with the cause ... As healers together, black and white, we are responsible for healing the mind, body and soul. (p. 522)

Key Terms

Assimilation: Attempts to remove cultural differences by having the Indigenous or minority group discard their own culture in favor of the culture of a dominant group.

Colonization: A process whereby a dominant group assumes control over the land and the economic, political, social, and cultural institutions of an Indigenous or pre-existing people.

Cultural racism: The values, beliefs, and practices of one culture are favored by the dominant group while other values, beliefs, and practices are ignored or suppressed.

Cultural renewal: Also cultural renaissance revival and revitalization of the suppressed cultural practices, language, and knowledge.

Cultural safety: Mainstream delivery of services to a cultural group in a way which does not perpetuate colonization or cultural racism, that is, where the safe service is defined by those who receive the service.

Decolonization: Process of undoing or healing the ill effects and changes implemented with colonization.

Genocide: Policy and practice aimed at eliminating a race of people.

Indigenous: The tangata whenua people of the land or original inhabitants of a country.

Pākehā: White settler in New Zealand.

Reconciliation: A movement to bring justice and equality to Aboriginal and Torres Strait Islander peoples in Australia.

Self-determination (tino rangatiratanga): Sovereignty, autonomy, the "unqualified authority," or political power of the Indigenous people to define and resource their priorities.

Social justice: A situation in which all social and cultural groups have the power to define and resource their priorities.

Universal applicability: Notion of universal truths where differences between peoples as individuals and groups are regarded as peripheral.

Resources

Dudgeon, P., Milroy, H., & Walker, R. (Eds.). *Working together: Aboriginal and Torres Strait Islander mental health and wellbeing principles and practice* (2nd ed.). Canberra: Commonwealth of Australia.
www.telethonkids.org.au/our-research/early-environment/developmental-origins-of-child-health/aboriginal-maternal-health-and-child-development/working-together-second-edition/

United Nations. (2008). *Declaration on the rights of Indigenous Peoples.* New York: UN Publishing.

The Canadian Labour Congress – for extensive information on human rights, racism and aboriginal issues: http://canadianlabour.ca/

The Australian Human Rights and Equal Opportunity Commission: www.humanrights.gov.au

Native Web Resources: www.nativeweb.org/resources

For information on Māori: www.maori.org.nz/

Peace Movement Aotearoa: www.converge.org.nz/pma. See also http://homepages.ihug.co.nz/~sai/racerenz.html for a useful article on race relations in New Zealand

HOW CAN COMMUNITY PSYCHOLOGISTS BEST WORK TOWARDS GENDER EQUITY?

16

Heather Gridley, Colleen Turner, Ronelle Carolissen, Sherine Van Wyk, and Monica Madyaningrum

Warm-up Questions

Before you begin reading this chapter, we invite you to reflect on the following questions:

1 Think of some ways that gender impacts on your life.

2 What would you be more (or less) able to do if you had been born (or assigned) a different gender?

3 Would this be the case if you had been born somewhere else in the world?

4 What are your culture or society's expectations or gender norms for people who identify as male or female? How rigid or flexible/fluid are these expectations as you experience them?

5 If you awoke one day to discover that gender equality and equity had miraculously been achieved worldwide, how would you notice?

Learning Objectives

In this chapter you will learn about

- The history of gender inequity and inequality in society and within psychology
- Community psychology's (CP) potential contribution to gender equity
- Feminist and more diversity-aware visions of wellness and liberation for people of all gender identities, locally and globally
- How we can participate in realising such visions and values, as community psychologists and in our personal lives

Introduction to Gender Equality

And she is carrying half a truth.
And she is carrying half a lie.
And she is carrying half of tomorrow.
And she is carrying half the sky.

This verse of a poem by Imtiaz Dharker (2015) is a poignant expression of the old saying "women hold up half the sky." More than 40 years since the peak of **feminism's** "second wave" and 20 years since the United Nations Conference on Women in Beijing, the basic aim of **equality** for women is far from being achieved. Today, more girls are being educated, and more women are living longer, are in paid employment, having fewer children, and engaging in politics. But while the lives of women have improved overall, there are many areas where advances have been slow or not achieved at all (United Nations, 2015a). There is still no country in the world where women's income is equal to men's, and women still shoulder most of the household responsibilities, including caring for children (United Nations, 2015a).

In 2000, the United Nations (UN) ushered in eight Millennium Development Goals (MDGs) in a concerted effort to promote human development and address inequality (United Nations, 2015b). The third Millennium Development Goal (MDG3) aimed "to promote **gender** equality and empower women." Six "Gender Indicators" for tracking progress towards this goal across sectors and nations were developed: education, infrastructure, property rights, employment, political participation, and violence against women. To build on the MDGs and realize those not yet achieved, the UN Member States in 2015 adopted 17 Sustainable Development Goals (SDGs) to be realized by 2030. The SDGs endeavor to address a number of global concerns, such as eradicating all forms of poverty (goal 1); promoting health and wellbeing for all (goal 3); gender equality and the empowerment of women and girls (goal 5); and reducing inequality within and among countries (goal 10). Central to all of these is the enactment of **power**.

In this chapter we examine CP's historical and potential contribution to gender equality and **equity**. What would a vision of wellbeing and liberation for women around the world be, and how can we know if we are part of the problem or part of the solution, as community psychologists and in our personal lives? If **sexism**, genderism and all forms of conscious and unconscious gendered entitlement are the problem, are feminisms the solution? Selected examples are used to anchor the chapter. We write from within our own communities in Australia, South Africa, and Indonesia, as feminist community psychologists working for change within and beyond our profession.

Historical Context

Why a Women's Movement?

Throughout history, every society has practiced some form of institutionalized disempowerment and oppression of women. Religious organizations often lead conservative backlashes on reproductive rights, blocking international aid funds for family planning programs, actively promoting homophobic and non-binary gender-devaluing discourses, and retaining narrow definitions of gender roles. The rise of religious extremism, encompassing Christian, Hindu, Muslim, and Jewish versions, saw heightened legal and social restrictions on women in 25 countries in the late 1990s/early 2000s (El Sadaawi, 2005). But more recently, sexual abuse scandals have challenged the patriarchal structures that enabled and even sanctioned abuse on a previously unimagined scale. And, in ongoing waves of consciousness-raising and collective action, women have practiced and continuously refined a range of social resistances to counter oppression. Resistance by women to systemic oppression is almost a definition of feminism.

Feminism's "first wave" centered around women's right to vote in Western democracies in the late 19th century and early 20th century. In the post-World War II Western (or Global Northern) world, the timing of so-called second-wave feminism paralleled the emergence of CP in the late 1960s. From the 1970s onwards, feminism drew on a range of perspectives, including liberal feminism (which emphasized equality with men), Marxist feminism (which made links with class and other forms of oppression), radical feminism (which argued that women should distance themselves from male norms), feminist psychology, postmodern feminisms, postcolonial feminisms (which highlighted the long-lasting political, economic, and cultural impacts of colonization on women in the Global South and postcolonial world), and feminisms within a range of cultural and geopolitical contexts (some African American women preferred to describe themselves as "womanist").

In the 21st century, new material feminisms have emerged, incorporating a post-humanist, post-constructionist stance to thinking about diversity and its intersections. These include trans-feminism and other more recently emergent models of gender non-conformity that envision more gender and variously other diverse future subcultures and societies. These non-conformity-embracing feminisms, or "diversity feminisms" represent a more recent, post-structural theoretical and social development, shifting further away from polarized traditions of binary, birth-assigned gender based on externally assessed judgements.

Individual and group activism against gender and all stereotyping confines are stressed in this "next wave." More pluralized notions of social **gender identity** in post-information age society are actively questioned, as is the readiness of people who espouse particular forms of diversity to embrace other diversities and personalized non-conformity. Gender is presented as falling along a continuum of bio-social experiences, rather than placed in a polar-opposed binary based on birth-assigned male or female anatomical gender, and/or on normatively defined social roles. (The Key Terms section at the end of this chapter outlines some of the language required to more meaningfully conduct discourse with professionals and gender non-conforming individuals who are now utilizing these more inclusive, more extensively "unconscious entitlement sensitive" diversity feminisms.)

These various feminisms all work towards the common goal of improving women's lives. Each has its own views on how improvements may be achieved and indeed what constitutes improvement. The vigorous ongoing debates among feminisms can confuse outsiders and frustrate feminist theorists and activists themselves – yet why would it be assumed, or even desirable, that all women, or all feminists, speak with a unified voice? bell hooks (**2000b**) challenged hegemonic feminism's notion of a shared female experience. She argued that it did not consider differences between women and that, in contrast to middle-class women, working-class women were compelled to work out of necessity. hooks further contended that feminism will not bring about real transformation if men and boys are not included in the feminist struggle: "we have to do so much work to correct the assumption deeply embedded in the cultural psyche that feminism is anti-male. Feminism is anti-sexism" (p. 12). This view suggests that both men and women, and arguably more so, **transgender** and gender diverse minority groups, suffer oppression if they deviate from prescribed powerful hegemonic patriarchal practices.[1]

---

[1] For a fuller introduction to feminist thought, see Tong (2014), or, for a straightforward girl-friendly version, Kaz Cooke's *Girl Stuff* (2016). Cooke lists the gains made by feminism in the 20th century from a teenager's perspective.

Community Psychology, Gender, and Feminisms

Within psychology, both feminist and community psychologists developed critiques of mainstream psychology, while in the 1970s within the wider community, feminism and CP were originally aligned with human rights movements like the gay liberation, civil rights, anti-apartheid, and peace movements. In Australia and Aotearoa/New Zealand in the same decade, Aboriginal and Maori activists (some of whom were also feminists) were making their presence felt. Similarly, in South Africa, gender activists were centrally involved in fighting against Apartheid and exploitation. The battle against exploitation continues today, often involving strong collaborations between women *and* men who identify with feminism.

Feminist psychologists directed their critique towards psychology's "mismeasure of women" (Tavris, 1992) and the individualization and pathologization of women's collective distress (e.g., Caplan, 1995). Women had not participated equally in psychology's establishment as a science, and feminists mistrusted its application to women's lives. As Weisstein (1968/1993) observed back in 1968, "Psychology has nothing to say about what women are really like ... essentially because psychology does not know" (p. 197).

The 1970s feminist slogan "the personal is political" meant psychology was (and still is) fertile ground for action, and that political questions could be seen as psychology's business. But some early attempts to paint women into the psychological picture were themselves criticized for perpetuating victim-blaming (e.g., by suggesting that women's "fear of success" was the real reason for the glass ceiling) or reinforcing gendered stereotypes of masculinity and femininity – and leaving oppressive, inequitable social and organizational structures unchallenged (Mednick, 1989). Examining texts and courses on the psychology of women, Crowley-Long (1998) concluded that "feminist psychology has adopted a much too narrow political focus" (p. 128) in drawing almost exclusively from liberal feminist frameworks and positivist methods, and not enough from radical and socialist alternatives. She argued that a broader frame of reference would be more inclusive of marginalized groups and more sensitive to the socioeconomic forces shaping the lives of women from diverse backgrounds. Her argument resonates even more strongly when considered from a global perspective.

Community psychologists' critique of mainstream psychology emerged in many countries from its parent sub-disciplines of community mental health (clinical psychology) and applied social psychology. In contrast to feminist critiques, their concerns focused less on measurement and therapy, and more on the settings where psychological research and practice took place – they set about broadening their applications (e.g., prevention and macro-level intervention) and taking account of contexts (ecology and community). Thus, they distanced themselves from "the personal" as reflecting psychology's traditional individualistic stance, and mostly took up "public" ahead of "private" causes as their intervention targets.

Anne Mulvey's (1988) landmark article noted that CP and feminism shared similar critiques of victim-blaming ideologies; pushed beyond individual, adjustment-oriented solutions; called for new paradigms beyond the fragmentation and mystification of traditional disciplines; and developed similar change models and strategies. Both focused on social policy, prevention ahead of "cure," advocacy, empowerment, and the de-mystification of experts. Feminist consciousness-raising groups resonated with community psychologists' support for self-help groups and consumer-based movements.

But shared values and goals, and the common experience of "swimming against the tide" of mainstream psychology, did not lead to much integration between the two emergent sub-disciplines.

Even now, references to CP rarely appear in feminist psychology literature, while feminist community psychologists have struggled to have "women's issues" acknowledged within CP agendas.

How Far Have We Come?

Fox and Prilleltensky (1997) brought together a range of critical perspectives from the margins of psychology, enabling the possibility of dialogue between community and feminist psychologies as well as other non-mainstream approaches. The special double issue of the *American Journal of Community Psychology* (Bond, Hill, Mulvey, & Terenzio, 2000) provided a rich menu of feminist research and action. The special issue was organized around seven themes linking CP with feminist theory and research: attention to diversity; contextualized understanding, speaking from the standpoints of oppressed groups; collaboration; multi-level, multi-method approaches; reflexivity; and action orientation. Angelique and Culley's (2003) examination of two key journals led them to be optimistic about CP's increasingly pro-feminist stance. For them, adopting a feminist paradigm means explicitly acknowledging one's worldview – particularly important in a globalized environment. Ayalar-Alcantar, Dello Stritto, and Guzmán (2008) celebrated the trailblazing contributions of 55 women within the Society for Community Research & Action (APA Division 27). More recently, a special issue of the *Journal of Community Psychology* (Angelique & Mulvey, 2012) documented and progressed the co-creation of a feminist CP.

How do the Core Principles of Community Psychology Advance Gender Equity?

What do CP's founding fathers (and mothers) have to say about women's experiences? How far do their principles/approaches take us?

Transforming Systems: Ecology and Complexity In a Globalized World

CP's primary departure point from mainstream psychology was/is its emphasis on the central importance of context to any understanding of human behavior. In practice, this might mean conducting research in naturalistic settings, working with family and community systems as well as individuals, or seeking sociopolitical as well as intrapsychic explanations for presenting problems. Feminist theorists similarly argue for more complex explanations and psychosocial understandings of psychological processes and functioning, as alternatives to reductionist approaches that narrow down and systematically decontextualize the phenomena to be studied.

Ecological models that promote holistic understandings of the interrelatedness of human experiences can be helpful in addressing structural inequalities based on gender. For example, changes occurring in women's lives that are related to their reproductive systems are often represented as purely biomedical problems (e.g., menopause) and psychological theories often add an "emotional disorder" layer (e.g., premenstrual syndrome, "empty nest syndrome"), necessitating therapeutic "treatment." An ecological perspective would take account of society's expectations and valuing of women at different points in their lives. Such a perspective would ensure that the demands of parenting adolescents, caring for ageing parents, renegotiating work roles, having less access to retirement benefits, or finding oneself devalued by the appearance of gray hair, would all be factored into any understanding of women's lives at mid-life – not to mention the freedom and energy that might be available to post-menopausal women. Ecological understandings thus invite researchers and practitioners to move away from single-factor causal models that promote medicalized solutions or individualized victim-blaming. And the next step is to embrace the complexity and tolerate the uncertainty required for the "dynamic co-creation of identities in multilayered contexts" as Angelique and Mulvey (2012, p. 1) described the "ongoing project" to develop a truly feminist CP. Such a project is particularly challenging in countries like Indonesia or Russia (and in some US states) where fundamentalist groups are increasingly demanding "zero tolerance" of what they describe as "uncertain" categories.

Families are perhaps the most obvious example of an ecological system with particular implications for women vis-à-vis men/partners and children. Patriarchal constructions implicitly or explicitly defined marriage as a hierarchical, male-headed, individualistic institution within which women and children were considered property. As family demographics and understandings of human diversity have shifted gradually, new family forms are demanding more complexity-sensitive research methods and understanding. Some obvious developments include dramatic increases in same-sex parenting and fostering, more transparent and openly polyamorous and multi-partner group-identified families, and parenting in transgender and gender transitioning contexts. Highly vocal social movements have successfully lobbied internationally for legalization changes, enshrining equality for any consenting adults seeking formal recognition of their marriages.

The notion of "family change" refers not only to those families clearly going through change (e.g., in the process of separation, or of gender transition of a child, sibling, or parent), but to all families who, on a daily basis, renegotiate their relationships to one another. Developing ways of respectfully engaging with a changing family ecology is essential for any services provided to parents, children and families. Yet women have historically and biologically been held responsible for children, and this continues to be the case. Where women do have access to income, they often experience the double burden of income-generation and domestic responsibilities. In East Timor, "there is very little progress in getting men to pour their own water, let alone share in domestic work" (International Women's Development Agency (IWDA) 2008, p. 5). In Australia, it has been estimated that fathers spend on average just one minute per weekday alone with their children (Craig, 2008) (see Box 16.1 to consider international care work).

From a feminist perspective, the downside of ecological and systems models is that they usually lack any power analysis and can risk promoting homeostatic "status quo" solutions to problems that require fundamental change. Between the rhetoric of terms like "ecology" and "prevention" and the reality that entrenched power is not easily given away, we need to keep asking what safeguards must be in place to ensure that interventions don't work against the groups they were intended to assist. Ecological conceptualizations must factor in social justice and human rights considerations if they are to pave the way for systems-level interventions that lead to social change. Theoretical models must involve naming of power differentials along with recognition of structural inequality as a primary cause of personal distress, whether these differentials and inequities arise from gender, race, class, age, sexuality, and/or other determinants.

Example: Moving Beyond Band-aid Interventions

Instead of merely addressing the symptoms of structurally entrenched inequalities and oppression, the Intervention with Microfinance for Aids and Gender Equity (IMAGE) Study (Kim et al., 2009) in the rural Limpopo province in South Africa is an example of an intervention that addressed an intersection between gender inequality, poverty, and health. Based on the model of the Grameen Bank, this community-based project loaned poor women money (i.e., microfinance) to start small businesses and also provided them with an HIV and gender training program. Compared to the control groups, those women who were in the IMAGE project challenged the acceptability of violence and reported a significant reduction in levels of intimate partner violence; participants also reported higher levels of self-esteem and self-efficacy skills and improved health-seeking behaviors (for a comprehensive discussion of the IMAGE study see Kim et al., 2009; World Health Organization 2015).

Prevention, Promotion, and Social Change

CP students soon become familiar with the "broken bridge" or "clifftop rescue" (see Chapter 6) metaphors of prevention – the notion that it is better to look upstream and repair the bridge or fence than to keep calling in emergency services to rescue those who fall into the water and need to be fished out downstream. But have we actually improved someone's quality of life if all we've done is remove a potential hazard, without questioning why it was allowed to fall into disrepair in the first place? Suicide prevention programs that focus on taking sheets from prisoners' beds or raising the safety rails on a bridge do nothing to address the poverty and desperation behind disproportionate incarceration rates among Indigenous communities or suicide rates among young men in rural communities.

An evidence-based prevention approach to depression in women of all ages would address the oppression and abuse that underpin much of the everyday experiences of women across a range of circumstances. But many approaches that claim to be "preventive" are narrowly focused on medical diagnostic explanations and ameliorative, intra-individual rather than systems-level solutions (McMullen & Stoppard, 2006). Individualized pathologization is all too evident in mental health initiatives that confine prevention to early identification of genetic predispositions to bipolar disorder, for example, or to early detection of symptoms to encourage speedier referral for treatment, often with antidepressant medication only.

Of course ambulances are still needed as well as fences and bridges. Prevention strategies can gain much from the experiences of those who have fallen off the metaphorical cliff. People living with HIV-AIDS have been heavily involved in designing and delivering prevention strategies, including "safe sex" education campaigns. Our vision of real primary prevention is the community center in the main street far from the river in flood – where women (and men and children) can sing, dance, work, and create.

Example: Homelessness Is Gendered

The introductory chapter of this book points out that the majority of the world's population is homeless or in insecure accommodation according to many definitions of homelessness. In many countries, formal housing systems fail to serve the bulk of the population, with whole communities living on the streets or in the bush. It is self-evident that homeless people – men, women, children – are without economic independence and/or the ongoing means to obtain adequate shelter.

The experience of homelessness is qualitatively different for men and women, in part because cultural and political assumptions, both explicit and implicit, continue to be promoted about what is "women's work." This work usually includes caring for children, husbands, older people, and extended family, and is often unpaid or poorly remunerated. Women's housing security often depends on the caring work they undertake within the family or their local or cultural community. Homelessness for older, socially female-identified people is thus often brought about by their lower, shared, or non-existent incomes over the life course and their long periods out of the paid workforce while raising children.

Women (including trans-women) are often not identified in homelessness statistics, which in themselves vary in definition, because they are less likely to "sleep rough" and more likely to find shelter in relationships or housing arrangements that expose them to sexual, physical, and/or economic abuse. Sex work is typically seen as "female work," and subject to the same problems characterizing such work: it is unpaid or poorly paid, but with the added problem of being illegal (usually), stigmatized, outside the mainstream economy – and unsafe.

A feminist CP analysis would factor in the prerequisites of economic independence for women when considering how to prevent women's homelessness. Those prerequisites include:

- access to education – still far from a universal right for women
- legislation and policy frameworks supporting paid work for women
- cultural beliefs, norms, and practices that support female-identified households outside of patriarchal structures.

For both **cisgender** and trans women, preventing homelessness can mean ensuring safety in leaving violent or abusive relationships. Women may find it difficult to leave a family situation when they have no economic supports of their own, and especially when they are responsible for children. It is very difficult to either earn a living or parent effectively without secure accommodation. Women leaving a male or female violent partner (with or without children) may need to escape and hide, and some even find themselves forced to live in their car. In other settings, accommodations "on the streets" are often less secure and safe for women and their children than the violent home they are fleeing.

Most developed countries have a system of child protection where the state has the authority to remove children from parent(s) who are not deemed able to care for them, due to violence or neglect of responsibility. For mothers, this situation may lead to an irresolvable choice between leaving children with a violent partner/parent or escaping with them to homelessness, which in turn leaves them vulnerable to child protection intervention. Many countries have refuge systems established from the 1970s onwards as safe houses for women fleeing domestic violence. In Australia these shelters are temporary and sometimes inaccessible due to long waiting lists. Others do not allow trans women or children (especially boys) over a certain age (often 12 years). This situation often has dire consequences, particularly for trans women.

A CP approach to preventing homelessness by enabling economic independence for women might be rights-based, ensuring that no group is without universal rights, including adequate housing and consideration of differing emotional recovery and safety support needs. The more difficult challenge is how to operationalize those rights. A cautionary tale from South Africa involves a woman who fought for the right of "access to reasonable housing" under the Constitution (De Vos, 2001). Despite Mrs. Grootboom winning her case, she died homeless in 2008 and her right to reasonable housing was never delivered by the Government (see http://constitutionallyspeaking.co.za/irene-grootboom-died-homeless-forgotten-no-c-class-mercedes-in-sight/).

In Australia and the UK, there has been a strong tradition of public housing for those with less access to economic resources. This tradition has considerably weakened over the last 20 years, and the focus has shifted towards supporting people and case-managing their economic, mental health, or substance abuse issues, sometimes in "safe" accommodation and other times wherever they are living. In contrast, "Housing First" models, where individuals with serious mental illness and co-occurring substance problems receive their own apartments with ongoing "wraparound" services available on site (but not necessarily mandated), have proved successful in a range of contexts (e.g., Nelson, 2010). Marybeth Shinn's meticulous research on homelessness over decades highlights how variables such as economic hardship cause homelessness, and illustrates how CP can contribute to evidence-based policy and solutions (Shinn & McCormack, 2017). She likens homelessness to a game of musical chairs: where then there is not enough to go round it is the poor and socially excluded who are left homeless (Shinn, 2009).

Community psychologists have a role at a number of levels in operationalizing the right to safe and secure accommodation and to the economic independence that supports women's ability to maintain that housing. I [Colleen] am a member of the Board of Management of a community housing organization. In this role, my CP background has been invaluable, especially in advising on how best to advocate for homeless women and children to legislators and policy-makers. For example, until recently, children accompanying their homeless parents (typically mothers) were not counted as homeless. This meant that the "no data no problem" factor made it easier for governments and policy-makers to deny or ignore problems for which there was limited statistical evidence. One of my organization's proudest achievements was being instrumental in having children counted in homelessness statistics, and then successfully attracting funding for a range of programs to support homeless families. But it should be noted that the programs were developed first, and were able to be scaled up when data were available to support the lived experience of many women and children, along with the practice wisdom of experienced housing workers.

Community, Networks, Partnership, Social Capital, and Sense of Community

There is increasing recognition in international development contexts that women's empowerment and education are the keys to real change in disadvantaged communities (United Nations, 2015a; Van der Gaag, 2008). Grass-roots community campaigns have often involved women fighting for the right to control their fertility, to limit the sale of war toys, or to bear witness to the "disappearance" of their children under repressive regimes.

The downside of community metaphors lies in concerns that a focus on public aspects of community may render women invisible, by prioritizing "public" over "private" concerns. The minimization of "domestic" violence by police and other authorities as less serious than other forms of crime is a prime example. The uncritical acceptance of "community" as an ideal can be problematic when it means the subordination of legitimate concerns to "the greater good." Women who were urged to leave the paid workforce to set up house in the post-World War II period were sacrificed to a narrow vision of community rebuilding. In such cases, a focus on community can have the effect of submerging women's voices beneath the louder notes of (usually male, often patriarchal) community leaders.

The policy and practice question then is: How do community-based organizations and local and national governments work with community members in ways that support the strengths of that community and address individual and collective needs (Turner, 2008). The following example from the Indonesian context highlights some possibilities for women's community participation, even within traditionally assigned gender roles.

Example: Community Networks as Platforms for Advocacy

Indonesia has recently been shifting toward a more democratic political system. Against this background, the concept of community participation is gaining widespread popularity in Indonesian community development practices. Encouraged by such a context, I [Monica] undertook doctoral research that examined the meaning of participation from the vantage point of a local community. Specifically, the study investigated the practice of community participation in a community-based program targeted to tackle discrimination and marginalization experienced by people with disabilities. This program was initiated by a local non-governmental organization (NGO) in a partnership with five villages in Bantul District, Yogyakarta.

Researching this program, I have learned that understanding the broader sociohistorical and political context of a partnership is critical in examining to what extent it has met its promise of promoting equality and access to decision-making. My conversations with villagers suggest that even a well-intended partnership can inadvertently foster existing inequalities between dominant and marginalized groups in a community, such as between "able" and "disabled" bodies, local bureaucrats, and regular villagers, and also between male and female community activists.

In these villages, community health cadres (trained volunteers)[2] are the backbone for community activities included in the program. Although not formally regulated as women-only positions, none of the community health cadres in these villages is male. It is highly likely that gender role stereotypes are behind this situation. In Indonesian culture, the assumption of the nurturing nature of women and the traditional division of labor in families (women as housewives) has conditioned women to take up various voluntary roles in their communities. Such a tendency is not confined to Indonesia, but is almost universally apparent (Musick & Wilson, 2008; Osborne, Baum, & Ziersch, 2009).

---

[2] Cadre is a term that is usually used to call those voluntarily working for community programs initiated by government, both at the local and national level. The word cadre seems to evoke a sense of being observant to authorities who own the programs, rather than the word volunteer. That is why government officials appear to prefer using the word cadre.

Historically, community health cadres were recruited by the government as non-paid fieldwork officers for national health programs. Thus, there is a common image that these cadres are the tool of the government whose main function is to ensure the delivery of government programs, whether or not the programs meet the needs of the targeted community. These cadres are usually depicted as a symbol of women's subordination within the patriarchal system, which positions women as dutiful servants of their community whose work does not need payment (Suryakusuma, 1996). However, my observation suggests that such depiction risks ignoring the women's agency as social actors in their locality. There are instances that indicate how these women tactfully function in their cadre role to promote issues which otherwise would have been overlooked by the decision makers in the community. For instance, one of the cadres is actively reviving what used to be a popular traditional art performance in the community. This activity can bring together youth and elder community members who are usually disengaged from the community life. With work taking up most of people's time, collective rituals and ceremonies that previously were important social gatherings are often missing from communities' routines.

This example indicates that women can have an opportunity to "hijack" the existing social spaces as a platform to advocate issues that matter most for them, and to restore a shared sense of community. It suggests the potential of initiating gradual changes through the existing social platform. Equally important however, are efforts to improve the quality of women's participation by ensuring that they have equal share in decision-making and are not confined in the "nurturing" roles. The next example confirms the importance of being vigilant about the quality of women's participation in their community.

Example: Promoting Environmental Sustainability Through Community Participation

Environmental sustainability is a social issue as much as it is about the physical environment. In the Bantul Region in Yogyakarta Province, Indonesia, where I [Monica] conducted my fieldwork, the social dimension of environmental sustainability is reflected in how people are dealing with the issue of disaster risk reduction (DRR). My field observations suggest that sense of community is central to the success of DRR programs. In addition, the observations indicate that gender significantly influences the way people experience their community.

Following the massive earthquake that hit the region in 2006, DRR has been a prioritized issue in Bantul. Geographically located in one of the world's most seismically active regions, the risks of earthquake and tsunami are ever-present. Therefore, local communities are a regular target for various DRR programs organized by either government or non-government organizations. The ultimate goals of such programs are to develop resilient local communities that can independently identify risks, mobilize local resources to mitigate risks, and promote better adaptation to the environment. Achieving these goals requires an inclusive process that fosters community members' willingness to participate in programs (Korstanje, 2014).

The participative nature of DRR is formally acknowledged in various speeches and discussions related to DRR activities in these villages; however, there were only a few occasions in which related actors (e.g., local community members, government officers, NGO staff) engaged in in-depth discussions about the nature of participation. Most of the time, the discussions focused on the technical aspects of DRR such as identifying disaster threats specific to the communities, developing evacuation maps, and establishing a legal body responsible for carrying out each village's DRR plan.

In these forums, usually professional practitioners (i.e., government officers and NGO staff) would present information and knowledge about DRR, with the community members invited as the targeted audience. For the practitioners, knowledge and technical skills related to the concept of DRR were perceived as the starting point. However, for community members, ensuring community involvement was the most crucial component. The practical utility of including different points of view in development initiatives is reflected further in considering that the majority of community activists involved were women.

As the region, in general, shifts toward a more industrialized society, it is becoming more difficult to attract community involvement in volunteer-based collective activities like the DRR programs. In this shifting context, such programs rely on a small number of mainly female volunteers, and the types of activities they engage in can reinforce existing stereotypes and power dynamics. Women would ordinarily have little or even zero involvement in the decision-making process in the programs. However, when it comes to the daily operations, they often carry most of the workload. At a glance, such a situation may create an impression that women have leading roles. But without ongoing critical analysis, this kind of participation may actually reinforce existing gender stereotypes and entrench gender-based inequality.

Power, Empowerment, and Depowerment

According to Burman (1997), traditional psychology's individual focus "has particular difficulty understanding power relations as socially constructed frameworks that may be expressed by individuals, but are created in larger social contexts" (p. 146). The operation of power is central to all feminist analyses. Why do so many men use violence against women? "Because they can," was how one police superintendent replied. Whether measured in terms of information, institutionalized authority, resources, decision-making, coercion, or privilege, power differentials can be seen to constrain or expand the choices available to women and men in a wide range of social contexts – not the pseudo-choice of coffee blends or ringtones, but real choices about how life is to be lived, individually and collectively.

Box 16.1 Women's Work – Whose Labor?

The Western world has become reliant on the skills of elite professional, educated women and expects them to continue in paid work, often for 50 or more hours per week. But neither the original 19th century "8-hour day" nor current campaigns factored in the second (domestic) shift worked by many women, or the "emotional labor" that is primarily women's work (Guy & Newman, 2004).

Poor women have always acted as housemaids, wet-nurses, or nannies to wealthy families. Globalization now means that women from poor countries such as the Philippines, Mexico, or Eastern Europe are forced by economic necessity to leave their own children behind (or sometimes, to prostitute them) to provide cheap immigrant labor, often illegal, in more affluent countries.

Similarly, men in South Asian countries often seek dangerous "slave labor" work in economically booming countries like Saudi Arabia, leaving their wives to carry the domestic load alone.

The exploitation of women in domestic work reproduces and widens the First World (minority) – Third World (majority) divide and makes real and reciprocal alliances between women structurally difficult, both within the "developed" world and between the minority and majority worlds (see Anderson, 2000). Privileged women of conscience, like Naomi Wolf (2001), can see the inequities operating in their daily lives:

> I learned that if I sat in a park with our baby and chatted with an immigrant

nanny who was wiping the drool of a white baby ... within minutes she would show me a photo of her own children far away, whom she might not have seen for years. And her eyes would fill with tears ... These women must often cross oceans and leave their children, big kids and small, with relatives. They often live in rooms at the margins of other people's families ... so that they (the children) can have school uniforms and good food, education and a better chance at life. (p. 219)

Power is not something we have, but something we swim in, a matter of discourse and practice rather than quantity. Feminist understandings of power have shifted from unitary notions of something bad when men have it and good when women have it, towards recognition of its multiple levels of operation. And like racism, its operation in sexist terms has become more subtle – it is rare, at least in Western society, for women to be openly referred to as property, yet the notion is far from dead. A range of gendered power disparities can still increase the risk of cis women, trans women and non-binary identifying individuals experiencing violence within relationships, and diminish their power to escape. Attitudes toward gender varied individuals can be particularly brutal, pathologizing, and often deadly.

The narrowing of gendered power differentials over the past 100 years in societies where women can now vote, be educated, earn an independent income, control their fertility, and participate in sports and other hitherto "unladylike" activities indicates that change, however slow, is possible. Related to the increase in women's education, Gakidou, Cowling, Lozano, and Murray (2010) estimate that 4.2 million child deaths have been prevented in the past 40 years worldwide, and that between 1990 to 2013, maternal mortality has also decreased by 45 percent (United Nations, 2015a). But the experiences of women under successive regimes in places like Afghanistan (and indeed in some US states where hard-won reproductive rights are being wound back) show how fragile such gains can be.

Horacek, 1994, *Unrequited Love*, Nos 1–100

Empowerment is a founding metaphor within both CP and feminism. But its critics have argued that it has been too easily reduced to simplistic notions of individual power. And conservative governments have co-opted the word "self-empowerment" as a counter to the more radical demands of minority groups for self-determination. We think empowerment is more usefully understood as a process rather than an active verb ("I cannot empower you, but our conversation or active engagement might be experienced as empowering to one or both of us"). Rape will not be eliminated by having all women learn self-defence skills; attention also needs to be directed towards "depowering the powerful," or at least towards creating space for more collaborative, inter-gender power-sharing partnerships.

As Perkins (1991) notes, "power does not have to be repressive – it can actually facilitate better, more satisfying lives for people" (p. 136). As feminist community psychologists from different backgrounds, the challenge for all five authors is to recognize both our relative privilege and relative powerlessness as springboards to action. We are aware of how our respective power and privilege may be useful to the communities we are working with. At other times, our own powerlessness enables us to firmly align ourselves with other women's experiences of oppression.

Diversity, Marginalization, Inclusion, and Intersectionality

Diversity is a complex term that often refers to cultural or ethnic diversity but can and should encompass gender, class, age, religion, languages, abilities, geography, and sexual orientation. It is often viewed in organizations and systems as "that which is different or other," or people and practices that do not conform to the norm. In most Western organizational contexts, like universities, White, male, heterosexual, and Christian values are considered the norm, and all forms of difference are tolerated but seldom affirmed. Affirmation of difference is seldom encouraged because assumptions are made that consensus alone promotes social inclusion in organizations or society. Yet post-constructionist feminist approaches encourage affirmation of difference as productive for organizations and society (Braidotti, 2013).

Diversity-affirming approaches are important as denial of difference with an emphasis on similarity and equality leaves "others," including multiply power-disadvantaged groups (consider Black, transgender, and/or Muslim "others" for example), to assimilate to the values in the organization (or society), resulting in a paradox for marginalized people in those organizations (Akhtar, 2014). This paradox arises because to participate at all, assimilation into the over-arching organizational culture requires individuals to deny the reality that group differences can be positive and desirable. Instead, marginalized people (if they choose to "assimilate") must accept and perform identities that do not necessarily resonate with their own personal, social, and cultural experiences. They are constantly enmeshed in a double bind that leaves them constructed as a liability and a disadvantage, even though the organization may superficially acknowledge that diversity is desirable.

Linked to the idea of difference is the idea that everybody must be treated "equally." Even though "equal treatment" sounds acceptable and just, it becomes unfair when it assumes that we live in a society without the deep inequalities all humans experience globally. Equity and equitable treatment is more desirable as it considers group needs and merit as opposed to merit only (Prilleltensky, 2012).

The equity/equality cartoon in Chapter 3 (p. 55) indicates that some people and groups need more resources than others so that key CP values of fairness and social justice can prevail in society. Affirmative action policies that emphasize equity as opposed to equality consider both merit and need by seeking to level playing fields and minimize continued inequalities for disadvantaged people such as women or older employees in job application and selection processes.

Such concerns apply to psychology too. Fine (2012) and many others have argued that dominant voices in mainstream psychology reflect White, male and heterosexual norms:

> We seem to have forgotten to ask critical questions like 'What kinds of evidence are being privileged? What are we not seeing?' in our rush to accept ever-narrowing notions of evidence-based practice in the face of irrefutable indicators of the gendered, raced, classed and sexualized collateral damage of economic and political crisis. (p. 3)

Psychology itself, therefore, needs to diversify the "voice" that authors (and author-izes) its claims to scientific status and pronouncements on the nature of evidence and "truth." While cultural diversity is given lip service, and guidelines warn against "bias" in research and practice, institutionalized practices often work against equal power distribution and opportunities for participation by diverse groups, interests, and individuals – the very communities we claim to serve.

Promoting diversity is no simple matter of token representation or assimilationist melting pots. Dimensions of diversity are commonly experienced as dimensions of inequality and discrimination, often with compounding effects. Crenshaw (1989) used the term **"intersectionality"** to describe the compounding effects of marginalization. She conceptualized identities in a grid-like fashion where multiple identities co-exist and intersect and can never exist in isolation of each other. Intersectionality challenges the notion that multiple aggregations of marginalization or privilege are listed additively. Multiple co-existing identity locations fundamentally shape individual subjectivities of race, class, and gender, even though race remains a marker of diversity. This means all women, for example, do not have the same oppressive experiences and power in patriarchal society, but that some, because of White privilege or middle class privilege, have more power than working class women (and men) of color.

During the 1990s, there was a vigorous debate between dominant forms of feminism and the increasingly visible feminisms of the non-Western world and of Indigenous women and women of color. Critics argued that Western liberal feminism had largely advantaged middle-class White women and had not necessarily had a flow-on effect to other social subgroups of women. Some reasons advanced included the fear that, in sharing newfound power, advantaged women risk losing favor, ground, or personal power. Meara and Day (2000) acknowledged that "in the short term a more inclusive feminism is likely to have more integrity and less power" (p. 260). White privilege has, for example meant that White women in the US and South Africa benefited most from affirmative action policies. Black men were the second group to benefit from such policies, and Black women derived the least benefit. This pattern of representation and power imbalance has also been observed at times in CP (Ayalar-Alcantar, Dello Stritto, & Guzmán, 2008; Gridley & Breen, 2007; Mulvey, 1988). For example, in the South African context, men and White women typically occupy high status posts in research, teaching, leadership, and publications, and women, often Black, are overrepresented as workers in less socially valued "frontline" community organizations (Carolissen & Swartz, 2009).

Affirming diversity within CP demands a commitment. First, to expand the range of voices represented in its publications, theory-building, and applications from token inclusion to a critical, sustainable mass. Next, beyond the "add voices" strategy, comes the promise and challenge of affirming the complexity of intersectionality – of recognizing that we are all more than the sum of our demographic dimensions, and that often, these dimensions are in conflict. And are we truly prepared for the field to be transformed by the inclusion *as equal partners* of multiple "others" we had assumed to have fewer resources or had defined by perceived deficits – homeless substance users, young single mothers, non-binary identifying persons, women in veils, refugees, Indigenous elders, clothing outworkers?

CP has taken steps towards affirming global and geographic diversity with international conferences in Puerto Rico (2006), Portugal (2008), Mexico (2010), Spain (2012), Brazil (2014), South Africa (2016), Chilé (2018), and Australia (2020). Participants experience the challenges of multilingual presentations, unfamiliar ways of being, and differing worldviews. Such events serve to de-center our discipline from its heavily North American, Caucasian, middle class assumptive base. But they are necessarily elite events, increasingly difficult to justify environmentally and in terms of their real effects on global and local diversity-based inequalities. Is this the best we can do for equity, social justice, and human rights?

Example: Intersectionality

In the post-1994 democratic South Africa, dominant discourses of national social inclusion suggest that South African children are "born free" and experience few impacts of legislated inequity in apartheid South Africa. However, Carolissen, Van Wyk, and Pick-Cornelius (2012) explored how a group of colored[3] adolescent girls talked about their intersectional experiences of race, gender, and class in their school and community. The girls' experiences represented a counternarrative to the inclusionary discourse associated with "rainbowism." A focus group interview as well as observations were conducted with 14 girls who participated in a pre-existing life-skills development program at a primary school, in a peri-urban area in Stellenbosch. Their reports of these experiences were often contradictory and involved girls both rejecting and re-inscribing micro-aggressions that impacted negatively on their identities.

Despite having grown up in a democratic South Africa, the young poor girls (aged 13–15) were found to have classed and gendered experiences, which were internalized and expressed as racialized experiences. They associated middle-class lifestyles with "Whiteness." One participant gave examples of upper middle-class colored men (sports stars and politicians) who married White women precisely because they had money and had acculturated themselves to becoming more desirable to White women through financially-acquired, middle-class power. Her responses imply that she and her peers would never be able to consider marrying middle-class colored men, because these men aspired both to Whiteness and to marrying White women. Some participants also said that middle-class colored children in their community thought they were White and better than themselves because they attended schools that were previously White.

In the group, girls were caught in a bind of both idealizing and rejecting Whiteness. They made observations that White people supported their children in further post-school education,

---

[3] We concur with scholars that race is a social construction and that there is no biological evidence for race (Soudien, 2012). The term 'colored' is a remnant of the apartheid system of racial categorization and oppression that ranked people according to their physical features as either White, colored, Indian, or Black. This racial classification entrenched White privilege and Black disadvantage, which denied the majority of South Africans access to resources. Although the democratic government of South Africa has attempted to dismantle the oppression and inequality by using the apartheid categories for redress, the legacy and deep internalization of apartheid race categories continue to shape the lives of all South Africans today (Bundy, 2014).

worked harder, and were wealthier. In contrast, the work ethic of colored people was questioned, with some girls suggesting application of a stereotype that colored people were "lazy" and just "get pregnant at school." This kind of comment reinscribed negative micro-aggressions to colored people like themselves, until another girl in the group rejected this view. She claimed that merit does not exist because inheritance has given White people farms and property and that White people buy drugs in their community. This shocked some girls because they couldn't believe that some White people are drug users.

When girls re-inscribe such micro-aggressions, they unwittingly collude with dominant social discourses and reinforce White supremacy. At the same time, they also display agency in resisting dominant discourses that devalue them. Young girls not only learn how to negotiate the spaces they physically inhabit, they also learn how to negotiate a neo-liberal world where a number of commodities such as branded goods and education have become desirable objects and markers of success associated with Whiteness. Such internalized attitudes are fundamental learning experiences their educators have to engage with when working with girls who experience multiple oppressions. The study's authors suggest that to work in anti-oppressive ways, we should engage learners on issues of power so we may start to build on the beginnings of resistance that are clear in these girls' responses.

Subjectivity and Reflexivity (Warning – you are about to enter big word territory!)

Notions of subjectivity and reflexivity are drawn from postmodern, poststructuralist, and social constructionist epistemologies that challenged the heavy reliance of psychology (and most modern sciences) on a positivist paradigm of "value-free," objective, measurement-focused research and a concomitant commitment to "evidence-based" practice. As the name suggests, poststructuralist approaches question the existence of a single human consciousness or reality, and hence emphasize plurality and tolerance of difference. While CP aspires to a more contextualized, ecologically valid and socially useful praxis, its entrenched North American hegemony has largely been impervious to the emergence in Europe and elsewhere of postmodern psychology. In contrast, critical psychology has been influenced by Marxist, feminist, Foucauldian (poststructuralist/postmodern) and psychoanalytic theories.

Critical, community, and feminist psychologies all agree on the need to be context specific in theory, research, and practice. Each seeks to prioritize voices that need to be heard or have been silenced on specific issues, which is where subjectivity comes into play – recognizing that truth claims based on notions of an objective, value-free science are unsustainable. Feminist psychologists were among the first to open up space for multiple subjectivities to be acknowledged within the discipline. Separating the universal "he" into the gendered subject "she or he," they exposed the supposedly impartial, depersonalized observer as just another form of the male gaze.

Poststructuralist approaches have drawbacks of their own, partly because they demand a new jargon that seems very academic, and risks alienating the very women whose perspectives they aim to include, and partly because their strategies of discourse analysis and deconstruction do not necessarily lead to advocacy for non-dominant groups or action for social justice, more equitable societies overall, or wider human rights. But within psychology, poststructuralist approaches can be a breath of fresh air in a discipline long dominated by adherence to a narrow and impoverished version of empirical science. They press us to ask questions like: Whose voices are privileged and whose are muted? Who is constructed as "other" vis-à-vis the subjectivities of "the experts" – authors, researchers, theory builders, and practitioners? And who benefits?

Visions and Values Guiding Feminist Community Work

We noted earlier that all forms of feminisms work towards the common goal of improving women's lives. We wonder what a world without sexism, or "genderism" as it has been redefined, would look, feel, smell like? The Revolutionary Association of Women of Afghanistan (RAWA – www.rawa.org) has struggled since 1977 for personal and political liberation, providing a striking example of the determination of women in enormously difficult circumstances to fight for their vision of a just society. And in the 21st century Pakistani schoolgirl Malala Yousafzai, who was shot in 2012 by the Taliban for her activism on girls' rights to education, has become the most recognizable face of the Global Partnership for Education (GPE – www.globalpartnership.org/).

Psychologists, or indeed any outsider working with communities, must recognize that in almost any community they are working with, for, or in, there will be identifiable women and others sharing more mixed gender identities. This seems obvious, but women are often invisible under "bigger issues" of poverty, HIV-AIDS, terrorism, immigration, and now, climate change, or more mainstream issues such as "the economy."

Beyond the acknowledgement that women and plural, mixed gender identities are already everywhere, the range of their voices and intersectional experiences should be sought out, considered and included so organizations themselves can affirm diversity by transforming organizational cultures. There is no one "women's voice" in any debate, but usually a multitude of voices, sometimes in harmony with each other and in dissent with other voices, and at other times in harmony with sections of their communities and not with each other. Not only must the voices of all genders be included, they must be given equality with already more entitled, enshrined male voices. After all, one of the most widely recognized goals of the various waves of women's and other equity movements has been for all humans to be treated equitably, in relation to those who hold societal privilege, especially those who have multiple marginalized identities.

The process of any activity is also historically important in feminist valuing. Consultation or action should, therefore, be planned and undertaken in accordance with clearly stated and transparent values that have been agreed to via ongoing inclusion of relevant voices. Equitable process is often bypassed in an era when the dominant consumer and corporate market-derived rhetoric defines equity as no more than a "level-playing field" on which unregulated competition is free to produce "winners and losers." Relationships built in the course of community action should be positive and sustaining – in both feminist and CP terms, the end never justifies the means.

For practitioners, CP and feminist work needs a balance between "ambulance" work such as counseling, the provision of soup kitchens, or crisis support, with proactive advocacy, structural reform, and/or social action – and scope for ongoing celebration of small and large successes. One activity supports and enables the other, in an action-research loop. Research, advocacy, or social reform without connection to people living with "the problem" risks being all head and no heart, while frontline work that is all heart risks futility and burnout. Some services operationalize this balance so that for each hour of service delivery, workers spend another on prevention or social action. Practice that encompasses "big picture" involvement like "Reclaim the Night" and other activist marches, or advocacy for rape law reform or transgender medical access can re-energize workers seeking channels for accumulating rage – and are likely to be more effective as actions for long-term change. (See Box 16.2 for an example of how CP theory and research connect to gender-based violence.)

Box 16.2 Putting Vision into Action: Stopping Gender-based Violence

Gender-based violence is one area in which American community psychologists like Cris Sullivan, Rebecca Campbell and Nicole Allen have long been active in both research and practice. Allen and Javdani (2017) draw on CP principles in their analysis of violence, emphasizing multiple layers of context. Sullivan and her colleagues have focused on evaluating community interventions for abused women and their children and improving community responses to gender-based violence (e.g., Sullivan, 2011).

Here we bring together the core CP principles examined in this chapter, and consider how they might advance gender equity in the particular case of violence. Gender-based violence is as public as the tools of war and as private as the family home. As such, it remains one of the most pervasive, yet least acknowledged, human rights abuses throughout the world, and the following quotes illustrate its entrenched nature over time and across cultures:

> It was impossible to find any historical period in which there were no formulae... specifying the conditions under which a wife was deserving of a good clout. (Dobash & Dobash, 1979, p. 31)

> This is my weapon, this is my gun; one is for fighting, the other for fun. (Traditional military drill chant, origin unknown)

> If your partner owns a gun, you could be the next target. (www.issafrica.org/about-us/press-releases/if-your-partner-owns-a-gun-you-could-be-the-next-target)

Quotes like these illustrate why a feminist CP approach emphasizes the need for fundamental social change to remove the cultural supports of violence against women and other marginalized people. How does each of our core principles apply to such a challenge?

- *Transforming systems:* Violence against the disempowered, including all socially marginalized women, must be located in its full social and historical context of gender and power. At the relational level, violence must be viewed in terms of its controlling effects rather than stated intentions. However, ecologically derived explanations such as "the cycle of violence" or "it takes two to tango" are challenged by feminists who argue that such models assign women a role in precipitating or maintaining

violent behavior patterns by their intimate partners.

- *Community, networks, and partnership:* Tackling violence is a community responsibility, not a private matter. Approaches that treat violence against women as an individual or a relationship problem lead to practices that are victim-blaming and unsafe. At the relational level, equal partnerships need to replace the still too internationally dominant patriarchal model based on power and control, now well past its use-by date. Community-level partnerships between cis women, cis men and gender nonconforming individuals committed to ending gender-based violence, need to be based on the "depowerment" principle – where the dominant group makes the changes and the less powerful group benefits. This requires firm accountability mechanisms and monitoring by all parties.

- *Prevention:* Raising the status of women is essential. A systems-wide approach addressing the "cultural facilitators" of violence against women is needed to ensure that legal, medical, and social responses serve to expand the options available to women experiencing violence. For example, Ackerson and Subramanian (2008) examined socioeconomic and demographic patterns in intimate partner violence (IPV) in India, and concluded that "challenging cultural norms to promote the status of women and increasing the educational and economic opportunities for all people could decrease the prevalence of IPV" (p. 81).

- *Power:* Questions that need to be asked of any theory of violence include: Does it deal with violence in terms of gender and power issues? Does it couch the problem in gender blind ways, like "the violent couple"? Does it encourage perpetrators to take responsibility for the violence? Does it blame the victim in any way? Does it directly confront the violence as a central issue OR as a side issue to a "larger" problem, a "by-product" of a bad relationship? Does it work to limit perpetrators' power by enforcing legal sanctions? Does it work to expand victims' options in housing, income support, job opportunities, legal redress, parenting support? How does it serve to narrow the gender/power gaps at global, community and interpersonal levels that facilitate violence against women?

- *Diversity/Intersectionality:* Respect for diversity is sometimes misinterpreted as cultural relativism, justifying a failure to intervene in the affairs of groups defined as "other." But violence is unacceptable in any form, and attention to diversity means working from within the perspectives of minority group women experiencing violence. Thus, Aboriginal women in remote communities may prefer to tackle alcohol profiteers to reduce levels of violence associated with substance abuse; in Aotearoa, parallel development models of service delivery aim to increase within-group accountability while promoting cultural as well as gender safety for Maori women (Te Puni Kōkiri, 2010); many African scholars and activists strongly oppose female genital cutting, yet challenge Western discourses and tactics in campaigns to end the practice (Nnaemeka & Ngozi Ezeilo, 2005).

- *Subjectivity/Reflexivity*: Violence is both a social construct and a (painfully) lived experience – feminist theories define it in terms of the social constructions of masculinity and femininity, the sets of traditions, habits and beliefs which permit some men to assume control over others, and thus, to assume the right to use violence in exercising that control. At the personal level, a person's subjective fear can be the best indicator of the dangerousness of a violent partner, regardless of any informal or professional risk assessment – yet her voice is often ignored, sometimes with fatal consequences.

Chapter Summary

We have not offered in this chapter a definitive conceptualization of a world without patriarchy, sexism, or **misogyny**, or a vision of wellbeing and liberation for under-entitled women and gender-varied individuals throughout the world. We leave that task for you, the readers, in your own contexts – because "feminism is a plant that grows only in its own soil" (Badran, 2002, cited in Van der Gaag, 2008, p. 16). Feminism's historical context reminds us that, in the words of a cigarette commercial, women "have come a long way baby." History also reveals that most changes are incremental and many gains fragile – as feminist community psychologists, we need to be vigilant about co-option by commercial interests (like tobacco companies!), erosion of hard-won rights, and the need to stay honest with ourselves about our relative power and privilege. Participants at a symposium discussing the UN MDG gender indicators wrote this song about empowerment (International Women's Development Agency (IWDA) 2006, p. 3):

> *It's girls in schools*
> *It's labor too*
> *It's being able to plan the kids*
> *And owning all our land*
> *Aspiring to be PM [prime minister]*
> *And having roads and water*
> *So that life in the future will be*
> *Better for our daughters*

Box 16.3 Exercise: From Rhetoric to Reality

Think back to the warm-up exercise at the start of this chapter – what specific aspects of gender equality and/or equity were part of your vision? Was it health, sexuality, work, spirituality, cultural safety, or any other issue impacting on the lives of women? What assumptions do you think you were making about gender identity as your vision took shape?

Deconstruction: Questioning the Text

Find a newspaper, magazine, or online article relating to your chosen issue. Read the text and try to answer the following questions.

1 What is the theme or topic, and how is it formulated (headlines, language, etc.)?

2 Whose voices are represented mostly? Women (or men) in positions of privilege? Are the voices of the people most affected represented in the text? In what ways do different actors and gendered identities enter the discourse (as victims, experts, competent, etc.)?

3 What kinds of discourses surround or are created within a particular text?

4 Are both equity and equality implicit in the text? Is patriarchy supported or subverted?

5 Where does the authority/authorship lie? Who can talk and who is talked about?

6 Who is cast as the expert? How is an expert position created and legitimated? What mechanisms are used to discredit alternative positions?

7 How is gender made relevant to the issues? Are gender relations visible in this text? What forms of masculinity and femininity are being made available here? Are any non-binary identities included or foregrounded?

8 What are the political implications of the text? Is there a transformative message there?

Action: Applying the Framework

In Box 16.2, we applied the principles of a feminist CP framework to the issue of violence against women. Think about the ways you would notice differences in the lives of women (and men and gender non-conforming groups) in your part of the world and elsewhere if your vision were realized, and list how each of those principles might (or might not) assist in working towards making your vision a reality.

Hint: Questions that need to be asked of any intervention include: Who is expected to change? Does it materially improve the lives of women? How many? Which women? How can you tell?

Key Terms

Cisgender: Refers to people whose gender identification and experiences are consistent with their birth-assigned sex. For example, cis female individuals were assigned female at birth and identify as women.

Gender: Refers to the attitudes, feelings, and behaviors attributed by a given culture to a person's assigned sex (often based on stereotypes of masculinity and femininity). Gender is defined along several dimensions, including how individuals are socialized and how they identify themselves. It is a variable set of practices. We all "do" gender within the parameters of our age, culture, social class, sexual orientation, personality, and circumstances. Behavior that is compatible with cultural expectations is referred to as "gender-normative." A much debated term.

Gender identity: Refers to "each person's deeply felt internal and individual experience of gender, which may or may not correspond with the sex assigned at birth, including the personal sense of the body (which may involve, if freely chosen, modification of bodily appearance or function by medical, surgical or other means) and other expressions of gender, including dress, speech and mannerisms" (International Panel of Experts, 2007, p. 6). As the Australian Psychological Society (2016) explains in recommending gender-affirming mental health practices, "[t]he majority of people are assigned as either male or female at birth, and will experience themselves as male or female accordingly. For some people, however, the presumed relationship between assigned sex and gender is incorrect."

Intersex: Refers to a group of people who are born with sexual features of both male and female reproductive organs, chromosomes, and/or genitals. The term refers to sex characteristics, not gender identity or sexual orientation.

Equality: In this chapter we have used equality, particularly between women and men, as the principle of "being of equal value" rather than "being the same as" or "identical." Treating everyone the same is not fair treatment.

Equal rights: Similarly this principle may require different actions or outcomes according to differing – but equally important – needs. For example, women have a right to (and need access to) appropriate medical care at the time they become mothers. Parents (and children) need, and therefore have equal rights to, a range of supports throughout childhood.

Equity: Ensuring people have what they need to be successful. In relation to gender, it means men and women should be given the same opportunities *despite their differences.*

Feminism(s): Various forms of feminism work towards a common goal of improving women's lives and dismantling patriarchal practices that impact on both men and women, and especially on gender non-conforming individuals and groups.

Intersectionality: Refers here to the complex interconnected inequities experienced by women across diverse cultures, abilities, and backgrounds. For example, an Aboriginal woman may be disadvantaged by being female AND by being Black.

Misogyny: Hatred and/or hostility towards all women.

Power: Central to all feminist analysis – traditionally measured in terms of individual or collective authority, information, resources, decision-making, coercion, and privilege, power is increasingly described in terms of discourse, relationship, and practice rather than quantity. In other words, power cannot be separated from how it is authorized and exercised.

Sex: Assigned at birth within the constraints of available legal categories (male, female, and, in some jurisdictions, intersex) on the basis of biological indicators including external genitalia, sex chromosomes, gonads, internal reproductive organs, and hormones.

Sexism: Any beliefs, attitudes, practices, and/or institutions in which distinctions between people's intrinsic worth are made on the basis of sex/gender. This discrimination can be systemic as well as individual.

Transgender (in text: **trans woman, trans man**): Used to refer to persons whose gender identity does not correspond with the sex assigned to them at birth, including but not limited to, transgender, transsexual, and genderqueer identities. Since individuals can express their gender identity in various ways that might differ from their birth-assigned category, these expressions and experiences are generally referred to as transgender spectrum experiences.

Resources

For an overview of global and economic issues affecting women:

http://womensissues.about.com and www.un.org/womenwatch/daw/daw/index.html

The APA Society for the Psychology of Women maintains an active website: www.apadivisions.org/division-35/

An amazing compilation is updated almost daily at the University of Maryland: www.umbc.edu/wmst/

An Australian site on, by, and for women with disabilities: http://www.wwda.org.au

Following a meeting held in Yogyakarta, Indonesia in 2006, experts from 25 countries with diverse backgrounds and expertise relevant to issues of human rights law unanimously adopted the Yogyakarta Principles on the Application of International Human Rights Law in relation to Sexual Orientation and Gender Identity: https://yogyakartaprinciples.org/

World Professional Association for Transgender Health: www.wpath.org/

BUILDING WELLBEING IN FAMILIES

17

Leslea Peirson, Glynis Clacherty, and Melissa L. Whitson

Warm-up Questions

Reflecting on your childhood, think about the resources you had in your family and in your community. You may have come from a family with many resources such as a house and a garden, a good school that was easy to get to, and a hospital nearby in case you were ill. You may have grown up without many conventional resources such as a comfortable house that you owned, money for family outings, or new clothes, but you had resources of another kind such as a wise grandmother or a neighbor who gave you help with homework or the occasional meal. All of the resources we have mentioned so far were external to you as a child. You may also have had internal resources such as self-confidence, intelligence, and the ability to laugh even though life was difficult. Think about how your family or members of your community helped to build your internal resources as a child.

Alternatively, think about someone you know who grew up with many difficulties but still "made it" in life. There are many examples of people in public life like this who survived extreme hardship as a child but grew up to become a happy, functioning, and contributing community member. What internal and external factors can you recognize that may have operated to protect this person from adversity and promote his/her wellbeing?

Learning Objectives

In this chapter you will learn about

- Traditional ways of understanding and reacting to families' realities and needs
- How using CP values and principles can help to reframe the ways that we think about and respond to families' realities and needs
- Some real-world examples of programs and policies that embody and activate CP values and principles in their efforts to address family adversity and support family wellbeing

Wellbeing of Children and their Families

In this chapter you will find out how the way we think about families and children and their needs has changed over the last few decades and how important it is that community psychology (CP) practice reflects these changes. Many of the services offered to families in the past were reactive and based at the micro level within the family, with little thought given to the impact of the context in which these families were trying to cope. Using the principles of CP, we focus on promoting **family wellbeing** within the many interacting contextual influences that hinder or help families to care for their children as best they can. We will also describe some **multi-focused, community-driven interventions** and social policies that build internal and external resources and promote family wellbeing.

Heterogeneity of Families

Before we start, here are a few introductory concepts. Families are not static entities. As they journey through life they experience many developmental and situational transitions. These transitions result in a dynamic context for family life that presents both opportunities and challenges. Families are also not identical; many children grow up in families that do not include two married, biological parents. Different family compositions can include single parent, grandparent, blended, LGBTQ, and multicultural families. This diversity can also impact the opportunities and challenges that families experience. Certain factors may be more or less important for different types and structures of families. Therefore, it is critical to expand our definition of "family" and develop programs that are inclusive and effective for all children and diverse families (Mercier & Harold, 2003). Ultimately, what constitutes family wellbeing is complex because of the difficulties of defining family (Robinson & Parker, 2008).

Globally, the most common challenge that families face is poverty. It is useful to remember that poverty is not exclusive to developing countries. For example, a recent review of child poverty in the US (Dreyer, Chung, Szilagyi, & Wong, 2016) showed that in spite of measures put in place during the recent economic recession, one in five children live below the official federal poverty level (FPL) and almost one in two is poor or near poor. Research tells us that poverty does create disadvantage for children (e.g., Blair & Raver, 2016; Chaudry & Wimer, 2016; Chopra & Sanders, 2005; Evans & Kim, 2007; Grantham-McGregor et al., 2007; Wise, 2016). But it is important that we do not assume that there is something inherent in the condition of poverty that predisposes poor children to a host of risks. "Deprivation and difficulty can also produce what Rutter and Silberg (2002) call 'steeling effects', in which coping with challenges produces strength and resilience" (Hardgrove, Enenajor, & Lee, 2011, p. 5).

Rather than assuming that families, and children in particular, are "disadvantaged" because they are poor, it is much more useful to look at families in the context of the balance of risk and protective factors in the interacting systems around them. Resilience, or the ability to bounce back from difficulty, is determined mainly by the balance between the stressors and developmental risks which children and families are exposed to on the one hand, and the protective factors that might be operating for them on the other. In everyday speech we often describe someone as "resilient," but it is important to understand that resilience is not a quality or set of characteristics within the individual. It is true that there are certain internal characteristics that will act as protective factors in relation to the developmental risks to which the child is exposed, but there are also many protective or compensatory factors that are external to the child. It is useful to call the internal factors assets, and the external factors resources (Fergus & Zimmerman, 2005). Practice identifying risk and protective factors and assets and resources using the story that is told in Box 17.1.

Box 17.1 Birth in a Refugee Camp: Identifying Risk and Protective Factors

The expectation of a baby often brings excitement and joy. For Palestinian refugees living in Lebanon, however, the birth of a newborn baby can cause anxiety, stress, and deep sorrow. Six decades after the first wave of refugees crossed the border into Lebanon, a quarter of a million Palestinians still remain in dilapidated, overcrowded camps with no rights to work, education, or health care.

Palestinian refugees currently reside in 12 UN camps (and many unregistered gatherings) across Lebanon. Over the years, the camps have become haphazard slums. Children are born into a world where opportunities are scarce and their earliest days are too often compromised by poor **health**. UN Relief and Works Agency (UNRWA) is the main provider of primary health care, but their clinic-based services are hugely overstretched. Doctors in these clinics are seeing an average of 107 patients per day as opposed to the recommended 70. According to a recent UNRWA survey, people living in the camps are suffering from severe poverty, with unemployment rates at 56%, food insecurity levels at 58% and 15% of the population affected by severe food shortages.

All of these factors greatly impact maternal and child health. Inadequate conditions and services for safe birth force mothers to give birth in unsafe conditions with little medical assistance. An NGO called Medical Aid for Palestine (MAP) is making strides through its Maternal and Child Health home visiting program, which brings healthcare right into the heart of the community. For the mothers we work with, MAP is a lifeline. For mothers and their newborn babies, MAP's targeted intervention fills in the gaps left by the chronically underfunded UNRWA, which is often unable to retain and motivate its staff.

To try to minimize the risks faced by pregnant women and their infants, MAP has introduced teams of community midwives and nurses who visit mothers and babies in their homes every day. Time is essential for understanding the risks that expectant mothers may face in the camp. While an average appointment at the UN Mother and Baby clinic is just five minutes, MAP-affiliated midwives are able to spend up to an hour with a mother, affording the necessary space and time to discuss problems and find solutions.

One of the mothers from the camps told me her story:

"This project was like a gift to me. I have had a very bad experience during my previous pregnancy, which ended with the death of my baby. When I got pregnant again my neighbor told her midwife about me, and two days later a midwife from the MAP project visited me. I told them that I previously had a difficult pregnancy and they visited me once a month. I had pre-eclampsia and hypertension. The midwife kept very close follow-up. I am very thankful that the midwife was here. The most important thing the midwife did for me was on the day I gave birth. It was the time for her visit and I told her that I was experiencing a severe stomachache. I didn't understand what was happening and I didn't want to go to the doctor. She encouraged me to go to the hospital, where I discovered that I was in labor. There was no way that I would have known this without her. I wish I had her support during my previous pregnancy. I didn't know anything about pregnancy before. Maybe my baby would still be alive if she had been there."

Written by Sara Halimah for Global Fund for Women Retrieved from https://imagining equality.globalfundforwomen.org/content/refugee-moms

1 Identify the risk factors for a baby born into this situation.

2 What protective factors can you identify?

It is important to remember that influences in human development are not one-way: people are influenced by various systems in their social contexts, and also influence those systems (consider the ecological model and systems thinking from Chapter 5). Their development, in other words, is not passive; it is a continuous process of adaptation to the physical, emotional, and sociocultural environments around them. Individual family members (including children) play a role within the balance of developmental risks and protective factors. This idea of active engagement is one that has become especially important in the study of childhood in recent years. One characteristic of this new way of thinking about children is that "children must be seen as actively involved in the construction of their own social lives, the lives of those around them and the societies in which they live. They can no longer be regarded as simply the passive subjects of structural determinations" (James & Prout, 1997, p. 4). One example of this idea of family members interacting with structural factors that seem to be out of their control is the work that Boyden (2003) has done with children involved in conflict situations. Boyden observed how, even in times of violence, children are not helpless victims but contribute to their own and to their families' coping. "The most resilient children in conflict zones are those who actively and creatively engage with their situation and adopt constructive approaches to the management of risk (and even) staying alive" (Boyden, 2003, p. 7). Thus, it is not only a balance of risk and protective factors in a particular context that affects a family's wellbeing, but also the individual family members' (including children) interactions and choices in terms of making use of relevant protective factors.

Nevertheless, in high-risk environments, protective factors must be obtainable if families are to make use of them. Helping to facilitate the process of resilience, therefore, depends very much on promoting the availability of such protective factors. The rest of this chapter looks at some of the approaches CP practitioners can use to think about reducing risk while supporting families to access protective factors in their journey towards wellbeing.

Before we move on though it is important to acknowledge that many readers of this book will not live in high-risk environments or routinely encounter adversity. They will be privileged with a host of protective resources around them. It is important if we are to work in CP to be aware of our privilege so we can identify potential biases and empathize with those who do not have access to the same assets and resources (refer to Chapter 3 for aspects to consider). In Box 17.2 we suggest an exercise to help readers "unpack their privilege."

Box 17.2 Unpacking Privilege

In McIntosh's (1990) insightful article "White Privilege: Unpacking the Invisible Knapsack" the author reflects on the concept of privilege and how members of dominant groups are afforded and take for granted many assets due to their privileged status. She goes on to identify 26 conditions that she attributes to her privilege as a White person. A few examples from this list include: "If I should need to move, I can be pretty sure of renting or purchasing housing in an area which I can afford and in which I would want to live," "I can arrange to protect my children most of the time from people who might not like them," and "I can easily buy posters, post-cards, picture books, greeting cards, dolls, toys and children's magazines featuring people of my race."

We encourage readers to consider their own privileged status and to generate other lists of unearned advantages that rest on social or economic class, religion, sexual or ethnic identity, age, ability, and gender. Although this exercise does not manifest the experience of subordination, it does cultivate an awareness of one's own privilege and what others who lack similar privilege may be subjected to or denied. McIntosh suggests that knowledge of systemic unearned advantage and privilege can be used to challenge the status quo and transform oppressive systems of power.

Reframing Our Notions of Families and Disadvantage: Towards an Agenda of Wellbeing

In this section of the chapter we examine traditional or neoliberal approaches to understanding and responding to families, particularly those families who encounter adversity. We also consider some of the challenges that arise from such ways of knowing and acting. The values and principles of CP are invoked to help reframe our notions and to better understand and respond to the realities and needs of families, especially those who are experiencing difficulties.

Individualism and Victim-blaming

The traditional approach to understanding families who experience problems is focused on a micro-level of analysis and looks either for difficulties within the family unit or within particular family members. The dominant worldview in Western cultures is that of individualism. The assumptions of this narrative that include initiative, independence, personal responsibility, and freedom of choice can be transferred onto families. Families are expected to be self-sufficient entities and when problems arise they are attributed to poor choices or deficits within the family. Not recognizing the broader forces that influence disadvantage leads to victim-blaming and a **doctrine of personal culpability** (Goldenberg, 1978; Ryan, 1971) and encourages social acceptance of the negative consequences for families (e.g., dislocation to segregated environments such as social housing or the streets, working at menial jobs, migration to the city). Furthermore, there is evidence suggesting that individualism is associated with negative outcomes, which in turn leads to more problems for families already experiencing difficulties (Lipset, 1996). For example, in conservative times of economic restraint, individualism allows us to blame families on public assistance for their problems and rationalizes cutbacks in social/public spending. Reductions in benefits and/or withdrawal of employment programs further increase the problems experienced by families and leave little hope for overcoming adversity.

The conventional approach to helping families is equally problematic. The response is often reactive, treating or assisting the family (e.g., counseling, assistance programs) after problems have occurred. Since individualism views the source of disadvantage within the context of the family, it is at this level that intervention is directed. The influences of community and societal level forces on family functioning are rarely considered. We try to change families, not situations of poverty, unemployment, poor housing, limited or inaccessible resources, and lack of social cohesion. We focus on the surface manifestations of disadvantage, not the deep causes (Joffe, 1996). As such, our efforts are ameliorative rather than transformative as we try to teach families how to live with adversity rather than working to change the unjust social conditions that lead to problems in the first place. This approach puts these families in a subordinate position to the rest of society and implies that they need to be repaired somehow or that their lives need to be managed by others.

Holistic, Strengths-based Ecological Perspective

Adopting a holistic perspective redirects our attention from a deficit orientation towards a focus on the strengths of families living in adverse conditions. An empowering or strengths-based focus identifies assets and capacities in families and offers hope and opportunities not only to families but also to service providers. Consider the following scenario. The Halabi family arrived in Canada in 2015 from a refugee camp in Greece after escaping the war in Syria. The family includes the parents of five children aged from two years to fifteen years, an elderly grandmother and an aunt. The family lost everything in the war and spent any savings they had getting to Greece. Mr. Halabi is a skilled metal worker and his wife is a seamstress but they speak only Arabic so it is unlikely they will find work until they have learned some English. Their eldest son and daughter have started school and are learning English quickly but now the weather is getting colder and they do not have coats and boots to walk to school so they often miss school. The family has found a small two-room apartment in a supported housing complex in the city, which is all they can afford. The two younger children have not found places at school yet as the local elementary schools have no programs for teaching English and the family cannot afford transport to the appropriate school. Mrs. Halabi spends most of her time indoors with her youngest child as she and her aunt have found it very difficult to adjust to the busy inner city area where they live. Mr. Halabi has not found work but leaves the house early and is away until late at night assisting in a local greengrocer run by a fellow Syrian who has lived in the area for some time. The elderly grandmother needs medical care but the family has little local knowledge about how to find a general practitioner. No one in the family feels at home yet and all of them carry the trauma of their past experiences. The six-year-old, little Sara, is the one Mrs. Halabi worries about the most, because she has stopped speaking since they left their home in Syria.

What does this description lead us to believe about the Halabis and the possibilities for improving their situation? The picture looks rather bleak for this family and it would not be unreasonable for a community service worker to feel powerless to assist in a meaningful way given the complexity of challenges. However, if the assessment was reframed to also consider the strengths of the Halabi family and their environment (e.g., the aunt is capable, supportive, and happy to care for the youngest child while Mrs. Halabi attends an English class and a cultural orientation program at a local support center; Mr. Halabi has made contact with a neighboring family who have a lot of local knowledge and contacts with local business owners; residents of the housing complex where the family lives have read about the problems of Syrian refugees and are willing to help with second-hand coats and boots for the family; a local health-related non-profit organization makes home visits to elderly people in the area), the situation and potential opportunities might appear quite different.

The value of holism allows us to contextualize the problems experienced by families over time and across multiple levels of analysis. It reflects the importance of focusing on the whole family in the context of the relationships, settings, and environments in which the family is embedded. Within families, members rely on one another for cognitive, emotional, psychosocial, and economic needs. Often the analysis stops there; looking at the individual or microsystem, but not beyond. The ecological principles (see Chapter 5) acknowledge that families are impacted not only by individual members and the family setting but also by other components of the microsystem (e.g., extended family, peer networks), the organizations they are connected to, the community environment, social norms and values, social and economic policies, and global and environmental issues. The problems associated with, or leading to, family difficulties do not always originate within the family or a particular member of the family, rather they often arise due to conditions or changes within broader structures that in turn influence the health and wellbeing of families. Consistent with this understanding, the focus of interventions targeting families should go beyond educational or skill-building programs offered to parents and children, to efforts aimed at altering or improving social and economic conditions within the contexts that surround the family. A good example of this approach is found in the Kwa Wazee program that is described in Box 17.3.

Box 17.3 Kwa Wazee: A Holistic Intervention

The Kwa Wazee community-based organization program in eastern Tanzania is a good example of a holistic intervention towards family wellbeing. There are many orphan children living with their aging grandparents in this area because many parents have died of AIDS. The program began with psychological support groups for grandparents and the orphan children they support, but it soon became clear that the project had to intervene at other levels too. So, the Kwa Wazee (a respectful term for an elderly person in the local language of Kiswahili) program now offers a small monthly pension (sourced from a community in Switzerland) to the grandparents, as there is no social assistance in Tanzania for elderly people. This small pension makes it possible for the grandparents to provide basic food, soap, and clothes to their grandchildren and thus improves their relationship. The program also provides each family with two goats, which if they build up into a herd can contribute to long-term sustainability of the families. An evaluation of the program (Hofmann, Heslop, Clacherty, & Kessy, 2008) showed that this macro-level contribution to livelihood was a huge factor in improving psychological wellbeing alongside the group counseling work that the project began with.

From Psychosocial Problems to Prevention and Promotion

Psychosocial Problems

Traditionally, psychological research and action have focused on psychosocial problems within individuals or the family unit (e.g., addictions, teenage pregnancy, child maltreatment, delinquency, and crime). Dysfunctions are conceived as emanating not from adverse economic conditions or individual attempts to cope with inequalities in social and economic power, but rather from inferior genes, poor parenting skills, lack of problem-solving skills, ineffective communication patterns, and so on. In essence, our understanding of disadvantage has been reduced to the psychosocial level or to the surface manifestations of the problem. This perspective has led to a treatment orientation that seeks to ameliorate difficulties at the personal or relational (within family) levels. This approach does not challenge the status quo, rather it attempts to reduce maladaptive behaviors or adapt the individual and/or family to enable them to function within established societal structures and norms.

Prevention and Promotion

The principles of prevention and promotion introduced in Chapter 6 invoke the value of health and are used to resist psychosocial problems and to encourage wellbeing. The term *health* has both a positive and negative meaning; the absence of disease or illness or "a state of complete physical, mental, and social wellbeing and not merely the absence of disease or infirmity" (World Health Organization, 2006, p. 1). It is the latter definition that is of interest to CP for it recognizes that health is a multidimensional concept that can and should take a positive form. The World Health Organization's *Ottawa Charter* (1986), states that "health is a positive concept emphasizing social and personal resources, as well as physical capacities" (p. 1) and calls for "coordinated action by all concerned: by governments, by health and other social and economic sectors, non-governmental and voluntary organizations, local authorities, industry and the media" (p. 2) in meeting the prerequisites for health which include "peace, shelter, education, food, income, a stable eco-system, sustainable resources, social justice and equity" (p. 1). These ideas continue to be relevant to public health today (Potvin & Jones, 2011), and are also of interest to CP as they reflect a competency orientation, the influence of the social context on health and wellbeing, cooperation across sectors at multiple ecological levels, and social ethics and emancipatory values.

Prevention and promotion aimed at families can reflect personal, collective, and relational dimensions. At a person/family-centered level, interventions can focus on the following: decreasing or dealing effectively with stress created by adverse living conditions; reducing the detrimental effects of physical vulnerabilities which may have contributed to, or resulted from, disadvantage; reducing or overcoming barriers to access of resources (e.g., cultural, economic, physical); increasing problem-solving, decision-making, social and coping skills; supporting relationships within the family; expanding perceived networks of social support; and developing self-esteem and self-efficacy (Albee, 1982; Robinson & Parker, 2008). Such efforts respond to the values of self-determination, caring and compassion, and health.

Interventions that foster collective wellbeing emphasize the role of broader structures in preventing psychosocial problems and promoting health. At an environmental level, efforts can be directed towards decreasing or removing stressors in socialization settings (e.g., schools, workplaces, health care); reducing the presence of risk factors in the environment that lead to increased physical vulnerabilities (e.g., poor prenatal care, exposure to hazardous substances, inadequate heating and ventilation); developing positive socialization practices (e.g., effectively preparing parents, teachers, employers, and others to assume their roles); expanding the strength, availability, and accessibility of social support resources; and increasing opportunities for positive relatedness to others and connections with formal and informal settings (Elias, 1987; Olson, 2007). At the societal level, through the unified action of all sectors, healthy public policies can be established to "[reduce] differences in current health status and [ensure] equal opportunities and resources to enable all people to achieve their fullest health potential [which] includes a secure foundation in a supportive environment, access to information, life skills and opportunities for making healthy choices" (World Health Organization, 1986, p. 1).

Promoting relational wellbeing requires that interventions, both in the personal and collective domains, respect differences among families, allow families to define their needs, promote acceptance and facilitate meaningful involvement of families in making decisions affecting their lives. In so doing, the values of respect for diversity and participation and collaboration are advanced. By recognizing the competencies that diverse forms of families bring, and how their decisions and strategies are often adaptive to their specific needs, interventions can make family relationships more flexible and stronger (Jones & Unger, 2000). Relational wellbeing may also be supported through interventions that encourage involvement and collective responsibility, such as mutual aid groups, community development initiatives, and social and political action. Hamber (2009) describes how survivors of the Northern Ireland and South African violence found value in an activist group. "There were individuals, for example, who joined the group as introverted and frequently ill, suffering from somatic complaints, who were slowly transformed into active, talkative and engaging members who developed a wide range of social relationships and networks as they became increasingly active and valued members of their community and society once again" (Hamber, 2009, p. 196). Imagine that the Halabi family mentioned earlier joined a Syrian solidarity group in their area that included refugees and local residents and involved activities for the whole family. What would the impact be?

From Social Isolation to Community

Social Isolation

Physical isolation or geographic separation can pose significant challenges for families (e.g., limited interaction with extended family or friends, lack of access to needed resources and services such as physicians, schools, and transportation). On the other hand, simply living in close proximity to others does not ensure that families are socially integrated, as we saw from the description of the Halabi family. Families may choose, or be forced, to become insulated from their neighbors and surrounding community for a variety of reasons such as a fear of crime or violence, suspiciousness, cultural or religious differences (especially for immigrants), the burdens of caring for children, or working multiple jobs.

As one of the structures of oppression, **containment** serves to intensify the social isolation experienced by disadvantaged families. Goldenberg (1978) describes containment as "limit[ing] the range of free movement available to a particular group ... increasingly restrict[ing] and narrow[ing] the scope of possibilities that can be entertained ... [and effectively] quarantining ... people from the possibilities of change" (p. 4–5). Families with limited economic resources are often forced to move into social housing or other lower-income neighborhoods. Poor conditions, absentee landlords, violence, stigma, and distance from important community resources such as quality schools, clinics, and grocery stores hamper the quality of life and the prospects for a better future for residents in these areas. Mobility issues can also contribute to social isolation. Not having a car or a reliable vehicle or other convenient and affordable means of travel can limit the possibilities available to families. Getting to work, taking children to be vaccinated, visiting community resources such as libraries, or taking family trips can be arduous journeys which may often be avoided, passed up, or impossible. Families may be excluded from participating in their communities if they are unable to pay for many services and opportunities such as recreational activities, summer camps, and training courses. Essentially the oppressive social and economic conditions experienced by some families trap or "contain" them in abject environments with limited opportunities for inclusion in the broader community.

Community

The values of caring, compassion and support for community structures involve empathy and concern for the welfare of others and emphasize the importance of networks and settings that facilitate the pursuit of personal and communal goals (Prilleltensky, Laurendeau, Chamberland, & Peirson, 2001). Although there are many caring and compassionate practitioners who have dedicated their working lives to helping families experiencing difficulties, there is not, nor will there ever be, a sufficient number of professionals trained to deal with the needs of the population (Albee, 1959). Nor is the traditional professional–client relationship the only, or best, context for responding to many of the problems associated with adversity. Families need more than therapy or other professional services; they need access to informal supports and strong community structures.

Informal relationships can provide families with ongoing general support as well as specific support related to particular stressors (Sarason, Sarason, & Pierce, 1990; Donald, Lazarus, & Moolla, 2014). Although adverse conditions may lead to a sense of exclusion, most disadvantaged families do not live in complete physical isolation from others. Psychological sense of community and social integration can be facilitated through mechanisms of connecting families to one another. For example, a recent evaluation (Hughes, Joslyn, Wojton, O'Reilly, & Dworkin, 2016) of the impact of a multi-systemic *Help Me Grow* intervention in Connecticut, US that includes a toll-free help-line, visits from care-workers, parenting education, and, most importantly, links for vulnerable families to community-based resources, shows that the program enhanced family functioning related to a number of protective factors and contributed to "parents feeling engaged, supported, educated and better equipped to meet their children's needs and foster healthy developmental outcomes" (p. 129).

In the context of immigration (one of the themes being explored in this book), the *Young Roots* program in London encourages young refugees and asylum seekers to attend regular weekly meetings in a center close to their homes. The aim of these meetings is to "reduce young refugees and asylum seekers' social isolation and enable them to make friends" (quote from *Young Roots* website http://youngroots.org.uk/london/). This may seem a simple aim but in the context of a move from social isolation to community, it is an important one.

The relationships formed within community support networks can provide families with a sense of belonging, emotional support, socialization, encouragement, advice, and tangible supports such as child care, money, clothing, meals and transportation as well as opportunities to reciprocate with support when others require assistance. Relational wellbeing may also be promoted through self-help and mutual-aid groups that deal with problems or issues affecting disadvantaged families and which provide connections to others and various specific supports in egalitarian, respectful, and reciprocal contexts. One good example of this is the village savings societies set up by non-governmental organizations (NGOs) in many developing countries to give women an opportunity to put in small amounts of money once a month and then borrow from the group savings for an emergency such as a trip to a hospital. The benefits of these village savings societies go beyond the economic; they become a community resource providing companionship and friendship as well as advice and support (USAID, 2014). See https://www.care.org.au/wp-content/uploads/2014/12/CARE-VSLA-Report-Uganda-Eco-Devel.pdf for a description of these groups.

In addition to social networks, developing the capacity to promote family wellbeing can occur through building support for the community structures that families interact with in their everyday lives. Ensuring a broad range of accessible, responsive, and publicly funded institutions is a critical factor in preventing problems and for promoting the wellbeing of all citizens (Prilleltensky, Laurendeau, et al., 2001). Included in this array would be health care services, schools and preschool interventions, transportation systems, waste management and water treatment facilities, libraries, cultural and recreational opportunities, police and other justice services, insurance and assistance programs, and many other vital resources and agencies. However, these structures that work for the common good are often the first to be cut back when they should in fact be increased in scope. For example, in many western countries the social support institutions that were put in place in times of economic growth are now threatened by neoconservative and neoliberal forces as governments seem intent on dismantling the welfare state and privatizing many community services (O'Neill 2005, Morgan Cumberworth, & Wimer, 2012) when families need them the most because of the economic recession. There is clear evidence that in times of recession families need extra support, not less, because reduced earnings and bread winners moving into unemployment can fundamentally change living arrangements and even family life decisions around marriage and child birth (Morgan et al., 2012). And it is often the children and elderly who suffer the most. The Population Association of America (2010) showed that in the US, children, adolescents, and old people are the most vulnerable to economic recession in both physical and psychological terms. In developing countries, of course, social service nets for poor families are very seldom a priority (see Box 17.3 on the Kwa Wazee project for an example of how a community-based service developed because of a lack of a state old age pension). Recognizing, valuing, protecting, maintaining, and expanding the welfare state are important steps towards promoting collective responsibility for the wellbeing of society's most vulnerable families.

From Powerlessness to Power

Powerlessness

Many children and families living in adversity lack both a sense of control and actual control over many aspects of their lives. Despair over the past and present and hopelessness for the future are created and maintained by their oppressive social context. Families with limited economic resources are often forced to live in public assisted housing, low-income neighborhoods, or are even homeless. They usually do not own their homes so they are subjected to the conditions imposed by governments and landlords. They usually cannot afford to register in skills-training programs or to send children to college or university. Without post-secondary education they are often relegated to menial, low-paying jobs with little opportunity for advancement or they must rely on public assistance benefits. The initiative of many families receiving public assistance benefits is repressed if income received from other sources is clawed back from support payments or there is a threat that benefits may be cut off entirely. These conditions and restrictions reflect the concept of containment which was described earlier in the chapter, and another structure of oppression, **compartmentalization**. "Compartmentalization is the process which encourages partial rewards at many levels but denies fulfillment at any one level" (Goldenberg, 1978, p. 11). Disadvantaged families are further disempowered if they cannot change their living situations without risking their access to shelter and means of survival. Under these circumstances, they lack choice and opportunity and are subordinated to others who control, monitor, and administrate their lives.

Families living with adversity also experience powerlessness in the contexts of service provision (e.g., mental health, physical health, legal, child welfare, education) and research. The traditional approach views professionals as expert technicians, as specialists who have expertise and are given authority to assess and treat families. Families, on the other hand, are viewed as clients, as passive recipients of services that are under professional control. Families who are unable to pay for private consultation, are without choice in terms of service options or specific practitioners. They are often on lengthy waiting lists to access services which are deemed appropriate by others and which are provided by agency-appointed staff. Families living with adversity are also often treated as passive objects of research. Traditional research has circumscribed the role of the family to that of a data source. In a number of qualitative studies we have been involved in, parents and young people have commented that researchers repeatedly come to them for information about the realities of disadvantaged living, but they are never certain about what happens to the knowledge they convey because their adverse situations persist.

Power

How can families that experience such an extreme lack of control acquire power and assert authority over their own lives? The principle of power emphasizes the values of participation, self-determination, and social justice. It is through the intertwining of these three values that families can gain both voice and choice.

The value of participation refers to respectful collaborative processes wherein all stakeholders have meaningful input into decisions that affect their lives (Prilleltensky, Laurendeau, et al., 2001). The practical experience of families living under adverse conditions must not be dismissed. Families should be involved in identifying their needs and determining appropriate responses. However, their participation must not be based on token strategies of inclusion, for this denotes a subordinated position. Instead, the power to define problems and shape solutions must be shared in value-based relationships of partnership (Nelson, Pancer, Hayward, & Peters, 2005; Nelson, Prilleltensky, & MacGillivary, 2001). Responding to the value of accountability, the principles of commitment and empowerment direct researchers, service-providers, and policymakers to work with families, and not for them. Through inter-disciplinary ties, community psychologists are learning how to promote the active participation of marginalized populations in decision-making processes. Feminist-oriented participatory action research and the application of traditional native teachings are two examples of approaches for involving the, often unheard, voices of disadvantaged groups. Box 17.4 describes a creative project with children and youth in South Africa that amplified the voices of another particularly marginalized group.

Box 17.4 Speaking Out Gives a Sense of Power (Psychological Empowerment)

An art-based project working with unaccompanied refugee children from Democratic Republic of Congo, Burundi, and Rwanda in inner city Johannesburg included a series of exhibitions in public places (Clacherty, 2015). The children expressed their life stories in and on suitcases using drawings, paintings, and prints and then exhibited these. The children attended the exhibitions allowing them to advocate for themselves about their lives and issues. Many of them had spent the last few years trying to be invisible because as foreigners they experienced a great deal of discrimination from local South Africans. But they wanted South Africans to understand why they had come to the country, as one Angolan boy of 15 said, "We made these suitcases for some of the people out there. There are rich people out there who live large. They don't know how poor people, like refugees, live. They don't know. They got to know" (Clacherty, 2019, p. 4). The public nature of the exhibitions moved the children from feelings of powerlessness and from a victim identity to alternative identities such as "artist" or simply, "young person." The sense of power and pride is evident in this quote from a 14-year-old girl. "It made me feel like a VIP, because the time we wanted to go into the art exhibition this (security) man chased us away – he thought we are the street kids. Diane (the project facilitator) came and said we were the ARTISTS! I liked that. We were the ARTISTS" (Clacherty, 2016, p. 159).

To acquire power, families living in adversity must have more than voice; they must also have choice. The value of **self-determination** refers to the ability of families to pursue chosen goals and direct their lives without facing formidable obstacles (Prilleltensky, Laurendeau, et al., 2001). Rather than having their lives externally orchestrated or regulated, families need to have control over decisions that affect their present and future wellbeing. Personal empowerment is enhanced when families maintain a sense of agency and experience autonomy in their everyday lives. Self-efficacy, which develops through having such control, acts as a protective mechanism against various risks and helps families cope with the daily stressors of living with adversity (Prilleltensky, Laurendeau, et al., 2001). However, self-determination is dependent upon the actualization of the third value connected to power, social justice.

In order for families to be able to make choices, options must exist and opportunities must be accessible. Social justice reflects the fair and equitable distribution of bargaining powers, responsibilities, and resources in society (Prilleltensky, 2012). This value blends the components of voice and choice, such that the needs of families living with adversity are identified by those who live the experience and there are programs and policies in place that respond to these needs. In the current conservative climate across the globe, which discriminates against disadvantaged families and other marginalized groups, social justice is brought about through social-change movements that promote the notion of collective wellbeing and a vision of a more just and caring society. There are many international, national, provincial/state, and local organizations that have been formed to address the issues of disadvantage, fight poverty, and advocate for equity in the division and distribution of global, societal, and regional resources. Many of these organizations work at a global level, for example the Global Campaign to End Immigration Detention of Children (www. endchilddetention.org) which has advocated successfully at national government and UN levels to make sure no child is ever held in detention apart from or with their family while their immigration status is being resolved (sadly, it has not stopped child detention in the US). Box 17.5 describes an international NGO that has developed an approach to advocacy for services at a local level.

Box 17.5 CARE: Striving Towards Social Justice at the Local Level

CARE, an International NGO that works globally with many families living in adverse circumstances, has developed a simple but effective approach to give communities access to social justice in the context of local services. The approach involves a series of workshops where families in a community interact with local service providers such as the staff from the health clinic, the government offices, law enforcement, and water and agricultural service providers. The community develops a set of expected actions (a checklist) that will show that service providers are doing their work (e.g., the health clinic should open on time and health service providers should treat patients with respect and kindness) and then rates the service providers against this checklist on a simple scorecard. The service providers go through a similar process rating the families, for example, health providers would rate the villagers' record of mosquito net use. The two groups then meet to look at the scores and make practical recommendations that service providers and villagers can follow, for example, "the clinic nurses will make sure they order enough mosquito nets for all pregnant women to get one and the villagers must use the nets." Regular follow up meetings are held to see if these contracts have been kept and to make new recommendations. In this way, the community holds the service providers accountable and the service providers are able to encourage the community to use their services to their full extent. The community scorecard process is a useful way of putting social justice into action and there is emerging evidence that the process can substantially change the wellbeing of vulnerable families (Chambers, 2014; Nigussie & Wales, 2014; Wild, 2014).

From Discrimination to Inclusion

Discrimination

What is a family? Each of us, no doubt, has our own opinion as to what constitutes the "ideal" family, which is shaped by personal experience and attitudes, social norms, and media influences. Families today take many forms and function under diverse circumstances. Although "recent studies have expanded the data base to many cohorts ... diverse families still tend to be evaluated in comparison to one standard" (Walsh, 1996, p. 268). Ideologically, we still romanticize the two-parent family model popularized in the conservative era of the 1950s. Although contemporary discourse reflects diversity and an acknowledgment of the different types of families, conservative values dominate and non-traditional families continue to be rejected (Leonard, 1997) and discriminated against by policies and social norms (Eichler, 1997; Nicholson, 1997). In turn, non-traditional families internalize this discrimination and are made to feel ashamed for their differences and responsible for their oppression (Goldenberg, 1978). Recent work by the *Young Lives* study conducted in Vietnam, Ethiopia, India, and Peru (Woodhead, Dornan, & Murray, 2013) shows that children are especially vulnerable to discrimination based on their economic inequality or other differences because their "[a]cute awareness of their relative disadvantage in comparison to others ... shapes the[ir] feelings of agency (or self-efficacy) that can help them cope with and possibly improve their situation" (p. 39). This awareness of differentness is illustrated in Box 17.6.

Box 17.6 Children's Sense of Their Economic Situation

A study in rural Andhra Pradesh highlighted the crucial significance of children's social context, their family and their peer relationships. What children often found most distressing about the lack of material goods was the sense of shame that came with "not having" or not "fitting in." For example, 13-year-old Kareena and her sister were keenly aware of their household's fragile economy, which Kareena attributed to her father's illness. Her mother could no longer afford to provide nutritious food for the family, who subsisted mainly on diluted 'dal' (a lentil stew). Kareena and her sister described how they attempt to conceal their poverty from other children by sitting apart during school lunches or covering their lunch box with a book while they ate (Boyden & Crivello, 2012). This research also drew attention to different ways that 12 to 15 year olds understood inequality, reflecting their position in the social hierarchy and the social expectations they were managing (Crivello, Vennam, & Komanduri, 2012).

Source: Extract from Woodhead, Dornan, & Murray (2013, p. 40). Reproduced with Permission from Young Lives.

Inclusion

The principle of inclusion calls upon the value of respecting diversity and the socioeconomic status of families. This diversity includes culture and socioeconomic status, as well as unique family structures such as single parent, blended, and LGBTQI families. Families should not be judged against a single standard; they should have the right to be different, and they should not be made to suffer because of their differences. The unique social identities of families need to be respected and accepted. Our notions about families guide our assumptions and the allocation of societies' resources. To promote equity, it is important that our policies and programs reflect the different types of families and respond to their varying needs.

For example, research has found that parents in nontraditional families have the same levels of knowledge and ability in parenting skills (Bronstein, Clauson, Stoll, & Abrams, 1993). Parenting programs can be geared towards reinforcing the strengths inherent in these families. Furthermore, at the organizational level, schools can support nontraditional families by including family structure diversity as a curricular topic to normalize the experiences of these families and providing support groups to children whose family is in a structural transition (e.g., divorce; Bronstein et al., 1993). Interventions like these can promote wellbeing and positive development for diverse families.

Interventions for Children and Families: Ecological and Empowerment Approaches

CP involves value-based thinking and action. In the previous section we discussed ways in which we understand families, wellness, and adversity. In this next section we focus more on the action component, describing some of the programs and policies that benefit children and families. Although creating equity from the beginning is the most effective way to address inequalities in health and wellbeing, interventions can still make a profound difference (Marmot, 2015a). A review of the literature indicates that there are numerous preventive interventions targeting children and families who face difficulties (Prilleltensky, Nelson, & Peirson, 2001). Given that these families are already experiencing adversity and may be at risk for additional problems, the types of interventions they encounter tend to be selective or indicated (Institute of Medicine (IOM) 1994). Many programs adopt a single focus (e.g., cognitive problem-solving, social decision-making, stress management, home visitation), are targeted at the micro-level (on children, parents, or families) and are of a relatively short duration. Numerous programs are also professionally driven or led and are implemented in a single context (e.g., home, school, or workplace). While there is substantial evidence that supports the effectiveness of many of these programs in realizing their goals, they do not respond to the range of values and principles promoted by CP. In order to advance personal, relational, and collective wellbeing for families and to support a transformative social agenda, we must look beyond traditional approaches to multi-focused, community-driven and policy-level interventions.

Multi-focused, Community-driven Programs

Multi-focused programs acknowledge the value of holism, recognizing that targeting a single contributing factor is unlikely to address the complexity of cumulative and interacting variables leading to and perpetuating adversity. Drawing on the ecological principle, multi-focused programs also recognize that factors beyond the immediate family, surrounding community, and macro-levels (e.g., policies, stigma), significantly influence the incidence and conditions of disadvantage. Although psychosocial problems may be addressed within multi-component interventions, this focus may be balanced by long-term efforts to develop social support and community capacity. Community development is a major component of many multi-focused programs, often resulting in the creation of neighborhood organizations. These organizations typically respond to the needs of families of preschool and elementary school-aged children, offering a variety of resources, including child care and family support (e.g., School of the 21st Century, Yale University, http://medicine.yale.edu/childstudy/zigler/21c/). Reciprocal informal support among neighbors is also stimulated by such interventions (Garbarino & Kostelny, 1992; Korbin & Coulton, 1996; Olson, 2007).

The fact that these programs are community-driven advances several additional values including self-determination, participation, respect for diversity, and accountability. While researchers and other professionals may be involved in the process, it is in partnership with community members who have a major voice in identifying their needs and wants as well as choice in determining what types of interventions are necessary and how they will be implemented (Nelson, Amio, Prilleltensky, & Nickels, 2000; Nelson et al., 2001; Peters et al., 2004). Program participants become involved and contribute to the management and delivery of their community projects in various ways, including formal and informal opportunities to express views and opinions, volunteering in the delivery of programs, participating on committees that provide advice to the project governing bodies and/or research teams, or sitting on governing bodies that make decisions about the projects and their programs.

Although most programs targeting families facing adversity are more narrowly focused and professionally directed, there is evidence that multi-component, community-driven interventions are becoming more common. Descriptions of proactive universal applications for families are beginning to emerge in the literature. While these programs are situated in high-risk communities, they fit the description of universal programs because the services and supports are available to all families in the area with children in the targeted age range and thus reduce stigma associated with such assistance.

Where Leslea lives, in Canada, there are notable examples of multi-focused, community-driven universal prevention programs being implemented with children and families living in socioeconomically disadvantaged communities. Better Beginnings, Better Futures (BBBF) is a longitudinal prevention research demonstration project that started in 1991 in eight culturally diverse, low-income, high-risk neighborhoods across the province of Ontario (Peters, 2003; Peters et al., 2004). Developed out of the 1990 World Summit for Children at the United Nations, the Community Action Program for Children (CAPC) is a national program with over 400 projects operating in more than 3,000 communities across Canada's provinces and territories (http://www.phac-aspc.gc.ca/hp-ps/dca-dea/prog-ini/capc-pace/index-eng.php). Common overriding goals of BBBF and CAPC are to prevent serious social, psychological, cognitive, and physical problems in at-risk families with young children, promote health and wellbeing, and strengthen community capacity to meet the needs of these families and enhance the environments in which they raise their children. The models followed in the programs incorporate a comprehensive, multi-level ecological framework emphasizing community empowerment and collaborative partnerships among parents, practitioners, researchers, decision-makers, and other citizens. There are many different activities offered across the project sites that are shaped with community input to meet the unique needs of residents. However, there are many similarities in supports and services across the programs including informal and professional home visitation for expectant parents and families with young children, drop-in centers, parent-training classes, social-skills training, literacy enrichment for children, collective kitchens, and recreational opportunities. Medium and long-term meta-evaluations on both programs (Nelson et al. 2012; Peters et al., 2010; Public Health Agency of Canada, 2009) have shown positive impacts for children (e.g., improved physical health, emotional wellbeing, language, cognitive development, and social competence), parents (e.g., improved parenting knowledge, skills, and empowerment), families (e.g., increased social support and improved family functioning), organizations (e.g., increased networking, partnerships, and collaboration), and communities (e.g., expanded resources and capacity, resident engagement). Economic evaluations of these two programs have also demonstrated positive impacts in terms of costs saved and costs avoided in relation to residual spending in the health, social, education, and justice systems (e.g., $2.50 saved for every dollar invested in Better Beginnings, Peters et al., 2016; Peters et al., 2010; Public Health Agency of Canada, 2009).

Glynis works with a multi-focused, community-driven program based in a completely different setting in rural Mozambique. The program, which is supported by CARE International in Mozambique, is currently present in two rural districts. It reaches over 3,000 families and began in 2013 as an Early Childhood Development program but has since expanded its focus. The key people in the program are men and women who are elected by a local village community to be Masungukate (which means "good advisor" in the local language). The Masungukate are trained in child development, health, and nutrition. They are all volunteers and serve neighbors in their local villages where they each visit six families that the community has identified as needing support once a week. One of the main motivators behind forming the program was that caregivers were often women left alone with the care of the children because their husbands had migrated, often as far away as neighboring South Africa, for work. The initial participatory research with women showed that they carried a heavy burden of stress and anxiety and often felt alone with the care of their children. The regular visits from the Masungukate have given them a supportive relationship that has become as important to them as the life-saving information the Masungukate bring about the need for mosquito nets to prevent malaria or how important it is to make sure their children are immunized.

But the program, as a good example of a multi-focused approach, goes beyond this to work in the macro-levels of economic health. One of the biggest stresses for the mothers and grandmothers is the need to find food for their children. They all have small farms and grow some maize for food but climate change has begun to impact this area and there has been no rain for at least two years so these farms are unproductive. Alongside the visits of the Masungukate, the initiative runs a farming program where local facilitators (also elected by the villagers) teach dry farming methods to increase crop yields and show women how to keep chickens for small production businesses. The women also belong to a group savings scheme. CARE has also facilitated the digging of new well points because many of the families had to walk for over an hour to fetch water for their everyday needs.

The Masungukate, with the help of the local community, have also built playgrounds made from simple materials. These have become a focus for young children in the village, with Masungukate on duty each weekday to supervise the play. Staff from a local community-based organization support the Masungukate through monthly reflection meetings and regular visits to the area. They have also organized for local government to bring officials to the distant villages to issue identity documents and birth certificates. An initiative to focus on orphan children of primary school age will soon be implemented, moving the focus beyond children under five years. Qualitative research suggests that the impact of this multi-focused, community driven program is to improve wellbeing for families, but the mixed-methods end line evaluation of this first phase of the project will tell us more about the impacts (See www.care.org.mz/childcare.php).

Another multi-focused, community-driven, universal prevention program was initiated in 1999 in the UK. Strikingly similar to some of the Canadian initiatives, the Sure Start program is described in Box 17.7.

Box 17.7 Program profile: Sure Start

Sure Start originated in 1999 and evaluated in 2012 as part of a national evidence-based campaign to address child poverty and social exclusion in the UK by bringing together services of early education, childcare, health, and family support. More than doubling the original goal of 250 programs, by the end of 2003 there were 524 local Sure Start programs operating in socioeconomically disadvantaged neighborhoods across the UK. In 2004, the initiative expanded with the formation of Sure Start Children's Centers. As of June 30th, 2015 there were 3,382 Children's Centers providing services to young children and their families across England and various other Sure Start services being offered to children and families in Northern Ireland, Scotland, and Wales. Although it originally targeted high-risk families by situating programs in the most deprived communities, Sure Start is an example of universal prevention, since services are available to all local families, regardless of economic status. The primary aim of Sure Start is to work with families with children, prenatally up to age four, to promote the physical, intellectual, and social development of infants and young children and to enhance family and community functioning. To advance this goal, the Sure Start programs concentrate on four main objectives: improving social and emotional development; improving health; improving children's ability to learn; and strengthening families and communities. Local programs are sensitive to diversity and are driven by the unique needs identified at the neighborhood level. However, there are core services that each Sure Start program is expected to provide, including outreach and home visiting; family and parent support; opportunities for quality play, learning, and childcare; primary and community health care; and support for children and parents with special needs. In terms of community participation, a key principle of the Sure Start approach is promoting the involvement of all local families in the design and implementation of services.

In addition to local evaluations of the 260 original programs and case studies of 26 of these programs, a team of academics and practitioners conducted a national process and impact evaluation of Sure Start. The first phase of the longitudinal evaluation began in January 2001 and the final report was released in 2012 (National Evaluation of Sure Start Team, 2012). With respect to child and family functioning when children were seven years old, and in comparison with families not living in areas served by Sure Start centers, the programs showed significant positive effects for all three parent and family functioning outcomes (use of harsh discipline, chaos in the home, and home learning environment). Significant effects were not observed across programs for any of the child specific (academic achievement, physical health, social and emotional development) or maternal wellbeing outcomes; however, the researchers indicated methodological challenges encountered by the evaluation may have limited the study's ability to detect strong causal inferences about the impact of the programs on children and their families. (Sure Start Services website: https://www.nidirect.gov.uk/articles/sure-start-services; National Evaluation website: http://www.ness.bbk.ac.uk/)

Social Policy Interventions

While multi-focused, community-driven approaches can respond to the needs of children and families for prevention, inclusion, support, sense of community, and personal empowerment, they cannot change the macro-social, economic, and political factors that significantly influence conditions of adversity (Febbraro, 1994). The patterns of poverty that are passed from one generation to the next can and will be broken when the poor have the means and opportunity to be healthy and well-nourished, educated, and skilled enough to fully participate in the decisions that affect their lives (UNICEF, 2000).

Preschools and early childhood interventions are an important avenue for establishing equity and equal educational opportunities for children from diverse social backgrounds. In general, equity includes both access and quality (Britto, Yoshikawa, & Boller, 2011), so high quality preschools that are available to all children represent a universal intervention that has been shown to have a high potential of reducing the school readiness gap for children from families of low socio-economic status (Burger, 2010; Melhuish, 2011). High quality preschool interventions have been found to increase positive cognitive, behavioral, social-emotional, and health outcomes for children from both lower- and middle-income families in the US and internationally (Nores & Barnett, 2010). However, reviews suggest that children from lower-income families benefit more. Benefits have also been demonstrated for those with special needs, dual-language learners and immigrants, and children from diverse racial/ethnic groups (Yoshikawa et al., 2013). Long-term effects of preschool interventions include individual and societal outcomes (e.g., high school education, higher educational level, higher income, and lower rates of crime, teenage pregnancy, and substance use; Barnett, 2011; Yoshikawa et al., 2013). Overall, several reviews of studies support the proposition that preschool interventions have substantial positive impacts on all children (Melhuish, 2011). For disadvantaged children, however, they are particularly important to establish equity in educational opportunity (Burger, 2010). Broadening the importance of preschool interventions to a macrosystem perspective, it is imperative that social policies reflect the importance of wellbeing and social justice in general to more fully support these programs (Nelson & Caplan, 2014; Olson, 2007).

The means and opportunity to pursue a healthy and satisfying life are bestowed through vehicles of social, economic, and health policy. To address socioeconomic inequalities and poverty, and to promote the wellbeing of children and families, social interventions must be mounted to advocate and develop policies that will ensure a more just and equitable distribution of resources among all members of society, nationally and globally.

There is a belief that the absolute wealth of a country produces health, but this notion does not consider the distribution of wealth. This idea neglects the importance of other structural factors such as race and gender and it fails to point to the need for broader emphasis on social, political, and economic activities like affordable housing and full employment policies. The importance of focusing on a transformative social justice agenda through equitable and responsive policies is supported by research on the social determinants of health. Wilkinson (1994, 1996, 1997), Marmot (2015b), and others (Ben Shlomo, White, & Marmot, 1996; Kaplan, Pamuk, Lynch, Cohen, & Balfour, 1996; Kennedy, Kawachi, & Prothrow-Stith, 1996) have argued from an economic perspective that in advanced industrial societies, a country's wealth status does produce health to some extent, but there is a point beyond which the relationship between wealth and health disappears, becoming instead a function of the relative gap between rich and poor. Furthermore, it is not just the health status of those individuals who exist at the polar extremes of poverty and wealth that is at stake, but rather we are all affected, as inequalities of morbidity and mortality have been found to apply across the socioeconomic gradient (Adler et al., 1994; World Health Organization, 2008). From this perspective, the focus of policy should not be relegated to wealth-generation strategies in the pursuit of improving health and the reduction of health-related problems, but on developing and instituting fundamental mechanisms for ensuring the equitable distribution of wealth and resources across the population. Social interventions promoting a model of collective responsibility will thus serve not only those children and families who are most vulnerable but the whole of society.

Certainly some efforts are working in the battle against poverty and the mission to improve wellbeing. However, there is still much more that needs to be done at the macro-sociopolitical level to address poverty and its consequences. To this end, there is an opportunity to learn from the numerous examples of policies that respond to the needs of children and families experiencing adversity. Social, economic, and health policies can redistribute income to those in lower socioeconomic classes through cash benefits and tax transfers, guarantee support payments to custodial parents, encourage nurturing caregiving environments for children by supporting parental leaves and early childhood care, protect children and adults from disease and disability through universal health coverage and immunization programs, advance learning and literacy through publicly funded education, and safeguard children and families from violent conflicts. Of further interest is a compelling message conveyed by comparative social policy studies that demonstrate greater reductions in economic inequalities among citizens when universal tax benefit and transfer strategies are adopted as opposed to targeting and means-testing such benefits (Baril, Lefebvre, & Merrigan, 2000; Council on Contemporary Families, 2014; Kamerman, 1996; Peters, Peters, Laurendeau, Chamberland, & Peirson, 2001). It is time for governments and citizenry alike to forcefully and collectively act on evidence and experience gained through these macro-level interventions to re-commit to or forge on with promises to eradicate child poverty and uphold obligations to promote the fundamental rights of every child (United Nations, 1991, 2007, 2014).

A good example of government and citizens acting together is the story of the Child Support Grant (CSG) in South Africa. The CSG is an important instrument of social protection, reaching over 10 million South African children each month. The story of this grant is one of community-driven policy change. When the grant was first introduced in 1998, it was for children under five years. In 2002, a network of over 1,300 organizations working in the child service field in South Africa formed the Alliance for Children's Entitlement to Social Security (ACESS). Using research that included the voices of children that had been gathered through participatory research and careful economic modeling to prove to the state that the grant was affordable, ACESS succeeded in getting the child support grant extended to children under seven years and subsequently to all children under 18 years. Recent research showed that the grant has proved to be a significant tool in supporting poor families to look after their children (UNICEF, 2012).

The importance and power of focusing not on economic growth but rather on social policy as a means of alleviating poverty and fighting oppression is further demonstrated by the remarkable transformations that occurred in the state of Kerala in India with respect to social development and population health. Beset by poverty, malnutrition, overcrowding, and other health and social problems, Kerala instituted a series of policies reflecting a campaign of social justice focused on ensuring a more equitable distribution of existing resources, goods, and services across the population. The approaches and advances in this state are profiled in Box 17.8.

Box 17.8 Social Justice through Transformative Policy: The Kerala Experience

India's Kerala State provides an excellent example of how engaging in broad structural reforms within a region's political economy can lead to important gains in the health status of its citizens. Some of the specific structural reforms that were accomplished as a result of various social movements over the course of a century, included amendments to the land tenure system, equalization of income, legislation to provide better social security, pensions and working conditions, free primary- and secondary-level education, increased production of high-yield crops and access to price-controlled food, enforcement of child labor laws, and increases in female participation in the labor force (Ratcliffe, 1978). By the end of the century, Kerala had successfully improved quality of life for its citizens to levels comparable to conditions in many developed nations (Franke & Chasin, 1995, 2000; Kannan, 2000; Parayil, 2000). Public health indices showed Kerala ahead of the rest of India with the lowest rates of diseases such as malaria and cholera; higher rates of immunization for child tuberculosis, polio, diphtheria-pertussis-tetanus, and measles; and greater access to and utilization of health professionals and facilities. Increased understanding of rights by the poor majority also led to raised political consciousness and persistent grassroots activity to force the government to listen to the poor and respond to their needs.

Recent data show many of the gains in the health status of Kerala's population were maintained through the first decade of the new millennium (Government of India, 2011). For example, the literacy rate held steady at 94 percent compared to 74 percent for all of India. At 12 per 1000 live births, the infant mortality rate in Kerala was much lower than the national rate (44 per 1000). Life expectancy at birth for those living in Kerala was 74 years compared to 67 years for all of India. The proportion of Kerala's population without homes was much lower than the national rate (0.04 percent vs. 0.15 percent), and for those with homes, the housing conditions were also rated more favorably in Kerala than across India (66 percent good and 28 percent livable condition vs. 53 percent good and 42 percent livable condition). Through structural changes based on equity considerations, rather than an emphasis on aggregate economic prosperity, Kerala managed to significantly improve the quality of life for the broad majority of its citizens.

Chapter Summary

In this chapter, through a traditional lens, we see that when families living in adversity are viewed in terms of deficits, blamed for their misfortunes, measured against narrow standards, discriminated against, and treated as passive recipients of services, they can become socially isolated, excluded, and powerless. However, viewed through a CP lens, we see that all families, even those experiencing difficulties have strengths, are impacted by forces at multiple ecological levels, reflect diversity, and have rights to power, inclusion, and self-determination. It is also evident that interventions that focus on multiple components, that involve participants as meaningful stakeholders, and promote equity and social justice can foster hope and social change and enhance opportunities for all children and families to become valued members of society, with their needs met. By focusing on values, principles, and interventions that support personal, relational, and collective wellbeing, we can work to transform unequal and unjust systems of power and privilege thereby improving not only the lives of children and families experiencing adversity, but society as a whole.

Key Terms

Community-driven interventions: Interventions that are guided by a community development philosophy in which local residents have a significant voice.

Compartmentalization: The process which encourages partial rewards at many levels but denies fulfillment at any one level.

Containment: Limiting the range of free movement available to a particular group, increasingly restricting and narrowing the scope of possibilities that can be entertained and effectively quarantining people from the possibilities of change.

Doctrine of personal culpability: A synonym for "blaming the victim."

Family wellbeing: A state of affairs in which everybody's needs in the family are met.

Health: A state of complete physical, mental, and social wellbeing, not merely the absence of disease or infirmity.

Multi-focused, community-driven interventions: Community-based interventions that have several different program components (e.g., preschool education for children, home visitation for parents, and so on).

Self-determination: The ability of individuals or collectives to pursue chosen goals and direct their lives without facing formidable obstacles.

Resources

Recommended Websites

- Better Beginnings, Better Futures is a major prevention policy research demonstration project that is being implemented and evaluated in Ontario, Canada: www.bbbf.ca
- Young Lives is an international study of childhood poverty following the lives of 12,000 children in Ethiopia, India (in the states of Andhra Pradesh and Telangana), Peru, and Vietnam over 15 years. Its aim is to shed light on the drivers and impacts of child poverty, and generate evidence to help policymakers design programs that make a real difference to poor children and their families. The website has a wealth of research data on children and families living in adversity: www.younglives.org.uk
- The Community Action Program for Children is a large-scale community-based prevention initiative with approximately 450 programs operating across Canada: www.phac-aspc.gc.ca/dca-dea/programs-mes/capc_main-eng.php
- Sure Start is large-scale prevention policy initiative that is being implemented and evaluated in the UK: www.ness.bbk.ac.uk
- OVCsupport.org is an information site with a wealth of the most up-to-date information on children and families facing HIV and other adversities.
- The Better Care Network website is a useful source of information for people working on issues related to children who lack adequate family care: www.bettercarenetwork.org
- The website of the United Nation's Children's Fund provides information on children's rights (including the United Nations Convention on the Rights of the Child) and other issues related to children living in poverty in developing nations, with links to UNICEF publications, speeches, frequently asked questions, and statistical information: www.unicef.org
- The Annie E. Casey Foundation in the US has a good site on disadvantaged children and families: www.aecf.org
- The Council on Contemporary Families has a lot of information about social policies affecting families. This is a very good resource for understanding research on family policies: https://contemporaryfamilies.org/

Recommended Books and Articles

Albee, G. W., Bond, L. A., & Monsey, T. (1992). *Improving children's lives: Global perspectives on prevention* (Volume XIV of the Primary prevention of psychopathology series). Thousand Oaks, CA: SAGE Publications.

Cicchetti, D., Rappaport, J., Sandler, I., & Weissberg, R. (Eds.). (2000). *The promotion of wellness in children and adolescents.* Washington, DC: Child Welfare League of America Press.

Donald, D., Lazarus, S., & Moolla, N. (2014). *Educational psychology in social context: Ecosystemic applications in Southern Africa* (5th ed.). Cape Town, South Africa: Oxford University Press.

Fergus, S., & Zimmerman, M. (2005). Adolescent resilience: A framework for understanding healthy development in the face of risk. *Annual Review of Public Health, 26,* 399–419.

Hardgrove, A., Enenajor, A., & Lee, A. (2011). *Risk and childhood poverty: Notes from theory and research.* Oxford: Young Lives.

Mrazek, P., & Haggerty, R. (1994). *Reducing risks for mental disorders: Frontiers for preventive intervention research.* Washington, DC: National Academy Press.

Prilleltensky, I. (2012). Wellness as fairness. *American Journal of Community Psychology, 49,* 1–21.

Prilleltensky, I. (2003). Poverty and power: Suffering and wellness in collective, relational and personal domains. In S. Carr & T. Sloan (Eds.), *Psychology and poverty* (pp. 19–44). New York: Kluwer/Plenum.

Prilleltensky, I., & Laurendeau, M.-C. (Eds.). (1994). Prevention: Focus on children and youth [Special issue]. *Canadian Journal of Community Mental Health, 13*(2).

Reynolds, A., Walberg, H., & Weissberg, R. (Eds.). (1999). *Promoting positive outcomes: Issues in children's and families' lives.* Washington, DC: Child Welfare League of America Press.

Ungar, M. (2008). Resilience across cultures. *British Journal of Social Work, 38*(2), 218–35.

Scott, J., & Ward, H. (Eds.). (2005). *Safeguarding and promoting the well-being of children, families and communities.* London: Jessica Kingsley Publishers.

Weissberg, R., Gullotta, T., Hampton, R., Ryan, B., & Adams, G. (Eds.). (1997a). *Enhancing children's wellness.* Thousand Oaks, CA: SAGE Publications.

Weissberg, R., Gullotta, T., Hampton, R., Ryan, B., & Adams, G. (Eds.). (1997b). *Establishing preventive services.* Thousand Oaks, CA: SAGE Publications.

Weissberg, R. P., & Kumpfer, K. L. (Eds.). (2003). Prevention that works for children and youth [Special issue]. *American Psychologist, 58*(6–7).

LGBTQ ISSUES IN COMMUNITY PSYCHOLOGY:
SHIFTING TERRAIN AND THE ONGOING STRUGGLE FOR FREEDOM FROM OPPRESSION

18

Lauren Munro and Robb Travers

Warm-up Questions

Before you begin reading this chapter, we invite you to reflect on the following questions:

1 What do you know about lesbian, gay, bisexual, transgender, and queer (LGBTQ) people and the challenges they face? If your knowledge level is very low, why do you think this is so?

2 How do LGBTQ issues affect you or people in your community?

Learning Objectives

This chapter provides an overview of some of the key issues related to LGBTQ identities and lived experience, the changing yet persistent nature of LGBTQ discrimination, and the global struggle for human rights.

In this chapter you will learn about

- The distinct differences between broader and more subtle forms of LGBTQ discrimination
- Some of the unique challenges facing LGBTQ individuals
- The complex factors and dynamics that contribute to resilience at individual and community levels
- How you can be an ally to LGBTQ individuals and communities

LGBTQ Issues in Community Psychology

Since D'Augelli (1989) and Harper and Schneider (1999; 2003) made their critical calls for a greater focus on **LGBTQ** issues in community psychology (CP), many researchers from diverse disciplines have responded, making valuable contributions to the literature. As this chapter will demonstrate, however, the shifting terrain of LGBTQ identities and communities, the varying forms of discrimination that still persist, and the unique contexts of different countries, present us with ongoing challenges as community psychologists for how to research and respond to the lived experience of LGBTQ individuals. This chapter addresses coming out, violence and discrimination, family, school, peer supports, homelessness, migration, resilience, and the ongoing struggle for human rights globally. Our aim is to situate these issues within a context of inequitable power relations, and forms of oppression that include **heteronormativity** and **cisnormativity**. Heteronormativity refers to the assumption that individuals will naturally be attracted to partners who are of the "opposite" gender. Cisnormativity refers to the assumption that **cisgender** individuals are normal or desirable, while **transgender** people are somehow inferior. We maintain that despite considerable advances in human rights protections for LGBTQ communities (particularly in Western democracies), power and oppression are still considerable forces that shape the lived experience of LGBTQ individuals globally.

LGBTQ: An Insufficient Acronym

As we draw attention to the issues facing gender and sexual minorities, we have chosen to use the acronym "LGBTQ" throughout this chapter. As Renn (2010) points out, "Political, social, and sometimes intellectual alliances of LGBTQ people have led to conflation of these distinct groups in campus contexts, where they are frequently treated as a monolithic community for the purposes of providing programs and services" (p. 135). We use LGBTQ with the acknowledgement that it is insufficient. Terminology varies across disciplines and societies, and within communities, ranging from GLBT (gay, lesbian, **bisexual**, transgender) to sexually diverse, or LGBTQQIP-2SAA (lesbian, gay, bisexual, transgender, queer, **questioning**, **intersex**, **pansexual**, **2-Spirit**, **asexual**, **ally**; see definitions in the Key Terms section at the end of this chapter). The shifting terrain of identity moves more quickly than academic publications and, thus, it would seem that we are always a step behind current discourse. Regardless of the length of an acronym, or the breadth of a chosen descriptor, the diversity of such a dynamic set of communities cannot be adequately summed up in a concise manner. How people identify their genders and sexualities varies depending on time, place, relationships, and myriad other factors. Some have reclaimed the word "queer" and use it to describe themselves and the broader LGBTQ community. We purposefully avoid using the term "**homosexuality**," (the exception being our section on legal decisions that use this language) because many LGBTQ individuals associate it with the historical pathologizing of their identities within mental health and medical professions (Drescher, 2015). While the term itself may seem value-free, it is laden with a history of fear, discrimination and pathologization, and it is therefore important to acknowledge that, for many, it is still a loaded term that has been used to hurt and humiliate. While we use the acronym LGBTQ to be consistent, we encourage you to consider the unique facets of various identities in relation to each issue raised in this chapter. As you read, you may come across terms in this chapter you are unfamiliar with. For this reason, we have included a glossary of key terms at the end of the chapter for easy reference.

The shifting terrain of identity presents numerous opportunities for community psychologists to grapple with issues of concern to identify communities, that, to date, have not received much attention in the literature, including pansexual, asexual, and **non-binary** individuals. We are also more than our sexual orientations and gender identities – we have intersecting identities inclusive of race, ability, social class, age, and so on. Intersectionality is concerned with analyzing how social and cultural categories intertwine to shape the unique and complex forms of oppression experienced by individuals (Knudsen, 2006). For example, individuals may face discrimination based on their gender, race, citizenship, sexuality, and a number of other intersecting identities simultaneously (Gray, Mendelsohn, & Omoto, 2015). Black men who have sex with men, for example, may feel torn between their various identities, leaving them vulnerable to anxiety, depression, and post-traumatic stress (Graham, Braithwaite, Spikes, Stephens, & Edu, 2009). Moreover, consider the impact of historical and ongoing colonization of Indigenous peoples and communities and how that intersects with, and magnifies, discrimination based on **gender minority** and **sexual minority** status.

Box 18.1 Black Lives Matter and the Toronto Pride Parade

In 2016, Pride Toronto appointed Black Lives Matter Toronto (BLMTO) as the "honored group" for the pride parade, one of the world's largest celebrations of LGBTQ culture and community. During the main parade, BLMTO staged a protest by halting the march until the Pride Toronto executive agreed to a list of demands, which included increased funding and support for Black queer youth, the elimination of police floats from the festival, and increased Black Deaf and hearing American Sign Language interpreters. After 30 minutes of protest, the executive director of Pride Toronto signed the list of demands. Negative reactions to the protest from inside and outside of the LGBTQ community were swift and enduring, described by some as divisive and as an interruption of celebration.

1 Why do you think some people, within and outside of the LGBTQ community, had negative reactions to this protest?

2 How does this action reflect the more politically-oriented origins of Pride?

The Changing Nature of Anti-LGBTQ Discrimination

Many jurisdictions internationally have made considerable advancements in LGBTQ human rights, including the decriminalization of same-sex sexual activity, the inclusion of sexual orientation and gender expression in human rights codes, same-sex partner benefits, and in many countries globally, same-sex marriage (Mack, 2005). However, things are more than what they seem, and discrimination still occurs. Historically, there has been a tendency in the literature to frame the discrimination faced by LGBTQ people as stemming from societal **homophobia** (Herek, 1990) and more recently, **transphobia** (Hill, 2002). While these terms have historic roots in relation to the fear and hatred of LGBTQ people, they do not adequately encompass the embedded social relations or the depth of oppression that allow for them to occur. We maintain that cisnormativity and heteronormativity shape the lives of LGBTQ people and we situate interpersonal violence and discrimination within these broader structural contexts. Such a broadened lens positions heteronormativity and cisnormativity as enabling constructs, which allows us to more accurately understand the complexities of multiple forms of discrimination facing LGBTQ individuals (Kitzinger, 2005). As a reminder, heteronormativity is the belief system that heterosexuality is the only and natural form of human sexuality and it allows for an understanding of "the myriad ways in which heterosexuality is produced as a natural, unproblematic, taken-for-granted phenomenon" (Kitzinger, 2005, p. 478). Jackson (2006) pointed out that Adrienne Rich's writings on "compulsory heterosexuality" in the 1980s laid the groundwork for conceptions of "heteronormativity" and contends that current definitions must acknowledge that "institutionalized, normative, heterosexuality regulates those kept within its boundaries as well as marginalizing and sanctioning those outside them" (p. 105).

We take up heteronormativity with attention to the ways in which assumed heterosexuality affects individual and interpersonal interactions and the ways in which this belief system underpins institutional and environmental contexts. Cisnormativity, on the other hand "describes the expectation that all people are cissexual, that those assigned male at birth always grow up to be men and those assigned female at birth always grow up to be women" (Serano, 2007). This assumption is so "pervasive that it otherwise has not yet been named" (Bauer et al., 2009, p. 356). Cisnormativity provides us with an understanding of why the possibility of even being transgender seems impossible (Namaste, 2000; Serano, 2007). Transgender is an umbrella term that can encompass anyone whose lived or felt experience of their gender differs from that assigned to them at birth.

Stigmatization, oppression, and discrimination towards LGBTQ individuals has been extensively documented (Matthews & Adams, 2009). Such discrimination is often seen in housing, employment, and custody rights, and may also take the form of verbal/sexual assaults, harassment, and homicide (Matthews & Adams, 2009). The ways that oppression manifests in the lives of LGBTQ individuals is complex and varies along lines of orientation, gender, class, race, and ability. For example, for bisexual individuals, **erasure**, invisibility, and the invalidation of their identities both within and outside of LGBTQ communities creates the conditions for poor psychological outcomes (Eady, Dobinson, & Ross, 2009). Trans people experience disproportionately high levels of overt violence and discrimination (Longman Marcellin, Scheim, Bauer, & Redman, 2013) and, as Lamble (2008) maintains, experiences of violence are deeply connected to issues of racism, classism, and **heterosexism**.

Certainly, physical harassment and individual acts of violence related to LGBTQ identities need to be taken seriously. Especially given that disclosure of violence is less common amongst LGBTQ persons, as the stigma of being a sexual minority can create a barrier to seeking help (Sylaska & Edwards, 2015). That being said, to focus only on overt forms of discrimination (e.g., violent assaults), obscures the daily, commonplace, and longer-term forms of subtle discrimination that are insidious and have been shown to have deleterious effects on LGBTQ wellbeing (Nadal et al., 2011). If we think of discrimination as occurring at *both* institutional and interpersonal levels, overt forms of violence and discrimination have likely lessened in many countries for many LGBTQ individuals.

Meyer's (2003) model of minority stress demonstrated that living in heterosexist, hostile, and homophobic environments can lead to adverse health and wellbeing outcomes for sexual minorities. Recently, there has been a focus on the more subtle forms of discrimination (i.e., microaggressions) that LGBTQ individuals face on a daily basis (Nadal et al., 2011; Munro, Travers, & Woodford, 2019; Woodford, Chonody, Kulick, Brennan, & Renn, 2015). The microaggressions framework adds depth to our understanding of the effects of more subtle forms of discrimination on wellbeing. For example, a colleague saying "homophobia is a thing of the past" or a classmate casually saying "that's so gay" also have considerable and adverse effects on LGBTQ individuals' wellbeing. In one study, heterosexism on university campuses was associated with decreased academic and social integration among sexual minorities (Woodford & Kulick, 2015). In a recently published paper, exposure to terms such as "no homo" or "that's so gay" was associated with increased drug and alcohol use among American LGBTQ college students (Winberg et al., 2018). One must be mindful of the myriad ways that oppression manifests. The tendency for the media to focus on more sensationalist forms of bullying, for example, can mean that the seemingly innocuous forms of homophobic and transphobic harassment, that Haskell and Burtch (2010) described as "gentle violence" (p. 95), are less visible and, as such, get left unacknowledged, and unaddressed.

We cannot hope to cover all of the issues pertaining to the health and wellbeing of LGBTQ people – for example, there is a rich body of research and community activism focused on LGBTQ people and HIV/AIDS that we simply do not have the space to examine – but we hope you will be inspired to explore beyond this chapter. In the following sections we will discuss coming out, school experiences, youth homelessness, global human rights, and LGBTQ resilience. Finally, we will close with a discussion of what it means to work in solidarity with LGBTQ communities.

Coming Out

Coming out is a process whereby people come to disclose their non-heterosexual sexual orientation or their non-cisgender identities. One of the precursors to coming out is defining one's own identity, which typically involves an understanding of one's sexual orientation and/or gender as different from expected societal norms, followed by a personal labeling as LGBTQ, and then potential disclosure of this identity to others (Kosciw, Palmer, & Kull, 2015). Although the general process presents itself differently for all LGBTQ individuals, coming out tends to occur during adolescence or early adulthood (Kosciw et al., 2015). However, identity formation (the process of self-discovery and exploration) and identity integration (acceptance and commitment to one's sexual identity) do not always occur in sync, creating further challenges with regards to coming out (Rosario, Schrimshaw, & Hunter, 2008). This process of identity integration is associated with increased psychological wellbeing for many individuals (Kosciw et al., 2015). Identity development discourse, however, has been criticized for an inherent assumption of linearity and a failure to recognize the diverse and dynamic coming-out processes, individual experiences, and the vulnerability of particular groups during this process; for many, coming out is not a one-time event but is done repeatedly in different social contexts (Rosario et al., 2008; Klein, Holtby, Cook, & Travers, 2014). For example, consider the ways in which cisnormativity and heteronormativity both necessitate and restrict the coming out process for LGBTQ individuals.

LGBTQ Youth and the School Experience

For LGBTQ youth, coming out in school may be paired with an increased risk of verbal and physical harassment, and/or physical assault, leading some to avoid school to reduce the likelihood of being victimized (Kosciw et al., 2015). School environments, however, can act as settings for social support through both ameliorative and transformative change efforts. In one example, school theatre programs benefited LGBTQ youth living in isolation and hopelessness in relation to their sexual identity, by providing a supportive community that allowed for personal empowerment, group solidarity, and trust building (Wernick, Kulick, & Woodford, 2014). School-based mentoring initiatives may also prove to be beneficial for LGBTQ youth. In a national US study, LGBTQ youth who did not have supportive family members, were more likely to be mentored by adults at school, indicating the importance of school environments (Johnson & Gastic, 2015).

Gay–straight alliances (GSAs) are an example of a school-based intervention that promotes the health and wellbeing of LGBTQ youth through offering structured spaces within schools for socializing and advocacy efforts between LGBTQ youth and their straight allies (Griffin Lee, Waugh, & Beyer, 2004; St. John et al., 2013; Poteat, Scheer, Marx, Calzo, & Yoshikawa, 2015). GSAs, depending on their context and focus, have the potential to create both ameliorative and transformative changes in the school environment depending on their structure and focus (Garcia-Alonso, 2004; Griffin et al., 2004). The focus of a GSA is typically context-specific – in schools where greater hostility is perceived, GSAs do more to advocate for support and collective social change (Poteat et al., 2015). Regarding their potential for ameliorative changes, in one US study, compared to heterosexual youth, LGBTQ youth in schools with GSAs reported less truancy, smoking, drinking, and suicide attempts, than those in schools without GSAs (Poteat, Sinclair, DiGiovanni, Koenig, & Russell, 2013). Teachers who lead GSAs report challenges associated with their efforts, including concerns for job security, and of losing credibility and being criticized for the recruitment of youth to a "gay lifestyle" (Valenti & Campbell, 2009). Despite these concerns, GSA advisors report choosing to be involved in these interventions because they genuinely care about the wellbeing of LGBTQ students (Valenti & Campbell, 2009). Regarding the "transformative change potential" of GSAs, when they are designed to support advocacy efforts on the part of students, they are more likely to achieve structural change in school environments (Russell, Muraco, Subramaniam, & Laub, 2009). Moreover, if they are nested within broader government, legislative, policy, and institutional supports, their efforts have the potential to be fully transformative (St. John et al., 2013). One notable example of very meaningful change is the impact GSAs have on suicide among young people. In the Canadian context, Saewyc, Konishi, Rose, and Homma (2014) found in a large population-based study of adolescents in British Columbia, that suicidal ideation decreased for all students (but especially for heterosexual males) in schools with GSAs.

LGBTQ Youth Homelessness

LGBTQ youth between 16 and 26 years of age are overrepresented among homeless youth in North America (Abramovich, 2012). While approximately 2 percent of the population self-identifies as LGBTQ (Tjepkema, 2008), 25–50 percent of homeless youth belong to this demographic (Josephson & Wright, 2000). Abramovich (2012) suggested a range of pathways to homelessness among LGBTQ youth, with the main one being ejection from the home due to family conflict; abuse, homophobia, and transphobia are the key drivers that result in youth leaving home out of desire or necessity (Abramovich, 2012; Public Health Agency of Canada, 2006). Once homeless, LGBTQ youth face new risks including anti-LGBTQ violence and discrimination, engagement in sex work, alcohol and drug use, despair, depression, and suicidality (Nyamathi et al., 2016). Furthermore, homeless transgender youth are denied access to shelters, and often forced to remain in dorms and use washrooms that correspond to the gender they were assigned at birth (Keuroghlian, Shtasel, & Bassul, 2015).

O'Brien, Travers, and Bell (1993) researched the conditions facing LGBTQ youth in Toronto's youth hostel, residential treatment center, and youth shelter systems. LGBTQ youth were told by staff and administrators to be silent about their sexual orientation, were denied accessible services and resources, and were subjected to severe hostility (O'Brien, Travers, & Bell, 1993). The authors argued for structural and transformative policy level changes as crucial elements in ensuring the ability of these systems to be able to adequately respond to the needs of LGBTQ youth. In 2010, Travers et al. queried more than 80 youth service providers across Toronto who reported that the youth social service system was actually less able to address the needs of LGBTQ youth almost 20 years later as a result of their coming out younger, a higher percentage of trans clients, an increasing ethno-racial diversity of clients, a fast-growing metropolitan area, and persistent government cutbacks to services.

Global Human Rights

The United Nations Human Rights Council (UNHRC) (2015) report on discrimination and violence against individuals based on their sexual orientation and gender identity reveals both challenges and successes for LGBTQ individuals and communities. The UNHRC (2015) reported that, between 2011 and 2015:

> 14 nations have adopted or strengthened anti-discrimination and hate crime laws, extending protection on grounds of sexual orientation and/or gender identity and, in two cases, also introducing legal protections for intersex persons. Three States have abolished criminal sanctions for homosexuality; 12 have introduced marriage or civil unions for same-sex couples nationally, and 10 have introduced reforms that, to varying degrees, make it easier for transgender persons to obtain legal recognition of their gender identity. (UNHRC, 2015, p. 3)

While these advances in legal protections demonstrate positive change, and are cause for celebration, they are eclipsed by ongoing violence and human rights violations against gender and sexual minorities. The International Lesbian, Gay, Bisexual, Trans and Intersex Association report on State Sponsored Homophobia (Carroll & Itaborahy, 2015) concluded that 75 countries still criminalize same-sex sexual acts. Of the states that criminalize same-sex encounters, eight officially legislate the death penalty, only five of which actually implement it (Mauritania, Sudan, Iran, Saudi Arabia, and Yemen).

Other countries subject individuals to violence, harassment, and abuse on the basis of perceived or actual gender and/or sexual orientation. Incidents of torture, arbitrary detention, mistreatment, and abuse by law enforcement agents, denial of rights to expression and assembly, and discrimination in healthcare, employment, housing, and education have all been documented (UNHRC, 2015). Even in places where LGBTQ people are protected by the law, individual acts of violence and discrimination compromise their ability to live free from discrimination, or simply to live at all:

- In 2012, Brazilian authorities documented 310 murders where homophobia or transphobia was a motive (UNHRC, 2015).

- Between January 2013 and March 2014, the Inter-American Commission on Human Rights ((IACHR) 2014) reported at least 770 acts of violence against LGBTQ people in 25 OAS (Organization of American States) member states (Argentina, Barbados, Belize, Bolivia, Brazil, Canada, Chile, Colombia, Cuba, Dominican Republic, Ecuador, El Salvador, Guatemala, Guyana, Haiti, Honduras, Jamaica, Mexico, Nicaragua, Panama, Paraguay, Peru, United States, Uruguay, and Venezuela), including 594 hate-motivated killings.
- A Europe-wide survey of 93,000 LGBTQ individuals revealed that a quarter of all respondents had been threatened with violence or attacked in the past 5 years. However, respondents rarely reported these incidents to police because they did not believe anything would change (European Union Agency for Fundamental Rights, 2013).
- The US Department of Justice (2014) reported single bias hate crime statistics that revealed the number of bias-motivated incidents related to sexual orientation (inclusive of acts against lesbian, bisexual, and trans individuals) ranks second only to racist incidents.
- On August 12th, 2016, 49 people were killed and 53 wounded in a hate-motivated mass shooting at a gay nightclub in Orlando, Florida.

Trans and gender-nonconforming individuals experience unparalleled levels of violence. Drawing on partnerships with trans organizations, activists, and internet research, the Trans Murder Monitoring (TMM) Project revealed a total of 2,115 reported killings of trans and gender variant people in 65 countries worldwide between January 1st, 2008 and April 30th, 2016 (TvT Research Project, 2016). This report highlights, "100 reported murders of trans and gender diverse people in 2016, which is the highest number in the first 4 months of the year registered by the TMM project since 2008" (TvT Research Project 2016, para. 2). Most countries do not systematically collect data on murdered trans people, and it is not possible to estimate the number of unreported murders. Region-specific data reveals that the highest numbers of trans murder cases have been found in countries where there are active trans movements and civil rights organizations that monitor abuses: Brazil (845), Mexico (247), Colombia (108), Venezuela (104), and Honduras (80) in Central and South America; the US (141) in North America; Turkey (43) and Italy (34) in Europe; and India (55), the Philippines (40), and Pakistan (35) in Asia (TvT Research Project 2016).

It is easy to falsely conclude that North America is a safe haven for LGBTQ people, though it is important to note that discrimination and violence are ever-present realities for LGBTQ people living there. In their research with Canadian LGBTQ newcomer (immigrant, refugee, and undocumented) youth, Munro et al. (2013) found that, while youth come to Canada seeking asylum and safety from homophobic and transphobic violence, they still encountered discrimination on the basis of their gender and sexual identities in a variety of settings including at work, while seeking support in social service organizations, in educational contexts, and within their diasporic communities. Those who came through the refugee system had to prove their sexual orientation or gender identity during the claims process by conforming to stereotypes about LGBTQ individuals and providing proof of relationships and involvement in LGBTQ events. In instances where youth were claiming refugee status on the basis of homophobic or transphobic persecution, there were high stakes hearings; if the authorities did not believe the veracity of their claims, they could be denied status and deported back to the countries they were fleeing (Munro et al., 2013).

The Advocate (2018) described 2016 and 2017 as tied for "the deadliest year on record for transgender Americans" with 27 reported homicides each year (para. 1). It is crucial that, as we take in these statistics, we note that most of the victims were women of color and, of those, the vast majority were Black transgender individuals. We must not lose sight of the ways that racism intersects with sexism and transphobia to create conditions of marginalization and vulnerability for trans women of color and, more specifically, Black trans women. In their report on anti-trans violence, the Human Rights Campaign (2018) reported that at least 22 trans people had been murdered since the beginning of 2018, though they noted that these numbers were published before the end of the year and that it is likely there are others that go unreported. Taken together, these stories and statistics serve as a reminder of where we, as community psychologists and citizens, still have a great deal of work to do.

Understanding Resilience in LGBTQ Individuals and Communities

This chapter has documented some of the complex challenges that continue to face LGBTQ communities and individuals both locally and globally. By now, it should be very obvious that while the literature is both complex and interdisciplinary, it remains largely risk/deficits focused (i.e., much of it attends to the identification of risk factors associated with the experience of marginalization and its negative outcomes). More recently, however, there have been efforts by many researchers to identify factors that protect some individuals against the effects of minority stress. Resilience theories attend to the degree to which protective factors mitigate sexual minority risk factors and promote positive adaptation amidst adversity (Shilo, Antebi, & Mor, 2014).

A recent review of the literature revealed that, while three domains (community, family, and individual) are present in LGBTQ resiliency research, the majority of studies focus on the individual level and very few speak to the interaction between domains (de Lira & de Morais, 2017). Viewing resiliency as an internal trait held by individuals ignores larger and more complex external forces and environments that may "blunt" resiliency on the part of some, while encouraging victim-blaming on the part of others (Masten & Obradović, 2006). Sexual orientation/gender identity oppressions are systemic and widespread social inequities that occur through the use of power granted to different groups in society (Case & Hunter, 2012). For example, an increasing body of literature shows that LGBTQ individuals with intersecting identities (e.g., Black, female, lesbian) face particular social circumstances that result in poorer self-rated health and wellbeing (Veenstra, 2011). We challenge the field of CP to think critically about what we already know about vulnerabilities shaped by social class, race, ability, power, and privilege and to focus on addressing deficits, while also attending to strengths.

Resiliency should be regarded, in part, as dependent on individual, familial, and community supports that provide protection against negative outcomes (Case & Hunter, 2012). One study, for example, explored resiliency in sexual minority women and revealed that, despite experiencing significant levels of family rejection, they were resilient to adverse mental health outcomes because they established strong peer and community connections (Zimmerman, Darnell, Rhew, Lee, & Kaysen, 2015). In the Ontario-based Trans PULSE Project, social and parental support for gender identity were associated with lower risk of attempted suicide for trans people of all ages (Bauer,

Scheim, Pyne, Travers, & Hammond, 2015). In an Israeli study, the role of community-level resilience factors in the lives of LGBTQ individuals and their support systems differed between age groups where, for youth, family support was a strong predictor of wellbeing and decreased adverse mental health outcomes (Shilo, Antebi, & Mor, 2015). Other social and community-level factors such as support from friends, LGBTQ connectedness, and having a romantic partner had more pronounced benefits in adults as compared to youth (Shilo et al., 2015). In a systematic review of parental influences on the health and wellbeing of sexual minority youth, the authors noted that the available literature focuses primarily on negative parental influences, risky sexual behaviors, substance use, and violence/victimization (Bouris et al., 2010). The review stresses the need for research that encompasses parental perspective and ways to support, promote, and assist in the health and wellbeing of LGBTQ youth (Bouris et al., 2010). Particularly exciting about all of these studies is that they broaden our collective understanding of what makes individuals *and* communities more resilient, signaling that meaningful change for LGBTQ people is indeed possible.

Working in Solidarity with LGBTQ Communities: What Can You Do?

There is always more to be done and it is important that we see the lives of LGBTQ people and communities as an integral part of the struggle for liberation and wellbeing. While your research or scholarship may not be explicitly focused on LGBTQ communities, it is important to remember that we are more than our gender and sexual orientations, and we may be members of multiple communities. To that end, have you considered whether LGBTQ people are represented within your research? Do you collect that kind of demographic information? Would it be valuable if you did? Rainbow Health Ontario offers a plethora of resources on LGBTQ research, including a fact sheet on designing surveys and questionnaires with LGBTQ people in mind. No single question will be adequate to capture diversity in gender and sexual identities, however, knowing what you need to know and reviewing best practices in LGBTQ research will ensure that you ask the questions in a more informed, sensitive and rigorous manner (see Box 18.2 for some questions for consideration).

Box 18.2 LGBTQ Inclusive Research: What Do You Need To Know?

- Are you trying to capture data on as many sexual minority people as possible? If so, you might measure attraction.

- Are you interested in knowing about sexual activity or STI risk? Then sexual behavior might be your focus.

- Do you need data on people who belong to specific communities? In that case identity may be more salient.

- Will your research account for people who do not fit within binary categories of male and female? Make sure you create space for them to identify.

- Are you conducting research with individuals from a variety of cultural backgrounds? Recognize that terminology may vary.

Adapted from Rainbow Health Ontario (2012)

In working with and for LGBTQ communities, it is imperative that we find ways to translate research into action. Consider the Trans PULSE Project, one of the most influential studies in the world in terms of its contributions to understanding the effects of social exclusion on trans people's health and wellbeing. Trans PULSE data were used extensively in the debates/decisions regarding the inclusion of gender identity and expression in the Canadian Human Rights Act as a protected ground from discrimination. The Trans PULSE Project was a "community-owned" research initiative driven by and governed by a majority trans investigative team. It is an example of how well-designed community-based research with the right partners at the table can yield high-quality data to shift power relations and effect change in the lives of community members (Travers et al., 2013).

Beyond research and academia, the role you play in identifying and responding to heteronormativity and cisnormativity in your day to day life is crucial (see Box 18.3 for an example). As explained in Chapter 1 (and discussed in more depth in Chapter 4) of this volume, being an ally involves not only recognizing the ways in which you have privilege but also using your social power to support marginalized groups in their efforts to gain power and create meaningful social change. This active component is essential. Reflecting on what it means to be an ally, McKenzie (2013) asserted, "It's not an identity. It's a practice. It's an active thing that must be done over and over again, in the largest and smallest ways, every day" (para. 9). In their research on LGBTQ ally development courses, Ji, Haehnel, Muñoz, and Sodolka (2013), found that delivering relevant content to students was not sufficient in generating allyship. Indeed, knowing is only half the battle; benefits were seen when instructors motivated students to engage in challenging learning activities to enhance their development as LGBTQ allies (Ji et al., 2013).

Box 18.3 Responding To Transphobia: What Would You Do?

Less than a week before Bill C-16, (federal trans rights legislation that added gender identity and gender expression to the Canadian Human Rights Act's list of prohibited grounds of discrimination), passed in the Canadian Senate, a woman-only spa in Ontario denied a trans woman entry to its facilities. Despite the spa having previously promoted itself as a "queer- and trans-friendly space," it became clear that their policy only allowed particular types of women to access their services – specifically the policy excluded anyone with "male genitalia."

Trans women and their allies rightfully named this policy as transphobic; a policy such as this suggested that womanhood is biologically-defined and excluded trans women who have not undergone gender-related surgeries.

1 How do policies that link gender to genitalia reinforce gender essentialism?

2 How might you be an ally in this situation? What actions could you take?

3 What connections exist between this issue and ongoing debates in the US about gendered washrooms?

Thinking about allyship as being inextricable from action creates space for us to consider the ways in which we challenge heterosexism and cissexism. Reflecting on citizen engagement, Walsh and Gokani (2014) assert that, "to become engaged in social justice we have to 'put our bodies where our mouths are' and, mediated by equal partnerships with other justice-seeking citizens, join the living work of social movements" (p. 30). Being an ally requires action, reflection, and a commitment to continual learning; in that spirit, we suggest reflecting on the following questions:

- Have I given myself the label of "ally" or am I acting in solidarity with LGBTQ people and movements that are inclusive of their needs?

- In what ways can I use my privilege to uplift the voices and work of LGBTQ people?
- Am I unintentionally reinforcing the same oppressive behaviors that I claim to be against?
- How often do I speak up against the routine discriminations (be they microaggressions or overt homophobia/transphobia) perpetrated by my friends, family, coworkers, or neighbors?
- Am I aware of how much space I take up in conversations with and about LGBTQ communities?
- How is my allyship grounded in action?

De Leon (2013) pointed out that "the original vision of allyship was calibrated to a society that would punish people who declared themselves as allies" (para. 13), citing job discrimination, loss of social status, criminalization on the basis of political beliefs, and violence as consequences for those who identified themselves as allies (to anti-racist movements in particular). This is contrasted with its usage today, where proclaiming oneself an ally is often rewarded socially and materially. With this in mind, it is important to be conscious of when being an ally becomes performative and to acknowledge that, at times, being an ally will mean risking your social status and leveraging the power and privilege to which you have access. Being an ally also requires that we recognize the ways in which privilege may initially obscure our understanding of an issue; it is crucial that we center the experiences of those who are most marginalized (see Box 18.4).

Box 18.4 Concluding thoughts on Black Lives Matter & the Toronto Pride Parade

Pride has its origins in protest. While there have been social gains in relation to LGBTQ rights in some places, as demonstrated in this chapter, there is still much to be done – particularly as it pertains to more marginalized members of the LGBTQ community. For example, some individuals (e.g., those that are White, cisgender, and/or affluent) may not have negative interactions or associations with police, though that has much to do with privilege and the relative safety it affords. Negative reactions from outside of the LGBTQ community reveal that some expect Pride to simply be a party, free from politics and open to all, but we must remember that the struggle for social justice is ongoing.

Given all that you've learned in this chapter, we have some points for you to reflect on as you move forward in your work in CP:

1 Given the advancement in human rights for LGBTQ communities in many parts of the world, why is discrimination and violence still commonplace?

2 What kinds of unique issues do you think trans people experience in their lives?

3 How can adopting an intersectional lens enhance our understanding of the oppression that LGBTQ people face?

4 Identify five concrete actions you can take to be an ally to LGBTQ people.

Chapter Summary

The aim of this chapter was to highlight some of the ways in which inequitable power relations and intersecting forms of oppression create unique challenges for LGBTQ individuals and communities. We also sought to complicate understandings of resilience, share stories of resistance, and offer strategies for working in solidarity with LGBTQ people. In doing so, we recognize that the richness and diversity of our communities means that we will never be able to cover it all – we encourage you, the reader, to engage in further exploration to understand these issues in local and global contexts. It is our hope that, as a field, CP will continue to recognize and respond to the injustices that both create and sustain barriers to health and wellbeing for LGBTQ communities.

Key Terms

2-spirit: A term used by some Indigenous people to describe individuals whose gender identity or sexual orientation embody aspects that are both "male" and "female," rather than a binary identity such as man/woman, gay/straight.

Asexual: Refers to individuals who do not experience sexual desire. Asexuality is its own spectrum, with individuals identifying differently on the grounds of romantic and aromantic identities; for example, of those who identify as asexual, many still experience attraction, but do not have a desire to engage in sexual activity related to those attractions.

Ally: Refers to individuals who do not identify as LGBTQ but are committed to working toward justice alongside LGBTQ community members. Historically, some gender and sexual minorities have used the "ally" label to be part of the LGBTQ community without having to come out.

Bisexual: A term used to refer to people whose emotional, romantic, and/or sexual attractions are not limited to one gender. For example, a bisexual individual may be attracted to men, women, and non-binary/trans individuals.

Cisgender: Sometimes abbreviated to "cis," refers to individuals whose gender assignment (typically decided at birth, based on the appearance of one's genitalia) matches their felt gender identity.

Cisnormativity: The assumption that cisgender individuals are normal or desirable. This can lead to erasure, which can then lead to the assumption that all bodies are cisgender.

Erasure: Erasure can occur in two forms, active and passive. Active erasure can range from discomfort with providing services, to refusal of services, sometimes even including intimidation or violence. Passive erasure refers to the processes by which individuals are rendered invisible through a lack of knowledge or the assumption that this knowledge is unnecessary or irrelevant. Both active and passive erasure result in barriers to care, which in turn reduce wellbeing. LGBT individuals and communities often experience erasure.

Gender minority: An umbrella term that is used to refer to individuals who do not identify as cisgender.

Heteronormativity: The assumption that individuals will be attracted to partners who are of the "opposite" gender, and that this is normal. This can lead to the erasure of lesbian, gay, or bisexual individuals, promoting the belief that all people are heterosexual or that non-heterosexuality is a form of deviance.

Heterosexism: Similar to racism and sexism, this term focuses on a system of oppression experienced by LGBTQ people which operates on multiple levels. It includes cultural heterosexism (institutional or systemic beliefs in the superiority of an exclusively heterosexual orientation) and psychological heterosexism (prejudice and stereotypes, harassment, and violence towards LGBTQ individuals).

Homophobia: A term used to describe heterosexual people's fear, contempt, and hatred of individuals who are not heterosexual.

Homosexuality: This is no longer the preferred term of the American Psychological Association or LGB communities due to its link to the Diagnostic and Statistical Manual of Mental Disorders (DSM), as well as the term identifying individuals solely on their sexual orientation. It has been used to refer to individuals who experience attraction to people of the same gender.

Intersex: A term used to refer to people whose reproductive or sexual anatomy does not fit within traditional definitions of female or male. It is important to note that the binary system of male/female results in the erasure of intersex identities and often leads to coercive gender assignments, and unnecessary surgeries (e.g., genital mutilation), for these individuals.

LGBTQ: Lesbian, gay, and bisexual refers to people who experience varying degrees of same-gender desire and attraction and who engage in same-gender sexual behavior, while transgender refers to a range of individuals who do not conform to traditional societal expectations and roles for each gender; LGB refers to sexual-orientation, while transgender refers to gender identity. The Q has historically been used to refer to individuals who are questioning their sexual orientation or gender identity or, more recently, to refer to those who identify as queer.

Non-binary: Non-binary is a term that is used to refer to individuals who do not identify with a binary gender (i.e., man or woman). Some, but not all, individuals who identify as non-binary also identify as transgender.

Pansexual: A label used by individuals whose feelings of sexual, romantic, or emotional attraction are not dependent on the gender identity of their partner(s). For example, someone who is pansexual would be romantically or sexually interested in men, women, transgender, and non-binary individuals.

Questioning: A label used by individuals who are still in the process of figuring out their gender and/or sexual identities and may identify as non-heterosexual.

Sexual minority: An umbrella term that is used to refer to individuals whose attractions or sexual behaviors do not fit within traditional conceptions of heterosexuality.

Transgender: Sometimes abbreviated to "trans," this term is used to describe those whose gender identity does not match the gender they were assigned at birth.

Transphobia: The hatred or fear of transgender people that often results in the stigmatization of trans identities. Transphobia may also become internalized and affect self-esteem and wellbeing of trans individuals.

Resources

- Amnesty International: www.amnestyusa.org/the-state-of-lgbt-rights-worldwide/
- International Lesbian, Gay, Bisexual, Trans and Intersex Association: https://ilga.org/
- National LGBTQ Task Force: www.thetaskforce.org/
- Rainbow Railroad: www.rainbowrailroad.com/
- Family Acceptance Project: https://familyproject.sfsu.edu/
- Egale Canada Human Rights Trust: https://egale.ca/
- Trans PULSE Project: http://transpulseproject.ca/

ABLEISM, PHYSICAL DISABILITY, AND COMMUNITY LIVING

19

Thilo Kroll and Glen White

Warm-up Questions

Before you begin reading this chapter, we invite you to reflect on the following questions:

1 What are your personal experiences with people with disabilities?

2 What – in your view – are the challenges and opportunities for people with disabilities to live independently in the community?

3 What do you think community psychologists can do to improve the lives of people with disabilities?

4 When thinking about the nature of disability, does it reside in the person, the environment, or at the intersection of person and environment? How would you support your answer?

Learning Objectives

The goal of this chapter is to provide you with an introduction to the contemporary understanding of disability and some of its accompanying challenges. To contextualize these issues, we focus on physical disabilities and the challenges that people with this type of disability face in their pursuit for inclusion, social participation, and independent living in the community. We will examine the concept of "ableism" as well as explore avenues for research and intervention by community psychologists to create empowering environments and support systems for people with physical disabilities. Ableism includes the normative attitudes and behaviors towards people with disabilities based on what personal characteristics and functional attributes are valued by the majority population. It can include explicit and overtly expressed behaviors of discrimination as well as unconscious forms of bias.

In this chapter you will learn about

- How disability can be understood and why it is not a person characteristic
- Independent living and housing for people with physical disabilities
- Homelessness and physical disability

Ableism

Over the past 20 years, there has been growing recognition of "able-ism" alongside other well recognized "-isms" such as sexism, heterosexism, racism, and ageism. While there are several attempts to define "ableism" it can be fundamentally characterized as the result of non-factual judgments about the overt or invisible characteristics, presumed (in)abilities, and (limited) capabilities of people with impairments and disabling conditions (Friedman & Owen, 2017). Ableist attitudes and behaviors are very much grounded in a view that disability is an attribute of a person rather than the product of social and environmental circumstances and individual characteristics. Thus, ableism is fundamentally labeling, stigmatizing, and discriminating as it segregates people with disabilities based on their physical, emotional, or cognitive functioning irrespective of the societal and environmental context in which they live. Ableism has been studied in a variety of contexts, including education, employment, built environment, and health care (e.g., Giese & Ruin, 2016; Mik-Meyer, 2016; Sutter, Perrin, Tabaac, Parsa, & Mickens, 2016). Ableist attitudes and practices prevent people with disabilities from full social and societal **inclusion** and participation.

Historically, we can identify a range of root causes and contextual factors for the emergence of ableism. For the US, and even longer for the UK and many other countries, we can trace the institutional history of disability and the othering of people with disabilities. But, we can also see examples that lay the early groundwork for attempts to facilitate participation in education, such as the work of educator Thomas Gallaudet, who advanced the education of the Deaf in the US. In early 19th century France, Louis Braille, who was blind himself and a lecturer at the National Institute for the Young Blind in Paris, invented and taught students a new tactile reading system consisting of embossed dots and dashes on cardboard. Institutions also rose up in Europe and the US to provide specially adapted education to children who were deaf, blind, or had intellectual disabilities. While well intended and clearly a step forward compared to the complete absence of education for these children in the centuries before, the institutional and segregated approach removed children from their families and social support networks at home. Furthermore, it primarily focused on providing a "remedy" or fix for what was not considered "normal" rather than focusing on empowerment and comprehensive social inclusion. It largely ignored the social and physical environment in their contribution to the disabling process.

Values, Theory, and Practice

Disability as a relational concept

For centuries a medicalized notion of "disability" has dominated public and professional perceptions. Disability was firmly seen as a personal attribute of functional physical or mental limitations and impairments irrespective of social, cultural, or physical context. In the wake of the civil rights movement of the 1960s an alternative view of "disability" began to take shape. This is now widely known as the "social model of disability," which introduced a shift in perspective from the individual to society (Oliver, 2013; Charlton, 2000). This "model" no longer regarded persons with disabilities as "deficient" but pointed to the stigmatizing, disabling, and exclusionary arrangements reflected in attitudes, behaviors, and practices of societies. These arrangements precluded equal and equitable participation through physical and social barriers. As early as 1967, a Norwegian parliamentary report (St melding 88 1966–1967) pointed to the need to not only adapt persons to the environment (the traditional rehabilitative approach) but also to adapt the environment to the person (Sosialdepartementet, 1967). For example, if a female wheelchair user cannot receive a mammogram when the machine is not designed to accommodate the wheelchair, the design needs to be improved to ensure that same diagnostic quality can be achieved. If a student with visual impairment cannot read the class handouts in 12-point font, this would have to be provided in alternative formats, such as large font, an audio file, or electronically to be read by screen reading software. If a woman with intellectual disabilities moves into her own home, she has the right to do this and the level and type of assistance that she requires to live independently and for inclusion in society will have to be designed around her needs and preferences. This relational understanding of disability as a multidimensional person and environment interaction is to date reflected in frameworks such as the WHO International Classification of Functioning, Disability and Health (WHO ICF; World Health Organization, 2001), human rights policy (UN Convention on the Rights of Persons with Disabilities), and international development (UN Sustainable Development Goals of the Agenda 2030).

Empowerment and Emancipation

Until the early 1960s, many disability groups in the US primarily functioned as organizations (e.g., National Paraplegia Foundation), where members would share potlucks, invite guest speakers, and organize other events. While members offered service to their organizations, little discussion took place about disability discrimination, or the lack of community accessibility. If these issues were discussed, usually there was no action plan component to address them. The understanding of disability organizations and their members about advocacy, empowerment, and emancipation was undeveloped. Most organizations viewed themselves more at the local level.

The US protests by Dr. Martin Luther King, Jr. and the civil rights movement started to have repercussions in the disability community. The strategies and actions developed by the civil rights organizers were soon adopted by the disability community. In the 1960s, Judy Heumann in New York, Ed Roberts in Berkeley, California, Max and Colleen Starkloff in St. Louis, Missouri, and Marca Bristo in Chicago, Illinois became emerging disability leaders fighting for their rights. They were joined by countless other advocates throughout the US. Together, they became successful role models of what could be achieved through personal and systems change advocacy. Similar activists spearheaded changes in other countries such as Sweden (Adolf Ratzka) and the UK (Paul Hunt, Mike Oliver, Vic Finkelstein).

Dr. Wade Blank, who served as a recreational director at a nursing home in the US, helped to get residents to move out of the facility and start their own community (Mountain State Centers for Independent Living, n.d.). In 1974, Dr. Blank helped to create the Atlantis Community, which served as a foundation for emerging disability community activists to take on discrimination and injustice toward people with disabilities using a variety of strategies, including grassroots education and mobilization for non-violent action, legislative policy advocacy, and legal challenges directed at state and local authority practices that violate the rights of people with disabilities. ADAPT (Americans Disabled for Accessible Public Transit) was birthed from the Atlantis Community and became a sustainable movement that empowered its members to employ civil disobedience to fight against discrimination and injustice. For example, ADAPT leaders learned where the American Public Transit Association (APTA) had its trade meetings and went to the convention sites. The bus operators refused to make public transportation wheelchair accessible. ADAPT organizers went to the convention sites, where the shuttle busses were located and chained their wheelchairs to the bus bumpers. This collective act of civil disobedience and the multiple arrests that ensued across the US during APTA meetings greatly empowered ADAPT members and eventually led to accessibility changes in the Americans with Disabilities Act (ADA) and accessible public transit systems (Rudolph, 2015).

Numerous US legislative rights have been established since these early protests. The Americans with Disabilities Act was signed into effect in 1990 and amended and expanded in 2009 and provides civil rights protections against discrimination to people with disabilities. Among the key provisions are the reasonable accommodations to employees with disabilities and general public accessibility requirements. Noting these successes, the US Congress amended Section 504 of the Rehabilitation Act of 1973. Part of these revisions included Title VII, which helped to establish the structure and process of Centers for Independent Living (CIL). As part of Title VII, the CILs were required to provide four core services: information and referral, peer counseling, independent living skills training, and advocacy. In 2014, the US Congress enacted the Workforce Innovation and Opportunity Act (WIOA) (PL 113-128) that added transition to the original four core CIL services. This transition focuses on both youth transitioning from school to post-secondary education or work and individuals with disabilities transitioning from nursing homes to home and community-based residences.

More recently, the move towards self-directed payment of personal assistance services in the US, under Medicaid, the UK, and Australia is an example of people with disabilities not only having equitable civil rights, but also choices about who they employ to provide assistance to them (see www.selfdirectedsupportscotland.org.uk for more details).

Despite these legal triumphs, ableist attitudes and practices have not completely vanished. While, overall, employer attitudes are positive towards hiring people with disabilities as a group, they still hold reservations towards some disability groups, such as people with intellectual or mental health disabilities. This finding has been consistent over decades (Song, Roberts, & Zhang, 2013; Hernandez, Keys, & Balcazar, 2000).

In considering physical disability, environments still lack in universal accessibility and some legal provisions have been implemented without regard to how people with disabilities can really act on them. It is one thing to have rights but another to be empowered and encouraged to put these provisions into real change. Legal challenges can seem daunting, especially in an unequal context of power. The right to self-direction in the choice of personal supports and assistance is important but difficult to implement when support mechanisms for self-direction are lacking. The right to live independently in the community just like everyone else is difficult to realize when too few affordable and accessible social and private housing options exist and when investment in this area is not supported. City planners still frequently design from an "ableist" point of view in that they develop blueprints for segregated accessible neighborhoods. This is currently reinforced, for example, by the trend to develop separate dementia-friendly communities, often at the outskirts of cities. While the need to adapt the environment to meet the accessibility needs of people with disabilities is now largely understood, the notion of choice for people with disabilities to live anywhere and how they wish to in principle is less appreciated.

Intersectionality

It is tempting to ignore complexities when adopting a particular lens or perspective on a topic, such as disability. We could focus on the functional limitations and immediate barriers that restrict social participation, but as lives are complex, we need to understand the multi-layered interactions of individual, social, economic, legislative, and political forces that maximize opportunities for participation or produce degrees of marginalization. We need to be mindful of **intersectionality**, i.e., how disability, education, economic, and political participation are inter-related. For example, Angel and Kroll (2012) compared the individual biographies of two young men with spinal cord injuries, one living in Washington DC (Thomas) and the other living in Aarhus (Henrik), the second largest city in Denmark. The two cases show clearly that it is not the type of disability but the complexity of personal life course histories, features of the social and physical environment, and educational and economic opportunities that enable or inhibit **independent community living**. The two examples demonstrate that while rehabilitation practices may be relatively comparable and functional, and have successful outcomes for both men, the inequity of accessibility and affordability of post-rehabilitation services, including assistive technology, environmental adaptation support (adapting homes) and personal assistance produced very different life opportunities and community engagement. Consider that Thomas was forced to move into a nursing home and he was deprived of educational resources and appropriate social support. Henrik, on the other hand, had the support of his family and educational and employment systems that provided him with opportunities for developing a self-directed, empowered life. In this case, the social and environmental barriers disempowered Thomas and deprived him of the choices, possibilities, and social engagement that were open to Henrik.

In 2016, the official poverty rate was 12.7 percent in the US, which amounted to 40.6 million people living in poverty. For people aged 18 to 64 years with a disability, the poverty rate was 26.8 percent, pointing to a dramatic economic disparity between people with and without disabilities (Semega, Fontenot, & Kollar, 2017). These percentages have been relatively stable over time and similar poverty rates for people with disabilities can be found for other OECD countries including Denmark (OECD, 2010). Clearly, the higher poverty rates found for people with disabilities as a group are linked to lower labor market participation, unemployment rates and under-employment among people with disabilities (Eurostat, 2017). The US Department of Labor Bureau of Labor Statistics reported in 2016 that unemployment rates were higher for persons with a disability than for those with no disability among all educational attainment groups and that in 2015, 32 percent of workers with a disability were employed part-time, compared with 18 percent for those with no disability.

While we have thus far focused on physical disabilities, it is important to recognize that the spectrum of disabilities and multiple impairments is much wider, and not all people with disabilities are visible in government statistics or in research that seeks to characterize their socioeconomic living circumstances. In an official report by a United Nations Expert Group on Disability Data, Statistics, Monitoring and Evaluation in 2014, the need for disaggregation of all census and population level data was mandated at a global scale as well as to make data capture and research more inclusive of people with disabilities (United Nations Department of Economic and Social Affairs (UNDESA) 2014). A particular disability group that has been underrepresented in research and society as a whole are people with intellectual disabilities, arguably underlining continued ableist social attitudes.

People with intellectual or developmental disabilities have faced not only substantial exclusion and marginalization in society but are often also "voiceless" in terms of research. Participatory approaches that involve them as equitable partners in social research are a way to inform a research agenda that is meaningful and significant to them, and not primarily to academics or practitioners. A study by Buettgen and colleagues presents a very good example of co-designed and implemented research on disability and poverty (Buettgen et al., 2012). The project involved several self-advocates with a developmental disability and academic researchers. The authors describe how they worked together to characterize the research problem, developed a shared understanding of the nature of the challenges in relation to disability and poverty, and devised a course of action to tackle the identified challenges. Examples like this are important as they demonstrate an approach that works with, rather than for, people with disabilities to design equitable and inclusive life opportunities.

Community psychologists can support people with disabilities as they prepare for labor market entry and moreover can provide assistance to people to maintain their employment status. The Capabilities Approach mostly represented by the work of economist Amartya Sen and philosopher Martha Nussbaum may be an interesting theoretical lens to apply to the work of community psychologists in relation to disability (Shinn, 2015; MacLeod, 2014; Munger, MacLeod, & Loomis, 2016). In short, the notion underpinning the Capabilities Approach (although with slightly different emphasis) is that human development depends on the freedom that individuals have to act according to their values given the resources they have available to them. It is not only the provision of rights but also creating opportunities so that individuals can achieve desired personally valued and meaningful outcomes, such as independent, inclusive living in accessible and chosen homes, full labor market participation without discrimination, or the choice of a health care provider based on quality and competence.

Inclusion, Independent Community Living, and Housing

In the previous section, we discussed some of the complexities that marginalize people with disabilities in society and that hinder inclusion and independent community living. The notion of inclusion refers to the full social and economic participation of people with disabilities. An inclusive attitude is arguably the opposite of an ableist or exclusionary mindset. In practice, inclusion is linked to universal design and accessibility and mainstreaming of social participation in education, employment, and all other life areas. Inclusion marks a clear departure from charity or therapeutic understandings of disability in favor of the aforementioned social or relational one. Simplican and colleagues introduced a socio-ecological model of social inclusion for people with intellectual and developmental disabilities that demonstrates how individual, interpersonal, organizational, community, and socio-political factors are linked to influence interpersonal relationships and community participation (Simplican, Leader, Kosciulek, & Leahy, 2015). Independent living is viewed alongside other adjacent and partially overlapping concepts such as social interaction, social capital, and community participation. David Gray and colleagues contributed to this debate by introducing the concept of community receptivity, which is understood as the readiness of communities to support public participation of people with disabilities while considering both environmental and social environments (Bricout & Gray, 2006). Independent community living has been an objective for disability advocates and many people with disabilities since the early days of the civic strife for equality. It is in many ways conceptually the precursor to the notion of inclusion.

As the disability-focused civil rights movement pushed for equal opportunities and rights in education, employment, and health, the ability to choose living arrangements and housing options that maximize independence became a key focus in the 1970s. Accessible, affordable, and available housing remains one of the major challenges across most countries to this day. As a group, people with disabilities have consistently ranked in economic surveys and censuses in the lower quartiles. Opportunities for full labor market participation are bound up with access to affordable and accessible housing. For many individuals with mobility impairments it is challenging to go and visit other individuals or families unless the meetings are arranged at a local venue that is accessible, such as a city park or a fast food restaurant. In many communities, a housing desert exists for those with mobility limitations who need housing and/or those with mobility limitations who wish to visit friends, co-workers, and family members in residences that offer basic physical accessibility. Instead of having unlimited housing options for visiting, architectural challenges exist that prevent individuals using wheelchairs, scooters, and even walkers from entering front entrances, moving around within the home as well as being able to use the restroom, if needed. In many cases this is exacerbated by inappropriate or unreliable transportation options (e.g., broken lifts, highly restricted paratransit service). According to Visitability.org, an organization established by Eleanor Smith, **Visitability** is referred to as basic home access or inclusive home design and requires a few essential features in every new home: (1) one zero-step entrance; (2) interior doors, including bathrooms, with 32 inches or more of clear passage space; and (3) at least a half bath (preferably a full bath) on the main floor (Visitability, 2018). Put another way, according to Maisel (2006), Visitability refers to design principles for one-family residences that incorporate simple access guidelines so individuals with physical disabilities can visit other's homes.

For his disability research, Hannigan (2013) visited ten residents of visitable homes in affordable housing developments around Philadelphia. In this qualitative study, Hannigan inquired as to what might be the advantages/disadvantages of having a home with visitable features. Many stated that the zero-step feature was a plus that allowed friends and family to visit; they also said it was a safer place for their children to play. Some mentioned though that fewer friends with mobility limitations visited them than expected. The wide doorways and hallways features of visitable homes did not receive much response. The first floor half bath was identified very positively with one participant stating an appreciation of the separation of public and private spaces. Another obvious benefit was that visitors who were older or had mobility limitations did not have to go upstairs to use the restroom. Nary (2014) provides helpful points on assessing wheelchair user's needs in preparing for an upcoming visit. The article also contains useful tips on low-cost changes to the built environment to accommodate adaptive equipment such as wheelchairs. While the concept of "Visitability" has been primarily applied to people with mobility impairments, it can be easily extended to other disability groups. The user-centered design of home and community environments that can be navigated safely and effectively by people with autism or dementia or people with vision or sight loss are equally important. Failure to adopt universal design approaches that places users at the center are fallbacks to ableist and exclusionary mindsets.

Another emerging concept is "usability" which places more emphasis on how useable a home is in contrast to its level of accessibility. Greiman, Ravesloot, Liston, Sanders, and Myers (2014) analyzed data from the 2011 American Housing Survey, which reported that 54.2 percent of individuals using a mobility device entered rental households with at least one step. Others responding to the survey said they do not have grab bars in the bathroom (44.9 percent), do not have a main floor bedroom (9.4 percent), and 6.2 percent stated they do not have a bathroom on the main floor. Homes with unusable features can affect the residents' independence and even participation in the community. Ravesloot and colleagues are currently conducting research to determine whether individuals with physical disabilities living in residences that are less useable also have a corresponding decrease in community participation.

The preceding paragraphs describe barriers and facilitators residents with mobility limitations face when visiting a home or making a home more useable. Living in an accessible and useable house or apartment is not the same as "feeling at home" or being able to "develop a sense of home." Recently, the Workforce Innovations Opportunity Act was passed in the US, which placed emphasis on a fifth core Independent Living (IL) service – transition, both from high school to work or post-secondary education, and from nursing homes to community-based living. The next section briefly presents an independent–interdependent living model for independent living and community participation (White, Simpson, Gonda, Ravesloot, & Coble, 2010).

Independent Living and Community Inclusion: Social Capital and Interdependence

The left-hand side of the independence model as shown in Figure 19.1 indicates that people with disabilities are beginning to receive basic Centers for Independent Living (CIL) services. In some cases, they become over-reliant on them – as noted by small arrows facing toward the CIL (see Figure 19.1).

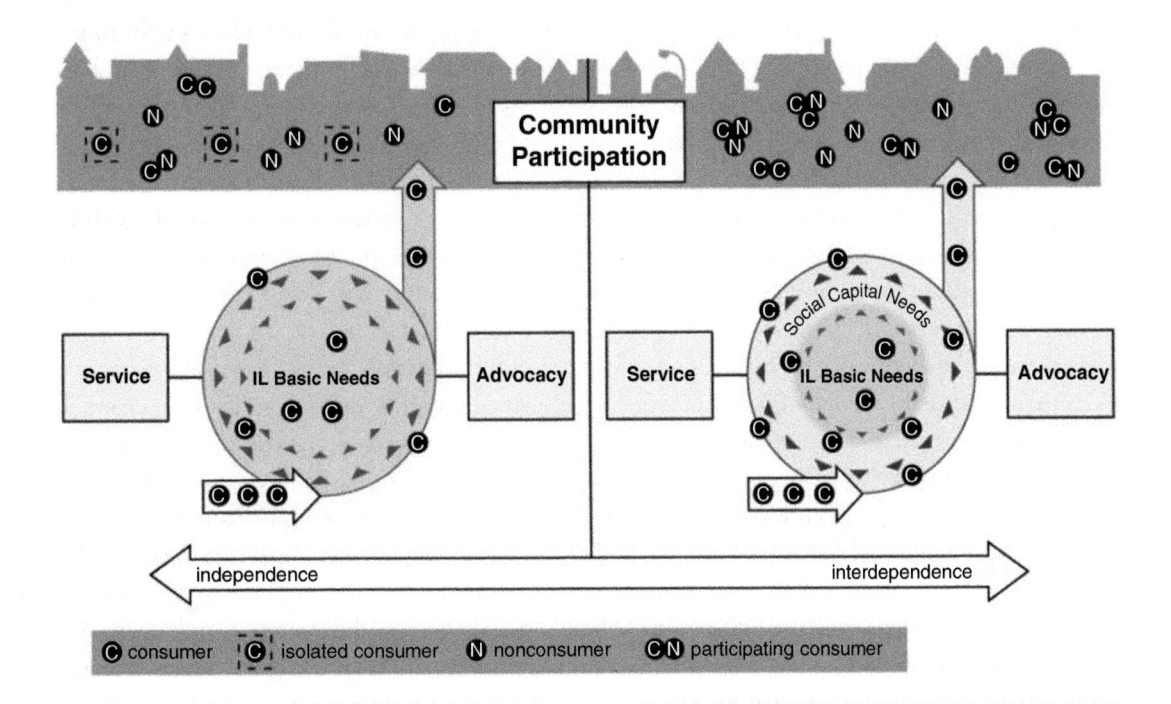

Figure 19.1 Model of the continuum of independence and interdependence

Source: White, Simpson, Gonda, Ravesloot, & Coble (2010, p. 238).

The independence model suggests that consumers will naturally participate in their communities if basic independent living (IL) services are met. While this approach can lead to improved community participation for some, it may not be sufficient for others, who may live an isolated "silo type" existence with an occupant status. This isolation from the community is characterized by the C or consumer, surrounded by a box with dashed lines. The IL model relies on consumer agency and empowerment alone but does not necessarily take a holistic or systemic view in that also the community and larger society have to change to make social inclusion a reality. Independent living arrangements cannot be viewed detached from the wider social and economic social environments that may prevent full societal participation. Inclusion differs from social integration in that the latter assumes that social arrangements and practices do not have to change and that it is sufficient to provide assistance and empowerment to people with disabilities.

Inclusion and participatory engagement of people with disabilities require a radical shift in the way societies and communities operate (Townley & Sylvestre, 2014). Inclusion means universal access and participation opportunities in communities for ALL people irrespective of disability, ethnicity, or gender. People with disabilities are an integral part of the fabric of human diversity of communities. A practical planning tool is the *Community Tool Box* (see http://ctb.ku.edu/en) developed by the University of Kansas, which includes a range of participatory planning tools for communities to design healthy communities and accessible environments. Inclusion is the result of processes that change communities in so far that people with disabilities are recognized as key stakeholders and change agents. Internationally, this notion is at the heart of inclusive local development (ILD) initiatives that seek to foster community design and capacity building through decentralized local dialogues involving people with disabilities in decision-making processes about services and infrastructure (see Handicap International, 2009). We would also like to refer to the significance of social and cultural capital here, which have been highlighted in their relevance for healthy community environments (Eicher & Kawachi, 2011). There has been a plethora of definitions of social capital but we describe it like Woolcock and Narayan (2000) as the "norms and networks that enable people to act collectively" (p. 226). Far more detailed explorations can be found elsewhere (e.g., Tzanakis, 2013) and in Chapter 4 of this book. Here we simply wish to highlight that social and cultural capital can be understood as closely linked with the promotion of participation and inclusion (Bates & Davis, 2004) as well as a prerequisite for self-determination (see also Walker et al., 2011) in the context of the **interdependence** model below.

The right-hand side of Figure 19.1 illustrates the interdependence model, which shows people entering and receiving basic CIL services *and* social capital services. In this model, the arrows in the gray central area point outward, indicating a supportive push toward social capital needs. In other words, the service is geared towards connecting individuals to their communities, their families, friends, peers, organizations rather than stressing solely their own skills irrespective of social context. This model stresses building social capital capacity among people with disabilities to help them participate in their communities to the fullest extent they are able. In reference to Woolcock and Narayan's (2000) characterization, this means that the community held norms have to shift from exclusion to inclusion and that the community networks need to include people with disabilities as integral partners.

Advocacy for accessible and affordable housing is critical but must further extend to advocate for the place-making conditions that enable people to develop a sense of living in an environment that is personally meaningful. At this point we may refer to Martin Seligman's work on human flourishing, in which he distinguishes five components, reflected in the acronym PERMA. Seligman (2011) postulates and has empirical support for these claims that people flourish if they can maximise **P**ositive emotions, feel **E**ngaged in activities, have positive **R**elationships, construct **M**eaning and have a sense of **A**chievement. Clearly, human flourishing and "feeling at home" extend beyond questions of built environment accessibility, and, arguably, human flourishing is linked to opportunities for social participation and community living. Place-making is both an individual as well as a collective task and involves the physical or built environment as well as the subjective perceptions and emotional responses of the persons who inhabit these environments (Friedmann, 2010; Cresswell, 2004).

Disability and Homelessness

In the UK, there is a massive shortage of affordable, accessible, and usable public housing options. The previous coalition government of Tories and Liberal Democrats introduced the so-called "bedroom tax" or under-occupancy penalty, which financially penalized people who receive housing benefits and who had a spare bedroom. However, many people with disabilities relied on this extra space for caregivers, or in some cases as storage space for assistive devices. The tax made it challenging to afford rent for many people with disabilities. In January 2016, the tax was ruled discriminatory.

In the US, Ho, Kroll, Kehn, and Pearson (2007) conducted focus groups as part of a larger study on the health and housing situation among low-income adults with physical disabilities. The 28 participants resided in the District of Columbia in a homeless shelter, a nursing home, or an inaccessible house or apartment. The participants reported threats to health in the homeless shelter including the lack of general accessibility, safety, and sanitation. Nursing home residents commented on having little privacy and autonomy, and those living in inaccessible apartments or houses were concerned about their social and economic life. All participants emphasized the importance of a barrier-free, clean living environment, as this was critical for them to feel safe, to maintain their health, and live independently.

There is mounting evidence about the impact of homelessness on physical and mental health (as noted throughout this book), either as a result of "sleeping rough," concomitant problems (e.g., mental illness, substance abuse), inappropriate diet, unsafe and poor sanitary conditions of homeless shelters or other sleep arrangements, and enduring stress resulting from having to manage a chaotic life with multiple daily challenges.

Globally, homelessness has been found to be associated with a higher prevalence of chronic health conditions (Fazel, Geddes, & Kushel, 2014). Yet, little research evidence exists on homelessness among people with physical and medical disabilities. In 2007, Ho et al. conducted semi-structured interviews in 13 homeless shelters in Washington DC and found considerable health-related challenges for people with disabilities who are homeless. The research with 83 participants, involved both quantitative and qualitative elements. The aims of the study were to describe the health service needs and related barriers for homeless individuals with mobility impairments requiring the use of a mobility device, such as a wheelchair or cane. Nearly three-quarters of participants perceived their health to be fair or poor, compared with only 19 percent of the general population of Washington, DC. In relation to unmet health service needs more than a third felt they did not have access to a case manager or social care support worker and more than a quarter struggled to gain access to physical therapy or durable medical equipment such as wheelchairs. Often the lack of transportation to facilities made access to therapy difficult. Researchers in the study also observed that several participants had defective and near unusable equipment. The study has highlighted the urgent need for research and practice development at the intersection of disability, poverty, and homelessness.

Box 19.1 People with Disabilities on Skid Row

Dr. Tom Seekins, Psychology Professor at the University of Montana, is exploring new ways of understanding the issue of homelessness and individuals with physical disabilities. He selected and analyzed Google Street View to determine density of people with mobility limitations in the Skid Row area of Los Angeles, the second largest US city, with almost 4 million residents, and over 58,000 people without housing. Using this technology Dr. Seekins sought to gain a preliminary understanding of homelessness by obtaining a sample from Skid Row, which specifically contains a population of about 18,000, and is estimated to have a homeless population ranging between 3000 and 6000 individuals.

Dr. Seekins and team incorporated a technological approach from wildlife biology called "mark and recapture" to estimate the size of an animal population. Thus, the Lincoln index, a statistical measure is used to estimate the total population size (N) by dividing the number of marked individuals in sample one (Kn) by the proportion of marked individuals in the second sample (k). The Lincoln index formula is

$$N = Kn/k$$

Dr. Seekins and his team demonstrated an innovative and practical approach to investigating the community psychology (CP) issue of homelessness. They were able to blend science and technology to learn more about the lived experience of people who are experiencing homelessness in a measurable, yet unobtrusive manner.

Questions for Your Consideration

1 What ideas do you have to blend science and technology to help individuals with disabilities who are homeless?

2 What are especially vulnerable points for persons with disabilities as they seek to maintain a continuity of community living?

Seekins, T., Rennie, B., & Hammond, J. (2014). Exploring the feasibility of using Google Street View to assess the accessibility of community environments: Developing definitions and observational protocol for image recognition and classification. *Research in Social Science and Disability.* 8, 125–41; Seekins, T., Rennier, B., & Hammond, J. (2014). Using Google Street View to assess community accessibility and participation: A demonstration. Unpublished paper. Research and Training Center on Rural Rehabilitation. Missoula, Montana.

Chapter Summary

In this chapter, we reviewed ableism in the context of health and housing for people with physical disabilities. We highlighted the need for accessibility and visibility considerations but also contend that pure focus on functional requirements in relation to the built environment is not sufficient. People with disabilities have been systematically deprived of developing their subjective sense of home in the sense of self-directed decisions about where and how to live. This is not just a matter of the built infrastructure but one of living in a place that has subjective value and meaning. CP plays a key role in how people with disabilities emotionally and socially construct their understandings of the environments that they inhabit. And, it helps empower people with disabilities to advocate for their right to a home, not only to housing. We also discussed the role of intersectionality between disability, housing, social capital, wellbeing, and health. CP has a specific responsibility of addressing the inequities that arise at these intersections in terms of diagnosing the challenges and fielding community derived solutions that empower people with disabilities and their communities (Bess, Prilleltensky, Perkins, & Collins, 2009). In addition, community psychologists can play a crucial role in helping people with disabilities feel empowered to decrease their marginalization in such areas as education, employment, transportation, and housing (Fawcett et al., 1994). The role of CP has recently been linked to understanding empowerment in the context of the Capabilities Approach, which views capabilities as the freedom to engage in socially valued roles and activities (Shinn, 2015).

Methodologically, community-based participatory research methods (CBPR) are closely associated with the values advocated in CP. As they involve community stakeholders from the outset of a research project and use a range of qualitative, observational, and creative modes of data collection, they are particularly appropriate for conducting disability-focused research in various settings while at the same time generating tangible change for those involved, thus stressing agency of all stakeholders (Hergenrather & Rhodes, 2008). This approach is consistent with the values advocated in CP to work closely with the value base of communities and to promote actions that seek to strengthen individuals, relationships, and communities in their capabilities and quality of life.

Thus, CP as a discipline focusing on individuals in diverse community settings is uniquely positioned to provide leadership in researching and advancing the inclusion and empowerment of people with disabilities in all areas of life in close collaboration with all community members.

Key Terms

Inclusion: This term refers to including people with disabilities in all aspects of life and enabling them to have similar roles to their peers without disabilities. Inclusion requires adequate policies and practices in communities that foster increased participation in social life roles such as being a student, worker, friend, community member, patient, spouse, partner, or parent. Inclusion requires accessible public resources such as transportation and libraries (see also Centers for Disease Control and Prevention, www.cdc.gov/ncbddd/disabilityandhealth/disability-inclusion.html).

Independent community living: Independent living is a "philosophy" that emphasizes equality opportunities, self-determination, and self-respect for people with disabilities. It contrasts with the view that people with disabilities are the subject of charity or medical care and other notions that portray them as sick, defective objects of professional interventions, or as a burden to others and society. Independent living emphasizes opportunities for making independent life decisions on where and how to live, employment, and personal and family relationships.

Interdependence: Interdependence moves away from complete "independence" towards recognizing the interdependence of people's relationships in societies. It stresses the fact that human lives are diverse and that distinct capabilities are found in every human being. However, these capabilities materialize in interconnections and relationships with others.

Intersectionality: Intersectionality steps away from a single lens on "disability" and emphasizes the interconnected influence of race, poverty, gender, and other characteristics in conjunction with disability to exercise power on individuals and communities.

Visitability: Refers to private housing that is designed in such a way that it can be lived in or visited by people who use wheelchairs, walkers, or find it difficult to negotiate steps. A house is visitable when it meets certain basic access requirements.

Resources

Books

Albrecht, G. L., Seelman, K., & Bury, M. (2001). *Handbook of disability studies*. Thousand Oaks: SAGE Publications.

Drum, C. E., Krahn, G. L., & Bersani, H. (Eds.). (2009). *Disability and public health*. Washington DC: American Public Health Association.

Garcia Iriarte, E., McConjey, R., & Gilligan, R (Eds.). (2016). *Disability and human rights: Global perspectives*. London: Red Globe Press.

Lollar, D., & Andresen, E. M. (Eds.). (2011). *Public health perspectives on disability: Epidemiology to ethics and beyond*. New York: Springer.

Shakespeake, T. (2014). *Disability rights and wrongs revisited*. Abingdon: Routledge.

Websites

- Centers for Disease Control and Prevention: www.cdc.gov/ncbddd/disabilityandhealth/index.html
- US Census: www.census.gov/people/disability/
- US Department of Health and Human Services: Administration for Community Living: https://acl.gov/programs/nidilrr/

ADDRESSING COMMUNITY-BASED CHALLENGES ARISING FROM MENTAL HEALTH PROBLEMS

20

LEARNING FROM EXPERIENCES OF PSYCHIATRIC CONSUMERS/SURVIVORS

Bret Kloos

Warm-up Questions

Before beginning the chapter, take a moment to reflect upon what information and assumptions you have about serious mental health problems:

1 What is the story that comes to mind when you think about life events for a person diagnosed with schizophrenia?

2 What is the nature of her or his difficulties?

3 How can her or his problems be addressed?

Learning Objectives

The goal for this chapter is to examine how action and research can help people with serious mental health problems achieve their hopes for liberation, wellbeing, and recovery. By now, you should expect that community psychology (CP) takes a different perspective on supporting people identified as having "problems."

In this chapter you will learn about

- Applying principles from earlier chapters to particular challenges faced by people diagnosed with serious mental health problems
- Challenging assumptions about mental health problems and seek alternatives in what might be helpful
- Oppression and issues of power that may exacerbate mental health problems and impede recovery
- Promotion of wellness and empowerment that goes beyond symptom reduction
- Using levels of analysis to identify structural impediments to social inclusion

Mental Health: A Community Psychology Perspective

While much is written about the treatment of mental health problems, this chapter focuses on what CP perspectives can contribute. In terms of **mental health promotion**, community psychologists can assist efforts to obtain resources and promote practices that advance wellbeing (e.g., housing, work, meaningful social relationships). In terms of liberation, the chapter provides examples of people with serious mental health problems challenging oppressive definitions of mental health deviancy and working to increase opportunities for their **self-determination**. In terms of prevention, mental health service providers can benefit from CP perspectives in seeking alternative ways to support persons with mental health problems, particularly with more work devoted to primary prevention.

The chapter begins by specifying what is meant by the terms **serious mental health problems** and **recovery**. Next, it briefly reviews historical contexts of how communities have responded to the needs of people with serious mental health problems and the needs for liberation. Third, it reports on the emerging role that people with serious mental health problems have in changing societies' responses. Finally, it presents examples of how liberation and wellbeing can be promoted in collaboration with people who have histories of serious mental health problems.

Definitions of Serious Mental Health Problems and Recovery

Serious Mental Health Problems

The term *serious mental health problems* refers to persistent psychiatric disabilities that can have a profound effect on a person's behavior, thinking, emotions and relationships. These include diagnoses such as schizophrenia, bipolar disorder and, severe depression. The designation of "serious" or "severe" is not meant to diminish the difficulties encountered by people with other psychiatric disabilities, but rather to refer to more extreme disturbances in living and everyday activities. The term also is associated with a high level of intervention that is typically prescribed to help people address the symptoms associated with these disorders. However, the term "serious mental health *problems*" underscores that the *social experience of these disabilities* is a major part of the difficulties faced by people experiencing these disorders, not solely symptoms (Stein, Dworsky, Phillips, & Hunt, 2005; Terry, Townley, Brusilovskiy, & Salzer, 2019).

Serious mental health problems "strike like a two-edged sword" (Corrigan & Penn, 1999, p. 765). They can profoundly disrupt personal functioning and have a simultaneously onerous set of consequences as communities respond to a person's problems. In terms of personal functioning, people may feel as if they have lost control of their lives. Thinking can be greatly distorted. For some people, beliefs of persecution or torment intrude, even when they doubt the authenticity of these feelings (e.g., being followed by government agents). A person's emotions can change drastically, leading to one becoming depressed and lacking enjoyment of previously rewarding activities. In other cases emotions can fluctuate to alarming highs and lows. The ability to complete previously easy tasks can be greatly diminished. Unlike many media portrayals, the symptoms of people who have the same diagnosis can vary widely. What is common in people's experiences is that these symptoms are unwanted, often frightening and dramatically disruptive. These experiences shake one's confidence in oneself and lower self-esteem. They contribute to difficulty in social situations, isolation, lost opportunities, and shattered personal dreams.

The social experiences of people with serious mental health problems often include encountering fear, discrimination, and prejudice from fellow citizens who learn of their disabilities (Brown & Rogers, 2014; Corrigan & Al-Khouja, 2018). Long-held expectations of participating in community life can disintegrate. Aspirations for careers, university degrees, intimate relationships, or making a commitment to a life partner are often lost or seem unattainable in the face of social responses to the personal difficulties associated with psychiatric disabilities. People with serious mental health problems have smaller networks of friends and support people (Brunt & Hansson, 2002; Townley, Miller, & Kloos, 2013) and often report being lonely and feeling isolated. Perhaps it is not surprising that those with serious mental health problems have difficulty getting jobs, making friends, or obtaining housing (Nelson, Kloos, & Ornelas, 2014). Furthermore, the quality of their housing is much lower than the general population and, as a group, they must find new housing twice as often as people without serious mental health problems (Newman, 1994). This chapter examines community responses that can foster nurturing social experiences in response to these oppressive social consequences.

While this chapter focuses on the experience of persons with serious mental health problems, community psychologists have also been active addressing a range of problems related to mental health. These have included prevention of depression, addiction, and suicide. See Box 20.1 for examples.

Box 20.1 Community Psychology Approaches to Mental Health

Clinical-community psychologists have developed educational tools to help people identify patterns of thinking that can contribute to depression and those that can help address stress (Muñoz et al., 1995; Muñoz & Bunge, 2016). Ricardo Muñoz and colleagues have adapted this approach for helping persons who may go to see a doctor but not a psychologist. In particular, this approach has been effective for Latino, Black, and other ethnic minority groups where there seeing a counselor or therapist may not be as widely accepted as a resource for addressing concerns. It has also been used with mothers who are feeling depressed after giving birth (Muñoz, Le, Clarke, & Jaycox, 2002). For a video clip of this work see: www2.psychology.uiowa.edu/faculty/ohara/videos/

Clinical-community psychologists have worked to identify the limitations of mental health services and develop options for community-based care, especially for ethnic minorities who have not found standard care accessible or approachable (e.g., Gone, 2004; Gone, 2013). This work has included new approaches to addressing post-traumatic stress (Pole, Gone, & Kulkarni, 2008), addictions (Mohatt et al., 2008), and suicide (Rasmus, Trickett, Charles, John, & Allen, 2019). Many community psychologists have worked with communities to develop approaches that reduce exposure to risk for developing addictions and to promote experiences and capacities that can protect youth (Oesterle et al., 2015). For further examples see: http://www.communitiesthatcare.net/

Recovery

The concept of *recovery* in mental health care has emerged with the acceptance of empirical findings that the course of serious mental health problems is not necessarily one of unavoidable decline and poor functioning (e.g., Harding, Zubin, & Strauss, 1987; Strauss & Carpenter, 1974). First, articulated by mental health consumers and ex-patients (e.g., Chamberlin, 1978; Deegan, 1988), recovery emphasizes personal goals of experiencing hope, healing, **empowerment**, and connection with others after life disruptions from serious mental health problems. Recovery has become increasingly accepted as an appropriate goal of mental health care in North America and some European countries (Davidson, 2016; Ornelas, Duarte, & Jorge-Monteiro, 2014) and has become a goal for mental health systems (http://www.mentalhealthcommission.gov/). Recovery has been defined as:

> A deeply personal, unique process of changing one's attitudes, values, feelings, goals, skills and/or roles. It is a way of living a satisfying, hopeful and contributing life even with limitations caused by an illness. Recovery involves the development of a new meaning and purpose in one's life as one grows beyond catastrophic effects of mental illness. (Anthony, 1993, p. 19)

It is important to note that proponents of recovery do not consider recovery to be synonymous with the notion of a cure. "Recovery is distinguished both by its endpoint – which is not necessarily a return to 'normal' health and functioning – and by its emphasis on the individual's active participation in self-help activities" (Jacobson & Greenley, 2001, p. 483). Recovery is about regaining a sense of purpose and self after a major life disruption. The concept of recovery is central to realizing liberation and wellbeing for those with serious mental health problems.

Community Contexts for Responding to Serious Mental Health Problems

There are competing tensions in how communities respond to people who experience disruptions in emotional, cognitive, and interpersonal life. In Western countries, people tend to emphasize the importance of individuals overcoming difficulties and value the "right" to live independently. Individuals expect that they should decide for themselves where to live, work, and with whom to have friendships. However, at the same time, we seek to maintain order and safety in our communities. When someone's behavior is too bizarre or appears dangerous, we rely on professionals to take control of the situation, "restore order" and, when appropriate, offer the person assistance. With serious mental health problems, the values of self-determination and social order come into conflict when a situation, behavior, or person is considered deviant rather than simply different. Judgements concerning deviancy often lead to decisions about the need for *social control* that are at odds with the cultural value of promoting *self-determination*. Communities differ in which problems they want to assist, which they will not tolerate, and which problems they will simply ignore. People with serious mental health problems inevitably are confronted with, and have to respond to, how their communities define and address deviance.

Designating a situation or person as deviant has far-reaching consequences for the person *and* for those making the judgement. The act of defining problems shapes how competing values are balanced. Defining someone as deviant because of some personal characteristic, such as mental or physical disabilities, injury, illness, race, or ethnicity devalues that person (Wolfensberger & Tullman, 1982; Corrigan, Bink, Fokuo, & Schmidt, 2015). Deviancy-based justifications are used to (1) detain people with serious mental health problems (e.g., disturbing the peace, involuntary psychiatric hospitalization); (2) take away individual rights (e.g., parental status, control of personal finances); and (3) restrict resources (e.g., welfare supplements). Examples are also readily available from everyday life; when we see a person talking to themselves, many of us go out of our way to avoid interaction.

Stigma about mental health problems is widely held, although the "negative stereotypes are not warranted and are often overgeneralized" (Corrigan & Penn, 1999, p. 766). Research has documented how stigmatizing views about mental health problems are also held by well-trained mental health professionals (Corrigan, 2005; Rao et al., 2009). Media representations of serious mental health problems fall into three main thematic categories: (1) people with serious mental health problems should be feared and thus excluded (e.g., the homicidal maniac); (2) they are child-like, irresponsible and need care from others (e.g., the innocent, child-like man who can't make good decisions for himself); and (3) they are rebellious free spirits who do not accept the norms of community living (Corrigan & Penn, 1999).

While stigma can translate into open discrimination, internalized negative images of oneself can destroy one's self-concept and radically limit personal goals, self-confidence, and the opportunities that one is willing to undertake. Thus, the experience of being categorized as a deviant can bring unintended consequences for the person's hopes for the future and sense of self. Box 20.2 presents one view of the pain and cost associated with being labeled deviant because of mental health problems, as well as some ideas about alternative responses.

Box 20.2 How Stereotypes About Deviance Can Oppress

To me, mental illness meant Dr. Jekyll and Mr. Hyde, psychopathic serial killers, loony bins, morons, schizos, fruitcakes, nuts, straight jackets and raving lunatics. They were all I knew about mental illness and what terrified me was that professionals were saying I was one of them. It would have greatly helped to have had someone come and talk to me about surviving mental illness – as well as the possibility of recovering, of healing and of building a new life for myself. It would have been good to have role models – people I could look up to who had experienced what I was going through – people who had found a good job or who were in love or who had an apartment or a house on their own or who were making a valuable contribution to society. (Deegan, 1993, p. 8)

Competing Tensions in Helping Professions

Before a brief discussion of historical context, I want to further ground our consideration of liberation and wellbeing for people with serious mental health problems in a dilemma frequently experienced by those in the helping professions. When social workers, nurses, mental health workers, psychiatrists, and psychologists are asked to help people experiencing serious mental health problems, they are conferred a social role of helping the person to fit into society. If a person is evaluated as being too vulnerable to take care of oneself, at risk of harming oneself, or a danger to others, the role of these mental health professionals is to ensure the safety of the person and those who may encounter that person in crisis. Thus, these helping professionals have the dual charge of being *agents of compassionate care* and *agents of social control*. Combining society's interest for compassionate care with interests in maintaining safety often puts these service providers in awkward situations where they have to choose one role over the other (e.g., when to involuntarily detain and hospitalize someone in the "best interest" of the community).

A Brief History of Community Responses to Mental Health Problems

Tension between the competing values of compassionate care and social control has existed throughout history for people with serious mental health problems. Severely aberrant behavior was often seen as a sign of demonic manipulation requiring exorcism or imprisonment (Fabrega, 1990). Native healers throughout the world have traditions of responding to emotional upset by restoring a balance of person, nature, and spirit (Asuni, 1990; Mohatt et al., 2008). In a few cases, communities have provided sanctuary to those who have been cast out due to judgements of deviance: the town of Gheel in Belgium has been a place of sanctuary where people with serious mental health problems have participated as citizens for several hundred years (Goldstein & Godemont, 2003). Although not given much consideration in historical accounts, it is likely that the most common practices of the "average person" living in communities of the past are those that continue today: ignoring or not associating with people who are considered deviant, hiding them from view, or actively ostracizing them from their communities.

The history of community responses to mental health care since the 18th century can be viewed as successive waves of periodic reform. In France, Phillipe Pinel unshackled those who were chained and asserted that hospital care should be provided rather than prison. Reformers of the 19th century argued that specialized institutions needed to be created by regional governments that would be dedicated to the care (and segregation) of people with serious mental health problems. In the US, Dorothea Dix advocated for the creation of state hospitals and sanatoriums. When 20th century regional mental hospitals mirrored the overcrowding and poor treatment of the prisons they were meant to replace (Linhorst, 2006), the mental hygiene movement took inspiration from Clifford Beers (1908), who spoke publicly about his mental health problems in the service of making reforms and policy changes. Beers' book, *A Mind That Found Itself*, recounted his journey to wellbeing after developing mental health problems. However, mental hygiene supporters emphasized training professionals as the primary means of reform (Rappaport, 1977). It would be another 60 to 70 years before people with serious mental health problems would re-emerge as powerful voices for the reform of societies' responses to serious mental health problems.

Between 1972 and 1982, the number of hospitals with over 1,000 psychiatric beds was reduced by 50–80 percent in Denmark, England, Ireland, Italy, Spain, and Sweden (Freeman, Fryers, & Henderson, 1985). Similar patterns occurred in North America and Australia (Carling, 1995; Newton et al., 2000). In many countries, community mental health centers were founded with the charge of developing care for serious mental health problems within the community contexts where people lived rather than at remote hospitals. However, caseloads for mental health professionals have increased, while resources for mental health services have been cut (Burns, 2004).

Have you noticed in this brief historical overview that past reforms have a consistent ameliorative focus with very little consideration of transformative possibilities for how serious mental health problems can be addressed? Over the past 300 years, a focus on illness-related deviance has replaced demonology as the major explanation of serious mental health problems. However, by framing serious mental health problems as being primarily about illness, community responses are limited to treatment and rehabilitation and are necessarily ameliorative in focus. With one's attention focused on matters of illness, one cannot see problems arising from the social experience of serious mental health problems. Within a treatment and rehabilitation paradigm, it is highly improbable that intervention efforts will address problems from overzealous social control, discrimination and stigma. A new paradigm is needed to help communities support recovery and participation in community life.

Changing the Balance? The Emergence of Consumer/Survivors in Society's Efforts to Address Serious Mental Health Problems

Over the course of these "modern" reforms in mental health practices, people with serious mental health problems were seldom included in formal deliberations and decisions about how communities can respond to the realities of mental health problems. By not including all stakeholders, these reforms often overlooked valuable resources for addressing mental health concerns, that is, the experience and input of people with serious mental health problems. However, during the past 30 years, the voices of people with serious mental health problems have become increasingly more influential and have greater prominence (e.g., Chamberlin, 1990; Everett & Boydell, 1994; Nelson, Janzen, Trainor, & Ochocka, 2008). In Box 20.3, Canadian psychiatric survivor David Reville describes a response by self-advocates to the issue of poverty.

Box 20.3 David Reville, The Voice of A Psychiatric Survivor

Many people with mental health challenges who had experience with the disempowering mental system rose up to advocate for **transformative change in community mental health**. It is useful and important to hear from these advocates directly. Here, we are featuring one of those people, David Reville, a survivor of the psychiatric system in Canada. His life story is a history of the rise of a national mad movement in Canada, but it is also the tale of a remarkable and inspirational individual who has refused to accept the stigmatizing labels associated with a mental health diagnosis. Now retired, he taught Mad People's History for 11 years at the School of Disability Studies at Ryerson University in Toronto. His chapter in *Mad Matters: A Critical Reader in Canadian Mad Studies* (2013), edited by LeFrancois, Menzies and Reaume, poses the question "Is mad studies emerging as a new field of inquiry?" Currently, he's asking himself whether he is writing a memoir. Below, David is sharing his thought regarding the issue of poverty that many psychiatric survivors are dealing with and the development of mental health consumer-run businesses as a form of resistance.

Laurie unlocks the front door at A-WAY Express Couriers on Danforth Avenue in Toronto. The camera follows her as she walks around the office turning on the lights. There's a voice-over.

"I'm a psychiatric survivor. I survived the mental health system. They told me I could never work. Most of us here were told that we'd never be able to work again. So we said 'Screw that. We'll start our own businesses.'" (From https://www.nfb.ca/film/working_like_crazy/). Many psychiatric survivors are desperately poor. They are poor because they have been shut out of the labor force, they are poor because social assistance rates are too low, they are poor because housing costs too much.

Poverty is just part of the problem; the other part is the social exclusion that goes with it. The philosopher Axel Honneth (1996) defines social exclusion as being deprived of social recognition and social value; socially excluded people seek full citizenship in the political sphere and an income large enough to participate fully in the life of the community in the economic sphere. Survivors didn't need philosophers to tell them what they needed. From the beginning, self-help groups looked for ways to get money into the hands of their members. Some of them started small businesses.

In 1973, Don Weitz traveled from Toronto to Vancouver to visit the Mental Patients Association. He returned home, inspired; he was going to start a Toronto version of the Mental Patient Association (MPA) if it killed him. And so, in 1977, Don and Alf Jackson founded Toronto's first survivor group. For a while, the group was called the Ontario Mental Patients Association but, after Judi Chamberlin (1978) published her amazing book – *On Our Own: Patient-Controlled Alternatives to the Mental Health System* – the name was changed to On Our Own. Right away, OOO looked for ways for its members to make some money. Here's Don:

We weren't going to beg or solicit. We were going into the flea market business. Alf approached a friend of his who found us a small stall in one of his flea market buildings, which cost us $10 or $20 a week. I had a pickup truck then, and Alf and I would go around the city and pick up stuff off the street at night and sometimes early morning ... we proved to ourselves and the public that we weren't a bunch of "mental incompetents." (Burstow & Weitz, 1988, p. 292)

In June, 1980, with the support of some community economic development (CED) money from the City of Toronto, OOO[1] opened the Mad Market, a used goods store that Don described as "a helluva lot more humane and empowering than any rehabilitation training, industrial therapy or sheltered work-shop" (Burstow & Weitz, 1988, p. 292).

The development of businesses by survivors is not just a strategy to fight poverty; it's also a strategy of resistance. Survivors were resisting the notion that mental illness means that you can't work; survivors were refusing the "permanently unemployable" label that used to be a pre-requisite of a disability pension in Ontario. And survivors were also saying that the mental health system had failed them. Many of us felt ripped off by vocational rehabilitation programs[2] that seemed to be about getting ready to work but not about actually working; or by training programs that led to other training programs, not jobs, or by placements that were time-limited – you'd work for a while and then you'd go back to looking again – or by placements that meant you were the lone survivor in a workplace suspicious of survivors. While I was still in the mental hospital, I got a placement as the pot washer in the kitchen of the women's residence at Queen's University in Kingston, Ontario. The other kitchen staff knew where I went after work. And, oh dear me, there I was with those big butcher knives in the pot room. It was months and months of funny looks. Some survivors, including Dr. Geoffrey Reaume,[3] now Associate Professor at York University, worked in sheltered workshops; they were paid maybe $10 a day; the work was mind-numbingly menial. Geoff spent many hours filling shampoo bottles. That was the best the mental health system could do?

Let's go back to where we began for a moment. To Laurie who is rejecting the system's negative judgment about her and other survivors. Laurie is the Executive Director of A-WAY Couriers, a survivor business started in 1987.[4] And, in case the talk about a voice-over didn't give it away, on this day Laurie's turning on the lights for the benefit of film directors (Laura Sky and Gwen Basen) and their cameras. If you were to watch the film for a while, you'd encounter Diana Capponi, the Executive Director of the Ontario Council of Alternative Businesses[5] (now called Working for Change: www.workingforchange.ca).

About a year earlier, Diana and Laurie[6] had been hopping mad. The Toronto Star was running a series on mental health and there was way too much talk about "the violent mental patient." They were determined to change the conversation. And that's when the idea for "Working Like Crazy" came to them. It would be a feature-length documentary and it would showcase people in survivor business. And showcase them it did. Diana and Laurie and Pat and Scott and Graham and Susan. And a supporting cast of survivors working in survivor business.

The first screening of the film was for a capacity crowd at the Centre for Addiction and Mental Health! Then, we took it across Ontario. For example, one of the stops I made was in Sault Ste. Marie, a northern

---

[1] In 1980, OOO began publishing Phoenix Rising: The Voice of the Psychiatrized. You can read a decade's worth of issues by going to http://www.psychiatricsurvivorarchives.com/

[2] My very first "activist" article was about how feeble psychiatric hospitals' vocational rehab programs were; the article was published in the Queen's University graduate quarterly Gavel in the fall of 1967.

[3] I was co-chair of A-WAY's board for 6 years; in 2017, I had the privilege of speaking at A-WAY's 30th anniversary. Learn more about A-WAY at https://www.awayexpress.ca/

[4] I see Dr. Reaume as the father of Mad Studies; he developed a course called Mad People's History for Ryerson's School of Disability Studies in 2002. When he went to teach York University in 2004, I developed and taught my own version of Mad People's History at Ryerson.

[5] After many years at OCAB, Diana went to work in the HR department of the Centre for Addiction and Mental Health, Canada's largest mental health teaching hospital. There, Diana was responsible for hiring hundreds of people with mental health and addictions histories. She died in 2014 at the age of 61.

[6] For how Diana and Laurie self-describe, see "self-labelling and identity," a webdoc I made for my Mad People's History course. https://www.youtube.com/watch?v=pxbw7dDMX60. For an extended interview with Diana, see https://www.youtube.com/watch?v=YDy6gROCJ-w. Danielle Landry, a mad activist who now teaches both A History of Madness and Mad People's History at Ryerson, edited and captioned the interview with the assistance of filmmaker Jonathan Balazs.

community about 400 miles north-west of Toronto. I screened the film three times, at a community mental health agency, at a community college and at a food bank. In 2001, "Working like crazy" went to England, Scotland and Ireland. Diana, Laurie, Laura Sky, Kathryn Church and Pat Fowler went with it. And they made connections with user groups and their allies that are still active today. Some of those connections have led to developments that could not have been imagined in 2001. For instance, some "service users" in Edinburgh took my online course in Mad People's History. They then developed their own version which they called Mad People's History and Identity. Somehow, they convinced Queen Margaret's University to take on both the course and the service user instructors. And they got the National Health Service to fund it. It's free. And they've been teaching it since 2014 (http://capsadvocacy.org/lothian-wide-projects/oor-mad-history/). Users come from as far away as Glasgow to take the course. How cool is that?

Happily, survivor business is well documented thanks to Dr. Kathryn Church, a mad-positive ally of the survivor movement. Her descriptions and analyses of survivor business in Ontario have appeared in three books on community economic development in Canada (Church, 1997; Church, Shragge, Fontan, & Ng, 2008).

Consumer/survivor movements have emerged in many cities around the world (Chamberlin, 1978; Brown & Rogers, 2014) and have dedicated themselves to bring together people with serious mental health problems for collective action and mutual support. The terms "consumer," "survivor," or "consumer/survivor" are used in North America by people with serious mental health problems to refer to themselves rather than the terms used by mental health professionals: "patient" or "client." In some European countries, the term "user" is preferred. The use of "consumer" or "user" is meant to emphasize the importance of individual choice in using services and the respect given to people who have rights and expectations about the services they use. The term "survivor" emphasizes the negative consequences that many people with serious mental health problems have experienced as a result of past mental health treatment; it is also a political statement about past mistreatment, individuals' resilience in living, and self-determination in current life choices. Some people with serious mental health problems have strong preferences for one term over the other and the identity that the terms represent. The term *consumer/survivor* was coined to include the political and personal perspectives of both terms. Regardless of the terms used, this new paradigm recognizes the value of using "people-first language" to promote citizenship and personhood over client or patient identities (Nelson, Kloos, & Ornelas, 2014).

Unlike past reforms, consumer/survivor movements have articulated needs and interests that argue for the priority of transformative approaches to change, those that will promote liberation, as well as ameliorative approaches that promote wellbeing (Chamberlin, 1978; Nelson, Kloos, & Ornelas, 2014). Priorities of the movements to challenge social conditions have included the need for affordable housing, employment opportunities, challenging discrimination (Ornelas et al., 2014; Goering & Tsemberis, 2014), and abolition of abusive practices of social control (Chamberlin, 1990; Nelson et al., 2008). The movements' priorities for change in care for persons with mental health problems include self-determination in treatment and life decisions, wellness and recovery planning, and advanced directives for treatment preferences (Copeland & Jonikas, 2014; O'Connell and Stein 2005).

The success of these consumer–citizen–professional collaborations can be seen in part through the growth of mutual aid, advocacy, and self-help organizations and their growing acceptance in treatment communities (Chinman, Kloos, O'Connell, & Davidson, 2002; Pistrang, Barker, & Humphreys, 2008), the formation of consumer/survivor advocacy movements with political clout (Nelson et al., 2008), representation at governmental agencies charged with policy and funding decisions (e.g., advisory panels, grant review panels), and the emergence of the recovery metaphor for interventions and accompanying practice.

From the ecological standpoint presented in Chapter 5, there are many niches where people with serious mental health problems can make contributions "inside" and "outside" formal mental health systems. These include roles as advocates, community leaders, guides for recovery, service providers, and advisors. *Advocates* have been successful in pursuing lawsuits to end practices judged to be abusive, in providing more resources to community services, in building collaborations with professionals and civic groups and in protesting negative media portrayals of serious mental health problems. *Community leaders* organize consumer/survivor initiatives and serve on policymaking boards of agencies or governments. The role of a *guide* recognizes the value of the lived experience in recovery journeys to wellbeing and liberation that only people with serious mental health problems can share. Mutual aid and self-help groups are founded on this principle and have grown greatly in the last 30 years. The role of a *service provider* has emerged in the past 20 years as consumer/survivor organizations have created their own services because of dissatisfaction with the services available (Mowbray, Lewandowski, Holter, & Bybee, 2006; Brown & Rogers, 2014). New services have included crisis respite services in lieu of emergency rooms, recovery-oriented case management services, and housing (Chamberlin, 1990; Davidson, 2016). Finally, people with serious mental health problems act as *advisors* to policymaking bodies by serving on committees and consult with community leaders to develop practices and policies that are more sensitive to the needs of people with serious mental health problems.

Community Psychology's Role in Supporting Persons with Mental Health Problems

What can CP offer in promoting the wellbeing and liberation of consumer/survivors? The chapter closes with consideration of concepts from community research and action that change how people understand how communities might provide support.

Resources For Changing How We View What Is Supportive

Promotion of Wellbeing and Health

Wellbeing is not restricted to the management of symptoms, but involves the development of personal resources to cope with everyday challenges and promote physical and mental health (see Chapter 6). The development of a goal of recovery from the consumer/survivor movement helps to extend CP's interest in wellness, or wellbeing, for persons with mental health challenges. In applying a wellbeing perspective to community mental health, individual and social processes of recovery become a central focus as people learn to use strategies that help maintain their wellbeing. One example of a self-help guide of wellbeing is WRAP – Wellness Recovery Action Plan, developed by Copeland from her personal experience (Copeland & Jonikas, 2014).

Social Inclusion and Community Integration

Involvement in meaningful activities and the development of valued social roles are crucial dimensions for recovery. Several community psychologists have focused on how to promote opportunities for **social inclusion** and **community integration** (Salzer & Baron, 2014; Terry et al., 2019). By engaging in community activities, individuals can gain significant social roles beyond being a mental health services client. Furthermore, employment, education, mutual help, or neighborhood organizations are contexts that promote interpersonal relations, personal development, and opportunities to help others and the community (see also Chapter 7 on this topic).

Focus on Strengths, Opportunities, and Resources

CP has long advocated for a focus on strengths as necessary to avoid deficit models of intervention (Rappaport, Davidson, Wilson, & Mitchell, 1975). In recovery processes, people can develop more positive personal identities and mental health system efforts can focus on strengths that help individuals develop. A focus on personal strengths leads to more opportunities to be involved in significant activities and develop valued social roles and relationships (Davidson, 2016).

Social Justice

Many of the challenges that consumer/survivors face in their daily life can be attributed to the effects of stigma, discrimination, unemployment, poverty, and social isolation (Nelson, Kloos, & Ornelas, 2014). As a guiding value of CP, social justice has focused on distributive justice (e.g., access to resources) and procedural justice (e.g., how decisions are made, ideally in an inclusive manner) (Prilleltensky & Nelson, 2009). Access to employment, education, housing or other resources that are available in the community for all citizens is a prerequisite for ensuring an improvement in the concrete living conditions of people with experience of mental health challenges (see a discussion on power and social justice in Chapter 4).

Multi-level Ecological Approaches

Fundamental to CP is consideration of phenomena at multiple levels of analysis (see Chapter 5). A focus on individuals alone obscures barriers to participation in community life and overlooks the social condition and limited opportunities that many persons with psychiatric disabilities face. An ecological orientation examines how different aspects of communities are interdependent, how they adapt to changes, how they distribute resources, and change over time (Kelly, 1966). Consumer/survivors and community members outside of the mental health system are often overlooked as resources for addressing mental health concerns (Trainor, Pomeroy, & Pape, 1999).

Resources for Changing How We Seek to be Supportive

Empowerment: Individual and Collective

Rappaport (1981) observed that those with least control in their lives were those that most needed it. From a CP perspective, empowerment includes the ability to make decisions that control your life, access to resources, and the ability to take action to realize your goals (see Chapter 4). Empowerment is not a purely internal state, such as simply feeling powerful, inspired, or confident (Christens, 2019). For many consumers, empowerment involves regaining the opportunity to direct their lives (Chamberlin, 1997; Deegan, 1997). These opportunities may include key decisions about where to live, how to pass the time, where to work, with whom they can relate, and the type of support and services they need and find most suitable. Regaining control over one's life helps to reduce feelings of helplessness and sense of victimization, while increasing feelings of personal self-efficacy.

Power: Oppression – Levels of Analysis and Intervention

Consideration of empowering processes and opportunities requires the examination of power relationships. For transformative change, we need to examine power across levels of analysis and identify potentially oppressive conditions that limit a person's capacity to exert actual influence on decisions (Rappaport, 1981; Serrano-García, 1994). Hierarchies of services often exclude those with disabilities from meaningful input in decisions about their lives using justifications about perceived lack of capacity of a "class" of persons (Kloos, 2010; Rappaport, 2000; White, 2010). Such exclusion is an act of oppression that limits the ability of individuals to make important decisions about their lives. Even more insidious are ideologies and myths to convince members of subordinated groups that they actually are inferior (Chamberlin, 1997; Corrigan & Al-Khouja, 2018; McDonald, Keys, & Balcazar, 2007). This sense of inferiority has been termed "internalized oppression." A transformative approach to mental health must address hierarchies of oppression as well as internalized oppression.

Liberation: Individual and Collective

The concept of liberation in social systems calls attention to the workings of power, to identify and challenge oppressive conditions, *and* to emphasize and support the capacities for oppressed people (Montero & Varas-Díaz, 2007; Nelson & Prilleltensky, 2010). In most mental health treatment systems, a liberation perspective seeks goals that many service providers and consumer/survivors endorse: better functioning, realization of recovery, and participation in community life. A liberation perspective will be needed among consumer/survivors and professionals to the extent that the system practices do not address conditions that mental health consumers view as oppressive. Mental health consumers have made important steps in raising critical awareness and understanding of oppressive circumstances in community mental health. Joint leadership by committed mental health professionals and consumers can guide efforts to change practices and policies; consumers are viewed as resources that have been under-utilized for making such changes (Brown & Rogers, 2014; Davidson, 2016).

Chapter Summary

Advocates and community members can support recovery and liberation by promoting collaboration between stakeholders as a means of realizing empowerment, focusing on strengths, and advancing social justice (Nelson, & Prilleltensky, 2010). Collaboration in mental health care means that consumers have the opportunity to make choices that may be different from those that professionals would make, and that those decisions would be respected. All of us have made bad choices or failed at some point in our lives. Deegan (1988) has called for mental health collaborations that allow for the dignity of failure in making decisions. Personal growth can occur when mental health professionals, friends, and family members support an individual to recover from problematic decisions. Not being allowed the opportunity to make a mistake will limit personal growth and recovery. Furthermore, the emergence of organized mutual help and consumer/survivor movements creates an effective lobby and significant precedent for sustaining changes at micro- and meso-levels of analysis. However, much work needs to be done at a macro-level of analysis to promote structural change that helps prevent serious mental health problems.

Key Terms

Community integration: Involvement in meaningful activities and the development of valued social roles in communities relevant to a person with experiences of mental health challenges.

Empowerment: Empowerment includes the ability to make decisions that control your life, raise concerns, work with others, gain access to resources, and the ability to take action to realize goals.

Mental health promotion: Activities that encourage the development of emotional wellbeing, coping, and interpersonal connectedness.

Peer support: Within mental health services, peer support refers to intentional efforts to connect persons with lived experience of mental health problems and recovery so that those farther along in recovery can offer unique insights and support to those who are having more difficulty.

Recovery: Recovery involves the development of a new meaning and purpose in one's life as one grows beyond catastrophic effects of mental illness. Recovery emphasizes personal goals of experiencing hope, healing, empowerment, and connection with others after life disruptions from serious mental health problems.

Self-determination: Having voice and decision-making power over your health, activities, and wellbeing.

Serious mental health problems: Persistent psychiatric disabilities that can have a profound effect on a person's behavior, thinking, emotions and relationships. These include diagnoses such as schizophrenia, bipolar disorder and, severe depression.

Social inclusion: For persons with serious mental health problems, being included in meaningful activities and valued relationships in settings outside of the mental health system that are important for those persons.

Transformative change in community mental health: Intentional efforts to shift perspective and power to include those with lived experience of mental health problems in decisions how services are structured, helping relationships, and choices that affects their lives.

Resources

Handling your psychiatric disability at work and school – Boston University Center for Psychiatric Rehabilitation: https://cpr.bu.edu/resources/reasonable-accommodations/jobschool
Community inclusion – Temple University Collaborative on Social Inclusion of Persons with Psychiatric Disabilities: http://tucollaborative.org/community-inclusion/resources/
Resources for Peer Support – *Ontario Peer Development Initiative*: www.opdi.org/

Additional Resources in different countries

- Canadian Mental Health Association: www.cmha.ca/
- Mental Health Australia: https://mhaustralia.org/
- Mental Health Ireland: www.mentalhealthireland.ie/
- National Empowerment Center (US): www.power2u.org/

Further reading on transformative change of mental health systems

Nelson, G., Kloos, B., & Ornelas, J. (Eds.) (2014). *Community psychology and community mental health: Towards transformative change.* New York: Oxford University Press.

RACISM AND APPLICATIONS OF CRITICAL RACE AND INTERSECTIONAL THEORIES IN COMMUNITY PSYCHOLOGY

21

Ciann L. Wilson, Natasha Afua Darko, Amandeep Kaur Singh, and Brianna Hunt

Warm-up Questions

Before you begin reading this chapter, we invite you to reflect on the following questions:

1 What is Critical Race Theory? What is Intersectionality Theory?

2 What responsibility does the field of community psychology (CP) have to acknowledge and address issues of racial injustice in contemporary society?

3 How have race and racism been discussed or framed in your education? How might an analysis of race inform your worldview?

4 Reflect on your own social location and think of various ways that Intersectional oppression impacts your life experiences. How might race impact your personal and professional relationships or daily interactions?

Learning Objectives

In this chapter you will learn about

- The historical construct of race while reflecting on the differences and similarities in manifestations of racism in several forms, including Indigenous erasure, anti-Blackness, and xenophobia
- Critical Race Theory, from its development to its salient critiques, and application to CP research and practice
- Intersectionality Theory and its relationship to Critical Race Theory
- How CP can use Critical Race Theory and Intersectionality Theory within research and praxis

Positionality of Authors

Western research has historically and contemporarily been written from the perspective of an unknown authority, one often assumed to be a white researcher who is an unbiased expert in what they are talking about (even when what and who they are talking about are cultures and peoples they do not actually know with any degree of familiarity). The activity of analyzing data pertaining to the lives and social interactions of others, while never having to name or reflect on your own social location and how that might impact your outlook on the world and the people you are researching, is an immense privilege. As such, an important practice is naming the positionality (i.e., social location with respect to **race**, gender, class, sexuality, ability, etc.) that informs the worldviews and perspectives being offered. In accordance with this practice, you will find the position statements of our team of authors below.

Ciann L. Wilson is an Associate Professor in Community Psychology at Wilfrid Laurier University. Ciann is of Afro-, Indo- and Euro-Jamaican ancestry. Her research interests build off her community-engaged work to include Critical Race Theory, anti-/de-colonial theory, African diasporic and Indigenous community health, sexual and reproductive wellbeing, and community-based research approaches. Her body of work aims to utilize research as an avenue for sharing the stories and realities of African diasporic, Indigenous, and racialized peoples and improving the health and wellbeing of these communities.

Natasha Afua Darko is a Black cis female. She is the daughter of Ghanaian immigrants. Her experiences with anti-Black racism have shaped her personal and professional experiences. Her community work focused primarily on health interventions for Black and racialized youth. Darko is deeply committed to anti-oppressive practices and inclusion.

Amandeep Kaur Singh is a South Asian (Punjabi-Sikh) cisgender woman, born and raised in Canada (Treaty 7). Her community and professional work focus on the experiences of racialized and marginalized communities in the access and accessibility of educational, cultural, and health services. She hopes to foster a collective space within her community and research for uplifting silenced voices in the opposition of white hegemonic narratives while recognizing the interconnected oppressions of racialized peoples and communities.

Brianna Hunt is a white cisgender woman who calls Treaty 1 territory her home. As an uninvited visitor on Turtle Island, Hunt works to acknowledge, analyze, and navigate her privilege within her academic and community work. As a queer scholar, Hunt's reflexive practice involves ongoing inquiry into the ways that her own identity shapes her work toward meaningful allyship with communities of color.

Introduction

In this chapter, we begin with a historical overview of the concept of race and explore how this concept shapes our relationships and interactions in North American society. We then provide a comprehensive overview of **Critical Race Theory (CRT)**, its historical underpinnings, main tenets and utility for analysis, gaps in the theory, and critiques. Specifically, we highlight that while the field of CP could greatly benefit from a critical analysis of race, a focus on race alone cannot account for the diverse, nuanced, and complex experiences of marginalized peoples. As such, we propose that in addition to a critical race lens, community psychologists should engage with an Intersectional theoretical framework. Throughout this chapter, you will find rich exemplars of Intersectional and race-based discrimination such as Indigenous erasure, anti-Black **racism**, and xenophobia. We will end by addressing how CRT and **Intersectionality** can be implemented within CP research and praxis.

Due in large part to their focus on social structures, CRT and Intersectionality are better frameworks about race and racism for informing CP than perspectives from the field of social psychology. The field of social psychology has a long tradition of understanding racism, prejudice, and discrimination, but from a micro-level of analysis that includes individual behavior and interpersonal relationships (e.g., contact hypothesis, which explores how intergroup contact between different racial or ethnic groups may impact relationships between these different groups) (Stangor, 2006). The inclusion of CRT and Intersectional frameworks in CP is also timely and important given the rise of white supremacy in countries around the world such as Canada, Brazil, the US, and across Europe. This re-emergence of emboldened white supremacy has political backative and a social media platform that makes these ideologies particularly virulent, violent, and harmful.

The Historical Concept of "Race"

Race continues to be a hotly debated topic within the intellectual community and broader society. The concept of race originated in the 15th century and was used to classify and group people into categories, classes, or kin, and was based on suggested likeness in observable characteristics and appearance (Banton, 2000; Omi & Winant, 1994; Wolf, Kahn, Roseberry, & Wallerstein, 1994). Race soon became a symbolic construct that served to hierarchically order groups of people (Wynter, 1995). More specifically, racial hierarchy was an instrument of colonization used to differentiate the ultimate human – the Western or white man – whose "natural place" atop the hierarchy was to be socially separate and apart from the other races of colonized people who were strung out in some arbitrary order along the hierarchy, based on perceived closeness to whiteness or European features and behaviors (Horne, 2015). The settler colonial "science" of race-making proliferated during the 18th century, and the variety of racial categories were numerous (Corcos, 1997). Some notable thinkers invested in this pseudo-science included the 18th century Swedish naturalist Carl Von Linne, who divided humanity into separate and static groups based on specific phenotypic or physical traits, temperament, geography, and political-moral behaviorisms (Corcos, 1997; Wolf et al., 1994): "Africans, were described as being Black, crafty and governed by impulse; Americans (Aboriginal peoples) reddish in color, obstinate and regulated by custom; and Europeans, white, gentle and governed by law" (Wolf et al., 1994, p.4). Today, these stereotyped traits, along with the concept of race, continue to shape the social, political, and economic fabric of our society. Ladson-Billings (1998) states that even when our notions of race fail to make sense, these concepts continue to be deployed, permeating our social and cultural world, and governing our interactions and experiences within it.

What is Critical Race Theory?

Critical Race Theory (CRT) was formed by activists and scholars who recognized the insidiousness of racism in American society. The theory was further inspired by African American struggles and intellectual tradition in the post-civil rights era of the 1970s (Crenshaw, 1993), at a time when the inseparability of the civil rights movement from law became evident. Other influential social movements that inform CRT include the Black Power and Chicano movements of the 60s and 70s (Delgado & Stefancic, 2001). CRT benefits from the insights made in the fields of critical legal studies and radical feminism (Ford & Airhihenbuwa, 2010; Delgado & Stefancic, 2001), and was developed by African American and other racialized law students in the US who were frustrated by the absence of race analyses in their discipline (Ladson-Billings, 1998). These students sought to draw attention to the ways in which racial hierarchies, racism, and power are institutionalized and engrained in the fabric of American society, designating whiteness as superior to Indigenous, Black, and people of color communities (Delgado & Stefancic, 2001). At its core, CRT focuses on the way in which the social construction of racial hierarchies that place Euro-Western men at the top as the arbiters of authority are embedded within institutions and structures that determine the differential treatment of non-white people within society, and the limited opportunities afforded to them. In essence, CRT challenges and is aimed at transforming the racial ideologies and racism operating within our society that determine the material conditions and subordination of racialized people. CRT provides an important lens through which we are able to observe how race and racism shape our social realities and our relationships with one another.

Many scholars from around the world in countries such as Canada, India, Spain, and the US have contributed to the body of CRT scholarship (Harris, 2001). For example, the late African American legal scholar, Dr. Derrick Bell, worked to examine and highlight the origins of CRT in social movements, and thus its practical application not only as a body of scholarship but as a political activist movement toward racial justice (Bell, 1984). The late Alan Freeman also wrote some seminal texts in the field of law that demonstrated how racism was embedded within American law (Delgado & Stefancic, 2001). Other notable scholars of color in the field include African American scholars Kimberlé Crenshaw and Angela Harris, Asian American scholars Mari Matsuda and Eric Yamamoto, Native American scholar Robert Williams, and Latin American scholars such as Richard Delgado, Francisco Valdes, and Margaret Montoya, to name a few (Delgado & Stefancic, 2001; Harré 2018).

In Canada, Dr. Carl James applies a CRT framework to his scholarship in the field of education, where he focuses on the educational and occupational inequities faced by Black youth (James, 2012). Another Canadian academic who frequently applies a CRT framework to his work is Dr. Rinaldo Walcott, whose research and publication focuses on Black, queer cultural politics, the history of colonialism, **multiculturalism**, and citizenship. His groundbreaking book *Black Like Who?: Writing Black Canada* provided a close reading of Black-Canadian cultural productions in hip-hop, film, sports, and literature. He argues that these creative outputs have in fact defined Canada and Canadian culture, despite mainstream Canada's erasure of the lived realities of Black people (Walcott, 2003). Today, CRT transcends the field of law and has grown in depth to be broadly applied in many fields, including: health, education, literature, sociology, political science, cultural studies, and history to explore how ideologies about race and racism shape our interactions and experiences (Harris, 2001).

The Tenets of Critical Race Theory

Delgado and Stefancic (2001, 2017) suggest some key tenets that underlie CRT. First, racism has been normalized in our society, and as a result, it permeates our institutions and interactions. Thus, racism is an "ordinary" part of everyday life experiences for people of color (p. 7). Second, the persistence of "white-over-color" ascendancy or white privilege are allowed to persist because people benefit physically and materially from the structures that reify this, so there is little incentive to eradicate it (p. 7). White people benefit materially from racial bias that privileges them, and non-white people are also motivated to "ascend to whiteness," in various ways. This can be phenotypically, through physical characteristics (i.e., the color of one's skin, where lighter skin tones and bright eye color – traditionally thought to be European features – are coveted in communities of color), or materially, where a belief that educational and/or class attainment brings one closer in proximity to whiteness. In turn, like a carrot dangling on a string, this goal of ascending to the pinnacle of whiteness (i.e., white skin, blond hair, blue eyes, and material and social affluence) motivates racialized people, and poor white people, to operate within the confines of the existing structures of power.

A third tenet of CRT is that race and "the races" are social constructs that are the product of racial ideologies and relations. They are not biologically determined or fixed. While people with similar physical features such as hair texture and skin color may have common places of origin, these genetically ordered traits do not extend to determine "intelligence, personality, or moral behaviours" (p. 8). However, in our racist society, these facts are ignored and races are created and endowed with a set of presumed characteristics.

Fourth, the dominant white settler society has strategically racialized different groups of people throughout history, at points when it has been convenient and to their benefit. For instance, the "one-drop rule" that demarcates anyone mixed with African blood as Black, afforded white settlers ownership of more slaves and thus enhanced wealth, whether or not these enslaved peoples were actually biracial or mixed with white. The same rule worked in reverse for Indigenous peoples, where one drop of white blood served to "dilute and disappear" the Native, leaving Indigenous peoples in a challenging position when trying to reclaim their ancestral culture, and territorial lands (Smith, 2008). White settlers have also recently absorbed previously ostracized ethnic groups such as white-passing Jewish communities into the fold, under the umbrella of whiteness. These examples demonstrate that the boundaries of whiteness are fluid; they shift and change ultimately to serve the dominant group. Furthermore, these examples demonstrate that at one time, the stereotypes about a group may depict them as reviled deviants in need of surveillance, repressive control, and sometimes even extermination, while at other points in history, when they serve the purposes of white expansionism, they are embraced.

A fifth tenet is that Indigenous people and people of color have important, valid, and unique perspectives to share about their lived experience, and those narratives are valuable and worthy of centering and telling, given their historical, social, and political treatment.

Sixth, no person has a singular, uni-dimensional identity. "Everyone has potentially conflicting, overlapping identities, loyalties, and allegiances" (Delgado & Stefancic, 2001, p. 9). A South Asian man may also identify as queer. A Muslim woman may be Black, and identify as an immigrant. This recognition is the concept of Intersectionality that we discuss in the following section.

Intersectionality: A More Critical Framework

The students of first-generation CRT scholars have explored the possible contributions that Intersectionality offers to our understandings of race and discrimination in research and practice (Crichlow, 2015). CRT has historically tended to privilege a race and class analysis, which can be viewed as quite limiting when accounting for multiple and complex identities. As a result, the application of an Intersectional lens has gained traction amongst proponents of CRT. Intersectionality as a theoretical framework emphasizes the simultaneity, irreducibility, and inseparability of systems of oppression such as racism, classism, misogyny, heteropatriarchy, and ableism, among others (Carastathis, 2014; Puar, 2011; see also Introduction to Part IV). Due to the interconnected nature of these systems, an Intersectional framework helps us better understand these multi-layered social divisions and complex manifestations of discrimination and oppression (Hill Collins & Bilge, 2016; The New School, 2014). An Intersectional analysis affords a more fulsome picture of the "interconnected nature of cis-normative-imperialist-white-supremacist-capitalist-patriarchy" (The New School, 2014). Intersectionality centers the realities and multiple social identities of marginalized people at the individual, community, societal, and structural levels of analysis (Bowleg, 2012). Rooted in social and activist movements, Intersectionality extends beyond a static analysis framework to include ongoing political action toward social justice. Intersectionality is an inherently political framework and serves as a call to action to dismantle various interlocking systems of oppression.

Intersectionality emerged out of Black feminist thought, CRT, and women of color activism in the 1960s and 1970s. By and large, African American women's work, voices, and lived experience laid the groundwork for what we now refer to as Intersectionality. Seminal texts include Sojourner Truth's penned essay in 1851 titled "Ain't I a Woman." The essay demanded equity for Black women within the anti-slavery movement (Brah & Phoenix, 2004). Another influential text, Frances Beal's essay, "Double Jeopardy: To be Black and Female" was published in 1969. This essay centered the erasure of Black women and their experiences by explaining the enactment of patriarchy and sexism prevalent within the Black Power movement, and the racism and Eurocentrism prevalent within the white feminist liberation movement (Beal, 2008). Informed by the ways in which their bodies were perceived and exploited in the enslavement era, Black women were never afforded the spoils of white femininity and fragility. While consigned to the same hard physical labor as their male counterparts, Black women were simultaneously expected to be submissive to men in accordance with heteropatriarchy.

Many scholars and activists cite The Comabahee River Collective Statement (CRCS) (Einstein, 1997) as a catalyst for Intersectionality in social movements. The CRCS is a document curated by a collective of Black feminists in 1977 that outlines how the systemic oppressions of racism, patriarchy, and capitalism interlock (Hill Collins & Bilge, 2016). In 1981, bell hooks denounced the feminist movement for solely catering to the needs of middle-class white women, while neglecting the needs of women of color and the poor. Angela Davis' volume *Women, Race and Class* (1983) focused on the interaction between race, gender, and class, and how these work together to shape inequality. The notion of interlocking systems of oppression that was developed in the CRCS was further explored by Patricia Hill Collins (2000) in what she called the "matrix of domination." This concept served as a major precursor to the theoretical framework of Intersectionality popularized by African American legal scholar, Kimberle Crenshaw (1989).

Integral to CRT and Intersectionality frameworks is a critique of the many manifestations of white supremacist logic, as it pertains to discrimination towards different groups. Harkening on the aforementioned racial hierarchy of the Euro-Western man's conception, which places him at the pinnacle, as the arbiter of all things, is the inherent view that "white is always right." The white man's perspective and way of thinking about the world is deemed superior, logical, and progressive, rather than emotional, illogical, and regressive. This worldview, which deems all other perspectives as degenerate, primal, or backwards, is the white supremacist logic that permeates every facet of society. It sanctions the view that other countries exploited by the West are "shithole" countries if not included in the white man's conception of the stolen territories under his domain.[1] An Intersectional framework allows us an analysis of the ways in which people can simultaneously be oppressed by one manifestation of white supremacist oppression, while still adhering to its logic. For instance, a Chinese woman can be confronted with racialized sexism and exotification directed at her person, while perpetuating anti-Black racism. In the sections below, we will unpack a few specific examples that highlight the complex and Intersectional experiences of racialized communities, demonstrating the continued relevance of CRT and Intersectional analyses in the contemporary moment.

Indigenous Erasure

For Indigenous people, white supremacist logic has manifested as itself what has been termed "erasure." This first took root when white settlers set their sights on the land of present-day North America and decided to use terra nullius, or *nobody's land*, and the doctrine of domination to imagine an erroneous, a-historical account of the "New World." In this re-imagination, Turtle Island was thought to be empty land, devoid of humanity, which Europeans were the "first" and only peoples to discover and inhabit. This marked the beginning of a long series of intentional acts of germ and physical warfare, which claimed the lives of one quarter of the Earth's population within the 150-year period post-European contact (Amadahy & Lawrence, 2009). Despite many attempts to sanitize and white-wash this history, it is the "largest holocaust that the world has ever known" (Amadahy & Lawrence, 2009, p. 106; Wright, 1993; Wynter, 1995). Only between two and five percent of the original 70–100 million Indigenous peoples of Turtle Island survived (Amadahy & Lawrence, 2009). These biological assaults were succeeded by state policies that served to control Indigenous peoples and exclude them from white settler societies and stolen land and resources. For instance, the Indian Act (1876) encouraged the extermination of Indigenous peoples through assimilation and the dissolution of Indigenous spiritual, political, and familial structures using violent state interventions such as the kidnapping of Indigenous children, their forced enrollment in residential schools (and more recently, the foster care system) where they were abused, and the displacement of Indigenous communities to reserves (Amadahy & Lawrence, 2009; Wright, 1993). The policy-driven dilution of Indigenous identity through interracial marriages between Indigenous women and white men, was another primary way that Indigenous peoples were intentionally defined into extinction, giving the governments of white settler nation-states such as Canada and the US advantageous access to millions of acres of stolen land for white settlement and exploitation. Ramifications of the Indian Act continue to impact the lives of countless Indigenous people today, including stark definitions of who is eligible to claim Indigenous identity. Other ramifications include lack of access to safe water and land for many Indigenous communities, absence of fair investigations and trials for missing and murdered Indigenous women and girls, and the unethical destruction of Indigenous land for corporate gain.

Anti-Black Racism

Anti-Black racism is characterized by particularly virulent and pervasive racial stereotypes and discrimination that shape behaviors, actions, and attitudes towards people of African descent (Mullings, Morgan, & Quelleng, 2016). Anti-Black racism in Canada, where we live and work, is often subtle and is generally not accompanied by overt racial slurs or explicitly prejudiced actions. However, it is deeply entrenched in Canadian institutions, policies, and practices, such that anti-Black racism is either functionally normalized or rendered invisible to the dominant society. Canadian anti-Black racism (much like that in the US) in its contemporary form continues the historical practices of racial segregation, economic disadvantage, and social division (Morgan & Bullen, 2015).

Canada's widespread reputation of having comprehensive and progressive human rights allows Canada to adopt a racialized rhetoric of community-blaming, especially in cases when the rights of Black people in Canada are being undermined (Mullings et al., 2016). Take for instance recent reports that police in Toronto, Canada's largest metropolis and industrial center, were more likely to injure or kill Black people than their white counterparts (Hayes, 2018). "While Black people made up only 8.8 percent of Toronto's population in 2016, the report found they were involved in seven out of 10 cases of fatal shootings by police during the latter period. It found that Black people (and specifically Black men) were overrepresented in everything from investigations into use of force and sexual assault by police, to inappropriate or unjustified searches and charges" (Hayes, 2018, para. 4). Also significant is that, in many of these cases of police brutality, the victims are also dealing with mental health related issues, serving as an example of systemic ableism.

Anti-Black racism underlies the legacy of the current social, economic, and political marginalization of Black people in Canada, who experience some of the highest rates of poverty and incarceration, lowest educational attainment, and poorest living and working conditions in the country. These factors are associated with various chronic diseases, including hypertension and obesity, substance abuse, and prolonged stress due to racism and exploitation (Mullings et al., 2016; Rodney & Copeland, 2009). Anti-Black racism is so pronounced in Canada that the United Nations issued an investigation and report warning of systemically entrenched anti-Black racism in the country (UN Human Rights High Commissioner, 2016). It is clear that despite Canada's international image as a bastion of human rights and dignity, the realities of anti-Black racism within the nation's borders continue to marginalize Black communities.

Xenophobia

Scholars of color from around the world have long been critical of the nuanced forms of racism directed at different racialized people in North America. In his critical and seminal text, *Orientalism*, published in 1978, Edward Said sheds light on the problematic underpinnings of Euro-Western discourses about Eastern cultures and peoples. Said was particularly critical of the ways in which Euro-Western racial formations informed the perception of Arabic, South Asian, Muslim, and other Brown people as barbarians and liars who were to be viewed with suspicion (Said, 1979). In this conceptualization, Eastern and other cultures are portrayed as exotic, mysterious, and dangerous foreign threats to the white-settler empire building project. Even before the

New York City World Trade Center attacks on September 11, 2001, and certainly after this event, Brown people were seen as "not belonging" in North America. Unwelcome foreigners to anti-immigrant proponents, Brown peoples' "rightful place" has always been perceived as elsewhere (Sharma & Wright, 2005). For people of Arabic or South Asian descent, this discrimination is expressed as Islamophobia, or negative attitudes and discriminatory practices towards Muslim people and/or Islam (Allen, 2010). Notably, inherent to Islamophobia is the convergence of racial, ethnic, and religious discrimination (Underwood, 2018). Following the 2001 attacks in New York City, a war on terror was launched, which manifested for many as a war on Islam (Husain & Howard, 2017). Today, a rise in anti-Muslim sentiments and hate crimes towards those mistaken to be Muslim (e.g., Sikh communities) also continue to be reported across Europe (Taras, 2013) and North America (Bhasin, 2012; Husain & Howard, 2017; Karam, 2012). According to Statistics Canada, hate crimes against Muslim communities in Canada increased by 61 percent between 2014 and 2015 (Leber, 2017). Reported hate crimes include both violent attacks and vandalism of mosques across the country (Leber, 2017). Unfortunately, the recent rise in Islamophobic sentiments is not unique to Canada. In the US, the Federal Bureau of Investigation indicated that anti-Muslim hate crimes rose by 67 percent between 2014 and 2015, representing the highest national rates since September 11, 2001 (Potok, 2016). Anti-Muslim discrimination is also evident within the systems that shape Canadian policies and practices. Islamophobic attitudes within Canada have been further exacerbated and normalized by policies such as Quebec's recent passing of Bill 62, which prohibits people from covering their faces when using public services (Steuter-Martin, 2017), and Bill 21 preventing public servants (e.g., teachers, police officers, judges) from wearing outward articles of faith or risk facing disciplinary measures. Policies such as Bill 62 and 21 encourage the social exclusion of those who choose to reflect their religious faith through the clothing they wear.

For South American communities, and particularly Mexican communities seeking to migrate to the US, xenophobic racism has meant being confronted with virulent anti-Mexican sentiments, that have most recently culminated in inhumane detention centers and the promise of a wall to be erected on the southern border of the US. An Intersectional analysis affords a deeper interrogation into the fact that prior to the arbitrary borders that box in the white-settler nation-states of Canada and the US, Indigenous peoples roamed from the territories of South America and present-day Mexico, all the way north to present-day Canada and back again. Historically, there was no separation between North and South America. By this account, many South American people are also Indigenous to the Americas, and any meaningful, Intersectional social justice movement in opposition to colonial processes and anti-immigration proponents must also address that there is no separation between North and South or "First" and "Third" worlds (Veracini, 2007).

For many Asian communities, with long histories in North America, xenophobic racism has meant dealing with being used for cheap labor while experiencing anti-immigration sentiment. The fear of the "Asian Invasion" or "Yellow Peril" rhetoric was popularized through media propaganda in North American society as early as the late 19th and early 20th centuries. For instance, the Canadian Parliament passed the Chinese Immigration Act of 1855 (also referred to as the Chinese head tax) to discourage Chinese people from entering Canada after the completion of the Canadian Pacific Railway. Building upon this act, the Chinese Immigration Act of 1923 (i.e., Chinese Exclusion Act)

---

[1] In early 2018, U.S. President Donald Trump wondered on camera "why are we having all these people from shithole countries come here?" (https://www.cnn.com/2018/01/11/politics/immigrants-shithole-countries-trump/index.html).

banned almost all forms of immigration from China (Holland, 2007; McEvoy, 1982). However, this fear was heightened within a larger geopolitical context when in the late 1940s, countries such as China were viewed as the second greatest communist threat after Russia. Similarly, during times of war such as post-Pearl Harbor in 1942, Japanese Americans and Japanese Canadians were forced to live in internment camps. As China continues to rise as an economic and political power in the world, an important site of technological advancement with a growing military and a population size unmatched by any other country, discourses perpetuating the idea that Asian cultures pose a threat to the dominance of the West abound through media propaganda.

Intersectional frameworks and practice rest on the recognition and acknowledgement that systems of oppression interlock for many racialized peoples in the West. Given the specific examples of Indigenous erasure, anti-Black racism, and xenophobia, it is crucial to recognize that forms and categories of racialized oppression are not mutually exclusive. Individuals, families, and communities that are Indigenous, Black, and Muslim-passing experience discrimination that rests on these multiple racialized and religious identities. Systems of oppression work together in a methodological fashion to disadvantage those who face discrimination based on any combination of race, culture, religion, gender, sexual identity, and ability, among other factors. Taking an Intersectional approach to research and practice allows researchers, scholars, and activists alike the opportunity to meaningfully address the multiple forms of oppression and systematic marginalization experienced by communities of color.

Critiques of and Debates within Critical Race Theory

As is the case with all theoretical frameworks, CRT is not without its criticism. Naturally, CRT has splintered and scholars have created different subgroups (e.g., Asian American, Latino, and queer contingents) of CRT in which they can center the communities they would like to prioritize (Delgado & Stefancic, 2001). Scholars report that these groups:

> continue to maintain relatively good relations under the umbrella of CRT, meeting together at periodic conferences and gatherings. Each has developed its own body of literature and set of priorities. For example, Latino and Asian scholars study immigration, theory and policy, as well as language rights and discrimination based on accent or national origin. A small group of Indian (i.e., Native American) scholars addresses indigenous people's rights, sovereignty, and land claims. (Delgado & Stefancic, 2001, p. 6)

However, one glaring challenge is that these groups have not built intentional alliances, nor have they prioritized the centering of an Intersectional framework in their work, which would afford them more opportunities for theoretical cross-pollination and a more nuanced analysis that highlights the problematic nature of white settlerism in all of its expressions (e.g., Indigenous erasure, anti-Black racism, xenophobia, sexism, transphobia, etc.).

Some scholars suggest that the heavy application of qualitative approaches to research, and the focus on individual narratives mentioned earlier that is common in CRT scholarship are anecdotal, at best, and not representative of, or generalizable to, larger sub-populations (Graham, Brown-Jeffy, Aronson, & Stephens, 2011). For example, a common methodological approach applied in

CRT scholarship is narrative storytelling that is used to highlight the lived experiences of participants. In response to criticism, proponents of CRT argue that the intention of CRT scholarship is to speak to the nuanced and specific experiences of racism of racialized groups and that this need not be generalizable, not even amongst different racialized groups. The uniqueness of the Black experience in North America does not allow us to understand the racism experienced by South Asian people who may be visibly Muslim, and vice versa. Further, proponents of CRT argue for the value of individual testimonial and lived experience, stating that the human experience is enough to warrant action when it comes to addressing racial injustice.

Scholars and theorists argue that Canada, and North America more broadly, are epicenters of exhaustive diversity due to the processes of colonialism, indentureship, and forced migration (Tuck & Yang, 2012). Others use a discourse of inclusive multiculturalism that deems a CRT framework neither necessary nor important in this presumed multicultural utopia. The discourse of multiculturalism used to describe large cities in Canada serve to recast these sites as benevolent and inclusive places where everyone who is seeking a fresh start is welcomed with open arms, thus challenging (optically at the very least) the relevance of, and need for, CRT. However, it is important to note that the rhetoric of multiculturalism in Canada stems from the long-standing historical conflicts between French and British colonial powers that erupted in the 1980s on the political stage (Gaztambide-Fernández, 2012). These conversations and resulting policies centered issues at the core of strife between white settlers in Canada, namely French versus English languages, customs, religion, and ultimately, physical and sociocultural territory. Policies resulting from these conversations were compiled in the country's *Multiculturalism Act* of 1988 (Bourhis, 2003; Boyd, 1999). The realities of racialized and Indigenous peoples were not part of the original conversations about multiculturalism, despite the role that multiculturalism and its counterparts – colorblindness and racelessness – play in the Canadian state's desire to appear modern, inclusive, and diverse. In this re-imagined multicultural Canada, there are equal opportunities for all under the myth of meritocracy. According to this myth, we can all assume wealth and the realizations of the "American dream" if we just pull up our bootstraps and work hard enough. If we fail, that too is a direct result of individual poor decisions, and not the persistence of structural discrimination.

Proponents of CRT argue that multiculturalism is a trivial celebration of diversity at a superficial level. The Canadian norm is to pretend that multiculturalism is a civil, normal, and utopic outcome to which all international societies should aspire, rather than the result of violent colonial globalization processes that continue to decimate entire cultures and communities in both the "New and Old worlds" (Wilson & James, forthcoming). The rhetoric of multiculturalism, much like superficial diversity or ethnic pluralism, are a-historical and mask the manifestations of racial apartheid that plague Canada's past and present (Goldberg, 2007; Richardson, 2008). This rhetoric both trivializes and seeks to erase Canada's participation in various colonial projects, including the insidious ways institutionalized racism continues to socially, politically, and economically disadvantage Black and Brown peoples. The rhetoric of multiculturalism in the contemporary Canadian consciousness is dangerous, precisely because it allows for the reimagining of European history and collective memory as existing separate and apart from past and continued racist oppression (James, 2001). In other words, white peoples imagined politically correct proclamations that they "do not see color" affords for the silencing, minimizing, and trivializing of experiences of racist violence (Sonn & Quayle, 2013).

Community Psychology and Critical Race Theory

CP utilizes diversity and inclusion as values that guide the field, as has been the case for over 30 years (Rappaport, 1977; see also Chapter 3). The values of diversity and inclusion are often defined as an understanding of differences among individuals based on race, ethnicity, gender, age, sexual orientation, physical and mental abilities, and other markers of identity (Tebes, 2010). CP scholars often highlight that their work is rooted in a fundamental respect for the equality of all peoples (Furman et al., 2018; Nelson & Prilleltensky, 2010). Many CP scholars explicitly reference personal and collective social justice orientations within their work. Despite these recognitions, the application of CRT and Intersectionality is too often absent from CP research (Furman, Singh, Darko, & Wilson, 2018), even in cases where research focuses explicitly on populations in which people of color are overrepresented. For example, many scholars that conduct research centered on those involved in Canadian child welfare and criminal justice systems often fail to apply a CRT or Intersectional framework.

Respect for diversity and inclusion are often mentioned as core CP values and principles that recognize the diverse needs of communities and populations through the research process (Furman et al., 2018; Nelson & Prilleltensky, 2010), without critically or concretely moving beyond this broad recognition. The principles of diversity and inclusion also fail to provide adequate guidance when navigating multiple and intersecting complexities (Bond & Mulvey, 2000; Furman et al., 2018). Furthermore, CP does not consistently employ a method of critical examination when it comes to diversity, nor does it examine how power, oppression, and marginalization are intertwined and impact marginalized people. Without tangible examination and actions, CP's aim to address the harm and distress resulting from inequity risks upholding and privileging Eurocentric discourse (Furman et al., 2018) and further perpetuating harmful and oppressive conjuncture. CRT and Intersectionality can serve as iterative frameworks for assisting researchers to remain conscious of racial inequity and Intersectional marginalization within research and practice (Ford & Airhihenbuwa, 2010).

Application of Critical Race Theory to Community Psychology Research

Finding research projects and manuscripts within CP that speak to race outside of the positioning of researchers or simple demographic information of participants is quite difficult. To challenge some of the dominant discourse within CP, CRT and Intersectionality can be a helpful tool for researchers and practitioners. One example in CP research is highlighted by Sonn and Quayle's (2013) reflective praxis paper, where they aim to understand racism by engaging with CRT and whiteness studies in their allied work with Community Arts Network Western Australia (CAN WA). CAN WA provides both opportunities for Indigenous arts and cultural expression and space for Indigenous peoples and local governments to build partnerships. Much of the collaborative work intends to create change and empower Indigenous groups through community cultural development. Significant outputs from this collaboration included performances and exhibitions which allowed community members to represent themselves while challenging dominant social narratives. In their process, Sonn and Quayle recognize how race continues to play a significant role in the structuring of relationships and partnerships with government, the allocation of privileges, and practices of exclusion. They also recognize that the work is not linear. It is both iterative and generative.

A further example of the illuminating potential of CRT within CP lies in the work of Reyes Cruz and Sonn (2011). Here, the authors highlight that CRT can be utilized from a decolonizing standpoint to address concepts of culture and diversity within CP. First, Reyes Cruz and Sonn (2011) use a case study to illustrate the experiences of marginalized Latino-American immigrants and the power inequities they face within the school system. This case study is centered on a school in the US Midwest, mandated to implement services in Spanish, where engagement of parents by the school district was merely symbolic. While parents demanded authentic participation and incorporation of their suggestions, the school district ultimately implemented a bilingual program that failed to respond to suggestions of the parents. In addition, institutional problems surrounding their treatment of students were disregarded by the school and blame was placed on the parents. This example highlights the ways that systems often work under a guise of meaningful participation and cultural inclusion, only to act in accordance with their own views on what constitutes appropriate participatory action and what types of knowledge are deemed valid. Using a critical lens allows us to observe the ways that systems place blame on individuals rather than acknowledging the shortcomings of institutions and structures.

Reyes Cruz and Sonn (2011) also highlight the importance of a critical lens when considering Sonn's own experiences as a Black person and immigrant from South Africa living and working in Australia. The authors address Sonn's experiences working within a white institution and being trained in a historically Eurocentric academic discipline. The favoring of Eurocentric thought within the institution stood in stark contrast to the doubt often cast on Indigenous ways of knowing and doing. According to Reyes Cruz and Sonn, CP research and understanding of culture should be placed within "critical frameworks that examine the dynamics of the social reproduction and contestation of inequality" (2011, p. 205).

Application of Critical Race Theory to Community Psychology Practice

The practical aspects of CP are too often overshadowed by research and theory (Prilleltensky, 2001). Despite values and principles of diversity, inclusion, transformative change, and social justice in CP (Nelson & Prilleltensky, 2010), actors in the field still struggle to put these values and principles into practice and provide guidance (Bond & Harrell, 2006). For example, much of CP scholarship focuses on the importance of community/academic partnership and collaboration. However, CP scholars may work on a collaborative research project without ever coming face to face with those people who are most impacted by their work. Additionally, researchers are often regarded as "experts" within collaborations, which are not devoid of power dynamics that privilege the perspectives of the researcher. As a result, researchers often fail to make outputs from their research accessible for a broader audience, and accessible for practical application in real-world settings and institutions. This practical application of CP research findings, is an essential part of the work of our discipline, which aims to be inclusive, center diversity and social justice, and create transformative change.

Community psychologists are called to consistently engage in critical **reflexivity**, regardless of their social location and status. The practice of critical reflexivity is often used by community psychologists to reflect on their power, privilege, and how they contribute to keeping people of color oppressed and marginalized (Reyes Cruz & Sonn, 2011). However, critical reflexivity requires more than just self-awareness, it requires that community psychologists consistently engage with how they contribute both individually and systemically to both oppression and liberation.

For instance, a study by Bond and Harrell (2006) highlights the need for critical reflexivity and self-awareness among community psychologists. They examined the types of diversity-related challenges that researchers in the field have encountered by requesting stories from researchers. As a part of their submission, researchers were asked to also identify their backgrounds (ethnic, race, geographic, gender, etc.) and to provide their positioning in their research. They received many submissions from white authors that were working within or with communities of color. However, it took several attempts by Bond and Harrell to get background and researcher positioning information, particularly from white authors. Bond and Harrell explained that "even within this group of professionals who have embraced the value for diversity within their work, [they] found several white authors falling into the assumption of 'white' as the default or norm against which to contrast" (2006, p. 161). Another issue that Bond and Harrell encountered during the peer-review process involved some reviewers' views of diversity-related research as being emotionally- or politically-charged, and thus too personal and invalid. Some reviewers suggested that these topics were messy and wanted to see more clear resolutions. In other words, they wanted to see more neat, tidy, and happy endings in the papers. This failure to recognize one's positionality and the white privilege inherent in dismissing the experiences and testimonies of individuals and communities as "less valid" or "not scientific enough" is problematic. White scholars often fail to recognize the inherent power and privilege that they hold in deciding that which counts as knowledge or scientific evidence, and that which does not.

Community psychologists must engage in critical practice through meaningful collaboration with people of color. One way to meaningfully involve people of color in CP practice is through building relationships over time and applying CRT to group model-building methods to address social and health issues (Frerichs et al., 2016). To address any issue that involves a racial hierarchy, a critical examination of how outcomes are affected by race and racism is necessary. CRT provides a framework for critical analysis centered around how race and racism are engrained in social structures and affect the lives of racialized folks. Using CRT to determine strategies that facilitate dialogue and mobilize around issues of racism within scholarship and beyond is essential. CRT also employs a narrative-based approach which may help to facilitate discussions about how specific communities want to combat a particular social or health issue. It is also important to note that it is impossible to achieve meaningful social transformation without consulting and collaborating with multiple contributors and stakeholders (Price, 2017).

Community psychologists need to critically engage with their positionalities, within research and community engagement, in order to foster genuine relationships with the communities in which they work. This engagement should continue throughout all phases of the research process, from inception to knowledge mobilization. Positionality statements within written work help readers to locate the authors within their writing. For this reason, we have included our own positionality statements at the beginning of the present chapter. Finally, in addition to critical analysis of positionality, researcher accountability is an important aspect of challenging racial hierarchies. Accountability measures in research include regular check-ins with community partners and stakeholders. These check-ins help researchers and community members to ensure that relevant community needs are being addressed and prioritized through CP research.

Chapter Summary

In CP, scholars acknowledge that in order to create real social change, structural inequalities must be addressed (Nelson & Prilleltensky, 2010). Similarly, critical race and Intersectional theorists also acknowledge these factors as they pertain to systemically entrenched oppression. Despite the possibility for cross-pollination of ideas, these two bodies of literature remain disparate fields. For example, the Society for Community Research and Action (SCRA) – Community Psychology, Division 27 of the American Psychological Association, has several committees and interest groups that focus exclusively on different aspects of diversity issues. These committees include an Indigenous interest research group, a research group focused on women, one centered around accessibility studies, a council on cultural, ethnic, and racial affairs, and many others that address issues of diversity within individual silos, without acknowledging the importance of intersections of discrimination. In one study, scholars recognize that work centering gendered experiences within SCRA itself includes no intersection with race or racism studies and demonstrates little variability within the group of women participants (Bond & Mulvey, 2000). Bond & Mulvey (2000) outline that the experiences of people of color have historically been viewed as a separate struggle, not to be conflated with gender or many other forms of discrimination within CP frameworks. Given these examples, it is clear that even within CP's largest institutions, those who are complexly marginalized may not find a seat at the table or know where to sit. Critical analysis of CP's contributions indicate that the field could greatly benefit from centering Critical Race and Intersectional frameworks, if for no other reason, than because Black, Indigenous and people of color communities have identified these frameworks as important for understanding their lived realities (Furman et al., 2018). In the work community psychologists do in their aims for social justice and social transformation, it is integral to recognize the unique experiences of those who are marginalized, and center Black, Indigenous, and people of color's lived experiences and their fight for their lives.

Key Terms

Critical Race Theory (CRT): A framework used to examine the ways in which the social construction of race and the resulting racist belief systems operate to disadvantage people of color socially, economically, legally, politically, etc.

Intersectionality: A framework that acknowledges that social categories (gender, race, sexual orientation, etc.) or identities are not distinct elements but rather interconnected, yielding complex experiences for multiply marginalized people.

Multiculturalism: An imagined society in which diverse and multiple cultural and/or ethnic groups coexist in equitable and utopic harmony. This may be referred to as cultural-pluralism.

Race: A symbolic construction used to refer to a class of people or kin based on suggested likeness in character and appearance.

Racism: Prejudice or discrimination directed against someone of a different race, with the notion that one's own race is superior.

Reflexivity: An iterative and continuous process of self-awareness and self-reflection by researchers between their positionality, values, biases, and experiences in relation to their research and community engagement, and vice-versa. It also includes a process of understanding the ways in which a researcher's positionality may contribute or recreate, both individually and systemically, oppression and liberation.

Resources

- Kimberlé Crenshaw: What is Intersectionality?: www.youtube.com/watch?v=ViDtnfQ9FHc
- Check out the Intersectionality Matters podcast with Kimberlé Crenshaw on #SoundCloud: https://soundcloud.com/intersectionality-matters
- The Combahee River Collective Statement: http://circuitous.org/scraps/combahee.html
- The 1619 Project – The New York Times: www.nytimes.com/interactive/2019/08/14/magazine/1619-america-slavery.html
- Check out the book "How to Be an Antiracist" by Ibram X. Kendi: www.ibramxkendi.com/how-to-be-an-antiracist-1
- A post-Charlottesville reading list to help explain American white supremacy: www.vox.com/culture/2017/8/15/16145380/post-charlottesville-reading-list-stamped-from-beginning-hitlers-american-model
- The Council on Cultural, Ethnic, and Racial Affairs (CERA) of the Society for Community Research and Action (SCRA): http://www.scra27.org/who-we-are/committees-and-interest-groups/cultural-ethnic-and-racial-affairs/

REFERENCES

Aaker, J., Drolet, A., & Griffin, D. (2008). Recalling mixed emotions. *Journal of Consumer Research, 35*(2), 268–78.

Aboriginal Male Health Summit (2008). *Inteyerrkwe* statement 2008. *Indigenous Law Bulletin 7*(7). Retrieved from http://classic.austlii.edu.au/au/journals/IndigLawB/2008/26.html

Abramovich, I. A. (2012). No safe place to go – LGBTQ youth homelessness in Canada: Reviewing the literature. *Canadian Journal of Family and Youth/Le Journal Canadien de Famille et de la Jeunesse, 4*(1), 29–51.

Ackerson, L. K., & Subramanian, S. V. (2008). State gender inequality, socioeconomic status and intimate partner violence (IPV) in India: A multilevel analysis. *Australian Journal of Social Issues, 43*, 81–101.

Adams, J., & White, M. (2005). Why don't stage-based activity promotion interventions work? *Health Education Research, 20*, 237–43.

Addams, J., & Waldm, L. D. (1910). *Forty years at Hull-House.* New York: Macmillan.

Adimora, A. A., Schoenbach, V. J., Martinson, F. E., Donaldson, K. H., Stancil, T. R., & Fullilove, R. E. (2003). Concurrent partnerships among rural African Americans with recently reported heterosexually transmitted HIV infection. *Journal of Acquired Immune Deficiency Syndromes, 34*(4), 423–9.

Adler, N., Boyce, T., Chesney, M., Cohen, S., Folkman, S., Kahn, R., & Syme, L. (1994). Socioeconomic status and health: The challenge of the gradient. *American Psychologist, 49*, 15–24.

Agyeman, J., Cole, P., Haluza-Delay, R., & O-Riley, P. (Eds.). (2009). *Speaking for ourselves: Environmental justice in Canada.* Vancouver, CA: The University of British Columbia Press.

Ahn, C. (2007). Democratizing American philanthropy. In INCITE! Women of Color against Violence (Eds.), *The revolution will not be funded* (pp. 63–76). Cambridge, MA: South End Press.

Akhtar, S. (2014).The mental pain of minorities. *British Journal of Psychotherapy, 30*(2), 136–53.

Alasuutari, P., Bickman, L., & Brannan, J. (2008). *The SAGE handbook of social research methods.* London: SAGE Publications.

Albee, G. W. (1959). *Mental health manpower trends.* New York: Basic Books.

Albee, G. W. (1982). Preventing psychopathology and promoting human potential. *American Psychologist, 32*, 150–61.

Albee, G. W. (1986). Toward a just society: Lessons from observations on the primary prevention of psychopathology. *American Psychologist, 41*, 891–8.

Albee, G. W. (1990). The futility of psychotherapy. *Journal of Mind and Behavior, 11*(3–4), 369–84.

Albee, G. W. (1996). Revolutions and counterrevolutions in prevention. *The American Psychologist, 51*(11), 1130–3.

Albee, G. W. (1998). The politics of primary prevention. *Journal of Primary Prevention, 19*, 117–27.

Aldarondo, E. (Ed.). (2007). *Advancing social justice through clinical practice.* London, England: Lawrence Erlbaum.

Aldrich, D., & Meyer, M. (2015). Social capital and community resilience. *American Behavioral Scientist, 59*(2), 254–69.

Alesina, A., & Glaeser, E. L. (2004). *Fighting poverty in the U.S. and Europe: A world of difference.* Oxford: Oxford University Press.

Alia, K. A., Freedman, D. A., Brandt, H. M., & Browne, T. (2014). Identifying emergent social networks at a federally qualified health center-based farmers' market. *American Journal of Community Psychology, 53*(3–4), 335–45.

Alinsky, S. (1971). *Rules for radicals.* New York: Vintage Books.

Allen, C. (2010). *Islamophobia.* Farnham, Surrey; Burlington, VT: Ashgate.

Allen, N. E., & Javdani, S. (2017). Toward a contextual analysis of violence: Employing community psychology to advance problem definition, solutions, and future directions. In M. A. Bond, I. Serrano-García, C. B. Keys, & M. Shinn (Eds.), *APA handbook of community psychology: Methods for community research and action for diverse groups and issues* (pp. 327–43). Washington, DC: American Psychological Association.

Almedom, A. M. (2005). Social capital and mental health: An interdisciplinary review of primary evidence. *Social Science & Medicine, 61*(5), 943–64.

Alsop, R., Bertelsen, M., & Holland, J. (2006). *Empowerment in practice: From analysis to implementation.* Washington, DC: The World Bank.

Alvaredo, F., Chancel, L., Piketty, T., Saez, E., & Zucman, G. (2018). *World inequality report 2018: Executive summary.* Retrieved from http://wir2018.wid.world/files/download/wir2018-summary-english.pdf

Alvesson, M., & Willmott, H. (Eds.). (1992). *Critical management studies.* London: SAGE Publications.

Alvesson, M., & Sköldberg, K. (2000). *Reflexive methodology: New vistas for qualitative research.* London: SAGE Publications.

Amadahy, Z., & Lawrence, B. (2009). Indigenous peoples and Black people in Canada: Settlers or allies? In A. Kempfs (Ed.), *Breaching the colonial contract: Anti-colonialism in the US and Canada* (pp. 105–36). Berlin: Springer. Retrieved from http://link.springer.com/chapter/10.1007/978-1-4020-9944-1_7

American Psychological Association (2009). *Report of the Task Force on gender identity and gender variance.* Retrieved from www.apa.org/pi/lgbt/resources/policy/gender-identity-report.pdf

American Psychological Association (2018). *The road to resilience.* Retrieved from www.apa.org/helpcenter/road-resilience.aspx

Amnesty International Publications. (2009). *Kenya the unseen majority: Nairobi's two million slum-dwellers.* Retrieved from https://www.refworld.org/pdfid/4a3660e82.pdf

Anderson, A., Binney, J., & Harris, A. (2015). *Tangata Whenua: A history.* Wellington: Bridget Williams Books.

Anderson, B. (2000). *Doing the dirty work? The global politics of domestic labour.* London: Zed Books.

Anderson, S., & Cavanagh, J. (2000). *Bearing the burden: The impact of global financial crisis on workers and alternative agendas for the IMF and other Institutions.* Washington, DC: Institute for Policy Studies.

Andery, A. A. (1984/2001). Psicologia na comunidade. In S. T. M. Lane & W. Codo (Eds.), *Psicologia Social - o homem em movimento* (pp. 203–20). São Paulo: Brasiliense.

Angel, S., & Kroll, T. (2012). Placing rehabilitation and recovery after spinal cord injury into a biographical context: A U.S. versus Danish case comparison. *Journal of Neuroscience Nursing, 44*(6), 298–306.

Angelique, H., & Culley, M. (2007). History and theories of community psychology: An international perspective of community psychology in the United States: Returning to political, critical, and ecological roots. In S. Reich, M. Riemer, I. Prilleltensky, & M. Montero (Eds.), *International community psychology: History and theories* (pp. 37–62). New York: Springer.

Angelique, H., & Kyle, K. (2002). Monterey declaration of critical community psychology. *The Community Psychologist, 35*(1), 35–6.

Angelique, H., & Mulvey, A. (Eds.). (2012). Co-creating feminist community psychology [Special issue]. *Journal of Community Psychology, 40*(1), 1–194.

Angelique, H. L., & Culley, M. R. (2003). Feminism found: An examination of gender consciousness in community psychology. *Journal of Community Psychology, 31*, 189–209.

Anthony, W. (1993). Recovery from mental illness: The guiding vision of the mental health service system in the 1990s. *Psychosocial Rehabilitation Journal, 16*(4), 11–23.

Appelbaum, L.D. (2001). The influence of perceived deservingness on policy decisions regarding aid to the poor. *Political Psychology, 22*(3), 419–42.

Arendt, H. (1958/1998). *The human condition* (2nd ed.). Chicago, IL: The University of Chicago Press.

Aristide, J. B. (2000). *Eyes of the heart: Seeking a path for the poor in the age of globalization.* Monroe, ME: Common Courage Press.

Arnstein, S. (1969). A ladder of citizen participation. *Journal of the American Institute of Planners, 35*(4), 216–24.

Ashkanasy, N., & Dorris, A. (2017). Emotions in the workplace. *Annual Review of Organizational Psychology and Organizational Behavior, 4*, 67–90.

The Aspen Institute. (1996). *Measuring community capacity building: A workbook in progress for rural communities.* Retrieved from www.aspeninstitute.org/publications/measuring-community- capacity-building

Asuni, T. (1990). Nigeria: Report on the care, treatment and rehabilitation of people with mental illness. *Psychosocial Rehabilitation Journal, 14*(1), 35.

Atallah, D. G., Contreras Painemal, C., Albornoz, L., Salgado, F., & Pilquil Lizama, E. (2018). Engaging critical community resilience praxis: A qualitative study with Mapuche communities in Chile facing structural racism and disasters. *Journal of Community Psychology, 46*(5), 575–97.

Atkinson, S., Bagnall, A.-M., Corcoran, R., South, J., Curtis, S., di Martino, S., & Pilkington, G. (2017). *What is community wellbeing? Conceptual review* (p. 68). London: What Works Wellbeing. Retrieved from https:// whatworkswellbeing.org

Aubry, T., Bernad, R., & Greenwood, R. (2018). A multi-country study of the fidelity of Housing First Programmes: Introduction. *European Journal of Homelessness, 12*(3), 17–31.

Aubry, T., Duhoux, A., Klodawsky, F., Ecker, J. &, Hay, E. (2016). A longitudinal study of predictors of housing stability, housing quality, and mental health functioning among single homeless individuals staying in emergency shelters. *American Journal of Community Psychology, 58*(1–2), 123–35.

Aubry, T., Nelson, G., & Tsemberis, S. (2015). Housing First for people with severe mental illness who are homeless: A review of the research and findings from the At Home–Chez soi Demonstration Project. *Canadian Journal of Psychiatry, 60*(11), 467–74.

Australian Bureau of Statistics (2016). *Estimates of Aboriginal and Torres Strait Islander Australians.* Retrieved from www.abs.gov.au/ausstats/abs@.nsf/mf/3238.0.55.001

Australian Psychological Society (1997). *Racism and prejudice: Psychological perspectives.* Melbourne: Australian Psychological Society.

Australian Psychological Society. (2016). Information sheet: Australian Psychological Society recommends mental health practices that affirm transgender people's experiences. Melbourne, Australia: APS. https:// www.psychology.org.au/getmedia/01982012-7605-4cbc-a14d-0cac47c2484b/Information-sheet-transgender-affirmation.pdf

Ayalar-Alcantar, C., Dello Stritto, M. E., & Guzmán, B. (2008). Women in community psychology: The trail-blazer story. *Journal of Community Psychology, 36*(5), 587–608.

Backer, T. E. (2002). *Finding the balance: Program fidelity and adaptation in substance abuse prevention: A state-of-the-art review.* Rockville, MD: Center for Substance Abuse Prevention, Substance Abuse and Mental Health Services Administration.

Baja, K. (2018). *Community Resilience Hubs: Shifting power to communities and increasing capacity.* Urban Sustainability Directors Network (USDN). Retrieved from www.adaptationclearinghouse.org/resources/resilience-hubs-shifting-power-to-communities-and-increasing-community-capacity.html

Baker, B. D. (2016). *Does money matter in education?* (2nd ed.). Washington, DC: Albert Shanker Institute. Retrieved from www.shankerinstitute.org

Bandura, A. (1997). *Self-efficacy: The exercise of control.* New York: W.H. Freeman and Company.

Banerjee, A., Karlan, D., & Zinman, J. (2015). Six randomized evaluations of microcredit: Introduction and further steps. *American Economic Journal: Applied Economics, 7*(1), 1–21.

Banton, M. (2000). The idiom of race – A critique of presentism. In L. Backs & J. Solomos. (Eds.), *Theories of race and racism a reader.* Abingdon: Routledge.

Barak, A., Boniel-Nissim, M., & Suler, J. (2008). Fostering empowerment in online support groups. *Computers in Human Behavior, 24*(5), 1867–83.

Baril, R., Lefebvre, P., & Merrigan, P. (2000 January). Québec family policy: Impact and options. *Choices: Family Policy, 6*(1), 1–52.

Baritz, L. (1974). *The servants of power: A history of the use of social science in American industry.* Westport, CT: Greenwood.

Barker, J. (1999). *Street-level democracy: Political settings at the margins of global power.* West Hartford, CT: Kumarian Press.

Barker, R. G. (1968). *Ecological psychology.* Stanford, CA: Stanford University Press.

Barker, R. G., & Gump, P. V. (1964). *Big school, small school.* Stanford, CA: Stanford University Press.

Barlow, M., & Campbell, B. (1995). *Straight through the heart: How the liberals abandoned the just society.* HarperCollins Publishers.

Barnett, R. (1997). *Higher education: A critical business.* Buckingham: Open University Press.

Barnett, W. S. (2011). Effectiveness of early educational intervention. *Science, 333,* 975–8.

Barrera, M. (1986). Distinctions between social support concepts, measures, and models. *American Journal of Community Psychology, 14*(4), 413–45.

Barrera, M. (2000). Social support research in community psychology. In J. Rappaport & E. Seidman (Eds.), *Handbook of community psychology* (pp. 215–45). New York: Kluwer Academic/Plenum Publishers.

Basran, G.S. & Zong, L. (1998). Devaluation of foreign credentials as perceived by visible minority professional immigrants. *Canadian Ethnic Studies Journal, 30*(3), 6–23.

Bates, P., & Davis, F. A. (2004). Social capital, social inclusion and services for people with learning disabilities. *Disability & Society, 19*(3), 195–207.

Batliwala, S. (2008). *Changing their world: Concepts and practices of women's movements.* Toronto, CA: Association for Women's Rights in Development (AWID).

Bauer, G. R., Hammond, R., Travers, R., Kaay, M., Hohenadel, K. M., & Boyce, M. (2009). "I don't think this is theoretical; this is our lives": How erasure impacts health care for transgender people. *Journal of the Association of Nurses in AIDS Care, 20*(5), 348–61.

Bauer, G. R., Scheim, A. I., Pyne, J., Travers, R., & Hammond, R. (2015). Intervenable factors associated with suicide risk in transgender persons: A respondent driven sampling study in Ontario, Canada. *BMC Public Health, 15*(1), 525.

Baym, N. (2007). The new shape of online community: The example of Swedish independent music fandom. *First Monday.* Retrieved from http://firstmonday.org/htbin/cgiwrap/bin/ojs/index.php/jfvfs/article/viewFile/2289/2046

Beaglehole, E. (1950). *Mental health in New Zealand.* Wellington, NZ: New Zealand University Press.

Beal, F. (2008). Double jeopardy: To be black and female. *Meridians: Feminism, Race, Transnationalism, 8*(2), 166–76.

Beehr, T., & O'Driscoll, P. (2002). Organizationally targeted interventions aimed at reducing workplace stress. In J. Thomas & M. Hersen (Eds.), *Handbook of mental health in the workplace* (pp. 103–19). London: SAGE Publications.

Beers, C. W. (1908). *A mind that found itself.* New York. Retrieved from www.gutenberg.org/files/11962/11962-h/11962-h.htm

Behrens, T. R., & Foster-Fishman, P. G. (2007). Developing operating principles for systems change. *American Journal of Community Psychology, 39*(3–4), 411–14.

Belfield, C., Bowden, B., Klapp, A., Levin, H., Shand, R., & Zander, S. (2015). *The economic value of social and emotional learning.* NY: Center for Benefit-Cost Studies in Education, Teachers College, Columbia University. Retrieved from http://cbcse.org/

Bell, D. A. (1984). The hurdle too high: Class-based roadblocks to racial remediation. *Buffalo Law Review, 33,* 1–34.

Ben Shlomo, Y., White, I. R., & Marmot, M. (1996). Does the variation in the socioeconomic characteristics of an area affect mortality? *British Medical Journal, 312,* 1013–14.

Benford, R. D., & Snow, D. A. (2000). Framing processes and social movements: An Overview and assessment. *Annual Review of Sociology, 26*(1), 611–39.

Benhabib, S. (1996). From identity politics to social feminism: A plea for the nineties. In D. Trend (Ed.), *Radical democracy: Identity, citizenship, and the state* (pp. 27–41). New York: Routledge.

Bennett, C., Anderson, L., Cooper, S., Hassol, L., Klein, D., & Rosenblum, G. (1966). *Community psychology: A report of the Boston conference on the education of psychologists for community mental health.* Boston: Boston University Press.

Bennet, E.M. (2005). Environmental degradation and ecologically minded alternatives. In G. Nelson & I. Prilleltensky (Eds.), *Community psychology: In pursuit of liberation and well-being* (pp. 468–85). London: Red Globe Press.

Bennett, E. M., & Hallman, D. (1987). The centrality of field experiences in training for social intervention. In E. M. Bennett (Ed.), *Social intervention: Theory and practice* (pp. 93–123). Lewiston, NY: The Edwin Mellen Press.

Benson, M. H., & Craig, R. K. (2014). The end of sustainability. *Society & Natural Resources, 27*(7), 777–82.

Berger, P. L., & Neuhaus, R. J. (1977). *To empower people: The role of mediating structures in public policy.* Washington, DC: American Enterprise Institute for Public Policy Research.

Bergold, J., & Seckinger, M. (2007). Community psychology between attitude and clinical practice: The German way. In S. Reich, M. Riemer, I. Prilleltensky, & M. Montero (Eds.), *International community psychology: History and theories* (pp. 238–62). New York: Springer.

Berry, J. W. (1997). Immigration, acculturation and adaptation. *Applied Psychology, 46,* 5–68.

Berry, J. W. (2001). A psychology of immigration. *Journal of Social Issues, 57,* 615–31.

Bess, K. D. (2015). Reframing coalitions as systems interventions: A network study exploring the contribution of a youth violence prevention coalition to broader system capacity. *American Journal of Community Psychology, 55*(3–4), 381–95.

Bess, K. D., Fisher, A. T., Sonn, C. C., & Bishop, B. J. (2002). Psychological sense of community: Theory, research, and application. In A. T. Fisher, C. C. Sonn, & B. J. Bishop (Eds.), *Psychological sense of community* (pp. 3–22). Boston, MA: Springer.

Bess, K.D., Prilleltensky, I., Perkins, D.D., Collins, L.V. (2009). Participatory organizational change in community-based health and human services: From tokenism to political engagement. *American Journal of Community Psychology, 43*(1–2), 134–48.

Bhana, A., Petersen, I., & Rochat, T. (2007). Community psychology in South Africa. In S. M. Reich, M. Riemer, I. Prilleltensky, & M. Montero (Eds.), *International community psychology: History and theories* (pp. 377–91). New York: Springer.

Bhasin, R. (2012). Sikhs have been living in fear of hate crimes since 9/11. *The Globe and Mail (Index-only),* p. 15. Retrieved from www.theglobeandmail.com/opinion/columnists/sikhs-have-been-living-in-fear-of-hate-crimes-since-911/article4468643/

Bhatia, S., & Sethi, N. (2007). History and theory of community psychology in India: An international perspective. In S. M. Reich, M. Riemer, I. Prilleltensky, & M. Montero (Eds.), *International Community Psychology: History and theories* (pp.180–99). New York: Springer.

Bickman, L., & Reich, S.M. (2015). Randomized control trials: A gold standard or gold plated? In S. Donaldson, C. Christie, & M. Mark (Eds.), *Credible and actionable evidence: The foundation for rigorous and influential evaluations* (2nd ed., pp. 83–113).Thousand Oaks, CA: SAGE Publications.

Bickman, L., & Rog, D. J. (Eds.). (2008). *The SAGE Handbook of Applied Social Research Methods* (2nd ed). Los Angeles: SAGE Publications.

Biglan, T. (2015). *The nurture effect: How the science of human behavior can improve our lives and our world.* Oakland, CA: New Harbinger.

Birman, D., Trickett, E., & Buchanan, R. M. (2005). A tale of two cities: Replication of a study on the acculturation and adaptation of immigrant adolescents from the former Soviet Union in a different community context. *American Journal of Community Psychology, 35*(1–2), 83–101.

Black, R., & Huygens, I. (2016). Pakeha culture and psychology. In W. W. Waitoki, J. S. Feather, N. R. Robertson, & J. J. Rucklidge (Eds.), *Professional practice of psychology in Aotearoa New Zealand* (pp. 49–66). Wellington: New Zealand Psychological Society.

Blair, C.B., & Raver, C. (2016). Poverty, stress and brain development: New directions for prevention and intervention. *Academic Pediatrics, 16*(3 Suppl), 30–6.

Blakeley, G. (2002). Social capital. In G. Blakeley & V. Bryson (Eds.), *Contemporary political concepts: A critical introduction* (pp. 198–213). London: Pluto Press.

Blakely, C. H., Mayer, J. P., Gottschalk, R. G., Schmitt, N., Davidson, W. S., Roitman, D. B., & Emshoff, J. G. (1987). The fidelity-adaptation debate: Implications for the implementation of public sector social programs. *American Journal of Community Psychology, 15*(3), 253–68.

Blanchard, A.L. (2007). Developing a sense of virtual community measure. *Cyber Psychology and Behavior, 10,* 827–30.

Blowers, A., & Leroy, P. (1994). Power, politics and environmental inequality: A theoretical and empirical analysis of the process of 'peripheralisation'. *Environmental Politics, 3*(2), 197–228.

Blyth, M. (2013). *Austerity: The history of a dangerous idea.* New York: Oxford University Press.

Bogart, K. (2015). Disability identity predicts lower anxiety and depression in multiple sclerosis. *Rehabilitation Psychology, 60*(1), 105– 9.

Bond, M. A. (1999). Gender, race, and class in organizational contexts. *American Journal of Community Psychology, 27*(3), 327–55.

Bond, M. A. (2007). *Workplace chemistry: Promoting diversity through organizational change.* Lebanon, NH: UPNE.

Bond, M. A. (2016). Leading the way on diversity: Community psychology's evolution from invisible to individual to contextual. *American Journal of Community Psychology, 58*(3–4), 259–68.

Bond, M. A., & Harrell, S. P. (2006). Diversity challenges in community research and action: The story of a special issue of AJCP. *American Journal of Community Psychology, 37*, 157–65.

Bond, M., Hill, J., Mulvey, A., & Terenzio, M. (Eds.). (2000). Feminism and community psychology [Special issue parts 1 & II]. *American Journal of Community Psychology, 27–8.*

Bond, M., & Mulvey, A. (2000). The history of women and feminist perspectives in community psychology. *American Journal of Community Psychology, 28*(5), 599–630.

Bond, M. A., Serrano-Garcia, I., & Keys, C. (Eds.). (2017). *Handbook of community psychology – Volume 1: Theoretical foundations, core concepts, and emerging challenges.* Washington, DC: APA Press.

Bond, M. A., Serrano-Garcia, I., & Keys, C. (Eds.). (2017). *Handbook of community psychology – Volume 2: Methods for community research and action for diverse groups and issues.* Washington, DC: APA Press.

Boonzaier, F., & van Niekerk, T. (2019). Introducing decolonial feminist community psychology. In F. Boonzaier, & T. van Niekerk (Eds.), *Decolonial feminist community psychology* (pp. 1–10). Berlin: Springer International Publishing.

Borgatti, S. P., Mehra, A., Brass, D. J., & Labianca, G. (2009). Network analysis in the social sciences. *Science, 323*(5916), 892–5.

Boulianne, S. (2015). Social media and participation: A meta-analysis of current research. *Information, Communication and Society, 18*, 524–38.

Bourdieu, P. (1986). The forms of capital. In J. F. Richardson (Ed.), *Handbook of theory and research for the sociology of education* (pp. 241–58). Westport, CT: Greenwood Press.

Bourdieu, P. (1998). *Practical reason: On the theory of action.* Stanford, CA: Stanford University Press.

Bourdieu, P., & Wacquant, L. (1992). *An invitation to reflexive sociology.* Chicago, IL: University of Chicago Press.

Bourhis, R. Y. (2003). Measuring ethnocultural diversity using the Canadian census. *Critical Ethnic Studies, 35*(1), 9–32.

Bouris, A., Guilamo-Ramos, V., Pickard, A., Shiu, C., Loosier, P. S., Dittus, P., ... Waldmiller, J. M. (2010). A systematic review of parental influences on the health and well-being of lesbian, gay, and bisexual youth: Time for a new public health research and practice agenda. *The Journal of Primary Prevention, 31*(5–6), 273–309.

Bowleg, L. (2012). The problem with the phrase women and minorities: Intersectionality – An important theoretical framework for public health. *American Journal of Public Health, 102*(7), 1267–73.

Boyd, M. (1999). Canadian, eh? Ethnic origin shifts in the Canadian census. *Canadian Ethnic Studies, 31*(3), 1–19.

Boyden, J. (2003). Children under fire: Challenging assumptions about children's resilience. *Children, Youth and Environments, 13*, 145–89.

Boyden, J., & Crivello, G. (2012). Political economy, perception and social change as mediators of childhood risk in Andhra Pradesh. In J. Boyden & M. Bourdillon (Eds.), *Childhood poverty multidisciplinary approaches.* London: Palgrave Macmillan.

Bradbury, H., & Reason, R. (2008). Issues and choice points for improving the quality of action research. In M. Minkler & N. Wallerstein, (Eds.), *Community-based participatory research for health: From process to outcomes* (2nd ed., 225–42). San Francisco, CA: Jossey-Bass.

Bradley, R., & Corwyn, R. (2002). Socioeonomic status and child development. *Annual Review of Psychology, 53*, 371–99.

Brah, A., & Phoenix, A. (2004). Ain't I a woman? Revisiting Intersectionality. *Journal of International Women's Studies, 5*(3), 75–86.

Braidotti, R. (2013). *The posthuman.* Cambridge: Polity Press.

Brazier, C. (1999 January/February). The radical twentieth century. *New Internationalist, 309*, 7–36.

Brecher, J., Costello, T., & Smith, B. (2000). *Globalization from below: The power of solidarity.* Boston, MA: South End Press.

Brechin, A. (2000). Introducing critical practice. In A. Brechin, H. Brown, & M. Eby (Eds.), *Critical practice in health and social care* (pp. 25–47). London: Open University Press.

Breda, C. S., & Riemer, M. (2012). Motivation for Youth's Treatment Scale (MYTS): A new tool for measuring motivation among youths and their caregivers. *Administration and Policy in Mental Health and Mental Health Services Research, 39*(1–2), 118–32.

Bregman, R. (2017). *Utopia for realists: And how we can get there.* London: Bloomsbury Publishing.

Bricout, J.C., & Gray, D.B. (2006). Community receptivity: The ecology of disabled persons' participation in the physical, political and social environments. *Scandinavian Journal of Disability Research, 8*(1), 1–21.

Brighouse, H. (2004). *Justice.* Cambridge, MA: Polity Press.

Britto, P. R., Yoshikawa, H., & Boller, K. (2011). Quality of early childhood development programs in global contexts: Rationale for investment, conceptual framework and implications for equity. *Social Policy Report, 25*(2), 1–23.

Brodsky, A., & Cattaneo, L. B. (2013). A transconceptual model of empowerment and resilience: Divergence, convergence and interactions in kindred community concepts. *American Journal of Community Psychology, 52*, 333–46.

Brodsky, A., Welsh, E., Carrillo, A., Talwar, G., Scheibler, J., & Butler, T. (2011). Between synergy and conflict: Balancing the processes of organizational and individual resilience in an Afghan women's community. *American Journal of Community Psychology, 47*(3–4), 217–35.

Brodsky, A.E. (2009). Multiple psychological senses of community in Afghan context: Exploring commitment and sacrifice in an underground resistance community. *American Journal of Community Psychology, 44*, 176–87.

Brodsky, A. E. (2017). Bridging the dialectic: Diversity, psychological sense of community, and inclusion. *American Journal of Community Psychology, 59*(3–4), 269–71.

Brodsky, A.E., Loomis, C., & Marx, C.M. (2002). Expanding the conceptualization of PSOC. In A.T. Fisher, C.C. Sonn & B.J. Bishop (Eds.), *Psychological sense of community: Research, applications, and implications* (pp. 319–36). Boston, MA: Springer.

Brodsky, A. E., Mannarini, T., Buckingham, S. L., & Scheibler, J. E. (2017). Kindred spirits in scientific revolution: Qualitative methods in community psychology. In M. A. Bond, I. Serrano-García, and C. B. Keys (Eds.), *APA Handbook of Community Psychology: Methods for community research and action for diverse groups and issues* (pp. 75–90). Washington, DC: American Psychological Association.

Brodsky, A. E., & Marx, C. M. (2001). Layers of identity: Multiple psychological senses of community within a community setting. *Journal of Community Psychology, 29*(2), 161–78.

Bronfenbrenner, U. (1977). Toward an experimental ecology of human development. *American Psychologist, 32*, 513–31.

Bronfenbrenner, U. (1979). *The ecology of human development.* Cambridge, MA: Harvard University Press.

Bronfenbrenner, U. (1986). Recent advances in research on the ecology of human development. In R. K. Silbereisen, K. Eyferth, & G. Rudinger (Eds.), *Development as action in context: Problem behavior and normal youth development* (pp. 287–309). New York: Springer.

Bronstein, P., Clauson, J., Stoll, M. F., & Abrams, C. L. (1993). Parenting behavior and children's social, psychological, and academic adjustment in diverse family structures. *Family Relations, 42*, 268–76.

Brown, L.D., & Rogers, S. (2014). The impact of mental health consumer-run organizations on transformative change. In G. Nelson, B. Kloos, & J. Ornelas (Eds.), *Community psychology and community mental health: Towards transformative change* (pp. 108–29). New York: Oxford Press.

Browne, K., & Nash, C. J. (Eds.). (2016). *Queer methods and methodologies: Intersecting queer theories and social science research.* Burlington, VT: Ashgate.

Brug, J., Conner, M., Harré, N., Kremers, S., McKellar, S., & Whitelaw, S. (2005). The transtheoretical model and stages of change: A critique. *Health Education Research, 20*, 244–58.

Brunt, D. & Hansson, L. (2002). The social networks of persons with severe mental illness in in-patient settings and supported community settings. *Journal of Mental Health, 11*, 611–21.

Bryan, A. E., & Arkowitz, H. (2015). Meta-analysis of the effects of peer-administered psychosocial interventions on symptoms of depression. *American Journal of Community Psychology, 55*(3–4), 455–71.

Buchanan, D. A., & Bryman, A. (2007). Contextualizing methods choice in organizational research. *Organizational Research Methods, 10*(3), 483–501.

Buettgen, A., Richardson, J., Beckham, K., Richardson, K., Ward, M., & Riemer, M. (2012). We did it together: A participatory action research study on poverty and disability. *Disability & Society, 27*(5), 603–16.

Buettner, D. (2010). *Thrive*. Washington, DC: National Geographic.

Building Movement Project. (2010). *Service delivery and social change: 2010 convening report*. Retrieved from www.buildingmovement.org/reports/entry/service_delivery_and_social_change_2010_convening_report

Bullard, R.D., Mohai, P., Saha, R., & Wright, B. (2007). *Toxic wastes and race at twenty, 1987-2007: Grassroots struggles to dismantle environmental racism in the United States*. Cleveland OH: United Church of Christ Justice and Witness Ministry.

Bullock, H., Williams, W., & Limbert, W. (2003). Predicting support for welfare policies: The impact of attributions and beliefs about inequality. *Journal of Poverty, 7*(3), 35–56.

Bundy, C. (2014). *Short-changed? South Africa since 1994*. Johannesburg: Jacana.

Burger, K. (2010). How does early childhood care and education affect cognitive development? An international review of the effects of early interventions for children from different social backgrounds. *Early Childhood Research Quarterly, 25*, 140–65.

Burman, E. (1997). Developmental psychology and its discontents. In D. Fox & I. Prilleltensky (Eds.), *Critical psychology: An introduction* (pp. 134–49). London: SAGE Publications.

Burns, T. (2004). Community mental health teams. *Psychiatry, 3*, 11–14.

Burstow, B., & Weitz, D. (1988). *Shrink resistant: The struggle against psychiatry in Canada*. Vancouver, BC: New Star Books.

Burt, R. S. (1992). *Structural holes*. Cambridge, MA: Harvard University Press.

Burton, M. (2003). Review of "Systemic Intervention: Philosophy, Methodology, and Practice" by Midgley, G. (2001). *Journal of Community & Applied Social Psychology, 13*(4), 330–3.

Burton, M. (2013). In and against social policy. *Global Journal of Community Psychology Practice, 4*(2), 2–15.

Burton, M., Boyle, S., Harris, C., & Kagan, C. (2007). Community psychology in Britain. In S. Reich, M. Riemer, I. Prilleltensky, & M. Montero (Eds.), *International community psychology: History and theories* (pp. 219–37). New York: Springer.

Burton, M., & Kagan, C. (2015). Theory and practice for a critical community psychology in the UK. *Psicología, Conocimiento Y Sociedad, 5*(2), 182–205.

Burton, M.H., Kagan, C., Duckett, P., & Siddiquee, A. (2011). *Critical community psychology*. Hoboken, NJ: Wiley Blackwell.

Butcher, H., Banks, S., Henderson, P., & Robertson, J. (2007). *Critical community practice*. Bristol: Policy Press.

Butterfoss, F. D., & Kegler, M. C. (2009). The community coalition action theory. In R. DiClemente, L. Crosby, & M. C. Kegler (Eds.), *Emerging theories in health promotion practice and research* (2nd ed., pp. 237–66). San Francisco, CA: Jossey-Bass.

Bywater, K. (2014). Investigating the benefits of participatory action research for environmental education. *Policy Futures in Education, 12*(7), 920–32.

Cabaj, M., & Weaver, L. (2016). *Collective Impact 3.0: An evolving framework for community change (Community Change Series)*. Waterloo, ON: Tamarack Institute.

Cahill, J. (1983). Structural characteristics of the macroeconomy and mental health: Implications for primary prevention research. *American Journal of Community Psychology, 11*, 553–71.

Caldarella, P., Shatzer, R. H., Gray, K. M., Young, K. R., & Young, E. L. (2011). The effects of school-wide positive behavior support on middle school climate and student outcomes. *RMLE Online, 35*(4), 1–14.

Calgary Anti-Racism Education, CARED (2019). *Racialization*. Retrieved from www.ucalgary.ca/cared/racialization

Cameron, R., & Miller, P. (2007). Mixed method research: Phoenix of the paradigm wars. Retrieved from https://www.anzam.org/wp-content/uploads/pdfmanager/1795_CAMERONROSLYN_260.PDF

Cammarota, J., & Fine, M. (Eds.). (2008). *Revolutionizing education: Youth participatory action research in motion*. New York: Routledge.

Campbell, R., & Wasco, S. M. (2000). Feminist approaches to social science: Epistemological and methodological tenets. *American Journal of Community Psychology, 28*(6), 773–91.

Campbell, R., Baker, C. K., & Mazurek, T. L. (1998). Remaining radical? Organizational predictors of rape crisis centers' social change initiatives. *American Journal of Community Psychology, 26*, 457–83.

Caplan, N., & Nelson, S. D. (1973). On being useful: The nature and consequences of psychological research on social problems. *American Psychologist, 28*, 199–211.

Caplan, P. (1995). *They say you're crazy: How the world's most powerful psychiatrists decide who's normal.* Massachusetts, Addison Wesley.

Cardazone, G. U., Sy, A., Chik, I., & Corlew, L. K. (2014). Mapping one strong 'Ohana: Using network analysis and GIS to enhance the effectiveness of a statewide coalition to prevent child abuse and neglect. *American Journal of Community Psychology, 53*(3–4), 346–56.

Carniol, B. (2010). *Case critical: Social services & social justice in Canada* (6th ed.). Toronto: Between The Lines.

Carling, P. J. (1995). *Return to community: Building support systems for people with psychiatric disabilities.* New York: Guilford Press.

Carlquist, E., Nafstad, H. E., & Blakar, R. M. (2007). Community psychology in a Scandinavian welfare society: The case of Norway. In S. Reich, M. Riemer, I. Prilleltensky, & M. Montero (Eds.), *International community psychology: History and theories* (pp. 282–98). New York: Springer.

Carolissen, R., & Swartz, L. (2009). Removing the splinters from our own eyes: A commentary on power and identity in South African community psychology. *Feminism & Psychology, 19*, 407–13.

Carolissen, R., Van Wyk, S., & Pick-Cornelius, M. (2012). "I want my family to be white": Coloured adolescent schoolgirls' articulations of identity in a South African peri-urban community. *Southern African Review of Education, 18*(1), 39–54.

Carr, S., & Sloan, T. (Eds.). (2004). *Poverty and psychology: From global perspective to local practice.* New York: Springer.

Carroll, A., & Itaborahy, L.P. for the International Lesbian, Gay, Bisexual, Trans and Intersex Association (2015). State Sponsored Homophobia 2015: A world survey of laws: criminalisation, protection and recognition of same-sex love (Geneva; ILGA, May 2015).

Carson, R. (2002). *Silent spring,* (40th Anniversary Edition). New York: Houghton Mifflin Harcourt.

Case, A. D., & Hunter, C. D. (2012). Counterspaces: A unit of analysis for understanding the role of settings in marginalized individuals' adaptive responses to oppression. *American Journal of Community Psychology, 50*(1–2), 257–70.

Cashman, S. B., Adeky, S., Allen, A. J., Corburn, J., Israel, B. A., Montaño, J., ... Eng, E. (2008). The power and the promise: Working with communities to analyze data, interpret findings, and get to outcomes. *American Journal of Public Health, 98*(8), 1407–17.

Cattaneo, L. B., Calton, J., & Brodsky, A. (2015). Status quo versus status quake: Putting the power back in empowerment. *Journal of Community Psychology, 42*(4), 433–46.

Caughy, M.O., O'Campo, P., & Brodsky, A.E. (1999). Neighborhoods, families and children: Implications for policy and practice. *Journal of Community Psychology, 27*(5), 615–33.

Cauthen, N. K., & Fass, S. (2008). *Measuring income and poverty in the United States.* New York: National Center for Children in Poverty, Columbia University, Mailman School of Public Health.

Center for Community Health and Development (CCHD). (2017a). The Community Tool Box: Lawrence, KS: University of Kansas. Retrieved from http://ctb.ku.edu/en/table-of-contents

Center for Community Health and Development (CCHD). (2017b). The Community Tool Box: Chapter 2: Other models for promoting community health and development. Lawrence, KS: University of Kansas. Retrieved from https://ctb.ku.edu/en/table-of-contents/overview/models-for-community-health-and-development

Center for Community Health and Development (CCHD). (2017c). The Community Tool Box: Chapter 7: Encouraging involvement in community work. Lawrence, KS: University of Kansas. Retrieved from: http://ctb.ku.edu/en/table-of-contents/assessment/assessing-community-needs-and-resources/conduct-concerns-surveys/main

Centers for Disease Control and Prevention (CDC). (2011). *Principles of community engagement* (2nd ed.). Washington, DC: NIH Publication.

Centers for Disease Control and Prevention (CDC). (2013). Community needs assessment. Retrieved from www.cdc.gov/globalhealth/healthprotection/fetp/training_modules/15/community-needs_pw_final_9252013.pdf

Centers for Disease Control and Prevention (CDC). (2017). African Americans, race/ethnicity, and HIV by group. Retrieved from www.cdc.gov/hiv/group/racialethnic/africanamericans/index.html

Cerullo, R., & Wiesenfeld, E. (2001). La concientizacion en el trabajo psicosocial comunitario desde la perspective de sus actores [Agents' perspectives on conscientization in psychosocial community work]. *Revista de Psicologia, 10*(2), 11–26.

Chamberlin, J. (1978). *On our own: Patient-controlled alternatives to the mental health system.* New York: McGraw-Hill.

Chamberlin, J. (1990). The ex-psychiatric patients' movement: Where we've been and where we're going. *The Journal of Mind and Behavior, 11*, 323–36.

Chambers, S. E., Canvin, K., Baldwin, D. S., & Sinclair, J. M. (2017). Identity in recovery from problematic alcohol use: A qualitative study of online mutual aid. *Drug and alcohol dependence, 174*, 17–22.

Chambers, V. (2014). 'CARE's experience with community scorecards in Tanzania – What works and why? *Country Case Study Note.* London: ODI.

Chan, W., Cattaneo, L. B., Mak, W., & Lin, W. (2017). From movement to movement: Empowerment and resilience as a framework for collective action in Hong Kong. *American Journal for Community Psychology, 59*(1–2), 120–32.

Chandra, A., Acosta, J., Meredith, L. S., Sanches, K., Stern, S., Uscher-Pines, L., Williams, M., & Yeung, D. (2010). *Understanding community resilience in the context of national health security: A literature review.* Santa Monica, CA: RAND Corporation. Retrieved from www.rand.org/pubs/working_papers/WR737.html

Chapman, B., & Sisodia, R. (2015). *Everybody matters: The extraordinary power of caring for your people like family.* New York: Penguin.

Charlton, J. I. (2000). *Nothing about us without us.* Berkeley, CA: University of California Press.

Chaskin, R. J. (2001). Building community capacity: A definitional framework and case studies from a comprehensive community initiative. *Urban Affairs Review, 36*(3), 291–323.

Chaskin, R. J., Brown, P., Venkatesh, S., & Vidal, A. (2001). *Building community capacity.* New York: A. de Gruyter.

Chaskin, R. J., & Karlstrom, M. (2012). *Beyond the neighborhood: Policy engagement and systems change in the New Communities Program.* New York: MDRC.

Chaudry, A., & Wimer, C. (2016). Poverty is not just an indicator: The relationship between income, poverty, and child well-being. *Academic Pediatrics, 3*(Suppl), S23–9.

Chaufan, C., Constantino, S., & Davis, M. (2011). 'It's a full time job being poor': Understanding barriers to diabetes prevention in immigrant communities in the USA. *Critical Public Health, 22*(2), 147–58.

Chávez, V., Duran, B., Baker, Q. E., Avila, M. M., & Wallerstein, N. (2008). The dance of race and privilege in CBPR. In M. Minkler & N. Wallerstein (Eds.), *Community-based participatory research for health: From processes to outcomes* (2nd ed., pp. 91–106). San Francisco, CA: Jossey-Bass.

Chavis, D. M. (2001). The paradoxes and promise of community coalitions. *American Journal of Community Psychology, 29*(2), 309–20.

Chavis, D. M., Florin, P., & Felix, M. (1992). Nurturing grassroots initiatives for community development: The role of enabling systems. In T. Mizrahi & J. Morrison (Eds.), *Community and social administration: Advances trends and emerging principles* (pp. 41–68). New York, NY: Haworth Press.

Chavis, D. M., & Pretty, G. M. H. (Eds.). (1999). Sense of community II [Special issue]. *Journal of Community Psychology, 27*(6), 635–42.

Chavis, D. M., Speer, P. W., Resnick, I., & Zippay, A. (1993). Building community capacity to address alcohol and drug abuse: Getting to the heart of the problem. In R. C. Davis, A. J. Lurigio, & D. P. Rosenbaum (Eds.), *Drugs and the community: Involving community residents in combatting the sale of illegal drugs* (pp. 251–84). New York: Routledge.

Checkland, P. (1999). *Systems thinking, systems practice.* Chichester: Wiley.

Checkoway, B. (1995). Six strategies of community change. *Community Development Journal, 30*(1), 2–20.

Chen, H.-T. (2005). *Practical program evaluation: Assessing and improving planning, implementation, and effectiveness.* Thousand Oaks, CA: SAGE Publications.

Cheng, S.-T., & Mak, W. (2007). Community psychology in a borrowed place with borrowed time: The case of Hong Kong. In S. M. Reich, M. Riemer, I. Prilleltensky & M. Montero (Eds.), *International Community Psychology: History and theories* (pp. 200–16). New York: Springer.

Chenoweth, E., & Stephan, M. J. (2011). *Why civil resistance works: The strategic logic of nonviolent conflict.* New York: Columbia University Press.

Cherniss, C. (1993). Role of professional self-efficacy in the etiology and amelioration of burnout. In W. B. Schaufeli, C. Maslach, & T. Marek (Eds.), *Series in applied psychology: Social issues and questions. Professional burnout: Recent developments in theory and research* (pp. 135–49). Philadelphia, PA: Taylor & Francis.

Cherniss, C., & Adler, M. (2000). *Promoting emotional intelligence in organizations.* Alexandria, VA: ASTD.

Cherniss, C., & Deegan, G. (2000). The creation of alternative settings. In J. Rappaport & E. Seidman (Eds.), *Handbook of community psychology* (pp. 359–77). New York: Kluwer Academic/Plenum Publishers.

Chetkovich, C., & Kunreuther, F. (2006). *From the ground up: Grassroots organizations making social change.* Ithaca, NY: ILR Press.

Chilisa, B. (2005). Educational research within postcolonial Africa: A critique of HIV/AIDS research in Botswana. *International Journal of Qualitative Studies in Education, 18*(6), 659–84.

Chilisa, B. (2011). *Indigenous research methodologies.* Thousand Oaks, CA: SAGE Publications.

Chilisa, B., & Kawulich, B. (2012). Selecting a research approach: Paradigm, methodology and methods. In C. Wagner, B. Kawulich, & M. Garner (Eds.), *Doing social research: A global context* (pp. 51–61). London: McGraw-Hill Higher Education.

Chinman, M., Acosta, J., Ebener, P., Burkhart, Q., Clifford, M., Corsello, M., ... Tellett-Royce, N. (2012). Establishing and evaluating the key functions of an interactive systems framework using an Assets-Getting to Outcomes Intervention. *American Journal of Community Psychology, 50*(3–4), 295–310.

Chinman, M., George, P., Dougherty, R. H., Daniels, A. S., Ghose, S. S., Swift, A., & Delphin-Rittmon, M. E. (2014). Peer support services for individuals with serious mental illnesses: Assessing the evidence. *Psychiatric Services, 65*(4), 429–41.

Chinman, M., Hunter, S. B., Ebener, P., Paddock, S. M., Stillman, L., Imm, P., & Wandersman, A. (2008). The getting to outcomes demonstration and evaluation: An illustration of the prevention support system. *American Journal of Community Psychology, 41*(3–4), 206–24.

Chinman, M., Kloos, B., O'Connell, M., & Davidson, L. (2002). Service providers' views of psychiatric mutual support groups. *Journal of Community Psychology, 30,* (4), 349–66.

Chipuer, H., & Pretty, G. H. (1999). A review of the sense of community index: Current uses, factor structure, reliability, and further development. *Journal of Community Psychology, 27*(6), 643–58.

Chomsky, N. (2000). *Rogue states: The rule of force in world affairs.* London: Pluto Press.

Chopra, M., & D. Sanders (2005). *Child health and poverty: CHIP Report 10.* Cape Town: Childhood Poverty Research and Policy Centre.

Christens, B. D. (2012). Toward relational empowerment. *American Journal of Community Psychology, 50*(1–2), 114–28.

Christens, B. D. (2019). *Community power and empowerment.* Oxford, New York: Oxford University Press.

Christens, B. D., Hanlin, C. E., & Speer, P. W. (2007). Getting the social organism thinking: Strategy for systems change. *American Journal of Community Psychology, 39,* 229–38.

Christens, B. D., & Inzeo, P. T. (2015). Widening the view: Situating collective impact among frameworks for community-led change. *Community Development, 46*(4), 420–35.

Christens, B. D., Inzeo, P. T., & Faust, V. (2014). Channeling power across ecological systems: Social regularities in community organizing. *American Journal of Community Psychology, 53*(3–4), 419–31.

Christens, B. D., Inzeo, P. T., Meinen, A., Hilgendorf, A. E., Berns, R., Korth, A., Pollard, ... Stedman, J. (2016). Community-led collaborative action to prevent obesity. *Wisconsin Medical Journal, 115*(5), 259–63.

Christens, B. D., & Perkins, D. D. (2008). Transdisciplinary, multilevel action research to enhance ecological and psycho-political validity. *Journal of Community Psychology, 36*(2), 214–31.

Christens, B. D., & Speer, P. W. (2006). Review essay: Tyranny/transformation: Power and paradox in participatory development. *Forum Qualitative Social Research, 7*(2).

Christens, B. D., & Speer, P. W. (2011). Contextual influences on participation in community organizing: A multilevel longitudinal study. *American Journal of Community Psychology, 47*(3–4), 253–63.

Christens, B. D., & Speer, P. W. (2015). Community organizing: Practice, research, and policy implications. *Social Issues and Policy Review, 9*(1), 193–222.

Chun Tie, Y., Birks, M., & Francis, K. (2019). Grounded theory research: A design framework for novice researchers. *SAGE Open Medicine, 7*(3), 1–8.

Church, K. (1997). Business (not quite) as usual: Psychiatric survivors and community economic development in Ontario. *Community Economic Development: In Search of Empowerment, 254*, 48.

Church, K., Shragge, E., Fontan, J. M., & Ng, R. (2008). While no one is watching: Learning in social action among people who are excluded from the labour market. In K. Church, N. Bascia, & E. Shragge (Eds.), *Learning through Community: Exploring Participatory Practices* (pp. 97–116). Dordrecht: Springer.

Clacherty, G. (2015). The Suitcase Project: Working with unaccompanied child refugees in new ways. In I. Palmary, B. Hamber, & L. Nùñez (Eds.). (2015). *Healing and change in the city of gold* (pp. 13–30). Switzerland: Springer International Publishing.

Clacherty, G. (2016). Understanding trauma and trauma intervention in new ways through an examination of the Suitcase Project, a project for unaccompanied refugee children in Hillbrow, Johannesburg. (Unpublished doctoral dissertation). University of the Witwatersrand, Johannesburg.

Clacherty, G. (2019). Art-based, narrative research with unaccompanied migrant children living in Johannesburg, South Africa. *Journal of Borderlands Studies*. DOI: https://doi.org/10.1080/08865655.2019.1621766

Clark, K. B. (1974). *Pathos of power*. New York: Harper & Row.

Clarkson, C., Jacobs, Z., Marwick, B., Fullagar, R., Wallis, L., Smith, M., … Pardoe, C. (2017). Human occupation of Northern Australia by 65,000 years ago. *Nature, 547*(7663), 306–10.

Cohen, S., Underwood, L. G., & Gottlieb, B. H. (Eds.). (2000). *Social support measurement and intervention: A guide for social and health scientists*. Oxford: Oxford University Press.

Coimbra, J., Duckett, P., Fryer, D., Makkawi, I., Menezes, I., Seedat, M., & Walker, C. (2012). Rethinking community psychology: Critical insights. *Australian Community Psychologist, 24*, 135–42.

Cole, E. R. (2009). Intersectionality and research in psychology. *American Psychologist, 64*(3), 170–80.

Coleman, J. (1988). Social capital in the creation of human capital. *The American Journal of Sociology, 94*, 95–120.

Collier, P. (2007). *The bottom billion: Why the poorest countries are failing and what can be done about it*. New York: Oxford University Press.

Collins, C. R., Neal, J. W., & Neal, Z. P. (2014). Transforming individual civic engagement into community collective efficacy: The role of bonding social capital. *American Journal of Community Psychology, 54*, 328–36.

Collins, P. H. (1991). *Black feminist thought: Knowledge, consciousness, and the politics of empowerment*. New York: Routledge.

Collins, P. H. (2008). *Black feminist thought: Knowledge, consciousness, and the politics of empowerment*. New York: Routledge.

Collins, P. H. (2010). The new politics of community. *American Sociological Review, 75*(1), 24.

Combahee River Collective. (1977/1995). Combahee River Collective statement. In B. Guy-Sheftall (Ed.), *Words of fire: An anthology of African American feminist thought* (pp. 232–40). New York: New Press.

Congressional Research Service (2018). *CRS annual report: Fiscal year 2017*. Library of Congress. Retrieved from https://fas.org/sgp/crs/

Connolly, P., & York, P. (2003). *Building the capacity of capacity builders*. New York: The Conservation Company.

Connors, E., & Maidman, F. (2001). A circle of healing: Family wellness in Aboriginal communities. In I. Prilleltensky, G. Nelson, & L. Peirson (Eds.), *Promoting family wellness and preventing child maltreatment: Fundamentals for thinking and action* (pp. 349–416). Toronto: University of Toronto Press.

Constantino, V., & Nelson, G. (1995). Changing relationships between self-help groups and mental health professionals: Shifting ideology and power. *Canadian Journal of Community Mental Health, 14*(2), 55–73.

Cook, J. R. (2015). Using evaluation to effect social change: Looking through a community psychology lens. *American Journal of Evaluation, 36*(1), 107–17.

Cooke, B., & Kothari, U. (2001). *Participation: The new tyranny?* London: Zed Books.

Cooke, K. (2016). *Girl stuff: Your full-on guide to the teen years*. Melbourne: Penguin Random House.

Copeland, M. E., & Jonikas, J. A. (2014). Wellness recovery action planning: The role of wellness promotion in a new paradigm of community mental health. In G. Nelson, B. Kloos, & J. Ornelas (Eds.), *Community psychology and community mental health: Towards transformative change* (pp. 133–51). New York: Oxford University Press.

Corasaniti, N. (2015, August 16). Donald Trump releases plan to combat illegal immigration. *New York Times*. Retrieved from https://www.nytimes.com

Corcos, A. F. (1997). *The myth of human races*. East Lansing: Michigan State University Press.

Corey, M., & Corey, G. (2003). *Becoming a helper*. Pacific Grove, CA: Brooks/Coles.

Corrigan, P. (Ed.). (2005). *On the stigma of mental illness: Practical strategies for research and social change*. Washington, DC: American Psychological Association.

Corrigan, P. W., Bink, A. B., Fokuo, J. K., & Schmidt, A. (2015). The public stigma of mental illness means a difference between you and me. *Psychiatry Research, 226*(1), 186–91.

Corrigan, P. W., & Penn, D. L. (1999). Lessons from social psychology on discrediting psychiatric stigma. *American Psychologist, 54*(9), 765–76.

Corrigan, P. W., & Al-Khouja, M. A. (2018). Three agendas for changing the public stigma of mental illness. *Psychiatric Rehabilitation Journal, 41*(1), 1–7.

Council for Reconciliation. (1995). *Going forward: Social justice for the First Australians – A submission to the Commonwealth Government*. Canberra: AGPS.

Council on Contemporary Families. (2014, January 6). *Was the War on Poverty a failure? Or are anti-poverty efforts simply swimming against a stronger tide?* (Brief Report). Retrieved from https://contemporaryfamilies. org/was-war-on-poverty-a-failure-report/

Cowen, E. (1991). In pursuit of wellness. *American Psychologist, 46*(4), 404–8.

Cowen, E. (1996). The ontogenesis of primary prevention: Lengthy strides and stubbed toes. *American Journal for Community Psychology, 24*(2), 235–49.

Cowen, E. L. (1985). Person centered approaches to primary prevention in mental health: Situation focused and competence enhancement. *American Journal of Community Psychology, 13*, 87–98.

Cowen, E. L. (1994). The enhancement of psychological wellness: Challenges and opportunities. *American Journal of Community Psychology, 22*(2), 149–79.

Cowen, E. L. (2000). Now that we all know that primary prevention in mental health is great, what is it? *Journal of Community Psychology, 28*(1), 5–16.

Craig, L. (2008). *Father care, father share in international perspective*. Retrieved from www.newstin.com/tag/ us/82125375

Cram, F. (1995). *Ethics and cross-cultural research*. [A draft paper.] Auckland: University of Auckland.

Crenshaw, K. (1989). Demarginalizing the intersection of race and sex: A Black feminist critique of antidiscrimination doctrine, feminist theory, and antiracist politics. *University of Chicago Legal Forum*, 139–67.

Crenshaw, K. (1990). Mapping the margins: Intersectionality, identity politics, and violence against women of color. *Stanford Law Review, 43*, 1241.

Crenshaw, K. W. (1993). Beyond racism and misogyny: Black feminism and 2 Live Crew. In M.J. Matsuda, C.R. Lawrence, R. Delgado, & K.W. Crenshaw (Eds.), *Words that wound: Critical race theory, assaultive speech, and the First Amendment* (pp. 111–32). Boulder, CO: Westview Press.

Cresswell, T. (2004). *Place: A short introduction*. Malden, MA: Blackwell.

Crichlow, W. (2015). Critical Race Theory: A strategy for framing discussions around social justice and democratic education. *Proceedings of the Higher Education in Transformation Conference, Dublin, Ireland*, (pp. 187–201).

Crivello, G., Vennam, U., & Komanduri, A. (2012). Ridiculed for not having anything: Children's views on poverty and inequality in rural India. In J. Boyden & M. Bourdillon (Eds.), *Childhood poverty: Multidisciplinary approaches*. London: Palgrave Macmillan.

Crow, D., Albright, E., & Koebele, E. (2016). Public information and regulatory processes: What the public knows and regulators decide. *Review of Policy Research, 33*(1), 90–109.

Crowley-Long, K. (1998). Making room for many feminisms: The dominance of the liberal political perspective in the Psychology of Women course. *Psychology of Women Quarterly, 22*, 113–30.

Crutchfield, L., & Grant, H. M. (2007). *Forces for good: The six practices of high-impact nonprofits*. San Francisco, CA: Jossey-Bass.

Culhane, D. (2010, July 11). Five myths about America's homeless. *The Washington Post*, p. B2.

Culley, M., & Angelique, H. (2003). Women's gendered experiences as long-term Three Mile Island activists. *Gender & Society, 17*(3), 445–61.

Culley, M., & Hughey, J. (2008). Power and public participation in a local hazardous waste dispute: A community case study. *American Journal of Community Psychology, 41*, 99–114.

Culley, M.R., & Angelique, H.L. (2011). Social power and the role of community psychology in environmental disputes: A tale of two nuclear cities. *American Journal of Community Psychology, 47*(3–4), 410–26.

Curwood, S. E., Munger, F., Mitchell, T., Mackeigan, M., & Farrar, A. (2011). Building effective community-university partnerships: Are universities truly ready? *Michigan Journal of Community Service Learning, 17*(2), 15–26.

D'Augelli, A. R. (1989). The development of a helping community for lesbians and gay men: A case study in community psychology. *Journal of Community Psychology, 17*, 18–29.

D'Andrade, R. (2008). *A study of personal and cultural values.* New York: Palgrave Macmillan.

Dahl, R. A. (1957). The concept of power. *Systems Research and Behavior Science, 2*(3), 201–15.

Dalton, J., Elias, M., & Wandersman, A. (2001). *Community psychology: Linking individuals and communities.* Stamford, CT: Wadsworth.

Dalton, J. H., Elias, M. J., & Wandersman, A. (2006). *Community psychology: Linking individuals and communities* (2nd ed.). Belmont, CA: Wadsworth Publishing.

Dalton, J., & Wolfe, S. (2012). Competencies for community psychology practice. *The Community Psychologist, 45*(4), 8–14.

Damon, W. (1995). *Greater expectations: Overcoming the culture of indulgence in America's homes and schools.* New York: The Free Press.

Davidson, H., Evans, S., Ganote, C., Henrickson, J., Jacobs-Priebe, L., Jones, D. L., ... Riemer, M. (2006). Power and action in critical theory across disciplines: Implications for critical community psychology. *American Journal of Community Psychology, 38*, 35–49.

Davidson, L. (2016). The recovery movement: Implications for mental health care and enabling people to participate fully in life. *Health Affairs, 35*(6), 1091–7.

Davidson, P. O. (1981). Some cultural, political and professional antecedents of community psychology in Canada. *Canadian Psychology, 22*(4), 315–20.

Davis, A. Y. (1983). *Women, race & class* (1st Vintage Books ed.). New York: Vintage.

Davis, L. W. (2010). *The effect of power plants on local housing values and rents* (09-AFC-3). Retrieved from http://docketpublic.energy.ca.gov/PublicDocuments/Regulatory/Non Active AFC's/09-AFC-3 Mariposa Energy/2010/October/TN 58732 10-07-10 The Effect of Power Plants on Local Housing Values - Rents.pdf

de Leon, A. (2013, October 16). We need to raise the bar on being an ally. *Bitch Magazine.* Retrieved from http://bitchmagazine.org/post/we-need-to-raise-the-bar-on-being-an-ally

de Lira, A. N., & de Morais, N. A. (2017). Resilience in lesbian, gay, and bisexual (LGB) populations: An integrative literature review. *Sexuality Research and Social Policy, 15*, 1–11.

De Vos, P. (2001). Grootboom, the right of access to housing and substantive equality as contextual fairness. *South African Journal of Human Rights, 17*, 258–76.

Deegan, P. (1988). Recovery: The lived experience of rehabilitation. *Psychosocial Rehabilitation Journal, 11*(4), 11–19.

Deegan, P. (1993). Recovering our sense of value after being labelled. *Journal of Psychosocial Nursing and Mental Services, 31*(4), 7–11.

Deegan, P. E. (1997). Recovery and empowerment for people with psychiatric disabilities. *Social Work in Health Care, 25*(3), 11–24.

DeFilippis, J. (2008). Paradoxes of community-building: Community control in the global economy. *International Social Science Journal, 59*(192), 223–34.

DeFilippis, J., Fisher, R., & Shragge, E. (2006). Neither romance nor regulation: Re-evaluating community. *International Journal of Urban and Regional Research, 30*(3), 673–89.

Delgado, R., & Stefancic, J. (Eds.). (1998). *The Latino/a condition: A critical reader.* New York: NYU Press.

Delgado, R., & Stefancic, J. (2001). *Critical Race Theory: An introduction* (2nd ed.). New York: New York University Press.

Delgado, R., & Stefancic, J. (2017). *Critical Race Theory: An introduction* (3rd ed.). New York: New York University Press.

Della Porta, D., & Diani, M. (1999). *Social movements: An introduction.* Oxford: Blackwell.

Denzin, N. K., & Lincoln, Y. S. (2017). *The SAGE handbook of qualitative research* (5th ed.). Los Angeles: SAGE Publications.

Department of Health. (2015). Charter of mental health principles: Mental Health Act 2014. Government of Western Australia, Office of Mental Health. Retrieved from https://mhas.wa.gov.au/assets/documents/13036-Charter-of-Mental-Health-Brochure-FINAL.pdf

DePiccoli, N. (2005). Sulla partecipazione (On participation). *Psicologia di Comunita, 2*, 27–36.

Dharker, I. (2015). *Half The Sky*. Retrieved from www.halfsky.org/blog/a-poem-by-imtiaz-dharker-half-the-sky

DiAngelo, R. (2018). *White fragility: Why it's so hard for white people to talk about racism*. Boston, MA: Beacon Press.

DiClemente, C., Nidecker, M., & Bellack, A. (2008). Motivation and the stages of change among individuals with severe mental illness and substance abuse. *Journal of Substance Abuse Treatment, 34*, 25–35.

Diemer, M. A., & Li, C. -H. (2011). Critical consciousness development and political participation among marginalized youth: Critical Consciousness and Political Engagement. *Child Development, 82*(6), 1815–33.

Diener, E., Lucas, R., Schimmack, U., & Helliwell, J. (2009). *Wellbeing for public policy*. New York: Oxford University Press.

Dimock, H. (1987). *Groups: Leadership and group development*. New York: Pfeiffer.

Dimock, H. (1992). *Intervention and empowerment: Helping organizations to change*. North York, ON: Captus Press.

Dittmer, L. (2019). *Building young people's capacity for critical and transcendent engagement: Examining the institution, the community, and the individual as protagonists of a school setting*. Retrieved from Theses and Dissertations (Comprehensive). 2135. https://scholars.wlu.ca/etd/2135

Doherty, S., & Mayer, S. E. (2003). *Capacity building programs for nonprofit programs*. Minneapolis, MN: Effective Communities.

Dobash, R. E., & Dobash, R. P. (1979). *Violence against wives: A case against the patriarchy*. New York: Free Press.

Dobles, I. (2015). Psicología de la liberación y psicología comunitaria latinoamericana: Una perspectiva. *Teoría y Crítica de la Psicología, 6*, 122–39.

Dohrenwend, B. P., & Dohrenwend, B. S. (1969). *Social Status and Psychological Inquiry: A Causal Inquiry*. New York: Wiley.

Dohrenwend, B. S. (1978). Social stress and community psychology. *American Journal of Community Psychology, 6*, 1–14.

Dokecki, P. (1992). On knowing the community of caring persons: A methodological basis for the reflective-generative practice of community psychology. *Journal of Community Psychology, 20*, 26–35.

Donald, D., Lazarus, S., & Moolla, N. (2014). *Educational psychology in social context: Ecosystemic applications in Southern Africa* (5th ed.) Cape Town, South Africa: Oxford University Press.

Donnor, J. K., & Ladson-Billings, G. (2017). Critical Race Theory scholarship and the post-racial imaginary. In N. Denzin & Y. S. Lincoln (Eds.), *The SAGE handbook of qualitative research* (5th ed., pp. 195–213). Los Angeles: SAGE Publications.

Dooley, D., & Catalano, R. (Eds.). (2003). Underemployment and its social costs: New research directions [Special issue]. *American Journal of Community Psychology, 32*(1), 1–7.

Dowling, M., & Cooney, A. (2012). Research approaches related to phenomenology: Negotiating a complex landscape. *Nurse Researcher, 20*(2), 21–7.

Dozois, E., Blanchet-Cohen, N., & Langlois, M. (2010). *DE 201: A practitioner's guide to developmental evaluation*. Quebec and British Columbia: The J.W. McConnell Family Foundation and the International Institute for Child Rights and Development.

Drescher, J. (2015). Out of DSM: Depathologizing homosexuality. *Behavioral Sciences, 5*(4), 565–75.

Dreyer, B., & Riemer, M. (2018). Community and participatory approaches to the environment. In K. O'Doherty & D. Hodgetts (Eds.), *Handbook of applied social psychology*. London: SAGE Publications.

Dreyer, B., Chung, P.J., Szilagyi, P., & Wong, S. (2016). Child poverty in the United States today: Introduction and executive summary. *Academic Pediatrics, 16*, 1–5.

Driskell, J., Salas, E., & Driskell, T. (2018). Foundations of teamwork and collaboration. *American Psychologist, 73*(4), 334–48.

DuBois, D. (2017). Prevention and promotion: Toward an improved paradigm. In Bond, M.A., Keys, C.B., & Serrano-García, I. (Eds.), *APA Handbook of community psychology: Theoretical foundations, core concepts, and emerging challenges* (pp. 233–52). Washington, DC: American Psychological Association.

DuBois, D. L., Holloway, B. E., Valentine, J. C., & Cooper, H. C. (2002). Effectiveness of mentoring programs for youth: A meta-analytic review. *American Journal of Community Psychology, 30*, 157–97.

DuBois, D. L., & Rhodes, J. E. (Eds.). (2006). Youth mentoring: Bridging science with practice [Special issue]. *Journal of Community Psychology, 34*(6), 657–76.

Dudgeon, P., Calma, T., Brideson, T., & Holland, C. (2016). The Gayaa Dhuwi (Proud Spirit) Declaration – A call to action for Aboriginal and Torres Strait Islander leadership in the Australian mental health system. *Advances in Mental Health: Promotion, Prevention and Early Intervention, 14*, 1–14.

Dudgeon, P., Garvey, D., & Pickett, H. (Eds.). (2000). *Working with Indigenous Australians: A handbook for psychologists*. Perth: Gunada Press.

Dudgeon, P., Milroy, H., & Walker, R. (Eds.). (2019). *Working together: Aboriginal and Torres Strait Islander mental health and wellbeing principles and practice* (2nd ed.). Canberra: Commonwealth of Australia.

Dudgeon, P., Mallard, J., Oxenham, D., & Fielder, J. (2002). Contemporary Aboriginal perceptions of community. In A. Fisher, C. Sonn, & B. Bishop (Eds.), *Psychological sense of community: Research, applications, and implications* (pp. 247–67). New York: Kluwer Academic/Plenum Publishers.

Dudgeon, P., & Pickett, H. (2000). Psychology and reconciliation: Australian perspectives. *Australian Psychologist, 35*(2), 82–7.

Dudgeon, P., & Walker, R. (2015). Decolonising Australian psychology: Discourses, strategies, and practice. *Journal of Social and Political Psychology, 3*(1), 276–97.

Dudgeon, P., Walker, R., Scrine, C., Shepherd, C., Calma, T., & Ring, I. (2014a). *Effective strategies to strengthen the mental health and wellbeing of Aboriginal and Torres Strait Islander people*. Australia: Australian Institute of Health and Welfare.

Dudgeon, P., Wright, M., Paradies, Y., Garvey, D., & Walker, I. (2014b). Aboriginal social, cultural and historical contexts. In P. Dudgeon, H. Milroy, & R. Walker (Eds.), *Working together: Aboriginal and Torres Strait Islander mental health and wellbeing principles and practice* (2nd ed., pp. 3–24). Canberra: Commonwealth of Australia.

Durie, M. H. (1996). Characteristics of Maori health research. In Te Rōpū Rangahau Hauora a Eru Pomare. (Ed.). *Hui Whakapiripiri: A Hui to discuss strategic directions for Māori health research* (pp. 32–41). Wellington: University of Otago, Te Rōpū Rangahau Hauora a Eru Pomare.

Durlak, J. A., & DuPre, E. P. (2008). Implementation matters: A review of research on the influence of implementation on program outcomes and the factors affecting implementation. *American Journal of Community Psychology, 41*(3–4), 327–50.

Dussel, E. (1992). *El encubrimiento del Otro: Hacia el origen del "mito de la modernidad."* La Paz: Plural Editores / Facultad de Humanidades y Ciencias de la Educación.

Dussel, E. (2008). *Twenty theses on politics*. Duke University Press. Retrieved from http://enriquedussel.com/txt/Textos_Libros/56.Twenty_theses_on_politics.pdf

Dutta, U. (2016). Prioritizing the local in an era of globalization: A Proposal for decentering community psychology. *American Journal of Community Psychology, 58*(3–4), 329–38.

Dutta, U. (2018). Decolonizing "community" in community psychology. *American Journal of Community Psychology, 62*, 272–82.

Dutta, U., Sonn, C. C., & Lykes, M. B. (2016). Situating and contesting structural violence in community-based research and action. *Community Psychology in Global Perspective, 2*(2), 1–20.

Eady, A., Dobinson, C., & Ross, L. E. (2011). Bisexual people's experiences with mental health services: A qualitative investigation. *Community Mental Health Journal, 47*(4), 378–89.

Eady, A., Dreyer, B., Hey, B., Riemer, M., & Wilson, A. (under review). *Reducing the risks of extreme heat for seniors: Communicating risks and building resilience*. Manuscript under review.

Eckersley, R. (2000). The mixed blessing of material progress: Diminishing returns in the pursuit of progress. *Journal of Happiness Studies, 1*, 267–92.

Eckersley, R. (2001). Culture, health, and well-being. In R. Eckersley, J. Dixon, & B. Douglas (Eds.), *The social origins of health and well-being* (pp. 51–70). New York: Cambridge University Press.

Economy, E., & Levi, M. (2014). *By all means necessary: How China's resource quest is changing the world.* New York: Oxford University Press.

Edmonson, A. C. (2012). *Teaming: How organizations learn, innovate, and compete in the knowledge economy.* San Francisco, CA: Jossey-Bass.

Edwards, M., & Gaventa, J. (Eds.). (2001). *Global citizen action.* New York: Lynne Rienner.

Eicher, C., & Kawachi, I. (2011). Social capital and community design. In A.L. Dannenberg, H. Frumkin, R.L. Jackson (Eds.), *Making healthy places: designing and building for health, well-being, and sustainability* (pp. 117–28). Washington DC: Island Press.

Eichler, M. (1997). *Family shifts: Families, policies, and gender equality.* Toronto: Oxford University Press.

Eisenstein, Z. (1978). The Combahee River Collective: The Combahee River Collective Statement. Retrieved from: http://circuitous.org/scraps/combahee.html.

El Sadaawi, N. (2005). Women, religion and postmodernism. In O. Nnaemeka & J. Ngozi Ezeilo (Eds.), *Engendering human rights: Cultural and socio-economic realities in Africa* (pp. 27–36). New York: Palgrave Macmillan.

Elias, M.J. (1987). Establishing enduring prevention programs: Advancing the legacy of Swampscott. *American Journal of Community Psychology, 15,* 539–53.

Elias, M. J. (1994). Capturing excellence in applied settings: A participant conceptualizer and praxis explicator role for community psychologists. *American Journal of Community Psychology, 22,* 293–318.

Elliott, J., Haney, T., & Sams-Abiodun, P. (2010). Limits to social capital: Comparing network assistance in two New Orleans neighbors devastated by Hurricane Katrina. *Sociological Quarterly, 51,* 624–48.

Embretson, S. E., & Reise, S. P. (2011). *Item response theory* (2nd ed.). Mahwah, NJ: Routledge Academic.

Emshoff, J. G., Darnell, A. J., Darnell, D. A., Erickson, S. W., Schneider, S., & Hudgins, R. (2007). Systems change as an outcome and a process in the work of community collaboratives for health. *American Journal of Community Psychology, 39*(3–4), 255–67.

Epp, J. (1988). *Mental health for Canadians: Striking a balance.* Ottawa: Minister of Supplies and Services.

Etzioni, A. (1960). Two approaches to organizational analysis: A critique and a suggestion. *Administrative Science Quarterly, 5,* 257–78.

Etzioni, A. (1996). *The new golden rule.* New York: Basic Books.

European Monitoring Centre for Drugs and Drug Addiction. (2015). *European drug report: Trends and developments.* Luxembourg: Publications Office of the European Union.

European Union Agency for Fundamental Rights. (2013). *EU LGBT Survey: Results at a glance.* Luxembourg: Publications Office of the European Union.

Eurostat. (2019). *Unemployment statistics.* Retrieved from https://ec.europa.eu/eurostat/statistics-explained/index.php/Unemployment_statistics

Euzébios Filho, A. (2016). About ideologies and income transfers in Brazil. *Psicologia & Sociedade, 28*(2), 257–66. Retrieved from: http://www.scielo.br/pdf/psoc/v28n2/1807-0310-psoc-28-02-00257.pdf

Evans, G. W., & Kim, P. (2007). Childhood poverty and health: Cumulative risk and stress dysregulation. *Psychological Science, 18*(11), 953–7.

Evans, M. D. R., Kelley, J., & Kolosi, T. (1992). Images of class: Public perceptions in Hungary and Australia. *American Sociological Review, 57,* 461–82.

Evans, S., Rosen, A., & Nelson, G. (2014a). Community psychology and social justice. In C. V. Johnson, H. L. Friedman, J. Diaz, Z. Franco, & B. K. Nastasi (Eds.), *Social justice and psychology. The Praeger handbook of social justice and psychology: Fundamental issues and special populations; Well-being and professional issues; Youth and disciplines in psychology* (pp. 143–63). Santa Barbara, CA: Praeger/ABC-CLIO.

Evans, S. D. (2012). *From amelioration to transformation in human services: Towards critical practice.* Saarbrucken, Germany: LAP LAMBERT Academic Publishing.

Evans, S. D. (2015). The community psychologist as critical friend: Promoting critical community praxis. *Journal of Community & Applied Social Psychology, 25*(4), 355–68.

Evans, S. D., Duckett, P., Lawthom, R., & Kivell, N. (2017). Positioning the critical in community psychology. In M. A. Bond, I. Serrano-García, & C. B. Keys (Eds.), *APA handbook of community psychology: Theoretical foundations, core concepts, and emerging challenges* (pp. 107–28). Washington, DC: American Psychological Association.

Evans, S. D., Hanlin, C. E., & Prilleltensky, I. (2007). Blending ameliorative and transformative approaches in human service organizations: A case study. *Journal of Community Psychology, 35*(3), 329–46.

Evans, S. D., & Kivell, N. (2015). The transformation team: An enabling structure for organizational learning in action. *Journal of Community Psychology, 43*(6), 760–77.

Evans, S. D., Kivell, N., Haarlammert, M., Malhotra, K., & Rosen, A. (2014b). Critical community practice: An introduction to the special section. *Journal for Social Action in Counseling and Psychology, 6*(1), 1–15.

Evans, S.D., Nelson, G., & Loomis, C. (2009). Critical perspectives on teaching and learning community psychology at Wilfrid Laurier University: Principles, strategies, and challenges. In C. Vázquez Rivera, M. Figueroa Rodríguez, W. Pacheco Bou, & D. Pérez-Jiménez (Eds.), *International community psychology: Shared agendas in diversity* (pp. 533–61). San Juan, Puerto Rico: University of Puerto Rico Press.

Evans, S. D., Prilleltensky, O., McKenzie, A., Prilleltensky, I., Nogueras, D., Huggins, C., & Mescia, N. (2011). Promoting strengths, prevention, empowerment, and community change through organizational development: Lessons for research, theory, and practice. *Journal of Prevention & Intervention in the Community, 39*(1), 50–64.

Evans, S. D., Raymond, C., & Perkins, D. D. (2014c). Organizational and community capacity building. In V. C. Scott & S. M. Wolfe (Eds.), *Community psychology: Foundations for practice* (pp. 189–219). Thousand Oaks, CA: SAGE Publications, Inc.

Evans, S. D., Rosen, A. D., Kesten, S. M., & Moore, W. (2014d). Miami thrives: Weaving a poverty reduction coalition. *American Journal of Community Psychology, 53*(3–4), 357–68.

Everett, B., & Boydell, K. (1994). A methodology for including consumers' opinions in mental health evaluation research. *Psychiatric Services, 45*(1), 76–8.

Fabrega, H. (1990). Psychiatric stigma in the classical and medieval period: A review of the literature. *Comprehensive Psychiatry, 31*(4), 289–306.

Fairweather, G. W., Sanders, D. H., Maynard, H., & Cressler, D. L. (1969). *Community life for the mentally ill: An alternative to institutional care.* Chicago, IL: Aldine Publishing Company.

Fals Borda, O. (1987). The application of participatory action-research in Latin America. *International Sociology, 2*(4), 329–47.

Fals Borda, O. (2001). Participatory (action) research in social theory: Origins and challenges. In P. Reason & H. Bradbury (Eds.), *Handbook of action research: Participative inquiry and practice* (pp. 27–37). London: SAGE Publications.

Fals Borda, O. (2003). La ciência y el Pueblo: Nuevas reflexiones sobre la investigación acción (participativa). In: N. A. Herrera & L. López (Eds.), *Ciencia, compromiso y cambio social* (pp. 301–20). Buenos Aires: El Colectivo / Lanzas y Letras / Extensión Libros.

Fanon, F. (1963). *The wretched of the Earth.* New York: Grove Press.

FAO, IFAD, & WFD. (2015). *Achieving zero hunger: The critical role of investments in social protection and agriculture.* Rome: FAO.

Fawcett, S. B., White, G. W., Balcazar, F. E., Suarez-Balcazar, Y., Mathews, R. M., Paine, A. L., … Smith, J. F. (1994). A contextual-behavioral model of empowerment: Case studies with people with disabilities. *American Journal of Community Psychology, 22*, 471–96.

Fawcett, S., Paine-Andrews, A., Francisco, V. T., Schultz, J. A., Richter, K. P., Quiñones, R. K. … Lopez, C. M. (1995). Using empowerment theory in collaborative partnerships for community health and development. *American Journal of Community Psychology, 23*(5), 677–97.

Fazel, S., Geddes, J. R., & Kushel, M. (2014). The health of homeless people in high-income countries: Descriptive epidemiology, health consequences, and clinical and policy recommendations. *Lancet, 384*(9953), 1529–40.

Febbraro, A. (1994). Single mothers "at risk" for child maltreatment: An appraisal of person-centred interventions and a call for emancipatory action. *Canadian Journal of Community Mental Health, 13*(2), 47–60.

Fedi, A., Mannarini, T., & Maton, K. I. (2009). Empowering community settings and community mobilization. *Community Development, 40*(3), 275–91.

Felner, R., & Adan, A. (1988). The School Transition Environment Project: An ecological intervention and evaluation. In R. Price, E. L. Cowen, R. P. Lorion, & J. Ramos-McKay (Eds.), *Fourteen ounces of prevention: A casebook for practitioners* (pp. 111–22). Washington, DC: American Psychological Association.

Feltham, C., Hanley, T., & Winter, L. A. (Eds.). (2017). *The SAGE handbook of counselling and psychotherapy* (4th ed.). London: SAGE Publications.

Fergus, S., & Zimmerman, M. (2005). Adolescent resilience: A framework for understanding healthy development in the face of risk. *Annual Review of Public Health, 26,* 399–419.

Fetterman, D. M. & Wandersman, A. (Eds.). (2005). *Empowerment evaluation principles in practice.* New York: Guilford Press.

Fettes, M. (1998). Indigenous education and the ecology of community. *Language Culture and Curriculum, 11*(3), 250–71.

Fine, B. (2010). *Theories of social capital.* London: Pluto Press.

Fine, M. (2000). *The politics of urgency.* Presentation at the Cross City Campaign for Urban School Reform's working meeting, "Changing urban high schools," Baltimore, MD. Retrieved from https://goo.gl/QgPXrP.

Fine, M. (2006). Bearing witness: Methods for researching oppression and resistance – A textbook for critical research. *Social Justice Research, 19*(1), 83–108.

Fine, M. (2012). Whose evidence counts? *Feminism & Psychology, 22,* 3–19.

Fine, M., Burns, A., Torre, M. E., & Payne, Y. (2008). How class matters: The geography of educational desire and despair in schools and courts. In L. Weis (Ed.), *The way class works: Readings on school, family and the economy.* New York: Routledge.

Firdion, J-M., & Marpsat, M. (2007). A research program on homelessness in France. *Journal of Social Issues, 63,* 567–87.

Fisher, A. T., Sonn, C. C., & Bishop, B. J. (2002). *Psychological sense of community: Research, applications, and implications.* Boston, MA: Springer.

Flaspohler, P., Lesesne, C. A., Puddy, R. W., Smith, E., & Wandersman, A. (2012). Advances in bridging research and practice: Introduction to the second special issue on the interactive system framework for dissemination and implementation. *American Journal of Community Psychology, 50*(3–4), 271–81.

Flaspohler, P., Wandersman, A., Keener, D., Maxwell, K. N., Ace, A., Andrews, A., & Holmes, B. (2003). Promoting program success and fulfilling accountability requirements in a statewide community-based initiative: Challenges, progress, and lessons learned. *Journal of Prevention & Intervention in the Community, 26*(2), 37–52.

Flicker, S., & Roche, B. & Guta, A. (2010). *Peer research in Action III: Ethical Issues.* Retrieved from: https://www.wellesleyinstitute.com/wp-content/uploads/2011/02/Ethical_Issues_WEB.pdf

Flicker, S., Travers, R., Guta, A., McDonald, S., & Meagher, A. (2007). Ethical dilemmas in community-based participatory research: Recommendations for institutional review boards. *Journal of Urban Health: Bulletin of the New York Academy of Medicine, 84*(4), 478–93.

Flora, C. B. (2004). Community dynamics and social capital. In D. Rickerl & C. Francis (Eds.), *Agroecosystems analysis* (pp. 93–107). Madison, Wisconsin: American Society of Agronomy, Inc., Crop Science Society of America, Inc., Soil Science Society of America, Inc.

Flores, J. M. (2009). Praxis and liberation in the context of Latin American theory. In M. Montero & C. C. Sonn (Eds.), *Psychology of liberation: Theory and applications* (pp. 11–36). New York: Springer.

Flynn, R. J., & Lemay, R. A. (1999). *A quarter-century of normalization and social role valorization: Evolution and impact.* Ottawa: University of Ottawa Press.

Fondacaro, M. R., & Weinberg, D. (2002). Concepts of social justice in community psychology toward a social ecological epistemology. *American Journal of Community Psychology, 30*(4), 473–92.

Fontana, L. (2014). Indigenous peoples vs peasant unions: Land conflicts and rural movements in plurinational Bolivia. *The Journal of Peasant Studies, 41*(3), 297–319.

Fook, J. (2012). *Social work: A critical approach to practice* (2nd ed.). Thousand Oaks, CA: SAGE Publications.

Ford, C., & Airhihenbuwa, C. (2010). Critical race theory, race equity, and public health: Toward antiracism praxis. *American Journal of Public Health, 100*(1), 30–5.

Forrester, J. W. (1971). *World dynamics.* Cambridge, MA: Wright-Allen Press.

Forrester, J. W. (1994). System dynamics, systems thinking, and soft OR. *System Dynamics Review, 10*(2–3), 245–56.

Foster, J. (2015). *After sustainability: Denial, hope, retrieval.* London: Routledge.

Foster-Fishman, P. G., & Behrens, T. R. (2007). Systems change reborn: Rethinking our theories, methods, and efforts in human services reform and community-based change. *American Journal of Community Psychology, 39*(3–4), 191–6.

Foster-Fishman, P. G., Berkowitz, S., Lounsbury, D., Jacobson, S., & Allen, N. (2001a). Building collaborative capacity in community coalitions: A review and integrative framework. *American Journal of Community Psychology, 29,* 241–61.

Foster-Fishman, P. G., Cantillon, D., Pierce, S. J., & Van Egeren, L. (2007a). Building an active citizenry: The role of neighborhood problems, readiness, and capacity for change. *American Journal of Community Psychology, 39,* 91–106.

Foster-Fishman, P. G., Fitzgerald, K., Brandell, C., Nowell, B., Chavis, D., & Egeren, L. A. V. (2006). Mobilizing residents for action: The role of small wins and strategic supports. *American Journal of Community Psychology, 38*(3–4), 143–52.

Foster-Fishman, P. G., Nowell, B., & Yang, H. (2007b). Putting the system back into systems change: A framework for understanding and changing organizational and community systems. *American Journal of Community Psychology, 39*(3–4), 197–215.

Foster-Fishman, P. G., Pierce, S. J., & Van Egeren, L. A. (2009). Who participates and why: Building a process model of citizen participation. *Health Education & Behavior, 36*(3), 550–69.

Foster-Fishman, P., Salem, D., Allen, N., & Fahrbach, K. (2001b). Facilitating interorganizational collaboration: The contributions of interorganizational alliances. *American Journal of Community Psychology, 29,* 875–905.

Foster-Fishman, P. G., & Watson, E. R. (2012). The ABLe Change Framework: A conceptual and methodological tool for promoting systems change. *American Journal of Community Psychology, 49*(3–4), 503–56.

Foster-Fishman, P., & Watson, E. (2017). Understanding and promoting systems change. In M. A. Bond, I. Serrano-García, C. B. Keys, & M. Shinn (Eds.), *APA handbook of community psychology: Methods for community research and action for diverse groups and issues* (pp. 255–74). Washington, DC: American Psychological Association.

Foucault, M. (1980). Truth and power. In C. Gordon (Ed.), *Michel Foucault – Power/Knowledge: Selected interviews and other writings 1972–1977* (pp. 109–33). New York: Random House.

Foucault, M. (1983). The subject and power. In H. Dreyfus & P. Rabinow (Eds.), *Michel Foucault: Beyond structuralism and hermeneutics* (2nd ed., pp. 208–26). Chicago, IL: University of Chicago Press.

Fowers, B. (2014). Values/Value Systems. In T. Teo (Ed.), *Encyclopedia of critical psychology* (pp. 2046–51). New York: Springer.

Fowler, P. J., & Todd, N. R. (2017). Methods for multiple levels of analysis: Capturing context, change, and changing context. In M. A. Bond, I. Serrano-García, C. B. Keys, & M. Shinn (Eds.), *APA handbook of community psychology: Methods for community research and action for diverse groups and issues* (pp. 255–74). Washington, DC: American Psychological Association.

Fox, D. R. (1991). Social science's limited role in resolving psycholegal social problems. *Journal of Offender Rehabilitation, 17,* 117–24.

Fox, D. R. (1999). Psycholegal scholarship's contribution to false consciousness about injustice. *Law and Human Behavior, 23,* 9–30.

Fox, D., & Prilleltensky, I. (Eds.). (1997). *Critical psychology: An introduction.* London: SAGE Publications.

Fox, D., Prilleltensky, I., & Austin, S. (Eds.). (2009). *Critical psychology: An introduction* (2nd ed.). Thousand Oaks, CA: SAGE Publications Ltd.

Francescato, D., Arcidiacono, C., Albanesi, C., & Mannarini, T. (2007). Community psychology in Italy: Past developments and future perspectives. In S. M. Reich, M. Riemer, I. Prilleltensky, & M. Montero (Eds.), *International community psychology: History and theories* (pp. 263–81). New York: Springer.

Franke, R., & Chasin, B. (1995). Kerala State: A social justice model. *Multinational Monitor, 16*(7–8). Available from http://multinationalmonitor.org/hyper/mm0795.08.html

Franke, R., & Chasin, B. (2000). Is the Kerala model sustainable? Lessons from the past, prospects for the future. In G. Parayil (Ed.), *Kerala: The development experience* (pp. 16–39). New York: Zed Books.

Frankfurt, H. G. (2015). *On inequality.* New Jersey: Princeton University Press.

Freedman, D. A., & Bess, K. D. (2011). Food systems change and the environment: Local and global connections. *American Journal of Community Psychology, 47*(3–4), 397–409.

Freedman, D. A., Ketcham, D., & Bess, K. D. (2011). Creating a community-engaged food security coalition: Contextual landscape, participatory planning, and relational change. *Arete, 32*(2), 33–60.

Freeman, H. L., Fryers, T., & Henderson, J. H. (1985). *Mental health services in Europe: 10 years on* (Public Health in Europe 25). Copenhagen: WHO Regional Office for Europe.

Freeman, J., & Johnson, V. (Eds.). (1999). *Waves of protest: Social movements since the sixties.* Boulder, CO: Rowman & Littlefield.

Freeman, J. (1999). On the origins of social movements. In J. Freeman & V. Johnson (Eds.), *Cycles of protest: Social movements since the sixties* (pp. 7–24). New York: Rowman & Littlefield.

Freire, P. (1970). *Pedagogy of the oppressed.* New York: Herder and Herder.

Freire, P. (1973). *Education for critical consciousness.* New York: Seabury.

Freire, P. (2006). *Pedagogy of the oppressed* (30th anniversary ed.). New York: Continuum.

Freitas, M. De F. Q. De (2000). Voices from the South: The construction of Brazilian community social psychology. *Journal of Community & Applied Social Psychology, 10*(4), 315–26.

French, J. R. P., Jr., Rodgers, W. L., & Cobb, S. (1974). Adjustment as person-environment fit. In G. Coelho, D. Hamburg, & J. Adams (Eds.), *Coping and adaptation* (pp. 316–33). New York: Basic Books.

Frerichs, L., Lich, K.H., Funchess, M., Burell, M., Cerulli, C., Bedell, P., & White, A. (2016). Applying critical race theory to group model building methods to address community violence. *Progress in Community Health Partnerships: Research, Education and Action, 10*(3), 443–59.

Frechtling, J. A. (2007). *Logic modeling methods in program evaluation* (Vol. 5). San Francisco, CA, Jossey-Bass.

Friedman, C., & Owen, A.L. (2017). Defining disability: Understandings of and attitudes towards ableism and disability. *Disability Studies Quarterly, 37*(1), 2.

Friedman, T. (2000). *The Lexus and the olive tree.* New York: Anchor.

Friedmann, J. (2010). Place and place-making in cities: A global perspective. *Planning Theory & Practice, 11*(2), 149–65.

Frumkin, P. (2002). *On being nonprofit: A conceptual and policy primer.* Cambridge, MA: Harvard University Press.

Fryer, D. (2008). Some questions about the history of community psychology. *Journal of Community Psychology, 36*(5), 572–86.

Fulbright-Anderson, K. (2006). Community change: Implications for complex community initiatives. In K. Fulbright-Anderson & P. Auspos (Eds.), *Community change: Theories, practice, and evidence* (pp. 9–17). Washington, D.C.: The Aspen Institute.

Fullan, M. (2005). *Leadership and sustainability.* Thousand Oaks, CA: Corwin.

Fullan, M. (2006). *Turnaround leadership.* San Francisco, CA: Jossey-Bass.

Fullan, M. (2008). *The six secrets of change. What the best leaders do to help their organizations survive and thrive.* San Francisco, CA: Jossey-Bass.

Fung, A., & Wright, E. O. (2003). *Deepening democracy: Institutional innovations in empowered participatory governance.* New York: Verso.

Furman, E., Singh, A. K., Darko, N.A., & Wilson, C. L. (2018). Activism, intersectionality, and community psychology: The way in which Black Lives Matter Toronto helps us to examine white supremacy in Canada's LGBTQ+ community. *Community Psychology in Global Perspective, 4*(2), 34–54.

Gaetz, S., Barr, C., Friesen, A., Harris, B., Hill, C., Kovacs-Burns, K., ... Marsolais, A. (2012). *Canadian definition of homelessness.* Toronto: Canadian Observatory on Homelessness Press. Retrieved from www.home-lesshub.ca/sites/default/files/COHhomelessdefinition.pdf.

Gakidou, E., Cowling, K., Lozano, R., & Murray, C. (2010). Increased educational attainment and its effect on child mortality in 175 countries between 1970 and 2009: A systematic analysis. *Lancet, 376* (9745), 959–74.

Galeano, E. (2001). *Las palabras andantes.* Buenos Aires, Argentina: Catálogos.

Gamble, A. (2001). Political economy. In G. Philo & D. Miller (Eds.), *Market killing: What the free market does and what social scientists can do about it* (pp. 170–76). London: Pearson Education.

Gamson, W. (1992). Social psychology of collective action. In A. P. A. D. Morris & A. P. C. M. Mueller (Eds.), *Frontiers in social movement theory* (pp. 53–76). New Haven, Conn: Yale University Press.

Gamson, W. A., & Modigliani, A. (1987). The changing culture of affirmative action. *Research in Political Sociology, 3*, 137–77.

Garbarino, J., & Kostelny, K. (1992). Child maltreatment as a community problem. *Child Abuse and Neglect, 16*, 455–64.

Garcia-Alonso, P. M. (2004). *From surviving to thriving: An investigation of the utility of support groups designed to address the special needs of sexual minority youth in public high schools* (Doctoral dissertation). Retrieved from Dissertation Abstracts International (UMI Number: 3126026).

García-Ramírez, M., de la Mata, M.L., Paloma, V., Hernández, S. (2011). A liberation psychology approach to acculturative integration of migrant populations. *American Journal of Community Psychology, 47,* 86–97.

García-Ramírez, M., Martinez, M., Balcazar, F., Suarez-Balcazar, Y., Albar, M.-J., Domínguez, E., & Santolaya, F. (2005). Psychosocial empowerment and social support factors associated with the employment status of immigrant welfare recipients. *Journal of Community Psychology, 33*(6), 673–90.

Garner, D.M. & Garfinkel, P.E. (1980). Socio-cultural factors in the development of anorexia nervosa. *Psychological Medicine, 10,* 647–56.

Gass, R. (2012). *What is transformation?* Oakland, CA: Social Transformation Project. Retrieved from http://stproject.org/resources/publications/what-is-transformation/

Gates, A. B. (2014). Integrating social services and social change: Lessons from an immigrant worker center. *Journal of Community Practice, 22*(1–2), 102–29.

Gaventa, J. (1980). *Power and powerlessness: Quiescence and rebellion in an appalacian valley.* Chicago, IL: University of Chicago Press.

Gaventa, J. (1995). Citizen knowledge, citizen competence and democracy building. *The Good Society, 5*(3), 28–35.

Gaventa, J. (2006). Finding the spaces for change: A power analysis. *IDS Bulletin, 37*(6), 23–33.

Gaventa, J. (2016). *Can participation 'fix' inequality? Unpacking the relationship between the economic and political citizenship.* Coady Innovation Series, No. 5. Retrieved from https://opendocs.ids.ac.uk/opendocs/handle/123456789/12127

Gaztambide-Fernández, R. A. (2012). Decolonization and the pedagogy of solidarity. *Decolonization: Indigeneity, Education & Society,1*(1). Retrieved from http://decolonization.org/index.php/des/article/view/18633

Gee, G., Dudgeon, P., Schultz, C., Hart, A., & Kelly, K. (2014). Aboriginal and Torres Strait Islander social and emotional wellbeing. In P. Dudgeon, H. Milroy, & R. Walker (Eds.), *Working together: Aboriginal and Torres Strait Islander mental health and wellbeing principles and practice* (2nd ed., pp. 55–68). Canberra: Commonwealth of Australia.

George, R. (2002). *Socioeconomic democracy.* London: Praeger.

Gergen, K. J. (2009). *Relational being: Beyond self and community.* New York: Oxford University Press.

Gerlach, L. P. (1999). The structure of social movements: Environmental activism and its opponents. In J. Freeman & V. Johnson (Eds.), *Cycles of protest: Social movements since the sixties* (pp. 85–98). New York: Rowman & Littlefield.

Gerschick, T. J., Israel, B. A., & Checkoway, B. N. (1990). *Means of empowerment in individuals, organizations, and communities.* Ann Arbor, MI: Program on Conflict Management Alternatives, University of Michigan.

Gibbs, A., Campbell, C., Akintola, O., & Colvin, C. (2015). Social contexts and building social capital for collective action: Three case studies of volunteers in the context of HIV and AIDS in South Africa: Social contexts and building social capital. *Journal of Community & Applied Social Psychology, 25*(2), 110–22.

Giese, M., & Ruin, S. (2016). Forgotten bodies – an examination of physical education from the perspective of ableism. *Sport in Society, 21*(1), 152–65.

Gifford, R. (2007). Environmental psychology and sustainable development: Expansion, maturation, and challenges. *Journal of Social Issues, 63*(1), 199–212.

Gil, D. G. (1998). *Confronting injustice and oppression: Concepts and strategies for social workers.* New York: Columbia University Press.

Gill, S. J. (2009). *Developing a learning culture in nonprofit organizations.* SAGE Publications.

Ginwright, S. A. (2007). Black youth activism and the role of critical social capital in black community organizations. *American Behavioral Scientist, 51*(3), 403–18.

Ginwright, S. (2010). *Building a pipeline for justice: Understanding youth organizing and the leadership pipeline* (No. 10). Retrieved from http://fcyo.org/media/docs/6252_FCYO_OPS_10_ScreenVersion.pdf

Gioia, D. A., & Pitre, E. (1990). Multiparadigm perspectives on theory building. *Academy of Management Review, 15*(4), 584–602.

Gitterman, A., & Shulman, L. (Eds.). (2005). *Mutual aid groups, vulnerable and resilient populations, and the life cycle.* New York: Columbia University Press.

Glouberman, S., & Zimmerman, B. (2002). *Complicated and complex Systems: What would successful reform of Medicare look like?* (Discussion Paper No. 8). Ottawa, Canada: Commission on the Future of Health Care in Canada. Retrieved from http://publications.gc.ca/collections/Collection/CP32-79-8-2002E.pdf

Glover, M., & Robertson, P. (1997). Facilitating development of Maori psychology. In H. Love, & W. Whittaker (Eds.), *Practice issues for clinical and applied psychologists in New Zealand* (pp. 136–46). Wellington: The New Zealand Psychological Society.

Glucker, A. N., Driessen, P., Kolhoff, A., & Runhaar, H. (2013). Public participation in environmental impact assessment: Why, who, and how? *Environmental Impact Assessment Review, 43,* 104–11.

Godsay, S., & Brodsky, A. (2018). "I believe in that movement and I beleive in that chant": The influence of Black Lives Matter on resilience and empowerment. *Community Psychology Global Perspectives, 4*(2), 55–72.

Goering, P., & Tsemberis, S. (2014). Housing First and system/community change. In G. Nelson, B. Kloos, & J. Ornelas (Eds.), *Community psychology and community mental health: Towards transformative change* (pp. 278–91). New York: Oxford University Press.

Goethe, J. W. (1906). The maxims and reflections of Goethe. New York: The Macmillian Company. Available: https://archive.org/details/maximsreflection00goetrich

Góis, C. W. L. (2003). *Psicologia comunitária no Ceará.* Fortaleza, Brazil: Instituto Paulo Freire de Estudos Psicossociais.

Góis, C. W. L. (2005). *Psicologia comunitária: Atividade e consciência.* Fortaleza: Publicações Instituto Paulo Freire de Estudos Psicossociais.

Goldberg, D. T. (2007). Raceless states from race, racialization and anti-racism. In *Canada and Beyond* (pp. 206–28). Toronto, ON: University of Toronto Press.

Goldenberg, I. I. (1978). *Oppression and social intervention: Essays on the human condition and the problem of change.* Chicago, IL: Nelson-Hall.

Goldstein, J. L., & Godemont, M. M. (2003). The legend and lessons of Geel, Belgium: A 1500-year-old legend, a 21st-century model. *Community Mental Health Journal, 39*(5), 441–58.

Goleman, D. (1998). *Working with emotional intelligence.* New York: Bantam.

Gone, J. P. (2013). A community-based treatment for Native American historical trauma: Prospects for evidence-based practice. *Spirituality in Clinical Practice, 1,* 78–94.

Gone, J. P. (2004). Mental health services for Native Americans in the 21st century United States. *Professional Psychology: Research and Practice, 35*(1), 10–18.

Goodman, D. (2001). *Promoting diversity and social justice: Educating people from privileged groups.* Thousand Oaks, CA: SAGE Publications.

Goodman, L., Litwin, A., Bohlig, A., Weintraub, S., Green, A., Walker, J., ... & Ryan, N. (2007). Applying feminist theory to community practice: A multilevel empowerment intervention for low-income women with depression. In E. Aldarondo (Ed.), *Advancing social justice through clinical practice* (pp. 265–90). London: Lawrence Erlbaum.

Goodman, R. M., Speers, M. A., McLeroy, K., Fawcett, S., Kegler, M., Parker, E., ... Wallerstein, N. (1998). Identifying and defining the dimensions of community capacity to provide a basis for measurement. *Health Education and Behavior, 2*(3), 258–78.

Gordon, C. (Ed.). (1980). *Michel Foucault – Power/Knowledge: Selected interviews and other writings 1972–1977.* New York: Random House.

Gore, A. (2006). *An inconvenient truth: The planetary emergency of global warming and what we can do about it.* New York: Rodale.

Gottlieb, B. H. (Ed.). (1981). *Social networks and social support.* Beverly Hills, CA: SAGE Publications.

Government of India. (2011). *Census of India 2011.* Ministry of Home Affairs. Retrieved from www.censusindia.gov.in

Graham, L. F., Braithwaite, K., Spikes, P., Stephens, C. F., & Edu, U. F. (2009). Exploring the mental health of black men who have sex with men. *Community Mental Health Journal, 45*(4), 272–84.

Graham, L., Brown-Jeffy, S., Aronson, R., & Stephens, C. (2011). Critical Race Theory as theoretical framework and analysis tool for population health research. *Critical Public Health, 21*(1), 61–93.

Gramsci, A. (1971). *Selections from the prison notebooks of Antonio Gramsci* (Q,. Hoare & G. Nowell Smith, Eds, Trans.). New York: International Publishers.

Granovetter, M. (1973). Strength of weak ties. *American Journal of Sociology, 78*(6), 1360–80.

Grantham-McGregor, S., Cheung, Y.B., Cueto, S., Glewwe, P., Richter, L., & Strupp, B. (2007). Child development in developing countries: Development potential in the first 5 years for children in developing countries. *The Lancet, 369,* 60–70.

Gray, A. (Ed.). (2001). *World health and disease.* Buckingham: Open University Press.

Gray, N. N., Mendelsohn, D. M., & Omoto, A. M. (2015). Community connectedness, challenges, and resilience among gay Latino immigrants. *American Journal of Community Psychology, 55*(1–2), 202–14.

Green, J. (1999). The spirit of willing: Collective identity and the development of the Christian Right. In J. Freeman & V. Johnson (Eds.), *Cycles of protest: Social movements since the sixties* (pp. 153–68). New York: Rowman & Littlefield.

Green, R. (2007). Gay and lesbian couples in therapy: A social justice perspective. In E. Aldarondo (Ed.), *Advancing social justice through clinical practice* (pp. 119–50). London: Lawrence Erlbaum.

Greenwood, R. M., Stefancic, A., Tsemberis, S., & Busch-Geertsma, V. (2013). Implementations of Housing First in Europe: Challenges in maintaining model fidelity. American Journal of Psychiatric Rehabilitation, 16, 290–312.

Greer, L. L., Van Bunderen, L., & Yu, S. (2017). The dysfunctions of power in teams: A review and emergent conflict perspective. *Research in Organizational Behavior, 37,* 103–24.

Greiman, L., Ravesloot, C., Liston, B., Sanders, P., & Myers, A. (2014). *Home usability: Life starts at home.* Presented at the National Association of Rehabilitation Research and Training Centers (NARRTC) National Conference, Alexandria, VA.

Gridley, H., & Breen, L. (2007). So far and yet. so near: Twenty-five years of community psychology in Australia. In S. Reich, M. Reimer, I. Prilleltensky, & M. Montero (Eds.), *International community psychology:History and theories* (pp. 119–39). NJ.: Kluwer/Springer.

Griffin, P., Lee, C., Waugh, J., & Beyer, C. (2004). Describing roles that Gay-Straight Alliances play in schools: From individual support to social change. *Journal of Gay & Lesbian Issues in Education, 1*(3), 7–22.

Gridley, H., & Turner, C. (2010). Gender, power and community psychology. In G. Nelson & I. Prilleltensky (Eds.), *Community psychology: In pursuit of liberation and well-being* (2nd ed., pp. 389–406). London: Red Globe Press.

Gruber, J., & Trickett, E. (1987). Can we empower others? The paradox of empowerment in the governing of an alternative public school. *American Journal of Community Psychology, 15,* 353–71.

Guba, E. G., & Lincoln, Y. S. (2005). Paradigmatic controversies, contradictions, and emerging confluences. In N. K. Denzin & Y. S. Lincoln (Eds.), The SAGE handbook of qualitative research (3rd ed., pp. 191–215). Thousand Oaks, CA: SAGE Publications.

Guldi, M., Page, M., & Stevens, A. H. (2006). *Family background and children's transitions to adulthood over time.* In S. Danziger & C. E. Rouse (Eds.), *The price of independence* (pp. 261–77). New York: Russell Sage.

Guta, A., Flicker, S., & Roche, B. (2013). Governing through community allegiance: a qualitative examination of peer research in community-based participatory research. *Critical Public Health, 23*(4), 432–51.

Guta, A., Flicker, S., Travers, R., St. John, A., Worthington, C., Wilson, C., ... Greene, S. (2014). *Supporting peer research assistants (PRAs)* (Fact Sheet No. 8). HIV CBR Ethics.

Gutiérrez, L. M. (1990). Working with women of color: An empowerment perspective. *Social Work, 35*(2), 149–53.

Guy, M., & Newman, M. (2004). Women's jobs, men's jobs: Sex segregation and emotional labor. *Public Administration Review, 64*(3), 289–98.

Habermas, J. (1971). *Knowledge and human interests.* Boston, MA: Beacon Press.

Hahn, A. (1994). *The politics of caring: Human services at the local level.* Boulder, CO: Westview Press.

Hall, M. F. (1995). *Poor people's social movement organizations.* London: Praeger.

Hall, P. D. (2013). Philanthropy, the nonprofit sector & the democratic dilemma. *Daedalus, 142*(2), 139–58.

Hallman, D. (1987). The Nestlé boycott: The success of a citizen's coalition in social intervention. In E. M. Bennett (Ed.), *Social intervention: Theory and practice* (pp. 187–229). Lewiston, NY: The Edwin Mellen Press.

Hamber, B. (2009). *Transforming societies after political violence: Truth, reconciliation, and mental health.* New York: Springer.

Hancock, A. (2016). *Intersectionality: An intellectual history*. New York: Oxford University Press.

Handicap International. (2009). *Inclusive local development: How to implement a disability approach at local level. PP Brief 1*. Retrieved from www.handicap-international.ch/sites/ch/files/documents/files/developpe-ment-local-inclusif_anglais.pdf

Hanleybrown, F., Kania, J., & Kramer, M. (2012). *Channeling change: Making collective impact work*. Stanford Social Innovation Review.

Hannigan, T. (2013). *A place for Visitability in the market place: A post-occupancy study*. Dissertation. Eastern University: Philadelphia, PA.

Hardgrove, A., Enenajor, A., & Lee, A. (2011). *Risk and childhood poverty: Notes from theory and research*. Oxford: Young Lives.

Harding, C. M., Zubin, J., & Strauss, J. S. (1987). Chronicity in schizophrenia: Fact, partial fact, or artifact? *Psychiatric Services, 38*(5), 477–86.

Hardt, M., & Negri, A. (2000). *Empire*. Harvard University Press.

Hargreaves, A., & Fink, D. (2006). *Sustainable leadership*. San Francisco, CA: Jossey-Bass.

Hari, J. (2015). *Chasing the scream: The first and last days of the war on drugs*. New York: Bloomsbury.

Harper, G. W., & Schneider, M. (1999). Giving lesbian, gay, bisexual, and transgendered people and communities a voice in community research and action. *The Community Psychologist, 32*(2), 41–3.

Harper, G. W., & Schneider, M. (2003). Oppression and discrimination among lesbian, gay, bisexual, and transgendered people and communities: A challenge for community psychology. *American Journal of Community Psychology, 31*(3–4), 243–52.

Harré, N. (2013, June 26–29). *Psychology and the infinite game*. Keynote presented at the 2013 Biennial Conference of the Society for Community, Research, and Action, Miami, FL.

Harré, N. (2016). Commentary of the special issue: Youth leading environmental change. *Ecopsychology, 8*(3), 202–5.

Harré, N. (2018). *Psychology for a better world*. Auckland, New Zealand: Department of Psychology, University of Auckland.

Harris, A. (2001). Foreword. In Delgado, R. & Stefancic, J., *Critical Race Theory – An introduction*. (pp. xvii–xxi). New York: New York University Press.

Harrison, M. I. (2005). *Open systems models: Vol. 8. Diagnosing organizations: Methods, models, and processes* (3rd ed.) Thousand Oaks: SAGE Publications.

Harvey, D. (2007). Neoliberalism as creative destruction. *The ANNALS of the American Academy of Political and Social Science, 610*(1), 21–44.

Harvey, D. (2010). Organizing for the anti-capitalist transition. *Interface: A Journal for and about Social Movements, 2*(1), 243–61.

Haskell, R., & Burtch, B. (2010). *Get that freak: Homophobia and transphobia in high schools*. Winnipeg, MB: Fernwood Publishing.

Hatch, J. (2017, March 22). Gender pay gap persists across faculty ranks. *Chronicles of Higher Education*. Retrieved from www.chronicle.com/article/Gender-Pay-Gap-Persists-Across/239553?cid=wcontent list_6_listtop.

Hawe, P. (2017). The contribution of social ecological thinking to community psychology: Origins, practice, and research. In M. A. Bond, I. Serrano-García, & C. B. Keys (Eds.), *APA handbook of community psychology: Theoretical foundations, core concepts, and emerging challenges* (pp. 87–106). Washington, DC: American Psychological Association.

Hawe, P., & Riley, T. (2005). Ecological theory in practice: Illustrations from a community-based intervention to promote the health of recent mothers. *Prevention Science, 6*(3), 227–36.

Hawe, P., Shiell, A., & Riley, T. (2009). Theorising interventions as events in systems. American Journal of Community Psychology, 43(3–4), 267–76.

Hawken, P. (2007). *Blessed unrest*. New York: Viking.

Hayes, M. (2018, July 21). Black people more likely to be injured or killed by Toronto Police officers, report finds. *The Globe and Mail Toronto*. Retrieved from www.theglobeandmail.com/canada/toronto/article-report-reveals-racial-disparities-in-toronto-polices-use-of-force/?fbclid=IwAR1tdALKa20lR_6fEkPmdd8G xUrQHMZaJJ1hQa3SR3f-f-fezj4XWCporh0

Heck, N. C., Flentje, A., & Cochran, B. N. (2011). Offsetting risks: High school Gay-Straight Alliances and lesbian, gay, bisexual, and transgender (LGBT) youth. *School Psychology Quarterly, 26,* 161–74.

Heckman, J. J., Moon, S. H., Pinto, R., Savelyev, P. A., & Yavitz, A. (2010). The rate of return to the High/Scope Perry Preschool Program. *Journal of Public Economics, 94*(1–2), 114–28.

Heller, H. (2016). *The capitalist university: The transformations of higher education in the United States since 1945.* London: Pluto Press. Retrieved from http://search.ebscohost.com/login.aspx?direct=true&db=nlebk &AN=1375766&site=ehost-live

Heller, K. (1989). The return to community. *American Journal of Community Psychology, 17*(1), 1–15.

Heller, K., Price, R. H., Reinhartz, S., Riger, S., & Wandersman, A. (1984). *Psychology and community change: Challenges of the future* (2nd ed.). Homewood, AL: Dorsey.

Herbert, A. M. L., & Morrison, L. E. (2007). Practice of psychology in Aotearoa: A Maori perspective. In I. M. Evans, J. J. Rucklidge, & M. O'Driscoll, (Eds.), *Professional practice of psychology in Aotearoa New Zealand* (pp. 35–47). Wellington, New Zealand: The New Zealand Psychological Society.

Herek, G. M. (1990). The context of anti-gay violence: Notes on cultural and psychological heterosexism. *Journal of Interpersonal Violence, 5,* 316–33.

Hergenrather, K.C., & Rhodes, S.D. (2008). Community-based participatory research: Applications for research in health and disability. In T. Kroll (Ed.), *Focus on disability: Trends in research and application* (pp. 59–87). Hauppage, NY: Novascience.

Henderson, P. (2007). Introduction. In H. Butcher, S. Banks, P. Henderson, & J. Robertson (Eds.), *Critical community practice* (pp. 1–13). Bristol: Policy Press.

Herman, E., & Chomsky, N. (2002). *Manufacturing consent: The political economy of the mass media.* New York: Pantheon.

Hernandez, B., Keys, C., & Balcazar, F. (2000). Employer attitudes towards workers with disabilities and their ADA employment rights: A literature review. *Journal of Rehabilitation, 66*(4), 4–16.

Herrnstein, R. J., & Murray, C. A. (1994). *The bell curve: Intelligence and class structure in American life.* New York: Simon & Schuster.

Hertzman, C. (1999). Population health and human development. In D. P. Keating & C. Hertzman (Eds.), *Developmental health and the wealth of nations: Social, biological, and educational dynamics* (pp. 21–40). New York: Guilford Press.

Hickman, G., & Riemer, M., & the YLEC Collaborative (2016). A theory of engagement for fostering collective action in Youth Leading Environmental Change. *Ecopsychology, 8,* 167–173.

Hill Collins, P. (2000). *Black feminist thought: Knowledge, consciousness, and the politics of empowerment.* New York, NY: Routledge.

Hill Collins, P., & Bilge, S. (2016). *Intersectionality.* Cambridge, UK; Malden, MA: Polity Press.

Hill, D. B. (2002). Genderism, transphobia, and gender bashing: A framework for interpreting anti-transgender violence. *Understanding and dealing with violence: A multicultural approach, 4,* 113–37.

Hillery, G.A. (1955). Definitions of community: Areas of agreement. *Rural Sociology, 20,* 111–23.

Hillier, J. (2002). Presumptive planning. In A. T. Fisher, C. C. Sonn, & B. J. Bishop (Eds.), *Psychological sense of community: Research, applications, and implications* (pp. 43–67). Boston, MA: Springer.

Hilson, G. (2002). An overview of land use conflicts in mining communities. *Land Use Policy, 19,* 65–73.

Himmelman, A. T. (1996). On the theory and practice of transformational collaboration: From social service to social justice. In C. Huxham, (Ed.), *Creating collaborative advantage,* (pp. 19–43). London: SAGE Publications.

Hirsch, E. L. (1999). Sacrifice for the cause: Group processes, recruitment, and commitment in a student social movement. In J. Freeman & V. Johnson (Eds.), *Cycles of protest: Social movements since the sixties* (pp. 47–64). New York: Rowman & Littlefield.

Hirsch-Kreinsen, H., Jacobson, D., Laestadius, S., & Smith, K. H. (2005). Low and medium technology industries in the knowledge economy: The analytical issues. In H. Hirsch-Kreinsen, D. Jacobson, & S. Laestadius (Eds.), *Low-tech innovation in the knowledge economy* (pp. 11–30). Frankfurt: Peter Lang.

Ho, P.-S., Kroll, T., Kehn, M., & Pearson, K. (2007). Health and housing among low-income adults with disabilities. *Journal of Healthcare for the Poor and Underserved, 18,* 902–15.

Hodges, S., Ferreira, K., & Israel, N. (2012). "If we're going to change things, it has to be systemic" Systems change in children's mental health. *American Journal of Community Psychology, 49*(3–4), 526–37.

Hofmann, S., Heslop, M., Clacherty, G., & Kessy, F. (2008). *Salt, soap and shoes for school, evaluation report: The impact of pensions on the lives of older people and grandchildren in the KwaWazee Project in Tanzania's Kagera region*. London: HelpAge International.

Holland, K. (2007). A history of Chinese immigration in the United States and Canada. *The American Review of Canadian Studies, 37*(2),150–160.

Hollander, E., & Offerman, L. (1990). Power and leadership in organizations. *American Psychologist, 45,* 179–89.

Hollingshead, A. B., & Redlich, F. C. (1958). *Social class and mental illness: Community study*. Hoboken, NJ: John Wiley & Sons Inc.

Hollway, W. (1991). *Work psychology and organizational behaviour*. London: SAGE Publications.

Holman, P., Devane, T., & Cady, S. (2007). *The change handbook: Group methods for shaping the future* (2nd ed.). San Francisco: Berrett-Koehler Publishers.

Holzkamp, K. (1983). *Grundlegung der Psychologie* [Foundation of psychology]. Frankfurt, Germany: Campus.

Honneth, A. (1996). *The struggle for recognition: The moral grammar of social conflicts*. MIT Press.

Hooghe, M. (Ed.). (2003). *Generating social capital: Civil society and institutions in comparative perspective*. New York: Palgrave Macmillan.

Hook, D. (2007). *Foucault, psychology and the analytics of power*. London: Palgrave Macmillan.

Hook, D., Mkhize, N., Kiguwa, P., & Collins, A. (2004). *Critical psychology*. Lansdowne: UCT Press.

hooks, b. (2000a). *All about love: New visions*. New York: HarperCollins.

hooks, b. (2000b). *Feminism is for everybody: Passionate politics*. Cambridge, MA: South End Press.

hooks, b. (2000c). *Feminist theory: From margin to center*. Pluto Press.

Horne, L. (2015, March 12). Real human being. *The New Inquiry*. Retrieved from http://thenewinquiry.com/essays/real-human-being/

Hossay, P. (2006). *Unsustainable: A primer for global environmental and social justice*. New York: Zed Books.

House, J. S., Schoeni, R. F., Kaplan, G. A., & Pollack, H. (2008). The health effects of social and economic policy: The promise and challenge for research and policy (pp. 3–26). In Schoeni, R. F., House, J. S., Kaplan, G. A., & Pollack, H. (Eds.), *Making Americans healthier: Social and economic policy as health policy*. New York: Russell Sage Foundation.

House, T. C. (2018). *Grading the states: A report card on our nation's commitment to public schools*. Retrieved from http://schottfoundation.org/report/grading-the-states

Howard, M. C., & Hoffman, M. E. (2018). Variable-centered, person-centered, and person-specific approaches: Where theory meets the method. *Organizational Research Methods, 21*(4), 846–76.

Howitt, D., & Owusu-Bempah, J. (1994). *The racism of psychology: Time for a change*. London: Harvester and Wheatsheaf.

Huang, Y., Shen, C., & Contractor, N. S. (2013). Distance matters: Exploring proximity and homophily in virtual world networks. *Decision Support Systems, 55*, 969–77.

Hughes, M., Joslyn, A., Wojton, M., O'Reilly, M., & Dworkin, P. (2016). Connecting vulnerable children and families to community-based programs strengthens parents' perceptions of protective factors. *Infants & Young Children, 29*(2), 116–29.

Hughey, J., & Speer, P.W. (2002). Community, sense of community, and networks. In Fisher, A. T., Sonn, C. C., Bishop, B. J. (Eds.), *Psychological sense of community*. The Plenum Series in Social/Clinical Psychology. Boston, MA: Springer.

Hughey, J., Speer, P. W., & Peterson, N. A. (1999). Sense of community in community organizations: Structure and evidence of validity. *Journal of Community Psychology, 27*(1), 97–113.

Hultman, K., & Gellerman, B. (2002). *Balancing individual and organizational values*. San Francisco, CA: Jossey Bass/Pfeiffer.

Human Rights Campaign (2018). *A national epidemic: Fatal anti-trans violence in America in 2018*. Retrieved from https://assets2.hrc.org/files/assets/resources/AntiTransViolence-2018Report-Final.pdf?_ga=2.229204124.1645033069.1549386441-1290127058.1549386441

Humphrey, G. (1924). The psychology of the gestalt. *Journal of Educational Psychology. 15*(7), 401–12.

Humphreys, K., & Rappaport, J. (1994). Researching self-help/mutual aid groups and organizations: Many roads, one journey. *Applied and Preventive Psychology, 3*, 217–31.

Humphreys, K. (1997). Individual and social benefits of mutual aid self-help groups. *Social Policy, 27*, 12–19.

Hunter, E. (1997). Double talk: Changing and conflicting constructions of Indigenous mental health. Paper presented to The National Conference on Mental Health Services, Policy and Law Reform into the Twenty First Century. University of Newcastle, 14 February.

Husain, A., & Howard, S. (2017). Religious microaggressions: A case study of Muslim Americans. *Journal of Ethnic & Cultural Diversity in Social Work, 26*(1–2), 139–52.

Huygens, I. (1996a). *Anti-racism education: Example of a partnership protocol.* Project Waitangi, Aotearoa, New Zealand.

Huygens, I. (1996b). *Gender safety: Example of a partnership protocol.* Men's Action, Hamilton and Women's Refuges, Aotearoa, New Zealand.

Huygens, I. (2011). Developing a decolonisation practice for settler-colonisers: A case study from Aotearoa New Zealand. *Settler Colonial Studies, 1*(2), 53–81.

Huygens, I., & Nairn, R. (2016). Ethics and culture: Foundations of practice. In W. W. Waitoki, J. S. Feather, N. R. Robertson, & J. J. Rucklidge (Eds.), *Professional practice of psychology in Aotearoa New Zealand.* Wellington: New Zealand Psychological Society.

Hyman, J. B. (2002). Exploring social capital and civic engagement to create a framework for community building. *Applied Developmental Science, 6*(4), 196–202.

Iasi, M. (2011). *Ensaios sobre consciência e emancipação.* São Paulo: Expressão Popular.

Ife, J. (1997). *Rethinking social work: Towards critical practice.* South Melbourne, Australia: Longman.

Ife, J. (2002). *Community development: Community-based alternatives in an age of globalisation* (2nd ed.). Frenchs Forest, NSW: Pearson Education Australia.

Iftikhar, S., Khadim, Z., Munir, S., & Amir, H. (2018). Role of microfinance in women empowerment and alleviating poverty: An overview. *Journal of Social Economics, 4*(2), 48–53.

Ikebe, S. (2016, January 21). The wrong kind of UBI. *Jacobin.* Retrieved from https://www.jacobinmag.com/2016/01/universal-basic-income-switzerland-finland-milton-friedman-kathi-weeks/

INCITE! Women of Color against Violence (Eds.). (2007). *The revolution will not be funded: Beyond the non-profit industrial complex.* Cambridge, MA: South End Press.

Indigenous Peoples' Health Research Centre. (2004). The ethics of research involving Indigenous peoples. Retrieved from http://iphrc.ca/pub/documents/ethics_review_iphrc.pdf

Institute for Work & Health. (n.d.). *Knowledge transfer and exchange.* Retrieved from www.iwh.on.ca/knowledge-transfer-and-exchange

Institute of Medicine (IOM). (1994). *Reducing risks for mental disorders: Frontiers for preventive intervention research.* Washington, DC: National Academy Press.

Interagency Council on the Homeless. (1994). *Priority: Home! The federal plan to break the cycle of homelessness.* HUD-1454-CPD. Washington, DC: U.S. Department of Housing and Urban Development.

Inter-American Commission on Human Rights. (IACHR). (2014). *Overview of violence against LGBTI persons: A registry documenting acts of violence between January 1, 2013 and March 31, 2014.* Annex to Press Release No. 153/14. December 17, 2014. Retrieved from http://www.oas.org/en/iachr/lgtbi/docs/Annex-Registry-Violence-LGBTI.pdf

Intergovernmental Panel on Climate Change (IPCC). (2007). Climate change 2007: Impacts, adaptation and vulnerability. Contribution of Working Group II to the Fourth Assessment Report of the Intergovernmental Panel on Climate Change. M. L. Parry, O. F. Canziani, J. P. Palutikof, P. J. van der Linden, & C.E. Hanson (Eds.). Cambridge: Cambridge University Press.

Intergovernmental Panel on Climate Change (IPCC). (2014) *Climate Change 2014: Impacts, Adaptations, and Vulnerability.* Retrieved from http://ipcc-wg2.gov

Intergovernmental Panel on Climate Change, IPCC. (2018): *Global warming of 1.5°C. An IPCC Special Report on the impacts of global warming of 1.5°C above pre-industrial levels and related global greenhouse gas emission pathways, in the context of strengthening the global response to the threat of climate change, sustainable development, and efforts to eradicate poverty.* Retrieved from www.ipcc.ch

International Panel of Experts (2007). *Yogyakarta principles on the application of international human rights law in relation to sexual orientation and gender identity.* Retrieved from www.yogyakartaprinciples.org/principles_en.pdf

International Women's Development Agency (IWDA). (2006). The harmonisation of gender indicators. *IWDA News (Spring Issue)*, *68*, 3.

International Women's Development Agency (IWDA). (2008). Literacy: A window into the future for women. *IWDA News (Winter Issue)*, *73*, 1.

Iscoe, I., Bloom, B. L., & Spielberger, C. D. (1977). *Community psychology in transition*. Paper presented at the National Conference on Training in Community Psychology, Austin, TX.

Ivey, A.E., Ivey, M.B., & Simek-Morgan, L. (1993). *Counselling and psychotherapy: A multicultural perspective* (3rd ed.). Boston: Allyn and Bacon.

Iwata, N., Turner, R. J., & Lloyd, D. A. (2002). Race/ethnicity and depressive symptoms in community-dwelling young adults: A differential item functioning analysis. *Psychiatry Research*, *110*(3), 281–89.

Jackson, S. (2006). Gender, sexuality and heterosexuality: The complexity (and limits) of heteronormativity. *Feminist Theory*, *7*(1), 105–21.

Jacobson, N., & Greenley, D. (2001). What is recovery? A conceptual model and explication. *Psychiatric services*, *52*(4), 482–85.

Jahoda, M. (1983). The emergence of social psychology in Vienna: An exercise in long-term memory. *British Journal of Social Psychology*, *22*(4), 343–9.

James, A., & Prout, A. (1997). *Constructing and reconstructing childhood: Contemporary issues in the sociological study of childhood*. London/Washington DC: Falmer Press.

James, C. E. (2001). Multiculturalism, diversity, and education in the Canadian context. The search for an inclusive pedagogy. In C. A. Grant & J. L. Lei (Eds.), *Global constructions of multicultural education: Theories and realities* (pp. 175–204). Mahwah, NJ: Lawrence Erlbaum.

James, C.E. (2012). Students "at risk": Stereotyping and the schooling of Black boys. *Urban Education*, *47*(2), 464–94.

Janzen, R., Nelson, G., Hausfather, N., & Ochocka, J. (2007). Capturing system level activities and impacts of mental health consumer-run organizations. *American Journal of Community Psychology*, *39*(3–4), 287–99.

Janzen, R., Nguyen, N., Stobbe, A., & Araujo, L. (2015). Assessing the value of inductive and deductive outcome measures in community-based organizations: Lessons from the City Kidz evaluation. *Canadian Journal of Program Evaluation*. *30*(1), 41–63.

Janzen, R., & Ochocka, J. (under review). Assessing research with Syrian refugee newcomers through a Community-Based Research Excellence Tool. Submitted to *Cultural Diversity and Ethnic Minority Psychology*. Special issue on collaborative and participatory research to promote engagement, empowerment, and resilience for immigrant and refugee youth, families, and communities.

Janzen, R., Ochocka, J., & Stobbe, A. (2016). Towards a theory of change for community-based research projects. *Engaged Scholar Journal: Community-Engaged Research, Teaching, and Learning*, *2*(2), 44–64.

Janzen, R., Ochocka, J., Turner, L., Cook, T., Franklin, M., & Deichert, D. (2017). Building a community-based culture of evaluation. *Evaluation and Program Planning*. *65*, 163–70.

Janzen, R., Seskar-Hencic, D., Dildar, Y., & McFadden, P. (2012). Using evaluation to shape and direct comprehensive community initiatives: Evaluation, reflective practice, and interventions dealing with complexity. *Canadian Journal of Program Evaluation*. *25*(2), 61–88.

Janzen, R., Walton-Roberts, M., & Ochocka, J. (2012). Waterloo region. In C. Andrew, J. Biles, M. Burstein, V.M. Esses, & E. Tolley (Eds.), *Immigration, integration and inclusion in Ontario Cities*. (pp.131–57). Montreal, PQ and Kingston, ON: McGill-Queen's University Press.

Jason, L. (2013). *Principles of social change*. Oxford; New York: Oxford University Press.

Jason, L. A., & Glenwick, D. S. (Eds.). (2016). *Handbook of methodological approaches to community-based research: Qualitative, quantitative, and mixed methods*. New York: Oxford University Press.

Jason, L. A., Keys, C. B., Suarez-Balcazar, Y., Taylor, R. R., & Davis, M. I. (Eds.). (2004). *APA decade of behavior. Vols. Participatory community research: Theories and methods in action*. Washington, DC, US: American Psychological Association.

Jason, L. A., Light, J. M., Stevens, E. B., & Beers, K. (2014). Dynamic social networks in recovery homes. *American Journal of Community Psychology*, *53*(3–4), 324–34.

Jenkins, J. C. (1999). The transformation of a constituency into a social movement revisited. In J. Freeman & V. Johnson (Eds.), *Cycles of protest: Social movements since the sixties* (pp. 277–302). New York: Rowman & Littlefield.

Jennings, J. (2007). Social capital, race, and the future of inner-city neighborhoods. In J. Jennings (Ed.), *Race, neighborhoods, and the misuse of social capital* (pp. 87–108). New York: Palgrave Macmillan.

Jervis, R. (2018, March 23). "I sit and cry all day": Suicide hotline calls double in Puerto Rico 6 months after Hurricane Maria. *USA Today*. Retrieved from www.usatoday.com/story/news/2018/03/23/mental-health-crisis-puerto-rico-hurricane-maria/447144002/

Ji, P., Haehnel, A. A., Muñoz, D. N., & Sodolka, J. (2013). The effectiveness of using new instructors to teach an LGBTQ ally development course. *Journal of Prevention & Intervention in the Community, 41*(4), 267–78.

Joffe, J. (1996). Looking for the causes of the causes. *Journal of Primary Prevention, 17*, 201–7.

Joffe, J. M., & Albee, G. W. (1988). Powerlessness and psychopathology. In G. W. Albee, J. M. Joffe, & L. A. Dusenbury (Eds.), *Prevention, powerlessness, and politics: Readings on social change* (pp. 53–6). Beverly Hills, CA: SAGE Publications.

Johnson, D., & Johnson, F. (2000). *Joining together: Group theory and group skills*. London, England: Allyn and Bacon.

Johnson, D., & Gastic, B. (2015). Natural mentoring in the lives of sexual minority youth. *Journal of Community Psychology, 43*(4), 395–407.

Johnson, G., Parkinson, S., & Parsell, C. (2012). Policy shift or program drift? Implementing Housing First in Australia. AHURI Final Report No. 184. Melbourne: Australian Housing and Urban Research Institute.

Johnson, J. (2019, August 5). *If inequality continues to grow at current rate, richest Americans will own 100% of US wealth in 33 years: Analysis. Common Dreams.* Retrieved from www.commondreams.org/news/2019/08/05/if-inequality-continues-grow-current-rate-richest-americans-will-own-100-us-wealth

Johnson, R. B., & Onwuegbuzie, A. J. (2004). Mixed methods research: A research paradigm whose time has come. *Educational Researcher, 33*(7), 14–26.

Johnson, R. C., & Raphael, S. (2009). The effects of male incarceration dynamics on acquired immune deficiency syndrome infection rates among African American women and men. *Journal of Law and Economics, 52*(2), 251–93.

Johnson-Hakim, S., & Boal, A. (2017). Putting your training to work: Finding a practice job. In J. J. Viola & O. Glantsman (Eds.), *Diverse careers in community psychology* (pp. 101–114). New York: Oxford University Press.

Jones, C. W., & Unger, D. G. (2000). Diverse adaptations of single parent, low-income families with young children: Implications for community-based prevention and intervention. *Journal of Prevention & Intervention in the Community, 20*, 5–23.

Jones, J. (1997). *Prejudice and racism* (2nd ed.). New York: McGraw-Hill.

Jordan, J., Kaplan, A., Miller, J. B., Stiver, I., & Surrey, J. (1991). *Women's growth in connection: Writings from the Stone Center*. New York: Guilford Press.

Joseph Rowntree Foundation, (2018, September 6). *How could Brexit affect poverty in the UK?* Retrieved from www.jrf.org.uk/report/how-could-brexit-affect-poverty-uk

Josephson, G., & Wright, A. (2000). *Ottawa GLBT wellness project: Literature review and survey instruments*. Retrieved from www.pinktriangle.org/wellness/main.html

Jost, J., & Major, B. (Eds.). (2001). *The psychology of legitimacy: Emerging perspectives on ideology, justice, and intergroup relations*. New York: Cambridge University Press.

Jost, J. T., & Banaji, M. R. (1994). The role of stereotyping in system-justification and the production of false consciousness. *British Journal of Social Psychology, 33*, 1–27.

Joyce, A., Wolfaardt, U., Sribney, C., & Aylwin, A. (2006). Psychotherapy research at the start of the 21st century: The persistence of the art versus science controversy. *Canadian Journal of Psychiatry, 51*, 797–809.

Kagan, C. (2007). Working at the "edge": Making use of psychological resources through collaboration. *The Psychologist, 20*(4), 224–7.

Kagan, C., & Burton, M. (2010). Marginalization. In G. Nelson & I. Prilleltensky, (Eds.), *Community psychology: In pursuit of liberation and well-being* (pp. 313–29). London: Red Globe Press.

Kagan, C., Burton, M., Duckett, P., Lawthom, R., & Siddiquee, A. (2011). *Critical community psychology*. Chichester, West Sussex: BPS Blackwell.

Kahn, S. (1982). *Organizing*. Toronto: McGraw Hill.

Kamya, H. (2007). Narrative practice and culture. In E. Aldarondo (Ed.), *Advancing social justice through clinical practice* (pp. 207–22). London: Lawrence Erlbaum.

Kanacri, B., González, R., Valdenegro, D., Jiménez-Moya, G., Saavedra, P., Andrés Mora, E., ... Pastorelli, C. (2016). Civic engagement and giving behaviors: The role of empathy and beliefs about poverty. *Journal of Social Psychology, 156*(3), 256–71.

Kaner, S. (2014). *Facilitator's guide to participatory decision-making* (3rd ed.). San Francisco, CA: Jossey-Bass.

Kangas, O., Jauhiainen, S., Simanainen, M., & Ylikännö, M. (2019). *The basic income experiment 2017–2018 in Finland Preliminary results* (No. 9). Helsinki: Ministry of Social Affairs and Health.

Kania, J., Hanleybrown, F., & Juster, J. S. (2014). Collective insights on collective impact. In *Collective insights on collective impact, 12*(4), 2–5. Retrieved from www.ssireview.org/supplement/collective_insights_on_collective_impact

Kania, J., & Kramer, M. (2011). Collective Impact. *Stanford Social Innovation Review, Winter 2011,* 36–41.

Kania, J., & Kramer, M. (2015, October). The equity imperative in Collective Impact. *Stanford Social Innovation Review.* Retrieved from https://ssir.org/equity_and_collective_impact/entry/the_equity_imperative_in_collective_impact

Kaniasty, K., & Norris, F. (1995). In search of altruistic community: Patterns of social support mobilization following Hurricane Hugo. *American Journal of Community Psychology, 23,* 447–77.

Kaniasty, K., & Norris, F. (2004). Social support in the aftermath of disasters, catastrophes, acts of terrorism: Altruistic, over-whelmed, uncertain, antagonistic, and patriotic communities. In R. Ursano, A. Norwood, & C. Fullerton (Eds.), *Bioterrorism: Psychological and public health interventions* (pp. 200–29). New York: Cambridge University Press.

Kannan, K. (2000). Poverty alleviation as advancing basic human capabilities: Kerala's achievements compared. In G. Parayil (Ed.), *Kerala: The development experience* (pp. 40–65). New York: Zed Books.

Kaplan, G., Pamuk, E., Lynch, J., Cohen, R., & Balfour, J. (1996). Inequality in income and mortality in the United States: Analysis of mortality and potential pathways. *British Medical Journal, 312,* 999–1003.

Kaplan, G.A., Ranjit, N., & Burgard, S. (2008). Lifting gates – lengthening lives: Did civil rights policies improve the health of African-American women in the 1960s and 1970s? In R. F. Schoeni, J. S. House, G.A. Kaplan, & H. Pollack (Eds.), Making Americans healthier: Social and economic policy as health policy. (pp. 145–69). New York: Russell Sage Foundation Publications.

Karam, N. (2012). *The 9/11 backlash: A decade of U.S. hate crimes targeting the innocent.* Berkeley, CA: Beatitude Press.

Katsiaficas, G. (1997). *The subversion of politics: European autonomous social movements and the decolonisation of everyday life.* Amherst, NY: Humanity Books.

Keating, D., & Hertzman, C. (1999). Modernity's paradox. In D. Keating & C. Hertzman (Eds.), *Developmental health and the wealth of nations* (pp. 1–17). New York: Guilford.

Kegan, R., & Lahey, L. (2016). *An everyone culture: Becoming a deliberately developmental organization.* Cambridge, MA: Harvard Business School Press.

Kellam, S. G. (2012). Developing and maintaining partnerships as the foundation of implementation and implementation science: Reflections over a half century. *Administration and Policy in Mental Health and Mental Health Services Research, 39,* 317–20.

Keller, C., Goering, P., Hume, C., Macnaughton, E., O'Campo, P., Sarang, A., ..., Tsemberis, S. (2013). Initial implementation of Housing First in five Canadian cities: How do you make the shoe fit, when one size does not fit all? *American Journal of Psychiatric Rehabilitation, 16*(4), 275–89.

Kelley, C. P., Mohtadi, S., Cane, M. A., Seager, R., & Kushnir, Y. (2015). Climate change in the Fertile Crescent and implications of the recent Syrian drought. *Proceedings of the National Academy of Sciences, 112*(11), 3241–6.

Kelly, J. G. (1966). Ecological constraints on mental health services. *American Psychologist, 21,* 535–9.

Kelly, J. G. (1971). Qualities for the community psychologist. *American Psychologist, 26,* 897–903.

Kelly, J. G. (1986). An ecological paradigm: Defining mental health consultation as preventive service. *Prevention in Human Services, 4*(3–4), 1–36.

Kemmis, S. (2008). Critical theory and participatory action research. In P. Reason & H. Bradbury (Eds.), *The SAGE handbook of action research: Participative inquiry and practice* (pp. 121–38). Thousand Oaks, CA: Sage.

Kennedy, B., Kawachi, I., & Prothrow-Stith, D. (1996). Income distribution and mortality: Cross sectional ecological study of the Robin Hood Index in the United States. *British Medical Journal, 312,* 1004–7.

Kennedy, S., & McDonald, J.T. (2006). Immigrant mental health and unemployment. *Economic Record, 82*(259), 445–59.

Kesten, S. M., Perez, D. A., Marques, D. S., Evans, S. D., & Sulma, A. (2017). Fight, flight, or remain silent? Juggling multiple accountabilities throughout the formative stage of a neighborhood revitalization initiative. *American Journal of Community Psychology, 60*(3–4), 450–58.

Keuroghlian, A. S., Shtasel, D., & Bassuk, E. L. (2014). Out on the street: A public health and policy agenda for lesbian, gay, bisexual, and transgender youth who are homeless. *American Journal of Orthopsychiatry, 84*(1), 66.

Khasnabish, A., & Haiven, M. (2012). Convoking the radical imagination: Social movement research, dialogic methodologies, and scholarly cocations.*Cultural Studies ←→ Critical Methodologies, 12*(5), 408–21.

Kidd, D., & McIntosh, K. (2016). Social media and social movements. *Sociology Compass, 10*(9), 785–94.

Kidd, S., Davidson, L., Frederick, T., & Kral, M. J. (2018). Reflecting on participatory, action-oriented research methods in community psychology: Progress, problems, and paths forward. *American Journal of Community Psychology, 61*(1–2), 76–87.

Kidder, L. H., & Fine, M. (1986). Making sense of injustice. Social explanations, social action and the role of the social scientist. In E. Seidman & J. Rappaport (Eds.), *Redefining social problems* (pp. 49–61). New York: Plenum Press.

Kiesler, C. A. (1992). U.S. mental health policy: Doomed to fail. *American Psychologist, 47*, 1077–82.

Kilmer, R.P., Cook, J.R., Crusto, C., Strater, K.P., & Haber, M.G. (2012). Understanding the ecology and development of children and families experiencing homelessness: Implications for practice, supportive services, and policy. *American Journal of Orthopsychiatry, 82*(3), 389–401.

Kim, J., & Bryan, J. (2017). A first step to a conceptual framework of parent empowerment: Exploring relationships between parent empowerment and academic performance in a national sample. *Journal of Counseling and Development, 95*, 168–79.

Kim, J., Ferrari, G., Abramsky, T., Watts, C., Hargreaves, J., Morison, L., & Pronyk, P. (2009). Assessing the incremental effects of combining economic and health interventions: The IMAGE study in South Africa. *Bulletin of the World Health Organization, 87*, 824–32.

Kimble, M. (2018, November). Austin's fix for homelessness: Tiny houses, and lots of neighbors. *CityLab.* Retrieved from www.citylab.com/design/2018/11/community-first-village-homeless-tiny-homes-austin-texas/575611/

King, D. K. (1988). Multiple jeopardy, multiple consciousnesses: The context of a Black feminist ideology. *Signs, 14*, 42–72.

King Jr., M.L. (1963). Letter from a Birmingham Jail. Martin Luther King , Jr., Research and Education Institute. Retrieved from https://kinginstitute.stanford.edu/king-papers/documents/letter-birmingham-jail

Kingsley, P. (2018, November 16). British austerity is "inflicting unnecessary misery," U.N. poverty expert says. *The New York Times.* Retrieved from www.nytimes.com/2018/11/16/world/europe/uk-un-poverty-austerity.html

Kirkby-Geddes, E., King, N., & Bravington, A. (2013). Social capital and community group participation: Examining "bridging" and "bonding" in the context of a healthy living centre in the UK: Social capital and community group participation. *Journal of Community & Applied Social Psychology, 23*(4), 271–85.

Kirst, M., Altenberg, J., & Balian, R. (2011). In search of empowering health research for marginalized populations in urban settings: The value of a transdisciplinary approach. In: M. Kirst, N. Schaefer-McDaniel, S. Hwang, & P. O'Campo (Eds.), *Converging disciplines.* New York: Springer.

Kirst, M., Lazgare, L. P., Zhang, Y. J., & O'Campo, P. (2015). The effects of social capital and neighborhood characteristics on intimate partner violence: A consideration of social resources and risks. *American Journal of Community Psychology, 55*(3–4), 314–25.

Kirton, J.D. (1997). *Paakeha/Tauiwi: Seeing the unseen: Critical analysis of links between discourse, identity, "blindness" and encultured racism.* Kirikiriroa/ Hamilton: Waikato Antiracism Coalition.

Kitzinger, C. (2005). Heteronormativity in action: Reproducing the heterosexual nuclear family in after-hours medical calls. *Social problems, 52*(4), 477–98.

Kivel, P. (2007). Social service or social change? In INCITE! Women of Color Against Violence (Eds.), *The revolution will not be funded: Beyond the non-profit industrial complex* (pp. 129–50). Cambridge, MA: South End Press.

Kivell, N. (2016). *What makes transformation transformative? Developing a theoretical framework to draw a line in the sand.* Unpublished manuscript, University of Miami, Florida.

Kivell, N., Evans, S., & Paterson, S. (2017). Community power structure analysis and the ethical considerations of "studying up". *American Journal of Community Psychology, 60*(3–4), 467–75.

Kivunja, C., & Kuyini, A. B. (2017). Understanding and applying research paradigms in educational contexts. *International Journal of Higher Education, 6*(5), 26.

Klein, K., Holtby, A., Cook, K., & Travers, R. (2015). Complicating the coming out narrative: Becoming oneself in a heterosexist and cissexist world. *Journal of Homosexuality, 62,* 297–326.

Klein, K., Ralls, R. S., Smith Major, V., & Douglas, C. (2000). Power and participation in the workplace: Implications for empowerment theory, research, and practice. In J. Rappaport & E. Seidman (Eds.), *Handbook of community psychology* (pp. 273–95). New York: Klewer Academic/Plenum.

Klein, K., & Riemer, M. (2011). Experiences of environmental justice and injustice in communities of people experiencing homelessness. *Ecopsychology, 3*(3), 195–204.

Klein, N. (2007). *The shock doctrine: The rise of disaster capitalism.* New York: Metropolitan.

Klein, N. (2015). *This changes everything: Capitalism vs. the climate.* Simon and Schuster.

Klein, N. (2018). *The battle for paradise: Puerto Rico takes on the disaster capitalists.* Chicago, IL: Haymarket Books.

Kloos, B. (2010). Creating new possibilities for promoting liberation, well-being, and recovery: Learning from experiences of psychiatric consumers/survivors. In G. Nelson & I. Prilleltensky (Eds.), *Community psychology: In pursuit of well-being and liberation* (2nd ed., pp. 453–76). London: Red Globe Press.

Kloos, B., Hill, J., Thomas, E., Wandersman, A., Elias, M. J., & Dalton, J. H. (2012). *Community psychology: Linking individuals and communities* (3rd ed.). Belmont, CA: Wadsworth Thomas Learning.

Knapp, M. R. J., McDaid, D., & Parsonage, M. (Eds.). (2011). *Mental health promotion and mental illness prevention: The economic case.* London: Department of Health.

Knoke, D., & Wood, J. (1981). *Organized for action: Commitment in voluntary associations.* New Brunswick, NJ: Rutgers University Press.

Knudsen, S. V. (2006). Intersectionality – A theoretical inspiration in the analysis of minority cultures and identities in textbooks. *Caught in the Web or Lost in the Textbook, 53,* 61–76.

Koch, M. (2011). *Capitalism and climate change: Theoretical discussion, historical development and policy responses.* New York: Springer.

Koger, S. M., & Du Nann Winter, D. (2010). *The psychology of environmental problems* (3rd ed.). New York: Psychology Press.

Konstantopolous, S., & Borman, G. (2011). Family background and school effects on student achievement: A multilevel analysis of the Coleman data, *Teachers College Record, 113*(1), 97–132.

Korbin, J. E., & Coulton, C. J. (1996). The role of neighbors and the government in neighborhood-based child protection. *Journal of Social Issues, 52,* 163–76.

Korstanje, M. E. (2014). Community-based disaster risk reduction. *International Journal of Disaster Resilience in the Built Environment, 5*(2), 213–16.

Korten, D. (2001). *When corporations rule the world.* West Hartford, CT: Kumarian Press.

Korten, D. C. (2015). *When corporations rule the world* (3rd ed). Oakland, CA: Berrett-Koehler Publishers.

Kosciw, J. G., Palmer, N. A., & Kull, R. M. (2015). Reflecting resiliency: Openness about sexual orientation and/or gender identity and its relationship to well-being and educational outcomes for LGBTQ students. *American Journal of Community Psychology, 55*(1–2), 167–78.

Kovach, M. (2010). Conversation method in Indigenous research. *First Peoples Child & Family Review, 5*(1), 40–8.

Kovach, M. (2017). Doing Indigenous methodologies – A letter to a research class. In N. Denzin & Y.S. Lincoln (Eds.), *The SAGE handbook of qualitative research* (5th ed., pp. 214–32). Los Angeles: SAGE Publications.

Kovel, J. (2007). *The enemy of nature: The end of capitalism or the end of the world?* London: Zed Books.

Kral, M. J., & Allen, J. (2016). Community-based participatory action research. In L. A. Jason & D. S. Glenwick (Eds.), *Handbook of methodological approaches to community-based research: Qualitative, quantitative, and mixed methods.* New York: Oxford University Press.

Krause, M., & Montenegro, C. R. (2017). Community as a multifaceted concept. In M. A. Bond, I. Serrano-García, & C. B. Keys (Eds.), *APA handbook of community psychology: Theoretical foundations, core concepts, and emerging challenges* (pp. 107–28). Washington, DC: American Psychological Association.

Kraut, R. (2007). *What is good and why: The ethics of well-being.* Cambridge, MA: Harvard University Press.

Krebs, P., Norcross, J., Nicholson, J., & Prochaska, J. (2018). States of change and psychotherapy outcomes: A review and meta-analysis. *Journal of Clinical Psychology, 74*, 1964–79.

Kretzmann, J. P., & McKnight, J. L. (1993). *Building communities from the inside out: A path toward findings and mobilizing a community's assets*. Chicago, IL: ACTA Publications.

Kubisch, A. C., Auspos, P., Brown, P., & Dewar, T. (2010). *Voices from the field III: Lessons and challenges from two decades of community change efforts*. Washington, DC: Aspen Institute.

Kuhn, T. (1962). *The structure of scientific revolutions*. Chicago, IL: University of Chicago Press.

Kuhn, R., & Culhane, D. P. (1998). Applying cluster analysis to test a typology of homelessness by pattern of shelter utilization: Results from the analysis of administrative data. *American Journal of Community Psychology, 26*(2), 207–32.

Kunreuther, F. (2002). Building movement into the nonprofit sector: Phase II. Retrieved from http:// www. buildingmovement.org/work/index.html

Kunruether, F., & Bartow, F. (2010). Catalysts for change: How California nonprofits can deliver direct services and transform communities (Part 2). Retrieved from http://buildingmovement.org/pdf/catalysts_part_two. pdf

Kunreuther, F., & Thomas-Breitfeld, S. (2015*)*. The new now. Retrieved from www.buildingmovement.org/?/ reports/entry/the_new_now_working_together_for_social_change

Labonte, R. (1994). Death of a program: Birth of a metaphor. In I. Rootman (Ed.), *Health promotion in Canada: Provincial, national and international perspectives*. Toronto, ON, Canada: Saunders.

Lacerda Jr., F. (2010). Notas sobre o desenvolvimento da psicologia social comunitária. In F. Lacerda Jr. & R. S. L. Guzzo (Eds.), *Psicologia e sociedade: Interfaces no debate sobre a questão social*, (pp. 19–41). Campinas: Alínea.

Lacerda Jr., F. (2013). Critical psychology in Brazil: A sketch of its history between the end of the 20th century and the early 21st century. *Annual Review of Critical Psychology, 10*, 110–49.

Lacerenza, C.N., Marlow, S.L., Tannenbaum, S.I., & Salas, E. (2018). Team development interventions: Evidence-based approaches for improving teamwork. *American Psychologist, 73*(4), 517–531.

Ladson-Billings, G. (1998). Just what is Critical Race Theory and what's it doing in a nice field like education? *The International Journal of Qualitative Studies in Education,11*(1), 49–64.

Lamble, S. (2008). Retelling racialized violence, remaking white innocence: The politics of interlocking oppressions in transgender day of remembrance. *Sexuality Research & Social Policy, 5*(1), 24–42.

Landry, R., Amara, N., & Lamari, M. (2001). Climbing the ladder of research utilization: Evidence from social science research. *Science Communication, 22*(4), 396–422.

Lane, S. T. M. (1996). Histórico e fundamentos da psicologia comunitária no Brasil. In R. H. de F. Campos (Ed.), *Psicologia social comunitária: Da solidariedade à autonomia* (pp. 17–34). Petrópolis: Vozes.

Langhout, R. D. (2015). Considering community psychology competencies: A love letter to budding scholar-activists who wonder if they have what it takes. *American Journal of Community Psychology, 55*(3–4), 266–78.

Langhout, R. D. (2016). This is not a history lesson; This is agitation: A call for a methodology of diffraction in US-based community psychology. *American Journal of Community Psychology, 58*(3–4), 322–8.

Langhout, R.D., Collins, C., & Ellison, E.R. (2014). Examining relational empowerment for elementary school students in a yPAR program. *American Journal of Community Psychology, 53*(3–4), 369–81.

Lawlor, J.A., & Neal, Z.P. (2016). Networked community change: Understanding community systems change through the lens of social network analysis. *American Journal of Community Psychology, 57*(3–4), 426–36.

Lawthom, R. (1999). Using the 'F' word in organizational psychology: Foundations for critical feminist research. *Annual Review of Critical Psychology, 1*, 67–82.

Lauffer, D.A. (2010). *Understanding your social agency* (3rd ed.). SAGE Publications.

Le, V. (2015). Why communities of color are getting frustrated with collective impact. Retrieved from https://nonprofitwithballs.com/2015/11/why-communities-of-color-are-getting-frustrated-with-collective-impact/

Leber, B. (2017). *Police-reported hate crime in Canada, 2015*. Statistics Canada. Retrieved from https:// www150.statcan.gc.ca/n1/pub/85-002-x/2017001/article/14832-eng.pdf

Leonard, P. (1997). *Postmodern welfare: Reconstructing an emancipatory project*. London: SAGE Publications.

Lerner, M. (1996). *The politics of meaning*. New York: Addison-Wesley.

Levine, M., & Levine, A. (1992). *Helping children: A social history*. Oxford University Press.

Levine, M., Perkins, D.D., & Perkins, D.V. (2005). *Principles of community psychology: Perspectives and applications* (3rd ed.). Oxford: Oxford University Press.

Levine, M., & Perkins, D.V. (1997). *Principles of community Psychology*. New York: Oxford University Press.

Levy, C.W. (1988). *A people's history of the independent living movement*. Lawrence, KS: Research and Training Center on Independent Living.

Levy, M. (2007). *Indigenous psychology in Aotearoa: Realising Māori Aspirations*. Hamilton, New Zealand: University of Waikato.

Lewin, K. (1946). Action research and minority problems. *Journal of Social Issues, 2*(4), 34–46.

Lexico (n.d.). Research. Retrieved from: https://www.lexico.com/en/definition/research

Lincoln, Y., Lynham, S., & Guba, E.G. (2017). Paradigmatic controversies, contradictions, and emerging confluences, revisited. In N. K. Denzin & Y. S. Lincoln (Eds.), *The SAGE handbook of qualitative research* (5th ed., pp. 108–50). Thousand Oaks: CA, SAGE Publications.

Linhorst, D. (2006). *Empowering people with severe mental illness*. Oxford: Oxford University Press.

Linney, J.A. (2000). Assessing ecological constructs and community context. In J. Rappaport & E. Seidman (Eds.), *Handbook of community psychology* (pp. 647–68). New York: Kluwer Academic/Plenum Publishers.

Lipset, S.M. (1996). *American exceptionalism: A double-edged sword*. New York: Norton.

Lofters, A., Slater, M., Kirst, M., Shankardass, K., & Quiñonez, C. (2014). How do people attribute income-related inequalities in health? A cross-sectional study in Ontario, Canada. *PLoS One, 9*(1).

Long, D.A., & Perkins, D.D. (2007). Community social and place predictors of sense of community: A multi-level and longitudinal analysis. *Journal of Community Psychology, 35*(5), 563–81.

Long, J., Harré, N., & Atkinson, Q.D. (2014). Understanding change in recycling and littering behavior across a school social network. *American Journal of Community Psychology, 53*(3–4), 462–74.

Longman Marcellin, R., Scheim, A., Bauer, G., & Redman, N. (2013). Experiences of racism among trans people in Ontario. *Trans PULSE e-Bulletin 7*.

Lord, J., & Church, K. (1998). Beyond "partnership shock": Getting to "yes," living with "no". *Canadian Journal of Rehabilitation, 12*, 113–21.

Lord, J., & Hutchison, P. (2007). *Pathways to inclusion: Building a new story with people and communities*. Concord, ON: Captus Press Inc.

Lorion, R.P., Iscoe, I., DeLeon, P.H., & VandenBos, G. R. (Eds.). (1996). *Psychology and public policy: Balancing public service and professional need*. Washington, DC: American Psychological Association.

Louzao, J. (2014). *Someday we'll be ready and we'll be enough: Building anti-authoritarian movements with the size and resilience to win*. Retrieved from https://mutualinspirationdotorg.files.wordpress.com/2014/09/somedaywellbereadyregular.pdf

Luce, S. (2012). Living wage policies and campaigns: Lessons from the United States. *International Journal of Labour Research, 4*(1), 11.

Luke, D.A. (2005). Getting the big picture in community science: Methods that capture context. *American Journal of Community Psychology, 35* (3–4), 185–200.

Lukes, S. (1974). *Power: A radical view*. London: Macmillan Press, Ltd.

Luthar, S.S., Sawyer, J. A., & Brown, P. J. (2006). Conceptual issues in studies of resilience. *Annals of the New York Academy of Sciences, 1094*(1), 105–15.

Lykes, M.B. (2017). Community-based and participatory action research: Community psychology collaborations within and across borders. In M. A. Bond, I. Serrano-García, C. B. Keys, & M. Shinn (Eds.), *APA handbook of community psychology: Methods for community research and action for diverse groups and issues* (pp. 43–58). Washington, DC: American Psychological Association.

Mack, L. (2005). *Human rights, LGBT movements and identity: An analysis of international and South African LGBT websites*. (Master's Thesis). Retrieved from OhioLINK Electronic Theses & Dissertations Center (Document number: ohiou1125527098).

MacLeod, J., & Nelson, G. (2000). Programs for the promotion of family wellness and the prevention of child maltreatment: A meta-analytic review. *Child Abuse and Neglect, 24*, 1127–49.

MacLeod, T. (2014). The Capabilities Approach, transformative measurement, and Housing First. *Global Journal of Community Psychology Practice, 5*(1), 1–10.

Macnaughton, E., Nelson, G., Goering, P., & Piat, M. (2016). The At Home/ Chez Soi Project: Moving evidence into policy. Available from the Mental Health Commission of Canada at www.mentalhealthcommission.ca

Macnaughton, E., Stefancic, A., Nelson, G., Caplan, R., Townley, G., Aubry, T., et al. (2015). Implementing Housing First across sites and over time: Later fidelity and implementation evaluation of a pan-Canadian multi-site Housing First program for homeless people with mental illness. *American Journal of Community Psychology, 55*(3–4), 279–91.

MacNeil, A.J., Prater, D.L., & Busch, S. (2009). The effects of school culture and climate on student achievement. *International Journal of Leadership in Education, 12*(1), 73–84.

Madara, E.J. (1990). Maximizing the potential for community self-help through clearinghouse approaches. *Prevention in Human Services, 7*, 109–38.

Madyaningrum, M.E., & Sonn, C. (2011). Exploring the meaning of participation in a community art project: A case study on the Seeming project. *Journal of Community & Applied Social Psychology, 21*(4), 358–70.

Mahon, R. (2008). Varieties of liberalism: Canadian social policy from the "golden age" to the present. *Social Policy & Administration, 42*(4), 342–361.

Maisel, J. (2006). Toward inclusive housing and neighborhood design: A look at Visitability. *Community Development: Journal of the Community Development Society, 37*(3), 26–34.

Manning, C. (2015). Same sex marriage is not equality, LGBT movement must continue. Retrieved from www.popularresistance.org/same-sex-marriage-is-not-equality-lgbt-movement-must-continue/

Marek, T., Schaufeli, W.B., & Maslach, C. (2017). *Professional burnout: Recent developments in theory and research*. New York: Routledge.

Markowitz, F.E. (2015). Involvement in mental health self-help groups and recovery. *Health Sociology Review, 24*(2), 199–212.

Marmot, M. (2015a). *The health gap: The challenge of an unequal world*. New York: Bloomsbury.

Marmot, M. (2015b). The health gap: The challenge of an unequal world. *Lancet* 386: 2442–4.

Marmot, M., & Allen, J. (2014). Social determinants of health equity. *American Journal of Public Health* 104 (S4): S517–19.

Marmot, M., & Wilkinson, R. (Eds.). (1999). *Social determinants of health*. New York: Oxford University Press.

Marmot, M., & Wilkinson, R. (Eds.). (2005). *Social determinants of health*. 2nd ed. London: Oxford University Press.

Marsella, A. (1998). Toward a "global-community psychology": Meeting the needs of a changing world. *American Psychologist, 53* (12): 1282–1291.

Marsick, V. J. (2000). From the learning organization to learning communities: Toward a learning society. Information Series No. 382. Columbus, OH: ERIC Clearinghouse on Adult, Career, and Vocational Education.

Martin, R. (2007). *The opposable mind*. Cambridge, MA: Harvard Business School Press.

Martín-Baró, I. (1986/1996). Toward a liberation psychology (A. Aron, Trans.). In A. Aron & S. Corne (Eds.), *Writings for a liberation psychology* (2nd ed., pp. 17–32). Cambridge: Harvard University Press.

Martín-Baró, I. (1980/2015). El papel del psicólogo en un proceso revolucionaio. *Teoría y Crítica de la Psicología* 6: 487–90.

Marvakis, A. (2011). La psicología (crítica) permanentemente en la encrucijada: Sirvientes del poder y herramientas para la emancipación. *Teoría y Crítica de la Psicología* 1, 122–130.

Marxuach, S. (2018, April 29). The social costs of the fiscal plan: Analysis by the Center for a New Economy. Noticel. Retrieved from www.noticel.com/opiniones/blogs/cne/the-social-cost-of-the-fiscal-plan/736222303

Masten, A.S. (2001). Ordinary magic: Resilience processes in development. *American Psychologist, 56*(3), 227–38.

Masten, A. S., & Obradović, J. (2006). Competence and resilience in development. *Annals of the New York Academy of Sciences, 1094*(1), 13–27.

Maton, K.I. (2000). Making a difference: The social ecology of social transformation. *American Journal of Community Psychology, 28*(1): 25–57.

Maton, K. I. (2008). Empowering community settings: Agents of individual development, community betterment, and positive social change. *American Journal of Community Psychology, 41* (1–2), 4–21.

Maton, K. I. (2017). *Influencing social policy: Applied psychology serving the public interest.* Oxford. New York: Oxford University Press.

Maton, K.I., Humphreys, K., Jason, L.A., & Shinn, B. (2017). Community psychology in the policy arena. In *APA handbook of community psychology: Methods for community research and action for diverse groups and issues,* ed. C.M. Bond, C. Keys, and I. Serrano-García, 275–95. Washington DC: American Psychological Association.

Maton, K.I., Salem, D.A. (1995). Organizational characteristics of empowering community settings: A multiple case study approach. *American Journal of Community Psychology, 23*(5), 631–56.

Matthews, C.R., & Adams, E.M. (2009). Using a social justice approach to prevent the mental health consequences of heterosexism. *The Journal of Primary Prevention, 30*(1), 11–26.

Matustik, M. (1998). *Specters of liberation: Great refusals in the New World Order.* Albany, NY: State University of New York Press.

Maxwell, J.A. (2012). *Qualitative research design: An interactive approach.* 3rd ed. Thousand Oaks, CA: SAGE Publications.

Maya Jariego, I. (2017). "But we want to work": The movement of child workers in Peru and the actions for reducing child labor. *American Journal of Community Psychology, 60* (3–4): 430–438.

Mayer, J.P., & Davidson II, W.S. (2000). Dissemination of innovation as social change. In *Handbook of community psychology,* ed. J. Rappaport and E. Seidman. Boston, MA: Springer.

Mayton, D., S. Ball-Rokeach, S. & Loges, W. (1994). Human values and social issues: An introduction. *Journal of Social Issues, 50* (4): 108.

Mayol, T. (2016, August 14). The solution to American poverty comes from Africa. Retrieved from https://news.yahoo.com/solution-american-poverty-comes-africa-080000664.html

Mazel, O. (2018). Indigenous health and human rights: A reflection on law and culture. *International Journal of Environmental Research and Public Health, 15* (4): 789.

Mazzei, P., & Sosa Pascual, O. (2017, October 21). "Days were lost": Why Puerto Rico is still suffering a month after Hurricane Maria. *Miami Herald.* Retrieved from www.miamiherald.com/news/weather/hurricane/article179744081.html

McAdam, D. (1999). *Political process and the development of black insurgency.* Chicago: University of Chicago Press.

McAfee, M., A.G. Blackwell, & J. Bell. (2015). *Equity: The soul of collective impact.* Oakland, CA: PolicyLink.

McAlevey, J. (2016). *No shortcuts: Organizing for power in the new gilded age.* New York: Oxford University Press.

McAlister, A. (2000). Action-oriented mass communication. In *Handbook of community psychology,* ed. J. Rappaport and E. Seidman, 379–396. New York: Kluwer Academic/Plenum Publishers.

McCammon, S.L. (2012). Systems of Care as asset-building communities: Implementing strengths-based planning and positive youth development. *American Journal of Community Psychology, 49* (3–4): 556–565.

McCarthy, J.D., & M.N. Zald. (1977). Resource mobilization and social movements: A partial theory. *American Journal of Sociology, 82* (6): 1212–1241.

McDonald, K.E., C.B. Keys, & F.E. Balcazar. (2007). Disability, race/ethnicity and gender: Themes of cultural oppression, acts of individual resistance. *American Journal of Community Psychology, 39* (1–2): 145–161.

McEvoy, F. (1982). "A symbol of racial discrimination": The Chinese Immigration Act and Canada's relations with China, 1942–1947. *Canadian Ethnic Studies = Etudes Ethniques Au Canada, 14*(3), 24–42.

McFarlane-Nathan, G.H. (1996). *The bicultural therapy project: Developing a psychological model for working with Maori.* Christchurch: Paper presented at the New Zealand Psychological Society Annual Conference.

McGillivray, M., & M. Clarke, (Eds.). (2006). *Understanding human well-being.* New York: United Nations University Press.

McHugh, M. (2014). *Feminist qualitative research. The Oxford handbook of qualitative research.* Oxford: Oxford University Press.

McKeever, B. S. (2019). The nonprofit sector in brief 2018: Public charities, giving, and volunteering. Retrieved from https://nccs.urban.org/publication/nonprofit-sector-brief-2018

McIntosh, P. (1990). White privilege: Unpacking the invisible knapsack. *Independent School, 49* (2): 31–36.

McKenzie, K., & T. Harpham, (Eds.). (2006). *Social capital and mental health*. London: Kingsley.

McKenzie, M. (2013, September 30). No more "allies." Black Girl Dangerous. Retrieved from www.blackgirl-dangerous.org/2013/09/no-more-allies/

McKenzie-Mohr, D. (2000). New ways to promote pro-environmental behavior: Promoting sustainable behavior: An introduction to community-based social marketing. *Journal of Social Issues, 56* (3): 543–554.

McKnight, J. (1995). *The careless society: Community and its counterfeits*. New York: Basic Books.

McLaren, P.L., & C. Lankshear, (Eds.). (1994). *Politics of liberation: Paths from Freire*. London: Routledge.

McMillan, D.W., & D.M. Chavis. (1986). Sense of community: A definition and theory. *Journal of Community Psychology* 14: 6–23.

McMullen, L.M., & J.M. Stoppard. (2006). Women and depression: A case study of the influence of feminism in Canadian psychology. *Feminism & Psychology, 16* (3): 277–288.

McNeely, J. (1999). Community building. *Journal of Community Psychology, 27*: 741–750.

McPhearson, T. (2013, January 20). Wicked problems, social-ecological systems, and the utility of systems thinking. Retrieved from http://www.thenatureofcities.com/2013/01/20/wicked-problems-social-ecological-systems-and-the-utility-of-systems-thinking/

McQuaig, L. (1998). *The cult of impotence: Selling the myth of powerlessness in the global economy*. Toronto: Viking.

McWhirter, E.H. (1994). *Counseling for empowerment*. Alexandria, VA: American Counseling Association.

McWhirter, E., & B. McWhirter. (2007). Grounding clinical training and supervision in an empowerment model. In *Advancing social justice through clinical practice*, ed. E. Aldarondo, 418–442. London: Lawrence Erlbaum.

Mead, A.T. (1995). The integrity of the human gene, genes and Whakapapa. In *New Zealand Health Research Council Consensus Development Workshop 'Whose genes are they anyway?'* Wellington: The use and misuse of human genetic information.

Meara, N., & J. Day. (2000). Epilogue: Feminist visions and virtues of ethical psychological practice. In *Practicing feminist ethics in psychology*, ed. M. Brabeck, 249–268. Washington DC: American Psychological Association.

Mednick, M. (1989). On the politics of psychological constructs. Stop the bandwagon, I want to get off. *American Psychologist, 44*: 1118–1123.

Melhuish, E.C. (2011). Preschool matters. *Science, 333*: 299–300.

Melucci, A. (1989). *Nomads of the present: Social movements and individual needs in contemporary society*. Philadelphia, PA: Temple University Press.

Menezes, I., P. Teixeira, & M. Fidalgo. (2007). Commnunity psychology in Portugal: From "revolution" to empowered citizenship. In *International community psychology: History and theories*, ed. S.M. Reich, M. Riemer, I. Prilleltensky, & M. Montero, 317–334. New York: Springer.

Mental Health Commission of Canada. (2014). New research results show that the Housing First approach contributes to ending homelessness. Retrieved from www.mentalhealthcommission.ca/English/article/32216/june-12-2014-new-research-results-show-housing-first-approach-contributes-ending-homel

Mercier, L.R., & R.D. Harold. (2003). At the interface: Lesbian-parent families and their children's schools. *Children & Schools, 25*: 35–47.

Mercy, J.A., M.L. Rosenberg, K.E. Powell, C.V. Broome, & W.L. Roper. (1993). Public health policy for preventing violence. *Health Affairs, 12* (4): 7–29.

Merrells, J., A. Buchanan, & R. Waters. (2019). "We feel left out": Experiences of social inclusion from the perspective of young adults with intellectual disability. *Journal of Intellectual & Developmental Disability, 44* (1): 13–22.

Mertens, D.M. (2009). *Transformative research and evaluation*. New York: Guilford Press.

Messinger, L. (2006). History at the table: Conflict in planning in a community in the rural American South. *American Journal of Community Psychology, 37*(3–4), 275–82.

Mészáros, I. (2009). *The structural crisis of capital*. New York: Monthly Review Press.

Meyer, I.H. (2003). Prejudice, social stress, and mental health in lesbian, gay, and bisexual populations: Conceptual issues and research evidence. *Psychological Bulletin 129*(5), 674.

Migration Policy Center. (2017, March 8). Frequently requested statistics on immigrants and immigration in the United States. Retrieved from www.migrationpolicy.org/article/frequently-requested-statistics-immigrants-and-immigration-united-states

Mik-Meyer, N. (2016). Othering, ableism and disability: A discursive analysis of co-workers' construction of colleagues with visible impairments. *Human Relations, 69*(6), 1341–63.

Miller, B.D., Blau, G.M., Christopher, O.T. & Jordan, P.E. (2012). Sustaining and expanding systems of care to provide mental health services for children, youth and families across America. *American Journal of Community Psychology, 49(1–2)*, 566–79.

Miller, R.L. (2017). The practice of program evaluation in community psychology: Intersections and opportunities for stimulating social change. In *APA handbook of community psychology: Methods for community research and action for diverse groups and issues*, ed. M.A. Bond, I. Serrano-García, C.B. Keys, and M. Shinn, 107–21. Washington, DC: American Psychological Association.

Miller, R.L., & M. Shinn. (2005). Learning from communities: Overcoming difficulties in dissemination of prevention and promotion efforts. *American Journal of Community Psychology, 35*(3–4), 169–83.

Miller, R.L., S.J. Reed, & V. Francisco. (2013). Accomplishing structural change: Identifying intermediate indicators of success. *American Journal of Community Psychology, 51*(1–2), 232–42.

Mills, C.W. (1956). *The power elite*. Oxford: Oxford University Press.

Minkler, M., & Wallerstein, N., (Eds.). (2008). *Community-based participatory research for health: From process to outcomes*. 2nd ed. San Francisco, CA: Jossey-Bass.

Minkoff, D.C. (2002). The emergence of hybrid organizational forms: Combining identity-based service provision and political action. *Nonprofit and Voluntary Sector Quarterly, 31*(3), 377–401.

Moane, G. (1999). *Gender and colonialism: A psychological analysis of oppression and liberation*. Basingstoke: Palgrave Macmillan.

Mohatt, G.V., Rasmus, S.M., Thomas, L., Allen, J., Hazel, K., & Marlatt, G.A. (2008). Risk, resilience, and natural recovery: a model of recovery from alcohol abuse for Alaska Natives. *Addiction, 103*(2), 205–15.

Monbiot, G. (2016, April 15). Neoliberalism – the ideology at the root of all our problems. *The Guardian*. Retrieved from www.theguardian.com/books/2016/apr/15/neoliberalism-ideology-problem-george-monbiot?CMP=fb_gu

Montaño, C., & Duriguetto, M.L. (2011). *Estado, classe e movimento social*. 3rd ed. São Paulo: Cortez Editora.

Montero, M. (1996). Parallel lives: Community psychology in Latin America and the United States. *American Journal of Community Psychology, 24*(5), 589–605.

Montero, M. (1998). Psychosocial community work as an alternative mode of political action. *Community, Work and Family, 1*, 65–78.

Montero, M. (2007). The political psychology of liberation: From politics to ethics and back. *Political Psychology, 28*, 517–33.

Montero, M. (2008). An insider's look at the development and current state of community psychology in Latin America. *Journal of Community Psychology, 36*(5), 661–74.

Montero, M., Varas-Díaz., N. (2007). Latin American community psychology: Development, implications, and challenges within a social change agenda. In *International community psychology: History and theories*, ed. S.M. Reich, M. Riemer, I. Prilleltensky, and M. Montero, 63–98. New York: Springer.

Moos, R.H. (1994). *The social climate scales: A user's guide*. 2nd ed. Palo Alto, CA: Consulting Psychologists Press.

Moos, R. H. (2003). Social contexts: Transcending their power and their fragility. *American Journal of Community Psychology, 31*, 1–13.

Morgan, A., & Bullen, D. (2015). *Civil and political wrongs: The growing gap between international civil and political rights and African Canadian life*. Toronto, ON: African Canadian Legal Clinic.

Morgan, P., Cumberworth, E., & Wimer, C. (2012). *The great recession and the American family*. Stanford, CA: Stanford Center on Poverty and Inequality.

Moritsugu, J., E. Vera, F. Wong, and K. Duffy. (2013). *Community psychology*. 5th ed. Boston: Pearson.

Moskell, C., & Allred, S.B. (2013). Integrating human and natural systems in community psychology: An ecological model of stewardship behavior. *American Journal of Community Psychology, 51,* 1–14.

Mountain State Centers for Independent Living. (2019). Retrieved from http://mtstcil.org/skills/il-2-background.html

Mowbray, C.T., Lewandowski, L., Holter, M. & Bybee, D. (2006). The Clubhouse as an empowering setting. *Health & Social Work, 31,* 167–179.

Mrazek, P.J., & Haggerty, R.J., (Eds.). (1994). *Reducing risks for mental disorders: Frontiers for preventive intervention.* Washington, DC: National Academy Press.

Mruck, K., & Breuer, F. (2003). Subjectivity and reflexivity in qualitative research – The FQS Issues. Forum Qualitative Sozialforschung / Forum: *Qualitative Social Research, 4*(2). Retrieved from http://www.qualitative-research.net/index.php/fqs/article/view/696/1504

Mulhall, S., & Swift, A. (1996). *Liberals and communitarians.* 2nd ed. Oxford: Blackwell.

Mullaly, B. (2002). *Challenging oppression: A critical social work Approach.* New York: Oxford University Press.

Mullings, D. V., Morgan, A. & Quelleng, H. K. (2016). Canada the great white north where anti-Black racism thrives: Kicking down the doors and exposing the realities. *Phylon, 53*(1), 20–41.

Mulvey, A. (1988). Community psychology and feminism: Tensions and commonalities. *Journal of Community Psychology, 16,* 70–83.

Munger, F., & Riemer, M. (2012). A process model for research collaborations and its application in environmental and sustainability fields. *Umweltpsychologie, 16*(1), 112–42.

Munger, F., & Riemer, M. (2014). Sustainability. In *Encyclopedia of Critical Psychology,* ed. T. Teo. New York: Springer.

Munger, F., MacLeod, T., & Loomis, C. (2016). Social change: Toward an informed and critical understanding of social justice and the capabilities approach in community psychology. *American Journal of Community Psychology, 57* (1–2): 171–80.

Muñoz, R.F., Le, H.N., Clarke, G., & Jaycox, L. (2002). Preventing the onset of major depression. In *Handbook of depression,* ed. I.H. Gotlib and C.L. Hammen, 343–59. New York: Guilford Press.

Muñoz, R.F., Ying, Y.W., Bernal, G., Pérez-Stable, E.J., Sorensen, J.L., Hargreaves, W.A., & Miller, L.S. (1995). Prevention of depression with primary care patients: A randomized controlled trial. *American Journal of Community Psychology, 23*(2), 199–222.

Muñoz, R.F., & Bunge, E.L. (2016). Prevention of depression worldwide: A wake-up call. *Lancet Psychiatry, 3*(4), 306–7.

Munoz, R.T., Brady, S., & Brown, V. (2017). The psychology of resilience: A model of the relationship of locus of control to hope among survivors to intimate partner violence. *Truamatology, 23*(1), 102–11.

Munro, L., Travers, R. St. John, A., Klein, K., Hunter, H., Brennan, D. & Brett, C. (2013). A bed of roses?: Exploring the experiences of LGBT newcomer youth who migrate to Toronto. *Ethnicity and Inequalities in Health and Social Care, 6*(4), 137–50.

Munro, L., Travers, R. & M.R. Woodford. (2019). Overlooked and invisible: Everyday experiences of microaggressions for LGBTQ adolescents. *Journal of Homosexuality,* Advance online publication. https://doi.org/10.1080/00918369.2018.1542205.

Murray, J., & Rosenberg, R. (2006). Community-managed loan funds: Which ones work? *Small Enterprise Development, 17*(3), 13–27.

Musick, M.A., & Wilson, J. (2008). *Volunteers: A social profile.* Bloomington, IN: Indiana University Press.

Myrdal, G. (1969). *Objectivity in social research.* New York: Pantheon Books.

Nadal, K. L., Issa, M. A., Leon, J., Meterko, V., Wideman, M., & Wong, Y. (2011). Sexual orientation microaggressions: "Death by a thousand cuts" for lesbian, gay, and bisexual youth. *Journal of LGBT Youth, 8*(3), 234–59.

Nafstad, H. E., Blakar, R. M., Carlquist, E., Phelps, J. M., & Rand-Hendriksen, K. (2007). Ideology and power: The influence of current neo-liberalism in society. *Journal of Community & Applied Social Psychology, 17*(4), 313–27.

Naidoo, L. (2012). Ethnography: An Introduction to definition and method. *An ethnography of global landscapes and corridors,* 1–8.

Nairn, M. (1990). *Understanding colonisation.* Auckland: Workshop material distributed by CCANZ Programme on Racism.

Nairn, M. (2000). *Decolonisation for Pakeha*. Auckland: Workshop material distributed by CCANZ Programme on Racism.

Nairn, R., Pega, F., McCreanor, T., Rankine, J., & Barnes, A. (2006). Media, racism and public health psychology. *Journal of Health Psychology, 11*(2), 183–96.

Namaste, V. (2000). *Invisible lives: The erasure of transsexual and transgendered people*. Chicago, IL: University of Chicago Press.

Narayan, D., Chambers, R., Shah, M. K. & Petesch, P. (2000). *Voices of the poor: Crying out for change*. Washington, DC: World Bank. Retrieved from http://documents.worldbank.org/curated/en/2000/01/1047447/voices-poor-crying-out-change.

Narayan, D., Patel, R., Schafft, K., Rademacher, A., & Koch-Schulte, S. (2000). *Voices of the poor: Can anyone hear us?* New York: Oxford University Press.

Nary, D. E. (2014). Making homes more "visitable" for wheelchair users and potential hosts. *Archives of Physical Medicine and Rehabilitation, 95*(10), 1995–6.

Natale, A., Di Martino, S., Procentese, F., & Arcidiacono, C. (2016). De-growth and critical community psychology: Contributions towards individual and social well-being. *Futures 78–79*, 47–56.

Nation, M., Crusto, C., Wandersman, A., Kumpfer, K. L., Seybolt, D., Morrissey-Kane, E., & Davino, K. (2003). What works in prevention: Principles of effective prevention programs. *American Psychologist, 58*, 449–456.

National Centre for Injury Prevention and Control. (n.d.). *Brief 1: Overview of policy evaluation*. Retrieved from www.cdc.gov/injury/pdfs/policy/Brief%201-a.pdf

National Evaluation of Sure Start Team. (2012). Full report on the impact of Sure Start local programmes on seven year olds and their families – 2012. Birkbeck, University of London. Retrieved from www.ness.bbk.ac.uk/impact/documents/DFE-RR220.pdf

National Health Care for the Homeless Council. (2012). *Universal solutions to prevent and end homelessness* (Policy Statement). Nashville, TN. Retrieved from www.nhchc.org/wp-content/uploads/2011/09/Universal-Solutions-20121.pdf

Navarro, V. (2009). What we mean by social determinants of health. *Global Health Promotion, 16*, 5–16.

Neal, J. W., & Christens, B. D. (2014). Linking the levels: Network and relational perspectives for community psychology. *American Journal of Community Psychology, 53*(3–4), 314–23.

Neal, J. W., & Neal, Z. P. (2011). Power as a structural phenomenon. *American Journal of Community Psychology, 48*(3–4), 157–67.

Neal, J. W., & Neal, Z. P. (2013). Nested or networked? Future directions for ecological systems theory. *Social Development, 22*(4), 722–37.

Neal, Z. P. (2014). A network perspective on the processes of empowered organizations. *American Journal of Community Psychology, 53*(3–4), 407–18.

Neal, Z. P. (2015). Making big communities small: Using network science to understand the ecological and behavioral requirements for community social capital. *American Journal of Community Psychology, 55*(3–4), 369–80.

Neal, Z. P. (2017). Taking stock of the diversity and sense of community debate. *American Journal of Community Psychology, 59*(3–4), 255–60.

Neal, Z.P., & Neal, J.W. (2014). The (in)compatibility of diversity and sense of community. *American Journal of Community Psychology, 53*, 1–12.

Neal, Z. P., & Neal, J. W. (2017). Network analysis in community psychology: Looking back, looking forward. *American Journal of Community Psychology, 60*(1–2), 279–95.

Nelson, G. (1994). The development of a mental health coalition: A case study. *American Journal of Community Psychology, 22*, 229–55.

Nelson, G. (2010). Housing for people with serious mental illness: Approaches, evidence, and transformative change. *Journal of Sociology and Social Welfare, 37*, 123–46.

Nelson, G. (2013). Community psychology and transformative policy change in the neo-liberal era. *American Journal of Community Psychology, 52*(3–4), 211–23.

Nelson, G., Amio, J., Prilleltensky, I., & Nickels, P. (2000). Partnerships for implementing school and community prevention programs. *Journal of Educational and Psychological Consultation, 11*, 121–45.

Nelson, G., & Caplan, R. (2014). The prevention of child physical abuse and neglect: An update. *Journal of Applied Research on Children: Informing Policy for Children at Risk, 5*, Article 3.

Nelson, G., Goering, P., & Tsemberis, S. (2012). Housing for people with lived experience of mental health issues: Housing First as a strategy to improve quality of life. In C.J. Walker, K. Johnson, & E. Cunningham (Eds.), *Community psychology and the socio-economics of mental distress: Global perspectives* (pp. 191–205). Basingstoke: Palgrave Macmillan.

Nelson, G., Janzen, R., Trainor, J., & Ochocka, J. (2008). Putting values into practice: Public policy and the future of mental health consumer-run organizations. *American Journal of Community Psychology, 42*, 192–201.

Nelson, G., Kloos, B., & Ornelas, J. (2014). Transformative change in community mental health: Synthesis and future directions. In G. Nelson, B. Kloos, & J. Ornelas (Eds.), *Community psychology and community mental health: Towards transformative change* (pp. 373–88) New York: Oxford University Press.

Nelson, G., & Lavoie, F. (2010). Contributions of Canadian community psychology. *Canadian Psychology, 51*(2), 79–88.

Nelson, G., Lavoie, F., & Mitchell, T. (2007). History and theories of community psychology in Canada. In S. Reich, M. Riemer, I. Prilleltensky, & M. Montero (Eds.), *International community psychology: History and theories* (pp. 13–36). New York: Springer.

Nelson, G., Lord, J., & Ochocka, J. (2001). *Shifting the paradigm in community mental health: Towards empowerment and community*. Toronto: University of Toronto Press.

Nelson, G., & MacLeod, T. (2017). The evolution of housing for people with serious mental illness. In J. Sylvestre, G. Nelson, & T. Aubry (Eds.), *Housing, citizenship, and communities for people with serious mental health illness: Theory, research, and policy perspectives* (pp. 3–22). New York: Oxford University Press.

Nelson, G., Pancer, S. M., Hayward, K., & Kelly, R. (2004). Partnerships and participation of community residents in health promotion and prevention: Experiences of the Highfield Community Enrichment Project (Better Beginnings, Better Futures). *Journal of Health Psychology, 9*(2), 213–27.

Nelson, G., Pancer, S.M., Hayward, K., & Peters, R. DeV. (2005). *Partnerships for prevention: The story of the Highfield Community Enrichment Project*. Toronto, ON: University of Toronto Press.

Nelson, G., Poland, B., Murray, M., & Maticka-Tyndale, E. (2004). Building capacity in community health action research: Towards a praxis framework for graduate education. *Action Research, 2*, 389–409.

Nelson, G., & Prilleltensky, I. (2005). *Community psychology: In pursuit of liberation and well-being*. London: Red Globe Press.

Nelson, G., & Prilleltensky, I. (2010). *Community psychology: In pursuit of liberation and well-being* (2nd ed.). London: Red Globe Press.

Nelson, G., Prilleltensky, I., & Hasford, J. (2013). Prevention and mental health promotion in the community. In D. Dozois (Ed.), *Abnormal psychology: Perspectives* (5th ed., pp. 467–85). Scarborough, ON: Prentice-Hall/Allyn & Bacon Canada.

Nelson, G., Prilleltensky, I., & MacGillivary, H. (2001). Building value-based partnerships: Toward solidarity with oppressed groups. *American Journal of Community Psychology, 29*, 649–77.

Nelson, G., & Riemer, M. (2014). Intervention. In Teo, T. (Ed.), *Encyclopedia of critical psychology*. New York: Springer.

Nelson, G., Stefancic, A., Rae, J., Townley, G., Tsemberis, S., Macnaughton, E., ... Goering, P. (2014). Early implementation evaluation of a multi-site Housing First intervention for homeless people with mental illness: A mixed methods approach. *Evaluation and Program Planning, 43*, 16–26.

Nelson, G., Westhues, A., & MacLeod, J. (2003). A meta-analysis of longitudinal research on preschool prevention programs for children. *Prevention and Treatment, 6* (December). Retrieved from http://journals.apa.org/prevention/volume6/toc-dec18-03.html

Nelson, G., Van Andel, A. K., Curwood, S. E., Hasford, J., Love, N., Pancer, M., & Loomis, C. (2012). Exploring Outcomes through Narrative: The Long-term Impacts of Better Beginnings, Better Futures on the Turning Point Stories of Youth at Ages 18–19. *American Journal of Community Psychology, 49*, 294.

Netto, J. P., & Braz, M. (2006). *Economia política: Uma introdução crítica*. São Paulo: Cortez.

Neufeldt, R., & Janzen, R. (under review). Learning from and with community-based and participatory action research: Constraints and adaptations in a youth-peacebuilding initiative in Haiti. *Submitted to the Action Research Journal*.

Newbrough, J. R. (1995). Toward community: A third position. *American Journal of Community Psychology, 23*(1), 9–37.

Newman, S. J. (1994). The housing and neighborhood conditions of persons with severe mental illness. *Psychiatric Services, 45*(4), 338–43.

Newton, L., Rosen, A., Tennant, C., Hobbs, C., Lapsley, H. M., & Tribe, K. (2000). Deinstitutionalisation for long-term mental illness: An ethnographic study. *The Australian and New Zealand Journal of Psychiatry, 34,* 484–90.

Nicholson, L. (1997). The myth of the traditional family. In H. Lindeman Nelson (Ed.), *Feminism and families,* (pp. 27–42). London: Routledge.

Nigussie, L., & Wales, J. (2014). CARE's experience with community scorecards in Ethiopia – What works and why. Country Case Study Note. London: ODI.

Nip, J. (2004). The relationship between online and offline communities: The case of the Queer Sisters. *Media, Culture, and Society, 26,* 409–29.

Nnaemeka, O., & Ngozi Ezeilo, J. (Eds.). (2005). *Engendering human rights: Cultural and socio-economic realities in Africa.* New York: Palgrave Macmillan.

Nores, M., & Barnett, W. S. (2010). Benefits of early childhood interventions across the world: (Under) investing in the very young. *Economics of Education Review, 29,* 271–82.

Norris, F. H., Stevens, S. P., Pfefferbaum, B., Wyche, K. F., & Pfefferbaum, R. L. (2008). Community resilience as a metaphor: Theory, set of Capacities, and strategy for disaster readiness. *American Journal of Community Psychology, 41*(1–2), 127–50.

Norris, T. (2001). America's communities movement: Investing in the civic landscape. *American Journal of Community Psychology, 29,* 301–7.

Norton, M. I., & Ariely, D. (2011). Building a better America – one wealth quintile at a time. *Perspectives on Psychological Science, 6*(1), 9–12.

Nosrati, E., & Marmot, M. (2019). Punitive social policy: An upstream determinant of health. *The Lancet, 394*(10196), 376–77.

Nowell, B. (2009). Profiling capacity for coordination and systems change: The relative contribution of stakeholder relationships in interorganizational collaboratives. *American Journal of Community Psychology, 44*(3–4), 196–212.

Nowell, B., & Boyd, N. M. (2014). Sense of community responsibility in community collaboratives: Advancing a theory of community as resource and responsibility. *American Journal of Community Psychology, 54*(3–4), 229–42.

Noy, D. (2008). Power mapping: Enhancing sociological knowledge by developing generalizable analytical public tools. *The American Sociologist, 39*(1), 3–18.

Nsamenang, A., Fru, F., & Browne, M. (2007). The roots of community psychology in Cameroon. In S. M. Reich, M. Riemer, I. Prilleltensky, & M. Montero (Eds.), *International community psychology: History and theories* (pp. 392–406). New York: Springer.

Nursing Council of New Zealand. (1996). *Guidelines for the cultural safety component in nursing education.* Wellington: Ministry of Education.

Nussbaum, M. (2003). Capabilities as fundamental entitlement: Sen and social justice. *Feminist Economics, 9*(2–3), 33–59.

Nyamathi, A. M., Reback, C. J., Shoptaw, S., Salem, B. E., Zhang, S., Farabee, D., & Khalilifard, F. (2016). Impact of community-based programs on incarceration outcomes among gay and bisexual stimulant-using homeless adults. *Community Mental Health Journal, 52,*(8), 1037–42.

O'Brien, J., & O'Brien, C. L. (1996). *Members of each other: Building community in company with people with developmental disabilities.* Toronto: Inclusion Press.

O'Donnell, C. R., & Ferrari, J. (Eds.). (2000). Employment in community psychology: The diversity of opportunity [Special issue]. *Journal of Prevention and Intervention in the Community, 19*(2), 1–131.

O'Malley, V. (2016). *The great war for New Zealand: Waikato 1800–2000.* Wellington: Bridget William Books.

O'Neill, P. (1976). Educating divergent thinkers: An ecological investigation. *American Journal of Community Psychology, 4,* 99–107.

O'Neill, P. (1989). Responsible to whom? Responsible for what? Some ethical issues in community intervention. *American Journal of Community Psychology, 17*, 323–41.

O'Neill, P. (2000). Cognition in social context: Contributions to community psychology. In J. Rappaport & E. Seidman (Eds.), *Handbook of community psychology*, (pp. 115–32). New York: Kluwer Academic/Plenum.

O'Neill, P. (2005). The ethics of problem definition. *Canadian Psychology/Psychologie Canadienne, 46*(1), 13–20.

O'Neill, P. (2005). The ethics of problem definition. *Canadian Psychology/ Psychologie Canadienne, 46*(1), 13–20.

O'Sullivan, D. (2017). *Indigeneity: A politics of potential: Australia, Fiji and New Zealand.* UK: Bristol University Press.

O'Brien, C. A., Travers, R., & Bell, L. (1993). *No safe bed: Lesbian, gay and bisexual youth in residential services.* Toronto, ON: Central Toronto Youth Services.

Ochocka, J., & Janzen, R. (2008). Blending commitment, passion and structure: Engaging cultural linguistic communities in collaborative research. In A. Williamson & R. DeSouza (Eds.), *Researching with communities*, (pp. 323–38). Waitakere City, New Zealand: Wairua Press.

Ochocka, J., & Janzen, R. (2014). Breathing life into theory: Illustrations of community-based research hallmarks, functions, and phases. *Gateways: International Journal of Community Research and Engagement, 7*, 18–33.

Ochocka, J., Janzen, R., & Nelson, G. (2002). Sharing power and knowledge: Professional and mental health consumer/survivor researchers working together in a participatory action research project. *Psychiatric Rehabilitation Journal, 25*(4), 379–87.

Ochocka, J., Moorlag, E., & Janzen, R. (2010). A framework for entry: PAR values and engagement strategies in community research. *Gateways: International Journal of Community Research & Engagement, 3*, 1–19.

O'Connell, M. J., & Stein, C. H. (2005). Psychiatric advance directives: Perspectives of community stakeholders. *Administration and Policy in Mental Health, 32*, 241–65.

OECD. (2010). Sickness, disability and work. Breaking the barriers – Denmark. Retrieved from www.oecd.org/els/soc/46460721.pdf

OECD. (2019). Poverty rate (indicator). Retrieved from https://data.oecd.org/inequality/poverty-rate.htm

Oesterle, S., Hawkins, J. D., Kuklinski, M. R., Fagan, A. A., Fleming, C., Rhew, I. C., ... & Catalano, R. F. (2015). Effects of Communities That Care on males' and females' drug use and delinquency 9 years after baseline in a community-randomized trial. *American Journal of Community Psychology, 56*(3–4), 217–28.

Ohmer, M. L. (2007). Citizen participation in neighborhood organizations and its relationship to volunteers' self- and collective efficacy and sense of community. *Social Work Research, 31*(2), 109–20.

Oliver, M. (2013). The Social Model of Disability: Thirty years on. *Disability & Society, 28*(7), 1024–26.

Oliver, M., & Barnes, C. (1998). *Social policy and disabled people: From exclusion to inclusion.* New York: Longman.

Olson, M. (2007). Strengthening families: Community strategies that work. *Young Children, 62*(2), 26–3.

Omi, M., & Winant, H. (1994). *Racial formation in the United States: From the 1960s to the 1990s.* New York: Routledge.

Ornelas, J., Duarte, T., & Jorge-Monteiro, M. F. (2014). Transformative organizational change in community mental health. In G. Nelson, B. Kloos, & J. Ornelas (Eds.), *Community psychology and community mental health: Towards transformative change* (pp. 253–77). New York: Oxford University Press.

Orr, M. (2007). Summing up: Community organizing and political change in the city. In M. Orr (Ed.), *Transforming the city: Community organizing and the challenge of political change* (pp. 252–60). Lawrence, KS: University Press of Kansas.

Ortiz, I., & Cummins, M. (2013). Austerity measures in developing countries: Public expenditure trends and the risks to children and women. *Feminist Economics, 19*(3), 55–81.

Ortlipp, M. (2008). Keeping and using reflective journals in the qualitative research process. *The Qualitative Report, 13*(4), 695–705.

Osborne, K., Baum, F. E., & Ziersch, A. (2009). Negative consequences of community group participation for women's mental health and well-being: Implications for gender aware social capital building. *Journal of Community & Applied Social Psychology, 19*, 212–24.

Ospina, S., Foldy, E., El Hadidy, W., Dodge, J., Hofmann-Pinilla, A., & Su, C. (2012). Social change leadership as relational leadership. In M. Uhl-Bien, & S. Ospina (Eds.), *Advancing relational leadership research: A dialogue among perspectives* (pp. 255–302). (Leadership Horizons Series). Greenwich, CT: Information Age Publishing.

Oxfam International (2018). *Richest 1 percent bagged 82 percent of wealth created last year – poorest half of humanity got nothing.* Retrieved from www.oxfam.org/en/pressroom/pressreleases/2018-01-22/richest-1-percent-bagged-82-percent-wealth-created-last-year

Paloma, V., García-Ramírez, M., & Camacho, C. (2014). Well-being and social justice among Moroccan migrants in southern Spain. *American Journal of Community Psychology, 54*, 1–11.

Pan, Z., & Kosicki, G. M. (1993). Framing analysis: An approach to news discourse. *Political Communication, 10*(1), 55–75.

Pancer, S. M. (1997). Program evaluation. In S. W. Sadawa & D. R. McCreary (Eds.), *Applied social psychology* (pp. 47–53). Englewood Cliffs, NJ: Prentice Hall.

Pancer, S. M. (2015). *The psychology of citizenship and civic engagement.* Oxford: Oxford University Press.

Pancer, S. M., & Cameron, G. (1994). Resident participation in the Better Beginnings, Better Futures prevention project: I. The impact of involvement. *Canadian Journal of Community Mental Health, 13*(2), 197–211.

Pancer, S. M., Nelson, G., Hasford, J., & Loomis, C. (2013). The Better Beginnings, Better Futures project: Long-term parent, family, and community outcomes of a universal, comprehensive, community-based prevention approach for primary school children and their families. *Journal of Community & Applied Social Psychology, 23*(3), 187–205.

Paradies, Y. (2016). Colonisation, racism, and indigenous health. *Journal of Population Research, 33*, 83–96.

Parayil, G. (Ed.). (2000). *Kerala: The development experience.* London: Zed Books.

Parker, I. (2007). *Revolution in psychology: Alienation to emancipation.* London: Pluto Press.

Parkhurst, M., & Preskill, H. (2014). Learning in action: Evaluating collective impact. *Stanford Social Innovation Review, 12*(4), 17–19.

Parris, T. M., & Kates, R. W. (2003). Characterizing a sustainability transition: Goals, targets, trends, and driving forces. *Proceedings for the National Academy of Sciences, 100* (24), 8068–73.

Partanen, A. (2016). *The Nordic theory of everything.* New York: Harper.

Paterson, S., McInerney, E., & Evans, S. D. (2019). *Using social network analysis as a tool in action research* (unpublished manuscript), University of Miami, Miami, FL.

Patterson, L. E. & Welfel, E. R. (2000). *The counselling process* (5th ed.). Belmont, CA: Brooks/Cole.

Patton, M. (2008). *Utilization-focused evaluation* (4th ed.). Thousand Oaks: SAGE Publications.

Patton, M. Q. (2014). *Qualitative research & evaluation methods: Integrating theory and practice.* Thousand Oaks, CA: SAGE Publications.

Pease, B., & Fook, J. (Eds.). (1999). *Transforming social work practice: Postmodern critical perspectives.* Sydney: Allen and Unwin.

Pees, R. C., Shoop, G. H., & Ziegenfuss, J. T. (2009). Organizational consciousness. *Journal of Health Organization and Management, 23*(5), 505–21.

Perilla, J., Lavizzo, E., & Ibáñez, G. (2007). Toward a community psychology of liberation. In E. Aldarondo (Ed.), *Advancing social justice through clinical practice* (pp. 291–312). London: Lawrence Erlbaum.

Perkins, D., Hughey, J., & Speer, P. (2002). Community psychology perspectives on social capital theory and community development practice. *Journal of the Community Development Society, 33*(1), 33–52.

Perkins, D., & Zimmerman, M. A. (1995). Empowerment theory, research, and application. *American Journal of Community Psychology, 23*(5), 569–79.

Perkins, D. D., García-Ramírez, M., Menezes, M., Serrano-García, I., & Stromopolis, M. (2016). Community psychology and public policy: Research, advocacy and training in international Contexts. *Global Journal of Community Psychology Practice, 7*(1), 1–8.

Perkins, D. D., Larsen, C., & Brown, B. B. (2009). Mapping urban revitalization: Using GIS spatial analysis to evaluate a new housing policy. *Journal of Prevention & Intervention in the Community, 37*(1), 48–65.

Perkins, J. (2005). *Confessions of an economic hit man.* New York: Plume.

Perkins, J. (2016). *The new confessions of an economic hit man* (2nd ed.). Oakland, CA: Berrett-Koehler Publishers.

Perkins, R. (1991). Women with long-term mental health problems: Issues of power and powerlessness. *Feminism and Psychology*, 1, 131–9.

Perry, M. J. (1996). The relationship between social class and mental disorder. *Journal of Primary Prevention*, 17, 17–30.

Perry, M., & Albee, G. W. (1994). On "the science of prevention." *American Psychologist, 49*, 1087–8.

Peters, R. DeV., Peters, J.E., Laurendeau, M.-C., Chamberland, C., & Peirson, L. (2001). Social policies for promoting the well-being of children. In I. Prilleltensky, G. Nelson, and L. Peirson (Eds.), *Promoting family wellness and preventing child maltreatment: Fundamentals for thinking and action* (pp. 177–219). Toronto: University of Toronto Press.

Peters, R. DeV., Bradshaw, A.J., Petrunka, K., Nelson, G., Herry, Y., Craig, W.W., ... Rossiter, M.D. (2010). The Better Beginnings, Better Futures project: Findings from grade 3 to 9. *Monographs of the Society for Research in Child Development, 75*(23), vii–viii, 1–174.

Peters, R.DeV., Petrunka, K., Khan, S., Howell-Moneta, A., Nelson, G., Pancer, S.M., & Loomis, C. (2016). Cost-savings analysis of the Better Beginnings, Better Futures community-based project for young children and their families: A 10-year follow-up. *Prevention Science, 17*(2), 237–47.

Peters, R.DeV., & Arnold, R. (2003). The Better Beginnings, Better Futures project: A universal, comprehensive, community-based prevention approach for primary school children and their families. *Journal of Clinical and Adolescent Psychology, 32*(2), 215–27.

Peters, R.DeV., Arnold, R., Petrunka, K., Angus, D. E., Belanger, J.-M., Boyce, W., ... Towson, S. (2004). *Better Beginnings, Better Futures: A comprehensive, community-based project for early childhood development: Highlights of lessons learned*. Kingston, ON: Better Beginnings, Better Futures Research Coordination Unit technical report. Available from http://bbbf.ca/Portals/15/pdfs/BB-Highlights.pdf

Peterson, N. A., & Zimmerman, M. A. (2004). Beyond the individual: Toward a nomological network of organizational empowerment. *American Journal of Community Psychology, 34*(1), 129–45.

Peterson, N. A., Speer, P. W., & McMillan, D. W. (2008). Validation of a brief sense of community scale: Confirmation of the principal theory of sense of community. *Journal of Community Psychology, 36*(1), 61–73.

Pew Research Center. (2013). *Changing patterns of global migration and remittances*. Retrieved from www.pewsocialtrends.org.

Pfeffer, J., & Salancik, G. R. (2003). *The external control of organizations: A resource dependence perspective*. Stanford University Press.

Phillips, D. (2000). Social policy and community psychology. In J. Rappaport & E. Seidman (Eds.), *Handbook of community psychology* (pp. 397–420). New York: Kluwer Academic/Plenum Publishers.

Pickett, K., & Wilkinson, R. (2015). Income inequality and health: A causal review. *Social Science & Medicine*, 128, 316–26.

Pilger, J. (2002). *The new rules of the world*. London: Verso.

Pilkington, E. (2017, September 9). A tale of two Irmas: Rich Miami ready for tumult as poor Miami waits and hopes. *The Observer*. Retrieved from www.theguardian.com/world/2017/sep/09/hurricane-irma-miami-florida-two-cities

Pinnington, E., Lerner, J., & Schugurensky, D. (2009). Participatory budgeting in North America: The case of Guelph, Canada. *Journal of Public Budgeting, Accounting & Financial Management, 21*(3), 455–84.

Piran, N. (2001). Re-inhabiting the body from the inside out: Girls transform their school environment. In D.L. Tolman & M. Brydon-Miller (Eds.), *From subjects to subjectivities: A handbook of interpretative and participatory methods* (pp. 218–38). New York: New York University Press.

Pistrang, N., Barker, C., & Humphreys, K. (2008). The contributions of mutual help groups for mental health problems to psychological well-being: A systematic review. In L.D. Brown & S. Wituk (Eds.), *Mental health self-help: Consumer and family initiatives* (pp. 61–85). New York: Springer.

Piven, F. F., & Cloward, R. (1978). *Poor people's movements: Why they succeed, how they fail*. New York: Vintage Books.

Pole, N., Gone, J. P., & Kulkarni, M. (2008). Posttraumatic stress disorder among ethnoracial minorities in the United States. *Clinical Psychology: Science and Practice, 15*(1), 35–61.

Ponce, A. N., & Rowe, M. (2018). Citizenship and community mental health care. *American Journal of Community Psychology, 61*, 22–31.

Ponterotto, J.G. (2005). Qualitative research in counseling psychology: A primer on research paradigms and philosophy of science. *Journal of Counseling Psychology, 52* (2): 126–136.

Portes, A. (1998). Social capital: Its origins and applications in modern sociology. *Annual Review of Sociology, 24*, 1–24.

Portes, A. (2014). Downsides of social capital. *PNAS, 111*: 18407–8.

Posavac, E. J., & Carey, R. G. (2007). *Program evaluation: Methods and case studies* (7th ed.). Upper Saddle River, NJ: Prentice Hall.

Poteat, V. P., Sinclair, K. O., DiGiovanni, C. D., Koenig, B. W., & Russell, S. T. (2013). Gay–Straight Alliances are associated with student health: A multischool comparison of LGBTQ and heterosexual youth. *Journal of Research on Adolescence, 23*, 319–30.

Poteat, V., Scheer, J., Marx, R., Calzo, J., & Yoshikawa, H. (2015). Gay-straight alliances vary on dimensions of youth socializing and advocacy: Factors accounting for individual and setting-level differences. *American Journal of Community Psychology, 55*(3–4), 422–32.

Potok, M. (2016, November 14). Anti-Muslim hate crimes surged last year fueled by hateful campaign. *Southern Poverty Law Center Hatewatch*. Retrieved from www.splcenter.org/hatewatch/2016/11/14/anti-muslim-hate-crimes-surged-last-year-fueled-hateful-campaign

Potvin, L., & Jones, C. M. (2011). Twenty-five years after the Ottawa Charter: The critical role of health promotion for public health. *Canadian Journal of Public Health, 102*, 244–48.

Power, A. (1996). Area-based poverty and resident empowerment. *Urban Studies, 33*, 1535–65.

Preskill, H., & Gopal, S. (2014). *Evaluating complexity: Propositions for improving practice*. Retrieved from www.fsg.org

Price, K. (2017). Queering reproductive justice toward a theory and praxis for building intersectional political alliances. In M. Brettschneider, S. Burgess, & C. Keating (Eds.), LGBTQ *politics: A critical reader* (pp. 72–88). New York: New York University Press.

Price, R. H., Van Ryn, M., & Vinokur, A. D. (1992). Impact of a preventive job search intervention on the likelihood of depression among the unemployed. *Journal of Health and Social Behavior, 33*, 158–67.

Prilleltensky, I. (1993). The immigration experience of Latin American families: Research and action on perceived risk and protective factors. *Canadian Journal of Community Mental Health, 12*(2), 101–16.

Prilleltensky, I. (1994). *The morals and politics of psychology: Psychological discourse and the status quo*. Albany, NY: State University of New York Press.

Prilleltensky, I. (2001). Value-based praxis in community psychology: Moving toward social justice and social action. *American Journal of Community Psychology, 29*(5), 747–78.

Prilleltensky, I. (2003). Understanding, resisting, and overcoming oppression: Toward psychopolitical validity. *American Journal of Community Psychology, 31*(1–2), 195–201.

Prilleltensky, I. (2004). Validez psicopolítica: El próximo reto para la psicología comunitaria [Psychopolitical validity: The next challenge for community psychology]. In M. Montero, *Introducción a la psicología comunitaria. Desarrollo, conceptos y procesos* [Introduction to community psychology: Developments, concepts and processes] (pp. 5–18). Buenos Aires, Argentina: Editorial Paidós.

Prilleltensky, I. (2008a). Migrant well-being is a multilevel, dynamic, and value dependent phenomenon. *American Journal of Community Psychology, 42*, 3–4, 359–64.

Prilleltensky, I. (2008b). The role of power in wellness, oppression, and liberation: The promise of psychopolitical validity. *Journal of Community Psychology, 36*(2), 116–36.

Prilleltensky, I. (2012). Wellness as fairness. *American Journal of Community Psychology, 49*(1–2), 1–21.

Prilleltensky, I. (2014). Meaning-making, mattering, and thriving in community psychology: From co-optation to amelioration and transformation. *Psychosocial Intervention, 23*(2), 151–4.

Prilleltensky, I., Dietz, S., Prilleltensky, O., Myers, N., Rubenstein, C., Jin, Y., & McMahon, A. (2015). Assessing multidimensional well-being: Development and validation of the I COPPE scale. *Journal of Community Psychology, 43*, 199–226.

Prilleltensky, I., & Fox, D. (1997). Introducing critical psychology: Values, assumptions, and status quo. In D. Fox & I. Prilleltensky (Eds.), *Critical psychology: An introduction* (pp. 3–20). London: SAGE Publications.

Prilleltensky, I., & Gonick, L. (1996). Polities change, oppression remains: On the psychology and politics of oppression. *Political psychology*, 127–48.

Prilleltensky, I., Laurendeau, M.-C., Chamberland, C., & Peirson, L. (2001). Vision and values for child and family wellness. In I. Prilleltensky, G. Nelson, & L. Peirson (Eds.), Promoting family wellness and preventing child maltreatment: Fundamentals for thinking and action (pp. 124–73). Toronto: University of Toronto Press.

Prilleltensky, I., & Nelson, G. (2002). *Doing psychology critically: Making a difference in diverse settings*. London: Red Globe Press.

Prilleltensky, I., & Nelson, G. (2009). Community psychology: Advancing social justice. In D. R. Fox, I. Prilleltensky, & S. Austin (Eds.), *Critical psychology: An introduction* (2nd ed., pp. 126–43). Thousand Oaks, CA: SAGE Publications.

Prilleltensky, I., Nelson, G., & Peirson, L. (2001). The role of power and control in children's lives: An ecological analysis of pathways toward wellness, resilience and problems. *Journal of Community & Applied Social Psychology, 11*, 143–58.

Prilleltensky, I., Nelson, G., & Sanchez Valdes, L. (2000). A value-based approach to smoking prevention with immigrants from Latin America: Program evaluation. *Journal of Ethnic and Cultural Diversity in Social Work, 9*(1–2), 97–117.

Prilleltensky, I., Peirson, L., Gould, J., & Nelson, G. (1997). Planning mental health services for children and youth: Part I—A value-based framework. *Evaluation and Program Planning, 20*(2), 163–72.

Prilleltensky, I., & Prilleltensky, O. (2006). *Promoting well-being: Linking personal, organizational and community change*. New York: John Wiley & Sons.

Prilleltensky, I., Sanchez Valdes, L., Walsh-Bowers R., & Rossiter, A. (2002). Applied ethics in mental health in Cuba: Dilemmas and resources. *Ethics and Behavior, 13*, 243–60.

Prilleltensky, I., Walsh-Bowers, R., & Rossiter, A. (1999). Clinicians' lived experience of ethics: Values and challenges in helping children. *Journal of Educational and Psychological Consultation, 10*(4), 315–42.

Prilleltensky, O. (2009). Critical psychology and disability studies: Critiquing the mainstream, critiquing the critique. In D. Fox, I. Prilleltensky, & S. Austin (Eds.), *Critical psychology: An introduction* (2nd ed., pp. 250–66). London: SAGE Publications.

Prochaska, J., Norcross, J., & DiClemente, C. (1994). *Changing for good*. New York: Avon Books.

Puar, J. (2011). I would rather be a cyborg than a goddess: Intersectionality, assemblage, and affective politics. Traversal eipcp. Retrieved from: http://eipcp.net/transversal/0811/-puar/en.

Public Health Agency of Canada. (2006). *Street youth in Canada: Findings from the enhanced surveillance of Canadian street youth, 1999-2003*. Ottawa: Government of Canada. Retrieved from http://tinyurl.com/3q7zbtk

Public Health Agency of Canada. (2009). Summative evaluation of the Community Action Program for Children: 2004–2009. Retrieved from www.phac-aspc.gc.ca/about_apropos/evaluation/reports-rapports/2009-2010/capc-pace/index-eng.php

Puddifoot, J. E. (1996). Some initial considerations in the measurement of community identity. *Journal of Community Psychology, 24*(4), 327–36.

Putnam, R. (1993). The prosperous community: Social capital and public life. *The American prospect, 13*(Spring), 35–42.

Putnam, R. D. (1995). Tuning in, tuning out: The strange disappearance of social capital in America. *PS: Political Science & Politics, 28*(4), 664–83.

Putnam, R. D. (2000a). Bowling alone: America's declining social capital. In L. Crothers & C. Lockhart (Eds.), *Culture and Politics* (pp. 223–34). New York: Palgrave Macmillan.

Putnam, R. D. (2000b). *Bowling alone: The collapse and revival of American community*. New York: Simon & Schuster.

Putnam, R. (Ed). (2002). *Democracies in flux: The evolution of social capital in contemporary society*. New York: Oxford University Press.

Putnam, R. D. (2016). *Our kids: The American dream in crisis*. New York: Simon & Schuster.

Quinn, R. (2015). *The positive organization*. Oakland, CA: Berrett-Koehler.

Quiñones Rosado, R. (2007). *Consciousness in action: Toward an integral psychology of liberation and transformation*. Cagua, Puerto Rico: Ilé Publications.

Rainbow Health Ontario. (2012). Designing surveys and questionnaires. *RHO Factsheet*. Toronto, Ontario. Retrieved from www.mun.ca/research/ethics/humans/icehr/LGBT_DevelopingStudyMeasures.pdf

Ramsden, I. (1991). *Kawa Whakaruruhau: Cultural safety in nursing education in Aotearoa*. Wellington: Ministry of Education.

Rao, H., Mahadevappa, H., Pillay, P., Sessay, M., Abraham, A., & Luty, J. (2009). A study of stigmatized attitudes towards people with mental health problems among health professionals. *Journal of Psychiatric and Mental Health Nursing, 16*(3), 279–84.

Raphael, D. (2008). *Social determinants of health: Canadian perspectives* (2nd ed.). Toronto: Canadian Scholars' Press.

Raphael, D., Bryant, T., & Mendly-Zambo, Z. (2018). Canada considers a basic income guarantee: Can it achieve health for all? *Health Promotion International*, 1–7. https://doi.org/10.1093/heapro/day058.

Rappaport, J. (1977). *Community psychology: Values, research, and action*. New York: Holt, Rinehart & Winston.

Rappaport, J. (1981). In praise of paradox: A social policy of empowerment over prevention. *American Journal of Community Psychology, 9*(1), 1–25.

Rappaport, J. (1987). Terms of empowerment/exemplars of prevention: Toward a theory for community psychology. *American Journal of Community Psychology, 15*(2), 121–48.

Rappaport, J. (1995). Empowerment meets narrative: Listening to stories and creating settings. *American Journal of community psychology, 23*(5), 795–807.

Rappaport, J. (2000). Community narratives: Tales of terror and joy. *American Journal of Community Psychology, 28*, 1–24.

Rappaport, J. (2005). Community psychology is (thank God) more than a science. *American Journal of Community Psychology, 35*(3–4), 231–8.

Rappaport, J., Davidson, W. S., Wilson, M. N., & Mitchell, A. (1975). Alternatives to blaming the victim or the environment: Our places to stand have not moved the earth. *American Psychologist, 29*, 525–8.

Rappaport, J., & Seidman, E. (2000). *Handbook of community psychology*. New York: Springer.

Rasmus, S. M., Trickett, E., Charles, B., John, S., & Allen, J. (2019). The qasgiq model as an indigenous intervention: Using the cultural logic of contexts to build protective factors for Alaska Native suicide and alcohol misuse prevention. *Cultural Diversity and Ethnic Minority Psychology, 25*(1), 44–54.

Rata, A., Liu, J.H., & Hanke, K. (2008). Te ara hohou rongo (The path to peace): Maori conceptualisations of inter-group forgiveness. *New Zealand Journal of Psychology, 37*(2), 18–30.

Ratcliffe, J. (1978). Social justice and the demographic transition: Lessons from India's Kerala State. *International Journal of Health Services, 8*(1), 123–44.

Raudenbush, S. W., & Bryk, A. S. (2002). *Hierarchical linear models: Applications and data analysis methods* (2nd ed.). Newbury Park, CA: SAGE Publications.

Ravitch, D. (2013). *Reign of error: The hoax of the privatization movement and the danger to America's public schools*. New York: Knopf.

Reardon, R., Lavis, J., & Gibson, J. (2006). *From research to practice: A knowledge transfer planning guide*. Toronto, ON: Institute for Work and Health.

Reason, P., & Bradbury, H. (2001). *Handbook of action research: Participative inquiry and practice* (2nd ed.). London: SAGE Publications.

Reich, J. A. (2005). *Fixing families: Parents, power, and the child welfare system*. New Jersey: Routledge.

Reich, S.M. (2010). Adolescents' sense of community on Myspace and Facebook: A mixed methods approach. *Journal of Community Psychology, 38*(6), 688–705.

Reich, S.M., Black, R.W., & Korobkova, K. (2014). Establishing connections and community in virtual worlds for children. *Journal of Community Psychology, 42*(3), 255–67.

Reich, S.M., Kay, J., & Lin, G. (2015). Nourishing a partnership to improve middle school lunch options: A community-based participatory research project. *Family & Community Health, 38*(1), 77–86.

Reich, S. M., Penner, E. K., Duncan, G. J. (2011). Using baby books to increase new mothers' safety practices. *Academic Pediatrics, 11*(1), 34–43.

Reich, S. M., Riemer, M., Prilleltensky, I., & Montero, M. (Eds.). (2007). *International community psychology: History and theories*. New York: Springer.

Reid, N. (2000, June). *Community participation: How people power brings sustainable benefits to communities.* Washington, DC: US Department of Agriculture, Rural Development, Office of Community Development.

Reinharz, S. (1984). Alternative settings and social change. In K. Heller, R. H. Price, S. Reinharz, S. Riger, & A. Wandersman, *Psychology and community change: Challenges of the future* (2nd ed., pp. 286–336). Homewood, IL: The Dorsey Press.

Reinharz, S. (1994). Toward an ethnography of "voice" and "silence." In E. J. Trickett, R. Watts, & D. Birman (Eds.), *Human diversity: Perspectives on people in context* (pp. 178–200). San Francisco, CA: Jossey-Bass.

Renn, K. A. (2010). LGBT and queer research in higher education: The state and status of the field. *Educational Researcher, 39*(2), 132–41.

Reville, D. (2013). Is mad studies emerging as a new field of inquiry? In B. LeFrancois, M. Menzies, & R. Reaume (Eds.), *Mad matters: A critical reader in Canadian mad studies* (pp. 170 – 80.) Toronto, ON: Canadian Scholars' Press.

Reyes Cruz, M., & Sonn, C. C. (2011). (De)colonizing culture in community psychology: Reflections from critical social science. *American Journal of Community Psychology, 47*(1-2), 203–14.

Richardson, C. (2008). *"Canada's Toughest Neighbourhood:" Surveillance, Myth and Orientalism in Jane-Finch* (Master's thesis, Brock University). Retrieved from http://jane-finch.com/articles/files/Richardson_Thesis.pdf

Rickel, A. (1987). The 1965 Swampscott Conference and future topics for community psychology. *American Journal of Community Psychology, 15*(5), 511–13.

Ridgway, P., & Zipple, A. M. (1990). The paradigm shift in residential services: From the linear continuum to supported housing approaches. *Psychosocial Rehabilitation Journal, 13*, 11–31.

Riemer, M. (2010). Community psychology, the natural environment, and global climate change. In G. Nelson & I. Prilleltensky (Eds.), *Community psychology: In pursuit of liberation and well-being* (2nd ed., pp. 498–516). London: Red Globe Press.

Riemer, M., Athay, M. M., Bickman, L., Breda, C., Kelley, S. D., & Vides de Andrade, A. R. (2012). The Peabody Treatment Progress Battery: History and methods for developing a comprehensive measurement battery for youth mental health. *Administration and Policy in Mental Health and Mental Health Services Research, 39*(0), 3–12.

Riemer, M., & Dittmer, L. (2016). The Youth Leading Environmental Change Project: An introduction to the special issue. *Ecopsychology. 8*(3), 163–6.

Riemer, M., & Harré, N. (2017). Environmental degradation and sustainability: A community psychology perspective. In M. A. Bond, I. Serrano-García, & C. B. Keys (Eds.), *APA handbook of community psychology: Methods for community research and action for diverse groups and issues* (pp. 441–56). Washington, DC: American Psychological Association.

Riemer, M., Lynes, J., & Hickman, G. (2014). Engaging youth in environmental change. A model for developing and assessing youth-based environmental engagement programmes. *Journal of Environmental Education Research, 20*(4), 552–74.

Riemer, M., & Reich, S. M. (2011). Community psychology and global climate change: Introduction to the special section. *American Journal of Community Psychology, 47*(3-4), 349–53.

Riemer, M., & Van Voorhees, C.W. (2014). Sustainability and social justice. In C. Johnson, H. Friedman, J. Diaz, B. Nastasi, & Z. Franco (Eds.), *Praeger handbook of social justice and psychology.* (pp 49–66). Westport, CT: Praeger Publishers.

Riemer, M., Van Voorhees, C. W., Dittmer, Alisat, S., Alam, N., Sayal, R., ... Schweizer-Ries, P. (2016). The Youth Leading Environmental Change Project: A mixed-method longitudinal study across six countries. *Ecopsychology, 8*(3), 174–87.

Riger, S. (1993). What's wrong with empowerment. *American Journal of Community Psychology, 21*(3), 279–92.

Riger, S. (2000). *Transforming psychology.* New York: Oxford University Press.

Riger, S. (2001). Transforming community psychology. *American Journal of Community Psychology, 29*(1), 69–81.

Ringwalt, C. L., Ennett, S., Johnson, R., Rohrbach, L. A., Simons-Rudolph, A., Vincus, A., & Thorne, J. (2003). Factors associated with fidelity to substance use prevention curriculum guides in the nation's middle schools. *Health Education & Behavior, 30*, 375–91.

Rittel, H., & Webber, M. (1973). Dilemmas in a general theory of planning. *Policy Sciences, 4*, 155–69.

Roberts, M., Norman, W., Minhinnick, N., Wihongi, D., & Kirkwood, C. (1995). Kaitiakitanga: Maori perspectives on conservation. *Pacific Conservation Biology, 2*(1), 7–20.

Robertson, N., & Masters-Awatere, B. (2007). Community psychology in Aotearoa/New Zealand: Me tiro whakamuri a kia hangai whakamua. In S. Reich, M. Riemer, I. Prilleltensky, & M. Montero (Eds.), *International community psychology: History and theories* (pp. 140–63). New York: Springer.

Robinson, E., & Parker, R. (2008). Prevention and early intervention in strengthening families and relationships: Challenges and implications. *Australian Institute of Family Studies, AFRC Issues, 2*, 1–13.

Robinson, W. L., Brown, M., Beasley, C. R., & Jason, L. A. (2016). Advancing prevention intervention from theory to application: Challenges and contributions of community psychology. In M. A. Bond, C. Keys, & I. Serrano-García (Eds.). *Handbook of Community Psychology.* Washington, DC: American Psychological Association.

Rodney, P., & Copeland, E. (2009). The health status of Black Canadians: Do aggregated racial and ethnic variables hide health disparities? *Journal of Health Care for the Poor and Underserved, 20*(3), 817–23.

Roffey, S. (2013). Inclusive and exclusive belonging: The impact on individual and community well-being. *Educational & Child Psychology, 30*(1), 38–49.

Roger, M., & White, B. (1997). *Pakeha process in the bicultural therapy project.* Paper presented at the Psychological Services Annual Conference, Department of Corrections, Rotorua.

Román, N. (2018). Puerto Ricans in the United States: 2010–2016. Data sheet. *New York: Centro for Puerto Rican Studies, Hunter College, City University of New York.* Retrieved from https://centropr.hunter.cuny.edu/research/data-center/data-sheets/puerto-ricans-united-states-2010-2016

Romero, A. J., Edwards, L. M., Fryberg, S. A., & Orduña, M. (2014). Resilience to discrimination stress across ethnic identity stages of development. *Journal of Applied Social Psychology, 44*(1), 1–11.

Rosa, A. (1997). *The courage to change: Salvadoran stories of personal and social transformation.* Unpublished MA thesis, Wilfrid Laurier University, Ontario.

Rosario, M., Schrimshaw, E. W., & Hunter, J. (2008). Predicting different patterns of sexual identity development over time among lesbian, gay, and bisexual youths: A cluster analytic approach. *American Journal of Community Psychology, 42*(3–4), 266–82.

Rosenhan, D. (1973). On being sane in insane places. *Science, 179*(4070), 250–8.

Ross, J. A., & Jaafar, S. B. (2006). Participatory needs assessment. *Canadian Journal of Program Evaluation, 21*(1), 131.

Ross, K. (2017). Making empowering choices: How methodology matters for empowering   r e s e a r c h participants. *Forum Qualitative Sozialforschung / Forum: Qualitative Social Research, 18*(3), 17.

Rossi, P., Lipsey, M., & Henry, G. (2018). *Evaluation* (8th ed.). Thousand Oaks, CA: SAGE Publications.

Rossiter, A., Prilleltensky, I., & Walsh-Bowers, R. (2000). Postmodern professional ethics. In B. Fawcett, B. Featherstone, J. Fook, & A. Rossiter (Eds.), *Postmodern and feminist perspectives in social work practice* (pp. 83–103). London: Routledge.

Roussos, S. T., & Fawcett, S. B. (2000). A review of collaborative partnerships as a strategy for i m p r o v i n g community health. *Annual Review of Public Health, 21*, 369–402.

Roy, A. L., Hughes, D., & Yoshikawa, H. (2013). Intersections between nativity, ethnic density, and neighbourhood SES: Using an ethnic enclave framework to explore variation in Puerto Ricans' physical health. *American Journal of Community Psychology, 51*, 469–79.

Rudolph, K. (2015). Denver Public Library Archives. Retrieved from https://history.denverlibrary.org/news/we-will-ride-origin-disability-rights-movement-denver-0

Runswick-Cole, K., & Goodley, D. (2013). Resilience: A disability studies and community psychology approach. *Social and Personality Psychology Compass, 7*(2), 67–78.

Russell, S. T., Muraco, A., Subramaniam, A., & Laub, C. (2009). Youth empowerment and high school gay-straight alliances. *Journal of Youth and Adolescence, 38*(7), 891–903.

Rutter, M., & Silberg, J. (2002). Gene-environment interplay in relation to emotional and behavioral disturbance. *Journal of Child Psychology and Psychiatry, 40*, 19–55.

Rutter, M., Maughan, B., Mortimore, P. & Ouston, J. (1979). *Fifteen thousand hours: Secondary schools and their effects on children.* Cambridge, MA: Harvard University Press.

Rutter, M. (1987). Psychosocial resilience and protective mechanisms. *American Journal of Orthopsychiatry*, *57*, 316–31.

Rutter, M. (1993). Resilience: Some conceptual considerations. *Journal of Adolescent Health, 14*(8), 626–31.

Rutter, M. (2012). Resilience as a dynamic concept. *Development and Psychopathology, 24*(02), 335–44.

Ryan, W. (1971). *Blaming the victim*. New York: Random House.

Ryan, W. (1994). Many cooks, brave men, apples and oranges: How people think about equality. *American Journal of Community Psychology, 22*, 25–35.

Ryerson Espino, S. L., & Trickett, E. J. (2008). The spirit of ecological inquiry and intervention research reports: A heuristic elaboration. *American Journal of Community Psychology, 42*, 60–78.

Sabin, K. M., & Johnston, L. G. (2014). Epidemiological challenges to the assessment of HIV burdens among key populations: Respondent-driven sampling, time–location sampling and demographic and health surveys. *Current Opinion in HIV and AIDS, 9*(2), 101.

Sachs, J. (2005). *The end of poverty: How we can make it happen in our lifetime*. Penguin UK.

Sachs, J. (2011). *The price of civilization: Reawakening American virtue and prosperity*. New York: Random House.

Saegert, S., and R.M. Carpiano. (2017). Social support and social capital: A theoretical synthesis using community psychology and community sociology approaches. In *APA handbook of community psychology: Theoretical foundations, core concepts, and emerging challenges*, ed. M.A. Bond, I. Serrano-García, and C. Keys, 293–314. Washington, DC: American Psychological Association.

Saegert, S., & Winkel, G. (1996). Paths to community empowerment: Organizing at home. *American Journal of Community Psychology, 24*, 517–50.

Saewyc, E. M., Konishi, C., Rose, H. A., & Homma, Y. (2014). School-based strategies to reduce suicidal ideation, suicide attempts, and discrimination among sexual minority and heterosexual adolescents in Western Canada. *International Journal of Child, Youth & Family Studies, 5*(1), 89–112.

Said, Edward. (1979). *Orientalism*. New York: Vintage Books.

Saforcada, E., Giori, V., LaPalma, A., Rodriguez, A., Ferullo, A. G., Rudolf, S., & Fuks, S. (2007). Community psychology in the river plate region (Argentina – Uruguay). In S. M. Reich, M. Riemer, I. Prilleltensky, & M. Montero (Eds.), *International community psychology: History and theories* (pp. 99–117). New York: Springer.

Salamon, L. M. (2010). Putting the civil society sector on the economic map of the world. *Annals of Public and Cooperative Economics, 81*(2), 167–210.

Salem, D., Foster-Fishman, P., & Goodkind, J. (2002). The adoption of innovation in collective action organizations. *American Journal of Community Psychology, 30*, 681–710.

Saleebey, D. (2002). *The strengths perspective in social work practice* (3rd ed.). Boston: Allyn and Bacon.

Salzer, M., & Baron, R. C. (2014). Who is John?: Community integration as a paradigm for transformative change in community mental health. In G. Nelson, B. Kloos, & J. Ornelas (Eds.), *Community psychology and community mental health: Towards transformative change* (pp. 228–49). Oxford: Oxford University Press.

Sampson, R. J. (2012). *Great American city: Chicago and the enduring neighborhood effect*. Chicago, Ill.: University of Chicago Press.

Sampson, R. J., Morenoff, J. D., & Earls, F. (1999). Beyond social capital: Spatial dynamics of collective efficacy for children. *American Sociological Review, 64*, 633–60.

Sampson, R. J., Raudenbush, S. W., & Earls, F. (1997). Neighborhoods and violent crime: A multilevel study of collective efficacy. *Science, 277*(5328), 918–24.

Sánchez, A. (2012). ¿Es posible el empoderamiento en tiempos de crisis? Repensando el desarrollo humano en el nuevo siglo [Is empowerment possible in times of crisis? Rethinking human development in the new century]. *Universitas Psychologica, 12*(1), 285–300.

Sandler, I. (2001). Quality and ecology of adversity as common mechanisms of risk and resilience. *American Journal of Community Psychology, 29*(1), 19–61.

Sandler, J. (2007). Community-based practices: Integrating dissemination theory with critical theories of power and justice. *American Journal of Community Psychology, 40*(3–4), 272–89.

Santens, S. (2017, December 6). Universal basic income will likely increase social cohesion. *Huffington Post*. Retrieved from www.huffpost.com/entry/universal-basic-income-wi_b_8354072?guccounter=1

Santrock, J. W. (2010). *Life-span development* (9th ed.). New York: McGraw-Hill.

Sarason, B. R., Sarason, I. G., & Pierce, G. (Eds.). (1990). *Social support: An interactional view*. New York: Wiley.

Sarason, S.B. (1972). *The creation of settings and the future societies*. San Francisco, CA: Jossey-Bass.

Sarason, S. B. (1974). *The psychological sense of community: Prospects for a community psychology*. San Francisco, CA: Jossey-Bass.

Sarason, S. B. (1976a). Community psychology and the anarchists insight. *American Journal of Community Psychology, 4*, 243–61.

Sarason, S. B. (1976b). Community psychology, networks, and Mr. Everyman. *American Psychologist, 31*(5), 317–29.

Sarason, S. B. (1978). The nature of problem solving in social action. *American Psychologist, 33*, 370–81.

Sarason, S. B. (1984). Community psychology and public policy: Missed opportunity. *American Journal of Community Psychology, 12*, 199–207.

Sarason, S. B. (1988). *The psychological sense of community: Prospects for a community psychology* (2nd ed.). Cambridge, MA: Brookline Books.

Sarkar, K., Dasgupta, A., Sinha, M., & Shanbabu, B. (2017). Effects of health empowerment intervention on resilience of adolescents in a tribal area: A study using the Solomon four-groups design. *Social Science & Medicine, 190*, 265–274.

Sasao, T., & Yasuda, T. (2007). Historical and theoretical orientations of community psychology practice and research in Japan. In S. M. Reich, M. Riemer, I. Prilleltensky & M. Montero (Eds.), *International Community Psychology: History and theories* (pp. 164–79). New York: Springer.

Saul, J. R. (2005). *The end of globalism*. Toronto: Viking Canada.

Saul, J. R. (2014). *On equilibrium: Six qualities of the new humanism*. Simon and Schuster.

Saul, J., Wanderman, A., Flaspohler, P., Duffy, J., Lubell, K., & Noonan, R. (2008). Research and action for bridging science and practice in prevention. *American Journal of Community Psychology, 41*(3–4), 165–70.

Schensul, J. J., & Trickett, E.J. (2009). Introduction to multi-level community based culturally situated interventions. *American Journal of Community Psychology, 43*(3–4), 232–40.

Schneider, J. (2006). *Social capital and welfare reform: Organizations, congregations, and communities*. New York: Columbia University Press.

Schneider, M., & Somers, M. (2006). Organizations as complex adaptive systems: Implications of complexity theory for leadership research. *The Leadership Quarterly, 17*(4), 351–65.

Schreiner, M., & Woller, G. (2003). Microenterprise development programs in the United States and in the developing world. *World development, 31*(9), 1567–80.

Schueller, S. M. (2009). Promoting wellness: Integrating community and positive psychology. *Journal of Community Psychology, 37*(7), 922–37.

Schwalbe, M. (2008). *Rigging the game: How inequality is reproduced in everyday life*. New York: Oxford University Press.

Schwartz, D. (1997). *Who cares: Rediscovering community*. Boulder, CO: Westview Press.

Schwartz, S. (1994). Are there universal aspects in the structure and contents of human values? *Journal of Social Issues, 50*(4), 19–46.

Scott, B.A., Amel, E.L., Koger, S.M., & Manning, C.M. (2016). *The psychology for sustainability* (4th ed.). New York: Psychology Press.

Scott, V. C., Alia, K., Scaccia, J., Ramaswamy, R., Saha, S., Leviton, L., & Wandersman, A. (2019). Formative evaluation and complex health improvement initiatives: A learning system to improve theory, implementation, support, and evaluation. *American Journal of Evaluation*, https://doi.org/10.1177/1098214019868022.

Scribner, R., Simonsen, N., & Leonardi, C. (2017). The social determinants of health core: Taking a place-based approach. *American Journal of Preventive Medicine, 52*(1), S13–19.

Seedat, M., Duncan, N., & Lazarus, S. (Eds.). (2001). *Community psychology: Theory, method and practice. South African and other perspectives*. Cape Town: Oxford University Press.

Seedat, M., & Lazarus, S. (2011). Community psychology in South Africa: Origins, developments, and manifestations. *Journal of Community Psychology, 39*(3), 241–57.

Seekins, T., Rennie, B., & Hammond, J. (2014a). Exploring the feasibility of using Google Street View to assess the accessibility of community environments: Developing definitions and observational protocol for image recognition and classification. *Research in Social Science and Disability, 8*, 125–41.

Seekins, T., Rennier, B., & Hammond, J. (2014b). Using Google Street View to assess community accessibility and participation: A demonstration. Unpublished paper. Research and Training Center on Rural Rehabilitation. Missoula, Montana.

Sehl, M. (1987). *The creation of a multi-ethnic housing cooperative: A social intervention*. Unpublished Master's Thesis, Wilfrid Laurier University, Waterloo, ON.

Seidman, E. (1983). Unexamined premises of social problem solving. In E. Seidman (Ed.), *Handbook of social intervention* (pp. 48–67). Beverly Hills, CA: SAGE Publications.

Seidman, E. (1986). Justice, values, and social science: Unexamined premises. In E. Seidman & J. Rappaport (Eds.), *Redefining social problems* (pp. 235–58). New York: Plenum Press.

Seidman, E. (1988). Back to the future, community psychology: Unfolding a theory of social intervention. *American Journal of Community Psychology, 16*(1), 3–24.

Seidman, E. (2012). An emerging action science of social settings. *American Journal of Community Psychology, 50*(1–2), 1–16.

Seidman, E., & Rappaport, J. (Eds.). (1986). *Redefining social problems*. New York: Plenum Press.

Seidman, S. (2017). *Contested knowledge: Social theory today* (6th ed.). Chichester: Wiley-Blackwell.

Selby, R. A. (Ed.). (2005). *Walking the talk: A collection of Tariana's papers*. Raukawa: Te Wananga o Raukawa.

Seligman, M. (2011). *Flourish: A visionary new understanding of happiness and well-being*. New York: Simon & Schuster.

Selket, K., Glover, M., & Palmer, S. (2015). Normalising post-mortems – whose cultural imperative? An Indigenous view on New Zealand post-mortem policy. *Kōtuitui: New Zealand Journal of Social Sciences Online, 10*(1), 1–9.

Semega, J. L., Fontenot, K. R., & Kollar, M. R. (2017). *Income and Poverty in the United States: 2016*. U.S. Census Bureau, Current Population Reports, P60-259. Washington, DC: U.S. Government Printing Office.

Sen, A. (1999a). *Beyond the crisis: Development strategies in Asia*. Singapore: Institute of Southeast Asian Studies.

Sen, A. (1999b). *Development as freedom*. New York: Oxford University Press.

Senge, P. & Scharmer, O. (2001). Community action research: Learning as a community of practitioners, consultants and researchers. In P. Reason & H. Bradbury (Eds.), *Handbook of action research: Participative inquiry and practice* (pp. 238–49). London: SAGE publications.

Senge, P. M. (1990). *The fifth discipline: The art and practice of the learning organization*. New York: Doubleday.

Serano, J. (2007). *Whipping girl: A transsexual woman on sexism and the scapegoating of femininity*. Berkeley, CA: Seal Press.

Serrano-García, I. (1994). The ethics of the powerful and the power of ethics. *American Journal of Community Psychology, 22*(1), 1–20.

Serrano-García, I., & Bond, M. B. (1994). Empowering the silent ranks: Introduction [Special issue]. *American Journal of Community Psychology, 22*(4), 433–45.

Sexual Orientation Laws. (2016). *A map of sexual orientation laws in the world*. The International Lesbian, Gay, Bisexual, Trans and Intersex Association (ILGA). Retrieved from http://ilga.org/what-we-do/lesbian-gay-rights-maps/

Shadish, W. R., Cook, T. D., & Campbell, D. T. (2002). *Experimental and quasi-experimental designs for generalized causal inference*. Boston, MA: Houghton Mifflin Company.

Shakespeare, T. (2006). *Disability rights and wrongs*. New York: Routledge.

Shaoul, J. (2001). Privatization: Claims, outcomes and explanations. In G. Philo & D. Miller (Eds.), *Market killing: What the free market does and what social scientists can do about it* (pp. 203–15). London: Pearson Education.

Sharma, N., & Wright, C. (2005). Decolonizing resistance, challenging colonial states. *Social Justice, 35*(3), 120–38.

Shields, S.A. (2008). Gender: An intersectionality perspective. *Sex Roles, 59*, 301–11.

Shilo, G., Antebi, N., & Mor, Z. (2015). Individual and community resilience factors among lesbian, gay, bisexual, queer and questioning youth and adults in Israel. *American Journal of Community Psychology, 55*(1–2), 215–27.

Shinn, M. (2009, October). How psychologists can help to end homelessness. *InPsych: Bulletin of the Australian Psychological Society 17*, 8–11.

Shinn, M. (2015). Community psychology and the capabilities approach. *American Journal for Community Psychology, 55*(3–4), 243–52.

Shinn, M. (2016). Methods for influencing social policy: The role of social experiments. *American Journal of Community Psychology, 58*(3–4), 239–44.

Shinn, M., Baumohl, J., & Hopper, K. (2001). The prevention of homelessness revisited. *Analyses of Social Issues and Public Policy, 1*(1), 95–127.

Shinn, M., & McCormack, M. M. (2017). Understanding and alleviating economic hardship: Contributions from community psychology. In M. A. Bond, I. Serrano-García, C. B. Keys, & M. Shinn (Eds.), *APA handbook of community psychology: Methods for community research and action for diverse groups and issues* (pp.345–60). Washington, DC: American Psychological Association.

Shinn, M., & Perkins, D. N. (2000). Contributions from organizational psychology. In J. Rappaport & E. Seidman (Eds.), *Handbook of community psychology* (pp. 615–42). New York: Kluwer Academic/Plenum.

Shinn, M., & Toohey, S. M. (2003). Community contexts of human welfare. *Annual Review of Psychology, 54*, 427–59.

Shirazi, R., & Biel, A. (2005). Internal-external causal attributions and perceived government responsibility for need provision: A 14-culture study. *Journal of Cross-Cultural Psychology, 36*(1), 96–116.

Shor, I. (1980). *Critical teaching & everyday life.* Chicago: University of Chicago Press.

Short, D. (2016). *Reconciliation and colonial power: Indigenous rights in Australia.* New York: Routledge.

Simplican, C. S., Leader, G., Kosciulek, J., & Leahy, M. (2015). Defining social inclusion of people with intellectual and developmental disabilities: An ecological model of social networks and community participation. *Research into Intellectual Disability, 38*, 18–29.

SIPRI (2015). *SIPRI military expenditure database.* Stockholm: SIPRI. Retrieved from www.sipri.org/research/armaments/milex/milex_database

Sisodia, R., Wolfe, D., & Sheth, J. (2007). *Firms of endearment: How world-class companies profit from passion and purpose.* Upper Saddle River, NJ: Wharton School Publishing.

Sloan, T. (1996). *Damaged life: The crisis of the modern psyche.* London: Routledge.

Sloan, T. (Ed.). (2000). *Critical psychology: Voices for change.* London: Red Globe Press.

Smail, D. (2001). De-psychologizing community psychology. *Journal of Community & Applied Social Psychology, 11*(2), 159–65.

Smale, A., Eddy, M., & Fahim, K. (2015; August 28). Europe reels from more migrant deaths on land and sea. *The New York Times.* Retrieved from www.nytimes.com

Smedley, B. D., & Syme, S. L. (Eds.). (2000). *Promoting health: Intervention strategies from social and behavioural research.* Washington, DC: National Academy Press.

Smit, B., & Wandel, J. (2006). Adaptation, adaptive capacity and vulnerability. *Global Environmental Change, 16*, 282–92.

Smith, A. (2008). Indigeneity, settler colonialism, white supremacy. In D. Martinez HoSang, O. LaBennett, & L. Pulido (Eds.), *Racial formation in the twenty-first century.* Berkeley, CA: University of California Press.

Smith, A. (2013). *Civic engagement in the digital age.* Washington, DC: Pew Research Center.

Smith, L.T. (1999). *Decolonizing methodologies: Research and Indigenous peoples.* London: Zed Books; Dunedin: University of Otago Press.

Smock, K. (2004). *Democracy in action: Community organizing and urban change.* New York: Columbia University Press.

Society for Community Research and Action (2018). Statement on the effects of deportation and forced separation on immigrants, their families, and communities. *American Journal of Community Psychology, 62*(1–2), 3–12.

Society for Community Research and Action (n.d.). *Who we are.* Retrieved from www.scra27.org/who-we-are/

Sofaer, S. (2000). *Working together, moving ahead: A manual to support effective community health coalitions.* New York: Baruch College, School of Public Affairs.

Solórzano, D. G., & Yosso, T. J. (2002). Critical race methodology: Counter-storytelling as an analytical framework for education research. *Qualitative Inquiry, 8*(1), 23.

Solty, I. (2013). The crisis interregnum: From the new right-wing populism to the Occupy movement. *Studies in Political Economy, 91*, 85–112.

Song, J., Roberts, E., & Zhang, D. (2013). Employer attitudes toward workers with disabilities: A review of research in the past decade. *Journal of Vocational Rehabilitation, 38*(2), 113–23.

Sonn, C. C., & Fisher, A. T. (2010). Immigration and settlement: Confronting the challenges of cultural diversity. In G. Nelson & I. Prilleltensky (Eds.), *Community psychology: In pursuit of liberation and well-being* (2nd ed., pp. 498–516). London: Red Globe Press.

Sonn, C. C., & Quayle, A. F. (2013). Developing praxis: Mobilising critical race theory in community cultural development. *Journal of Community & Applied Social Psychology, 23*, 435–48.

Sonn, C. C., & Quayle, A. F. (2014). Community cultural development for social change: Developing critical praxis. *Journal for Social Action in Counseling and Psychology, 6*(1), 16–35.

Sonn, C.C., G. Stevens, and N. Duncan. (2013). Decolonisation, critical methodologies and why stories matter. In *Race, memory and the apartheid archive*, ed. G. Stevens, N. Duncan, and D. Hook, 295–314. London: Palgrave Macmillan.

Sosialdepartementet. (1967). *Stortingsmelding St 88 (1966-1967). Om utviklingen av omsorgen for funksjonshemmede*. Oslo. Retrieved from www.stortinget.no/no/Saker-og-publikasjoner/Stortingsforhandlinger/Lesevisning/?p=1966-67&paid=3&wid=c&psid=DIVL2473&s=True

Sou, G. (2019). *After Maria: Everyday recovery from disaster*. University of Manchester. Retrieved from www.hcri.manchester.ac.uk/research/projects/after-maria/.

Soudien, C. (2012). *Realising the dream: Unlearning the logic of race in the South African school*. Cape Town: HSRC Press.

Speer, P. (2002). *Social power and forms of change: Implications for empowerment theory*. Unpublished manuscript.

Speer, P., Newbrough, J., & Lorion, R. (2008). The assessment of power through psychopolitical validity [Special issue]. *Journal of Community Psychology 36*(2), 113–268.

Speer, P.W., & Christens, B.D. (2014). Community organizing. In *Foundations of community psychology practice*, ed. V. Chien and S. Wolfe, 220–36. Thousand Oaks, CA: SAGE Publications.

Speer, P.W., & Hughey, J. (1995). Community organizing: An ecological route to empowerment and power. *American Journal of Community Psychology 23*(5), 729–48.

Speer, P.W., Hughey, J., Gensheimer, L., & Adams-Leavitt, W. (1995). Organizing for power: A comparative case study. *Journal of Community Psychology 23*(1), 57–73.

Speer, P.W., Tesdahl, E.A., & Ayers, J.F. (2014). Community organizing practices in a globalizing era: Building power for health equity at the community level. *Journal of Health Psychology, 19* (1), 159–169.

Speth, J.G. (2008). *The bridge at the edge of the world: Capitalism, the environment, and crossing from crisis to sustainability*. New Haven, CT: Yale University Press.

St. John, A., R. Travers, L. Munro, R. Liboro, M. Schneider, and C.L. Greig. (2014). The success of Gay–Straight alliances in Waterloo region, Ontario: A confluence of political and social factors. *Journal of LGBT Youth, 11*(2), 150–70.

Staggenborg, S. (1999). The consequences of professionalization and formalization in the Pro-Choice movement. In *Cycles of protest: Social movements since the sixties*, ed. J. Freeman and V. Johnson, 99–134. New York: Rowman & Littlefield.

Stahlhut, D. (2003). The people closest to the problem. *Social Policy, 34*(2-3), 71–74.

Stansfeld, S. (1999). Social support and social cohesion. In *Social determinants of health*, ed. M. Marmot and R. Wilkinson, 155–178. New York: Oxford University Press.

Stangor, C. (2006). *Principles of social psychology – 1st International Edition*. Victoria, BC: BCcampus.

Starnes, D.M. (2004). Community psychologists—Get in the arena. *American Journal of Community Psychology, 33*(1), 3–6.

Steele, C. (2011). *Whistling Vivaldi: How stereotypes affects us and what we can do*. New York: WW Norton & Company.

Steger, M. (2013). *Globalization: A very short introduction*. 3rd ed. London: Oxford University Press.

Stein, C., D. Dworsky, R. Phillips, and M. Hunt. (2005). Measuring personal loss among adults coping with serious mental illness. *Community Mental Health Journal, 41*, 129–39.

Steinitz, V., & Mishler, E.G. (2009). Critical psychology and the politics of resistance. In *Critical psychology: An introduction*, ed. D. Fox, I. Prilleltensky, and S. Austin, 2nd ed., 390–409. London: SAGE Publications.

Steuter-Martin, M. (2017, October 24). *Breaking down Bill 62: What you can and can't do while wearing a niqab in Quebec. CBC News*. Retrieved from www.cbc.ca/news/canada/montreal/bill-62-examples-ministry-release-1.4369347

Stiglitz, J.E. (2002). *Globalization and its discontents*. New York: Norton.

Stiglitz, J. (2011). Of the 1%, by the 1%, for the 1%. *Vanity Fair*. Retrieved from www.vanityfair.com/news/2011/05/top-one-percent-201105

Stiglitz, S. (2017). Debt, austerity, growth: There is another way. Retrieved from www.youtube.com/watch?v=_1vcWhyJ9uQ&feature=youtu.be

Stivala, A., G. Robins, Y. Kashima, and M. Kirley. (2016). Diversity and community can coexist. *American Journal of Community Psychology, 57*: 243–254.

Stoecker, R. (2003). Are academics irrelevant? Approaches and roles for scholars in community based participatory research. In *Community-based participatory research for health*, ed. M. Minkler and N. Wallerstein, 98–112. San Francisco, CA: Jossey-Bass.

Stoecker, R. (2013). *Research methods for community change: A project-based approach*. Thousand Oaks, CA: SAGE Publications.

Stokols, D. (2018). *Social ecology in the digital age: Solving complex problems in a globalized world*. London: Academic Press/Elsevier.

Stone, W., & Hughes, J. (2002). *Social capital: Empirical meaning and measurement validity. Research paper No. 27*. Retrieved from https://aifs.gov.au/publications/archived/1119

Stout, L. (1996). *Bridging the class divide and other lessons for grassroots organizing*. Boston: Beacon Press.

Strauss, J.S., & Carpenter, W.T. (1974). Characteristic symptoms and outcomes in schizophrenia. *Archives of General Psychiatry, 30*, 429–34.

Stroh, D.P. (2015). *Systems thinking for social change: A practical guide to solving complex problems, avoiding unintended consequences, and achieving lasting results*. White River Junction, Vermont: Chelsea Green Publishing.

Stromquist, N.P. (1998). The impact of structural adjustment in Africa and Latin America. In *Gender, education and development: Beyond Access to empowerment*, ed. C. Howard and S. Bunwaree, 17–32. London: Zed Books.

Sue, D.W., & Sue, D. (1990). *Counselling the culturally different: Theory and practice*. New York: John Wiley & Sons.

Sullivan, C.M. (2011). Evaluating domestic violence support service programs: Waste of time, necessary evil, or opportunity for growth? *Journal of Aggression and Violent Behavior, 16*, 354–60.

Sullivan, E.V. (1984). *A critical psychology*. New York: Plenum Press.

Suryakusuma, J.L. (1996). The state and sexuality in new order Indonesia. In *Fantasizing the feminine in Indonesia*, ed. L.J. Sears, (pp. 92–119). Durham, NC: Duke University Press.

Sutter, M., Perrin, P. B., Tabaac, A. R., Parsa, L., & Mickens, M. (2016). Do ableism and ageism predict college students' willingness to provide care for a family member with a chronic condition? *Stigma and Health, 2*(2), 110–120.

Swan, P., & Raphael, B. (1995). *Ways forward: National consultancy report on Aboriginal and Torres Strait Islander mental health*. Canberra: Department of Health and Ageing, Australia.

Swartz, T.T. (2008). Family capital and the invisible transfer of privilege: Intergenerational support and social class in early adulthood. In *Social class and transitions to adulthood*, ed. J.T. Mortimer, (pp. 11–24). San Francisco, CA: Jossey-Bass.

Swift, C., & Levin, G. (1987). Empowerment: An emerging mental health technology. *Journal of Primary Prevention, 8*, 71–92.

Swim, J., Clayton, S., Doherty, T., Gifford, R., Howard, G., Reser, J., …, Weber, E. (2009). *Psychology and global climate change: Addressing a multi-faceted phenomenon and set of challenges. A report by the American Psychological Association's task force on the interface between psychology and global climate change*. Washington, DC: American Psychological Association.

Sylaska, K. M., & Edwards, K. M. (2015). Disclosure experiences of sexual minority college student victims of intimate partner violence. *American Journal of Community Psychology, 55* (3–4), 326–335.

Szakos, K., & Szakos, J. (2007). *We make change: Community organizers talk about what they do – and why.* Nashville, TN: Vanderbilt University Press.

Szasz, T.S. (1960). The myth of mental illness. *American Psychologist, 15*(2), 113–118.

Szreter, S., & Woolcock, M. (2004). Health by association? Social capital, social theory, and the political economy of health. *International Journal of Epidemiology, 33*, 650–667.

Tamasese, K. (1993). Interface of gender and culture. In L. W. Nikora (Ed.), *Cultural justice and ethics* (pp. 8–11). Waikato: New Zealand Psychological Society: National Standing Committee on Bicultural Issues.

Tangata Tiriti – Treaty People. (2016). *Workshop evaluations 2011 - 2018.* Retrieved from www.treatypeople.org

Taras, R. (2013). "'Islamophobia never stands still': Race, religion, and culture." *Ethnic and Racial Studies, 36*(3), 417–33.

Tarrow, S. (1998). *Power in movement: Social movements and contentious politics.* New York: Cambridge University Press.

Tavris, C. (1992). *The mismeasure of woman.* NY: Touchstone/Simon & Schuster.

Taylor, C. (1992). *Multiculturalism and "the politics of recognition".* Princeton, NJ: Princeton University Press.

Taylor, P. J. (1996). What's modern about the modern world-system? Introducing ordinary modernity through world hegemony. *Review of International Political Economy, 3*(2), 260–86.

Taylor, V., & Whittier, N. E. (1992). Collective identity in social movement communities: Lesbian feminist mobilization. In A. P. A. D. Morris & A. P. C. M. Mueller (Eds.), *Frontiers in social movement theory* (pp. 104–30). New Haven, Conn: Yale University Press.

Taylor-Gooby, P. (2004). Open markets and welfare values: Welfare values, inequality and social change in the silver age of the welfare state. *European Societies, 6*(1), 29–48.

Te Awekotuku, N. (1991). *He Tikanga Whakaaro: Research ethics in the Māori community.* Wellington: Manatu Maori.

Te Puni Kōkiri. (2010). *Arotake Tūkino Whānau: Literature review on family violence.* Wellington: Te Puni Kōkiri.

Tebes, J. K. (2010). Community psychology, diversity, and the many forms of culture. *American   Psychologist, 65*(1), 58–59.

Tebes, J. K. (2012). Philosophical foundations of mixed methods research: Implications for research practice. In L. Jason & D. Glenwick (Eds.), *Methodological approaches to community-based research* (pp. 13–31). Washington, DC: American Psychological Association.

Tebes, J. K. (2017). Foundations for a philosophy of science of community psychology: Perspectivism, pragmatism, feminism, and critical theory. In M. A. Bond, I. Serrano-García, C. B. Keys, & M. Shinn (Eds.), *APA handbook of community psychology: Methods for community research and action for diverse groups and issues* (pp.21–40). Washington, DC: American Psychological Association.

Tebes, J. K., Thai, N., & Matlin, S. (2014). Twenty-first century science as a relational process: From Eureka! to team science and a place for community psychology. *American Journal for Community Psychology, 53*, 475–90.

Temm, P. B. (1990). *The Waitangi Tribunal: The conscience of the nation.* Auckland: Random Century.

Teo, T. (1999). Methodologies of critical psychology: Illustrations from the field of racism. *Annual Review of Critical Psychology, 1*, 119–34.

Teproff, C. (2016). Miami's No. 1. Its prize? The biggest gap between rich and poor. *Miami Herald.* Retrieved from www.miamiherald.com/news/local/community/miami-dade/article106325122.html

Terry, R., Townley, G., Brusilovskiy, E., & Salzer, M. S. (2019). The influence of sense of community on the relationship between community participation and mental health for individuals with serious mental illnesses. *Journal of Community Psychology, 47*(1), 163–75.

The Advocate. (2018). *Violence against the transgender community in 2018.* Retrieved from www.hrc.org/resources/violence-against-the-transgender-community-in-2018

The New School. (2014, October 13). *bell hooks and Laverne Cox in a public dialogue at The New School* [Video file]. Retrieved from www.youtube.com/watch?v=9oMmZlJijgY

Thomas, D. R., Neill, B., & Robertson, N. (1997). Developing a graduate program in community psychology: Experiences at the University of Waikato, New Zealand. *Journal of Prevention and Intervention in the Community, 15*(1), 83–96.

Thompson, J. (1984). *Studies in the theory of ideology*. Berkeley, CA: University of California Press.

Tjepkema, M. (2008). Health care use among gay, lesbian and bisexual Canadians. *Health reports, 19*(1), 53–64. Retrieved from: http://thebridgebrant.com/wp-content/uploads/2014/03/Health-care-among-LGBT-Canada-stats-Can.pdf

Tolan, P., Chertok, F., Keys, C., & Jason, L. (1990). *Conversing about theories, methods, and community research*. Washington, DC: American Psychological Association.

Tolan, P. E., Keys, C. E., Chertok, F. E., & Jason, L. A. (1990). *Researching community psychology: Issues of theory and methods*. Washington, DC: American Psychological Association.

Tong, R. (2014). *Feminist thought: A more comprehensive introduction* (4th ed.). Boulder, CO: Westview Press.

Toporek, R., Gerstein, L., Fouad, N., Roysircar-Sodowsky, G., & Israel, T. (Eds.), (2005). *Handbook for social justice in counseling psychology: Leadership, vision, and action*. London: SAGE Publications.

Toro, P. A. (2007). Toward an international understanding of homelessness. *Journal of Social Issues, 63*, 461–81.

Toro, P. A., Tompsett, C. J., Lombardo, S., Philippot, P., Nachtergael, H., Galand, B., ... Harvey, K. (2007). Homelessness in Europe and the United States: A comparison of prevalence and public opinion. *Journal of Social Issues, 63*, 505–24.

Townley, G., & Sylvestre, J. (2014). Toward transformative change in community mental health: Introduction to the special issue. *Global Journal of Community Psychology Practice, 5*(1), 1–8.

Townley, G., Kloos, B., Green, E. P., & Franco, M. M. (2011). Reconcilable differences? Human diversity, cultural relativity, and sense of community. *American Journal of Community Psychology, 47*, 69–85.

Townley, G., Miller, H., & Kloos, B. (2013). A little goes a long way: Assessing distal social support for individuals with psychiatric disabilities. *American Journal of Community Psychology, 52*, 84–96.

Townley, G., Pearson, L., Lehrwyn, J. M., Prophet, N. T., & Trauernicht, M. (2016). Utilizing participatory mapping and GIS to examine the activity spaces of homeless youth. *American Journal of Community Psychology, 57*(3–4), 404–14.

Trainor, J., Pomeroy, E., & Pape, B. (1999). *Building a framework for support: A community development approach to mental health policy*. Toronto: Canadian Mental Health Association/National.

Travers, R., Guta, A., Flicker, S., Larkin, J., Lo, C., McCardell, S., & van der Meulen, E. (2010). Service provider views on issues and needs for lesbian, gay, bisexual, and transgender youth. *Canadian Journal of Human Sexuality, 19*(4), 191–8.

Travers, R., Pyne, J., Bauer, G., Munro, L., Giambrone, B., Hammond, R., & Scanlon, K. (2013). "Community control" in CBPR: Challenges experienced and questions raised from the Trans PULSE project. *Action Research, 11*(4), 403–22.

Trickett, E. J. (1984). Toward a distinctive community psychology: An ecological metaphor for the conduct of community research and the nature of training. *American Journal of Community Psychology, 12*(3), 261–79.

Trickett, E. J. (1986). Consultation as a preventive intervention: Comments on ecologically based case studies. *Prevention in Human Services, 4*(3–4), 187–204.

Trickett, E. J. (1994). Human diversity and community psychology: Where ecology and empowerment meet. *American Journal of Community Psychology, 22*, 583–92.

Trickett, E. (1996). A future for community psychology: The contexts of diversity and the diversity of contexts. *American Journal of Community Psychology, 24*, 209–29.

Trickett, E. J., Barone, C., & Watts, R. (2000). Contextual influences in mental health consultation. In J. Rappaport & E. Seidman (Eds.), *Handbook of community psychology* (pp. 303–30). Boston, MA: Springer.

Trickett, E. J., Beehler, S., Deutsch, C., Green, L. W., Hawe, P., McLeroy, K., ... Trimble, J. E. (2011). Advancing the science of community-level interventions. *American Journal of Public Health, 101*(8), 1410–19.

Trickett, E. J., Kelly, J. G., & Todd, D. M. (1972). The social environment of the high school: Guidelines for individual change and organizational redevelopment. In S. E. Golann & C. Eisdorfer (Eds.), *Handbook of community mental health* (pp. 331–406). New York: Appleton-Century-Crofts.

Trickett, E. J., Kelly, J. G., & Vincent, T. A. (1985). The spirit of ecological inquiry in community research. In E. Susskind & D. Klein (Eds.), *Community research: Methods, paradigms, and applications* (pp. 283–333). New York: Praeger.

Trickett, E. J., Watts, R., & Birman, D. (Eds.). (1994). *Human diversity: Perspectives on people in context*. San Francisco, CA: Jossey-Bass.

Trochim, W. M., Cabrera, D. A., Milstein, B., Gallagher, R. S., & Leischow, S. J. (2006). Practical challenges in systems thinking and modeling in public health. *American Journal of Public Health, 96*(5), 538–46.

Trout, L., McEachern, D., Mullany, A., White, L., & Wexler, L. (2018). Decoloniality as a framework for indigenous youth suicide prevention pedagogy: Promoting community conversations about research to end suicide. *American Journal of Community Psychology, 62*(3–4), 396–405.

Truth, S. (1851). Ain't I a woman? *Women's Convention*. Akron. Retrieved from https://sourcebooks.fordham.edu/mod/sojtruth-woman.asp

Tsemberis, S. (1999). From streets to homes: An innovative approach to supported housing for homeless adults with psychiatric disabilities. *Journal of Community Psychology, 27*(2), 225–41.

Tsemberis, S. (2010). *Housing first: The pathways model to end homelessness for people with mental illness and addiction*. Center City, MN: Hazelden.

Tsemberis, S., & Eisenberg, R. F. (2000). Pathways to housing: Supported housing for street-dwelling homeless individuals. *Psychiatric Services, 51*(4), 487–93.

Tsemberis, S., Gulcur, L., & Nakae, M. (2004). Housing First, consumer choice, and harm reduction for homeless individuals with a dual diagnosis. *American Journal of Public Health, 94*(4), 651–6.

Tseng, V., & Seidman, E. (2007). A systems framework for understanding social settings. *American Journal of Community Psychology, 39*, 217–28.

Tseng, V., Chesir-Teran, D., Becker-Klein, R., Chan, M. L., Duran, V., Roberts, A., & Bardoliwalla, N. (2002). Promotion of social change: A conceptual framework. *American Journal of Community Psychology, 30*(3), 401–27.

Tuck, E., & Yang, K. W. (2012). Decolonization is not a metaphor. *Decolonization: Indigeneity, Education & Society, 1*(1). Retrieved from http://decolonization.org/index.php/des/article/view/18630/15554

Tucker, C. M., Wippold, G. M., Williams, J. L., Arthur, T. M., Desmond, F. F., & Robinson, K. C. (2017). A CBPR study to test the impact of a church-based health empowerment program on health behaviors and health outcomes of black adult churchgoers. *Journal of Racial and Ethnic Health Disparities, 4*(1), 70–8.

Tufekci, Z., & Wilson, C. (2012). Social media and the decision to participate in political protest: Observations from Tahrir Square. *Journal of Communication, 62*, 363–79.

Turner, C. (2008). Editorial: Introduction to the special issue on place based research and intervention. *Australian Community Psychologist, 20*, 5–7.

Turner, S., Merchant, K., Kania, J., & Martin, E. (2012, July). Understanding the value of backbone organizations in collective impact: Part 2. Retrieved from www.ssireview.org/blog/ entry/understanding_the_value_of_backbone_organizations_in_ collective_impact_2

TvT Research Project. (2016). *Trans Murder Monitoring results: TMM IDAHOT 2016 update. Transrespect versus Transphobia Worldwide*. Retrieved from http://transrespect.org/en/research/trans-murder-monitoring/

Tyler, F. (2007). *Developing prosocial communities across cultures*. New York: Springer.

Tyler, F. B., Sussewell, D. R., & Williams-McCoy, J. (1985). Ethnic validity in psychotherapy. *Psychotherapy: Theory, Research, Practice, Training, 22*(2S), 311.

Tzanakis, M. (2013). Social capital in Bourdieu's, Coleman's and Putnam's theory: Empirical evidence and emergent measurement issues. *Educate, 13*(2), 2–23. Retrieved from http://www.educatejournal.org/index.php/educate/article/view/366

US Department of Justice (2014). *Uniform Crime Reports, 2014 Hate Crime Statistics*. Retrieved from www.fbi.gov/about-us/cjis/ucr/hate-crime/2014

US Interagency Council on Homelessness (USICH). (2010). *Opening doors: the Federal strategic plan to prevent and end homelessness*. Retrieved from www.usich.gov/PDF/OpeningDoors_2010_FSPPreventEndHomeless.pdf

UN Human Rights High Commissioner (2016). OHCHR | Canada: UN expert panel warns of systemic anti-Black racism in the criminal justice system. Retrieved from www.ohchr.org/en/NewsEvents/Pages/DisplayNews.aspx?NewsID=20736&Langl D=E

Underwood, A. (2018, April 6). What most Americans get wrong about Islamophobia. *Vox*. Retrieved from www.vox.com/2018/4/6/17169448/trump-islamophobia-muslims-islam-black-lives-matter

UNESCO. (n.d.). *Migrant/Migration*. Retrieved from www.unesco.org/new/en/social-and-human-sciences/themes/international-migration/glossary/migrant/

UNICEF. (2012). *The South African child support grant impact assessment: Evidence from a survey of children, adolescents and their households.* Pretoria: UNICEF South Africa.

United Nations. (1991). *United Nations Convention on the Rights of the Child.* (Minister of Supply and Services Canada, Catalogue No. S2–210/1991E). Hull, Québec: Communications Branch, Human Rights Directorate, Department of Canadian Heritage.

United Nations. (2007). *The millennium development goals report 2007.* Available from www.un.org/millenniumgoals/pdf/mdg2007.pdf

United Nations. (2014). *The millennium development goals report 2014.* Retrieved from www.undp.org/content/dam/undp/library/MDG/english/UNDP_MDGReport_EN_2014Final1.pdf

United Nations. (2015a). *The world's women 2015: Trends and statistics.* New York: United Nations, Department of Economic and Social Affairs, Statistics Division.

United Nations. (2015b). *Transforming our world: The 2030 agenda for sustainable development.* Retrieved from www.un.org/ga/search/view_doc.asp?symbol=A/RES/70/1&Lang=E

United Nations Department of Economic and Social Affairs (UNDESA). (2014). Disability data and statistics, monitoring and evaluation: The way forward – A disability-inclusive agenda towards 2015 and beyond. Retrieved from https://www.un.org/disabilities/documents/egm2014/EGM_FINAL_08102014.pdf

United Nations Human Rights Council (UNHRC). (2015). *Discrimination and violence against individuals based on their sexual orientation and gender identity.* Retrieved from www.refworld.org/docid/5571577c4.html

United Nations High Commissioner for Refugees. (1991). *Background note on the Safe Country concept and refugee status.* Retrieved from https://www.unhcr.org/excom/scip/3ae68ccec/background-note-safe-country-concept-refugee-status.html

USAID. (2014). *Final evaluation of the International Rescue Committee's ESPOIR project in the North and South Kivu provinces of the Democratic Republic of Congo (DRC).* Kivu: USAID.

US Department of Labor, Bureau of Labor Statistics. (2016). *Persons with a disability: Labor force characteristics – 2015.* Washington, DC: Author. Retrieved from https://www.bls.gov/news.release/pdf/disabl.pdf

Valenti, M., & Campbell, R. (2009). Working with youth on LGBTQ issues: Why Gay-Straight Alliance advisors become involved. *Journal of Community Psychology, 37*(2), 228–48.

Van der Gaag, N. (2008). *The no-nonsense guide to women's rights.* Oxford: New Internationalist Publications.

Van Genugten, W., & Perez-Bustillo, C. (Eds.). (2001). *The poverty of rights: Human rights and the eradication of poverty.* London: Zed Books.

Van Voorhees, C. & Perkins, D. D. (2007, June). *Is ecological research ecological? Is research validity valid?* Paper presented at the biennial meeting of the Society for Community Research and Action, Pasadena, CA.

Vasey, A. (2018). The state of cities reducing poverty. Retrieved from http://www.tamarackcommunity.ca/latest/the-state-of-cities-reducing-poverty

Veenstra, G. (2011). Race, gender, class, and sexual orientation: Intersecting axes of inequality and self-rated health in Canada. *International Journal for Equity in Health, 10*(1), 3.

VeneKlasen, L., & Miller, V. (2002). *A new weave of power, people & politics: The action guide for advocacy and citizen participation.* Oklahoma City, OK: World Neighbors.

Vera, E., & Speight, S. (2007). Advocacy, outreach, and prevention: Integrating social action roles in professional training. In E. Aldarondo (Ed.), *Advancing social justice through clinical practice* (pp. 373–90). London: Lawrence Erlbaum.

Veracini, L. (2007). Settler colonialism and decolonisation. *Borderlands E-Journal, 6*(2). Retrieved from www.borderlands.net.au/vol6no2_2007/veracini_settler.htm.

Verba, S., & Nie, N. (1972). *Participation in America: Political democracy and social equality.* New York: Harper and Row.

Varda, D. M. (2018, February 6). Are backbone organizations eroding the norms that make networks succeed? *Nonprofit Quarterly.* Retrieved from https://nonprofitquarterly.org/2018/02/06/backbone-organizations-eroding-norms-make-networks-succeed/

Viola, J., & McMahon, S. (2011). *Consulting and evaluation with nonprofit and community-based organizations.* Sudbury, MA: Jones & Bartlett.

Viruell-Fuentes, E. A., Miranda, P. Y., & Abdulrahim, S. (2012). More than culture: Structural racism, intersectionality theory, and immigrant health. *Social Science Medicine, 75*(12), 2099–106.

Visitability. (2018). *Basic access to homes*. Retrieved from https://visitability.org/

Von Bertalanffy, L. (1968). *General system theory: Foundations, developments, applications*. New York: Braziller.

Waitoki, W. W., Feather, J. S., Robertson, N. R., & Rucklidge, J. J. (Eds.). (2016). *Professional practice of psychology in Aotearoa New Zealand*.(3rd ed.) Wellington, New Zealand: New Zealand Psychological Society.

Walcott, R. (2003). *Black like who?: Writing Black Canada*. London, Ontario: Insomniac Press.

Walker, C., Burton, M., Akhurst, J., & Degirmencioglu, S. M. (2015). Locked into the system? Critical community psychology approaches to personal debt in the context of crises of capital accumulation. *Journal of Community & Applied Social Psychology, 25*(3), 264–75.

Walker, H., Calkins, C., Wehmeyer, M. L., Walker, L., Bacon, A., Palmer, S.B., ... Johnson, D. R. (2011). A social-ecological approach to promote self-determination. *Exceptionality, 19*, 6–18.

Walker, R. (1990). *Ka whawhai tonu matou: Stuggle without end*. Auckland: Penguin.

Wallerstein, N., & Duran, B. (2008). The theoretical, historical, and practice roots of CBPR. In M. Minkler & N. Wallerstein (Eds.), *Community-based participatory research for health: From process to outcomes* (2nd ed, pp. 25–46). San Francisco, CA: Jossey-Bass.

Walsh, R. T. (1996). The evolution of the research relationship in community psychology. *American Journal of Community Psychology, 15*, 773–88.

Walsh, R. T., & Gokani, R. (2014). The personal and political economy of psychologists' desires for social justice. *Journal of Theoretical and Philosophical Psychology, 34*(1), 41–55.

Wandel, J., Riemer, M., de Gómez, W., Klein, K., de Schutter, J., Randall, L., ... Singleton, C. (2010). *Homelessness and global climate change: Are we ready? A report from the study on the vulnerability to global climate change of people experiencing homelessness in Waterloo Region*. Waterloo, ON: Author.

Wandersman, A., & Florin, P. (2000). Citizen participation and community organizations. In J. Rappaport & E. Seidman (Eds.), *Handbook of Community Psychology* (pp. 247–72). New York: Springer.

Wandersman, A., Duffy, J., Flaspohler, P., Noonan, R. K., Lubell, K., ... Saul, J. (2008). Bridging the gap between prevention research and practice: The interactive systems framework for dissemination and implementation. *American Journal of Community Psychology, 41*(3–4), 171–81.

Wandersman, A., Snell-Johns, J., Lentz, B., Fetterman, D. M., Keener, D. C., Livet, ... Flaspohler, P. (2005). The principles of empowerment evaluation. In D.M. Fetterman, & A. Wandersman (2005). *Empowerment evaluation principles in practice* (pp. 27–41). New York: Guilford Publications.

Wang, M. T., & Degol, J. L. (2016). School climate: A review of the construct, measurement, and impact on student outcomes. *Educational Psychology Review, 28*(2), 315–52.

Warren, M. R., Thompson, J. P., & Saegert, S. (2001). The role of social capital in combating poverty. In S. Saegert, J. P. Thompson, & M. R. Warren (Eds.), *Social capital and poor communities* (pp. 1–28). New York: Russell Sage Foundation.

Wasserman, S., & Faust, K. (1994). *Social network analysis: Methods and applications*. Cambridge: Cambridge University Press.

Watkins, M., & Shulman, H. (2008). *Toward psychologies of liberation*. New York: Palgrave Macmillan.

Watts, R. J. (1992). Elements of a psychology of human diversity. *Journal of Community Psychology, 20*(2), 116–31.

Watts, R. J. (2017). Utopian vision: A grand solution for a scholarly dilemma. *American Journal of Community Psychology, 59*(3–4), 280–83.

Watts, R. J., Diemer, M. A., & Voight, A. M. (2011). Critical consciousness: Current status and future directions. *New directions for child and adolescent development, 134*, 43–57.

Watts, R. J., & Serrano-García, I. (2003). The quest for a liberating community psychology: An overview. *American Journal of Community Psychology, 31*(1–2), 73–8.

Watts, R. J., Williams, N. C., & Jagers, R. J. (2003). Sociopolitical development. *American Journal of Community Psychology, 31*, 185–94.

Watzlawick, P., Beavin, J. H., & Jackson, D. D. A. (1967). *Pragmatics of human communication: A study of international patterns, pathologies, and paradoxes*. New York: Norton.

Watzlawick, P., Weakland, J., & Fisch, R. (1974). *Change: Principles of problem formation and problem resolution*. New York: Norton.

Weber, M. (1978). *Economy and society*. Berkeley, CA: University of California Press.

Weber, O., & Geobey, S. (2012). *Final report: Social finance and nonprofits: The Contribution of social finance to the sustainability of nonprofit organizations and social enterprises.* Waterloo, ON: EDC. Retrieved from www. researchgate.net/profile/Olaf_Weber2/publication/

Wei, W. W. S. (2013). Time series analysis. In T. D. Little (Ed.), *The Oxford handbook of quantitative methods in psychology: Vol. 2.* New York: Oxford University Press.

Weick, K. E. (1979). *The social psychology of organizing* (2nd ed.). Reading, MA: Addison-Wesley.

Weick, K., & Quinn, R. (1999). Organizational change and development. *Annual Review of Psychology, 50,* 361–86.

Weinberg, R. (2001). *Incorporating mental health policy research and advocacy in clinical training: The Florida Mental Health Institute predoctoral psychology internship.* Unpublished paper, University of South Florida and Florida Mental Health Institute, Florida.

Weiner, E. (2008). *The geography of bliss.* New York: Twelve.

Weinstein, R. (2002). Overcoming inequality in schooling: A call to action for community psychology. *American Journal of Community Psychology, 30,* 21–42.

Weisbrot, M. (1999). *Globalization: A primer.* Washington, DC: Center for Economic and Policy Research. Retrieved from www.cepr.net/GlobalPrimer.htm

Weiss, C. H. (1972). *Evaluation research: Methods for assessing program effectiveness.* Englewood Cliffs, N.J.: Prentice-Hall.

Weissberg, R. (1999). *The politics of empowerment.* Westport, CT: Praeger.

Weisstein, N. (1968/1993). Psychology constructs the female, or the fantasy life of the male psychologist (with some attention to the fantasies of his friends, the male biologist and the male anthropologist). Reprinted in *Feminism and Psychology, 3,* 195–210.

Wellman, B. (2002). Little boxes, globalization, and networked individualism? In M. Tanabe, P. van den Besselaar, & T. Ishida (Eds.), *Digital cities II: Computational and sociological approaches* (pp. 10–25). Berlin: Springer.

Wepa, D. (Ed.). (2015). *Cultural safety in Aotearoa New Zealand.* Cambridge University Press.

Wernick, L., Kulick, A., & Woodford, M. (2014). How theater within a transformative organizing framework cultivates individual and collective empowerment among LGBTQ youth. *Journal of Community Psychology, 42*(7), 838–53.

West, E. (2018). *Beyond the non-profit industrial complex.* Retrieved from https://truthout.org/articles/beyond-the-non-profit-industrial-complex/

Wheatley, M. J. (1992). *Leadership and the new science: Learning about organization from an orderly universe.* San Francisco: Berrett-Koehler.

Whitaker, R. (2002). *Mad in America: Bad science, bad medicine, and the enduring mistreatment of the mentally ill.* Cambridge, MA: Perseus Books.

White, G. (2010). Ableism. In G. Nelson & I. Prilleltensky, (Eds.), *Community psychology: In pursuit of liberation and well-being* (2nd ed., pp. 405–25). London: Red Globe Press.

White, G. W., Simpson, J. L., Gonda, C., Ravesloot, C. R., & Coble, Z. (2010). From Independence to interdependence: A conceptual model for better understanding community participation of centers for independent living consumers. *Journal of Disability Policy Studies, 20*(4), 233–40.

Wiesenfeld, E. (1996). The concept of "we": A community social psychology myth? *Journal of Community Psychology, 24*(4), 337–46.

Wild, L. (2014). CARE's experience with community scorecards in Malawi – What works and why? *Country Case Study Note.* London: ODI.

Wilkes, R. (2000). The last word. In P. Dudgeon, D. Garvey, & H. Pickett (Eds.), *Working with Indigenous Australians: A handbook for psychologists* (pp. 519–22). Perth: Gunada Press.

Wilkinson, D. (2007). The multidimensional nature of social cohesion: Psychological sense of community, attraction, and neighboring. *American Journal of Community Psychology, 40,* 214–29.

Wilkinson, R. G. (1994). The epidemiological transition: From material scarcity to social disadvantage? *Daedalus, 123*(4), 61–77.

Wilkinson, R. G. (1996). *Unhealthy societies: The afflictions of inequality.* London: Routledge.

Wilkinson, R. G. (1997). Socioeconomic determinants of health. Health inequalities: Relative or absolute material standards? *British Medical Journal, 314*(22), 591–4.

Wilkinson, R. G., & Pickett, K. (2009). *The spirit level: Why more equal societies almost always do better.* London: Allen Lane.

Wilkinson, R. G., & Pickett, K. E. (2017). The enemy between us: The psychological and social costs of inequality. *European Journal of Social Psychology, 47*(1), 11–24.

Wilkinson, R. G., & Pickett, K. (2019). *The inner level: How more equal societies reduce stress, restore sanity and improve everyone's well-being.* London: Penguin Press.

William, L. (1999). Participatory research, knowledge, and community-based change: Experience, epistemology, and empowerment. *Research in Community Sociology, 9,* 3–40.

Williams, D., Ducheneaut, N., Xiong, L., Zhang, Y., Yee, N., & Nickell, E. (2006). From tree house to barracks: The social life of guilds in World of Warcraft. *Games and Culture, 1*(4), 338–61.

Williams, L. D. (2014). Understanding the relationships among HIV/AIDS-related stigma, health service utilization, and HIV prevalence and incidence in Sub-Saharan Africa: A multi-level theoretical perspective. *American Journal of Community Psychology, 53*(1–2), 146–58.

Willis, G. B., & Artino, A. R. (2013). What do our respondents think we're asking? Using cognitive interviewing to improve medical education surveys. *Journal of Graduate Medical Education, 5*(3), 353–56.

Wilson, C., & Flicker, S. (2014). Arts-based methods. In D. Coghlan & M. Brydon-Miller (Eds.), *The SAGE Encyclopedia of Action Research.* Los Angeles: SAGE Publications.

Wilson, S. (2008). *Research is ceremony: Indigenous research methods.* Black Point, N.S: Fernwood Publishing.

Winberg, C., Coleman, T., Woodford, M. R., McKie, R. M., Travers, R., & Renn, K. A. (2018). Hearing "That's so Gay" and "No Homo" on campus and substance use among sexual minority college students. *Journal of Homosexuality.* Advance online publication. doi: 10.1080/00918369.2018.1542208.

Wirihana, R., & Smith, C. (2014). Historical trauma, healing and well-being in Māori communities. *MAI Journal, 3*(3), 1–14.

Wiscovithc, J., & Sosa Pascual, O. (2018, May 24). Puerto Rico government did not prevent most hurricane María-related deaths. *Centro de Periodismo Investigativo.* Retrieved from http://periodismoinvestigativo. com/2018/05/puerto-rico-government-did-not-prevent-most-hurricane-maria-related-deaths/

Wise, P. (2016). Child poverty and the promise of human capacity: Childhood as a foundation. *Academic Pediatrics, 16*(3 Suppl), 37–45.

Withorn, A. (1984). *Serving the people: Social services and social change.* New York: Columbia University Press.

Wodak, R., & Meyer, M. (2015). *Methods of critical discourse studies.* London: SAGE Publications.

Wolf, E. R., Kahn, J. S., Roseberry, W., & Wallerstein, I. (1994). Perilous ideas: Race, culture, people [and Comments and Reply]. *Current Anthropology, 35*(1),1–12.

Wolf, N. (2001). *Misconceptions: Truth, lies and the unexpected on the journey to motherhood.* Chatto & Windus: London.

Wolfensberger, W. (1972). *The principle of normalization in human services.* Toronto: National Institute on Mental Retardation.

Wolfensberger, W., & Tullman, S. (1982). A brief outline of the principle of normalization. *Rehabilitation Psychology, 27,* 131–45.

Wolff, T. (2001). Community coalition building – contemporary practice and research: Introduction. *American Journal of Community Psychology, 29*(2), 165–72.

Wolff, T. (2016). Ten places where collective impact gets it wrong. *Global Journal of Community Psychology Practice, 7*(1).

Wolff, T., Minkler, M., Wolfe, S. M., Berkowitz, B., Bowen, L., Butterfoos, F. D., ... Lee, K. S. (2017, January 9). Collaborating for equity and justice: Moving beyond collective impact. *Nonprofit Quarterly.* Retrieved from https://nonprofitquarterly.org/2017/01/09/collaborating-equity-justice-moving-beyond-collective-impact/

Wong, N. T., Zimmerman, M. A., & Parker, E. A. (2010). A typology of youth participation and empowerment for child and adolescent health promotion. *American Journal of Community Psychology, 46*(1–2), 100–14.

Wong, Y. L. I., & Hillier, A. E. (2001). Evaluating a community-based homelessness prevention program: A geographic information system approach. *Administration in Social Work, 25,* 21–45.

Woodford, M. R., & Kulick, A. (2015). Academic and social integration on campus among sexual minority students: The impacts of psychological and experiential campus climate. *American Journal of Community Psychology, 55*(1–2), 13–24.

Woodford, M. R., Chonody, J. M., Kulick, A., Brennan, D. J., & Renn, K. (2015). The LGBQ microaggressions on campus scale: A scale development and validation study. *Journal of Homosexuality, 62*(12), 1660–87.

Woolcock, M., & Narayan, D. (2000). Social Capital: Implications for development theory, research, and policy. *World Bank Research Observer, 15*(2), 225–49.

World Health Organization. (1986). *Ottawa Charter for Health Promotion: An international conference on health promotion*. Retrieved from www.who.int/healthpromotion/conferences/previous/ottawa/en/.

World Health Organization. (2001). *International Classification of Functioning, Disability and Health (ICF)*. Retrieved from www.who.int/classifications/icf/en/

World Health Organization. (2006). *Constitution of the World Health Organization* (45th ed.). Retrieved from www.who.int/governance/eb/who_constitution_en.pdf

World Health Organization. (2008). *Closing the gap in a generation: Health equity through action on the social determinants of health*. Commission on Social Determinants of Health Final Report. Geneva, Switzerland.

World Health Organization. (2014). *Social determinants of mental health*. Geneva, Switzerland: World Health Organization and Calouste Gulbenkian Foundation.

World Health Organization. (2015). *The intervention with microfinance for AIDS and gender equity (IMAGE) study*. Retrieved from www.who.int/violenceprevention/about/participants/Intimite_partner_violence.pdf

Worldwatch Institute. (2013). *State of the World 2013: Is sustainability still possible?* Washington: Island Press.

Worline, M., & Dutton, J. E. (2017). *Awakening compassion at work: The quiet power that elevates people and organizations*. Oakland, CA: Berrett-Koehler Publishers.

Worton, S. K., Nelson, G., Loomis, C., Pancer, S. M., Hayward, K., & Peters, R. D. (2018). Advancing early childhood development and prevention programs: A Pan-Canadian knowledge transfer initiative for Better Beginnings, Better Futures. *Australian and New Zealand Journal of Family Therapy, 39*(3), 347–63.

Wright, R. (1993). *Stolen continents*. Toronto, ON: Penguin Books Canada Ltd.

Wynter, S. (1995). 1492: A new world view. In V. Lawrence Hyatt & R. Nettleford (Eds.), *Race, discourse, and the origin of the Americas: A new world view*. Washington, DC: Smithsonian Institution.

Yates, B. T. (1998). Formative evaluation of costs, cost-effectiveness, and cost-benefit: Toward cost-procedure-process-outcome analysis. In L. Bickman & D. J. Rog (Eds.), *Handbook of applied social research methods* (pp. 285–314). Thousand Oaks, CA: SAGE Publications.

Yilmaz, R. (2016). Knowledge sharing behaviors in e-learning community: Exploring the role of academic self-efficacy and sense of community. *Computers in Human Behavior, 63*, 373–82.

Yoshikawa, H., Weiland, C., Brooks-Gunn, J., Burchinal, M. R., Espinosa, L. M., Gormley, W. T., ... Zaslow, M. J. (2013). *Investing in our future: The evidence base on preschool education*. New York: Society for Research in Child Development and Foundation for Child Development.

Yoshino, K. (2007). *Covering: The hidden assaults on our civil rights*. New York: Random House.

Zakocs, R. C., & Edwards, E. M. (2006). What explains community coalition effectiveness? A review of the literature. *American Journal of Preventive Medicine, 30*, 351–61.

Zimmerman, L., Darnell, D. A., Rhew, I. C., Lee, C. M., & Kaysen, D. (2015). Resilience in community: A social ecological development model for young adult sexual minority women. *American Journal of Community Psychology, 55*(1–2), 179–90.

Zimmerman, M.A. (2000). Empowerment theory: Psychological, organizational, and community levels of analysis. In J. Rappaport & E. Seidman (Eds.), *Handbook of community psychology* (pp. 43–63). New York: Springer.

Zimmerman, M. A., & Eisman, A. B. (2017). Empowering interventions: Strategies for addressing health inequities across levels of analysis. In M. B. Bond, I. Serrano-García, C. Keys, & M. Shinn (Eds.), *APA Handbook of community psychology: Methods for community research and action for diverse groups and issues*. (pp. 173–91). Washington DC: American Psychological Association.

Zimmerman, M. A., Eisman, A. B., Reischl, T. M., Morrel-Samuels, S., Staddard, S., Miller, A. L., Hutchinson, P., Franzen, S. & Rupp, L. (2018). Youth empowerment solutions: Evaluation of an after-school program to engage middle school students in community change. *Health Education & Behavior, 45*(1), 20–31.

AUTHOR INDEX

SUBJECT INDEX